KV-675-298

Windows NT™ Server 4.0 SECRETS®

by Valda Hilley

IDG
BOOKS
WORLDWIDE

IDG Books Worldwide, Inc.
An International Data Group Company

Foster City, CA ♦ Chicago, IL ♦ Indianapolis, IN ♦ Southlake, TX

Windows NT™ Server 4.0 SECRETS®

Published by
IDG Books Worldwide, Inc.
An International Data Group Company
919 E. Hillsdale Blvd. Suite 400
Foster City, CA 94404

Library of Congress Catalog Card No.: 96-076234

ISBN: 1-56884-717-3

Printed in the United States of America

10 9 8 7 6 5 4 3 2 1

1B/SS/QY/ZW/FC

Distributed in the United States by IDG Books Worldwide, Inc.

Distributed by Macmillan Canada for Canada; by Contemporanea de Ediciones for Venezuela; by Distribuidora Cuspide for Argentina; by CITEC for Brazil; by Ediciones ZETA S.C.R. Ltda. for Peru; by Editorial Limusa SA for Mexico; by Transworld Publishers Limited in the United Kingdom and Europe; by Academic Bookshop for Egypt; by Levant Distributors S.A.R.L. for Lebanon; by Al Jassim for Saudi Arabia; by Simron Pty. Ltd. for South Africa; by Pustak Mahal for India; by The Computer Bookshop for India; by Toppan Company Ltd. for Japan; by Addison Wesley Publishing Company for Korea; by Longman Singapore Publishers Ltd. for Singapore, Malaysia, Thailand, and Indonesia; by Unalis Corporation for Taiwan; by WS Computer Publishing Company, Inc. for the Philippines; by WoodsLane Pty. Ltd. for Australia; by WoodsLane Enterprises Ltd. for New Zealand. Authorized Sales Agent: Anthony Rudkin Associates for the Middle East and North Africa.

For general information on IDG Books Worldwide's books in the U.S., contact our Consumer Customer Service Department at 800-762-2974. For reseller information, including discounts and premium sales, contact our Reseller Customer Service department at 800-434-3422.

For information on where to purchase IDG Books Worldwide's books outside the U.S., contact IDG Books Worldwide's International Sales department at 415-655-3078 or fax 415-655-3281.

For information on foreign language translations, contact IDG Books Worldwide's Foreign & Subsidiary Rights department at 415-655-3018 or fax 415-655-3281.

For sales inquiries and special prices for bulk quantities, contact IDG Books Worldwide's Sales department at 415-655-3200 or write to the address above.

For information on using IDG Books Worldwide's books in the classroom or for ordering examination copies, contact IDG Books Worldwide's Educational Sales department at 800-434-2086 or fax 817-251-8174.

For authorization to photocopy items for corporate, personal, or educational use, contact the Copyright Clearance Center, 222 Rosewood Drive, Danvers, MA 01923, or fax 508-750-4470.

 is a trademark under exclusive license to IDG Books Worldwide, Inc., from International Data Group, Inc.

Windows NT™
Server 4.0
SECRETS®

Welcome to the world of IDG Books Worldwide.

IDG Books Worldwide, Inc., is a subsidiary of International Data Group, the world's largest publisher of computer-related information and the leading global provider of information services on information technology. IDG was founded more than 25 years ago and now employs more than 8,500 people worldwide. IDG publishes more than 270 computer publications in over 75 countries (see listing below). More than 90 million people read one or more IDG publications each month.

Launched in 1990, IDG Books Worldwide is today the #1 publisher of best-selling computer books in the United States. We are proud to have received eight awards from the Computer Press Association in recognition of editorial excellence and three from *Computer Currents'* First Annual Readers' Choice Awards, and our best-selling . . .*For Dummies*® series has more than 25 million copies in print with translations in 30 languages. IDG Books Worldwide, through a joint venture with IDG's Hi-Tech Beijing, became the first U.S. publisher to publish a computer book in the People's Republic of China. In record time, IDG Books Worldwide has become the first choice for millions of readers around the world who want to learn how to better manage their businesses.

Our mission is simple: Every one of our books is designed to bring extra value and skill-building instructions to the reader. Our books are written by experts who understand and care about our readers. The knowledge base of our editorial staff comes from years of experience in publishing, education, and journalism — experience which we use to produce books for the '90s. In short, we care about books, so we attract the best people. We devote special attention to details such as audience, interior design, use of icons, and illustrations. And because we use an efficient process of authoring, editing, and desktop publishing our books electronically, we can spend more time ensuring superior content and spend less time on the technicalities of making books.

You can count on our commitment to deliver high-quality books at competitive prices on topics you want to read about. At IDG Books Worldwide, we continue in the IDG tradition of delivering quality for more than 25 years. You'll find no better book on a subject than one from IDG Books Worldwide.

John J. Kilcullen

John Kilcullen
President and CEO
IDG Books Worldwide, Inc.

Credits

Senior Vice President and Group Publisher
Brenda McLaughlin

Acquisitions Editor
John Osborn

Managing Editor
Andy Cummings

Development Editor
Cynthia Putnam

Copy Editor
Colleen Brosnan

Technical Reviewer
Matthew Hayden

Production Director
Andrew Walker

Supervisor of Page Layout
Craig A. Harrison

Project Coordinator
Phyllis Beaty

Reprint Coordination
Tony Augsburger
Theresa Sánchez-Baker
Elizabeth Cárdenas-Nelson

Media/Archive Coordination
Leslie Popplewell
Melissa Stauffer
Jason Marcuson

Production Staff
Diann Abbott
Mick Arellano
Vince Burns
Laura Carpenter
Tom Debolski
Renée Dunn
Ritchie Durdin
Mary Ellen Moran
Stephen Noetzel
Chris Pimentel
Andreas F. Schueller
Elsie Yim

Proofreader
Mary C. Oby

Indexer
Ty Koontz

Book Design
Liew Design

Cover Design
Liew Design

To my husband Glenn, who constantly encourages me to be all that I can be.
To my daughter, Sidney, a budding young story writer.
And to my mother for always being there.

About the Author

Valda Hilley is the author of *Windows® 3.1 Configuration SECRETS®* and *Internet Gizmos®*. She is a Microsoft Certified Professional and an engineer and systems consultant who has worked with microcomputers for nearly twenty years.

Preface

Windows NT 3.1, released in 1992, represented a milestone in operating system development. However, despite its advanced technology and new features, Windows NT 3.1's release was met with a lukewarm reception from the Windows community. Reviewers cited its unproved status as a 1.0-version product (despite the 3.1 moniker) and its appetite for RAM and CPU resources (the minimum RAM requirement was 16MB which was rarely installed and very expensive at the time). All of this on the wings of a less-than-aggressive marketing effort by Microsoft helped to keep Windows NT out of the limelight in its initial release.

Since the release of Version 3.5, Windows NT is fast becoming the de facto standard for both small business and corporate computing environments. As such, the issues of installing, configuring, optimizing, and maintaining Windows NT can seem overwhelming. My goal for this book is to provide you with information that will help you manage your systems.

This book gives you the means to maximize the software and hardware investment you have made in Windows NT. It shows you how to take control of your Windows NT environment and optimize it to its maximum potential. Your productivity with any computing task depends greatly on a solid and well-tuned configuration, but we have discovered that things don't always work the way you expect. Turning that situation around and getting Windows NT to work for you is the primary theme of this book. After reading this book you will be able to do the following:

■ Determine the hardware requirements for implementing Windows NT.

■ Track down bottlenecks in your systems.

■ Understand how various aspects of your computer and operating system affect overall performance.

■ Determine various tradeoffs to optimize your core applications.

■ Access hardware requirements for core applications.

■ Troubleshoot problems with your applications.

As this project developed, I discovered that this book couldn't hold all the information available to help you with Windows NT. As with any reference guide, you will not find all the secrets, workarounds, tips, and insider information necessary to solve every potential problem. However, you will find tools to help you with most of your problems.

This book is designed in manageable sections. As a reference work, I don't expect you to read it from cover to cover. Just use what you need and share the rest. As you get more experience or your computing environment changes, you'll more than likely find yourself coming back to those sections you skipped the first time. Keep this book handy so that you can find it easily when you need it!

After you have read some of the the chapters, get the CD from the back of this book and schedule some uninterrupted time to experiment with the enclosed programs and utilities. I have put together useful and interesting programs, and I hope you take every possible opportunity for using them.

As much as I like to teach, I can be taught. If you disagree with a method, let me know. If you would like to see a topic covered that I haven't covered, tell me what it is and about your specific application. Use the feedback form on the CD to make your point. Or send email to NT_MAVEN@CPRESS.COM. For updates upon final release of Windows NT Server 4.0, visit my Web site at http//: www.cpress.com/discover_nt.

Acknowledgments

A book like this isn't just born out of the sweat of its author. Numerous people pitched in and provided support during the development and writing of *Windows NT Server 4.0 Secrets*. First of all, I want to thank IDG Books for giving me this opportunity and allowing me complete freedom while providing hearty assistance in all matters relating to the book — from editorial to production.

I'd also like to thank the following people:

My development editor, Cindy Putnam, who survived the numerous bumps we encountered during the course of producing this book. I'm sure it's a better book because of her efforts.

Matt Hayden, my technical editor, who gave me solid support and feedback throughout the book. Matt's a Windows NT expert in his own right and his contributions to this book were invaluable.

Arthur Knowles, my associate and my own personal Windows NT guru, who answered my questions, provided information, and watched me sweat over the details.

And to the rest of my associates, who provided moral support, encouraging words, and advice: Jeff Bankston, James Blakely, Sean Daily, Sue Mosher, Nik Simpson, and Michael Browning. Thanks!

I'd also like to thank my Internet provider, One Net Communications, Inc. in Cincinnati, OH for providing me with all the bandwidth I needed to get through this project. They are solid group of Internet and communications experts.

Big thanks to Executive Software, Octopus Technologies, Somarsoft, Camellia Software, and Hewlett Packard.

Last but certainly not least, thanks to Microsoft (the TechNet Group and those beta repro dudes), for supplying me with an overabundance of information.

(The Publisher would like to give special thanks to Patrick J. McGovern, without whom this book would not have been possible.)

Contents at a Glance

Contents

Part II: Windows NT Server Installation and Setup 93

Chapter 4: Preparing to Install Windows NT Server 95

Part I

Getting to Know
Windows NT Server

Chapter 1

Inside Windows NT Server

In This Chapter

▶ Windows NT and its advantages

▶ Important features of Windows NT's design

▶ New additions to Windows NT version 4.0

▶ Key differences between Windows NT Workstation and Windows NT Server

At first glance, Microsoft's Windows NT resembles the familiar Windows 3.x interface. But what is visible to users is only a small part of Windows NT — a host of powerful features lie beneath the surface. This chapter describes these features under the graphical user interface. It provides an overview by introducing the Windows NT components and showing how they interrelate.

Creating an Advanced LAN Operating System

When Microsoft threw Windows NT onto the drawing board, it had a number of critical concerns for large-scale network installations. Some of these concerns were

- Assuring network security and reliability without reducing resource availability

- Providing efficient network administration and management to facilitate the twin goals of security and availability

- Making the software modular to meet the needs of businesses in moving toward a client/server architecture

- Designing the architecture to allow Windows NT to remain hardware independent

- Fully supporting connectivity in a heterogeneous, multi-vendor, multi-protocol environment

- Supporting virtual access to all network resources with a single logon

■ Providing a robust and fully functional enterprise network with an open platform to support full compatibility with hardware and software products on the market, without incurring any penalties in performance and response time.

Windows NT meets these concerns head on. It is a preemptive, 32-bit multi-tasking operating system with security and networking services as principal components.

Key Features of Windows NT

Windows NT is a unique and powerful operating system. The major design goals used in Windows NT's development were reliability, performance, portability, compatibility, scalability, and security.

To gain a better understanding of Windows NT, let's examine some of these features more closely and find out what they mean and how they are implemented inside Windows NT.

Reliability

Superior reliability allows Windows NT to be used as a foundation for mission-critical applications. It's especially ideal for a client workstation and network server, where both types of systems need to be up and running as much as possible. Windows NT improves on previous versions of Windows as well as other operating systems by offering the following reliability features:

■ **Internal Client-Server system model.** Windows NT prevents user applications from interfering with important operating system services by running these services in a protected layer called *Kernel Mode*. Windows NT Kernel Mode and its services operate inside the processor's Ring 0, where user applications, which run in *User Mode*, cannot directly access or interfere with them. User Mode applications, which run in processor Ring 3, cannot access important operating system functions directly. They are instead forced to communicate with Windows NT's lower-level services using a message-passing methodology rather than being able to access directly (and therefore potentially corrupt) the Kernel Mode's address space. This method of communication between processes provides an enormous increase in overall system reliability but incurs some performance penalties (due to the overhead of the message-passing technique).

■ **32-bit flat-memory model.** A true 32-bit operating system, Windows NT provides a 32-bit flat memory model that allows the operating system to access 4 GB (over 4 billion bytes) of memory, and individual applications to access up to 2 GB of private address space. Because this design keeps individual applications physically protected from one another in memory, it prevents one program from overwriting another's memory space accidentally, the most common cause of system lockups.

■ **Preemptive multi-tasking model.** Windows NT uses preemptive multi-tasking that guarantees all running applications adequate CPU resources at all times. It also prevents individual applications from monopolizing the CPU or halting the entire system if they become unstable or cease execution. This allows Windows NT to continue functioning in circumstances that would bring other operating systems to a grinding halt.

■ **Transactional File System (NTFS).** Windows NT NTFS file system is an advanced and extremely robust file system that provides superior reliability. As a transactional file system, Windows NT is able to reverse incomplete or invalid write operations that occur as a result of hardware or software failure (for example, a power outage in the middle of writing a file). Due to this design, Windows NT is far less susceptible than other file systems to corruption or damage by errant applications.

Performance

Windows NT was also designed to be a high-performance operating system. Several of its built-in features contribute to this:

■ **True 32-bit design.** All of Windows NT was written using 32-bit code, which provides an inherent speed advantage over operating systems containing 16-bit technology. Windows 95, by contrast, continues to employ 16-bit code for some of its functionality.

■ **Multi-tasking and multi-processing features.** Windows NT's preemptive multi-tasking allows smooth and even simultaneous execution of all running processes. Its multi-processor support allows the operating system to become instantly more powerful by spreading processes and even individual threads of execution within processes across multiple CPUs.

■ **RISC CPU support.** Windows NT was designed from the outset to support several different types of high-powered RISC processors such as the PowerPC, DEC Alpha AXP, and MIPS CPUs. This allows Windows NT to run not only on Intel-based personal computers, but on high-performance workstation-level systems as well.

Portability

In the past, operating systems have usually been designed around a single hardware platform, such as Intel's x86 family of processors. Unfortunately, this prevents the operating system from being able to take advantage of newer, more powerful hardware designs and chip types. Portability in

Windows NT means that it isn't tied to any single architecture or technology; it can be ported to different types of hardware without being completely rewritten. Windows NT offers the following portability features:

- **Modular, micro-kernel architecture.** Windows NT has a modular, layered design that prevents hardware dependence. The only hardware-specific code resides in the Hardware Abstraction Layer (HAL), which comprises only a small portion of the entire operating system. The HAL operates at the lowest level, translating low-level operating system functions into instructions that are understandable by the specific hardware used in the system. In the future, additional HALs can be written by Microsoft or by hardware manufacturers as new processors are designed. This universal design allows Windows NT to run on an unprecedented number of different systems, from notebook PCs to multi-CPU superservers.

- **Installable file system support.** Another feature of Windows NT that increases its portability is its ability to support multiple file systems. Currently, it supports FAT (File Allocation Table, used in DOS systems), HPFS (High Performance File System, used by OS/2; this is not supported natively by Windows NT 4.0 and enabling HPFS support requires special procedures to activate), NTFS (NT File System, introduced with Windows NT), CDFS (CD-ROM File System), and Macintosh File System (Mac name space support is found in the Windows NT Server product). Again, due to Windows NT's modular nature, support for additional file systems can be easily added in the future.

Compatibility

A key element in the acceptance of any operating system is its ability to work with existing applications. To this end, Microsoft designed Windows NT to be able to run a wide variety of different applications and interact with a number of different foreign operating systems.

- **Application subsystem design.** Windows NT supports MS-DOS, Windows 3.x (Win16), Windows 95 and Windows NT (Win32), POSIX, and OS/2 1.x character-mode applications. Again, the modular design of Windows NT makes it possible to support additional APIs by simply adding new subsystems. An OS/2 Presentation Manager subsystem is also available as a separate add-on product for Windows NT.

- **Windows-On-Windows (WOW) subsystem.** WOW provides excellent Win16 compatibility by completely emulating a Windows 3.1 environment and offers the choice of running individual Windows 3.x applications in a shared or separate memory space. This support allows separate Win16 applications to communicate as seamlessly under Windows NT as they did under Windows 3.x, using inter-process communications features such as DDE and OLE.

- **Windows 95 Explorer interface.** The long-awaited inclusion of the innovative Windows 95 interface in Windows NT makes the Win95 to WinNT upgrade path a seamless one for Windows 95 users. During installation, Windows NT 4.0 allows Win95 users to do a one-way migration, which preserves their Win95 application and desktop configurations.

- **Interoperability with NetWare.** Windows NT's NetWare support includes native support for IPX/SPX protocol and inclusion of both NetWare 3.x and 4.x native clients (Client Services for NetWare or CSNW). It also offers the capability (in Windows NT Server) to share NetWare file and print resources to non-NetWare clients (Gateway Services for NetWare or GSNW) or appear to NetWare clients as a NetWare 3.x Server (File and Print Services for NetWare or FPNW) or NetWare 4.x Server (Directory Service Manager for NetWare or DSMN). Windows NT Server can import NetWare user accounts and logon scripts, as well as provide NetWare-compatible logons and logon scripts for NetWare Clients via FPNW.

- **Interoperability with UNIX.** Windows NT communicates with UNIX systems through its native support of the TCP/IP protocol suite, TCP/IP printing, and the inclusion of basic TCP/IP connectivity applications such as FTP, Telnet, and Ping. Third-party products are also available to allow Windows NT and UNIX systems to share files on shared network volumes.

- **Interoperability with Macintosh.** Windows NT offers an unprecedented level of support for Apple Macintosh systems. Both the Workstation and Server versions support AppleTalk, the protocol used in Macintosh networks. Windows NT Server allows the creation of Macintosh name space on NTFS volumes to enable Mac/PC file sharing. It also allows Macintosh systems to print to non-PostScript printers connected to the Windows NT network.

Scalability

Another important aspect of Windows NT is that it is a *scalable* operating system. This means that it can be used on a wide range of systems, from personal computers to large systems with multiple processors. These systems may have very little or nothing in common other than that they can all run Windows NT. A summary of Windows NT's scalability features follows:

- **Multi-platform support.** Due to its layered, micro-kernel architecture and use of the Hardware Abstraction Layer (HAL), Windows NT is essentially open-ended in its ability to support more powerful processors developed in the future. This allows the same operating system to be used on systems of virtually any size or power, with no effective limits.

- **Multi-processor support.** Support for multiple CPUs in a single system allows Windows NT to scale to the number of available processors on the system and become instantly more efficient as the number of processors is increased.

- **Scalable security model.** Windows NT's support for two different security models — the workgroup and domain models — enables the same product to address the needs of small and large businesses alike, on networks as small as two PCs or as large as 20,000. The domain networking model also offers several sub-models from which organizations can choose for managing users and resources across the enterprise.

Security

Some of Windows NT's most important and touted features relate to the area of security. From the beginning, Microsoft intended Windows NT to be a secure operating system on which businesses and government could rely to protect their data. Windows NT's security goes far beyond that of previous personal computer operating systems, providing security that is on a par with many minicomputer and mainframe systems. To accomplish this, Windows NT offers several layers of system security, including

- **Domain security model.** Windows NT's domain security model is a sophisticated network access scheme that allows administrators to implement strict security measures about who receives access to what information and resources on the network. Special Windows NT Servers called *domain controllers* are responsible for authenticating user logon requests, and no user can gain access to network resources without first being authenticated by a domain controller. Security information on a Windows NT system is stored in a special security database known as the SAM (Security Account Manager) database, which is continually replicated among all Windows NT Servers acting as domain controllers.

- **NTFS file system.** Windows NT includes a special file system, NTFS, that complements its security design. NTFS is tightly integrated with Windows NT's other security features, allowing administrators to utilize a variety of different access levels for users and user groups, down to the directory and file level. File-level permissions allow administrators to set unique permissions on individual files on NTFS volumes — even different files residing in the same directory (folder).

- **Discretionary access control.** Windows NT allows administrators and owners of system objects to have complete control over who gets what kinds of access to those objects (for example, a file or a printer). This type of security, where the owner of a resource has discretion over who may access the resource and how, is known as *discretionary access control*. This level of security gives resource owners and system administrators an enormous amount of flexibility in controlling access to their data and resources.

- **Fault tolerance features.** Windows NT includes significant *fault tolerance* features. Fault tolerance refers to the ability of a system to withstand various kinds of equipment failure. Windows NT includes several features that help to protect the computer and its data in the event of such failures. The first feature is its software support (in NT Server) for several types of RAID (Redundant Array of Inexpensive Disks), which uses technologies such as disk mirroring or disk striping with parity to offer data-redundancy on hard disks. With RAID, drive information can be recovered in the event of a failed hard disk. Another fault tolerance feature is Windows NT's built-in support for Uninterruptible Power Supply (UPS) devices. This support allows the system to communicate with the UPS and perform such tasks as notifying users and automatically shutting down the system in the event of a power outage.

- **Government C2 certification.** Windows NT is a class C2-certified operating system. C2 is a strict government standard that defines specific security features that must be present in US government installations. Any system applying for C2 status must have these features, and the system must pass a long and arduous testing process conducted by the government.

- **Audit trails.** Windows NT allows the tracking of many system events, including all security-related events that occur on a system. This process is known as *auditing*. These events are recorded in a log file, which may be examined by the system administrator. Auditing can reveal break-in attempts and other attempted security breaches and provides administrators a good record of who has accessed the system and how.

- **Ctrl+Alt+Del logon feature.** Part of Windows NT's security is a feature that is designed to break "password-grabbing" programs. These types of programs present a fake logon screen to a user in hopes of capturing a user name and password (for later use by some unauthorized party). In Windows NT, a user must press the Ctrl+Alt+Del keys before Windows NT will present the logon screen and allow the user to enter a name and password. You may know this key sequence as a system reboot or program shutdown command under MS-DOS and Windows 3.x. However, in Windows NT, Ctrl+Alt+Del is used to "wake up" the Windows NT logon manager. It guarantees that the Windows NT logon screen is genuine and not a password-capture program. This works because software cannot be written to capture and process the Ctrl+Alt+Del keyboard sequence.

Additional Features

Along with the features that meet Microsoft's design goals are a number of addtional features:

- **New platform support for PowerPC.** Windows NT Server offers unprecedented choice in hardware platforms, adding the PowerPC to the currently supported platforms: Intel x86, Pentium, DEC Alpha AXP, and MIPSRx400.

■ **Licensing and license management tools.** With the Windows NT Server 3.51 release, Microsoft extends the licensing model to include a Per Server (concurrent) licensing option. Windows NT Server 3.51 includes tools that assist network administrators in managing Client Access Licenses for Windows NT Server and all BackOffice products.

■ **Per file and per directory compression.** NTFS compression on a file and directory basis improves hard drive utilization.

■ **Remote Access Service (RAS) compression.** Added support for RAS software compression between Windows for Workgroups and Windows NT Server results in better throughput than modem compression, lowers the interrupt rate, and diminishes the risk of overruns.

■ **Network client administration for Windows 95.** This feature allows over-the-network installation of Windows 95 from a server-created startup disk.

■ **New device support.** Drivers included on the CD-ROM support more than 2,000 devices.

■ **Improved performance.** File server performance is up to 200 percent faster and uses 4 to 6 megabytes less memory.

■ **New IPX stack.** Multiple network and SPX II support improves performance.

■ **Gateway Service for NetWare.** This service allows users to access NetWare servers without running dual stacks at the client.

■ **Migration Tool for NetWare.** Migration Tool for NetWare aids network administrators by copying user accounts and files from NetWare Servers to a Windows NT Server while maintaining security.

■ **New TCP/IP transport stack.** Rewritten from the ground up, this stack is faster and smaller than the previous stack.

■ **Dynamic Host Configuration Program (DHCP).** DHCP assigns IP addresses dynamically from a centrally managed pool of addresses. It relieves administrators of the burden of assigning IP addresses to individual workstations and maintaining those addresses.

What's New in Version 4.0?

If you're upgrading from a previous version of Windows NT, you're probably anxious to know what new features await you in version 4.0. You'll be happy to know that there are a variety of major enhancements and additions in 4.0, changes that go well beyond a simple "facelift" of the Program Manager-style interface. We'll explore each of these important additions and changes in the following sections.

Windows 95 interface

The most anticipated change in Windows NT 4.0 is the addition of the
Windows 95-style Explorer interface, which has gained widespread acceptance and support due to Windows 95's popularity. This addition finally puts
Windows NT on a par with Windows 95 in terms of ease-of-use and interface
simplicity. In fact, the integration of the Windows 95 interface into Windows
NT is so well done that the two have become cosmetically indistinguishable
from one another. Figure 1-1 shows the Windows NT 4.0 desktop.

Figure 1-1: The Windows NT 4.0 desktop.

The Windows 95 interface gives Windows NT users a more integrated
desktop, one that blends the desktop and file system together into one
coherent unit. No more going to File Manager to manage drives and Program
Manager to manage icons; now you can perform all important system
operations from the same desktop, without the need for special applications. The new interface also introduces a variety of desktop features and
on-screen elements that will be unfamiliar to Windows NT users who have
never used Windows 95 before.

These features and screen elements are summarized in Table 1-1.

Table 1-1	New Windows NT 4.0 Interface Features
Screen element	*Description*
The Windows NT Desktop	The desktop is a dynamic area that can contain a variety of screen elements including files, folders, and program shortcuts. It can, therefore, act as a launching pad for applications as well as a folder for storage (which may in turn contain subfolders that appear on the desktop). The Windows NT desktop maps to an actual folder (or directory) on the hard disk and is located in the C:\<*winnt_root*>\PROFILES\ <*username*> folder, where <*winnt_root*> is the Windows NT installation directory, and <*username*> is the currently logged-on user.
Shortcut	A shortcut is identical to a Windows 3.x icon. It acts as a pointer to an application, which if double-clicked, launches the application.
Folder	A folder represents one of two things: a directory on the hard disk, or a desktop folder that contains files or shortcuts.
Taskbar	The taskbar is an ever-present, movable screen bar that houses the Start button (see next entry), shows all running applications and currently open desktop folders, and displays the time and a volume control icon.
Start Button	The Start button is part of the taskbar. Clicking the Start button opens a menu that allows access to all Windows NT 4.0 programs; recently edited documents; settings such as Control Panel and Printers folders; and a Find, Help, and Run Option, as well as a Shutdown command.
Recycle Bin	The Recycle Bin functions as a disposal unit for unwanted files, folders, and shortcuts. You drag and drop items onto the Recycle Bin to delete them; however, they are retained in the Recycle Bin until the Bin is emptied manually by the user or becomes larger than its configured maximum size.
My Computer	The My Computer icon represents the computer being used. Double-clicking the icon shows all of the primary system components, including icons representing all system drives, any network-attached drives, and the Control Panel and Printers folders.
Network Neighborhood	The Network Neighborhood icon is present when networking is enabled on your Windows NT system. Double-clicking this icon reveals a list of all known networks, servers, and network shares. The icons represented in this list may be used to map drives and printers locally using the mouse.

While developing the Explorer (Windows 95-style) interface, Microsoft did an unprecedented amount of research on what kinds of features might make Windows easier to navigate and control. The result was a user interface that is powerful, yet surprisingly simplistic in appearance. Above all, the interface has been designed to make Windows NT easier to use, without hindering or limiting its power in any way. By combining this interface with the power of the Windows NT operating system, the Windows world now has a product capable of suiting the needs of both regular users and power users.

Application Programming Interfaces

Among the new additions in Windows NT 4.0 are new Application Programming Interfaces (APIs) for software developers. APIs allow developers to incorporate Windows NT 4.0 features into their applications. These new APIs include both Windows NT versions of existing APIs presented in Windows 95 and completely new APIs developed specifically for Windows NT 4.0.

Table 1-2 lists Windows NT 4.0's new APIs.

Table 1-2	New Windows NT 4.0 APIs
API name	*Capabilities/Features*
Telephony API (TAPI) and Unimodem	Allows for integration of computers and telephone equipment such as voice mail, fax, and so on. The Unimodem specification allows all applications to share a modem driver (as is done with printers). This API also includes functionality required for use of Microsoft Exchange and The Microsoft Network.
Cryptograph API (CAPI)	Allows developers to create custom data encryption features in their products. This is a new Windows NT feature and is not present in the Windows 95 product.
Distributed Component Object Model (DCOM, a.k.a. Network OLE)	Extends the OLE specification (which allows Windows applications on a single PC to share data objects) to include applications running on different computers across the network. This is another new feature in Windows NT 4.0 and does not exist in Windows 95.
DirectX API support	A collection of multimedia APIs important for games and graphics applications. These APIs allow hardware acceleration for this type of software, even with multiple applications running simultaneously.

(continued)

Table 1-2 *(Continued)*

API name	Capabilities/features
Disk Defragmentation API	This new API assists disk utility developers in creating disk defragmentation (optimization) utilities for Windows NT volumes. This was a difficult task in previous versions of Windows NT. It forced applications to be tied to particular versions and required Service Pack updates to Windows NT.
Internet Server API (ISAPI)	The Internet Server API is used by Internet-related applications running on Windows NT Server such as the Perl-like scripting language included in the Internet Information Server (IIS) product (IIS is shipped with and incorporated into Windows NT Server 4.0).

Networking features

The Windows NT 4.0 product improves on Windows NT networking in several key areas. This includes better integration with the Internet and NetWare 4.x and tools to administer a Windows NT Server from a Windows NT 4.0 workstation.

Table 1-3 lists the new Windows NT 4.0 networking features:

Table 1-3   New Windows NT Networking Features

Feature	Description
NetWare 4.x and NDS Support	Windows NT 4.0 now includes a NetWare Directory Services (NDS)-aware client redirector, which supports execution of NetWare 4.x logon scripts. (Note that Novell has also developed a NetWare 4.x Client for Windows NT 4.0.)
WINS/DNS Integration	Windows NT now includes a TCP/IP name resolution feature which integrates the Windows Internet Name Services (WINS) and the Internet-standard Domain Name Services (DNS) standards. This is a significant improvement and means (among other things) that Windows NT 4.0 workstations can access a Windows NT 4.0 Server across the Internet. It removes any need for network administrators to manually maintain LMHOSTS files (which map machine names to their TCP/IP addresses).

Feature	Description
Peer Web Services	Peer Web Services allow you to create a personal Internet (or Intranet if used internally only) World Wide Web server on your Windows NT computer.
Distributed Component Object Model (DCOM, a.k.a. Network OLE)	This feature extends the OLE specification (which allows Windows applications on a single PC to share data objects) to include applications running on different computers across the network. This is a new feature in Windows NT 4.0 and does not exist in Windows 95.
Domain Logon via Dial-Up Networking	Windows NT 4.0 includes a new feature that allows you to log on to a Windows NT Domain using Dial-Up Networking. This provides an easy way for remote domain clients to obtain authentication from a domain server without the problems that existed in previous versions of Windows NT.
Windows NT Server Administration Tools (a.k.a. The Nexus Tools)	Windows NT Server administration applications (using the Windows 95-style interface), such as User Manager for Domains and Server Manager for Domains, allow graphics administration of a Windows NT Server from a Windows NT 4.0 (or Windows 95) system.
Enhanced Metafile-based (EMS) Print Spooling	EMS print spooling allows faster network printing by offloading the majority of print-job rendering to the print server rather than to the client PC.

Relocation of Win32 graphics components

One of the most important and controversial changes in Windows NT 4.0 involves the restructuring of the Windows NT graphics subsystem, which is part of the Win32 subsystem.

An unfortunate side effect of Windows NT's internal client/server architecture is a performance penalty for graphics applications. This occurs because these kinds of applications, which run in User Mode, continually request low-level graphics functions residing in Kernel Mode. As a result, Windows NT must constantly switch the processor back and forth between User Mode and Kernel Mode (an event known as *context-switching*). This switching back and forth creates overhead and imposes a severe performance penalty for graphics-intensive applications. In order to combat this problem, it was necessary for Microsoft to incorporate several of the key graphics-related components of Windows NT directly into the Windows NT Executive (which runs in Kernel Mode). Specifically, three components were moved: the Windows Manager, Graphics Device Interface (GDI), and Graphics Device Drivers (GDD).

The advantage of this relocation is that graphics applications such as CAD software, imaging software, and games run significantly faster under Windows NT 4.0 than under previous versions of Windows NT. The potential disadvantage to this move is that these graphics functions now have direct access to low-level system services, and Windows NT's reliability could be compromised if a vendor's graphics driver had problems. However, the magnitude of the performance benefits is such that this trade-off is generally considered worthwhile.

Other features

In addition to those already mentioned, Windows NT 4.0 includes a host of other new features, including

- **486 emulation.** For RISC-based machines, the MS-DOS and Windows 3.x subsystems of Windows NT 4.0 provide Intel 80486-level emulation. For the first time, this allows RISC machines to run Windows 3.x 386 Enhanced mode applications; previous support was only for standard-mode applications. This feature also significantly improves the performance of x86-based applications running on RISC-based Windows NT systems.

- **Hardware profile support.** Like Windows 95, Windows NT 4.0 now supports hardware profiles that allow users to select different hardware configurations at system startup. Each profile includes information on which video resolution, services, and drivers should be used for that configuration. This is especially useful for laptop users who use docking stations or attach to an office network.

- **System Policy Editor.** First introduced with Windows 95, the System Policy Editor has also found its way into the Windows NT 4.0 product. This application allows administrators to set system "policies" for Windows NT 4.0 Workstation, including what features users see and don't see, what environmental features they can modify, etc.

- **Faster graphics and user interface.** One of the more important (and controversial) structural changes to Windows NT 4.0 is the incorporation of the Graphics Device Interface (GDI) and User layers of the Windows NT environment out of the Win32 subsystem and into the Windows NT Executive. This was done to provide faster execution of applications, especially those that make heavy use of graphics. Incorporation of GDI and User into the Windows NT Kernel allows these subsystems to respond many times faster to these applications than was possible under Windows NT 3.x.

- **Joystick support.** Windows NT 4.0 includes built-in support for joysticks, a previously missing feature that prevented Windows NT from being a viable platform for games in the past.

- **Internet Explorer 2.0.** Another Windows 95 favorite, the Internet Explorer 2.0 is also included in Windows NT 4.0. The Internet Explorer is a World Wide Web (WWW) browser that seamlessly integrates with the Windows NT 4.0 desktop, allowing users to, among other things, place shortcuts to their favorite Web sites right on the Windows NT desktop.

- **The Microsoft Network.** Although The Microsoft Network is not included with the shipping version of Windows NT 4.0, users may download a free add-on that allows Windows NT to access The Microsoft Network (MSN), Microsoft's on-line service. Like other online services such as CompuServe, America Online, and Prodigy, MSN offers a variety of informational services including file downloads, e-mail, news, discussion forums, information databases, and the like. As with the Internet Explorer, MSN has the advantage that it integrates seamlessly with the Windows NT 4.0 desktop and uses a Windows 95/NT-style metaphor for its interface. Users can place shortcuts to on-line areas such as chat rooms and file download areas right on the Windows NT desktop.

- **CD-ROM enhancements.** Windows NT 4.0 includes several enhancements to the CD-ROM File System (CDFS), including support for the CD-XA (eXtended Audio) format and the AutoPlay feature introduced in Windows 95. AutoPlay enables an AutoPlay-aware CD-ROM application to start automatically as soon as the CD-ROM is inserted in the drive.

- **Microsoft Plus.** Microsoft has incorporated many of the features found in Windows 95's optional Microsoft Plus! package into Windows NT 4.0. These features include special screen savers, background wallpaper graphics, and some new system utilities. One screensaver in particular, "3D Maze," is an OpenGL-based application that astoundingly demonstrates Windows NT's graphics capabilities.

- **Device drivers and support.** As with any new version of Windows, Windows NT 4.0 further extends the list of supported hardware devices. This support has been updated to include many of today's most popular printers, CD-ROM drives, tape drives, video displays, network interface cards, and so on. A formal list of supported devices, known as the NT Hardware Compatibility List (HCL), is available from Microsoft.

- **New desktop accessories, utilities, and games.** Last but not least, what would a new version of Windows be without cool, new desktop accessories and games? Windows NT 4.0 includes a variety of new utilities and desktop accessories, such as a phone dialer, HyperTerminal (a new communications program), WordPad (a combination of Write and Notepad), a CD player application, Paint (a 32-bit successor to PaintBrush), and much more. Also included are a few new games: FreeCell (a card game), Pinball (a 3-D pinball game), and Hover! (a 3-D virtual-reality maze game).

Features removed from Windows NT 4.0

The Windows NT 4.0 product is somewhat unusual in that the list of features *removed* from Windows NT 4.0 is nearly as extensive as the list of features added. Some Windows NT 3.x users may be in for a surprise when they upgrade to Windows NT 4.0, because a variety of older devices and technologies have been purposefully excluded from version 4.0.

The most significant omission is the removal of support for PCs based on the 386 processor. The 486 processor is now the minimum CPU required for a Windows NT system. Support for 5.25-inch floppy disk drives and some older SCSI host adapters has also been removed. Finally, support has been removed for the OS/2 High Performance File System (HPFS). However, it is possible to re-enable HPFS support using some special tricks.

Although support for a number of older SCSI host adapters has been removed in Windows NT 4.0, support driver disks can be created from the \retired directory found on the Windows NT CD-ROM.

Differences between Windows NT 4.0 and Windows 95

Misconceptions about the differences between Windows NT and Windows 95 abound these days. So if you're feeling confused about how Windows NT and Windows 95 differ, you're definitely not alone. It is somewhat unfortunate that Microsoft has done very little in their marketing campaigns to clear up this confusion or clarify for users the differences between these sibling versions of Windows.

In this section, we'll discuss exactly how the Windows 95 and Windows NT products compare and what the strengths and weaknesses of each system are.

A Path Not Taken

The most important differences between Windows NT and Windows 95 are related to their basic design and structure. These differences arise from the two system's different design goals and priorities, as set forth by Microsoft during their development. Specifically, Windows NT sacrifices some compatibility with Windows 3.x and DOS applications in order to maintain its design goal of reliability. Windows 95, on the other hand, has compatibility with existing DOS and Windows 3.x applications as its primary design goal, which is sometimes accomplished at the expense of reliability. This is a common theme we will see as we compare the two systems — for almost every advantage there is a corresponding trade-off or disadvantage. As such, the question of which operating system is better can only be answered after examining the environment in which it will be used.

Windows NT is a 32-bit operating system through and through. Unfortunately, the same cannot be said for Windows 95. Although much of Windows 95's code is 32-bit, a significant amount of 16-bit code remains. This was done for several reasons, one of which was better compatibility with existing Windows 3.x (16-bit) applications. The developers of Windows 95 went to great trouble to ensure that existing MS-DOS and Windows 3.x applications would run the same under Windows 95 as they did under Windows 3.x. This was necessary for Windows 95 to gain acceptance as the successor to the Windows 3.x product line. Still other code was left 16-bit for a more obvious reason: developmental time constraints imposed by Windows 95's shipping deadline.

Note

Although Windows 95's usage of 16-bit code is fairly well-known, the ramifications of this were not well understood until a recent news item regarding Intel's Pentium Pro, Intel's latest-generation processor which is specifically optimized for use with 32-bit code. While testing Windows 95 on a variety of new Pentium Pro systems, several independent testing labs discovered that Pentium Pro systems actually ran Windows 95 *slower* than comparable Pentium systems. This slow-down was immediately attributed to Windows 95's continued use of 16-bit code, which the Pentium Pro does not handle as efficiently as the original Pentium processor.

Another distinction between Windows 95 and Windows NT relates to their differing methods of supporting 16-bit MS-DOS and Windows applications. The different methods are related directly to each operating system's basic design. As you already have heard, Windows NT completely removes DOS from the core operating system, providing support via an MS-DOS compatibility subsystem known as a Virtual DOS Machine (VDM).

Windows 95, on the other hand, provides more intrinsic support for MS-DOS applications. Windows 95 does not completely remove MS-DOS from the core operating system services as does Windows NT. As with the DOS/Windows arrangement found in Windows 3.x, DOS can be found lying just underneath the surface in Windows 95. Although the DOS included in Windows 95 is a far superior, improved MS-DOS, it is DOS nonetheless. This continued presence becomes evident when working with Windows 95 for any period of time, from its "restart in DOS-mode" shutdown menu option to its ability to run DOS applications in "exclusive" mode by unloading virtually all of the Windows 95 operating system from memory. The bottom line? Windows NT provides excellent MS-DOS and Windows 3.x compatibility (roughly 95 percent of existing MS-DOS and Windows 3.x applications run on Windows NT), but Windows 95's support is better. This makes sense when you consider that one of Windows 95's primary design goals was DOS and Windows 3.x compatibility, whereas Windows NT has a much broader range of design goals (of which DOS and Windows 3.x support is only one).

MS-DOS and Windows 3.x compatibility is one of the few areas in which Windows 95 is superior to Windows NT. It should be noted that it is unlikely that Windows NT will ever catch up to Windows 95 in this department, because major improvements in compatibility would almost certainly require a major compromise of system stability (such as allowing direct hardware access). Because such changes would be in direct conflict with Windows NT's primary goals, it is unlikely that they will be made.

Longevity

Windows 95 is in many ways a transitional operating system, acting as a bridge for users to cross over from the 16-bit world of DOS and Windows 3.x to the world of 32-bit Windows applications. Because of its design limitations, Windows 95 does not have the same opportunity as Windows NT for longevity in the marketplace. Unlike Windows NT, Windows 95 maintains an architecture that is inherently tied to the Intel x86 processor family. Windows NT's broader hardware support and ability to easily incorporate new technologies (such as new processors, file systems, and APIs) positions it as the operating system of both today and tomorrow.

As a bridge between Windows 3.x and Windows NT, Windows 95's major contribution may be that of bringing Windows 32-bit applications to the masses. This may, in turn, pave the way for long-term acceptance of Windows NT on the desktop. It should be noted that as of this writing, Windows 95 may have at least one version left in it. Microsoft has shown previews of an upgrade to Windows 95 which is currently under development and slated for a 1997 release (to be named Windows 97, perhaps?).

Hardware Requirements

One of the key differences between Windows 95 and Windows NT is in their minimum requirements for system hardware. Any system running Windows NT 4.0 requires 12 MB RAM minimum, whereas Windows 95 can run in only 8 MB of RAM.

Note

Despite the stated minimums, I have seen Windows NT load and run in 8 MB and Windows 95 in 4 MB; however, these are not ideal situations. Anemic environments such as these cause either system to load at an excruciatingly slow pace due to the heavy usage of virtual memory (hard disk space used as if it were RAM). Also, the number of applications you are effectively able to multi-task is greatly reduced. Although the minimum RAM recommended for Windows NT and Windows 95 is 12 MB and 8 MB respectively, for best performance, a Windows NT Workstation system should contain 16 MB or more, and a Windows 95 system should contain 12 MB of RAM or more.

Owners of either system should have at least 150 MB of hard disk space free prior to installation. Although the actual amount of disk space occupied by either operating system will range from 65 to 105 MB depending on the options chosen, the system will also need space for a disk paging file (which allows the system to use hard disk space as additional RAM). You'll probably also want to have some space left over to put a few applications on your new system!

Finally, having experimented with both Windows NT and Windows 95 on a wide variety of different hardware configurations, I recommend that you not consider anything less than a 486/25 MHz or 386/40 MHz processor for Windows 95, and nothing less than a 486/50 MHz processor for Windows NT. And as with any computer system, more is better, if you can afford it.

Table 1-4 lists both Microsoft's and the author's recommended minimum configurations for both Windows NT and Windows 95.

Table 1-4	Windows NT and Windows 95 Hardware Configurations	
Operating system	*Recommended minimums (Microsoft)*	*Recommended minimums (Author)*
Windows 95	Any 80386-based system with 4 MB RAM, VGA display, 65 MB free disk space	80486/25 MHz or 386/40 MHz or faster system, at least 12 MB RAM, Super VGA display (640x480x256 colors), 130 MB free disk space
Windows NT Workstation 4.0	Any 80486-based system, 12 MB RAM, a CD-ROM drive, VGA display, 100 MB free disk space	80486/50 MHz or better CPU, at least 16 MB RAM, a 4x or faster CD-ROM drive, a Super VGA display (640x480x256 colors), 150 MB free disk space

Note

RISC-based system installations will require additional hard disk space over Intel-based installations. For RISC systems, add approximately 25 percent to the overall free disk space requirement.

Choosing Between Windows 95 and Windows NT 4.0

Usually, the answer to the question "Windows 95 or Windows NT?" can be determined by the needs of the particular user. The hardware present in the system can also be a determining factor, since the two platforms have distinctly different minimum requirements. Computers with minimal RAM or CPU resources (for example, a 386 or 486 PC with 8 MB of RAM) will have only one real choice: Windows 95. In addition, there are many users who do not require the power and wealth of features found in Windows NT, and for these users, Windows 95 is often sufficient.

In order to help with this decision-making process, Table 1-5 offers a comparison of each system's strengths and weaknesses.

Table 1-5	Windows NT and Windows 95 Feature Comparison	
Feature	*Windows 95*	*Windows NT*
Performance	Can be faster than Windows NT when running a single application due to lower operating system overhead; slower on 32-bit optimized processors than Windows NT due to usage of some 16-bit code	Can be slower than Windows 95 with a single application running, faster with a heavy application load due to more efficient multi-tasking features; faster than Windows 95 on 32-bit optimized processors due to 100 percent 32-bit design
Reliability	Although stability is much better than Windows 3.x, and bad applications can generally be shut down, the operating system is not completely protected and crashed applications can interfere with the operating system and each other	Extremely reliable operating system; provides superior memory protection, which prevents errant applications from interfering with the operating system or with one another; far less prone to system lockups than Windows 95
Multi-processor support	None; single processor only	Supports up to 32 concurrent processors
Multi-platform support	Intel x86 family only	Supports Intel 486 or later processors, as well as MIPS, PowerPC, and DEC Alpha
32-bit application support	Full support for Win32 API	Full support for Win32 API and 32-bit POSIX applications
Compatibility (with Legacy Applications)	Best compatibility with MS-DOS and Windows 3.x applications	Excellent compatibility with MS-DOS and Windows 3.x applications; also supports POSIX and OS/2 1.x character-mode applications
Laptop computer support	Excellent support, including laptop power-saving features and PC Card (PCMCIA) support	Poor support; no power-savings features supported and limited PC Card (PCMCIA) support
Fault tolerance features	None	Support for UPS interface as well as software RAID levels 0, 1 and 5 (in Windows NT Server)
Internet connectivity	Excellent Internet connectivity features, including Internet e-mail support (Exchange) and World Wide Web browser (Internet Explorer)	Excellent Internet connectivity features, including Internet e-mail support (Exchange) and World Wide Web browser (Internet Explorer)
Data compression	Yes; requires you to compress entire partition	Yes; allows you to selectively compress individual files and directories

Choosing Between Windows NT Workstation and Windows NT Server

Windows NT comes in two different flavors: Windows NT Workstation (formerly called Windows NT in version 3.1), and Windows NT Server (formerly called Windows NT Advanced Server in version 3.1). Both of these products have a unique set of features and strengths and are intended for use in different applications.

Table 1-6 compares the features available in Windows NT Workstation and Windows NT Server.

Table 1-6	Comparison of Windows NT Workstation and Server	
Feature	**Windows NT Workstation**	**Windows NT Server**
Application performance	Optimized for maximum responsiveness of foreground applications	Optimized for server applications and evenly distributed performance of all background tasks
Maximum number of processors	2	32 (systems using more than 4 CPUs require a custom HAL supplied by the hardware vendor or Microsoft)
Maximum number of simultaneous Remote Access Server connections	1	256
Maximum number of simultaneous network client connections to system	10	Unlimited
Domain security model support	No (by itself; requires presence of Windows NT Server to use domain security)	Yes
Macintosh file and printer sharing allowed	No	Yes (NTFS volume required for Macintosh-accessible volumes)
RAID support (Disk Fault Tolerance)	None (RAID 0 disk striping, a non-fault tolerant RAID level, is supported)	RAID 1 (disk mirroring and duplexing) and RAID 5 (disk striping with parity)
Built-in Internet server applications	No	Yes; Internet Information Server (includes a World Wide Web, Gopher, and FTP server)

Although they differ in terms of features and focus, both Windows NT Workstation and Windows NT Server share the same basic construction and code base. This has several advantages, because applications that work on one system generally work on the other, and they can both be upgraded with the same Service Pack updates.

Generally speaking, Windows NT Workstation 4.0 should be used in the same situations where one might use any other client operating system such as Windows 95 or Windows 3.x. It should also be used for high-performance, workstation-level systems doing advanced graphics, CAD, or computational work.

Windows NT Server should be used on systems that act as network servers, such as file, print, application, or communication servers. It should also be used in situations where one of Windows NT Server's unique features is required, such as the ability to create a Macintosh-accessible disk volume or provide multiple Remote Access connections to the system.

Summary

This chapter covered:

▶ Key features of Windows NT

▶ Features new to version 4.0

▶ Differences between Windows NT 4.0 and Windows 95

▶ How to choose between Windows 95 and Windows NT 4.0

▶ How to choose between Windows NT Workstation and Windows NT Server

Chapter 2

Redefining the Enterprise Network

T raditionally, the enterprise network has consisted of a network of clients (either dumb terminals or PCs with emulators) connected to one or more wholly dedicated servers. This arrangement, designed to suit the hierarchy, asserted the primacy of the server that held all data and applications. In this setup, the client workstations didn't have anything to offer one another, so there was no need for them to be able to see each other across the network wire.

However, with the advent of smaller, more powerful computers, the centralized Information System (IS) mode has become outdated. With powerful networking built into the operating system, suites of applications, and plenty of room to store data, Windows NT offers users many ways to network. Right out of the box, it's a good network citizen, since it connects to NT Server, NetWare, and a host of other operating systems. Combine that with each workstation's ability to share files and directories with other network users, and the network ceases to be a centralized entity. Instead, it becomes a web of interconnections that empowers users and increases productivity.

Everybody's a Peer

In a workgroup model, users share and manage resources that are distributed among multiple computers. In fact, the resources and the administration of a workgroup environment are distributed throughout the network. In a sense, each user is a network administrator who manages his or her own machine.

For practical purposes, think of a workgroup as a set of machines, logically grouped together under a single name (the workgroup name). Computers in this logical group can be used to send messages to the single name and have multiple machines receive the message. These computers can also be used for *browsing* — the ability to list the machines in a group. For example, browsing occurs when you use programs such as File Manager to establish network drive connections. Having computers in workgroups helps to organize the machines on the screen, thus making it easier to locate the correct machine to make the connection.

In a workgroup network, each computer maintains its own security and has its own user accounts and groups; therefore, each computer must be administered separately. Each individual user is responsible for granting access rights and permissions, issuing passwords, and establishing resource share points.

Examples of workgroup computers are MS-DOS workgroup clients, Windows for Workgroup computers, and Windows NT Workstation or Server computers participating in a workgroup.

The workgroup model works well for small groups that do not have a lot of servers or accounts that need to be maintained. Users in this model log on to their local machine. A user enters a user name and password for remote server logon when accessing other computers in the workgroup or when accessing a computer in a domain.

The workgroup "binds" the machines together via broadcast packets, which it sends periodically. These broadcasts ensure that the browser information (list of workstations in your domain) stays up-to-date and remains accurate.

You should use workgroups in the following situations:

- If there is no centralized security in your environment
- If there is no centralized server and no client-server-based application, such as SNA Server
- If users are comfortable with network commands and procedures

Table 2-1 summarizes the advantages and disadvantages of using a workgroup type of network.

Table 2-1   Workgroup Advantages and Disadvantages

Advantages	*Disadvantages*
Each user is in full control of his or her workstation and resources.	No centralized control. No method for establishing or enforcing security rules or regulations.
	If a user forgets the administrator password, there is no way to regain administrator control of the machine.

Advantages	Disadvantages
Less expensive. The operating system can be Windows for Workgroups or Windows NT.	Intangible cost of requiring users to be part-time system administrators.
No need for a network administrator because administrative tasks fall to each workstation user.	Additional training and responsibility required at the user level. Additional impact on user's time, associated with network management, not line of business.
Easiest to establish and administrate. You simply install the machines and let the users do the administration.	

Keep in mind that you should use the NetBEUI protocol. If you are using TCP/IP or IPX, all workstations in a workgroup must reside on a single subnet. Also, you should have no more than 50 workstations to a workgroup to help reduce broadcast traffic.

Grouping Computers

The domain concept adds central administration to the workgroups' function of collecting machines together for messaging and browsing. Whereas each workgroup machine has its own security information and requires each user to manage his or her workstation, a domain has a single machine, the primary domain controller (PDC), which serves as the single security point.

To avoid problems that might occur if the primary domain controller were lost, additional servers [the domain servers or backup domain controllers (BDC)] can be added. The security information automatically replicates from the PDC to the BDCs on a periodic basis.

Because there is a centralized security system, more security options can be made available. These options include

- Centralized administration
- Required user logons
- Logon scripts
- Home directories
- Control of logon time and location

All of these features can help to increase the security of your network and its data, as well as make user operations easier and more controlled by automatically performing certain tasks during the logon script. Table 2-2 lists the advantages and disadvantages of a domain.

Table 2-2	Domain Advantages and Disadvantages
Advantages	*Disadvantages*
Centralized security management.	Designated system administrator(s).
Individual users must work within the constructs of security policy.	
Fewer employees need to be trained as system administrators.	More expensive. The operating system must be Windows NT Server.
Greater security and control of security options.	More tasks to install and harder to recover from forgotten administrator passwords, absent employees, and so forth.

You should use domains in the following situations:

■ If centralized security exists or is preferred in your environment

■ If you run client-server-based applications, such as SQL Server or SNA Server

■ If users are comfortable with network commands and procedures

If you're using NetBEUI or SPX/IPX, all machines in a given domain must be in the same subnet.

If it is configured properly, a Windows NTS machine can also be used for an SQL Server, SNA Server, and so on. However, Windows NTS should not be used as a user workstation.

Whenever possible, it is best to have at least one BDC per domain.

Windows NT Workstations in a Domain

For each Windows NT Workstation on your network, you can have the workstation participate in a Server domain or a workgroup. In most cases, you will want each Windows NT Workstation to join a domain for two purposes:

■ To get access to the domain accounts

■ To allow users to log on to the domain at the initial logon screen of the workstation

A Windows NT workgroup workstation can be part of a domain for browsing purposes only and yet maintain its own security. This is analogous to LAN Manager stand-alone servers and is accomplished by configuring the computer to be in a workgroup and assigning the workgroup name the same name as the domain.

How a Windows NT Workstation joins a domain

A Windows NT Workstation that participates in a domain does not actually get a copy of the domain's user database, but it can use user accounts and global groups from its domain (and any domain trusted by that domain) via pass-through authentication.

Joining a domain can be done in two ways; each way requires domain administrator privileges because the domain accounts are shared to the workstation (not just anyone should get access to the domain accounts).

To join a domain if the user at the workstation has domain administrator privileges

1. Use the network Control Panel applet to change to the requested domain.

2. Create a computer account in that domain by providing a domain administrator account name and password in the dialog box. The user can also provide the information in the setup program if the computer is being installed.

To join a domain if the user at the workstation does not have domain administrator privileges

1. The domain administrator gives the user permission to join the domain by adding the computer to Server Manager.

2. The user changes domains with the network Control Panel applet or installs the workstation with that domain name. Because the computer account has already been created, the bottom portion of the Change Domains dialog box can be ignored.

Initial logon at a Windows NT domain workstation

After a Windows NT computer has joined a domain, the From field on the initial screen will list the computer, the domain, and any trusted domains as places where logon accounts may exist. Remember that accounts in each of these security systems are different even though they may share the same name.

Users log on to the security system where their account exists. Remember: The user name and password of the user — not where the user is authenticated for initial logon — will affect server logons.

Server logon from a Windows NT domain workstation

When a user in the domain attempts to connect to a Windows NT domain workstation, and the workstation knows the domain name, the workstation communicates with a Server in the domain to authenticate the user via pass-through authentication. The Windows NT domain workstation takes the user and group information returned from the server to create an access token for the user.

If the workstation does not know the domain name, it looks in its own separate local user account database to authenticate the account and creates an access token locally.

Using accounts at a Windows NT domain workstation

In addition to the user accounts and local groups on a Windows NT Workstation, a domain workstation has access to the domain global accounts and local user accounts. Local groups on the workstation can contain each of these domain accounts as well as local user accounts.

Understanding Domains

The basic unit of security and centralized administration in Windows NT is the domain, a logical grouping of servers and workstations. A Windows NT domain network consists of one or more domains housed at one site or

---

LAN Manager Servers

A LAN Manager for OS/2 Server can also participate as a backup or member server in a domain but not as the primary controller. A LAN Manager Server can also be configured as a stand-alone in a domain so that it appears in browse lists but does not share user account information. If a LAN Manager Server tries to start as a primary domain controller, all of the server computers will send a response prohibiting the server from doing so.

The LAN Manager for OS/2 backup/member Servers maintain a copy of the same accounts as the domain controllers in the domain. However, just as Windows NT Workstations participating in a domain, only domain global groups, not domain local groups, can be used on the server.

LAN Manager Server logons for remote access from Windows NT clients work seamlessly. However, LAN Manager Servers cannot respond to an initial logon request from a Windows NT client because they do not have all of the security information needed to allow the user to log on. A LAN Manager Server can authenticate the initial logon requests of other clients such as LAN Manager MS-DOS and OS/2 clients, as well as Windows for Workgroups clients.

spanning different sites. The minimum requirement for a domain is one server running Windows NT Server, which serves as the primary domain controller (PDC) and stores the master copy of the domain's user and group database. A domain can include other servers running Windows NT Server and acting as backup domain controllers (BDCs). It can also include Windows NT Server computers running as standard servers, LAN Manager 2.x Servers, Windows NT Workstation clients, and other clients, such as those running Windows for Workgroups and MS-DOS.

Domain concepts

In order to understand the details of domain implementation, you need to understand basic domain components — accounts, servers, and domains — and the interaction between these components.

Windows NT security requires users to be identified to the system. Therefore, each person who regularly uses the network must have a user account on a domain in the network. Guest access may be allowed for users without user accounts who need limited access to the network.

The scope of an account (user or group) has normally only applied to a workgroup workstation or a single domain. With Windows NT Server security, the security context has now been expanded to include trusted domains and computers in the domain that do not have an exact copy of the domain-wide account database (that is, Windows NT domain workstations and LAN Manager 2.x Servers).

To accommodate this expansion, the server has two types of accounts: local and global. The name refers to where the account can be used rather than what the account contains. These types of accounts are discussed in detail in the section, *Groups*.

Assigning Accounts

In order to identify users to the system, an administrator creates user accounts by assigning user names to new user accounts. When this happens, Windows NT generates a security identifier (SID) for each new account. Each user account SID uniquely identifies the user, regardless of when or where the account was created. This information is stored in the Security Account Manager (SAM) database in the Windows NT Registry and includes such data as

- The user name that identifies an individual account

- The account's password

- Groups of which the account is a member

- Initialization information, including home directory and logon script

- Restrictions on how the user can use the network

Each user account requires approximately 1 K in the SAM. The database is located on the PDC for the domain or on a PDC in the master domain. The password information for the account is stored doubly encrypted for security purposes.

Windows NT Server 4.0 allows a user to maintain a single user account to gain access to the domain, including other servers in the domain. If trust relationships are established, that single user account can also gain access to servers in other domains that trust the account domain.

The user account database is replicated between the PDCs and all BDCs in the domain on a regular basis. The replication allows the logon process to be handled by the PDC or any BDC, which increases throughput and helps eliminate bottlenecks during the logon process.

Machine Accounts

When a workstation, server, or BDC is added to a domain, Windows NT generates an account for the machine name. The machine accounts serve various purposes, including linking BDCs with the PDC and pairing up the trusting and trusted domains.

Groups

To simplify administration of user accounts that have similar resource needs, the administrator can categorize the user accounts into *groups*, which makes granting access rights and resource permissions easier. Instead of performing many individual actions to grant certain rights or permissions, the administrator can perform a single action that gives a group — and all the present and future members of that group — that right or permission. Changing access rights is a simple task; changing the rights of the group will automatically change the rights of all group members. Group accounts are also stored in the SAM. The size of a group account may vary, based on the number of user accounts associated with the group. A good rule of thumb is that each group account requires 4 K in the SAM.

Windows NT Server provides built-in local groups and the ability to create custom global groups. Administrators should use built-in local groups whenever possible.

Local Groups

Local groups define permissions to resources only within the domain in which the local group exists. Hence, the term *local* defines the scope of the resource permissions granted to users within the group. Local groups may contain users and global groups from the local domain (but not other local groups), as well as users and global groups from trusted domains. However, a local group can only be assigned permissions and rights in its home domain.

Local groups are local to the security system in which they are created. With a Windows NT workgroup workstation, this means the group will only be used on the workstation itself. With a server domain group, this means the group will only be used on the servers in the domain.

Not only are local groups an effective way of collectively assigning user rights and permissions for a set of users within the home domain, but they can also be used to gather numerous global groups and users from other domains. This allows an administrator to change access to domain resources globally with a single modification to the local group permissions.

The best group strategy to implement in the multiple master domain model is to create local groups in the resource domains. Those local groups will hold the global groups from the account domains.

Default Local Groups

Windows NT automatically creates default user groups during installation. The default user groups make it easy for the system administrator to assign users rights, that is, give users different levels of control over the computer. This level of control is sometimes referred to as the *privilege level* of a user. Table 2-3 lists the default user groups for Windows NT Workstation and Server. As the table shows, the groups are quite similar.

Table 2-3	Default User Groups
Windows NT Workstation	***Windows NT Server***
Administrators. An account that gives its members full access to the system. If an administrator has not been given access permissions to a resource, he or she can take ownership of the resource and get full access.	Administrators. An account that gives its members full access to the system. If an administrator has not been given access permissions to a resource, he or she can take ownership of the resource and get full access.
Users. An account for normal operations such as running programs and managing files.	Users. An account for normal operations such as running programs and managing files.
Guests. An account that controls access permissions for people who use the system infrequently.	Guests. An account that controls access permissions for people who use the system infrequently.
Replicator. An account used by the replicator server to maintain security during file replication.	Replicator. An account used by the replicator server to maintain security during file replication.
Backup operators. An account that allows users to back up and restore files to a backup medium regardless of the permissions of the user.	Backup operators. An account that allows users to back up and restore files to a backup medium regardless of the permissions of the user.
Power users. Same as a user account with the added ability to share resources and create non-administrator accounts.	Server operators. Allows users to share resources at the server (printers and files), lock the server, back up and restore files, and shut down the server.

(continued)

Table 2-3 *(Continued)*

Windows NT Workstation	Windows NT Server
Account operators. Allows users to modify and change user and group accounts. Certain accounts such as Administrators, Server, Account, Print, and Backup Operators cannot be modified by a user with this privilege level.	
Print operators. Allows users to manage printers and printer shares in the domain.	

Besides these default groups, which refer to the privilege level of a user, there is a second type of default group that contains no members. This type of group refers to how computer resources are accessed. The groups have no members because they apply to any account that is using the computer in a specified way. These four groups include

- **Interactive users.** Users who only log on to the computer interactively.

- **Network users.** Users who connect to the computer over the network.

- **Everyone.** Every user who accesses the computer, including interactive and network users.

- **Creator/owner.** The user who created or took ownership of a resource.

Global Groups

Global groups are groups that can be utilized in other domains. In fact, global groups, because they have no user rights associated with them, are powerless until they are assigned to a local group or to a user right. Note that global groups defined in a domain can be exported to Windows NT Workstations in that domain. Windows NT Workstations support local groups and can, therefore, make use of global groups defined in either the workstation's own domain or from other domains.

A global group can only contain user accounts that are locally defined in the domain in which the global group exists. By using trust relationships, users within a global group can access resources outside of their locally-defined domain. Global groups are quite suitable, therefore, for large, multi-domain networks. Global groups can provide an inclusive list of all user accounts within a domain that require a particular type of access to resources that exist within another domain.

An administrator creates multiple global groups (in each master domain) to accommodate all users in the network. It helps to distribute the users among the master domains according to organization within the company rather than alphabetically.

Note

A local group and a global group sharing the same name are two separate entities, each with their own distinct security identifier. Permissions assigned to one group do not apply to the other group sharing the same name.

Default Global Groups

The default global groups for a server domain are a good example of when global groups are used. The Domain Administrators global group is created and added to the Administrators local group on every Windows NT Workstation and LAN Manager Server that is added to the domain. The administrators for the domain can then also administrate the Windows NT Workstations and LAN Manager Servers in the domain.

The other default global group is the Domain Users group which provides an easy way to give user privileges on Windows NT domain workstations and LAN Manager Servers to all of the user accounts in the domain.

Trust relationships

Windows NT Server domain models are flexible and allow you to extend a network easily. The single domain model is the building block of a network; trust relationships between domains allow network designers to implement the most appropriate design for their enterprise. Trust relationships are simple to initiate and administer with Windows NT Server User Manager for Domains.

A trust relationship is an administration and communications link between two Windows NT Server domains. Domains use trust relationships to share account information and validate the rights and permissions of users and global groups residing in the trusted domain. A user has only one user account in one domain, yet can access all servers on the network.

Windows NT Server domain models make use of trust relationships to facilitate

- Centralized administration in multiple domain models

- Simplified administration by combining two or more domains into a single administrative unit

- The ability for users to log on from domains where they don't have accounts

- The ability for users from one domain to be permitted to use resources in another domain, even if they do not have a user account in the resource domain

- An increased number of user accounts in a master domain by locating machine and resource accounts in other domains

- A domain structure that serves a large organization, for example, 100,000 users

The "trusting" domain allows the remote user accounts and global groups in the "trusted" domain to use the resources of the trusting domain. Consider, for example, giving your neighbor a house key; you are trusting your neighbor, and your neighbor is trusted.

In a two-domain example, where one is an account domain and the other is a resource domain, the only time that a one-way trust relationship makes sense is when the account domain is the trusted domain, and its users can use the resources in the resource domain (which is the trusting domain).

A two-way trust is where both domains trust each other equally. This allows users to log on from either domain to the domain that contains their account. Using this implementation, each domain can have both accounts and resources, and remote user accounts and global groups may be used from either domain to grant rights and permissions to resources in either domain. In other words, both domains are trusted domains.

Depending on the goals of a domain model, one-way and two-way trust relationships can be used. A domain can make use of up to 128 incoming trust relationships and an unlimited number of outgoing trust relationships.

Multiple Trust

In the multiple-trust model, all domains trust all other domains. This model is the simplest to understand but, if many domains are involved, is the most complex to administer.

The multiple-trust model is scalable as the organization grows: It can support as many as 10,000 users for each domain. Because each domain has full control over its own user accounts, the multiple-trust model can work well for a company without a centralized management information services (MIS) department. If, however, the organization has many domains, there can be a very large number of trust relationships to manage. Because domain administration is decentralized, it is harder to assure the integrity of global groups that other domains might use.

Ideally, one user ID or password allows access to all of a user's resources. If you want to take advantage of Microsoft's Client Services for NetWare, in which the Windows NT user name and password are passed through to NetWare, set up the user account on NetWare with the same account name and password as in Windows NT. If there is no capability to send the user's password to other systems (such as Banyan Vines and some databases), the next best thing is to at least have a consistent full-name property within each company organization.

The Complete Trust Model

The complete trust model consists of several domains with each domain performing its own administration. In other words, no single domain exerts any control over the others. Each domain has its own controller. The complete trust model illustrates the range of domain models available, but it is not recommended in a practical implementation.

Because each domain is administered independently, there is no centralized security authority in the data processing environment. Rights to resources in one domain are based on mutual trust relationships. Unfortunately the number of trust relationships that must be established and maintained grows geometrically {n(n-1)}as additional domains are added. Thus with five domains, the number of trust relationships is 20; with ten domains, 90 trust relationships must be created; and at 20 domains, the number of trust relationships is 380.

If you want to use this model, implement it only on a NetBEUI network on a single subnet network. The amount of maintenance needed to the LMHOSTS file to implement this scenario can be prohibitive.

Domain Models

A *domain model* is a grouping of one or more domains, with administration and communications links between the domains (trust relationships), for the purpose of user and resource management.

Single domain model

In the single domain model, there is only one domain. Because there are no other domains, there are no trust relationships to administer. This is the best model for organizations with fewer than 10,000 users in which trust among departments is not an issue. It offers centralized management of all user accounts, and local groups have to be defined only once. In an organization with multiple domains where there is no need to share information among domains, the best configuration is often multiple single domains.

If you anticipate significant growth in your organization, consider a more flexible model, such as the multiple master domain model described later in this section. If your organization grows beyond 10,000 users, the single domain model can no longer support all your users, and there might be a great deal of administrative work involved in reconfiguring your user database.

The single domain model is best for networks with a small number of machines. To achieve reasonable logon times (that is, 486/66 server with five-second logon times), the number of workstations with a single domain controller can be no larger than 30. With one additional backup domain controller, the number of machines can be 100. This domain model can be extended to include up to 10,000 users; however, you would need approximately 50 servers.

When creating a single domain model, keep in mind the following guidelines:

- If you're using the NetBEUI protocol, all machines in the domain must be on the same subnet network. Domain servers use broadcast messages to

communicate with each other. Because NetBEUI is not a routable protocol, all of the domain servers must be on the same subnet network to
communicate with each other.

■ If you're using TCP/IP protocol, you can combine multiple subnet
networks to form a single domain. The routers must be configured to
support NetBIOS broadcasts. In addition, special consideration must be
given to the LMHOSTS file configuration information.

■ A workstation machine must be able to access a domain server to be
permitted to log on. However, links between routers may sometimes be
unpredictable (especially long-haul links such as telephone lines).
Design the router network to allow for fault-tolerant paths between any
subnet network and a domain server. Another option is to place a
backup domain controller in each subnet network. Thus, even if the
router links fail, users will still be able to log on. This solution is the
most robust in terms of assuring ability of logging on to the domain, it
may be cost effective depending on the cost of the connection between
routers, and it provides the fastest response time because the user will
be logged on to the network by the backup domain controller in his or
her local subnet. Although this solution may increase the amount of data
flowing between subnets on an average basis, it will greatly reduce the
need for bandwidth to support the "feeding frenzy" at logon time.

Single master domain model

The single master domain model is comprised of several domains, one of
which acts as the central administrative unit for user accounts. All user and
machine accounts are defined in this master domain, and all users log on to
their accounts in the master domain. Resources, such as printers and file
servers, are located in the other domains. Each resource domain establishes
a one-way trust with the master (account) domain, enabling users with
accounts in the master domain to use resources in all of the other domains.

The benefit of the single master domain model is its flexibility of administration. The network administrator can manage the entire multi-domain network, as well as its users and resources, by managing only a single domain.
For example, in a network requiring four domains, it might at first seem to
make sense to create four separate user account databases, one for each
domain. However, by putting all user accounts in a single database on one of
the domains and then implementing one-way trust relationships between
these domains, you can consolidate administration of user and machine
accounts. You can also administer all resources or delegate these to local
administrators. Users need only one logon name and one password to get
access to resources in any of the domains.

This model balances the requirements for account security with the need
for readily available resources on the network because users are given
permission to resources based on their master domain logon identity.

The single master domain model is particularly suited for

■ Centralized account management. User accounts can be centrally managed; you can add, delete, or change user accounts from a single point.

■ Decentralized resource management or local system administration capability. Department domains can have their own administrators, who manage the resources in the department. Resources can be grouped logically, corresponding to local domains.

The single master domain model requires careful placement of BDCs. Consider the following:

■ Resource domains that have a WAN connection to the master account domain controller should consider having an on-site BDC for local authentication so that accounts can log on in the event that the WAN link becomes unavailable.

■ Resource domains that have a LAN connection to the master account domain controller do not require an on-site BDC.

Multiple master domain model

With the multiple master domain model, there are two or more single master domains. Like the single master domain model, the master domains serve as account domains, with every user and machine account created and maintained on one of these master domains. Like the single master domain model, the other domains on the network are called resource domains; they don't store or manage user accounts but do provide resources such as shared file servers and printers to the network.

In this model, every master domain is connected to every other master domain by a two-way trust relationship. Each resource domain trusts every master domain with a one-way trust relationship. The resource domains can trust other resource domains but are not required to do so. Because every user account exists in one of the master domains and each resource domain trusts every master domain, every user account can be used on any of the master domains.

Users log on to the domain that contains their account. Each master domain contains one PDC and at least one BDC per 2,000 user accounts to validate user logons and provide fault tolerance.

The multiple master domain model incorporates all of the features of a single master domain, in addition to accommodating

■ Organizations of more than 40,000 users. The multiple master domain model is scalable to networks with any number of users.

■ Mobile users. Users can log on from anywhere in the network, anywhere in the world.

- Centralized or decentralized administration schemes.

- Organizational needs. Domains can be configured to mirror specific departments or internal company organizations.

This model works best when computer resources are grouped in some logical fashion, such as by department or by location. Because a multiple master domain model can support as many as 10,000 users per master domain, it works well for large organizations. Because all of the master domains trust each other, only one copy of each user account is needed.

The administrative requirements for a multiple master domain model can be considerably greater than for a single domain or master domain model. Local and global groups might have to be defined several times, there are more trust relationships to manage, and not all user accounts reside in the same domain.

Choose the multiple master domain model if more than a certain limit of users are to be defined to the security system. The documented limit per domain is 10,000 users. Practically, however, the number is 500 users for a single domain controller and 1000 per each additional backup domain controller installed.

The protocol issues for the multiple master domain model are the same as the single master domain model.

Choosing the Right Domain Model

Earlier in this chapter, I discussed the differences between a workgroup and a domain as they pertain to Windows NT. It's important to choose a Windows NT domain model carefully because

- It is very difficult to change a domain structure once it is implemented.

- Site boundaries depend on the domain structure in place. If sites span more than one domain, these domains must trust each other so that users and Windows NT services can be authenticated across the site.

If Windows NT Server is already implemented in your company, you should study the domain model currently in use. You need to know how many Windows NT domains your company has and what kind of Windows NT domain model your company supports. Find out how it is structured, how trust relationships are set up, why that model was chosen, and where the domain controllers are located.

Base the domain model that you select on the number of users in the organization and how you want to manage your organization. In addition, topology and location considerations will influence how domains are specifically implemented and where different resources are physically located.

Designing and building a domain strategy can be a challenging task, since there are few limits in the Windows NT software itself to dictate decision points. Other aspects of the computing environment must be considered to provide guidelines for the choices and decisions needed.

Remember that the process of design and selection is recursive. Decisions made earlier in the process must be verified in light of information available later in the process. Therefore, you should anticipate making several passes through the process until all decisions match with the information available at all steps.

Once the choices and configurations are determined, implementation of the domain can begin. Designing the implementation of the domain strategy contains fewer decisions than the initial selection of the domain strategy, but there are certainly still a number of choices to make.

Implementation of any computer system solution should follow a few key steps:

1. **Planning.** Do as much as possible on paper before starting any task. Erasing is far easier than rerouting wiring.

2. **Preparation.** Prestaging components and tools expedites the installation. It also provides one last sanity check before the installation itself.

3. **Installation.** The installation should be straightforward and orderly if the proper planning and preparation were done.

4. **Checkout.** Once installed, the installation should be checked to ensure that it was successful and the system works.

Domain strategies

How you configure your network into domains depends on your administrative resources and the size of your network.

Each Windows NT Server domain structure, no matter how simple or complex, originates from one of four basic designs or models. These models are derived from the ability to link domains logically using trust relationships. Models can be used in combination to fit any business need or environment. Here are a few key concepts to keep in mind:

■ First, machines in a domain do not have to be physically related, especially if the protocol being used is routable, such as TCP/IP or SPX/IPX.

■ Second, in a trust relationship, the trusting domain (or the resource domain) contains the resource(s); the trusted domain (or the account domain) contains the user definitions. No matter where the resources are located, the user always logs on to his or her home domain (the trusted domain).

- Finally, trust is usually one-way and not transitive. If domain A trusts domain B, it does not imply that domain B trusts domain A. Two-way trust can be established, but it must be established explicitly. Also, if domain A trusts domain B and domain B trusts domain C, it does not imply that domain A trusts domain C.

Management and administration

Windows NT allows you to manage user accounts centrally or decentrally for your organization. With centralized management, there is usually one SAM and, therefore, one master domain where all user account information is stored. Users are defined once on the network and given permissions to resources based on their logon identity in the central user database. The single domain model and single master domain models are centrally managed. A multiple master domain model can also be managed centrally by giving designated administrators to appropriate administrative groups.

With decentralized management, there is more than one SAM containing information about different user accounts in the organization. You can create trust relationships to enable domains to access resources in other domains. The multiple master domain model and the single domain models can use decentralized management.

When planning for your domain model, you'll need to establish administrative policies and procedures for

- Managing and monitoring domain(s) and accounts.
- Managing and monitoring resources.
- Establishing addressing and naming conventions.

How many domains do you need?

The number of users in a domain is a function of the size of the SAM database. Table 2-4 can help you to determine the number of domains you need. Note that the single domain model and the single master domain model can accommodate at least 26,000 user accounts if both user accounts and machine accounts are stored in the database.

Location considerations

You should consider the following items before setting up a domain model:

- Where will users log on? Ensure adequate access to an authenticating BDC.

Table 2-4	PDC/BDC Hardware Requirements		
SAM file size	*Number of user accounts*	*Minimum CPU needed*	*Required RAM* +
5 MB	Up to 3,000	486DX/33	32 MB
10 MB	7,500	486DX/66	32 MB
15 MB	10,000	Pentium, MIPS, Alpha AXP	48 MB
20 MB	15,000	Pentium, MIPS, Alpha AXP	64 MB
30 MB	20,000 to 30,000	Pentium, MIPS, Alpha AXP	128 MB
40 MB	30,000 to 40,000	Pentium, MIPS, Alpha AXP	166 MB

+RAM memory should equal at least 2.5 times the size of the SAM.

■ Do users need to be able to log on from more than one location? If so, their account cannot be tied to that location, implying a single master domain or multiple master domain model.

■ What are the availability requirements?

■ Does a user need to be able to log on if the WAN to the central location is down (for example, if all data is central and no local processing can be done)?

■ How fast are the WAN links? The speed of the links needed between locations should be determined by the usage of resources across the links and the frequency of changes to user and group settings.

Locating backup domain controllers

The most important location considerations are where to locate BDCs that will act as account logon servers and how to plan account replication traffic across WAN links. If your WAN speed or bandwidth is too low, you must arrange for logon to occur at a local BDC.

Think of your networked organization in terms of sites. A site is a well-connected LAN — it can be separated by fast links such as bridges and routers, but not asynchronous WAN links such as T1, 56K, or ISDN. In most cases, sites correspond to physical locations such as Seattle, Paris, New York, and so on. Is your networked organization one location (a well-connected LAN), or does it consist of several locations connected by WAN links?

The physical distribution of BDCs is determined by several factors: line speed, link reliability, administrative access, protocol, user authentication requirements, the number of users to be supported at a site, and locally available resources.

Replication over WAN and RAS

Consideration should be given to the amount of traffic that account replication places on the WAN or a RAS dial-up line. In particular, avoid doing full synchronization across WAN links. Full synchronizations are required when first setting up a new PDC or bringing a new location online. Full synchronizations are also initiated when more than 2,000 changes happen to users or groups within a short period of time (less than one hour). Synchronizations are configurable by increasing the size of the change log. If you anticipate high change activity, you may want to increase the value of this parameter.

An important part of administration is managing the amount of network traffic so that response time remains acceptable. When the PDC is located across a WAN or modem link, you can estimate the amount of traffic and time needed to replicate SAM changes to and from the PDC and then schedule this traffic to meet the needs of the site.

How many BDCs do you need?

The ratio of workstations to servers in a domain is a way of maintaining a level of responsiveness during the logon process. Additional BDCs (also called domain servers) allow for more users to log on simultaneously. One BDC can support up to 2,000 user accounts.

The server configuration in Table 2-5 is for a 486/66 with 32 MB of RAM, running Windows NT Server.

Table 2-5	BDCs per Number of User Accounts
Number of workstations	*Number of BDC servers*
10	1
100	1
500	1
1,000	1
2,000	1
5,000	2
10,000	5
20,000	10
30,000	15

Consider performing the initial setup of all BDCs on-site or over high-speed links, because each new BDC will need a full synchronization with the PDC. At many companies, BDCs are set up at the same site as the PDC and then shipped to the intended location. This is the most efficient alternative for sites that have only low-speed or RAS access.

Implementing Your Domain Model

For ease of administration, the preferred domain model is the single domain model. If the single domain model cannot be used, the second choice should be the single master domain model. If neither of these is available, an administrator can use trust relationships to centralize all user administration into a single domain, eliminating the need to administer each domain separately.

Domain selection matrix

It is useful to view the characteristics of the domain models side by side to match the characteristics and benefits of each implementation model to the needs of your organization. If the needs of your organization change over time, you can review the matrix in Table 2-6 to determine if the implementation model should change. Conversely, if you have established an implementation model already, you might review this chart to see which additional benefits or trade-off decisions are related to an alternative domain model strategy.

Table 2-6	Domain Selection Matrix			
Domain attribute	*Single domain*	*Single master domain*	*Multiple master domain*	*Independent single domains with trust relationships*
Less than 40,000 users/domain	X	X		
More than 40,000 users/domain			X	
Centralized account management	X	X	X	
Centralized resource management	X			
Decentralized account management			X	X
Decentralized resource management		X	X	X
Central MIS	X	X	X	
No central MIS				X

Setting up the domain

If you did your homework and laid out a well-defined plan, setting up your domain structure should be very straightforward. The following list describes general guidelines for implementing a domain network:

■ First install the master domain controllers. Next, install the domain servers. Once the domain server and controller machines are in place, install the workstations or associate the workstations with each domain.

■ With the domains in place, establish the trust relationships using Windows NT Server Manager. Then define groups within this domain. Defining groups after you establish trust relationships allows you to create local groups in this domain that may contain global groups from a trusted domain.

Finally, check out the domain structure by making sure that

■ The domain controller replicates user database updates to all domain servers.

■ Data replication is working.

■ Workstations are capable of logging on to the system and gaining access to the resources needed.

Keeping your existing workgroup model

If you decide to keep your workgroup model and have more than ten network clients, you should upgrade to Windows NT Server. You can even upgrade an existing Windows NT Workstation to Windows NT Server, as long as you install Windows NT Server and operate it in server mode. This will keep all of your existing user accounts, groups, shares, and software configurations intact but still allow more network clients to connect and better provide for centralized administration of the network — at least as far as your file, print, and application server is concerned.

Unless you know all of the Windows NT Workstation administrator accounts, you still cannot administer other Windows NT Workstation network clients remotely as you can with Windows NT Server in a domain model. However, it does offer a network model that is easier to maintain, when compared to a peer-to-peer model. And it offers you increased client connectivity, as well as the ability to use SQL Server and other Windows NT application servers. It even includes the ability to exceed the one-user RAS limitation so you can support multiple remote client connections. It also includes the ability to create a striped set with parity and other fault-tolerant capabilities not included in Windows NT Workstation.

Windows NT Server is a good match for small networks that are based on the workgroup model because it provides increased connectivity options. However, it is not the perfect match if you need more than one server, because once you add another server, you lose the few centralized administration capabilities that you had. In addition, you cannot run applications like System Management Server which requires the domain model.

If you need more than one server, you may want to consider migrating to a domain model.

The domain model also offers you several more advantages when compared to a workgroup model. First, it provides centralized administration. With a domain model, you can remotely administer any Windows NT domain client. You can create one user account that can be used by any network client. These network clients can include MS-DOS, Windows for Workgroups, LAN Manager, or Windows NT clients. You can further group these user accounts into local groups (which are only accessible on the local domain) or global accounts (which are accessible on any domain). If you decide to use global accounts from multiple domains, you have two choices: You can import global accounts from any domain to which you have administrative access, which requires that you have multiple administrative accounts. Or you can establish a trust relationship to share a user account and global account database among one or more domains.

Another benefit of a domain model is the directory replicator service, which allows you to automate the copying of your logon scripts to your backup domain controllers. This prevents a bottleneck in user authentication because the domain controller (backup or primary) with the fastest response time will be used to authenticate the user. Because each domain controller also includes a copy of the user logon script, courtesy of the directory replicator service, any domain controller can perform the user authentication.

Note

Only a Windows NT Server can export a directory tree, although any Windows NT Server or Windows NT Workstation can import a directory tree.

The major benefit of domains is that you can install software that requires the domain model to operate. This includes the System Management Server which you can use to automate the installation of shared applications and network client operating systems and even to provide centralized inventory capabilities.

If you use a Windows for Workgroups, Windows NT, or Windows NT Server computer operating in server mode as your server, you can install Windows NT Server as a primary domain controller on a new computer, or you can upgrade the existing computer if the hardware platform will support Windows NT Server. This computer will become your replacement server. However, there are a few complications in this process that you should consider.

Note

Although you can leave your current workgroup server online during this upgrade process, I do not recommend it. If you leave it online, some user may change a data file which will cause your replacement server's copied data files to be out of sync. If you have connected users and attempt to change the computer name, you will have to disconnect all of your connected users and possibly cause loss of data.

If you plan to completely replace your current workgroup server with a new computer as transparently as possible, both of these computers must have their names changed. This is required because computer names must be unique within a domain. So if your workgroup computer is called *Server* and your new replacement server is called *NTServer*, after the installation, you must rename the workgroup server to a new name (maybe *OldServer*), and rename the replacement server to *Server*. The domain name of your new server should be the same as your current workgroup name.

Once you have created a new server with the appropriate computer and domain names, you have to copy the shared data and applications. This is easily performed by connecting from your new domain controller to the workgroup computer and copying all of the shared data. If you upgrade an existing workgroup computer, all of the data will already reside on the server.

Complications can arise with shared data. If you have a Windows for Workgroup computer, all you need to do is recreate the shared directories. If you have a Windows NT Server, it can be a bit more complicated if you are using more than the share level permissions provided by Windows for Workgroups. If, for example, you have your data on an NTFS partition and have assigned any directory or file permissions, all of this permission information will be lost as part of the upgrade and have to be recreated manually.

Tip

To make life a little easier in copying and recreating the sharepoints, I have included a program that you can run on your workgroup computer to create a data file containing your existing shared directory names. You run the same program and read the data to create the shares on your new server. This program will be in the TOOLS directory of the CD-ROM accompanying this book.

All of the directory and file permission information will be lost because when you upgrade a Windows NT Workstation or a Windows NT Server operating in server mode, you cannot upgrade and use the user account database. In fact, when you upgrade any of the platforms mentioned before, you will have to replace all of the configuration information. It is not a software upgrade; rather, it is a replacement.

Note

Not only will you lose the user account database, but you will also lose access to any striped sets, volume sets, or any fault-tolerant partitions. This occurs because the existing NT operating system files and all of the Registry files will be deleted prior to installing Windows NT Server. The Registry files contain the user accounts, the system partition information, and any security information.

The only other item to consider is related to network protocols and configuration. You will need to install the same protocols that your clients are currently configured to use. If one of these is TCP/IP, your new server must use the old server's IP address and import any LMHOSTS files that it may have been using. Your old server will have to have a new IP address allocated for its use.

After you have created your new server, you must complete the following steps on the server:

1. Create new user accounts and local and global groups. This is required because all of your user account information is lost during the installation.

2. Create your new shared directories and assign new user- or group-level permissions for the new sharepoints.

3. Take ownership of any directories and files if you upgraded a Windows NT Workstation or Windows NT Server operating in server mode. Then reassign the directory and file permissions based on your new user accounts.

Once these steps are completed, you must perform the following step on your network client computers:

4. Change from a workgroup to a domain. This is accomplished on a Windows for Workgroups or Windows NT Workstation computer by running the Control Panel Network applet. On a Windows for Workgroups computer, you will also want to specify that the computer will be logging on to a domain. This option is accessible by clicking on the Advanced button.

Note

The preceding step does not have to be performed immediately. Your current clients will be able to connect to existing shared resources as long as they have a current user identification and password. Since you will be changing all of your network passwords (probably to your user's user names) and requiring that the users change their passwords at first logon, this could cause a bit of user anxiety. Plan for this by distributing a mail message to all of your users before you upgrade your server.

On your Windows NT clients, change any shared directory permissions to use the accounts from the domain rather than the local database. This will prevent a user from requiring two separate passwords — one for the domain account and one for the shared directories on the NT Workstation. This step does not have to be performed immediately. As long as the user has a valid user identification and password on the NT Workstation, they can continue to supply it when prompted or use the Connect As option in the Connect to Network Drive dialog box.

Summary

This chapter examined the concepts and issues surrounding Windows NT Server and the development of a domain strategy. The ability to collect multiple servers into a domain and establish a single security identity makes it easier to manage servers and ensure security policies on all servers. This chapter covered

▶ Windows NT Workstations in a domain

▶ Domain strategies

▶ Setting up the domain

▶ Migrating to a domain model

Chapter 3

Designing the Windows NT Network

In This Chapter

▶ Networking basics

▶ Identifying your network needs

▶ Determining a network strategy for Windows NT

▶ Selecting network topologies

▶ Building a Windows NT internetwork with wide area connections

---

Today's businesses depend on enterprise-wide networks as critical tools. You must carefully plan, design, and implement a network so that it aligns with your company's business and technology concerns. Instead of viewing a network as a high-technology toy, think of it as a competitive and strategic tool with distinct advantages. This chapter shows you how to design and implement a Windows NT network to fit your organization's business functions.

A Networking Primer

A *network* consists of two or more computers that are connected together by physical media and are running software that enables the computers to communicate with one another. Each local area network has certain common characteristics. The following sections discuss LAN topologies, cabling media, and transmission techniques.

LAN configurations

LANs are configured according to the method of operation:

■ **Peer to peer.** A network where each workstation can share some, all, or none of its resources with other workstations.

■ **Resource sharing.** With resource sharing, one or more centralized servers send and receive files and contain the resources that the workstations use. The workstations cannot access other workstations' resources; they do all the processing.

■ **Client/server.** Client/server computing splits an application into client (workstations) and server components. At the front end, the client part of the application accepts input from the user, prepares it for the server, and issues a request to the server. At the back end, the server receives requests from clients, processes them, and provides the requested service to the client. The client then presents the data or other results to the user through its own interface.

An overview of network architecture

The primary goal of a network is to marry miscellaneous hardware and software components into a functioning system. The manner in which a mirage of network components comes together is defined by standards and specifications. The term *standard* as it applies to computer networks is often ambiguous, especially when you consider that there are many standards in existence and that many computer manufacturers deviate from those standards to create their own proprietary components. The problems arise when products from one manufacturer have to communicate with proprietary products from another manufacturer.

To alleviate the problems caused by computer manufacturers using different standards for hardware components, there are software standards known as *protocols*. Protocols allow communication between different networks by regulating data formats.

When you see the term *network architecture,* it refers to the combination of standards and protocols needed to create a functioning network. A network architecture is also a standard; it defines the rules of a network and how its components interact.

Topologies

Every network must be connected via some sort of transmission medium or cabling. The placement of cables and connections is referred to as *topology*. Your network topology defines the physical layout of your network cables as well as how your network clients physically connect to the network. There are three basic topology implementations, along with various deviations, used in today's networks. They are the star, ring, and linear bus; each has different strengths and weaknesses.

Linear bus topology

A linear bus topology connects each computer to a single cable. At each end of the cable is a terminating resistor, or a *terminator*. A signal is passed back and forth along the cable past the workstations and between the two terminators.

The "bus" carries a message from one end of the network to the other. As the bus passes each workstation, the workstation checks the destination address on the message. If the address in the message matches the workstation's address, the workstation receives the message. If the address doesn't match, the bus carries the message to the next workstation, and so on.

One type of bus network, called a local bus, is shown in Figure 3-1. A local bus uses a T-connector to connect the cable to the workstation's network adapter card. A terminator is connected to the last T-connector at each end of the network.

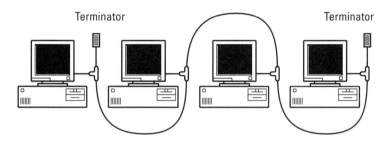

Figure 3-1: A local bus network connects the network cable directly to each computer using T-connectors.

A bus network, as shown in Figure 3-2, uses drop cables to connect each workstation to the main "backbone" cable.

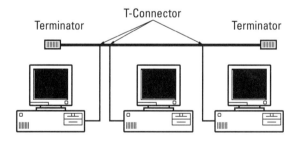

Figure 3-2: A regular bus network uses drop cables to connect each computer to the network cable.

Bus topology is passive, meaning that workstations only listen for data being sent on the network and are not responsible for moving data from one workstation to the next. If one workstation fails, it doesn't affect the entire LAN. On the other hand, if the *connection* to one workstation comes loose or if a cable breaks, the entire cable segment (the length between two terminators) loses its connectivity, causing the entire segment to be nonfunctional.

Its primary flaw is that if one piece of the network cable is faulty, the entire network fails. Isolating the fault requires that you perform a binary test by splitting the bus into two separate sections to determine which half has the cable break. Once you have determined which half has the break, you must split that segment into two equal parts and continue this process until the cable break has been found.

Table 3-1 lists some advantages and disadvantages of bus networks.

Table 3-1   Advantages and Disadvantages of Bus Networks

Advantages	*Disadvantages*
Failure of a single workstation doesn't affect the entire LAN	Cable break can affect large number of users
Easy cable connections; flexible	Limited cable length and number of workstations
Inexpensive cable and connectors	Difficult to isolate network cabling errors
	Performance degradation is not graceful
Requires the least amount of cable	Fault diagnosis and isolation are very difficult
Wiring layout is extremely simple making it very reliable	The trunk can be a bottleneck when network traffic is heavy
It is very easy to extend	

Star topology

In a network using a star configuration, each workstation is connected to a special device called a *hub,* as shown in Figure 3-3. The hub provides a common connection so that all of the computers can communicate with one another.

Star bus topology uses signal splitters in the hub to send out signals in different directions on the cable connections. Both active and passive hubs are allowed. Active hubs can transmit a stronger signal to feed a longer cable and/or more signal splitters.

If a single cable fails between the hub and workstation, only that workstation is affected. The other workstations continue their network activity without experiencing any problems. However, if a hub fails, all of the workstations connected to that hub fail. This is easily diagnosed, because all of the users connected to that failed hub are clamoring for your attention, making it clear that the problem is with the hub itself rather than an individual workstation.

Star Network

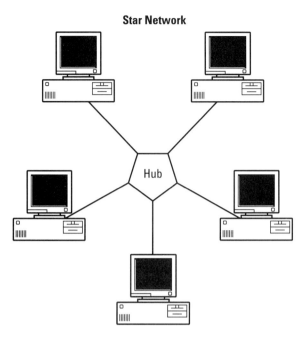

Figure 3-3: Each computer on a star network is connected to a hub.

Tip

Planning for this type of disaster requires that you have a spare hub available to replace a failed hub. This is one reason why it makes sense to use the same type of hub throughout your network installation. In addition, it is a good idea to use smart hubs. A smart hub supports the Simple Network Management Protocol (SNMP) which can be used to query the hub about its performance and, in many cases, reboot it without physically walking over to the hub and cycling the power.

Table 3-2 lists some advantages and disadvantages of star bus topology.

Table 3-2 Advantages and Disadvantages of Star Networks	
Advantages	*Disadvantages*
Easy to add new workstations	Failure of hub cripples the workstations connected to the hub
Central monitoring and network management	
Cable layouts are easy to modify	
Provides centralized control, allowing defective communication lines to be identified more easily	Requires large amounts of cable, which adds to the overall expense

Token Ring topology

On a Token Ring network, shown in Figure 3-4, workstations are situated on a continuous network loop on which a "token" is passed from one workstation to the next. Although the name *Token Ring* implies a ring, the Token Ring is physically laid out as a star. Workstations are centrally connected to a hub called a Media Access Unit (MAU) and are wired in a star configuration. Workstations use a token to transmit data and must wait for a free token from the hub in order to transfer messages.

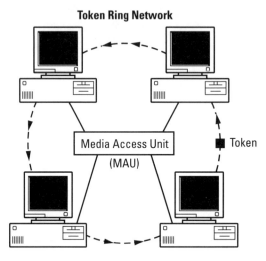

Figure 3-4: A computer communicates on a Token Ring network by "grabbing" the token and sending it around an electric ring.

The token contains the address of the sender and the address of the recipient. When the recipient has copied the information from the received message, it returns the token to the originating workstation to verify that the message was received. The original sender then passes the token to the next workstation in the ring so that workstation can send information over the network.

Table 3-3 lists some advantages and disadvantages of a Token Ring topology.

Table 3-3	Advantages and Disadvantages of Token Ring Networks	
Advantages	**Disadvantages**
Cable failures affect a small number of users	Costly wiring and connections
Equal access for all workstations	
Graceful performance degradation as the size of the network grows	

Network Protocols

Previous sections defined network architecture as the combination of standards and protocols used in a particular network. Another characteristic of network architecture is that it is broken into layers — each with a specific responsibility or task to perform. Each layer can communicate with the layer directly above or below it, and it is the protocol that defines how communication between layers occurs.

The layering of protocols to create network architectures is fundamental to standards-based networking. All networks are built on layers of protocols, and these layers are the foundations for network architectures. Still there is a problem. A number of diverse protocols are incompatible with other protocols. It seems that every computer company had a better idea, and that better idea spawned proprietary communication and networking standards. To get a handle on this "tower of Babel," a handful of organizations and committees collaborated to develop a reference model for computer networking known as OSI (Open Systems Interconnection).

The OSI model was established by the International Standards Organization in 1984. This model, shown in Figure 3-5, separates computer communications into distinct functions that are represented by layers. Like all layered protocols, each OSI layer functions independently of the layers immediately above and below it. Despite this separation of states, each layer can communicate with the layer directly above or below it. Although a layer can communicate with the layer immediately adjacent to it, it cannot skip over a layer to communicate with another layer.

The OSI model has seven layers: physical, data link, network, transport, session, presentation, and application. The lower layers — physical, data link, network, and transport — provide real-time data communication services. The upper layers — session, presentation, and application — provide end-user services. Table 3-4 briefly explains the roles or functions of each of the seven layers.

OSI

7	Application
6	Presentation
5	Session
4	Transport
3	Network
2	Data Link
1	Physical

Figure 3-5: The OSI model.

Table 3-4	The Seven-layered OSI Model
Layer number and name	*Function*
7–Application	The application layer provides communication-based services to end users. High-level system-independent activities occur at this level, and such activities are managed by a component of the local operating system. Unlike the other layers of the OSI model, the services of the application layer are directly available to the end users. Functions include file transfer, message handling, directory management, remote job execution, and terminal emulation.
6–Presentation	The presentation layer determines the form used to exchange data between networked computers. It can be called the network's translator. At the sending computer, this layer translates data from a format received from the application layer into a commonly recognized, intermediary format. At the receiving end, this layer translates the intermediary format into a format useful to that computer's application layer. The presentation layer also manages network security issues by providing services such as data encryption. It also provides rules for data transfer and provides data compression to reduce the number of bits that need to be transmitted.

Layer number and name	Function
5–Session	The session layer sits between the upper layers, which are oriented toward applications, and the lower layers, which are oriented toward real-time data communications. The session layer provides services for the management and control of data between multiple simultaneous connections, synchronizing and managing the dialog between communicating applications. Session layer management services include the ability to start, halt, abandon, or restart activities.
4–Transport	The transport layer ensures that the data will be handled reliably, regardless of the underlying layers. It is the last line of defense. It handles end to end, or node to node, connection management error control and flow control. Common transport layer protocols are OSI's Transport Class 0, Class 1 and 4, Internet's Transmission Control Protocol (TCP), and Novell's Sequenced Packet Exchange (SPX).
3–Network	The network layer uses the data link services from the underlying layer to provide data transmission services across the network. The network layer provides the rules that dictate how computers communicate across multiple network segments, including the containment of messages into packets with addresses. It is responsible for reliably transmitting the data from end to end. The network layer is particularly concerned with routing and provides data transmission services to the transport layer. Common network layer protocols are CNLS, CONS, IP, and IPX.
2–Data link	The data link layer organizes the bits into frames of data so that they can be transmitted as electrical signals by the physical layer. Error detection and correction occurs at this level. Often the data link layer contains two sublayers designed to handle the differences between physical networks used for LAN and WAN communications. Refer to the sidebar titled *Project 802* for more information on the data link sublayers.
1–Physical	The physical layer provides the mechanical and electrical interface specification for how a computer attaches to a physical medium, so that the computer can transmit bit-oriented data, that is, coaxial and twisted-pair cable. It includes physical connectors to the electrical voltage to be used to transmit bits.

Project 802

Another networking model was developed by the Institute of Electrical and Electronic Engineers (IEEE.) As local area network (LAN) products proliferated, and with them a need for consistency, IEEE began to define LAN standards. Its project was called 802, for the year and month it began (February 1980).

Project 802 defines LAN standards for the physical and data link layers of the OSI model. Although the published IEEE 802 standards actually predate the ISO standards, both were in development at roughly the same time and shared information, which resulted in two compatible models.

The 802 standards committee agreed with most of the OSI model but decided that more detail was needed at the data link layer. The 802 project divided the data link layer into two sublayers: Media Access Control (MAC) and Logical Link Control (LLC).

As Figure 3-6 indicates, the Media Access Control sublayer is the lower of the two sublayers, providing shared access for the computers' network adapter cards to the physical layer. The MAC layer communicates directly with the network adapter card and is responsible for delivering error-free data between two computers on the network.

The Logical Link Control sublayer, the upper sublayer, manages data link communication and defines the use of logical interface points [called Service Access Points (SAPs)] that other computers can reference and use to transfer information from the LLC sublayer to the upper OSI layers.

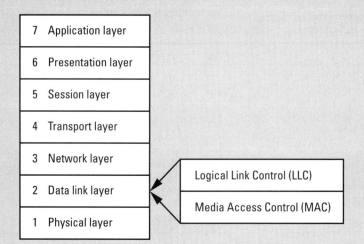

7 Application layer	
6 Presentation layer	
5 Session layer	
4 Transport layer	
3 Network layer	
2 Data link layer	Logical Link Control (LLC)
1 Physical layer	Media Access Control (MAC)

Figure 3-6: IEEE Project 802 defined the Logical Link Control and Media Access Control sublayers.

Project 802 resulted in a number of documents, including three important standards for network topologies:

- 802.3 defines standards for bus networks, such as Ethernet, that use a mechanism called Carrier Sense Multiple Access with Collision Detection (CSMA/CD).

- 802.4 defines standards for token passing bus networks. (The ArcNet architecture is similar to this standard in many ways.)

- 802.5 defines standards for Token Ring networks.

 Note IEEE defined functionality for the LLC layer in standard 802.2 and defined functionality for the MAC and physical layers in standards 802.3, 802.4, and 802.5.

LAN cabling media

The LAN industry has standardized three primary physical media that can be used at the physical layer: coaxial cable, twisted-pair cable, and fiber optic cable. Transmission rates that can be supported on each of these physical media are measured in millions of bits per second, or Mbps. The choice of cabling media is influenced by several factors, such as bandwidth, distance, security, electromagnetic and radio frequency interference, and cost. Characteristics for each medium are discussed in the following sections.

Coaxial Cable

Coaxial (or coax) cable, as shown in Figure 3-7, has a conductive center wire surrounded by an insulating layer, a layer of wire mesh (shielding), and a non-conductive outer layer. Coaxial cable is resistant to interference and signal weakening that other cabling, such as unshielded twisted-pair cable, can experience. Coax is generally better than unshielded twisted-pair cable over longer distances and for reliably supporting higher data rates with less sophisticated equipment.

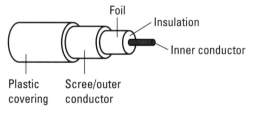

Figure 3-7: Coaxial cable.

Coaxial cable grades and fire codes

Coaxial cables come in two grades: PVC and plenum. The cable grade that you should use to connect workstations depends on where the cables are going to be routed in your office.

PVC (polyvinyl chloride) is a chemical used to construct the insulation and the cable jacket for most types of coaxial cable. PVC coaxial cable is flexible and can easily be routed in the exposed areas of an office.

A *plenum* is the short space in many buildings between the false ceiling and the floor above and is used to circulate warm and cold air through the building. Fire codes are very specific on the type of wiring that can be routed through this area.

Plenum cabling refers to coax cable that contains special materials in its insulation and cable jacket. It is certified to be fire resistant and produces a minimum amount of smoke to minimize poisonous chemical fumes. It can be used in the plenum area and in vertical runs (for example, in a wall) without conduit. Plenum cabling is not as flexible as PVC cable and is more expensive.

Table 3-5 lists some advantages and disadvantages of coaxial cabling.

Table 3-5   Advantages and Disadvantages of Coaxial Cabling

Advantages	*Disadvantages*
Low maintenance costs	Limited distance and topology
Simple to install and tap	Low security; easily tapped
Better resistance to signal noise over longer distances	Difficult to make major changes to the cabling topology
	Cable cost is higher than that of twisted pair, although electronic support components are less expensive

Twisted-pair Cable

Twisted-pair cable, as shown in Figure 3-8, consists of two insulated strands of copper wire twisted together. A number of twisted-wire pairs are often grouped together and enclosed in a protective sheath to form a cable.

Shielded Twisted-pair Cable

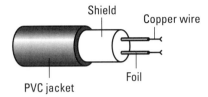

Unshielded Twisted-pair

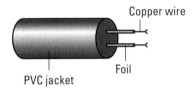

Figure 3-8: Twisted-pair wire and cable.

- **Shielded twisted-pair (STP).** Like UTP cable, STP cable includes two pairs of wire twisted around each other. But unlike UTP, it has shielding wrapped around each individual pair as well as a layer of shielding around both pairs. This shielding provides better signaling capabilities than UTP and should be used in electrically noisier environments. A shielded twisted-pair cable is less subject to electrical interference and supports higher transmission speeds over longer distances than unshielded twisted-pair cable.

- **Unshielded twisted-pair (UTP).** This particular cable uses two pairs of wire twisted (the more twists, the better the signaling capability) around each other to provide a resonant magnetic field to increase signal quality. In appearance, it looks just like your phone cable. Unshielded twisted-pair wire is commonly used for telephone systems and is already installed in most office buildings.

Tip

There are actually five different categories of UTP cabling. Levels 1 and 2 are low-grade cables designed for voice-only transmissions. Level 3 is the minimum required level for 10-MB networks. Level 4 supports up to 16-MB networks. Level 5 supports up to 100-MB networks. When you choose your network cable, purchase Level 5 UTP cable because approximately 75 percent of your installation cost is for the labor of pulling the cables. Level 5 cable will provide the longest service life and make your network cabling Ethernet-ready if you decide to migrate to this medium later.

Table 3-6 lists some advantages and disadvantages of twisted-pair cabling.

Table 3-6	Advantages and Disadvantages of Twisted-pair Cabling	
Advantages	**Disadvantages**	
Well-understood technology	Susceptible to noise	
Easy to add computers to network	Limited maximum bandwidth	
Least expensive medium	Distance limitations	
Same medium as telephones	Easiest to tap	
Pre-existing phone wire may be in place to connect workstations	Requires expensive support electronics and devices	

Fiber Optic Cable

Optical fibers carry digital data signals in the form of modulated pulses of light. An optical fiber, as shown in Figure 3-9, consists of an extremely thin cylinder of glass, called the core, surrounded by a concentric layer of glass, known as the cladding.

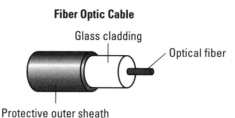

Fiber Optic Cable

Glass cladding

Optical fiber

Protective outer sheath

Figure 3-9: Fiber optic cable.

There are two fibers per cable — one to transmit and one to receive. Optical fiber cable transmissions are not subject to interference and are very fast (currently transmitting about 100 Mbps with demonstrated rates of up to 200,000 Mbps).

Fiber optic cable is the best cable to use for electrically noisy environments because it carries pulses of light rather than electrical pulses. It should be used as the backbone of a computer network to provide the fastest and most error-free data path between servers. Like coax cable, fiber optic cable has a core, made of glass rather than copper, surrounded by several layers to protect the glass core.

Tip

You can also use fiber optic cables to provide an electrically isolated method of joining two physical segments. For instance, rather than use electrical cables to span two segments in different buildings, use a pair of fiber optic cables. That way you have isolated the two networks from electrical interference rather than joining the two networks with a "lightning rod."

Table 3-7 shows some advantages and disadvantages of fiber optic cabling.

Table 3-7	Advantages and Disadvantages of Fiber Optic Cabling	
Advantages	**Disadvantages**
High bit rates	More expensive than other cabling types
Lowest transmission loss over longer distance	Cabling is inflexible; can't be bent sharply
Not subject to interference	Lack of standard components
Good for network "backbones"	Limited (practically) to high-traffic, point-to-point service
Supports voice, data, video	Requires skilled installation and maintenance
Difficult to tap	High installation costs

Guidelines for Cabling

Before cabling, create a to-scale cabling diagram, preferably on computer (so you can make changes easily). Show all cable runs, repeaters, and wiring closets. Indicate types of cabling and post this on the wall. Also consider what cabling changes may be needed in the future.

When running cable, consider the following:

- Get high-quality cable that is clearly labeled as RG-58/A-AU (Ethernet) or 73-ohm RG-62/A-AU (ArcNet, 3270, and so on).

- Be cautious when pulling and pushing cable to avoid damaging it. A kink can cause reflection problems.

- Keep cabling away from fluorescent lights, motors, power wires, and electronic devices to avoid electromagnetic energy.

- Don't run cable under carpet.

- Put a label on all cabling parts, including wall plates, and all parts in the wiring closet.

- Run two lengths of cable instead of one so it will be easier in the future to replace faulty cable with the second run.

■ With twisted-pair, don't share the same conduit as phone wire; the ringer signal creates a destructive voltage. Also for twisted-pair, don't use silver satin cable. Twisted-pair should conform to IBM's Type 3 standard: two pairs of 24-gauge solid copper wire.

Access methods

So far you have seen that you can install a LAN with several different topologies. Beyond the cabling and physical layout of the LAN, the computers have to access the cabling to send and receive data. Computers access the LAN using a predefined set of rules or protocols known as a media access method. Media access methods regulate how computer data enters and exits the network cabling. There are three access methods, but only two — CSMA/CD (Carrier Sense Multiple Access with Collision Detection) and token passing — are widely used. The third method, polling, is used primarily in mainframe and minicomputer networking systems.

Ethernet networks all use a CSMA/CD algorithm to send data across the wire. In this algorithm, the network adapter is required to listen (carrier sense) before sending data. If two or more computers (multiple access) send data at the same time, a data collision occurs and is detected by the computer (collision detection). When a collision occurs, the computers will pause for a random time before retransmitting their data. Token Ring networks use a token-passing algorithm. Only one computer will have the token that permits it to send data on the network. Once the data has been sent, the token is released for the next computer to use to send data.

Types of Local Area Networks (LANs)

The most common types of LANs are

■ **Ethernet.** Uses a linear bus topology and thin or thick coaxial cable or twisted-pair cable. Ethernet lines operate at 10 Mbps.

■ **Token Ring.** Combines star and ring topologies and can operate at bandwidths of 4 or 16 Mbps.

■ **ArcNet.** Uses a star or bus topology and generally operates at 2.5 Mbps, although ArcNetplus operates at 20 Mbps.

Ethernet

In the late 1960s, the University of Hawaii developed a *wide area network* called ALOHA. (A wide area network extends LAN technology across a larger geographical area.) The university needed to connect various computers that were spread throughout its campus. A key feature of that network design was called the Carrier Sense Multiple Access with Collision Detection (CSMA/CD) access method. Carrier Sense means that the network card listens to the cable for a quiet period during which it can send messages.

Multiple Access refers to multiple computers using the same network cable. Collision Detection is a safeguard against messages colliding in transit.

This early network design was the foundation for today's Ethernet. In 1972, Xerox Corporation created Experimental Ethernet, and in 1975, it introduced the first Ethernet product. The original version of this networking product was designed as a 2.94-Mbps system to connect over 100 workstations on a 1-kilometer cable.

Ethernet networks can be wired with different types of cable, each with its own benefits and drawbacks. Three popular specifications for Ethernet topologies follow:

- The 10-Base2 specification (referred to in this book as *thinnet*) refers to an Ethernet baseband LAN that uses thinnet cabling. Thinnet coaxial cable can carry a signal up to approximately 200 meters (about 607 feet). Beyond that distance, the signal must be regenerated and amplified by a device called a repeater. There is also a minimum cable length. The cable between computers must be at least 0.5 meters (20 inches) long. A thinnet network was designed to be an economical way to support a small department or workgroup. It is also easy to configure and to install.

- The 10-Base5 specification (referred to in this book as *thicknet*) is an Ethernet baseband LAN using thicknet cabling. Thicknet can carry a signal for 500 meters (about 1,640 feet) before needing a repeater. Thicknet was designed to support a backbone for a large department or even all of the workstations in an entire building.

- The 10-BaseT specification (referred to in this book as *twisted-pair*) is an Ethernet baseband LAN using an unshielded twisted-pair (UTP) cable, commonly called twisted-pair. This cabling medium can carry a message for 100 meters (about 328 feet) between a workstation and the hub to which the workstation is connected.

The following sections describe each of these three Ethernet topologies.

Thinnet (10-Base2)

This network is called thinnet, or thin wire, because of the thin, inexpensive coaxial cabling (RG-58) it uses. IEEE calls this network 10-Base2 because it transmits at *10* Mbps over a *base*band wire and can carry a signal roughly *2* x 100 meters (actual distance is 185 meters).

Thinnet networks generally use a local bus topology, as described in *Linear bus topology* earlier in this chapter. IEEE standards for thinnet don't allow a drop cable to be used from the bus T-connector to a workstation. Instead, a T-connector fits directly on the network adapter card. A BNC barrel connector may be used to connect thinnet cable segments together, thus extending a length of cable. For example, if you need a length of cable that is 30 feet long, but all you have is a 25-foot length and a 5-foot length of thinnet cable, you can use a BNC barrel connector to join the two cable segments together. The use of barrel connectors, however, should be kept to a minimum.

A single thinnet network can support a maximum of 30 nodes (workstations and repeaters) per cable segment. A *segment* is the length of cable between two terminators. A terminator must be connected to each end of a LAN for the network to function. Using repeaters, a thinnet network can combine as many as five cable segments to support up to 150 computers (based on the IEEE 802.3 specification).

Thicknet (10-Base5)

Although IEEE calls this 10-Base5 — referring to its main specifications of *10* Mbps, *base*band, and 500-meter (*5* x 100) segments — it is commonly known as thicknet because of the cabling it uses. (It is also called Standard Ethernet.)

Thicknet generally uses a bus topology and can support as many as 100 nodes (workstations, repeaters, and bridges) per backbone segment. The backbone, or trunk segment, is the main cable from which drop cables are connected to workstations, repeaters, and bridges. Unlike thinnet, this type of network uses drop cables connected to external transceivers to connect workstation network adapter cards to a cable segment.

Thicknet cable transmits at a rate of 10 Mbps and can carry a signal for 500 meters (1,640 feet), excluding drop cables, before needing a repeater. A maximum of five backbone segments can be connected using repeaters (based on the IEEE 802.3 specification). The length of drop cables is not used to measure the distance supported on the thicknet cable; only the end-to-end length of the thicknet cable segment itself is used. The minimum cable length between connections (or taps) on the thicknet cable segment, excluding drop cables, is 2.5 meters (about 8 feet).

Drop cables are typically 3/8-inch shielded-pair cable and can be as long as 50 meters (about 164 feet). Drop cables are connected by AUI (Attachment Unit Interface) connectors on the network adapter card at one end and the main backbone cable at the other (through the use of an external transceiver).

Twisted-Pair (10-BaseT)

10-BaseT is an Ethernet baseband LAN that uses unshielded twisted-pair cable to connect workstations. Most networks of this type are configured in a star pattern but internally use a bus signaling system like other Ethernet configurations.

Typically, the hub of a 10-BaseT network serves as a repeater and often is located in a work closet of the building (for example, in a phone closet). Each workstation or server is located at the end-point of a cable connected to the hub. Each computer has two pairs of wire; one pair is used to receive data, and one pair is used to send data. Wires can be up to 100 meters (about 328 feet) from the repeater to the computer. The minimum cable length between computers is 2.5 meters (about 8 feet).

Token Ring

A Token Ring network is an implementation of IEEE standard 802.5, the standard for the Token Ring access method. The access method, more than the ring shape, distinguishes Token Ring networks from other LANs. Token Ring networks are generally used in IBM shops, because it is the easiest network to connect to IBM mainframes. Token Ring networks can operate at either 4 Mbps or 16 Mbps.

Caution

Data on the ring is transmitted at either 4 or 16 Mbps, depending on the actual implementation. In order for workstations to communicate with each other, all network cards must be configured alike to communicate at either 4 or 16 Mbps on the network. You cannot mix and match transmission rates in a single ring. A ring must be all 4 Mbps or all 16 Mbps. Mixing transmission speeds in a single ring can bring the entire ring down.

A single Media Access Unit (MAU) can support up to 260 workstations with a maximum cable length of 100 meters between the MAU and workstation when utilizing STP cable. When you use UTP cable, this capability drops to 72 workstations with a maximum cable length of 45 meters between the MAU and workstation. You should consider breaking up your segments whenever you reach 40 to 60 percent of your network bandwidth.

As described earlier in this chapter, a token is passed around the ring to which the computers are connected. The computer that grabs the token is able to send data over the network. When the token returns to its source with an acknowledgment from the destination, the source relinquishes the token and continues passing it around the ring, allowing another workstation to send data out on the network. (The other common access method for LANs, the CSMA/CD access method, is described in the previous section on Ethernet.)

Network computers are connected by shielded and/or unshielded twisted-pair cable to a wiring concentrator. Each computer can be up to 100 meters (about 328 feet) from the MAU using shielded wire, or 45 meters (about 148 feet) using unshielded wire. The minimum shielded or unshielded cable length is 2.5 meters (about 8 feet).

Each MAU can support as many as 72 workstations that use unshielded wire, or up to 260 workstations using shielded wire. Each ring can have as many as 33 MAUs.

A Token Ring is an efficient design for moving data on a network. On small- to medium-sized networks with heavy data traffic, Token Rings are more efficient compared to most Ethernet installations. On the other hand, the direct routing of data supported by Ethernet networks tends to fare better when a network includes a large number of computers with light to moderate traffic.

ArcNet

The Attached Resource Computer Network (ArcNet) was developed by Datapoint Corporation in 1977. It was designed as a token-passing bus architecture, transmitting at 2.5 Mbps. ArcNetplus, a successor to the original ArcNet, supports data transmission rates of 20 Mbps.

ArcNet technology predates IEEE Project 802 standards, but most closely maps to 802.4, the standards for token-passing bus networks using broadband cable. ArcNet, however, is a baseband network and can have a star or bus topology.

ArcNet is an easy-to-install, inexpensive network. It typically uses coaxial cable and includes both active and passive hubs. Active hubs regenerate signals. Passive hubs split strong signals into multiple, weaker signals. Each workstation is connected by cable to a hub. The maximum cable length is from 120 meters (about 393 feet) to 606 meters (about 1,988 feet), depending on the type of cable and hub connection.

Table 3-8 summarizes the specifications for the architectures discussed in the previous sections.

Note

The following table provides the minimum standards required to conform to IEEE specifications. A particular implementation of the network architecture may differ from the information in this table.

Table 3-8   Summary of Network Architecture Specifications

	Ethernet	IEEE 802.3	Twisted-pair	Token Ring	ArcNet
Topology	Local bus	Bus	Star	Ring/star	Series of stars
Cable type	RG–58	Thicknet; 3/8-inch shielded-pair drop cable	Unshielded twisted-pair	Shielded or unshielded twisted-pair	RG–62 or RG–59
Impedance	50 Ω	50 Ω			
Terminator resistance	50 Ω±2 Ω	50 Ω±2 Ω	85–115 Ω UTP; 135–165 Ω TP	100–120 Ω UTP, 150 Ω TP	RG–59: 75 Ω RG–62: 93 Ω

	Ethernet	*IEEE 802.3*	*Twisted-pair*	*Token Ring*	*ArcNet*
Maximum cable segment length	185 meters (about 606 feet)	500 meters (about 1,640 feet)	100 meters (about 328 feet)	From 45 to 200 meters (about 148 to 656 feet); depends on cable type	Depends on cable but on average: W-W:120 meters (393 feet) A-A: 606 meters (1,988 feet); P-W or P-A: 30 meters (98 feet) A-A: 0.3 meters (about 12 inches) jumper[1]
Minimum length between computers	0.5 meters (about 23 inches)	2.5 meters (about 8 feet)	2.5 meters (about 8 feet) between repeater hub and computer	2.5 meters (about 8 feet)	Depends on cable
Maximum connected segments	5	5	Star pattern doesn't support connected segments	33 Media Access Units (MAUs)	Doesn't support connected segments
Maximum computers per segment	30	100	N/A	Unshielded: 72 workstations per concentrator; Shielded: 260 workstations per concentrator	Depends on cable used

[1]W-W = workstation to workstation; A-A = active hub to active hub;
P-W = passive hub to workstation; P-A = passive hub to active hub

Planning a Windows NT Network

Building a successful Windows NT network requires planning. You will build on the networking fundamentals presented earlier in this chapter as you plan and develop your Windows NT network.

Know your users

Before you can actually plan your network and site, you need to define who your users are and what they do. This information enables you to build profiles that describe users and their needs in detail and helps you to plan and meet their data needs.

Assessing user needs means identifying the types of applications and services that your users require, such as e-mail, database access, and connections to the Internet. You'll probably need to dig up organization charts and various departmental lists so that you can determine the flow of information and types of applications with which users work. You can also solicit feedback from users and management. After you identify user needs, map them to the features available in Windows NT and Microsoft Back Office components or other business critical applications. Table 3-9 illustrates how you might group users.

Table 3-9	Mapping User Needs to Features	
Function	*User needs*	*Available feature*
Field personnel	Remote connectivity to access e-mail	
News wire application for news and weather forecasts	Remote connectivity	
Research and development	E-mail connectivity to the Internet	Internet Mail Connector
Sales	Connectivity to other locations through X.400	X.400 connector

You can use this data to help group users according to software, hardware, and training requirements; the amount of server disk space that they need; the amount of network traffic; and so on.

Know where your users are

At this point you know who your users are and what your users need, but do you know where they reside? You may have users clustered in a small region or dispersed over a large geographical area. If your users are spread over miles and time zones, you need to know how they make their network connections. Use a spreadsheet to build a geographic profile for your organization. The geographic profile includes all locations where your company has an office or any other facility.

For example, you might create a spreadsheet with column headings that identify physical locations, types of users at each location, and available network connections. Table 3-10 shows such a spreadsheet.

Table 3-10			**Sample Spreadsheet**					
Location	*Windows NT*	*Windows 95*	*Windows 3.1x*	*MS-DOS*	*Macintosh*	*OS/2*	*Novell*	*Type of con-nection*
Cincinnati	4	10	3	1	3	2	1	T1
San Diego	6	5	1	1			1	ISDN

Segment your network

All data that moves on a LAN is transmitted, carried, and received. In the simplest LAN, the data travels directly from the transmitter to the receiver. In more complex situations, the data must travel through routers or bridges. Each part of the network that connects into a router or bridge forms a *segment* of the network.

Almost every network contains multiple physical segments due to the limitations imposed by the technical specifications of your network implementation. A network split into separate segments can improve performance. However, when you split a network into segments, networked workstations cannot access any resources beyond their local segment without a router or bridge.

Start your site layout with a drawing of your logical network. (If there are no routers or bridges within your site, your drawing can be a simple straight line.) Label each router with the protocols that it routes between segments. Within a site, you need one or more protocols routed between every segment of your network. Your Windows NT machine has to support at least one of these common protocols so that all clients can communicate with all servers in the site. If you do not have at least one common protocol, you will have problems with service and application access.

Every segment of your network is in a physical location. For example, one segment can serve a building or a floor in that building. Add information to your drawing about the location of each segment.

Choosing a Network Topology

Designing a topology for your organization includes conceiving and drawing plans for the number of sites, site boundaries, number of servers per site, and the links between them. Determining the right number of sites, size, and links requires analysis of various factors such as the available network bandwidth, the type of physical links, the amount of internetwork traffic, the types of network protocols, operating systems in use, and costs.

To determine the topology, you must decide where to locate resources in the infrastructure. During the requirements analysis phase, you identified the resources and applications needed. The underlying network determines — to a great extent — the topology for an organization and its configuration. Site boundaries, site links, message routing, directory replication, and system administration depend on network topology. The key factors affecting network topology are

■ Network size

■ Network bandwidth

■ Network type and links

■ Network traffic patterns

■ Network protocols

Sizing your network

An organization can have networks of different sizes: a single local area network (LAN) that connects a few computers for sharing files and printers; a mixed internetwork of LANs that connects computers company-wide; a metropolitan area network (MAN) that connects LAN segments within a campus, industrial park, or city; or a wide area network (WAN) that links all of the computers of a worldwide organization.

Designing and configuring organizations for networks of different sizes requires careful consideration. For example, for a large network you may need to set up multiple sites. In that case, you must consider how to move data over WAN links and how to configure the organization to provide the information and application services. On the other hand, an organization for a small network could consist of one or a few sites and may not require data replication over a WAN link.

Using network bandwidth efficiently

Network bandwidth is the data transmission capacity over a network link. Within a site, servers require higher bandwidth connections than servers in different sites because servers within a site communicate over synchronous RPCs. When configuring links between sites, be aware of the available bandwidth so that you can choose the most appropriate site link (site or X.400 connector), set directory replication schedules, and set costs appropriately.

Net available bandwidth is the effective bandwidth that is available after bandwidth consumption by other applications is taken into consideration. The net available bandwidth on a network link between two servers — not the total available bandwidth — is the decisive factor for determining whether servers can be placed in the same site. Therefore, you must be aware of the net bandwidth available after allowing for other applications that share the same link.

The client/server architecture used by Windows NT Server provides an excellent way to use bandwidth. With Windows NT Server, the server processes data and transmits only the results. In contrast, a file-based system transfers data files back and forth over a link. In addition to this inherent advantage in Windows NT Server, think about conservation measures that you can take to minimize network traffic. For example, to minimize network traffic during regular business hours, you can configure services and applications to run after business hours, when bandwidth consumption is lower.

Minimizing costs

When considering bandwidth, you should make sure that network links between servers have enough bandwidth to handle not only the common load due to message, public folder, and directory replication traffic, but also bursts in traffic. You also need to consider the costs of providing that bandwidth.

Table 3-11 lists the approximate costs for connecting to the Internet over some common network links in the United States. Use this table as a guideline for factoring bandwidth costs into your budget. The cost is based on bandwidth and availability. For example, both the PPP and dedicated PPP dial-up lines have the same bandwidth (up to the speed of the modem used). However, dedicated PPP dial-up lines are more expensive because they are available 24 hours a day.

Table 3-11	Bandwidth Costs	
Network link	*Bandwidth*	*Approximate cost*
PPP dial-up line	Modem speed (2.4, 19.2, to 38.4 Kbps)	$20-30 per month
SLIP dial-up line	Modem speed (2.4, 19.2, to 38.4 Kbps)	$20-30 per month
Dedicated PPP/SLIP	Modem speed (2.4, 19.2, to 38.4 Kbps)	$200-300 per month
56-K line	56 Kbps	$150-300 per month
PPP ISDN	128 Kbps	$70-100 per month plus equipment
T1	1.544 Mbps	$1,500-2,000 per month
T3	44.184 Mbps	$65,000-80,000 per month

Choosing a Protocol

Most LANs today typically run a multitude of network protocols and transports. For your topology design, you'll need to know what type of network protocols and transports you have so that you can configure the site links appropriately.

Right-out-of-the-box Windows NT provides you with several choices of transport protocols. Each of these choices has its good and bad aspects, which you should consider carefully before making a final decision on which protocol to implement. Of course, if you are planning to integrate Windows NT into an existing network, your choices may already be made.

Microsoft provides three transport drivers (that is, protocols) with Windows NT: TCP/IP, NWLink, and NBF. Windows NT also ships with the Data Link Control (DLC) protocol, which does not provide transport layer services. The terms TCP/IP, NWLink, and NBF refer respectively to the Windows NT transport drivers that implement the Internet TCP/IP, Novell SPX/IPX, and IBM NetBEUI network protocol suites.

Windows NT installs NWLink by default, primarily because IPX is the most common protocol in PC networks and has relatively simple configuration requirements. As a rule, you should use the minimum protocols necessary, because multiple protocols usually result in higher memory requirements for clients, more complex client configuration, and network administration.

Transport driver characteristics

As mentioned previously, your computing environment determines which protocol characteristics you need and which are most important. The applicability and importance of these characteristics depend on factors such as

- Network size
- Number of locations
- Node type (homogeneous or heterogeneous)
- Internet connectivity requirements

Interoperability

The availability of a protocol on a variety of operating systems and hardware platforms provides the advantage of interoperability. Windows NT provides native support for NetBEUI, TCP/IP, and SPX/IPX through the NBF, TCP/IP, and NWLink transport drivers.

- NetBEUI is limited almost exclusively to Microsoft and IBM PC networks: Microsoft LAN Manager, Windows NT, Windows for Workgroups, LAN Manager for UNIX, and IBM PCLAN and LAN Server environments.

- TCP/IP is available on a wide variety of operating systems such as Windows NT, UNIX, NetWare, VMS, VM, MVS, MS-DOS, Macintosh, and OS/2. It is the protocol of the global Internet. NetWare/IP enables NetWare users to run TCP/IP-only networks, accessing NetWare services without requiring SPX/IPX. However, NetWare/IP is not native IP for NetWare; it emulates the IPX stack to NCP, which still requires an underlying IPX (or emulated IPX) layer. In comparison, Windows NT provides true protocol-independent networking, running SMBs over its transport drivers without emulation requirements.

- IPX is the native protocol of Novell NetWare, although SPX/IPX is also available on other operating systems. Microsoft provides NWLink for Windows NT, TGV provides IPX for DEC VMS, and Novell offers IPX on UnixWare.

Easy Configuration and Administration

No matter what size of network you manage, you still need a client configuration that is simple and easy to administer. If your site is large, you have many clients to configure; and if your site is small, you might not have enough support personnel to maintain even a minimum number of clients. All three protocols implemented under Windows NT are self-tuning. You simply install them, configure them, and let them do their jobs. However, there may be times when you want to tweak the configuration to meet special requirements in your network. Microsoft provides access to certain tuning parameters for manual configuration in special situations.

- NBF requires little or no initial configuration or network administration.

- TCP/IP is potentially difficult to configure due to the relative complexity of its multi-part naming scheme and the fact that a default gateway (router) must be identified for each station. To reduce the client configuration burden, Windows NT supports the Dynamic Host Configuration Protocol (DHCP), an open standard that transparently provides dynamic negotiation of client configuration. DHCP clients require no manual IP configuration, and administrators do not have to assign IP addresses manually. However, DHCP does require proper planning and administration of DHCP servers.

- NWLink requires little or no initial client configuration on small non-routed networks. The node ID component of the IPX address is simply the 6-byte MAC address of the NIC. This simple node ID eliminates the need for manual client configuration. Configuring a server's external and internal networks is more complex, however.

Network Segmentation

When administering large networks, you must be able to differentiate between multiple interconnected networks. Hierarchical network addresses provide the ability to manage a hierarchy of subnetworks within networks, allowing smarter forwarding and security. Creating smaller segments with fewer stations produces more manageable networks with reduced traffic levels. This ability may not be critical for small networks.

- NetBEUI uses a single-part naming scheme and, therefore, has no facility for differentiating between multiple interconnected networks.

- TCP/IP uses a multi-part naming scheme that allows very large multi-location networks to be logically segmented into multiple levels of subnets. Network administrators can use the network ID component of the IP address in conjunction with a subnet mask to configure and manage subnetworks within subnetworks. IP uses subnetworks to logically segment large networks into separate, smaller, interconnected subnetworks.

- IPX uses a simple two-part naming scheme that allows large multi-location networks to be logically segmented into multiple subnets. However, the IPX network ID is not hierarchical; it does not divide into subcomponents.

Routing Capabilities

Multi-location networks require routing capabilities, although single location networks have little use for such capabilities. Routable protocols do not generally allow broadcast packets to traverse routers, thereby reducing network congestion. Both IP and IPX are natively routable; they do not require encapsulation for routing. Both employ Interior Gateway Protocols (IGPs) to exchange routing information among routers within an autonomous network (that is, a group of nodes controlled by a single administrative authority). One of the most common IGPs is the Routing Information Protocol (RIP), which uses a vector-distance algorithm to determine optimum routes. The RIP implementations used in IP and IPX are based upon the XNS RIP developed by Xerox Corporation's Palo Alto Research Center (PARC).

- NetBEUI is not routable. NBF does support a simple form of routing known as Token Ring Source Routing; it is offered only on Token Ring networks. However, source routing is not actually implemented at the Open Systems Interconnection (OSI) Network Layer.

- TCP/IP provides full internetwork routing support. In addition to RIP, IP can also use other IGPs such as Cisco Systems' Interior Gateway Routing Protocol (IGRP) and the IETF's Open Shortest Path First (OSPF) protocol. NWLink enables Windows NT to perform static IP routing but does not support dynamic IGPs such as RIP and OSPF. Dynamic routing must be implemented with third-party routers.

- IPX provides full internetwork routing support. NWLink uses RIP over IPX (RIPX) to implement route and router discovery services used by SPX and NBIPX. When NWLink loads, it sends out a RIPX request for a network number to be used for addressing at the IPX level. NetWare servers respond with a RIP packet containing the network number of the local network. If there is no RIPX response, NWLink uses 0 for the network number and indicates that the IPX packet is for the local subnet.

Performance

Protocol performance is typically dependent on the efficiency and tuning of the transport driver implementation rather than the protocol itself.

- NBF is tuned for small LAN communication and, therefore, is very fast. Its performance across WANs is poor.

- TCP/IP is not as fast as NBF on small LANs.

- NWLink is not so fast as NBF on small LANs.

  IPX/SPX protocols have some significant performance limitations in a routed (wide area) network, which is why Novell has been modifying them with "packet burst" and "SPX II" changes. IPX is only slightly faster than TCP/IP for file and print operations, and only slightly slower than TCP/IP for application services.

Determining Site Boundaries

Site planning builds on the work done during enterprise (network) planning. When planning a new network, you look at issues and try to plan them to meet your current and future needs, minimize impact on your existing network, and stay within your budget. Site planning has the same goals.

The following details are needed to plan a site:

- **Logical network layout.** As discussed earlier in the chapter, locating servers on the same LAN segments as the users reduces traffic across bridges and routers.

- **Types of users and their needs.** Planning for server hardware and gateways requires knowing which users plan to use what services.

- **Special service needs.** Special services, such as gateways, news feeds, and other applications affect planning for server loading and hardware.

- **Remote client access.** Planning for remote clients includes deciding on the type and quantity of remote services that your site must support.

- **Connections to other sites and message systems.** Depending on the type of connections, special network protocols or hardware may be required on some servers.

There are several factors that determine where to draw site boundaries. Some are necessary conditions that all Windows NT Server computers must satisfy to be placed in the same site; others are optional guidelines that ease administration, minimize cost, provide more security, and increase performance.

Caution

It is extremely important to plan the number of sites and their boundaries very carefully. Redefining sites includes reinstalling and reconfiguring the sites and all of the related system information.

Necessary conditions

To be placed in the same site, all servers must meet the following conditions:

- **Synchronous remote procedure calls (RPC) connectivity.** The network link must be permanent. A site's boundary cannot span a connection that does not support synchronous RPC.

- **Adequate available bandwidth.** The bandwidth threshold is somewhat arbitrary. It must be enough to support the volume of data transmitted within the site. Considerations include message volume, as well as directory and public folder replication.

- **Same Windows NT security context for all servers.** Within a site, all Windows NT Server services must run under the same security context so that they can authenticate each other. This means that servers within a site must belong to either the same Windows NT domain or to domains that trust each other. All Windows NT services within a site use the same service account to simplify security.

Within a site, all Windows NT Server services communicate through RPC. Remote Procedure Calls (RPCs) can use named pipes, NetBIOS, or Windows Sockets to communicate with remote systems. This allows servers to communicate with each other efficiently and independently of the type of network. RPC supports the following network protocols transparently:

- IPX/SPX through Microsoft NWLink

- NetBEUI

- TCP/IP

Optional conditions

In addition to the necessary conditions listed in the preceding section, you can also consider the following factors for determining the number of sites and boundaries:

- **Site administration.** It is easier to administer servers that are grouped within a single site. When you make a change on one server, the changes are propagated to all servers within a site automatically. For ease of configuration and administration, keep the number of sites to a minimum and make sites as large as possible. Place servers that you want to administer collectively in the same site. If you want to split administration duties, use different sites.

- **Cost.** To control costs, place servers that are connected through an expensive link in separate sites. Another cost consideration is the number of servers per site. In some cases, it might be more cost effective to have more lower-cost servers than a few, higher-cost servers. You have to weigh performance versus cost.

- **Performance.** To maximize performance in your site, draw site boundaries so that servers connected through links with similar bandwidth are placed within a site. For example, if you have three servers — Cincinnati, San Diego, and Atlanta — and the link between Cincinnati and Atlanta is very fast but the link to San Diego is much slower, place San Diego in a separate site.

  There are other factors that affect performance at the site and server levels, such as the number of servers per site. The more servers in a site, the more RPC-generated network traffic occurs.

- **Directory replication.** Directory replication occurs more often within a site than between sites because it is assumed that the network bandwidth between sites is lower than within a site. If you want automatic, frequent replication between servers, place them in the same site (as long as they meet the necessary conditions described in the preceding section). On the other hand, if you want to control when replication occurs, place servers in different sites.

Linking Sites

Once you have decided on the number of Windows NT Server sites that make up your organization and the site boundaries, you need to decide how to link the sites.

Tip

If two sites are connected through a slow link, configure directory replication between these two sites so that the slow link is used only occasionally. This minimizes the use of that link and improves performance.

Methods of connecting sites

You can connect sites using either the X.400 mail-based method or an RPC method.

RPC connections can be either over a LAN or WAN or asynchronously through RAS. RAS can be configured over a modem, RS-232 null-modem cable, X.25 network, modem pool, security hosts and switches, SNA, and ISDN.

To establish communication between any two sites, you can have one or more connections. This can be used to balance the load or as a cost-control measure.

Wireless Local Area Networks (LANs)

LANs can connect using wireless technology, which consists of transmitters and receivers. The transmitter unit connects to a standard Ethernet cable and broadcasts the signals to computers around it. There are three techniques for wireless data transmission:

- **Narrow-band (or single-frequency) radio.** This transmission technique can penetrate walls and spread over a wide area, but it interferes with other radio frequencies.

- **Spread spectrum radio.** This transmission technique uses a wide range of frequencies, avoiding the interference problems associated with narrow-band transmission.

- **Infrared light.** The infrared light technique can transmit data at very high rates, but this technique is susceptible to obstructions (such as strong light sources) within a typical office building. Infrared transmission serves best as a backbone between buildings.

Wireless LANs operate at speeds between 128 Kbps and 1.544 Mbps.

Wide Area Networks (WANs)

Creating a wide area network with Windows NT Server is easy. You can follow the conventional method of using a router or bridge to connect two networks located at physically different locations, or you can use RAS.

Tip

For your first wide area network, I suggest that you use the RAS software. This service is included with Windows NT Server and is, therefore, the least expensive alternative for creating a wide area network. It can support up to 256 simultaneous client connections, although to support this, you will require a third-party adapter from a manufacturer such as DigiBoard. If you do plan on supporting 256 simultaneous connections, this server should not perform any other network action. With the remote access service, you can use an X.25 adapter card to connect you to an X.25 source which is low speed but provides worldwide connectivity from a local phone number; you can use a pair of modems, which requires calling a standard phone number (just like your bulletin board access); or you can use an ISDN adapter.

Metropolitan Area Networks (MANs) and WANs

LANs can grow or expand into metropolitan area networks (MANs) and wide area networks (WANs) by using remote connection or high-speed, fiber optic backbones. A remote connection can link two or more LANs in two buildings that are nearby or on opposite sides of the world. Fiber optic backbones, even though they can provide high speeds (from 10 through 100 Mbps), are currently used only in MAN connections. There are several types of WAN links:

- **Dial-up phone lines.** These are the same copper, voice-grade wires used for voice communication. They are relatively slow but provide an inexpensive way to transfer data that is not time critical. You can increase transmission speed by using modems at both ends of the link that use the same encoding and compression technology. With this method, transmission speeds of up to 57.6 Kbps are possible.

- **Packet-switching networks (leased lines).** These lines provide full-time connections between LAN segments and use a packet delivery method (X.25 and frame relay) to transfer data in small pieces (packets) of information. A packet-switching network, also referred to as a *cloud*, is a complex web of interconnections and switching equipment. The connections are called *virtual connections* because they appear to users as dedicated lines, even though they transfer packets for multiple destinations on the same high-speed line. Public Data Networks (PDNs) companies such as AT&T, Tymenet, GE, and Sprint provide packet-switching networks for a fee.

- **Microwave connections.** These wireless connections use waves at the microwave frequency and generally connect buildings in a campus or an industrial park.

- **Satellite connections.** These wireless connections interconnect LANs over a wide area. AT&T Tridom, Comsat General Corporation, and GTE Spacenet Corporation offer satellite links. These connections make good backup connections because you pay only for the time you actually use the connection (plus a flat fee).

- **Campus backbones.** These connections interconnect LANs by using backbone coaxial or fiber optic cable.

MAN and WAN links range from 19.2 Kbps through 9.6 Gbps. On the low end of the range (from 19.2 Kbps through 128 Kbps), you must place servers in different sites and connect through X.400 connectors. On the high end of the range (above 128 Kbps), servers can exist in the same sites and link through either site or X.400 connectors.

Windows NT Remote Access Server

Remote Access Server is a Windows NT service that allows a remote workstation to connect to a network. You can use the following connection methods with RAS:

- Modem

- X.25 network, directly or through a modem and packet assembly and disassembly (PAD)

- Modem pool

- ISDN

- SNA

- Security hosts and switches

- RS-232 null-modem cable

Cross Reference

Refer to Chapter 14, *Using Remote Access Service,* for detailed information on installing and configuring RAS.

Using a RAS connector

You use the RAS connector when you don't have a permanent connection and you can connect through RAS.

The advantages are that the administrator controls when connections happen. Also, RAS works over slow, non-permanent links. The disadvantage is that data transfer is dependent on the speed of the modem, so it might be slow.

X.25 Networks

An X.25 RAS connection is a low-speed (about 9600 bps), packet-based connection (just like your LAN). The primary advantage of an X.25 network is that it is cheaper to implement than the regular modem-to-modem or ISDN-to-ISDN connection when supporting a large number of RAS clients. This is because you can use an X.25 connection from just about anywhere in the world just by dialing a local access number.

There are two parts to this process and two ways to implement an X.25 RAS connection. You can use an X.25 network adapter (such as that manufactured by Eicon) to X.25 network adapter connection. Or you can use an X.25 network adapter on the server, and a modem on the client. The client will dial a local access number to gain access to the X.25 network. These network packets will then be routed to your network server. Once this has occurred, a two-way communication linkage will be established, and the user can perform any desired network action, such as printing a file or running an application.

X.25 is also a good choice for a network that has to maintain a low-cost, low-usage (particularly at 9600 bps) communication linkage between two remote locations. However, it is not for the security-minded as the X.25 network can be easily tapped by potential hackers.

High-speed Modems

The most common RAS connection is based on high-speed modems. You can use your standard 14400 or 28800 modems to provide data transfers in the 57600-bps to 115200-bps range. Although this is not the fastest data transfer rate, it is an acceptable data transfer rate for infrequent network usage and works extremely well for distributed applications (such as SQL Server). However, as in most software packages, there are issues to consider.

The first thing of which you should be aware is that a reliable modem connection is based on the quality of the phone line. The faster the baud rate, the cleaner the line has to be to obtain error-free data transmissions. Reliable 28800 connections are almost impossible to achieve with local phone lines. Long-distance connections seem to perform better, probably because many of them are based on fiber optic phone lines.

Next, consider the UART (Universal Asynchronous Receiver Transmitter) on which your COM port is based. If you have the standard 16450, the best that you can achieve is a 38400-bps data transmission. If you have a 16550 UART, the best that you can achieve is a 57600-bps data transfer rate. To obtain any higher data transfer rate, you must use either an internal modem with a buffered 16550 UART or another buffered UART supported by Windows NT Server. The best solution that I have found is to use a DigiBoard adapter, which can support from 2 to 256 UARTs and includes a dedicated CPU to offload the work from the CPU on your motherboard.

To obtain the higher data transfer rates, modify the SERIAL.INI file located in the SystemRoot\System32\RAS directory. Change the MAXCONNECTBPS and IntialBps parameters to the highest DTE rate (from 38400 to 57600 for a 14400 modem, and from 57600 to 155200 for a 28800 modem). Configure your client software similarly. Otherwise, you will only achieve the data transfer rate of the slowest RAS configuration.

You should also test your RAS configuration to determine whether the hardware or software compression performs better. This will depend on the speed of your CPU. For most computers, the software compression will outperform the hardware compression, but you need to test this on your hardware platforms to be sure.

And lest we forget, consider the cost associated with local and long-distance access. This will vary from state to state and your phone company, but you should consider it in your budget.

The ISDN Connection

An ISDN connection can offer the best performance when compared to either an X.25 or modem connection. This is because ISDN is a digital-based connection; therefore, the quality of the connection is superior to the average modem connection and much faster than an X.25 connection. However, ISDN uses a proprietary phone connection so it is not acceptable for mobile computer users. It does perform well for sites where your local phone company supports ISDN phone lines. An ISDN connection can support one or two 64-KB connections (some phone companies use 8 KB as overhead so you may only get 56 KB). In theory, this can give you up to a 128-KB (possibly only 112-KB) data transfer rate.

Like an X.25 connection, ISDN requires a proprietary adapter, which will increase your WAN expense. You should also consider the monthly fee and the per minute access fees. These fees vary from state to state.

You can use a router or bridge with an ISDN connection to provide an additional benefit that a RAS connection cannot perform for you. This is the ability to dial up and connect to a remote network node based on user demand. A RAS connection must either be user initiated or permanent. A router or bridge (depending on the manufacturer) can automatically dial up a remote node when it detects a request for an external server in its internal database. This can decrease your phone bill quite a bit over a dedicated connection to your remote server.

Some routers can use either a regular phone line or a digital leased line. Regular phone lines offer a limited bandwidth and increased cost based on whether you dial local or long-distance phone numbers. For a constant communication linkage, I recommend a leased line. Leased lines vary in cost from location to location so you should check with your phone company for the specific cost associated with connecting your sites. Leased lines also come in various types and speeds. (See Table 3-11).

ISDN service is not available in every state so you should check with your local phone company before deciding to use this alternative.

Characteristics of common network links

Tables 3-12, 3-13, and 3-14 group the most common network links in three categories: low-to-medium bandwidth, medium-to-high bandwidth, and very high bandwidth. When choosing the appropriate bandwidth range, consider the number of servers, message volume, and the amount of traffic generated by users and system services. As a rule of thumb, you should design sites so that servers can connect through links that are in the medium-to-high and very high bandwidth range. However, in some cases, you may be able to use links in the low-to-medium bandwidth range if you have low message volume.

Be aware that some of these links are available in ranges of bandwidth rather than just at a discrete bandwidth. For example, frame relay links range from 64 to 512 Kbps. If you have a frame relay connection between two servers at 64 Kbps and a high message volume, you should consider placing them in different sites. On the other hand, if you connect them at 512 Kbps, you can place them in the same site.

Another important characteristic of network links is reliability. For example, satellite connections have very high bandwidth but, in some cases, may not be as reliable as an Ethernet link with a lower bandwidth. Because servers in the same site require permanent connections, it may be better to choose a link with lower bandwidth if its reliability is better than that of a higher bandwidth link.

Table 3-12	Low-to-medium Bandwidth Connections		
Network link	*Bandwidth*	*Common use*	*Description*
Dial-up phone line	2.4, 19.2, to 57.6 Kbps	Single user; remote connections to LANs and WANs	Copper, voice-grade wire. Bandwidths of up to 57.6 Kbps are possible when used with high-speed modems that are configured with the same encoding and compression technology on both ends.

Network link	Bandwidth	Common use	Description
X.25 (leased lines)	19.2, 56, and 64 Kbps	WANs	Provides permanent connections between LAN segments. X.25 is an international standard for sending packets over public data networks. Access to an X.25 network is through leased or dial-up lines.
Frame relay (leased lines)	64 to 512 Kbps	WANs	Provides permanent connections between LAN segments. Frame relay is a method for sending packets over private and public data networks. It provides better performance than X.25 because it reduces some of the overhead used in X.25. Sprint, CompuServe, Tymenet, Williams Telecommunications, and other carriers offer frame relay services.
Fractional T-1	64 Kbps	WANs and redundant links	A fraction of a T-1 line. Fractional T-1 makes T-1 service at 64 Kbps more affordable. You can add channels to expand bandwidth up to a full T-1 line.

Table 3-13	Medium-to-high Bandwidth Connections		
Network link	**Bandwidth**	**Common use**	**Description**
Integrated Services Digital Network (ISDN)	128 to 150 Kbps	LANs and WANs	High-speed, digital dial-up lines based on the ISDN standard. Personal computer users benefit the most from these lines. They provide connections to data services, databases, and international networks at reasonably fast rates.
T-1	1.544 Mbps	High-use WAN links	A high-quality digital line that runs over two twisted copper wires. T-1 is commonly used to build private voice and data networks. Its bandwidth of 1.544 Mbps can be divided into 24 64-Kbps channels, each carrying one voice or data transmission.

(continued)

Table 3-13 *(Continued)*

Network link	Bandwidth	Common use	Description
ArcNet	2.5 Mbps	LANs	ArcNet links have a star or bus topology and use a token-passing access method with coaxial cable.
Token Ring	4 or 16 Mbps	LANs	Token Ring links combine star and ring topologies and use a token-passing access method with shielded or unshielded twisted-pair cable.
Thin Ethernet	10 Mbps	Single LANs	Thin Ethernet links have a linear bus topology and use a Carrier Sense Multiple Access with Collision Detection (CSMA/CD) access method with thin or twisted-pair cable.
Thick Ethernet	10 Mbps	Multiple LANs	Same as thin Ethernet but with thick or twisted-pair cable.
Fiber optic	10 to 100 Mbps	High-use MAN links	Fiber optic cable that usually follows the Fiber Distributed Data Interface (FDDI) standard. It is used for backbone connections in MANs. Large networks with many LAN segments and heavy traffic benefit from FDDI fiber optic cable.

Table 3-14   Very High Bandwidth Connections

Network link	Bandwidth	Common use	Description
Satellite connections	128 Kbps to 1.544 Mbps	Wireless WANs (often used as backup connections)	Wireless connections that provide global data links. AT&T Tridom, Comsat General Corporation, and GTE Spacenet Corporation offer satellite links.
Microwave connections	1.544 Mbps	Wireless LANs	Wireless connections that use waves at the microwave frequency.

Network link	Bandwidth	Common use	Description
T-3	44.184 Mbps	High-use WAN links	Similar to T-1 but has higher bandwidth and can be divided into 28 T-1 channels.
Asynchronous Transfer Mode (ATM)	100, 200, and 400 Mbps to 9.6 Gbps	WANs	
LAN-to-WAN connections			Data transfer technology that provides a way to send packets of information simultaneously from many sources across a high-speed line, where it is reassembled and transferred to each destination point. ATM supports voice and video. ATM can be used on existing fractional T-1, T-1, T-3, and SONET as its physical medium.

Planning for Mobile User Access

In planning your Windows NT network, you must evaluate the needs of your mobile users. By understanding your users' access requirements, you can plan for connection issues. This includes managing remote access, ordering sufficient modems and ISDN or X.25 connections for the expected volume of traffic, building in flexibility for future growth, and considering security. When planning for mobile users, you should ask the following questions:

- What remote communications programs will be used for your Windows NT Server clients? Remote access, Dial-Up Networking, AppleTalk?

- What remote access communications programs will be used on your network? Windows NT RAS Server?

- How many remote clients do you plan to have?

- How often will the remote clients connect to the network?

- What kind of security do you plan to implement for remote clients?

Assessing the mobile computer user's needs

As you plan remote access hardware requirements, you need to examine your mobile user traffic patterns. The following factors can affect your decisions:

- Number of remote clients
- Frequency of connections
- Volume of data sent and received
- Time of calls
- Convenience for remote clients
- Connection speed

Many mobile users can be served by one RAS server, unless they call frequently. If all mobile users call the server at the same time, you need more lines to handle the load or a way to encourage them to spread out their calls over a longer time period.

If you want to support multiple connections in the site, decide if you need a *hunt system* in your organization's phone system. With a hunt system, a call to a single phone number is switched to an available modem. The alternative is for each modem to have a separate phone number. A hunt system makes it easier and quicker for mobile users to connect.

A more important consideration is the speed of the connections. A remote client connecting at 9600 bits per second (bps) keeps a connection busy longer than a remote client connecting at 19,200 bps. This speed is limited in asynchronous connections by the types of modems used and the highest transfer rates at which the two can connect. In X.25 connections, the speed is limited by either the bandwidth of the leased line or the modem speed of the PAD (if a PAD is used), whichever is lower.

Determining the number of connections

In order to meet the needs of your mobile users, you must have enough connections available. Several factors can influence just how many connections you need to provide. Keep in mind that

- All Microsoft Windows and DOS users now have clients capable of mobile use. This implies that the number of potential mobile or remote computer users is not entirely limited by the operating system they run.
- The number of portable and home computers is increasing. With so many companies implementing telecommuting programs, it's not uncommon to have large percentages of the workforce working beyond the corporate walls.

Obviously, there are limits to the number of mobile users that you can support with a single Windows NT machine. With the growing number of mobile computer users, you need to employ other mechanisms to help cut down on the number of discrete connections you provide. The following options can decrease the number of connections needed:

- High-speed connections, such as X.25 and ISDN

- Compression of all messages (but not attachments) by the mail system

- Compression of all data across a RAS connection by the RAS client and server

Remote connections to Windows NT

To access Windows NT domains or workgroups, Windows NT clients need network access to the Windows NT Server. If they are at a remote location, they need some means of connecting to the network so that they can send remote procedure calls (RPCs) to the Windows NT Server just as if they were on a LAN.

All Windows NT clients have the capability to start and end communications programs that allow the client or network operating system to connect to the network. You do not have to use this software to make the network connection — it is provided as a convenient default. When making connections from the client side, you have the following choices:

- **MS-DOS Shiva**. This is included with the client and can connect to Windows NT RAS Servers and Shiva LAN Rovers.

- **Windows 16-bit Shiva.** This is included with the client and can connect to Windows NT RAS Servers and Shiva LAN Rovers.

- **Windows NT Remote Access Service (RAS).** This is included with the operating system.

- **Windows 95 Microsoft Dial-Up Networking.** This is included with the operating system.

On the network half of remote access to Windows NT, you have three options:

- **Windows NT RAS Server.** This is built into Windows NT Servers and supports connections from RAS, PPP, and Shiva clients.

- **Shiva LAN Rover.** This supports connections from Shiva, RAS, and ARA clients.

- **Other.** This includes any remote access server software that is compatible with RAS or the network software that is currently used by your remote workstations.

Summary

Windows NT is a powerful and flexible network operating system. When properly designed and implemented, it becomes a valuable business platform. This chapter began with an overview of networking fundamentals and covered the following topics:

▶ Network architecture

▶ Planning Windows NT sites

▶ Choosing a network topology

▶ Choosing network protocols

Part II

Windows NT Server
Installation and Setup

Chapter 4

Preparing to Install Windows NT Server

In This Chapter

▶ Evaluating and planning the installation process

▶ Making decisions about partitions and file systems

▶ Preparing your hardware for Windows NT

▶ Fine-tuning your hardware before you install Windows NT

▶ Avoiding complications during installation

Windows NT Server is a huge system, and your investment in it is substantial. Your expectations of this advanced network operating system are probably high, too. Getting the most out of an enterprise network built around Windows NT servers and workstations is the result of good planning and execution. This chapter lays the groundwork for a solid Windows NT Server installation.

You should approach installing Windows NT as a three-phase process:

■ Planning the installation

■ Preparing the hardware

■ Installing and configuring

Planning the Installation

Installing and configuring Windows NT Server is no trivial task. However, the thought of installing Windows NT shouldn't send you into a state of bewilderment, especially if you've taken time to plan the installation and to prepare your hardware properly. Spend a day or so prepping your system for Windows NT, and you'll increase the odds of having a glitch-free installation.

Begin the planning phase by surveying your current computer system. Take a good look at the environment into which you're introducing Windows NT Server:

1. What types of applications do your users need?

2. What operating systems are currently running?

3. What network operating systems are running?

   - Windows NT Server
   - NetWare version 3.x
   - NetWare version 4.0
   - LAN Manager version 2.x
   - Windows for Workgroups version 3.11
   - AppleTalk
   - Banyan Vines
   - PC-NFS

4. What are your network protocols?

   - NetBIOS Extended User Interface (NetBEUI)
   - Novell's Internetwork Packet Exchange/Sequenced Packet Exchange (IPX/SPX)
   - Transmission Control Protocol/Internet Protocol (TCP/IP)
   - System Network Architecture (SNA)

5. If your new NT machine is joining an existing network, what is the name of the new NT machine and the name for the workgroup or domain that this machine will join?

   - What is the name of your organization?
   - What are the names of your sites?
   - What are the names of your domains?
   - What are the names of your Windows NT Server computers?

6. How many Windows NT domains does your organization have?

7. What kind of Windows NT domain does your enterprise support?

   - Single domain model
   - Master domain model
   - Multiple master domain model
   - Complete trust model

Cross Reference

If domain planning is in order, refer to Chapter 2, *Redefining the Enterprise Network* and Chapter 3, *Designing the Windows NT Network*.

Making decisions about Windows NT's environment

It's important to analyze and plan your Windows NT installation carefully because there are some decisions that you cannot change except by reinstalling Windows NT. For example, you have to select an operating mode before you install Windows NT Server software; that is, you have to decide whether this installation should function as a domain controller (either primary or backup) or as an application server. Once you make the selection, the only way to change your selection is to reinstall Windows NT Server.

Here are the decisions you need to make about the Windows NT computer before you set up:

- Do you want a domain controller or server?

- How will you partition the disk where you want to install Windows NT?

- What file system will you use on the Windows NT disk partition?

- What directory should hold the Windows NT system files?

Partitioning the disk

Before you arbitrarily carve up the disk into partitions, you need to devise a partitioning scheme. Windows NT offers a number of disk management techniques that you can use to organize and protect data on your disks:

- You can choose the number of physical disks and logical disk partitions your system will have. You can also choose whether you want to use volume sets or stripe sets to organize data across partitions.

- You can choose from among several fault-tolerance options to ensure data reliability on your system.

- You can employ other data backup and recovery techniques, such as tape backups and use of uninterruptible power supplies, to further safeguard against data loss.

A physical disk can support one or more logical partitions with each partition or set of partitions formatted as a volume for a particular file system and assigned a drive letter.

The operating system uses the primary partition of a physical disk. Each disk can have as many as four partitions, one of which may be an extended partition.

You can subdivide extended partitions into logical drives; primary partitions can't be subdivided. Besides logical drives, the free space in an extended partition can also contain volume sets or other kinds of volumes for fault-tolerance purposes. As long as the disk does not contain the boot partition, it can serve entirely as an extended partition.

Disk striping is another way to increase disk performance. This method increases both read and write performance since multiple I/O commands can be active on the drives at the same time. A striped set can have from two to 32 disks. If the disks are different sizes, the smallest is used as the common partition size. The remaining free space can be used individually or in a volume set.

You can create a partition that consumes as little as 1 MB or as much as the entire hard disk. Windows NT Server requires a partition on a permanently attached hard disk with about 90 to 100 MB of free space to store its files.

When planning your disk partitioning scheme, consider the following:

- If you're hosting other operating systems on the same disk on which you plan to install Windows NT, place them on separate partitions.

- If you plan to use a single disk system to function as a server, work-station, and application server, divide the disk into at least three partitions:

  Partition 1   Operating System

  Partition 2   Applications

  Partition 3   Data

- Allocate a sufficient amount of disk space to the partition holding the operating system. To calculate how much space to allow, consider the amount of space used by the operating system files, virtual memory paging files, temporary files, and print spooling. Plan for the worst case.

- Windows NT looks for the files it needs to load itself on the system partition. On an x86-based computer, the operating system starts from the active system partition on the first internal hard disk. So Windows NT looks for certain files in the root directory of the C drive (Disk 0) when you start your computer. Even if you place the bulk of its files on a secondary partition, Windows NT must be able to locate its system files on the primary partition.

Selecting a file system for the Windows NT partition

When IBM introduced its first personal computer running MS-DOS, the computer shipped with a 16-bit 8088 processor chip and two low-density floppy disks. The MS-DOS file system, FAT (named for its file allocation table), provided more than enough power to format these small disk volumes and to manage hierarchical directory structures and files. Along came double-density disks and then high-density disks. The FAT file system continued to serve as the primary file system even as hardware and software power increased year after year. However, file searches and data retrieval took significantly longer on large hard disks than on the original low-density floppy disks of the first IBM personal computer.

The FAT file system has been improved over the years to work more effectively with larger disks and more powerful personal computers. With MS-DOS version 4.0, the FAT entries grew from 12 bits to 16 bits in size, thus allowing for partitions larger than 32 MB.

In 1990, IBM introduced a high-performance file system (HPFS) as part of the OS/2 operating system version 1.2. Software engineers designed HPFS specifically for large hard disks on 16-bit processor computers. Not long after the birth of HPFS, IBM introduced HPFS386. This file system became a part of Microsoft LAN Manager and took advantage of the 32-bit 80386 processor chip.

Because of features such as speed and universality, FAT and HPFS are popular and widely used file systems. The new Windows NT file system, NTFS, offers compatibility with these two file systems, plus advanced functionality (such as fault tolerance, data recovery, and security) for corporations interested in greater flexibility and in data security.

NTFS is also designed for optimal performance on today's personal computers, which include a variety of very fast processor chips and can accommodate multiple, huge hard disks.

Disk Anatomy

Each hard disk, as shown in Figure 4-1, is divided into top and bottom layers, rings on each layer called tracks, and sections within each track called sectors. A *sector* is the smallest physical storage unit on a disk, typically 512 bytes in size. The Format command organizes the disk into tracks and sectors for use by a particular file system. Unless you specify a particular sector size, Format evaluates your disk and determines an appropriate sector size for you.

As a file is written to the disk, the file system allocates the appropriate number of sectors to store the file's data. For example, if each sector is 512 bytes and the file is 800 bytes, two sectors are allocated to the file. If the file is appended, for example, to twice its size (1600 bytes), another two sectors are allocated. If *contiguous* sectors (sectors that are next to each other on the disk) are not available, the data is written elsewhere on the disk, and the file is considered to be fragmented. *Fragmentation* becomes an issue when the file system must search several different locations to find all the pieces of the file that you want to read. The search causes a delay before the file is retrieved. Allocating larger sectors reduces the potential for fragmentation but increases the likelihood that sectors will have unused space.

(continued)

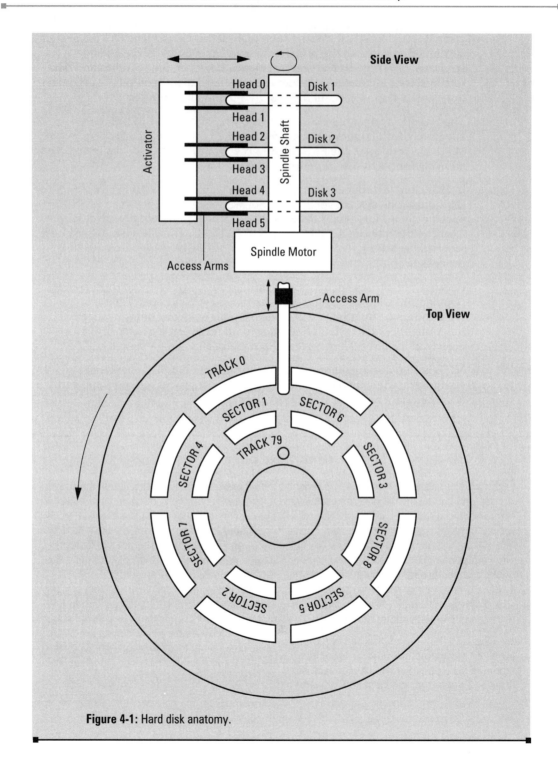

Figure 4-1: Hard disk anatomy.

The way in which data is retrieved depends on the indexing methods used by the file system. The following text provides details about FAT, HPFS, and NTFS, including how each stores, indexes, and retrieves data on the disk.

Guidelines for selecting a file system for Windows NT

As described in the previous section, Windows NT can use any one of three file systems: the file allocation table (FAT), the high-performance file system (HPFS), or the Windows NT file system (NTFS). Each file system has its own advantages and disadvantages.

- **File allocation table (FAT).** FAT is the lowest common denominator among PC file systems. It allows access to files when your computer is running MS-DOS or OS/2. What you don't get with FAT is the capability to use the security features of Windows NT. Also, FAT cannot support extremely large files and is less robust than NTFS; for example, it does not have automatic disk restore features.

- **High-performance file system (HPFS/HPFS386).** HPFS ensures file compatibility if you want to switch between Windows NT and OS/2 on your hard disk. It supports long filenames and provides better error correction than the FAT file system.

  So what's wrong with HPFS? Again, you lose out on the security features of Windows NT. You also lose compatibility with MS-DOS- and Windows 3.1-based applications when you store files with long filenames or with long directory names in their paths.

- **Windows NT file system (NTFS).** NTFS supports complete Windows NT security, so you can specify who is allowed various kinds of access to a file or directory. It also keeps a log of activities to restore the disk in the event of power failure or other problems. Unlike FAT, it supports file and directory names of up to 255 characters and supports extended file attributes. NTFS automatically generates correct MS-DOS filenames so that files can be shared with MS-DOS users. It allows a program designed to run under other operating systems such as MS-DOS access to NTFS files when it runs under Windows NT.

Note

NTFS is recognized only by Windows NT. When the computer is running another operating system (such as MS-DOS or OS/2), that operating system cannot access files on an NTFS partition on the same computer.

NTFS takes the best parts of both FAT and HPFS and improves upon those designs. From FAT, NTFS borrowed the "simplicity yields performance" philosophy. Performance increases when the number of disk transfers is minimized for common operations. From HPFS, NTFS borrowed techniques for speed and flexibility. For example, NTFS uses B-trees similar to those used by HPFS to maximize performance.

NTFS supports both long and short (eight-plus-three) filenames for compatibility with MS-DOS, HPFS, and other networked clients, including OS/2, UNIX, AppleShare, and NFS. NTFS also provides for multiple extended attributes and allows future applications to define other extended attributes.

Deciding which file system to support with your Windows NT installation requires consideration of many factors. If you plan to use only the Windows NT Workstation operating system, make a single partition and format it with NTFS.

If you plan to use NTFS and have access to another operating system, you must have at least two disk partitions. Format the C drive with a file system that Windows NT and your other operating system can use, such as FAT. Format the other partition for NTFS. You can place the Windows NT files on any uncompressed partition with sufficient free space. The following guidelines will help you make the best decision:

- **Running with DOS.** If you want to run both MS-DOS and Windows NT on the same computer, you must first install MS-DOS. Installing MS-DOS later might overwrite the boot sector on the hard disk, making it impossible to start Windows NT without using the Emergency Repair process. Make sure that the system partition (the C drive) is formatted with the appropriate file system. For example, if you already have MS-DOS installed and want to keep it, preserve the C partition and keep the file system as FAT. You can place the Windows NT files on any uncompressed partition with sufficient free space.

- **Running with Windows 3.1.** Treat this situation the same as if you were running Windows NT alongside DOS.

- **Running with Windows 95**. In addition to using FAT on local drives, Windows 95 can access files on HPFS or NTFS partitions on remote drives. However, there is no built-in support in the release of Windows 95 for adding either of these file systems as another installable file system under Windows 95. Therefore, Windows 95 cannot access either an HPFS or NTFS partition on a local disk drive by using the file system drivers provided with Windows 95.

- **Running with OS/2.** You can format an unformatted partition with either the NTFS or FAT file system. Choose FAT if you want to access files on that partition when running Windows NT, MS-DOS, or OS/2 on this computer. Choose NTFS if you want to take advantage of the features in NTFS.

- **Running with Macintosh.** Macintosh clients must use NTFS. Services for Macintosh are included with Windows NT Server. These services give Macintosh users access to files residing on a Windows NT Server. Since these files are available to Windows NT network users, the file server can be easily used for sharing files across platforms.

Establishing a new file system

There are three ways to establish a new file system on a disk partition:

- Specify the file system for the boot partition during the installation process.

- Use the FORMAT utility and specify the file system for the partition.

- Use the CONVERT utility to convert a partition from FAT or HPFS to NTFS. This leaves the existing files intact.

Caution

With the Windows NT FORMAT utility, you can format a partition as an NTFS volume by entering **/FS:NTFS** at the command line.

Using the FORMAT utility destroys all existing files on the partition.

Using the CONVERT Utility

With the CONVERT utility, you can convert an existing partition from FAT or HPFS to NTFS without destroying files. However, you cannot convert from NTFS to another file system. To convert a partition to the NTFS file system, type the CONVERT command as follows:

```
CONVERT E: /FS:NTFS
```

where *E:* is the partition that you want to convert. The CONVERT utility can be used on the boot partition of non-RISC-based computers, as well as on secondary partitions. However, the CONVERT utility cannot convert the boot partition while it is in use. Instead, if you specify the active partition, an entry is added to the Registry so that the CONVERT utility is run the next time that the system is booted.

Warning

You must not convert the boot partition to NTFS on a RISC-based computer. This is because the firmware on RISC-based computers loads the first system files in the Windows NT boot process, and the firmware understands only the FAT file system. Converting the boot partition would make the computer unable to boot. If you want to use NTFS on a RISC-based computer, create a small boot partition (1 MB or larger) to hold the HAL.DLL and OSLOADER.EXE files. The rest of the disk can be used as an NTFS partition. The installer correctly puts the HAL.DLL and OSLOADER files on the boot partition.

If someone mistakenly converts the RISC-based boot partition to NTFS, run the ARCINST.EXE utility from the install CD-ROM and reformat the boot partition as FAT.

The CONVERT utility works in only one direction, so you cannot use it to change your file system from NTFS back to FAT or HPFS format. Instead, you must reformat the NTFS drive using the FORMAT command. (Be sure to back up any files that you want to preserve before using the FORMAT command.)

Remember that you cannot use the Windows NT FORMAT command on the system partition. If Windows NT is installed on the system (NTFS) partition, you can reformat the drive by following these steps:

1. Start Windows NT Setup.

2. Choose Custom Installation.

3. When Setup prompts you to select the partition where you would like to install Windows NT, highlight the NTFS drive, and type **p** to delete the partition.

4. Continue using the Setup program to recreate and format the partition.

After running Setup, you can change file systems on any partitions. However, to preserve data when you convert an NTFS partition to any other file system, you must back up all of the files, reformat the partition (which erases all files), and then restore the files from the backup. You must also back up data before repartitioning a hard disk.

Tip

Also, if you convert the file system on an existing partition to NTFS, the conversion does not take place until all of Setup is complete and you reboot your computer with Windows NT. If you quit Setup before it finishes running, the file system on that partition is not converted.

As a general rule, always use the FAT file system for the system partition on a new installation. You can convert the partition to NTFS later using the CONVERT.EXE program. Installing Windows NT to the FAT file system ensures that you can access the partition from an MS-DOS boot disk — just in case you run into a problem during installation.

Deciding on a directory for Windows NT files

If you did not choose to upgrade an existing installation of Windows NT 3.1 and Setup detects a version of Windows NT in the directory where you want to place the new Windows NT files, Windows NT asks if you want to choose another directory. If you choose another directory, Setup automatically configures your computer so that you can run both versions of Windows NT. If you install Windows NT into a directory that contains a previous installation of Windows NT, Setup overwrites the earlier version without preserving any custom settings or user accounts.

Note

If you want to replace an existing version of Windows NT and retain your system settings and security accounts, be sure to choose the option that Setup provides for upgrading Windows NT.

Taking Stock of Your Hardware

In Chapter 1, *Inside Windows NT Server,* I described an ideal or optimum hardware setup for running Windows NT. If you're fortunate enough to work one of those high-end systems into your budget, fine. If not, read on.

A basic hardware configuration

If you're not planning to run Windows NT on a state-of-the-art powerhouse machine, here's a basic configuration on which you can install it:

- 386 or higher microprocessor

- VGA or higher resolution video display adapter

- One or more hard disks with 90 MB of free space (on a single disk drive)

- A single high-density floppy drive

- One or more network adapter cards

- 16 MB of RAM

- A mouse or other pointing device (optional, but recommended)

- One or more CD-ROM disk drives (optional, but recommended)

There are many situations in which the minimum hardware configuration can serve your needs. There's no sense in spending money to add more hardware or to replace existing hardware with bigger, better, faster equipment — unless you need it. Wait until you have Windows NT installed and running, and then use Performance Monitor to analyze and tune your system resources. This gives you the opportunity to make intelligent decisions about upgrading hardware based on how your organization uses NT, what resources are bottlenecks, and which system components are performing below your expectations. Once you have analyzed your network's performance and determined your objectives, draft a performance plan and translate that into hardware requirements for your business or enterprise.

(I have a small Windows NT network set up as a pilot system to support this book. It is running on a 486-66 DX/2 ISA local bus, with 16 MB RAM, a 1 GB IDE hard drive, a SCSI drive, an IDE CD-ROM, and a sound system. It supports three other computers as an application server, file server, mail server, and gateway to the Internet. Most of the time, I'm self-hosted. This setup is more than adequate for evaluating and using Windows NT.)

Tip

Don't install more than 16 MB of RAM on an ISA machine to boost performance. When accessing memory above 16 MB, Windows NT Virtual Direct Memory Access (DMA) uses a technique called *double buffering* to compensate for the limitations inherent in the 24-bit DMA hardware used by 16-bit Industry-Standard Architecture (ISA) bus PCs. Double buffering usually provides performance that is within a few percent of the 32-bit hardware that DMA used with 32-bit bus architectures such as Extended Industry-Standard Architecture (EISA) or Micro Channel Architecture (MCA). In general, Windows NT will continue to take full advantage of additional RAM in PCs with ISA, EISA, MCA, and other 32-bit bus architectures up to a maximum of 4 GB.

A few ISA-based PCs have unusually poor secondary cache schemes. On these computers, increasing memory beyond 16 MB will actually degrade, rather than improve, performance. This problem is a hardware limitation of these particular computers and is not specific to Windows NT.

Does your hardware have the right stuff?

Microsoft provides Hardware Compatibility lists for Windows NT 3.1 and Windows NT 4.0 These lists are posted on CompuServe in Library 1 of the WINNT forum and at FTP server location FTP.MICROSOFT.COM (advsys/winnt/winnt-docs/hcl). For your convenience, the list is available in Word for Windows format and in a Windows Help file. The hardware listed in these files is fully supported by Windows NT.

The Hardware Compatibility list is updated approximately every two months. It's possible that a piece of hardware you purchase is supported and just has not made it onto the current list. The best thing to do if you do not see your hardware on the list is to ask the manufacturer about the compatibility status. Absence from this list does not necessarily mean that the hardware will not work with Windows NT, only that it is untested or not supported at this time.

If you'd like Windows NT to support your hardware, you can put in a request to Microsoft by filling out the form, HWFEED.TXT. It is in Library 1 of the WINNT forum. You can mail it via CompuServe to the Internet address listed in the form. Information from these forms is compiled by the development team to help determine where support is needed most.

Also, because many drivers are written by third-party companies, contact your vendor to indicate that you need a driver for their hardware to run under Windows NT.

Evaluating Your Hardware

Preparing to install Windows NT requires that you give your system a thorough checkup. NT is an advanced operating system that pushes your hardware to its limits. So you'd be wise to make sure that your hardware is up to the task.

Ever watch late-night TV and see those commercials for exercise machines that promise to whip your body into some kind of new technology of its own? If you read the fine print that accompanies those ads, it usually says,

"Consult your physician before using the XKG40 body blaster." And so it is with Windows NT Server: Check your hardware before installing. In other words, compile system information, obtain service reports, and run diagnostics.

Compile extensive system information

Before installing Windows NT, gather as much information about it and its peripherals as possible. Even if this means hunting down the manuals and data sheets to every component and add-on, do it. Once you've collected the manufacturers' data, probe the inner workings of the machine for still more information. Find out everything you can, including the following information:

■ Interrupt assignments, including DMA channels and I/O assignments

■ Hardware configuration, including identification of the latest processors, BIOS type and date, CPU and math coprocessor, clock/calendar base, extended and expanded memory size, video type, mode, base address, RAM size, serial and parallel ports and addresses, mouse, game ports, hard (local or network) and floppy drives and capacities, sound cards, and scanner

■ Device drivers, including DOS and user-installable drivers

■ First MB memory map base and upper memory block allocation, including system ROM, video RAM, and EMS page frame

■ DOS memory map, including address, size, owner, type, hooked vectors and programs in upper memory

Armed with the manufacturers' data and the system information generated from your investigative probe, you can install hardware and software more easily and with a much greater chance of first-time success.

BIOS Information Stored in the CMOS

Sophisticated operating systems like Windows NT use automatic detection routines to identify a computer's hardware settings. To get this information, the operating system reads the computer's BIOS settings, which are extracted from the *CMOS* (a form of memory). Sometimes, the detection routines get carried away. Perhaps the routines decide that the CMOS settings don't suit the operating system, for example, so they alter the settings or, in extreme cases, wipe the CMOS clean.

How do you know if this happens to your computer? Often the changes that an autodetection routine makes are very subtle. If it were not for a conversation I had with a colleague, I would not have suspected anything of the sort going on with my system. Here's a sign that the CMOS has been seduced:

(continued)

(continued)

If a piece of software or hardware worked fine a week ago, the hardware checks out, and the only change you've made to your system is that you've installed or upgraded a major piece of software, check your BIOS settings.

There are several good CMOS saver programs on the market, including the PC-Tools and Norton recovery programs. They allow a user to save a copy of the CMOS registers to a file in case the battery dies, the automatic detection routines mess around with the settings, or some other mishap occurs.

To perform its tasks, the BIOS needs to know various parameters (the hardware configuration). These parameters are permanently saved in a little piece (64 bytes) of CMOS RAM (also known as CMOS). The CMOS power is supplied by a little battery, so its contents will not be lost after the PC is turned off. CMOS memory has a tendency to get erased as the battery gets old or become inaccessible if you forget the password. Write down your current setup options and put them somewhere safe — taped to the inside or the outside of the case, for instance. Especially remember the hard disk settings; they are the most important.

Using MSD to Generate System Reports

Because MS-DOS is a single-tasking operating system (where only one application at a time can access the system hardware) and Windows is a multi-tasking operating system (where multiple applications can access the system hardware), a hardware configuration that works with MS-DOS may not necessarily work reliably with Windows. The three most common causes of system failure or inconsistent hardware functionality are shared interrupts, overlapped I/O addresses, and upper memory conflicts.

MSD is a useful tool for gathering information about your computer and its hardware/software environment. You can use MSD to help you do the following:

- Check for possible interrupt conflicts.
- Check for memory conflicts between the network card and other devices in the system.
- Identify hardware that must be reinstalled or reconfigured.

For example, you can use MSD to identify how memory is used in the range between 640 K and 1 MB. By determining where you have free blocks in the upper memory area, you can avoid conflicts when loading device drivers into this range.

You also can use MSD to examine the computer's communication ports, memory, type of video card, disk drives installed, and so on. MSD allows you to view the contents of configuration files such as CONFIG.SYS, AUTOEXEC.BAT, and all of the Windows initialization (INI) files. In addition, you can print out a report.

To start MSD

1. Exit Windows. MSD reports are less accurate when MSD runs within Windows. Run MSD from DOS instead.

Both DOS and Windows will install MSD. Check the file dates to determine which is the latest and delete the older one.

2. At the DOS command prompt, type the following line and press Enter:

```
C:\path\MSD
```

where *path* indicates the directory path to MSD.EXE. Usually, the path is \WINDOWS, unless you removed MSD from the Windows directory. (If you installed Windows for Workgroups in a directory other than \WINDOWS or on a drive other than C, make the necessary changes to the *path* option.)

MSD also has command-line options you can use when starting the program. The syntax for MSD is as follows:

```
MSD [/B] [/I] [/F <FILENAME> | /P <FILENAME> | /S [<FILENAME>]] [/?]
```

Table 4-1 explains each of the command line options.

Table 4-1	Command Line Options for the MSD Utility
Option	**Description**
/B	Starts MSD in black-and-white mode. Use this option if your computer has a monochrome or LCD monitor.
/I	Specifies that no initial hardware detection be performed. Use this option if MSD fails to start correctly.
/F<FILENAME>	Writes a complete MSD report to the specified filename. Requests information such as name, company, address, telephone number, and comments.
/P<FILENAME>	Writes a complete MSD report to the specified filename without requesting any information.
/S<FILENAME>	Writes a summary MSD report to the specified filename. If no filename is specified, the report is displayed on-screen.
/?	Displays the MSD command options.

Use a comprehensive diagnostics program

Gathering system information is only part of the system checkout procedure. I also recommend that you use a comprehensive diagnostics program to run a battery of tests on the overall system. A thorough testing of system components may save you time and trouble by identifying any component that is not performing the way it should and that may be on its way to failure. It's a good idea to run the following tests:

- System Board Tests that test CPU, math coprocessor, interrupt controller, interval timer, DMA controller, CMOS clock, EISA, and MCA

- RAM (Memory) Tests to test Base, Extended, and Expanded Bus noise

- Video Adapter Tests to test Video RAM Mono, CGA, EGA, and VGA modes

- Hard Drive Tests (non-destructive) to test controller random, linear, and butterfly cylinder access

- Floppy Drive

- CD-ROM Tests to test eject and play CD random, linear, and butterfly sector access

- Serial and Parallel Port Tests to test data path internal and external loopback

Preparing Your Hardware

After checking your hardware for adequacy and malfunctions, you should prepare the system to accept Windows NT. The following section describes some of the hardware preparation steps that you should take.

The hard drive

Hard drives are the cornerstone of your system. They hold data. Without data, you have no computer system, you have no information, you have no business. Everything else in the computer system can go as long as the hard drive is intact.

The first thing that you have to do is prepare the hard drive to store information. That is, you have to be sure that the drive is low-level formatted.

Low-level Formatting

Low-level formatting is probably one of the most misunderstood aspects of hard drives. Let's start by saying that every hard drive (MFM, ESDI, IDE, and SCSI) can be low-level formatted. This is a vital step in preparing any drive for service and must be accomplished before a DOS partition or DOS format (a high-level format) is applied. Most of the current drives (IDE and SCSI) are already low-level formatted at the factory. Therefore, it should not be necessary to perform an LL format on these drives when installing them for the first time. However, there may be some circumstances (virus damage, old age, unrecoverable files, Track 0 data, and so on), where it may be desirable to LL format the drive again.

The problem is that no two IDE or SCSI drives are the same, and each needs its own LL-formatting utility to ensure that the drive hardware is formatted properly. The wrong utility can easily overwrite vital tracking information that cannot be recovered. As a consequence, the familiar DEBUG routine to invoke a classic BIOS LL formatter simply does not work for IDE and SCSI drives. If you have to perform LL formatting yourself, contact tech support for your drive manufacturer and see about obtaining the LL format utility for your particular drive. In many cases, the drive manufacturer already has a selection of utilities in a CompuServe forum, an Internet FTP site, or on their own BBS.

Defragmenting the Hard Drive

Before installing Windows NT, you should check the fragmentation level of your disk and refragment it if necessary. If your disk is too fragmented, there may not be enough room for Windows NT Setup to create essential system files. If this occurs, Setup will not be able to convert a volume at the conclusion of installation. Before trying to convert the volume again, either delete some files or back up and reformat the drive.

Testing Disks

Always run CHKDSK before using any other disk tool. If you get a clean bill of health from CHKDSK, then proceed with using a more intense disk tool.

Caching Disk Controllers and Drives

Windows NT supports caching disk controllers and drives only if one of the following is true:

- The controller has a driver that specifically supports caching (several of these exist, including DPT and IBM SCSI Caching Adapter).

- Write-through is activated (that is, write caching is disabled) by setting it either manually or by default when the computer starts. (Certain applications are data-sensitive and require that write-through is active. Examples of this are SQL Server-based applications and NTFS partitions.)

- The entire cache option is turned off, by setting it either manually or by default when the computer starts.

If you use a caching controller or drive in other situations, you risk losing data if the computer is rebooted or a power failure occurs before the cache has flushed itself. You can minimize risk by waiting at least one minute (less if you know the maximum time that the cache waits before flushing itself) after all system activity stops before rebooting. The disk activity light is a good indicator of how write caching is being done on your system. This guideline applies to the initial Windows NT installation as well as shutdown. Note that an unexpected power failure at any time can potentially corrupt data on the disk, possibly to the extent that the disk becomes unreadable. You can reduce this risk by making the delay time that write data is cached before being flushed to disk as short as possible.

Setting up the LAN card

If you want to access other systems, you need some type of adapter. An adapter can be as simple as a serial port and a modem or as complex as a dedicated network adapter, associated cables, and device drivers. The two basic types of network adapters are those that utilize I/O port access only and those that utilize I/O port access plus a dedicated buffer located in the upper memory area. Generally speaking, many of the network adapters that contain an upper memory buffer can also contain a dedicated processor to offload processing from the host CPU. Many network adapters also utilize DMA to transfer data from the adapter to system memory. As with any adapter that requires an I/O range, dedicated interrupt, or DMA channel, conflicts can occur. To avoid conflicts, be sure that none of the adapter's I/O, interrupt, upper memory addresses, or DMA channels are shared with any other adapter on the system.

Warning

If a network card cannot be found during the installation process, you may be unable to install Windows NT Server. A resource conflict, such as using IRQ 3 for your network adapter when you also have your second communication (COM2) port using IRQ 3, may cause the failure. You can avoid this failure by selecting a different IRQ for your network card before you begin the installation. Table 4-2 lists some common default settings. There are other options as well, which we will examine as part of the installation process a little later on.

Table 4-2	Default Network Card Settings
Card name	*Default settings*
3Com	
EtherLink II	IRQ=3, IOBaseAddress=0x300, Transceiver=On board, MemoryMapped=OFF
EtherLink II /TP	IRQ=3, IOBaseAddress=0x300, Transceiver=On board, MemoryMapped=OFF
EtherLink II/ 16	IRQ=3, IOBaseAddress=0x300, Transceiver=On board, MemoryMapped=OFF
EtherLink II/ 16 TP	IRQ=3, IOBaseAddress=0x300, Transceiver=On board, MemoryMapped=OFF
EtherLink/ MC	No settings required
EtherLink 16/16 TP	IRQ=5, IOBaseAddress=0x200, MemoryMappedAddress=0xd0000, MemorySize=16, Transceiver=On board, Zero Wait State=OFF
EtherLink 3 ISA 509	IOBaseAddress=0x200

Card name	Default settings
EtherLink 3 EISA	No settings required
EtherLink 3 MC	No settings required
AMD	
AM2100/AM1500T/ PCnet	IRQ=3, DMA channel=3, IOBaseAddress=0x300
Compaq	
32-bit NetFlex Controller	No settings required
32-bit DualSpeed Token-Ring Controller	No settings required
DayStar	
Digital LocalTalk	IOBaseAddress=0x340
Digital LocalTalk MC	No settings required
Digital Equipment Corporation	
EtherWorks LC	IRQ=5, MemoryAddress=0xd0000, IO Port Address=Primary
EtherWorks Turbo	IRQ=5, MemoryBaseAddress=0xd0000, IO Port Address=Primary
EtherWorks Turbo/TP	IRQ=5, MemoryBaseAddress=0xd0000, IO Port Address=Primary
EtherWorks Turbo EISA	No settings required
DECpc	No settings required
DigiBoard	
PC/8i	MemoryBaseAddress=0xd0000, IOBaseAddress=0x220, IRQ=disabled
PC/Xem	MemoryBaseAddress=0xd0000, IOBaseAddress=0x224, IRQ=disabled
C/X	MemoryBaseAddress=0xd0000, IOBaseAddress=0x228, IRQ=disabled
PCMCIA - ISA/MC ISDN and PCIMAC/4	IRQ=disabled, IOBaseAddress=0x320, MemoryBaseAddress=0xd0000, SwitchType=AT&T
IBM	
Token Ring 16/4	IO Port Address=Primary
Token Ring 16/4A	No settings required
Intel	
Ether Express 16 LAN	IRQ=3, IOBaseAddress=0x300, IOChannelReady=Late, TransceiverType=Thin Net

(continued)

Table 4-2 *(Continued)*

Card name	Default settings
Network Peripherals	
FDDI EISA	No settings required
FDDI MC	No settings required
Novell	
NE1000	No settings required
Novell/Anthem NE1500T	No settings required
Novell/Anthem NE2100	No settings required
NE2000	IRQ=3, IOBaseAddress=0x300
NE3200	No settings required
Proteon	
P1390	IRQ=5, IO Port Address=0xa20, DMA channel=5, Cable Type=STP, Card Speed=16
P1990	No settings required
SMC/Western Digital	
8003EP	IRQ=2, MemoryBaseAddress=0x0, IO Port Address=0x200
8013EWC	IRQ=2, MemoryBaseAddress=0x0, IO Port Address=0x200
8013WB	IRQ=2, MemoryBaseAddress=0x0, IO Port Address=0x200
8013EA	No settings required
SMC/WD ISA	IRQ=2, MemoryBaseAddress=0xd0000, IO Base Address=0x300
SMC/WD MC (WD8003EA,WD8003WA, WD8013WPA, WD8013EPA)	No settings required
Ungermann-Bass	
Ethernet NIUps (MC)	No settings required
Ethernet NIUps/EOTP (short)	No settings required
Ethernet NIUpc (long)	IRQ=5, IOBaseAddress=0x368, MemoryMappedAddress=0xd8000
Ethernet NIUpc/EOTP (short)	IRQ=5, IOBaseAddress=0x368, MemoryMappedAddress=0xd8000
MIPS and Olivetti	No settings required

Network Adapter Card Interrupts

The IRQ that you assign to a network adapter card should be unique; that is, it should not be used by any other device in the system, including an active serial or parallel port — even if no device is currently attached to the port. Most newer x86-based computers let you disable the built-in serial or parallel ports. After you disable a port, you can assign its associated IRQ to another device, such as a network card. For example, if you use only a network printer, you can usually disable the built-in parallel printer ports for both LPT1 and LPT2. Network software does not use these interfaces when the underlying devices are redirected.

COM1 (IRQ 4) and COM2 (IRQ 3) are usually poor choices for network adapter cards because most x86-based computers come with two active serial ports. For example, a typical computer with a mouse on COM1 and a modem on COM2 cannot use IRQ 3 or IRQ 4 for a network adapter card. IRQ 5 is often a safe choice, because x86-based computers usually do not have two parallel printer ports.

If you have two or more COM ports on your computer, you might find that a network adapter card (especially an EtherLink II card) will conflict with one port. Two common symptoms are that the workstation service fails to start and that an error attributed to the network adapter card is logged in Event Viewer.

Assigning I/O port base addresses

IBM-compatible systems have 65,536 individual I/O addresses or ports. These I/O ports can be accessed individually or in series, depending on the CPU used. An 80386, for example, can read or write four bytes to four sequential I/O ports in a single access whereas an 80286 requires two separate read or write requests for the same action.

Most devices have unique default I/O port base addresses. In the rare case that an I/O port appears to be in conflict, it can usually be moved to another setting without harm. Table 4-3 shows some common I/O port addresses:

Table 4-3	Common I/O Port Addresses
I/O address	*Used for*
3F8	COM1
2F8	COM2
3E8	COM3
378	LPT1
278	LPT2

Interrupt Isolation

IBM-compatible computer systems have two types of interrupts: hardware interrupts, which are generated by individual peripherals, and software interrupts, which are generated by the CPU. Interrupts provide a means to serve some type of data request, such as a request to read or write data from a hard disk.

ISA peripherals use edge-level interrupts, and EISA and MCA peripherals use trigger-level interrupts. Edge-level interrupts are not sharable. Trigger-level interrupts are priority based and may be shared. Table 4-4 lists the default system interrupts.

An *active interrupt* is an interrupt with an associated interrupt handler, such as the BIOS or device driver. MSD cannot detect interrupts that have been allocated by a peripheral but are not currently in use. Therefore, to gain an accurate IRQ listing, run MSD with a clean boot (that is, no memory manager, no device driver, and so on), run it with all of the associated device drivers but no memory manager, and finally run it with the memory manager. Compare each listing to gain as accurate a report as possible. Table 4-5 shows typical IRQs and I/O addresses from a PC-AT.

Table 4-4	Default System Interrupts	
Interrupt	*Normal usage*	*Additional possibilities*
0	Timer (DRAM refresh)	
1	Keyboard	
2	Cascade	Mouse, 8-bit network adapter[1]
3	COM2	COM4
4	COM1	COM3
5	LPT2	8-bit SCSI, sound card[2]
6	Floppy controller	
7	LPT1	Sound card[3]
8	System clock	
9[4]		
10		Network adapter
11		Adaptec SCSI adapter
12		
13	Math coprocessor	
14	Hard disk controller	
15		

[1] Due to the lack of free low-end IRQs, many 8-bit network adapters use IRQ 2 for network access. However, because IRQ 2 is also the cascade interrupt, network access may be sporadic on some systems.

[2] FutureDomain and Trantor SCSI 8-bit SCSI cards are often configured to use IRQ 5 for non-DOS operating systems. Most MS-DOS configurations use I/O polling instead of an IRQ. A peripheral that utilizes I/O polling continually queries the status of an I/O port waiting for an event to be signaled. The Media Vision Pro Audio Spectrum 16 uses IRQ 5 for the Creative Labs Sound Blaster-compatible section of the adapter. Some Sound Blaster compatibles also use this IRQ.

[3] Many sound cards, such as the Creative Labs Sound Blaster and the Media Vision Pro Audio Spectrum series, use IRQ 7. This hardware configuration can cause problems if Windows is configured to use MS-DOS interrupt-driven print services instead of polled I/O-driven services.

[4] If a device such as a serial port or network card is configured to use IRQ 2, in most cases Windows must be configured to use IRQ 9 for the device since IRQ 2 is utilized as the cascade interrupt.

Table 4-5		IRQs from a PC-AT		
IRQ	**Address**	**Description**	**Detected**	**Handled by**
0	1B2C:003C	Timer Click	Yes	Default Handlers
1	1B2C:0045	Keyboard	Yes	Default Handlers
2	1B2C:0057	Second 8259A	Yes	Default Handlers
3	1B2C:006F	COM2: COM4:	No	Default Handlers
4	1B2C:0087	COM1: COM3:	Yes	Default Handlers
5	1B2C:009F	LPT2:	No	Default Handlers
6	1B2C:00B7	Floppy Disk	Yes	Default Handlers
7	0070:06F4	LPT1:	Yes	System Area
8	1B2C:0052	Real-Time Clock	Yes	Default Handlers
9	F000:DF4A	Redirected IRQ2	Yes	BIOS
10	1B2C:00CF	(Reserved)		Default Handlers
11	1B2C:00E7	(Reserved)		Default Handlers
12	1B2C:00FF	(Reserved)		Default Handlers
13	F000:DF54	Math Coprocessor	Yes	BIOS
14	1B2C:0117	Fixed Disk	Yes	Default Handlers
15	1B2C:012F	(Reserved)		Default Handlers

Choosing an interrupt

The most common conflict when installing a network adapter is inadvertently sharing an interrupt with another installed device. Worse yet, many cards ship with default configurations that are certain to conflict with installed devices.

As mentioned before, there are hardware interrupts and software interrupts. Hardware interrupts allow I/O operations to be performed simultaneously with processing by allowing a peripheral device to signal the CPU when an event occurs. This interrupt causes the CPU to attend to the needs of the peripheral device and then return to normal operations. This process keeps the CPU from waiting for a device to complete an operation, such as printing a single character, before it continues with the task at hand. When the printer is ready, it sends an interrupt to the CPU, and the CPU sends the next character to print. Software interrupts work much the same way but involve a program executing an instruction that works with the BIOS or the operating system, instead of a hardware interrupt that works with the CPU. The following discussion pertains to hardware interrupts. Software interrupts will be discussed later in this chapter in the section, *Base I/O Addresses, Software Interrupts, and Potential Conflicts.*

In the context of hardware interrupts, the term *peripheral device* includes more than the usual peripherals like printers, modems, and mice. Devices such as the keyboard, disk controllers, real-time clock, and the system timer (an oscillator) also generate hardware interrupts. In addition, parity errors generate a hardware interrupt but are outside the normal priority scheme that is the subject of this discussion. The CPU has only two classes of interrupts: maskable and non-maskable. Maskable interrupts are prioritized, and non-maskable interrupts are not. Parity errors are the only common non-maskable interrupt. (Because this discussion revolves around the prioritization of maskable interrupts, the parity error (NMI) has no bearing.)

A single interrupt controller on the PC and XT handles eight levels of priority. On the AT, IBM added a second interrupt controller. The way in which IBM implemented this second controller changes the way that interrupts are handled, making the AT and subsequent systems work differently than the PC and XT.

(Please note that references made to AT systems are meant to apply to all 80286, 80386 (SX and DX), and 80486 systems. Consider AT to mean any 286 system or above.)

Interrupts are processed in order of priority. On the PC, there are eight interrupts or levels of priority, from 0 through 7. The lower the number, the higher the priority. On the AT, IBM cascaded all the high-order interrupts (all interrupts on the second controller, from 8 through 15) into interrupt 2 on the first controller. This changes the order of priority to a rather odd scheme:

0 -1, 2/9 -15, 3-7.

Notice here that interrupt 2 is the same as interrupt 9. Interrupt 2 was a normal interrupt on an XT, but on an AT system, it is very special. The cascade interrupt is wired to the second interrupt controller and functions as a gateway for the high-order interrupts. In short, there is no interrupt 2 on an AT system.

Selecting network card interrupts

When assigning an interrupt to your network card, follow these two guidelines: avoid using interrupt 2, and avoid using any interrupt that is in use by any other device, active or otherwise. Many video cards use interrupt 2 or 9 but can be configured not to use any interrupt at all.

Certain systems with EISA or Micro Channel expansion slots may be able to share interrupts. The information presented in this section is common to ISA systems, but you may have additional options if you are using an EISA or Micro Channel system.

In addition to those interrupts listed as available, interrupts for devices not physically installed are usually available as well. For example, if you do not have an LPT2 port installed, installing a network card on interrupt 5 makes sense. If the network card and driver support it, I usually recommend putting the network card on interrupt 5 (if there is no LPT2 port installed) or interrupt 10, 11, or 12.

Address Conflicts

Determining an I/O conflict in an ISA or mixed EISA/ISA/VL- bus system can be very difficult, particularly because most manufacturers do not list all of the associated I/O ports that their adapter card uses. MCA-, EISA-, and PCI-based systems can limit some of the problems that are associated with configuring a system and determining I/O port usage. However, the associated data files that these systems use to list the adapter I/O ports may be incomplete because there is a file size limit. If the listed I/O ports exceed the file size, the manufacturer has to determine which I/O ports to drop from the list.

When you are attempting to determine an I/O conflict, be aware that most manufacturers list only the starting I/O, or base, address and not the entire range. If the adapter is an 8-bit adapter, then eight I/O ports most likely start from the base address; 16- and 32-bit adapters often function similarly. For example, most 16-bit adapters with a starting I/O address of 0300 actually use the range 0300 to 030F. If another peripheral is configured to use any I/O address in the same range, an I/O overlap will occur, and the peripheral devices may operate sporadically.

Only one method guarantees that you will find the problem adapter — or at least one method has always worked for me. That method is to build a clean system. A *clean system* is one that has only the video adapter and the disk adapter installed. If the problem still exists after you build a clean system, swap either the video or disk adapter and try again. If the problem still exists with different video and disk adapters, perhaps the motherboard is the problem. When the system functions as expected, add each peripheral back into the system, one at a time, to determine the cause of the I/O conflict. You can also use this method to identify interrupt or upper memory problems. After you identify the troublesome peripheral, examine the configuration options, modify the peripheral settings, reinstall the peripheral, and then test the system.

Keep in mind that every system is different. Sometimes, even two supposedly identical systems from the same manufacturer may be slightly different. Do not accept the claims of your friends, acquaintances, or the manufacturer that peripheral X and peripheral Y always work together without incident. Always make sure that you can return a peripheral if it does not function correctly in your system.

Table 4-6 lists some of the more common I/O ports for IBM-compatible computers.

Table 4-6   Common I/O Ports for IBM-Compatible Computers

Ports	Description
0000–000F	DMA controller
0020–002F	Peripheral interrupt controller 1
0030–003F	Peripheral interrupt controller 2
0040–004F	Timer
0050–005F	Timer
0060–006F	Keyboard
0070–007F	Real-time clock
0080–008F	DMA page registers
0090–009F	DMA page registers
00A0–00AF	Peripheral interrupt controller 2
00B0–00BF	Peripheral interrupt controller 2
00C0–00CF	DMA controller 2
00D0–00DF	DMA controller 2
00F0–00FF	Math coprocessor
01F0–01FF	WD1003-compatible fixed disk controller
0200–020F	Game I/O adapter
0270–027F	Parallel port 2
02B0–02BF	Alternate EGA
02C0–02CF	Alternate EGA

Ports	Description
02D0–02DF	Alternate EGA
02E0–02EF	Data acquisition GPIB
02F0–02FF	Serial port 2
0300–030F	Prototype adapter card
0310–031F	Prototype adapter card
0360–036F	PC network adapters
0370–037F	Parallel port 1
0380–038F	SDLC or Bisync #2
0390–039F	Cluster adapter
03A0–03AF	Bisync #1
03B0–03BF	Monochrome display adapter
03C0–03CF	EGA adapter
03D0–03DF	CGA adapter
03F0–03FF	Floppy disk controller and serial port #1

Assigning Memory Buffer Addresses

No two devices can share memory buffers. Use Microsoft NT Diagnostics (MSD) to make sure that the buffer address for your network adapter card is not already used by another device, such as a SCSI adapter card or hard disk controller. Check the installation guide for your computer or peripherals to verify the setting of the memory buffer address.

Some SCSI and network adapters use conflicting memory addresses, such as an Adaptec or Future Domain SCSI adapter and a Digital EtherWorks Turbo TP network adapter. To resolve these memory-address conflicts, you have to reconfigure the hardware by changing jumpers.

Many devices, especially network cards, use memory-mapped I/O to allow programs to write to the device using standard memory transfers. This feature makes the device appear as a block of memory, and the program reads from or writes to that memory, rather than directly to or from the device. Most network cards use a 16 K RAM buffer to implement memory-mapped I/O. The default location for that buffer is D000–D3FF, but most manuals list only the starting address rather than the full range. Different cards use different-sized buffers, so one card could use D000–D3FF whereas another could use D000–D7FF. You should be aware of the size and location of your network card's RAM buffer (if any) when configuring the system for Windows.

Base I/O Addresses, Software Interrupts, and Potential Conflicts

As mentioned, software interrupts involve a program executing an instruction that works with the BIOS or the operating system, in the same way that a hardware interrupt works with the CPU. For devices that use interrupt-driven I/O, the device has a base I/O address that contains a pointer to the code required to handle the interrupt. This code is often contained in a BIOS ROM on the card in question, but it also may be contained in the system BIOS, application program or device driver, or in the operating system itself.

As a logical consequence, no two devices can share the same base I/O address. Because the base I/O address is just that, a "base" address, care must be taken not to overlap. If a given device uses 32 bytes for its interrupt vectors, no other device may use a base I/O address within that range.

If, for example, the controller for your CD-ROM drive uses a base I/O address of 300h and uses 32 bytes of interrupt vectors, the next (sequential) available base I/O address would be 320h. If you assign your CD-ROM controller a base I/O address of 300h and assign your network card a base I/O address of 300h as well, strange things may happen. In this specific example, the result could be to disable the entire network segment when you boot the machine. The device driver for the CD-ROM loads, the driver for the network card loads at the same address, and the network card driver ends up executing code meant for the CD-ROM drive. I can testify that this specific combination has proved to be deadly to one of my company's networks, not once, but twice.

Warning

VGA cards

As with hardware interrupts, Windows uses software interrupts that weren't widely used in other programs. For instance, on systems with a VGA or Super VGA adapter, Windows uses the standard VGA reset port at 2E8h. Prior to Windows, very few programs used the VGA reset port. Note what happens with a network card using a default base address of 2E0h on a system with a VGA card: The network card uses at least 16 bytes of interrupt vectors, which overlaps the VGA reset port. When Windows uses the software interrupt to reset the VGA card, it clobbers the network card's software interrupts, which results in a spontaneous disconnect from the network. Consequently, you *must* not use an I/O address of 2E0h on systems with a VGA card.

Using I/O base address 360h may conflict with the parallel port

When choosing your network card settings, avoid using an I/O base address of 360h, because this address can conflict with an installed parallel port. Normally, a network card uses a 16-byte I/O buffer at a specified base address. Certain network cards, however, may use a 32-byte buffer, which can cause problems.

IBM's original PC architecture calls for the first parallel port to be located at 3BCh, the second at 378h, and the third at 278h. Most systems implement the first parallel port at 378h, though. Whether it's at the first or second port, a parallel port addressed at 378h is overrun by a network adapter that uses a base address of 360h with a 32-byte buffer. Reserving the range of 360h–37Fh overruns the parallel port by eight bytes. In this case, the only solution is to change the I/O address for the network card. However, when changing settings to avoid a conflict with the parallel port, be careful not to create a new situation in which other devices conflict.

SCSI devices

The SCSI and CD-ROM drive support built into Windows NT requires that CD-ROM drives provide SCSI parity to function properly. For many drives, this is a configurable option or is active by default. To find specifics on how SCSI parity is configured for your drive, see the documentation for your CD-ROM drive. Examples of drives that do not provide or support SCSI parity are the NEC CDR-36 and CDR-37 drives.

If you have trouble with a SCSI drive, make sure that the SCSI bus is set up properly (refer to your hardware documentation for specific details):

■ The ends of the SCSI bus must have terminating resistor packs (also called terminators) installed. If you have only internal or only external SCSI devices, the SCSI adapter and the last device on the cable are probably the terminators. If you are using both an external and an internal SCSI device, the adapter probably is in the middle of the bus. If so, it is best to terminate the devices and remove the terminators on the SCSI adapter.

■ If you disconnect a device that has terminators installed (such as an external CD-ROM drive), be sure to install terminators on whatever device becomes the last one on the bus.

■ For the SCSI adapter to operate effectively, termination power must be provided on the SCSI bus either by the adapter or by a SCSI device connected to the bus. Some adapters provide termination power with no configuration options. Others do not provide termination power (for example, Future Domain 1660 and Trantor 128 and 130B). Still others provide termination power only if a jumper is set on the adapter (for example, Future Domain 850M).

■ If you have a SCSI hard disk drive that uses removable media, such as a cartridge drive, make sure that media is mounted on the drive before running Setup. If no media is on the drive, errors may occur during Setup that prevent installation of Windows NT.

Tip

If you're having a problem with SCSI hardware, check this list:

1. Every SCSI device requires a unique ID (including the controller).

2. Every SCSI bus requires a terminator on each end and at least one terminator power source.

3. External cables must be a minimum of one foot (0.3 m) and a maximum of 20 feet (6 m).

4. Every SCSI device, except the fixed disk drives, requires a software driver for DOS/Windows to recognize it.

5. ASPI and CAM drivers are incompatible; do not load them in the wrong order. Use Automatic installation to load them in the correct order.

6. Power-on all external SCSI peripherals first; your PC should be powered-on last.

7. Not all SCSI peripherals are compatible with all SCSI controllers.

Getting to the Heart: The System BIOS

The system BIOS, or Basic Input Output System, is the final layer between the operating system and hardware peripherals that are installed in the computer. It provides an interface between the underlying hardware and the operating system in the form of a library of interrupt handlers. For instance, each time a key is pressed, the CPU (central processing unit) performs an interrupt to read that key. This is similar for other input/output devices (serial and parallel ports, video cards, sound cards, hard disk controllers, and so on). The BIOS is also responsible for booting the computer by providing a basic set of instructions. It performs all of the tasks that need to be done at start-up time.

Many, but not all, computers use a system BIOS that can configure individual system components to optimize the computer system. These configuration options are generally divided into sections.

Most AMI BIOS, for example, have three separate sections:

■ **Standard CMOS setup**. This section is used to configure the default CMOS settings, which include the system date and time, the hard disk drive settings, the floppy drive settings, the video display settings, and the keyboard settings. This information is stored in the 64-bit CMOS RAM area. (At a minimum, all AT class computers also have this configuration.)

■ **Advanced CMOS setup**. This section is used to configure the advanced CMOS settings, which include selectable keyboard options, memory test options, memory parity options, Num Lock enable/disable, floppy seek enable/disable, Weitech coprocessor support, system boot sequence (A: then C:, or C: then A:, and so on), internal and external CPU cache options, password options, and ROM shadowing options.

■ **Advanced chipset setup**. This section is used to configure such motherboard system components as the Dynamic Random Access Memory (DRAM) speed, the DRAM RAS precharge, the DRAM CAS write pulse width, the DRAM interleave, external cache options, keyboard and I/O bus speeds, and I/O recovery options.

Begin BIOS tuning by looking at the memory-specific options. System memory is not accessed as a single block; instead, it is divided into columns and rows. To access a specific byte of memory, the hardware needs to specify the individual column and row. Specifying the column and row, as with all memory access implementations, is transparent to the software that is executing on the system. The *row access strobe* (RAS) and *column access strobe* (CAS) are memory timing options. DRAM must be refreshed at periodic intervals to maintain the state of the stored data. Depending on the clock speed and DRAM speed of the system's CPU, the system may require a faster or slower RAS and CAS.

Another option to consider is the DRAM interleave. When you interleave memory, sequential data access occurs to separate banks of memory. A two-way interleave, for example, allocates even address accesses to one bank and odd address accesses to another bank. This arrangement is particularly useful because after the CPU accesses a particular bank of memory, it cannot access that bank again until the DRAM has been refreshed. Interleaving the memory provides for sequential accesses without waiting for the refresh cycle. The system can use slower and, therefore, less expensive memory without sacrificing performance.

The next items to consider are the I/O bus speed and I/O recovery select options. The ISA bus design has a maximum clock speed of 8 MHz; however, to increase system performance, manufacturers have made modifications that enable users to select the bus speed. The bus speed is generally based on a fraction of the system CPU's clock speed. For example, on a 486/33, a setting of Clk/4 supplies a bus speed of 8.33 MHz. Yet some peripherals can handle clock speeds of 12.5 to 16 MHz, and such speeds offer significant performance increases. After all, if you can increase the bus speed from 8 MHz to 16 MHz, you can theoretically double the data transfer rate from the system memory to peripheral devices.

Increasing throughput sounds ideal, but there is a catch. If a device cannot respond quickly enough, either a data loss or a system lockup can occur. The I/O recovery select option can prevent such problems. This option provides a delay between back-to-back I/O requests to a peripheral so that the device can complete its current task before accepting and processing another task.

How to get to the BIOS setup

When the system is powered on, the BIOS performs diagnostics and initializes system components, including the video system. This is commonly referred as POST (Power-On Self Test). Afterwards, the computer proceeds to the final boot-up stage by calling the operating system. Just before that, you can interrupt the boot process to access the BIOS Setup program. Usually, you enter the Setup program by pressing a special key combination (Del, Esc, Ctrl+Esc, or Ctrl+Alt+Esc) during boot up. (Some BIOS's allow you to enter Setup at any time by pressing Ctrl+Alt+Esc.)

You can bypass the extended CMOS settings by holding the [INS] key down during boot-up. This is really helpful, especially if you bend the CMOS settings right out of shape and the computer won't boot properly anymore.

Avoiding Complications

Even though you have taken time to plan your Windows NT installation you should take precautionary measures to avoid potential complications. This section points out some of the situations or anomalies that could impact the installation process.

Upgrading when third-party system software is present

If you are using third-party system software that installs its own services, such as network redirectors, contact the software vendor to determine if any of these services should be disabled before upgrading.

Running Windows NT 4.0 on PCI bus systems

PCI peripherals are auto-configuring. Each PCI card has configuration settings stored in on-board memory and provides this information to the system during the system boot phase. The information supplied by the PCI cards is then used by the BIOS to automatically configure each PCI device around the other resources already in use by other peripherals. Non-PCI cards, such as ISA cards, can be used in a PCI system. However, they may require extra configuration, via a utility supplied with the system, so that the PCI cards can be automatically configured around the ISA cards.

It is interesting to note that the card connector on a PCI motherboard to which the PCI expansion cards can be plugged in is significantly shorter than an expansion slot used by an ISA expansion card.

To run Windows NT on a PCI bus system, it may be necessary to enable the interrupts either via the CMOS screen or by switching jumpers on the motherboard.

The Windows NT 4.0 family supports only the PCI bus specification; it does not support PCMCIA.

ROM shadowing on multiprocessor systems

If you encounter persistent installation problems on multiprocessor systems, try installing with ROM shadowing disabled. Refer to the section on altering BIOS settings, *Getting to the Heart: The System BIOS,* presented earlier in the chapter.

Installing Windows NT on an ESDI disk drive with more than 1024 cylinders

In some cases, Windows NT installation on disk drives with more than 1024 cylinders proceeds normally until the first boot from the hard drive where Windows NT is installed. The Windows NT Boot Loader will load various files and then produce a Fatal System Error: 0x0000006b, with the message that Phase 1 Process Initialization failed. Following this message will be some type of hexadecimal dump, and the system will be locked up. If you experience this difficulty, the following information can help.

Microsoft has tested the ESDI controllers listed in README.WRI using a hard drive with a capacity exceeding 516 MB (MB=1,048,576 bytes) formatted. The MS-DOS limit of 1024 cylinders creates a situation where special BIOS mapping on the controller is used to change the geometry of the drive. ESDI drives are capable of being prepared with various values of sectors per track (spt) such as 53 or 63 spt geometry during a low-level format, as shown in the following example:

1024 cylinders x 15 heads x 53 spt x 512 bytes per sector = 398 MB formatted capacity

Or

1024 cylinders x 15 heads x 63 spt x 512 bytes per sector = 472 MB formatted capacity

Thus, using 63 spt will yield 74 MB more space. Windows NT is perfectly compatible with either geometry and, depending on the drive or controller, can access the remaining cylinders beyond 1024. This space can be partitioned and formatted but not accessed by MS-DOS. However, some controllers can successfully remap the remaining cylinders beyond 1024 so that either MS-DOS or Windows NT can use the entire capacity. For example:

1632 cylinders x 15 heads x 53 spt x 512 bytes per sector = 634 MB formatted capacity

IDE/ESDI drive support

The Windows NT IDE/ESDI (Integrated Device Electronics/Enhanced Small Device Interface) drive support is limited to two disk drives per controller. Windows NT supports a second IDE/ESDI controller added to Compaq computers only or built in, like the Gateway 2000 VESA local bus computers. If you need to configure from two to six IDE or ESDI controllers in one system, contact your technical support representative for details on how to do so.

Summary

You can save yourself or your company a lot of time, money, and heartache by planning the installation process for Windows NT. I know how easy it is for a computer enthusiast to get a new piece of software and drop everything just to load it on to the system. Don't do this with Windows NT. Take a day to plan your system and prepare your hardware.

In this chapter, I discussed some of the decisions, plans, and preparation techniques that you should use before installing Windows NT. I also discussed ways that you can fine-tune your platform before you install Windows NT. This chapter also presented you with

▶ Guidelines for choosing a disk partitioning scheme

▶ Differences and advantages between Windows NT-supported file systems

▶ Information on how to use your system BIOS to fine-tune your hardware

Chapter 5

Installing Windows NT Server

In This Chapter

▶ Installing Windows NT Workstation and Windows NT Server

▶ Upgrading from a previous operating system

▶ Reinstalling NTS

▶ Choosing network protocols

▶ Setting up a primary or backup domain controller

Windows NT's install process is fairly straightforward. However, there are many decisions you have to make along the way. Making the wrong decision can cause problems with the installation. This chapter takes you through the installation process step by step, providing guidelines to help you make appropriate decisions and pointing out paths to help you steer clear of pitfalls.

Ready..., Set..., Install

You've thoroughly planned your installation, checked and prepped your hardware, and now you're ready to install Windows NT or NT Server.

Cross Reference

If you do not have the required information on hand, or you're not sure about what you need to do to prepare for a successful installation, refer to Chapter 4, *Preparing to Install Windows NT Server*.

Before you install, make sure you do the following:

- **Check your hardware settings.** Unlike MS-DOS, Windows NT does not allow shared interrupts on the ISA expansion bus. However, you can share interrupts on EISA, MCA, and PCI busses. Make sure to resolve I/O, DMA, or upper memory conflicts before you start the installation process.

- **Check your network card.** Note the type of network adapter in your computer, the card's interrupt request (IRQ) number, base I/O address, and other settings.

Caution

If a network card cannot be found during the installation process, you may be unable to install Windows NT Server. A resource conflict, such as selecting IRQ 3 for your network adapter when you already have your second communication (COM2) port using IRQ 3, may cause the installation to fail. You can avoid this by selecting a different IRQ for your network card before you begin the installation.

- **Check the Windows NT Server computer name.** Also, if the computer is to act as a domain controller or a server, you must know the name of the Windows NT Server domain.

- **Check the domain or workgroup name.** If this computer is to join an existing domain controller, you need to know the name of the domain or workgroup.

- **Check your printer.** If you have a printer connected directly to your computer, record the printer model and port used by the printer.

- **Obtain your OEM drivers.** If you have proprietary or unsupported hardware, you should assemble these driver diskettes before you begin your installation. During the installation, Setup gives you a chance to install OEM (Original Equipment Manufacturer) drivers.

Tip

You can find many OEM drivers for Windows NT Server (for example, disk controller drivers, video drivers, printer drivers, and so on) in the DRIVLIB subdirectory on the CD-ROM that accompanies this book. Even if you have an OEM diskette, check the CD-ROM to see if it contains a newer version.

- **Check the Hardware Compatibility List (HCL).** This booklet is included with your source media package and includes a listing of every hardware platform that Microsoft has tested to ensure compatibility with Windows NT Server.

  The Hardware Compatibility List contains a list of computers and peripherals that have been tested and have passed compatibility testing with Windows NT. In this document, you may find specific BIOS requirements for your particular hardware platform, or even for peripherals (such as video or SCSI adapters). If your hardware platform is not listed by name, don't despair; it only means that the platform has not been tested for complete compatibility. In this case, look through the list of peripherals to see if you can identify any problem areas (such as an unsupported network adapter) that you should consider before installation. Some computers may be sold with peripherals that are not yet supported by the Windows NT operating system or that require a device driver supplied by the manufacturer. It's impossible to test every computer and/or device in all possible configurations, so you'll have to refer to the SETUP.TXT file on the installation media for additional compatibility information when installing Windows NT.

  Check for updates of the Hardware Compatibility List for Windows NT on the Internet:

  ftp.microsoft.com

  cd\bussys\winnt\winnt-docs\hcl

The following list shows a breakdown of the hardware categories in the HCL. Check the category listing to see if a specific type device or peripheral is covered by the list. If you discover that some element of your system is not covered on the list, contact the manufacturer to determine the status of drivers for use with Windows NT.

x86 Architecture Uniprocessor Computers	Hard Drives
x86 Architecture Multiprocessor Computers	Storage Cabinets
	RAID Systems
MIPS(r) RISC Architecture Computers	Video Capture Adapters
	Video Display Support
MIPS RISC Multiprocessor Architecture Computers	Network Adapters
Digital Alpha AXPTM RISC Architecture Computers	Uninterruptible Power Supplies
	Multimedia Audio Adapters
Digital Alpha AXP RISC Multiprocessor Architecture Computers	Modems
	Hardware Security Hosts
Processor Upgrade Products	ISDN Adapters
SCSI Host Adapters	Multi-port Serial Adapters
SCSI CD-ROM Drives	X.25 Adapters
Non-SCSI CD-ROM Drives	Third Party Remote Access Servers
SCSI Tape Drives	
Other Tape Drives	Keyboards
SCSI Removable Media	Pointing Devices
SCSI Scanners	Printers
Disk Controllers	

Tip

If you plan on installing Windows NT from your CD-ROM, check to see if it is listed in the HCL. If it is a SCSI CD-ROM, see if your SCSI controller is listed. If it is an IDE CD-ROM, Windows NT does support the ATAPI interface and proprietary CD-ROM controllers from Sony, Panasonic, and Mitsumi. If the installation process does not autodetect your CD-ROM controller, try to install these manually, one at a time. If they all fail, you may have to install using the MS-DOS method (WINNT.EXE) discussed later in this chapter.

■ **Read the additional information.** The following files contain more details about various hardware and software that may affect your installation:

SETUP.TXT contains specific information about various hardware platforms and peripherals, which is often not mentioned in the Hardware Compatibility List. SETUP.TXT can be found in the root directory of the CD-ROM.

README.WRI gives general information about Windows NT, including information on specific hardware and software.

PRINTER.WRI has information about specific printer problems or components.

NETWORK.WRI provides information about networks, including information on network adapter cards and network interoperability.

Tip

README.WRI is a compressed file located in the installation subdirectory (I386 for Intel processors). You can manually expand the README.WRI file by running the MS-DOS expand program (located in your MS-DOS or Windows 3.x installation directory). For example,

```
EXPAND X:\I386\README.WRI C:\TEMP\README.WRI
```

where *X:* is the drive letter of your CD-ROM drive.

- **Check for free disk space.** Windows NT Server requires about 90 MB for a complete installation (this includes the minimum paging file size). If Setup cannot find enough free space on a single disk drive, the installation program halts, prompting you to reformat your disk drive in order to continue the installation. You can always exit the installation by pressing the F3 key, deleting some files, and then restarting the installation process.

- **Check for unsupported partition schemes.** Windows NT 3.51 and higher supports only OnTrack Disk Manager for accessing enhanced IDE drives greater than 512 MB. If you have a different manufacturer's partitioning program, it is possible that Setup will fail to detect your drive or will require you to repartition and reformat it as part of the installation process.

Note

When you buy an IDE hard drive that holds more than 528 million bytes (504 megabytes), be sure it comes with OnTrack Disk Manager. Disk Manager installs a custom boot sector on the drive that allows MS-DOS to see the drive's full capacity. Chapter 4, *Preparing to Install Windows NT Server,* discusses using OnTrack Disk Manager in detail.

Windows NT versions 3.1 and 3.5 do *not* support OnTrack Disk Manager. However, Windows NT 3.51 and 4.0 are compatible with Disk Manager's boot sector program.

Seagate hard drives come with a disk manager called Microhouse EZ Drive, which was not supported on Windows NT 3.5 and is not supported on Windows NT 3.51 and higher.

■ **Check for compressed files.** If you use Microsoft DriveSpace or Microsoft DoubleSpace to compress files on Windows 95 or MS-DOS, Windows NT cannot install on to a compressed partition.

Setup at a glance

At first glance, installing Windows NT Workstation or NT Server resembles installing Windows for Workgroups or Windows 95. The basic steps when installing Windows NT on a computer for the first time are as follows:

1. Start the Setup program. How you start Setup depends on what kind of hardware you have and whether you are running Setup from floppy disks, a CD-ROM compact disc, or a shared network directory.

2. Choose Custom or Express Setup.

3. Specify whether you're upgrading an existing Windows NT installation or performing a new installation. If it is a new installation, choose the disk partition, file system, and directory for the Windows NT Server system files to be installed on your computer.

4. Provide identification information about your user name, computer name, and other identifiers. Specify whether this computer has a security role in the domain.

5. Choose the local language you want to use.

6. For Custom Setup, choose the options you want to install. (All options are installed with Express Setup.)

7. Set up your network adapter card, and select the default network protocol.

8. Optionally, specify the Windows NT Server domain for which this computer serves as the primary or backup domain controller.

9. Set up the locally installed printer, if you have one.

10. Set up a password for the administrator's account for the local computer.

11. For Custom Setup, set up a paging file for virtual memory, and specify the installed programs on your hard disk that you want to set up to run with Windows NT. (These tasks are done automatically in Express Setup.)

12. Set the local time, specify video adapter settings, and create an Emergency Repair disk.

Preparing to Run the Windows NT Install Program

Windows NT ships on a set of disks or on a CD-ROM with three boot disks. Depending on the source media and your hardware configuration, you can choose from any of three installation methods for Windows NT Workstation and Windows NT Server:

- Installing from 3.5-inch floppy disks. Windows NT 4.0 Setup only supports 3.5-inch Setup floppies.

- Installing from a compact disc drive. CD-ROM installations require a local CD-ROM drive.

- Installing from a shared network directory.

Note

The installation process for Windows NT Workstation and Windows NT Server are identical, except where noted in the descriptions of the Setup process.

The floppy disk and CD-ROM installation methods have at least one element in common: the Windows NT Setup Boot Disk. The Windows NT Setup Boot Disk accompanies the CD-ROM and is also Disk #1 of the set of disks used for the floppy installation. This disk contains these key files:

- **SETUPLDR,** which is required to start the Setup process

- **NTDETECT.COM,** which detects if there is a SCSI adapter in the system

- **SETUPAPP.EXE,** which is the Setup application itself

- **TXTSETUP.INF,** which contains the instructions for Setup

- **Drivers** for the most popular SCSI devices defined by the *.SYS files on the boot disk

Caution

Disks formatted with DMF (Setup Disk #4 and beyond) cannot be copied to a standard high density 3.5-inch disk using the MS-DOS DISKCOPY or Windows COPY command.

Because DMF is a new format, many existing disk utilities such as Norton Disk Doctor, Central Point's PC Tools, and Microsoft's ScanDisk, do not recognize DMF and may try to write over the file on the installation disks. Therefore, you should *not* attempt to use disk utilities to diagnose DMF-formatted disks.

Installing Windows NT from a set of floppy disks is the same as installing from a CD-ROM, only much slower. In either case, you begin with your computer turned off, insert the Windows NT Server Setup Boot Disk in drive A, and then turn on your computer. When Setup asks for Setup Disk #2, and then Setup Disk #3, insert the disk in drive A. If you do not have a CD-ROM drive, Setup continues to prompt you for disks until the process is complete. If Setup detects a compatible CD-ROM drive, it asks for the Windows NT Server compact disc. Insert it in the CD-ROM drive, and then proceed through the setup process.

RISC Processor Installation

Installation on a RISC processor follows the same basic format as on an Intel processor with a few minor differences. The first "gotcha" is that each RISC-based computer differs a bit in how you run a program from the CD-ROM drive, so refer to your operating manual to determine the particulars. The basic process is as follows:

1. Insert the Windows NT Server CD-ROM in your CD-ROM drive.

2. Restart the computer.

3. When the ARC menu appears, choose the Run a Program option from the menu.

4. Type **CD:*SYSTEM*\SETUPLDR** (where *SYSTEM* is the RISC computer type, Alpha, MIPS, or PPC), and press Enter. Note that this process varies from RISC computer to RISC computer. In some cases, you must supply a full qualified device name. Check the system's documentation for specifics.

5. At this point, the installation process is exactly the same as the process for the Intel x86 platform.

In order to install Windows NT Server on a RISC processor, you must have a system partition of at least 2 MB, and the partition must be formatted as FAT.

If you have only a floppy disk drive or diskette media, you must install Windows NT using the floppy disks. If you have a local CD-ROM, you naturally would install from the CD-ROM. However, the network share installation method offers some benefits and options that may affect your decision to use a particular installation method.

First, the network share method allows you to install Windows NT across any MS-DOS supported network. This is a relatively fast installation, because the files are transferred across the network and simply moved around on the hard disk during the local setup. There is no need for floppy disks other than one for the boot floppy. In addition, this method allows multiple machines to run the network Setup at the same time and does not require a network supported by Windows NT.

Second, it enables you to install Windows NT from a CD-ROM device that might be supported under MS-DOS but not under Windows NT.

There are four different options for installing from a network share:

- Install from a network distribution share and have Setup create the three 3.5-inch Setup boot disks necessary to complete NT Setup.

- Install from a network distribution share and have Setup copy the Setup boot files onto the user's local hard disk.

- Install from a CD-ROM drive by having Setup first create the three 3.5-inch Setup boot disks necessary to complete NT Setup.

- Install from a CD-ROM drive and have Setup copy the Setup boot files onto the user's local hard disk.

Installing Windows NT over a Network

To install Windows NT from a network, you perform the following procedure from the local x86-based computer where you want to install Windows NT. You can also use this method to install Windows NT on x86-based computers with SCSI or CD-ROM devices that are supported under MS-DOS but are not supported by Windows NT.

This method uses a program called WINNT.EXE to prepare an x86-based computer for running Windows NT Setup. You can use WINNT.EXE to either upgrade your existing Windows NT operating system or to install Windows NT for the first time.

Before you can execute a network installation, you must make the installation files accessible by copying the files to a shared directory. You can set up the shared directory using any type of network, such as Microsoft LAN Manager 2.1, Novell NetWare, or Banyan VINES. Just make sure that the directory containing the Windows NT files is accessible from MS-DOS.

Before copying the master Windows NT files onto a network directory, be sure that

- The network is operational.

- You have read-write permission to the network directory where you want to copy the Windows NT files, and other users have read access to that directory.

To copy the master Windows NT files onto a network computer

Share the \I386, \MIPS, and \ALPHA directories of the Windows NT Workstation or Server compact disc in the CD-ROM drive connected to a network computer.

Or

1. Connect to the drive where you want to install the Windows NT master files.

2. Create the shared directory on the drive that will contain the Windows NT master files.

3. In Program Manager, choose the Command Prompt icon, and then use the XCOPY command to copy the Windows NT files to the shared directory that you created. The correct syntax is as follows:

```
XCOPY /S <CDROM>:\<PLATFORM> <SHARE_DIRECTORY>
```

For example,

```
XCOPY /S F:\I386 \\WINNT35.SRC\X86
```

The Setup program copies the files to the specified target directory. You can now connect to this shared directory and follow the procedures for installing Windows NT from the network, as described next.

Preparing to run WINNT.EXE

You need three blank, formatted, high-density floppy disks of the correct size for your computer's drive A and an additional disk of the same size for formatting during Setup.

Label the formatted disks as follows:

- Setup Boot Disk
- Setup Disk #2
- Setup Disk #3

Label the fourth disk

- Emergency Repair Disk

To use the WINNT Setup, the user must connect to the network share and change into the directory that contains all of the Windows NT files. Following are four options for running WINNT.EXE:

- **Running WINNT.EXE from DOS.** If you are using WINNT, use your existing MS-DOS-based network software to connect to the shared network directory that contains the Windows NT Server master files.

- **Running WINNT.EXE from Windows or Windows NT.** If you are using WINNT or WINNT32, use File Manager to switch to the network directory that contains the master files for the new version of Windows NT Server.

- **Running WINNT.EXE if Windows NT 3.1 or 3.5x is already installed.** You can run a program called WINNT32.EXE to upgrade the operating system or install a new version.

- **Running WINNT.EXE from a non-NT-supported CD-ROM.** If you have an unsupported local CD-ROM device, insert the Windows NT Workstation or Server compact disc in the drive. Then, while running MS-DOS, change to the CD drive:\I386 directory on the CD-ROM drive. For example, if the CD-ROM drive is drive E, change to the E:\I386 directory.

Running WINNT.EXE

Here are the WINNT Setup instructions needed for you to run WINNT.EXE:

1. Create a Setup boot floppy, identical to the boot floppy used in the floppy or CD-ROM installation.

2. Connect to the shared directory containing the NT master files. Start WINNT Setup by typing **WINNT** at the MS-DOS command prompt and pressing Enter. If your computer is running Windows NT Server, double-click WINNT32.EXE in the directory that contains the Windows NT Server master files.

   Next, WINNT downloads the complete Windows NT source directory onto the local partition in the WIN_NT.~LS directory.

3. Confirm the Windows NT source directory by typing the path for the directory where the NT master files are stored (the same directory as in Step 2.)

4. To create the three startup disks required for Setup, insert the blank, formatted, high-density floppy disk labeled Setup Disk #3 in drive A when prompted. After copying files to Setup Disk #3, WINNT Setup prompts you to insert Setup Disk #2, and then Setup Boot Disk in drive A.

After WINNT Setup copies the files to the local hard drive, it instructs you to leave the boot floppy in the drive and press Enter to restart the computer.

Windows NT Setup now runs just like the CD-ROM-based installation. However, instead of copying the files from the CD-ROM, Setup simply moves the files into the appropriate target directories on the hard disk.

Note

Make sure you keep the Setup and Emergency Repair disks that WINNT creates during installation. If you have problems with your installation, you may need these disks to repair your operating system.

The WINNT.EXE utility supports the following command line switches:

```
WINNT [/S[:]SOURCEPATH] [/T[:]TEMPDRIVE] [/I[:]INFFILE] [/O[X]] [/X
| [/F] [/C]] [/B]
```

These options are described in Table 5-1.

Table 5-1	WINNT.EXE Command Line Options
Option	*Purpose*
/S[:]sourcepath	This option specifies the source location of Windows NT files and must be a full path. By default, this is the current directory.
/T[:]tempdrive	This option specifies the drive to contain the temporary setup files, the \WIN_NT.~LS directory. If this option is not specified, Setup attempts to locate a local drive with enough free space.
/I[:]inffile	This option specifies the filename of the setup information file, which is DOSNET.INF by default.
/X	This option specifies that the Setup boot floppy is not created.
/F	This option specifies that files are not verified as they are copied to the Setup boot floppy.
/C	This option skips the free-space check on the Setup boot floppy.
/O	This option specifies that only boot floppies are created.
/OX	This option creates boot floppies for CD-ROM- or floppy-based installation.
/B	This option specifies floppyless operation.

Installing Windows NT Server

No matter which installation method you use, make these last-minute checks before installing or upgrading Windows NT version 4.0:

- **SCSI devices must be on for Setup.** You should ensure that all SCSI devices are on.

- **Disconnect UPS serial connections.** UPS serial-monitoring cable connections should be disconnected during Setup. Windows NT attempts to automatically detect devices connected to serial ports, which could cause problems with UPS equipment connected to a serial port.

- **Copy third-party drivers to the boot floppy.** If Setup is being run on a system that has a SCSI device installed that is not supported by one of these drivers, copy the proper Windows NT device driver onto the boot floppy before starting the Setup process.

Setup starts in Text mode

Start the Windows NT Setup process by rebooting the system with the boot floppy. The boot floppy loads and executes the Windows NT Setup Loader (SETUPLDR), which in turn executes NTDETECT.COM to determine the hardware configuration of the system. During the detection process, NTDETECT.COM displays the message,

```
Windows NT Setup is inspecting your computer's hardware configuration.
```

After the detection process, Setup Loader loads and executes the Windows NT Setup program (SETUPAPP.EXE).

Choosing the Setup Mode

Much like Windows 3.1 Setup, you can choose to do an Express or Custom Setup of Windows NT. Express Setup is the "no brainer" way to install Windows NT. Express Setup asks you the minimum number of questions and installs all optional Windows NT components. It automatically configures your hardware settings and other components.

Microsoft says that "Custom Setup is designed for experienced users who want or need more control over how Windows NT is installed on their computers." However, I recommend that you use Custom Setup, regardless of your experience level. (If you happen to be an inexperienced user, you won't gain experience or learn much of anything using Express Setup.) With Custom Setup, you step through each option and choose to override default values or accept recommended settings for the following:

- Detection of special disk controllers. Windows NT Setup can detect SCSI adapters, CD-ROM drives, and special disk controllers for use with Windows NT.

- The directory where the Windows NT files install.

- The video display, mouse, keyboard, and keyboard layout.

- The Windows NT components you want to install, and the existing applications you want to set up to run with Windows NT.

- The virtual memory settings and local printer connections for your computer.

- Any additional network adapters or other network components you want to install and configure during Windows NT Setup.

Setup Probes Your System

After choosing the setup mode, Windows NT Setup probes your system in an attempt to determine what, if any, SCSI devices exist in the system. At this point Setup allows you to install device drivers from third-party hardware vendors. If Setup detects a SCSI device, it offers you a choice between a CD-ROM-based installation and a floppy drive installation.

After the SCSI detection routine, Setup continues checking your hardware configuration, looking for machine type, display adapter type, mouse, and keyboard information.

Note

What if you have a flawed Pentium processor? The Setup program also has been changed to automatically detect the Intel Pentium processor's floating-point division error. If Setup detects the error on your system, it prompts you to indicate whether you want to disable the floating-point hardware on the processor. If you choose not to have the floating-point hardware disabled during Setup, you have the option of doing so after Windows NT is installed using a command-line utility called PENTNT. See Appendix C, *The Windows NT Command List,* for more information on this utility.

After completing the hardware detection, Setup loads the file systems that Windows NT supports and proceeds to determine the target drive and directory for the Windows NT installation. First, Setup checks the system's local hard drives for an installation of Windows 3.x on the system by searching for WIN.COM. If it finds a version of Windows 3.x, Setup asks you whether or not it should install over Windows 3.x, storing the Windows NT files in the \WINDOWS\SYSTEM32 directory. If you decide not to install NT on top of Windows 3.x, or if Setup does not find an installation of Windows 3.x, Setup brings up a screen showing disk configuration information. This screen allows you to create and delete partitions and to select the partition on which to install Windows NT.

Specifying Hard Disk Partitions

Hard disks can be partitioned. Each partition can have a different file system, such as file allocation table (FAT) or Windows NT file system (NTFS). If you want more than one file system, you must have more than one partition on the hard disk before you install Windows NT Workstation or Windows NT Server.

Note

A RISC-based computer can have several system partitions that are configurable by the manufacturer's configuration program; each system partition must be formatted for the FAT file system. If you want to use NTFS, you must create at least one FAT system partition of at least 2 MB plus a second partition large enough to contain all of the files you want to protect with NTFS. For information about setting up more than one system partition on a RISC-based computer, see your hardware documentation.

If you plan to use only the Windows NT Workstation Server operating system

- On a new x86-based computer, make a single partition and format it with NTFS.

- On an existing system that contains files you want to keep, leave the existing partitions intact and place the Windows NT files on any partition with sufficient free space.

If you want to use another operating system such as MS-DOS, Windows 3.1, Windows for Workgroups 3.11, or Windows 95 in addition to Windows NT Workstation or Server

- Make sure the system partition (drive C) is formatted with the appropriate file system. For example, if you already have MS-DOS installed and want to keep it, preserve the C partition and keep the file system as FAT. You can place the Windows NT files on any uncompressed partition with sufficient free space.

Note

If you plan to use NTFS and have access to another operating system, you must have at least two disk partitions. Format drive C with a file system that Windows NT and your other operating system can use, such as FAT. Format the other partition with NTFS. You can place the Windows NT files on any uncompressed partition with sufficient free space.

Selecting a File System

Once you select the partition on which to install Windows NT, Setup gives you the choice of either keeping the existing file system or converting the partition to NTFS (if the partition is currently formatted as FAT). If the installation partition is formatted as High Performance File System (HPFS), you have a choice of converting or reformatting the partition.

Tip

When bringing up a new system, I recommend that you use the FAT file system initially. This allows you to get the operating system installed and to test network connections from all sides.

In general, format NT Workstations with FAT (to maintain compatibility with other file systems) and format NT Servers with NTFS (to take advantage of the high levels of security and performance).

Here are the advantages of NTFS:

- Supports upper- and lowercase letters in file and directory names.
- Supports Unicode in filenames.
- Allows you to set permissions on directories and files.
- Provides faster access to large sequential files.
- Supports file and directory names up to 254 characters long.
- Provides Macintosh compatibility.
- Supports both long and short (eight-plus-three) filenames for compatibility with MS-DOS, HPFS, and other networked clients, including OS/2, UNIX, AppleShare, and NFS.
- Offers data security on fixed and removable hard disks (an important feature for corporate users and other power users).
- Provides a recovery system that is more reliable than either FAT or HPFS, and meets POSIX requirements.

Table 5-2 summarizes the key features of FAT, HPFS, and NTFS as implemented on Windows NT.

Once you have chosen a file system, Setup runs CHKDSK on the system's drives to ensure that there are no problems that may cause trouble during Setup.

After the CHKDSK has completed, Setup starts copying the core Windows NT files — those that are necessary to bring up the graphic mode portion of Setup — into the selected destination path. When the necessary files and the Registry information needed to boot Windows NT and continue Setup are in place, a blue screen appears requesting that you remove the boot floppy from drive A and reboot the system.

The graphic mode portion of setup

The graphic mode portion of Setup is much like the graphic mode portion of the Windows 3.x Setup, in that Setup is running under Windows NT.

To set up graphic mode

1. Enter a name and company name. Windows NT uses the names to identify you for various operations. You must type a response and verify your response for Setup to continue.

2. Enter a Product Identification number. Technical support representatives use this number to identify your system. Look for it either on the inside back cover of your Installation Guide or on your registration card. You must type a response and verify your response for Setup to continue.

Table 5-2	Comparison of FAT, HPFS, and NTFS		
File system	**FAT**	**HPFS**	**NTFS**
Filename	Eight-plus-three ASCII characters, one period delimiter) allowed; on Windows NT 3.5 and higher, 255 Unicode characters, multiple periods (delimiters) allowed	254 bytes of double-byte characters, multiple periods (delimiters) allowed	255 Unicode characters, multiple periods (delimiters) allowed
File size	232 bytes	232 bytes	264 bytes
Partition	232 bytes	241 bytes	264 bytes
Maximum path length	64; on Windows NT 3.5 and higher, no limit	No limit	No limit
Attributes	Only a few bit flags, plus a few bytes of extended attribute information on Windows NT 3.5 and higher	Bit flags plus up to 64K of extended attribute information	Everything, including data, is treated as file attributes
Directories	Unsorted	B-tree	B-tree
Philosophy	Simple	Efficient on larger disks	Fast, recoverable, and secure
Built-in security features	No	No	Yes

Choosing a Security Role

Deciding on the security role for a Windows NT Server installation is a very important decision and not easily changed. You cannot change the status of a machine from server to domain (or vice versa) without reinstalling Windows NT Server.

What is the difference between a domain controller (DC) and a server?

■ A server does not get a copy of the domain account database but does have access to it.

■ A server maintains its own local user account database.

■ A server does not process domain logons.

■ A server has the same built-in user groups as Windows NT Workstations (including Power Users).

■ You can configure a server as a member of a domain or workgroup.

Why use a server?

- A server does not have to spend resources processing domain logons. Domain controllers spend part of their time processing logons and replicating the security database.

- Servers allow you to mix and match security accounts. They can be created in the local security database and assigned to local resources. Any of the domain accounts (and accounts from trusted domains) can be assigned to local resources if the server is a member of a domain.

- A server is easier to move to a different domain than a backup domain controller. A backup domain controller must be reinstalled in the new domain, but the server can change its domain membership without reinstalling Windows NT.

Selecting a License Mode

Microsoft has introduced a new philosophy concerning product licensing. They've reasoned that because network solutions are comprised of servers that contain information and provide services as well as clients that access information and services, servers and clients should be licensed separately.

This new licensing philosophy is called the *Microsoft BackOffice licensing model.* Components are licensed separately, so you purchase only what you need to build a network solution for your company's particular requirements. Each server requires a license, and each client computer accessing a server also requires a license (called a Client Access License).

The license agreements for certain Microsoft BackOffice server products (such as Windows NT Server, SQL Server, and SNA Server) also provide the flexibility of two licensing modes:

- **Per Server.** With Per Server licensing, each Client Access License is assigned to a particular server and allows one connection to that server for basic network services (file, print, and communications).

- **Per Seat.** The Per Seat licensing mode requires a Client Access License for each computer that accesses Windows NT Server for basic network services. Once a computer is licensed in the Per Seat mode, it can access any Windows NT Server computer installed on the network at no additional charge.

Caution

Client Access Licenses are separate from the desktop operating system software you use to connect to Microsoft server products. Purchasing Microsoft Windows for Workgroups, Windows NT Workstation, or any other desktop operating system (such as Macintosh) that connects to Microsoft server products does not constitute a legal license to connect to those Microsoft server products. In addition to the desktop operating system, Client Access Licenses must also be purchased.

During Windows NT Server Setup, a detailed Choose Licensing Mode dialog box appears giving you the following choices:

■ Obtain online Help describing the two licensing modes: Per Server and Per Seat

■ View online versions of the Windows NT Server Client Access License and Server License agreements

■ Select the licensing mode that best suits your network or business requirements

■ Agree to the terms and conditions of the license agreement

When Windows NT Server is installed, a Licensing icon is added to the Control Panel. If you have administrative authority for your local server or for your server's domain, you can double-click the Licensing icon to display the Choose Licensing Mode dialog box. In this dialog box, you can perform a one-time, one-way licensing mode change from Per Server to Per Seat. This change is currently possible only with Windows NT Server 3.51 and 4.0, SQL Server, and SNA Server. You cannot legally change the licensing mode from Per Seat to Per Server.

Notice that if you select the Per Server licensing mode for those server products, you must specify the number of computers that can concurrently connect to the server on which the product is installed.

What's in a Computer Name?

You must provide a name to identify your computer on the network. This name must be 15 characters or fewer and must not be the same as any other computer name, domain name, or workgroup name on the network.

Caution

Each computer on a network must have a unique name. The machine name *must not* be the same as the domain name if this is a Windows NT Server installation. If you specify a computer name that is the same as another computer on the network or the same as a workgroup or a domain, Windows NT Server cannot start network services.

Don't play games with the computer name

Many people use the names of their favorite characters, cars, or movies as computer names. Although this may provide unique names, it's a strategy that doesn't hold out over long periods and numerous machines. Be conventional when naming computers; use department or division names so that users browsing the network will have an idea of a particular server's function.

Note

If you're going to run logon scripts, do not use spaces in the computer names of the domain controllers in the network.

What not to use in a computer name

Do not use the characters in Table 5-3 in computer names because they can cause unexpected results when the computer is accessed over the network.

Table 5-3	Unusable Characters	
Character	*Name*	*Keystroke*
*	Bullet	Alt+0149
¤	Currency sign	Alt+0164
|	Broken vertical bar	Alt+0166
§	Section sign	Alt+0167
¶	Paragraph sign	Alt+0182

What language do you speak?

Setup next asks for the Language, or Locale, of the system. This information is used for formatting date, time, and currency information.

Windows NT Options

If you chose to run Custom Setup, a dialog box now appears with a selection of optional tasks that Setup can perform. These tasks include installing optional components such as accessories and games, configuring network settings, setting up locally connected printers, and setting up applications on your hard disk to run with Windows NT.

Note

If you're installing Windows NT Server, choosing whether to install network services is not an option. You must install network functionality. Therefore, the network option appears grayed out indicating that Setup installs the services by default.

Printer Configuration

Next, you have a chance to set up a default printer. You should do this only if you have a printer attached to the system locally or need to print to non-Windows NT print shares. Windows NT does not require a local printer driver as long as you're printing to a Windows NT print share. If you're setting up to print to a non-Windows NT network printer, temporarily assign that printer to LPT1. Once Setup installs the network components, you can redirect printing to the network print share using the Network option.

Network Configuration

Setup proceeds to install network components (1) when installing Windows NT Server, or (2) if you directed Setup to install network support under Windows NT Workstation. If Setup is running as a Custom Installation, Setup notifies you that it is ready to detect the system's network card automatically and pauses, allowing you to initiate the detection process or bypass automatic detection and make a manual selection.

Once Setup has determined the type of network card, it displays a dialog box with its findings and requests approval. At this time, you can choose to override the automatic detection and make a selection from the list of supported network cards.

Under an Express Installation, Windows NT automatically searches for a network card and makes the appropriate selection. With the network card determined, Setup presents a dialog box showing the detected network card's settings: the I/O (input/output) port address, the memory address setting for the card, and the IRQ (interrupt request) setting.

Secret

If a network card causes the auto-detection code to hang, you have the following options:

- Rerun a Custom Setup and bypass the auto-detection code. Then manually select your adapter.

- Install the MS Loopback adapter until you can isolate the trouble with your adapter.

- As an extra measure of safety, install the Loopback adapter in addition to your network card. Windows NT Server must have a functioning network adapter in order to log you on locally. Installing the Loopback adapter allows you to log on if your network card fails.

Networking services overview

Next, Setup installs the network services necessary to support the card, default workstation, and server components. Once Setup successfully copies these files, it installs the rest of the files necessary for Windows NT and then starts the Network Control Panel applet. The Network Settings dialog box displays the installed network hardware and software configuration information.

Choosing protocols

Windows NT Setup adds the basic software you need to begin working on the network immediately. However, you may want to install additional network services on your Windows NT computer. Network *services* are components that add networking capabilities to Windows NT.

A network *protocol* is a set of rules that allows computers on a network to communicate with each other. Two computers must use the same network protocol (speak the same language) to communicate.

Protocols communicate through other layers of software that control the flow of information. How network protocols and other layers of network software work together is determined by network *bindings*. Windows NT automatically binds network protocols to all appropriate layers.

The following protocols or services are available under NTS:

- **DLC protocol.** The Data Link Control (DLC) protocol allows access to IBM mainframe computers or printers attached directly to the network.

- **NetBEUI protocol.** NetBIOS extended-user interface is the standard protocol for the NetBIOS interface; it is for local area networks (LANs) of 20 to 200 workstations.

- **Network Monitor Agent.** This provides performance counters for the network adapter card and an agent that can be used by other monitoring software to analyze traffic on a LAN.

- **NWLink IPX/SPX Compatible protocol and Gateway Service for NetWare networks.** These are the transport protocols used in Novell NetWare networks and the service that allows access to files, directories, and printers on NetWare servers.

- **Remote Access Service.** This service allows remote computers to dial in to a LAN.

- **Services for Macintosh.** This service manages file and printer sharing for Windows NT and Apple Macintosh computers.

- **TCP/IP and related components.** A suite of Transmission Control Protocol/Internet Protocol (TCP/IP) protocols is used for communicating in heterogeneous interconnected networks. For Windows NT Server, you can also install Dynamic Host Configuration Protocol (DHCP) servers and Windows Internetwork Name Service (WINS) servers to support dynamic configuration and name resolution services.

Choosing the protocols to use in a network requires evaluating several elements of the network, such as the number and types of computers, special hardware or software used, and compatibility and integration into existing networks.

Follow these guidelines in choosing the protocols to install:

- For a small, isolated network, you should probably use NetBEUI or the NWLink IPX/SPX Compatible Transport. If you have no other server types, use NetBEUI. If you have a NetWare server, use IPX/SPX and the Gateway/Client Services for NetWare, which are discussed in Chapter 13, *Coexisting with NetWare*.

- For a large network, you, as the network administrator, should determine the network protocol(s) to use based on network components and your company's requirements.

Because NetBEUI is very fast for small LAN communications but provides poorer performance for WAN (wide area network) communications, one recommended strategy for setting up a network is to use both NetBEUI and another protocol, such as TCP/IP, on each computer that may need to access computers across a router or on a WAN.

When you install both protocols on each computer and set NetBEUI as the first protocol to be used, Windows NT uses NetBEUI for the communication between Windows NT computers within each LAN segment and TCP/IP for communication across routers and to other parts of your WAN.

Note

You *must* install the NetBEUI protocol if your computer communicates with other computers on an existing Microsoft network that uses NetBEUI with Windows NT 3.x, Windows for Workgroups 3.11, or LAN Manager 2.x. If you do not have NetBEUI installed when your network requires it, your computer cannot communicate with other computers on your network.

Unlike NetBEUI and TCP/IP, the Data Link Control protocol is not designed to be a primary protocol for use between PCs. You should use Data Link Control with Windows NT only under the following circumstances:

■ If you need Windows NT computers to access IBM mainframe computers

■ If you are setting up a printer that attaches directly to a network cable, instead of to a serial or parallel port on a print server

Domain Controller Settings

Windows NT allows a system to exist as a member of a workgroup or a domain when running Windows NT Workstation or NT Server. By this point in the installation process, you should have made a decision about the domain or workgroup status for this computer. If you choose a workgroup, Setup prompts you for the local user account information (user name and password).

If you choose domain, Windows NT Server installation requires that the machine either join an existing domain or become a domain controller in a new domain.

When a computer becomes a controller in a new domain, it becomes the primary domain controller (PDC) and you need to supply a domain name and administrator password. When joining an existing domain, the Windows NT Server computer becomes a backup domain controller (BDC). In this case, you must provide an administrator name and password for authentication in order to receive a copy of the user database.

Setting up a primary or backup domain controller

After you enter your choices for the network configuration settings, Setup displays another dialog box. It gives you the choice of identifying the domain for the Windows NT Server computer to serve as a backup domain controller or creating a new domain for which the computer serves as the primary domain controller.

To create a new domain

1. In the Domain Settings dialog box, select the Controller In New Domain option.

Caution

After Setup is finished, the only way that a Windows NT Server computer can join a different domain is if you reinstall Windows NT Server. You can, however, choose the Network option in Control Panel to define a new, unused domain name for a primary domain controller.

2. In the appropriate box, type the correct domain name. Domain names cannot contain spaces (blank characters).

3. Click on the OK button.

To join a domain as a backup domain controller

1. Select the Backup Domain Controller option.

2. In the appropriate box, type the correct domain name. Domain names cannot contain spaces (blank characters).

3. Click on the OK button if a computer account already exists for this computer. If this computer does not have an account in the domain you want to join, select the Create Computer Account in Domain check box to create an account. Then press the OK button.

Administration Password

Windows NT Setup asks you to specify a password for the special Administrator user account. This account enables you or someone you designate to log on to the computer with maximum access. Then, if the computer is not joining a domain, Setup asks you to specify the user name and password for a local account. NT requests this user name and password each time you log on. The user name may have up to 20 characters containing any upper- or lowercase characters except the following:

" / \ [ ] : | = , + * ? < >

A password can contain up to 14 characters and is case-sensitive (for example, Windows NT distinguishes between the passwords Cpress and cpress).

Caution

If you lose the Administrator account password for your computer, there is no way to recover it. If no other Administrative accounts have been created, you have to reinstall NT Server and set a new password to log on as Administrator.

Virtual Memory

If you selected Custom Setup, Windows NT displays a configuration screen for virtual memory with a minimum and recommended size displayed for the drive. This is where you specify the target drive and size for the Windows NT page file. As a general rule, you should set the page file size to equal the sum of the machine's available RAM plus 12 MB. For example, if you have 16 MB RAM, then specify 28 MB as the page file size. If you used Express Setup, Windows NT automatically sets virtual memory size to this recommendation.

Final stages of setup

When you reach this stage of setup, you're in the home stretch. The next few steps should be very familiar because they are identical to Windows 3.1 setup. Setup does the following:

- Creates Program Manager groups.

- Searches for applications, if selected.

- Creates the Emergency Repair disk, saving the default configuration information (necessary to restore Windows NT) on the Emergency Repair diskette.

- Sets the system's time zone setting. Unless the system happens to be in the Greenwich mean time zone, you must select the correct time zone.

Completing Setup

After you follow the instructions to create the Emergency Repair disk, Setup completes these final installation steps:

1. If the computer serves as a backup domain controller, Setup replicates security account information from the primary domain controller. This can take a while, depending on the size of the security database.

Note

Canceling the database replication at this time simply postpones database replication until the next time you restart the computer.

2. When Setup is finished running, you'll get a message asking you to restart your computer. Remove any disks from the floppy disk drives and choose the Reboot button to start Windows NT.

Starting Windows NT on an x86-based computer

Windows NT starts in the following sequence on an x86-based computer:

1. During installation, Windows NT alters the system's boot record to look for and run a program called NTLDR.

2. NTLDR reads BOOT.INI and builds a menu of the operating systems that you can start. (The BOOT.INI file is described in the next section, *If Windows NT Doesn't Start.*)

3. NTLDR runs NTDETECT.COM, which builds a list of the system's hardware components.

4. When the Boot Loader menu appears, press Enter. You can select an operating system from the menu or let the time-out count down to 0 to start the default operating system.

Note

If you don't see the menu and the default operating system starts automatically, the time-out value has been set to 0 in BOOT.INI.

5. The low-level components of Windows NT load, and then Windows NT initializes the drivers and starts the services based on information stored in the Registry.

6. The high-level components of Windows NT load, and then the Welcome screen is displayed so that you can log on. When the Welcome logon message appears, press Ctrl+Alt+Del to log on. In the Welcome dialog box, type and confirm your password, and then click on the OK button.

Caution

For an x86-based computer, NT Setup copies the following files to the root directory on the C drive: BOOT.INI, BOOTSECT.DOS (if another operating system is on your computer), NTLDR, and NTDETECT.COM. Also, if you have a SCSI disk that is not visible from MS-DOS (that is, not seen by the BIOS), the NTBOOTDD.SYS file is copied. *Never* delete these files — Windows NT cannot start without them.

For a RISC-based computer, HAL.DLL and OSLOADER.EXE are copied to the \OS\WINNT directory on your system partition. These files should never be deleted.

All the files mentioned in the preceding paragraph are read-only, hidden system files. If any of these files is missing on your system, you can use the Emergency Repair disk to restore them.

If Windows NT Doesn't Start

If Windows NT does not start, make sure that the statements in BOOT.INI (found in the root directory of your system partition) refer to the correct path for the \SYSTEMROOT directory.

BOOT.INI is a system text file that has two sections: The first section specifies the default operating system to start and a time-out value indicating how long to wait before starting automatically. The second section specifies the other operating systems that you can start. For example, I have configured one of my systems to run either Windows NT Server or Windows 95, so the BOOT.INI file looks like this:

```
[boot loader]
timeout=30
default=multi(0)disk(0)rdisk(0)partition(1)\winnt35
[operating systems]
multi(0)disk(0)rdisk(0)partition(1)\winnt35="Windows NT
Server"
c:\="Windows 95"
```

Preserving the Startup Configuration

Just because Windows NT starts successfully after installing doesn't mean your job is over. You should immediately take steps to ensure that Windows NT starts again and again, and that you can recover in case it fails to start. Back up your configuration directory (\SYSTEMROOT\SYSTEM32\CONFIG) and remember to maintain current backups each time you change your configuration and accounts. This way, you can use the Repair option in Windows NT Setup to restore the system, and then you can restore the configuration from your backup.

If you made changes to a system that previously started Windows NT successfully and it doesn't start now, you can return to your previous configuration by choosing the Last Known Good Configuration option at system startup. If Windows NT still won't start, use the Repair process described in Chapter 6, *Troubleshooting Startup Problems*, to recover the system.

Upgrading from a Previous Operating System

The previous sections assumed that you plan to install Windows NT on a clean system (no existing operating system) or that you plan to install Windows NT in its own directory. The following sections discuss situations in which you might be upgrading from a previous version of Windows NT or Windows.

Upgrading from Windows NT 3.x

When you start Windows NT Setup to install NT 4.0, Setup searches for any existing version of Windows NT and offers you the opportunity to upgrade it.

Upgrading your current installation preserves the following information:

- Local security accounts
- Network adapter settings, protocols, and service configuration (including settings for Remote Access Service (RAS) and services for Macintosh servers)
- Custom program groups, desktop settings, and other preferences set using the Control Panel
- Preferences set for administrative tools and accessories
- Custom settings made using Registry Editor

Before upgrading the servers (also known as backup domain controllers or BDCs), you should first upgrade the primary domain controller (PDC) to Windows NT Server 4.0. If you upgrade a server that is not the primary domain controller first, all of the new security information installed for version 4.0 gets replaced with old security information when the server is restarted, because the server automatically replicates all information from the existing domain controller.

If you are using either WINNT or WINNT32 to upgrade from source files on a network directory, Windows NT Setup temporarily needs space on your hard disk to create the local source files for the upgrade process. The space required is about 100 MB. Windows NT Setup warns you if it cannot find sufficient free space.

If you are using the Windows NT compact disc or 3.5-inch floppy disks to upgrade the operating system, you need about 10 MB of free space.

During the upgrade process, Setup automatically copies new files and new versions of existing files required by the system and makes changes to system settings and program groups required for the new version. You do not have to configure network adapters, printers, and other settings as you did when you first installed Windows NT. The only actions you must perform during the upgrade are

- Confirming the drive and directory containing your existing Windows NT installation

- Providing new information for configuring Microsoft TCP/IP if this network protocol is already included in your previous Windows NT installation

- Supplying a new Emergency Repair disk

The upgrade process in Windows NT Setup is a safe operation. However, Setup may not be able to complete an upgrade if there is insufficient space on the drive containing your existing Windows NT installation or if other problems occur with the system.

If Setup cannot perform an upgrade, a message explains the reason so that you can quit Setup and correct the problem. After you correct the problem, start Windows NT Setup again and choose the upgrade option once more. You can retry upgrading Windows NT an unlimited number of times.

If Setup still cannot complete the upgrade, start Windows NT Setup again and choose the option of installing a new version of Windows NT. However, the new Windows NT installation does not preserve your custom settings or security account information.

If Windows NT Setup warns you that it cannot proceed with the upgrade, your previous version of the Windows NT operating system remains intact.

You can upgrade Windows NT 3.5 systems to Windows NT Server 4.0. However, you cannot upgrade the computer to be a primary or backup domain controller. You can only upgrade the computer to be a server that does not participate in validating users.

Upgrading from MS-DOS

When upgrading an MS-DOS-based system, the Windows NT Setup program installs the Windows NT Boot Loader to allow you to boot to Windows NT or DOS.

Upgrading from Windows 3.x

You can install Windows NT into the same directory as an existing version of Windows 3.x. Windows NT places its system files in a \<WINDOWS ROOT>\SYSTEM32 directory. The Windows NT Setup program also places common files, such as *.BMP files, in the \<WINDOWS ROOT> directory.

If you choose not to install Windows NT into the same directory as Windows 3.x, Windows NT cannot access the Windows 3.x Program Manager groups. Also, Windows NT won't run applications installed in Windows 3.x, because it won't know where to find the program's various components. In addition, OLE (Object Linking and Embedding) and DDE (Dynamic Data Exchange) applications won't know how to edit or play objects embedded or linked in applications under Windows NT.

The information that NT needs to recognize and run OLE and DDE is stored in the Registry of the Windows version where the application is installed. In this case, the necessary information is in the Windows 3.x Registry (REG.DAT), not the Windows NT Registry. For this reason, Windows NT won't be able to find the component OLE server and client DLL (Dynamic Link Library).

Installing Windows NT into a directory other than the Windows 3.x directory requires that you reinstall all of the Windows 3.x applications under Windows NT in order to get OLE and DDE. It is important to reinstall all of the applications into the same directory (on top of themselves), because the goal is to install the necessary OLE and DDE information and files in the Windows NT Registry.

Migrating Windows 3.x configurations to Windows NT

If you installed Windows NT Server into an existing Windows 3.x directory (including Windows for Workgroups), you have the opportunity to migrate a portion of your Windows 3.x settings when you first log on as a new user (this option is not available for the Administrator user name). If you choose to preserve Windows 3.x system and program settings, Windows NT Server migrates the following:

■ All program groups that do not already exist in Windows NT Server. For example, a program group named Spreadsheets would migrate, although the Main program group (because it already exists) would not. The location of each program group icon and each group window when the icon is opened remain the same as in Windows 3.x, unless the display resolutions differ between Windows NT Server and Windows 3.x.

■ File associations

■ Settings for your Windows-based applications

■ Information used for object linking and embedding

■ Desktop configuration settings, with the exception of screen savers

Shared directories from Windows for Workgroups on the local computer and connections to other resources are not preserved in Windows NT Server.

When Windows NT is installed on top of Windows 3.x, *.INI file data, *.GRP file data, and REG.DAT data is migrated into the Windows NT environment. Currently, the migration process is only one way, from Windows 3.x to Windows NT, and happens only the first time that a user name logs in after Setup.

Migration Begins when You Log On

This portion of the migration process occurs just once — the first time every new user name logs on to a Windows NT system that has been installed over Windows 3.x. However, the Administrator and System user names are exempt from the migration.

Table 5-4 lists the sections and variables that are migrated from the WIN.INI during this stage.

Table 5-5 lists the sections and variables that are migrated from the CONTROL.INI during this stage.

All sections and variables from WINFILE.INI are migrated during this stage.

Table 5-4	WIN.INI File Sections
Section	*Purpose*
[Windows]	Affects several elements of the Windows environment.
[desktop]	Controls the appearance of the desktop and the position of windows and icons.
[extensions]	Associates specified types of files with corresponding applications.
[intl]	Describes how to display items for countries other than the United States.
[TrueType]	Describes options for using and displaying TrueType fonts.
[sound]	Lists the sound files assigned to each system event.
[colors]	Defines colors for the Windows display.

Table 5-5	CONTROL.INI File Sections
Section	**Purpose**
[Current]	Specifies the current color scheme.
[Color Schemes]	Defines the colors for each element of specific color schemes, as set by choosing the Color icon.
[Custom Colors]	Defines the custom colors in the color palette, as set by choosing the Color icon.
[Patterns]	Defines the color values for the bitmap patterns, as set by choosing the Desktop icon.
[MMCPL]	Specifies values related to the multimedia items in the Control Panel.
[Screen Saver.*]	Specifies the density, warp speed, and password-protection values for the screen saver.

The following sections and variables from the SYSTEM.INI are also migrated during this stage:

```
[boot]
SCRNSAVE.EXE
```

All of the Windows 3.x Program Manager group files, as identified by the list of groups in the PROGMAN.INI file, are migrated during this stage. If the name of the group, as contained within the *.GRP file and not the *.GRP filename, is the same as the name of a Windows NT Personal *or* Common group, then NT does not migrate the group. Obviously, the Main, Accessories, Games, and Startup groups cannot migrate, unless their names have been changed, because these groups already exist in Windows NT.

Items that are not migrated

The following information is *not* migrated, because it would potentially cause problems:

- [Ports], [Devices], and [PrinterPorts] sections of WIN.INI. These are actually migrated during the first stage of the migration process to keep Windows 3.x applications happy, but Windows NT ignores them.

- Persistent shares and users from Windows for Workgroups.

- Default domain and user ID from Windows for Workgroups or the LANMAN.INI.

- Per user profiles maintained by WINLOGIN.

- Any changes that the user has made to Main, Startup, Games, and Accessories groups in Windows 3.x.

- MS-DOS drive letters. Local drive letters should be configured using Windows NT Disk Administrator.

- The Program Manager Auto Arrange, Minimize on Run, and Save Settings on Exit options from PROGMAN.INI are not migrated because the Windows NT Program Manager stores these in the Registry as REG_DWORD instead of as text strings.

- Font information for character mode command windows.

Potential problems

Some icons that have been migrated may appear as black "blobs" under Windows NT. To correct this problem, edit the properties of the icon and press OK to restore the icon to the correct image.

Booting Multiple Operating Systems

If you are installing Windows NT on a computer currently configured to start either OS/2 or MS-DOS using the Boot command, Windows NT Setup sets up your system so that you can run Windows NT or whichever of the two operating systems (MS-DOS or OS/2) you last started before running Windows NT Setup.

If the alternate operating system does not start, make sure that the statements in BOOT.INI (found in the root directory of your system partition) specify the correct path for that operating system.

The file BOOTSECT.DOS contains the boot record for the alternate operating system (whether or not the alternate is MS-DOS). Startup fails if the system cannot find BOOTSECT.DOS in the root directory of the system partition.

If you have OS/2 Boot Manager installed on your computer and want to continue to use it after Windows NT Server installation is complete, you need to reenable it. Start Disk Administrator from the Administrative Tools group in Program Manager. Select the OS/2 Boot Manager partition, and then select Mark Active from the Partition menu. To return to booting Windows NT Server, use FDISKPM in OS/2 to make the Windows NT Server partition available.

Reinstalling Windows NT Server

In most cases, you should choose the option to upgrade your existing installation when you run Windows NT Setup instead of reinstalling the operating system. When this is not possible, reinstalling Windows NT Server is the same as first-time installation unless you are reinstalling on a computer that belongs to a domain or on a domain controller. In these cases, additional steps are required to maintain security settings.

Before reinstalling Windows NT Server on a computer that belongs to a domain, the domain administrator must delete the computer account for the computer and create a new one. For security reasons, the Windows NT Net Logon service periodically changes the passwords of computer accounts (passwords change on the domain controller and on the computer simultaneously so that they always match). If you reinstall Windows NT Server without creating a new computer account, passwords on the computer and domain controller conflict, preventing you from logging on to the domain from that computer.

Reinstalling Windows NT Server on a domain controller requires extra steps to ensure preservation of the user accounts database:

1. Use Server Manager to temporarily promote another Windows NT Server domain controller to be the primary domain controller. This step automatically demotes the original primary domain controller to backup domain controller status.

2. Reinstall Windows NT Server on the original primary domain controller, making it a backup domain controller.

   As soon as you restart the computer, the security database on the new primary domain controller begins to replicate to this backup domain controller. This may take a few minutes, depending on the type of computer hardware and the number of user accounts.

3. Use Server Manager to promote this computer back to primary domain controller.

Summary

You've got Windows NT Server installed and running, but your job as system administrator is just beginning. This chapter covered the following:

▶ Installing Windows NT over a network without the Windows NT boot floppies

▶ Selecting a security role (domain or server)

▶ Selecting a license mode

▶ Installing networking services

▶ Diagnosing problems if Windows NT fails to start

▶ Preserving the startup configuration

▶ Reinstalling Windows NT Server

Chapter 6

Troubleshooting Startup Problems

In This Chapter

▶ Common installation errors

▶ An in-depth look at the boot process

▶ Errors during booting the machine

▶ Common network errors

▶ Common service and application errors

▶ Using Event Viewer to monitor system errors

Even with Windows NT's intelligent installation process, self-tuning environment, and ability to run applications from different operating systems, you can still encounter problems. There are potential problems with the installation process, booting Windows NT, and using applications. This chapter provides a road map to some of the problems that can occur with Windows NT.

Installation Errors

If you encounter errors during installation of Windows NT, odds are that the problem is caused by one of the following:

■ **Incorrect Hardware.** The system may not have the equipment required to run Windows NT. Before starting installation of Windows NT, make sure that there is enough free hard disk space and enough physical memory; that the CPU, keyboard, video card, mouse, and network card are all *supported;* and that you have any additional information you need, such as the IRQ setting for the network card.

Cross Reference

See Chapter 4, *Preparing to Install Windows NT Server,* for more information on avoiding installation pitfalls.

■ **Corrupted media.** The second possible problem is that the installation media — the diskettes or CD-ROM — are corrupted. In this event, a screen message would tell you to insert a diskette (which is already in the drive) or tell you that the loaded diskette is not formatted properly. The best course of action is to return the media to the supplier immediately for a new set.

The Windows NT Boot Process

From the time you turn on the machine until you see the logon prompt, the system is going through a series of processes. This boot process is governed by four key files: NTLDR, BOOT.INI, NTDETECT.COM, and NTOSKRNL.EXE. Windows NT boots according to the following sequence of events (on x86-based systems):

1. System performs POST (Power On Self Test).

2. System runs Find Boot Device and Load Boot Record.

3. Windows NT attempts to find NTLDR.

4. NTLDR reads BOOT.INI and displays possible operating system selections.

5. The user selects the operating system for NTLDR to load.

6. NTLDR runs NTDETECT.COM.

7. NTDETECT.COM builds a list of hardware for NTLDR.

8. NTLDR loads NTOSKRNL.EXE (or BOOTSECT.DOS if MS-DOS or OS/2 is selected).

9. NTOSKRNL loads and initializes Windows NT using information from the Registry.

Boot sequence details

Windows NT boots in a number of stages. Some stages are specific to Windows NT, and some are specific to the hardware platform, such as the POST routine. The following sections discuss the boot process specific to each platform and conclude with a discussion of the portion of the Windows NT boot sequence that is platform independent.

The Intel Boot Process

When powered on, an Intel-based machine's CPU runs in real mode. The Power On Self Test (POST) routine begins in this mode and is responsible for determining the amount of memory and whether required hardware components are present (such as a keyboard). The routine also allows adapter cards to initialize. This is usually about the time many of us go to get coffee, but if you watch a machine boot up, you'll notice a series of information that appears on the screen. Typically, you can identify the POST routine by the on-screen count of the memory installed in the system.

When the POST routine is completed, the CPU begins to process any commands at software interrupt nineteen hex (19h), the reboot computer interrupt. This routine attempts to locate the boot device by first checking drive A for a disk; if it doesn't find a disk in drive A, it checks the hard disk C (depending on CMOS settings). The system uses two steps to determine whether drive C serves as a boot device:

1. The first sector of the hard disk contains the Master Boot Record (MBR), which is loaded into memory. The MBR contains a program that scans the partition table (the remaining portion of the MBR) for a specific flag to locate the active partition in the partition table.

2. Next, the boot record for the active partition is loaded into memory. The boot record starts at the first logical sector in the active partition. The program located in the boot record loads the first layer of the program necessary to start the operating system. When Windows NT is installed, the boot record is changed to support the booting of the Windows NT operating system.

Note The system saves the boot record as BOOTSECT.DOS regardless of which operating system was installed on the system prior to the installation of Windows NT.

If for some reason no active partition is found on drive C, processing passes to the ROM BASIC. In remote boot situations where the operating system image is loaded from a server, the POST routine on the network adapter card redirects this interrupt to the ROM on the network adapter card.

The Remoteboot service (also called Remote Program Load, or RPL) makes it possible to boot a workstation over the network using software on the server's hard disk instead of the workstation's hard disk. The workstation's network adapter card must have an RPL ROM chip on it. Each RPL ROM chip is made for a specific type of network adapter; it cannot be interchanged. This RPL network adapter broadcasts a request for boot records. The server responds by automatically establishing a connection and loading the MS-DOS startup files into the workstation's memory.

Note Windows NT does not currently support being booted remotely.

The boot process starts to differ here from the way in which the system would boot if only the MS-DOS operating system were installed. At this stage in the MS-DOS boot process, the program located in the boot record would load IO.SYS into RAM and MSDOS.SYS and then pass control to the SYSINIT portion of IO.SYS.

As noted before, Windows NT replaces the boot record during installation. The new boot record is instructed to find, load into memory, and execute NTLDR, which *must* be located in the root directory of drive C.

You can tell when NTLDR starts executing, because the screen clears and displays the following message:

```
Windows NT
Portable Boot Loader
```

NTLDR controls the Boot Loader Operating System selection process and requires NTDETECT.COM, BOOT.INI, and BOOTSECT.DOS to be in the root directory of the boot drive. In addition, if the system is booting from a SCSI drive, the file NTBOOTDD.SYS must also be in the root directory. You create NTBOOTDD.SYS during Setup (if the boot drive is a SCSI device) by copying the appropriate SCSI driver into the root directory and naming the driver NTBOOTDD.SYS.

Once NTLDR is started, it proceeds through the following steps:

- Switches the processor to 32-bit flat model mode. When Intel computers first boot, they are running in real mode, like an old 8088 or 8086 processor. Because NTLDR is mostly a 32-bit program, it must switch the processor to 32-bit flat model mode before it can perform the rest of its functions.

- Starts the appropriate mini-file system. During this portion of the boot sequence, NTLDR loads a small version, with limited functionality, of the file systems in use on the system. NTLDR supports FAT, HPFS, and NTFS. The mini-file systems are contained within NTLDR and allow NTLDR to access files as well as change directories on the boot drive.

- Reads the BOOT.INI and displays the operating system selections. The BOOT.INI is a standard text file and can be edited using any text editor. However, the BOOT.INI is marked read only, so you have to change the attribute to edit the file. In addition, by using the Control Panel System applet, it is possible to change the timeout= and default= values in the BOOT.INI.

- Allows the user to select an operating system.

- Loads the correct operating system. If MS-DOS, OS/2 1.x, or OS/2 2.0 is selected from the NTLDR menu, NTLDR loads the hidden file BOOTSECT.DOS into memory. NTLDR then switches the processor back to real mode and jumps to the start of the boot sector program contained in BOOTSECT.DOS. From this point on, the boot sequence is the same as for the other operating system.

Note

NTLDR currently supports loading multiple versions of Windows NT and *one* other operating system. If Windows NT is selected, NTLDR executes NTDETECT.COM.

- Executes NTDETECT.COM. NTDETECT.COM collects information on the hardware components installed in the machine. It then builds a list of these components and returns this information to NTLDR. Currently, NTDETECT.COM can collect information about machine identification, bus/adapter type, video, keyboard, communication port, parallel port, floppy drive, and mouse.

To determine if any selection other than Windows NT appears in the NTLDR menu, Setup searches the boot drive for certain files. If it finds MSDOS.SYS or IBMDOS.COM, MS-DOS or PC-DOS becomes the alternate selection. If OS2 is found, OS/2 is a menu item for the other operating system.

Currently, both the Central Processor and the Floating Point Coprocessor are detected by the Windows NT Kernel (NTOSKRNL.EXE) and the Hardware Abstraction Layer (HAL.DLL).

After NTDETECT.COM has given NTLDR the list of installed hardware, the Windows NT boot process continues, as described in the section, *Loading Windows NT*.

Note

If the system is not 100 percent PC-compatible (for example, if the system has more than one I/O bus or has more than one central processor), OEMs must provide their own version of NTDETECT.COM.

The ARC-Based Boot Process

On Advanced RISC Computer (ARC)-based systems, the resident ROM firmware selects a boot device by reading a boot precedence table from non-volatile RAM. In some cases, the non-volatile RAM may not be valid or may be blank. In these instances, the firmware either queries the user for the boot device or defaults to a floppy/hard disk sequence. For a hard disk boot, the firmware reads the first physical sector of the boot drive (the Master Boot Record) to determine if a bootable partition is present. If it finds a bootable partition, Setup reads the first sector of the partition into memory and examines the BIOS Parameter Block (BPB) to determine whether it recognizes the volume's file system as one that the firmware supports. If it recognizes a supported file system, Setup searches the root directory of the volume for OSLOADER.EXE, loads the program if found, and passes control to it.

Note

If the file system is *not* supported by the firmware, the system cannot boot, because the ARC specification requires that the system partition always be formatted with the FAT file system.

ARC-based systems do not use the Boot Loader menu and functionality that is implemented by NTLDR on x86-based systems because the NTLDR functionality is built into the system firmware. Instead, OSLOADER.EXE handles the initial stages of loading Windows NT.

In addition, ARC-based systems do not need NTDETECT.COM. The ARC POST routine collects the hardware information and passes it to OSLOADER.EXE when necessary.

In order to display information regarding the boot process, the video hardware is initialized by the Windows NT HAL (Hardware Abstraction Layer).

MIPS boot screen

Upon system power on, the machine will go through its Power On Self Test (POST) routine and should display the following information on the screen:

```
Testing Memory 32768 KB...OK
Testing Memory Controller...OK
Testing Interrupt Controller...OK
Testing Keyboard Controller...OK
Testing Serial Controller...OK
Testing Parallel Controller...OK
Testing Floppy Controller...OK
Testing SCSI Controller...OK
Testing Ethernet .........OK
Testing APPR.............OK
Testing Loop.............OK
Initializing Firmware...........
```

Based on the information supplied by the POST routine, it is possible to tell if a particular hardware component is functioning correctly before booting Windows NT.

ARC multiboot screen

If you have the correct version of the system's ARC firmware (for more information on the ARC firmware, see the earlier section, *The ARC-Based Boot Process*), the following screen should appear:

```
ARC Multiboot Version 248
ACTIONS:
Boot Windows NT
Boot an alternate OS
Run a program
Execute Monitor
```

You will be instructed to use arrow keys to select entries and to press Enter to enable them.

- **Boot Windows NT.** This option allows Windows NT to be booted.

- **Boot an alternate OS.** This allows a different operating system, or another version of Windows NT, to be booted.

- **Run a program.** When this option is selected, a full ARC pathname must be specified to the executable.

- **Execute Monitor.** This executes the system monitor, which is similar to the MS-DOS Debug utility.

MIPS boot

The R4000 system supports three types of resets:

- **Power-On Reset.** This reset starts when the power supply is turned on.

- **Cold Reset.** This restarts all clocks, but the power supply remains stable. The processor operating parameters do not change.

■ **Warm Reset.** This restarts the processor but does not affect the clocks.

Loading Windows NT

The following stages occur no matter on what platform Windows NT is booting.

■ **Kernel Load**. During this stage, the Windows NT kernel (NTOSKRNL.EXE) and the Hardware Abstraction Layer (HAL) are loaded into memory but not initialized. Next, a copy of the system hive, HKEY_LOCAL_MACHINE\SYSTEM, from the Registry is loaded into memory.

■ **Kernel Initialization**. This stage of the boot process is signified by the screen turning blue. This is when NTOSKRNL.EXE is initialized and control is passed to it. In addition, all of the drivers that were loaded during the Kernel Load stage are initialized.

After all of the drivers are successfully loaded and initialized, the NTOSKRNL.EXE performs some housecleaning by freeing memory blocks used by the device drivers.

■ **Service Load**. This stage is when Session Manager (SMSS.EXE) is started. Session Manager first reads and executes the list of programs in the Session Manager section of the Registry. One of the default entries is AUTOCHK.EXE, the boot time version of CHKDSK that automatically performs a check on each partition.

When the check disk information starts appearing on the blue screen, it is a clear indication that Session Manager has started. Of course, if this information does not appear, it is possible that the autocheck line was removed from the BootExecute Registry entry.

After all of the checks have been successfully performed on the system's hard drives, Session Manager sets up the Pagefiles.

Note

Windows NT supports multiple Pagefiles (up to 16) which should be located on separate physical drives for maximum performance.

■ **Windows Start.** When the Win32 subsystem is started, it automatically starts WINLOGON.EXE, which starts its System entries.

By default, WINLOGON.EXE starts the Local Security Authority subsystem (LSASS.EXE) and the print spooler (SPOOLSS.EXE). Next, the welcome screen appears with the Ctrl+Alt+Del logon message. The Service Controller (SCREG.EXE) is then executed.

Bypassing the Logon Message

You can set up the system to bypass the Ctrl+Alt+Del logon message so that you can automatically log on to Windows NT.

To automatically log on to Windows NT

1. Start RegEdit32 (REGEDT32.EXE) and edit the following key:

```
\HKEY_LOCAL_MACHINE
\SOFTWARE
    \Microsoft
            \Windows NT
                    \CurrentVersion
                            \Winlogon
```

2. Assign the appropriate strings to the following values of the \Winlogon key:

```
DefaultDomainName
DefaultUserName
DefaultPassword
```

3. Add a value called AutoAdminLogon to the ...\Winlogon key. This value should have a data type of REG_SZ and a value of 1 (just the character 1).

The next time the system is shut down and restarted, the system automatically logs on to Windows NT and brings up the Program Manager ready for use.

Creating the Control Set

Once the Service Controller has started, it makes a final pass through the Registry looking for items with a start value of 0x2. However, at this point, the loading sequence is different from that of the device drivers that were loaded earlier in the process. All services with a 0x2 start value have certain dependencies — DependOnGroup and/or DependOnService entries — that determine their load order. This is necessary because these services are loaded in parallel for better performance, whereas the device drivers were loaded serially. Each service must have its dependencies started before it is able to start.

At this point, the Clone ControlSet is copied to the LastKnownGood ControlSet. The boot will not be considered good until a user successfully logs on to the system. After a successful logon, the Clone ControlSet will be copied to the LastKnownGood ControlSet.

Troubleshooting the Boot Process

Even when Windows NT has been installed properly or has been running glitch-free for some time, there are still some problems that can occur during the boot process. This section describes some of these problems and possible solutions.

Errors on first boot

As a final phase in Windows NT's installation process, Windows NT attempts to boot. If Windows NT fails to boot immediately after installation, there are two possibilities:

- A component of the system was not configured correctly during the installation process.

  An installation checklist helps prevent this problem, but things can go wrong. Since the network card is the most likely problem, remove the network card briefly and try booting again before putting the card back in. If the boot is successful, log on as Administrator and use the network Control Panel to modify the configuration of the network adapter. Make sure that there is no IRQ conflict. Once you have made the modification, shut down the system, put the card back in, and reboot. If problems continue, you may have the wrong device driver for the network adapter or a hardware problem. The SCSI adapter is typically the next most likely candidate for problems.

- Files from the installation media were corrupt. The best course of action is to return the media to the supplier immediately for a new set.

Missing system files

If you want to delve deep into the Windows NT boot process, try renaming the system files one by one and making a note of the problems that occur and their corresponding error messages. In case you're not up for fun and games, Table 6-1 lists a few of the boot problems that can occur due to missing or corrupted files.

Table 6-1	Error Messages	
Missing file	*Error message*	*Comments*
NTLDR	BOOT: Couldn't find NTLDR. Please insert another disk.	If NTLDR is missing from the root of the C drive, Windows NT cannot boot. To fix, copy NTLDR from the installation media onto the hard disk.
NTDETECT.COM	Fatal System Error: 0x00000067-Configuration Initialization Failed.	This message appears if the boot fails right after switching to the blue screen. Check the BOOT.INI file for errors. If no errors exist in BOOT.INI, you may need to restore the NTDETECT.COM file to the hard drive. Simply copy the file from the installation media.

(continued)

Table 6-1 *(Continued)*		
Missing file	**Error message**	**Comments**
BOOTSECT.DOS	Couldn't open boot sector file multi(0)disk(0) rdisk(0)partition(1): \bootsect.dos.	This appears in a dual boot configuration when attempting to boot the second operating system. BOOTSECT.DOS is a hidden file that contains specific information about the hard drive's physical lay out. Therefore, this type of error is not easily fixed. You can try copying the BOOTSECT.DOS file from a machine that has exactly the same type of hard disk, partitioning, and directory structure. If the system does not boot using this new file, your only solution is to strip Windows NT from the system, reformat the hard drive using the previous operating system, and reinstall Windows NT.

Bad or missing BOOT.INI

If the system automatically boots into Windows NT without giving the Boot Loader choices, BOOT.INI is either bad, missing, or the time= entry is set too low.

If the path for the default= line in the [Boot Loader] section of the BOOT.INI file does not match any of the paths in the [operating systems] section, a new menu selection, NT (default) [debugger enabled], appears. This entry is highlighted, using the default= line in the [Boot Loader] section. It will be loaded, or loading will be attempted, if the time expires. This additional selection means that a line has been changed in the BOOT.INI.

Incorrect path statement to Windows NT

If part of the path statement to Windows NT is incorrect, you receive the following error message:

```
OS Loader V2.10 loading file
scsi(0)disk(0)rdisk(0)partition(1)\nt\system32\ntoskrnl.exe
The system did not load because it cannot find the following file:
<winnt root>\system32\ntoskrnl.exe
Please re-install a copy of the above file.
Boot failed
```

The second line of the error message varies depending on system hardware and the path where Windows NT is installed. This error message can be caused by a damaged BOOT.INI file, or NTOSKRNL.EXE may indeed be missing.

Unrecognized device or partition

When you install Windows NT on a system that has an unusual partitioning scheme or if Windows NT does not recognize the partition type, you might receive one of the following error messages:

```
OS Loader V2.10 The system did not load because of a computer disk
hardware configuration problem.
Could not read from the selected boot disk. Check boot path and disk
hardware.
```

Both of these messages indicate a possible problem with the BOOT.INI file's path statement. Windows NT might be able to process BOOT.INI to the point where NT starts to load (indicated by the blue loader screen), but it fails when it gets to the path statement. The solution is to boot to another operating system and search the directory structure for a file that has been marked improperly. Then manually edit the BOOT.INI file and try to boot again.

Check the Windows NT documentation about hardware disk configuration and your hardware reference manuals for additional information.

Errors booting MS-DOS or OS/2

If the machine is dual booting and there is a problem with booting into MS-DOS or OS/2, there are three strong possibilities:

- The BOOT.INI file that contains the path to the boot record is incorrect. An example would be that the BOOT.INI file points to c:\ as the path to the previous operating system, but it was really d:\. BOOTSECT.DOS is a hidden file. Use the ATTRIB command to see if it exists. If this file is missing, restore it from the Emergency Repair disk or copy it — *from an identical machine*. It is important that the machine from which you are copying the BOOTSECT.DOS is identical in terms of the hard disk layout and capacity. Information in the BOOTSECT.DOS describes the hard disk layout (number of heads, cylinders, tracks, sectors, and so on). Always rehide the BOOTSECT.DOS so that you do not delete it accidentally.

- The BOOT.INI file may not exist. Another possibility is that the BOOT.INI may have been accidentally deleted.

- The boot partition may be NTFS, which is not supported by MS-DOS or OS/2. Operating systems prior to Windows NT cannot read an NTFS volume successfully. If you intend to have dual boot machines, the boot partition must be FAT for MS-DOS, or FAT or HPFS for OS/2. If you are not dual booting, save the user some time and set the default time in the BOOT.INI to 0 so that the system automatically starts Windows NT.

Errors during boot of Windows NT

If an existing Windows NT machine that was successfully booting Windows NT suddenly starts having problems booting Windows NT, something has changed in the environment. The most probable cause is a change in the

Registry. Because Windows NT no longer boots, there is no way that the Regedit program can help in this situation. The only solution is to recover the original Registry from the Emergency Repair disk. If this still does not fix the problem, there could be a hardware error in either an adapter or in memory.

Starting and Quitting Windows NT

Under Windows NT, Ctrl+Alt+Del is used as a Security Attention Sequence (SAS). Ctrl+Alt+Del must be used prior to entering logon information. In addition, you can use the sequence at any time to bring up the Windows NT Security dialog box. The Security dialog box allows users to log off, shut down, change their password, lock the workstation, or select the task list.

Note

The Ctrl+Alt+Del keys were chosen because they could not be easily intercepted by any other program and because they prevent users from inadvertently rebooting the system.

Forgotten password

Users do forget their passwords. As system administrator, you must help the user get back into the system. There are two possible scenarios:

- The user's workstation is not part of a domain. In this case, Windows NT uses only the local security database for user authentication. To regain access, you should first try using the default Administrator (no password) account to get into the system. If this account is still valid, you should be able to enter the system and change the user's account information. If the Administrator account is not available, use the Emergency Repair disk, as described earlier in this chapter, to restore the Registry and then use the Administrator account.

- The workstation is part of a domain. In domain structures, the domain server performs user authentication. Anyone with administrator privileges in the domain can establish a new password for the user. As a precaution, have an Administrator account on every domain and a stand-alone machine with a password that is known only to the support team.

Troubleshooting Network Problems

Network problems can be the toughest to troubleshoot because there are so many different components, and the path causing the problem may not be active when the troubleshooting engineer arrives. The most common problems are as follows:

- Loose adapter cable. The first rule of troubleshooting network problems is to make sure that the network is plugged into the network adapter card. It sounds silly, but it is always worth checking.

■ Network adapter failure. Check the event log for system errors related to the network adapter, the workstation, and the server components. Use ping and/or nbping to determine if the machine is getting out on the wire and how far. If ping is unable to talk to its closest neighbor, you may want to enlist the help of a LAN protocol analyzer to determine if packets are getting onto the net. If not, work forward from the network control card to isolate the faulty component. If the machine is getting to the wire but not its nearest neighbor, use the analyzer to look for congestion, jitter (token ring), and broadcast storm.

■ IRQ conflict with new adapter. If you suspect an IRQ conflict, disable the mouse in the Registry by setting the start value to 0x4. You may also want to disable the serial ports.

■ Protocol mismatch. If two machines are active on the same network but still cannot communicate, it may be that they are using different protocols. For successful communications, both must be using the same protocol. If machine A is only speaking NetBEUI and machine B is only speaking TCP/IP, the two machines are not able to establish a successful connection. Use the network Control Panel to determine which protocols are supported.

There are two important things to remember about Windows NT and protocols: First, Windows NT does not use the DLC protocol to establish workstation or server sessions. DLC is used only for mainframe and network printer traffic. Second, NetBEUI is not routable. If the network uses TCP/IP, IPX, or XNS routers, machines on different sides of the router cannot establish communications.

■ External network problems. If the hardware on the local machine checks out, there may be an external network error. Use ping or nbping to isolate the problem. Attempt to ping the closest neighbor in increasing distances until a problem is seen. Also use a LAN protocol analyzer to help locate jitter (token ring only), congestion, and broadcast storms.

Problems with Services

Windows NT uses several internal software routines to provide support for other applications. These routines are called *services.* Some services are critical to the operation and performance of Windows NT functions, and many services are dependent on one another. The most common problem with services is that they simply don't start when they're supposed to, or they don't start at all.

Service doesn't start

There are two ways to start services: automatically and manually. If an automatic service won't start, check the event log for a record of the failure. It is very likely that the service failure is due to a prerequisite component not starting.

It may be possible to get more information from the service if you start it manually. Use the Services Control Panel to attempt to start the service manually. The service may display a message box that provides more information than the event log.

Using Event Viewer to monitor services

Every significant incident (system-wide or application-specific) that occurs under Windows NT requires a user or users to be notified. For critical events, such as when the power is interrupted while using the UPS service, Event Viewer immediately notifies the user. For most other non-critical events, Windows NT places the information in an event log file to supply information on events without disturbing a user's work.

The Windows NT Event Logging service is configured to start automatically every time the system starts. You can disable the Event Logging service from starting in the Control Panel Services applet.

When you first start Event Viewer, by default it displays the event logs on the local system. You can use the Log menu's Select Computer option to view the event logs on any of the following systems:

- A Windows NT workstation

- A Windows NT Advanced Server

- A LAN Manager 2.x server, for which the current user has administrative privileges

You can use the Event Viewer utility, located in the Administrative Tools group, to view the event log files generated by the events that occur on a system. The Event Viewer allows event logs to be viewed, sorted, filtered, and searched for specific details. Event Viewer also has the capability to archive log files in a variety of formats for later examination. Table 6-2 shows an example of what Event Viewer displays.

Windows NT categorizes events in three classes and stores them in three separate logs as follows:

- **System.** The System log records events logged by the Windows NT system components. This includes such things as the failure of a driver or other system component to load during the boot process.

- **Security.** The Security log contains records regarding security events on the system. Event Viewer logs security information if you have enabled auditing through User Manager.

Note

When viewing a LAN Manager 2.x server, the System log displays the LAN Manager server's error log, and the Security log displays the LAN Manager server's audit log.

Table 6-2	Event Viewer Information
Item	*Description*
Date	This is the date on which the event occurred.
Time	This is the time at which the event occurred.
Source	This identifies the software that logged the event, which can either be an application or a system component.
Category	This is a classification of the event; it is generated by the source of the event. Every event does not have an entry in the Category column. Some event sources do not classify the event or place an entry in the Category column.
Event	This is a unique number that is specified by the source of the event. The source of the event can use this number to identify the event. It may also be meaningful to product support representatives for the company that supplied the software used to log the event.
User	This is the user name of the user who was logged on at the time the event occurred. A user entry of "N/A" indicates that the software logging the event did not specify a user name.
Computer	This is the computer name for the computer on which the event occurred.

■ **Application.** The Application log records events that are logged by applications. If you installed Windows NT on top of Windows 3.1, the Application log also contains information regarding the status of the migration of Windows 3.1 configuration information to the Windows NT Registry.

All three of the preceding event log files are located in \<WINNT ROOT>\SYSTEM32\CONFIG*.EVT.

Event Viewer displays events according to their date and time. By default, Event Viewer displays all events from the most recent to oldest events. It is possible to change the order to display events from oldest to most recent under the View menu.

The Windows NT Event Viewer logs five types of events. These events are listed in Table 6-3.

General System Errors

General system errors manifest themselves in several ways. For example, you're working along fine when the system locks up suddenly. Or an important data file appears as garbage when you open it. This section describes some of the errors you might encounter.

Table 6-3	Event Types
Event type	**Description**
Error	This event type indicates a significant problem, such as data loss. Typically, if a service or device driver failed to load during the Windows NT boot sequence, the system logs it as an error.
Information	This event type is infrequent, yet significant. It describes the successful operation of a major server service. For example, when a service is manually started through Control Panel Services, it may log an event here indicating that it started successfully.
Security	This event type indicates an audited security access that was successful, such as logging onto the system or opening a file.
Failed Access	This event type indicates an audited security access attempt that failed, such as someone trying to access a file without appropriate permission.
Warning	This event type indicates an event that may not be significant at the moment but may lead to future problems. An example of a warning would be a message indicating that a drive is low on free space.

Frozen system

In theory, Windows NT is not supposed to freeze, but sometimes it does. When a system is frozen, not even the mouse moves. This indicates that interrupts have been turned off. Only one type of component can turn interrupts off: device drivers. The only recovery for the problem is to power cycle the machine. If the problem persists, collect a list of device drivers active on your machine and check on CompuServe to see if there are any known problems with those drivers.

Corrupt disk

Disk corruption under Windows NT should be a thing of the past. NTFS provides *hot fixing* (fixing a machine without taking it offline or powering it down) of clusters and has a recovery transaction log. All allocated objects on the disk are part of the file structure on NTFS, and the file table is duplicated to prevent single point of failure. With HPFS, it is possible to corrupt the disk if either the super block, the spare block, or the FNODE for the root directory are lost. If one of the special sectors is corrupted, the disk may be unusable.

FAT does not provide hot fixing. If a sector corruption occurs in the FAT table, large sections of the disk could be lost. Software such as Norton Utilities, third-party tools from Symantec, can be used to help recover some of the problems. To use these tools, boot back into MS-DOS to avoid any drive access restrictions imposed by Windows NT.

The blue screen of death

Extremely serious errors within Windows NT are known as *blue screens*. These are unresolved errors within the kernel itself.

If you received a blue screen core dump, look at the error code first and compare it with the listing of common errors in *The Windows NT Resource Kit, Volume 3: Windows NT Messages*. You may also want to look in the Event Viewer logs for any additional information about the error. Some of the more common error codes include

- **F002.** This error code indicates that a parity error or non-maskable interrupt occurred. In most cases, this error is memory related, although some network and video adapters can also generate this error. If you receive this error, run a system diagnostic on the computer and check your BIOS memory refresh rates and cache settings. This error is sometimes caused by a poorly seated SIMM. Try removing each SIMM, cleaning it with an eraser, and then reinstalling it.

- **0000001E.** This unhandled kernel exception usually indicates a problem with the file system. If you receive this error, look for possible causes at the bottom of the blue screen for the stack dump. For instance, if you see RDR.SYS listed, there is a problem with the network redirector, and you should check your network adapter settings. If you see NTFS.SYS or FASTFAT.SYS, you have an error in your NTFS or FAT partitions, and you should run the CHKDSK.EXE program with the /F (to fix any errors) option on all of your drives.

- **0000000A.** This is a catastrophic error and generally indicates an interrupt, I/O, or DMA conflict. Check your hardware to make sure you are not sharing any IRQs or having any other resource conflicts.

- **0x0000007B.** This error code indicates that your boot drive is inaccessible. Possible causes are disk drives greater than 1024 cylinders, unsupported disk partitioning schemes, accidental compression of the boot drive with an MS-DOS compression program in a dual boot environment, or a boot sector virus. This can also be caused by some MS-DOS-based disk utilities.

- **Couldn't Find NTLDR.** This message is displayed if the file NTLDR is missing from the root of drive C. You can copy the file to C:\ from either the Windows NT CD-ROM or floppy disks.

  To copy NTLDR from the Windows NT compact disc

  1. Make the CD-ROM drive your current drive.

  2. At the command prompt, type **COPY \I386\NTLDR C:\.**

  To copy NTLDR from floppy disk

  1. Insert Windows NT Setup Disk #2 in your disk drive and make that drive the current drive.

  2. At the command prompt, type **EXPAND NTLDR.$ C:\NTLDR.**

- **0x00000069 or 0x00000067.** This initialization error indicates that Windows NT is unable to communicate with the hard drive controller. Try the following:

  - Slow down the direct memory access (DMA) transfer rate on the controller.

  - Make sure that both ends of the SCSI bus are terminated.

  - Make sure that there are no conflicts for interrupt requests (IRQs) or memory addresses.

  - Make sure that you are not using a faulty or unsupported driver.

  - Make sure that NTDETECT.COM is in the root of the boot drive partition.

  - Make sure that there are no missing Windows NT system files.

- **NMI Hardware Error.** This error is caused by a hardware problem. In some cases, the computer's memory can be at fault, leading to an error that does not appear when running MS-DOS or Windows 3.x but does appear when running Windows NT. Memory errors can occur when the access rate does not match the requirements of the system board or when the access rate varies between SIMM modules or chips on a module. Cache memory access rates that are too slow can also cause this problem.

  Check that contacts for all boards and memory modules are clean, boards and memory modules are properly seated, and the computer is free of dust. If these steps do not correct the problem, take the computer to the dealer or hardware repair technician for complete diagnostics.

Restoring the System

With all the things that can go wrong with your Windows NT installation, sometimes it's just smarter to revert to a configuration that you know works. This is what is meant by restoring the system. You restore a system to the state in which it last worked.

What about "Last Known Good"?

The boot process uses a *ControlSet* (stored in the System portion of the Registry), which lists general boot process information and services to load. The *LastKnownGood* is the last known control set that successfully booted Windows NT. This option is useful if the system is no longer booting, due to an incorrect entry in the Registry or inappropriate driver selection.

If an incorrect driver selection or Registry entry causes the system to fail to boot, the LastKnownGood can be used to boot the system. In order to get the option to use the LastKnownGood, hold down the spacebar as soon as Windows NT has been selected from the Boot Loader menu. This brings up a choice of configurations — ControlSets — for the boot process to use. The choices are

■ Use Current Configuration

■ Use Last Known Good Configuration

■ Reboot

Restoring a system to an MS-DOS or WIN 95 boot machine

One recommendation made in Chapter 4, *Preparing to Install Windows NT Server*, was to install Windows NT so that you can boot from a FAT partition, and after everything checked out, convert the partition to NTFS. Just in case a problem develops or you decide to remove Windows NT from a machine, here's a way to clean Windows NT off the system and revert to DOS or Windows 95. (These instructions assume that the partition was not converted to NTFS.)

As stated earlier in this chapter when describing the Windows NT boot process, Windows NT replaces the boot record during installation. The new boot record looks for and loads NTLDR into memory for execution. To rid a system of Windows NT, you must remove the Boot Loader, which is controlled by NTLDR.

To remove the Windows NT Boot Loader

1. Boot the system from an MS-DOS boot disk that contains the SYS.COM file. The FORMAT /S command does not copy this file as a part of the formatting process so you need to select SYS.COM for separate copying.

2. At the A: prompt, enter the following command to copy system files to the hard drive:

```
sys c:
```

3. After you have transferred the system files, remove the system disk from the diskette drive and reboot the system from the hard drive.

4. After rebooting, you may want to free up space on the hard drive by deleting the following files:

```
c:\pagefile.sys
c:\boot.ini
c:\nt*.*
c:\bootsect.dos (this is marked as hidden, system, and read only)
\<winnt root>\system32 subdirectory
```

If the boot drive was converted to NTFS, the only way to return to booting just MS-DOS is to reformat the drive and reinstall MS-DOS.

Using the Repair Disk Utility

Microsoft added a new administrative tool in Windows NT 3.51 called the Repair Disk Utility (RDISK.EXE). This utility enables you to update your repair information, which is contained in your SystemRoot\Repair subdirectory, or to create a new repair disk. If you did not create a repair disk during the installation process, this utility is your only alternative (aside from the tape backup application) for protecting yourself from a system failure. Windows NT Server does not automatically install the Repair Disk Utility as an icon when you install Windows NT Server so you have to install the icon yourself.

You can use the repair disk with the three installation disks to repair a failed installation of Windows NT. It also is useful for restoring the Registry (which is what the repair information includes) when you make a mistake with the Registry Editor or install software that prevents your system from functioning properly.

Before you make any system modifications, use the Repair Disk Utility to back up your Registry. Make a new repair disk before you edit the Registry; at the very least, update the local repair information. In fact, it is a good practice to keep at least three repair disks at a time so that you will always have one you can use to restore your configuration.

Running Repair Disk

After you create the program item for the Repair Disk Utility, it is a good idea to run it and back up your system configuration. When you run the application, the Repair Disk Utility dialog box appears, as shown in Figure 6-1.

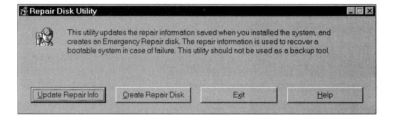

Figure 6-1: The Repair Disk Utility dialog box.

The Repair Disk Utility dialog box has four buttons:

- **Update Repair Info.** Use this option to update the Registry information contained in the SystemRoot\Repair directory. After you click this button, you are asked whether you want to create a new repair disk.

- **Create Repair Disk.** Click this button to format a high-density floppy disk and copy the same repair information as described for the Update Repair Info button. This repair disk is used by the repair process to restore your Registry.

- **Exit.** Click this option to exit the application.

- **Help.** Use this option to display brief descriptions of the Repair Disk Utility button actions.

The information contained in the SystemRoot\Repair directory consists of uncompressed copies of your AUTOEXEC.NT and CONFIG.NT files and the compressed files listed in Table 6-4.

Table 6-4	**Key Registry Components**	
Filename	*Registry key*	*Description*
default._	HKEY_USERS\DEFAULT	The default system profile
sam._	HKEY_LOCAL_MACHINE\SAM	The security account manager
security._	HKEY_LOCAL_MACHINE\Security	The security database
software._	HKEY_LOCAL_MACHINE\Software	Software configurable settings
system._	HKEY_LOCAL_MACHINE\System	System-specific configuration settings

SystemRoot\Repair does not include all your local profiles. If you want to back up local profiles, copy them manually from the SystemRoot\System32\Config subdirectory (where SystemRoot is the root directory where you installed Windows NT Server).

There is one additional file not shown in the SystemRoot\Repair directory unless you enable the Show Hidden/ System Files option with File Manager. This file is called SETUP.LOG, and you should never delete it. The Windows NT Setup program uses SETUP.LOG during an upgrade. If the setup program cannot find enough free space during the upgrade, it prompts you to delete some files in your current installation. The files listed in SETUP.LOG are the files that the setup program deletes to make room for the upgrade. If this file is missing and you have insufficient disk space, the setup program can continue only if you format your hard disk.

Using the Emergency Repair disk to restore a system

The Emergency Repair disk performs the following steps:

- Runs CHKDSK on the partition containing Windows NT system files.

- On x86-based systems, also runs CHKDSK on the system partition.

- Verifies that each file in the installation is good, through a checksum. If files are missing or corrupt, they are restored from the installation disks.

- Replaces the default system and security/sam Registry hives, subject to user confirmation.

- Reinstalls Boot Loader, that is, the boot sector, BOOT.INI, NTLDR, and so on.

To restore an x86 system

1. Reboot from the Setup disk, and choose R for Repair on the appropriate screen.

2. Follow the instructions on the screen, inserting the Emergency Repair disk or Windows NT disks as requested.

3. When you reach the final message, remove the Emergency Repair disk and press Ctrl+Alt+Del to restart the system.

To restore a RISC system

1. Start the Windows NT Setup program as instructed in the manufacturer's documentation.

2. Follow the instructions on the screen, inserting the Emergency Repair disk or Windows NT disks as requested.

3. When you reach the final message, remove the Emergency Repair disk and press Enter to restart the system.

The Emergency Repair disk is *machine specific* and should *not* be used on a system on which it was not created.

Application Errors

Windows NT seamlessly runs many different types of applications on the same graphical desktop. It runs applications written for existing operating systems such as MS-DOS, OS/2, and Windows 3.1x and Windows 95. It also runs applications written for newer application programming interfaces such as POSIX and Win32.

Windows NT supports this variety of applications through the use of environment subsystems. Environment subsystems are Windows NT processes that emulate different operating system environments. The Windows NT executive provides generic services that all environment subsystems can call to perform basic operating system functions. The subsystems build on the executive's services to produce environments that meet the specific needs of their client applications.

Troubleshooting MS-DOS applications

MS-DOS applications do not run under their own environment subsystems. Instead, Windows NT supports them with special Win32 applications called *virtual (MS-)DOS machines (VDM)*. VDMs provide MS-DOS applications with an execution environment that looks like native MS-DOS.

Each MS-DOS application runs in its own VDM to mimic the single-tasking nature of native MS-DOS. It can access memory just as it would on a native MS-DOS system. Its attempts to access hardware devices directly are intercepted and processed by appropriate *virtual device drivers*, which translate those attempts into Windows NT API (application programming interface) calls. Running MS-DOS applications in separate VDMs increases the overall robustness of Windows NT. The worst that an MS-DOS application can do is to crash its own VDM, which has no negative impact on other applications or Windows NT as a whole. Because each MS-DOS application has a single thread, applications can be preemptively scheduled for execution just like any other process in the system. The failure of one process does not affect the others. The potential problems with MS-DOS applications under Windows NT stem from the following:

- Applications written for MS-DOS often try to manipulate the computer's hardware directly. They expect free access to the computer's memory, including the areas where operating system code and data structures reside. These needs conflict with the requirement for Windows NT to be a secure operating system.

- MS-DOS is a 16-bit operating system. It accesses memory using segmented addresses. Windows NT accesses memory using flat, or unsegmented, memory addresses.

- The application programming interface for MS-DOS relies on Intel 80x86-specific machine instructions that invoke software interrupts. Windows NT is a portable operating system designed to run on processors that do not support the Intel 80x86 instruction set.

Windows NT restricts access to vital system resources and process memory and imposes security limitations. These restrictions can cause some MS-DOS programs (ill-behaved ones) to fail. When an MS-DOS program attempts to perform a function that violates a restriction imposed by Windows NT, a message box providing information about the violation appears. There are two main types of error: direct hardware access and software interrupt access. The virtual MS-DOS environment provided by Windows NT allows MS-DOS programs to simulate direct hardware access via the use of a virtual device driver (VDD). Some VDDs are provided with Windows NT, but not for all hardware combinations. In addition, direct access to some devices such as hard disks could seriously compromise system security and integrity.

Windows 3.1 applications

All Win16 applications share a single VDM in order to emulate the native Windows 3.1 environment in which multiple Win16 applications coexist in a single address space. It also allows the WOW (Windows On Windows) layer to mimic the non-preemptive multi-tasking environment expected by Win16 applications. Each Win16 application does get its own thread; however, the WOW layer ensures that only one Win16 application's thread is active at any given time, so the effect is the same as if only one thread has been used.

Running all Win16 applications in the same VDM provides maximum compatibility with the native Windows 3.1 environment. However, compatibility has a cost. It forces the WOW VDM to have the same weaknesses as Windows 3.1. It allows Win16 applications to inadvertently (or intentionally) access memory that belongs to other Win16 applications or to WOW, with potentially disastrous effects. It also allows a single Win16 application that does not yield control of the processor effectively to crash all other Win16 applications. Even so, a crashed Win16 application does not affect the other VDMs, nor does it affect applications running under other subsystems.

Much of what was said earlier about MS-DOS is true for Windows 3.1 applications as well. There is one major difference between the Windows 3.1 environment and MS-DOS. In MS-DOS, each program receives its own address space. If it fails or corrupts the space, no other applications in the system are affected. Windows 3.1 applications all run in the same address space. This is done to provide the same environment that the application experienced under Windows 3.1. There is only one message stream. If an application stops responding to messages, it not only stops responding to commands, but it can also prevent other Windows 3.1 applications from continuing to process messages as well. While running Windows NT, if it appears that some applications continue to work (Win32, MS-DOS, OS/2, and POSIX) but Windows 3.1 applications do not, this is very likely the situation. If there is a problem, the best option is to contact the developer.

OS/2 and POSIX applications

OS/2 and POSIX applications are treated very much like MS-DOS applications in that each receives its own memory space. OS/2 programs come in two varieties: character mode and Presentation Manager (PM). The initial release of Windows NT does not support running PM programs. When you start a PM program, the following message appears:

```
The system cannot find the file OS2SM (indicates a PM program).
```

Or

```
Error ordinal not found DOSCALLS.xxx (indicates a VIO program).
```

In this case, contact the developer of the application and determine if there is a Windows NT-compatible version of the application.

Although Microsoft did not include support for PM-based applications in the base Windows NT product, support for this environment is available via an add-on product known as the Presentation Manager Subsystem for Windows NT (PMNT). Many long-time users of Windows NT are completely unaware of this product. It is often only by word-of-mouth that users ever become aware of its existence.

Secret

Although it offers improvements over the basic OS/2 support provided in Windows NT, the Presentation Manager Subsystem for Windows NT still supports only 16-bit applications (specifically, those developed for PM under OS/2 versions 1.2 and 1.3). There is no support under Windows NT for any applications written for OS/2 version 2.0 or later (including OS/2 Warp and Warp Server).

Win32 applications

Win32 programs run in their own memory space. A poorly written application can attempt to access system resources in such a way that a violation occurs. The best solution is to record the violation and contact the vendor that supplied the software.

Using Dr. Watson

The Windows NT retail product includes Dr. Watson, also referred to as the Windows NT Post Mortem Debugger, which is similar in functionality to the Windows 3.1 Dr. Watson utility.

Under Windows NT, Dr. Watson is configured automatically to catch any Win32 application errors and generate a log file containing fault information about the offending application. The following data is generated in the Dr. Watson log file:

- Exception information, such as exception number and name

- System information, such as machine name, user name, and OS version

- A state dump for each thread, including a register dump, disassembly, stack walk, and symbol table

The Dr. Watson log file, DRWTSN32.LOG, is located by default in the \<winnt root> directory.

In addition to the information in the Dr. Watson log, the Windows NT application log (which can be viewed through Event Viewer) also contains a record regarding the application error.

Enabling Dr. Watson

When you install Windows NT, it enables Dr. Watson by default. To disable Dr. Watson, change the following Registry value from a 1 to 0 (zero):

```
\HKEY_LOCAL_MACHINE
    \SOFTWARE
        \Microsoft
            \Windows NT
                \CurrentVersion
                    \AeDebug:Auto
```

To enable Dr. Watson, change the Auto value from 0 to 1. This launches whatever debugger or application is under ...\AeDebug:Debugger. For Dr. Watson, the ...\AeDebug:Debugger value should contain:

```
drwtsn32 -p %ld -e %ld -g
```

Note

When Dr. Watson is enabled, it does not appear as an icon on the desktop or in the Task List. However, when a Win32 application causes an application error, Dr. Watson pops up and generates a log.

Summary

Installing Windows NT Server is usually a painless operation. Because Windows NT and NT Server run on so many different hardware configurations and platforms, it's impossible to have it start or run glitch-free on every system. This chapter provided a troubleshooting hit list that covered the following:

▶ Understanding startup problems and solutions

▶ Using Event Viewer to track down problems with services

▶ Troubleshooting network problems

▶ Restoring a system to its previous working condition

▶ Using Dr. Watson

Chapter 7

Working with the Registry

In This Chapter

▶ Using Registry Editor and Windows NT Diagnostics

▶ Viewing the Registry for a remote computer

▶ Editing Registry value entries

▶ Maintaining the Registry

As a system administrator, you face an enormous challenge in managing hardware, operating systems, and applications on personal computers. In Windows NT, the Registry helps simplify the burden by providing a secure, unified database that stores configuration data in a hierarchical form, allowing you to use the administrative tools in Windows NT to provide local or remote support easily. This chapter explains the inner workings of the Registry and how to use it.

An Overview

Windows NT Registry is a central, secure repository for information that describes the hardware configuration, installed system and application software, user and group account security, desktop settings and profiles, file associations, and applications that support Object Linking and Embedding (OLE). Starting at boot time, this database is populated by a variety of Windows NT or NTS system modules and is added to or modified by the configuration tools in Control Panel, the Windows NT Setup applet, User Manager or User Manager for Domains, third-party configuration tools, and software installation procedures.

The Registry provides several benefits to an administrator:

■ It collects all configuration information while accommodating the data and storage needs of system components. The Registry replaces the complex and fragmented collection of initialization and configuration files used in Windows 3.x and provides all of the data required to describe and operate a specific workstation or server.

- It allows discretionary access control to local and remote configuration data. Each key in the Registry can be protected by an Access Control List (ACL), which allows some users to modify Registry contents and grants other users read-only access to the same data.

- It records and preserves security and desktop information on an individual basis. Although Windows NT currently supports only one interactive user, it is common for workstations and servers to have multiple concurrent network connections. In the Registry, you will find a permanent record of per-user, per-application, and per-machine configuration information.

- You can use the Registry to determine all of the hardware components installed on a local or remote system, the BIOS revision levels for motherboards and video adapters, the number and type of SCSI adapters, the devices installed on each adapter, and IRQ/address and DMA channel assignments for specific components. On the software side, you can see installed applications and system configuration data set by various Windows NT applets.

Understanding the Registry

The Registry is simply a database that you view and manipulate through a program called the Registry Editor. The Registry Editor uses a hierarchical structure to display four *subtrees,* shown in Figure 7-1, through which you access the contents of the database. At first glance, the hierarchical structure displayed in the Registry Editor looks very similar to File Manager's hierarchical directory structures. The difference is in the kinds of information contained in the Registry and the impact that manipulating the Registry has on your system.

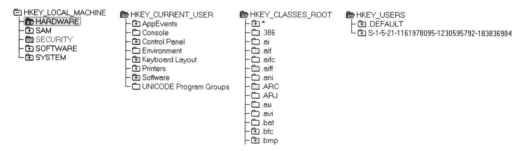

Figure 7-1: The four subtrees in the Windows NT Registry.

Under Windows 3.x, whenever you started the system, connected to a network, and ran an application, the system hunted for and read several configuration files to set up its operating environment. In contrast, Windows NT stores and checks the configuration information in only one location — the Registry. The Registry contains the following types of configuration information:

- Application data

- Hardware data

- Device driver data

- Network protocols and adapter card settings

- AUTOEXEC.BAT, CONFIG.SYS, WIN.INI, SYSTEM.INI, CONTROL.INI, LANMAN.INI, PROTOCOL.INI, and miscellaneous INI files.

Several Windows NT components and applications use the Registry. They are

- **Setup.** Whenever you run the Windows NT Setup program or other setup programs for applications or hardware, the Setup program adds new configuration data to the Registry.

- **Hardware Detector.** Each time you start a Windows NT machine, the Hardware Detector places hardware configuration data in the Registry. This information includes a list of hardware detected in your system.

- **Windows NT Kernel.** During system startup, the Windows NT Kernel extracts information from the Registry, such as the device drivers to load and their load order. The NTOSKRNL.EXE program also passes information about itself to the Registry, such as its version number.

- **Device drivers.** Device drivers send and receive load parameters and configuration data from the Registry. This data is similar to what you might find on the DEVICE=lines in the CONFIG.SYS file under MS-DOS. A device driver must report system resources that it uses, such as hardware interrupts and DMA channels, so that the system can add this information to the Registry. Applications and device drivers can read this Registry information to provide users with smart installation and configuration programs.

- **Administrative tools.** The administrative tools in Windows NT, such as those provided in Control Panel and in the Administrative Tools program group, can be used to modify configuration data. The Registry Editor is helpful for viewing and occasionally making detailed changes to the system configuration. You can also use the Windows NT Diagnostics program (WINMSD.EXE) to view configuration information stored in the Registry.

Basic Registry Anatomy

The first step in mastering the Registry is understanding the design and layout of the database. Learning how to interpret the database, relate keys and values to specific hardware or software components, and modify and add keys and values is an essential survival skill for system and network administrators. Because the Registry contains data critical to system operation, such as data accessed by loaded device drivers and client or server processes, be careful when performing modifications.

The Registry is comprised of thousands of individual data items that describe every aspect of a specific operating system installation, from the hardware to valid users to customized logon messages and performance-monitoring profiles. These data items are organized into keys and optional values. Keys are grouped so that related information can be accessed and cross-referenced.

Each area of the Registry has a standard set of keys that are common across all Windows NT installations. Within these keys, system-specific values describe hardware components, operating system components, and bootable configurations. Then the variations begin. For example, if a network card is installed, there are several entries that describe the hardware type (such as NE2000 and EtherExpress), the IRQ and base address, loaded driver, and related network services. Additional entries indicate the protocols that have been bound to the network driver for that card. Another common variation is the type of graphics adapter installed or the type and mode of a sound card or SCSI adapter.

Standard keys

If you compare one key with another, you will find standard keys with a significant variation in value entries. Each hardware component causes multiple subkeys to be placed in the hardware, software, and ControlSet keys. If one system has several applications and another has only a couple, the system with many will have more keys in the software section. Likewise, if one system is a domain server, there will be many entries in the users area, as compared to only one or two entries for a stand-alone workstation with a single dedicated user and only two network connections.

The Registry is one database, structured like a hierarchical file system. It is presented in four views called subtrees. Each Registry subtree contains keys that hold configuration data about a specific computer and each of its users. These subtrees describe hardware and software configuration, security data, all connected-user operating environments (profiles), the currently logged on user, and file associations used for Object Linking and Embedding. Each view has a name that begins with HKEY, which stands for Handle to a Key. A handle is a programming construct used to access Windows NT objects.

HKEY_LOCAL_MACHINE

The most important subtree is HKEY_LOCAL_MACHINE, because this is where hardware, software, and security information is stored. It contains information about the local computer system, including hardware and operating system data such as bus type, system memory, device drivers, and startup control data. This subtree is where you most often make changes to the Registry. It contains five main keys — HARDWARE, SAM, SECURITY, SOFTWARE, and SYSTEM — described in detail in the following sections.

HKEY_LOCAL_MACHINE\HARDWARE

This database describes the physical hardware in the computer, the way that device drivers use the hardware, and mappings and related data that link kernel-mode drivers with various user-mode code. All data in this subtree is recreated whenever the system is started. The Description key describes the actual computer hardware, for example, the make of motherboard, type of video adapter, SCSI adapters, serial ports, parallel ports, sound cards, network adapters, and so on. The DeviceMap key contains miscellaneous data in formats specific to particular classes of drivers. The ResourceMap key describes which device drivers claim which hardware resources. The Windows NT Diagnostics program (WINMSD.EXE) can report on this database's contents in an easy-to-read form.

All information in HKEY_LOCAL_MACHINE\HARDWARE is disposable, meaning that the settings are computed each time the system is started and then discarded when the system is shut down. Hardware configuration changes are reflected in the HARDWARE key at the next boot. Applications and device drivers use this subtree to read information about the system components.

Tip

Do not try to view or edit the data in HKEY_LOCAL_MACHINE\HARDWARE; much of the information appears in binary format, making it difficult to decipher. Instead, use Windows NT Diagnostics (discussed later in this chapter) to view hardware data in an easy-to-read format for troubleshooting.

The HKEY_LOCAL_MACHINE\SAM and HKEY_LOCAL_MACHINE\SECURITY subtrees

The Security Accounts Manager (SAM) and SECURITY keys have no visible information, as they point to site security policies such as specific user rights, as well as information for user and group accounts and for the domains in Windows NT Server. This information is in User Manager, and it also appears in the lists of users and groups when you use the Security menu commands in File Manager. You create, modify, and remove keys and values in these two keys with either User Manager or User Manager for Domains.

Caution

The information in this database is in binary format. You should not use Registry Editor to change it. Errors in this database may prevent users from being able to log on to the computer — which is another reason why system administrators should not allow typical users to log on as members of the Administrator group.

The HKEY_LOCAL_MACHINE\SOFTWARE subtree

This is the per-computer software database. This key contains data about software installed on the local computer, along with miscellaneous configuration data. The entries under this handle, which apply for anyone using this particular computer, show what software is installed on the computer and also define file associations and OLE information.

The HKEY_LOCAL_MACHINE\SYSTEM subtree

This database controls system startup, device driver loading, Windows NT services, and operating system behavior. The SYSTEM key describes bootable and nonbootable configurations in a group of ControlSets, where each ControlSet represents a unique configuration. Within each ControlSet, two keys describe operating system components and service data for that configuration. This key also records the configuration used to boot the running system (CurrentControlSet), along with failed configurations and the LastKnownGood configuration (Select).

HKEY_CURRENT_USER

A third subtree, HKEY_CURRENT_USER, contains the user profile for the user who is currently logged on, including environment variables, personal program groups, desktop settings, network connections, printers, and application preferences.

HKEY_CLASSES_ROOT

The last subtree, HKEY_CLASSES_ROOT, contains information on file associations (equivalent to the Registry in Windows for MS-DOS) and data required to support Microsoft's Object Linking and Embedding technology. This last subtree is a clone of data contained in the HKEY_LOCAL_MACHINE view and is separated primarily for usability reasons, because the machine subtree is so large and complex.

The Classes subkey defines types of documents, providing information on filename-extension associations and OLE that can be used by Windows shell applications and OLE applications. HKEY_CLASSES_ROOT displays the same information as stored under this subkey.

Note

The OLE information must be created by the specific application, so you should not use Registry Editor to change this information. If you want to change filename-extension associations, use the Associate command in File Manager.

HKEY_USERS

The HKEY_USERS subtree describes a default operating environment and contains one top-level key for each user logged on either interactively or via a network connection. It contains all actively loaded user profiles, including HKEY_CURRENT_USER, which always refers to a child of HKEY_USERS, and the default profile. Users who are accessing a server remotely do not have profiles under this key on the server; their profiles are loaded into the Registry on their own computers.

Value entries

Registry data is maintained as value entries under the Registry keys. As shown in Figure 7-2, Registry Editor displays data in two panes. The value entries in the right pane are associated with the selected key in the left pane.

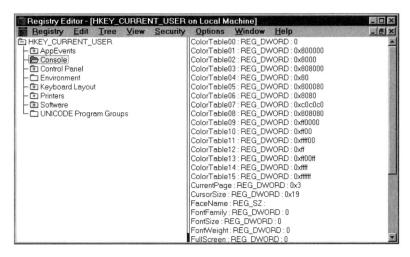

Figure 7-2: Registry key structure.

A value entry has three components, which always appear in the following order: the name of the value, the data type of the value, and the value itself, which can be data of any length. Table 7-1 lists the data types currently defined and used by the system.

Table 7-1	Data Types for Registry Entries
Data type	*Description*
REG_BINARY	Raw binary data. Most hardware component information is stored as binary data. It can be displayed in Registry Editor in hexadecimal format or via the Windows NT Diagnostics program (WINMSD.EXE) in an easy-to-read format.
REG_DWORD	Data represented by a number that is four bytes long. Many parameters for device drivers and services are this data type and can be displayed in Registry Editor in binary, hex, or decimal format. For example, entries for service error controls: ErrorControl : REG_DWORD : 0x1.
REG_EXPAND_SZ	An expandable data string, which is text that contains a variable to be replaced when called by an application. For example, for the following value, the string %SystemRoot% is replaced by the actual location of the directory containing the Windows NT system files: File : REG_EXPAND_SZ : %SystemRoot%\file.exe.
REG_MULTI_SZ	A multiple string. Values that contain lists or multiple values in human-readable text are usually this type. Entries are separated by null characters. For example, the following value entry specifies the binding rules for a network transport: bindable : REG_MULTI_SZ : dlcDriver dlcDriver non non 50.
REG_SZ	A sequence of characters representing human-readable text. For example, a component's description: DisplayName : REG_SZ : Messenger.

Hives

The Registry is divided into parts that define a discrete body of keys, subkeys, and values as shown in Figure 7-3. These parts are called *hives* and are rooted at the top of the Registry hierarchy. Table 7-2 shows the standard hives for a Windows NT computer.

By default, all hives are stored in the SystemRoot\SYSTEM32\CONFIG subdirectory, which also includes SYSTEM.ALT and the .LOG files, which are backup hive files. Whenever a new user logs on to a computer, the system creates a new hive for that user. Because each user profile is a separate hive, each profile is also a separate file. (If you prefer, you can store profile hives in other directories.) You can copy a user profile as a file and view, repair, or copy entries using Registry Editor on another computer.

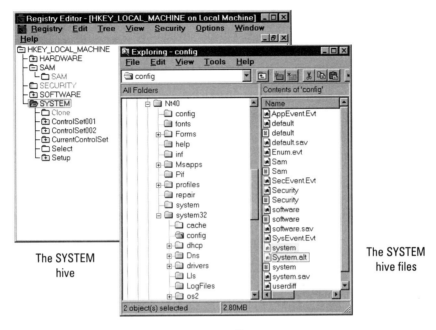

The SYSTEM hive

The SYSTEM hive files

Figure 7-3: The SYSTEM hive and its associated files.

Table 7-2	Standard Hive Files
Registry hive	**Filenames**
HKEY_LOCAL_MACHINE\SAM	SAM and SAM.LOG
HKEY_LOCAL_MACHINE\SECURITY	SECURITY and SECURITY.LOG
HKEY_LOCAL_MACHINE\SOFTWARE	SOFTWARE and SOFTWARE.LOG
HKEY_LOCAL_MACHINE\SYSTEM	SYSTEM and SYSTEM.ALT
HKEY_CURRENT_USER	USER### and USER###.LOG or ADMIN### and ADMIN###.LOG
HKEY_USERS\.DEFAULT	DEFAULT and DEFAULT.LOG

By default, all hives are stored in the SystemRoot\SYSTEM32\CONFIG subdirectory, which also includes SYSTEM.ALT and the .LOG files, which are backup hive files. Whenever a new user logs on to a computer, the system creates a new hive for that user. Because each user profile is a separate hive, each profile is also a separate file. (If you prefer, you can store profile hives in other directories.) You can copy a user profile as a file and view, repair, or copy entries using Registry Editor on another computer.

Using the Registry Editor

When you install Windows NT or Windows NTS, the system sets appropriate Registry values for the local hardware and software configuration. Although the standard tools do a good job of maintaining configuration information, there are many entries for which no graphical user interface exists. In this case, adjustments to system configuration or operation must be made by directly editing the configuration database.

Caution

The full path name for the Registry Editor is %systemroot%-\system32\regedt32.exe where %systemroot% normally is the directory in which Windows NT is installed. The Registry Editor is not loaded as an icon at installation. Note that there is another file in the %systemroot% directory, called REGEDT.EXE, that exists for compatibility with Windows applications. Do not use the older version to access the Registry — it may trash your system.

With the Registry Editor, you can load either the local or a remote Registry, if you have a valid user name and necessary rights and permissions on the target system. When the database is in place, you can display, add, modify, and delete keys and values in the database, protect keys with an ACL, modify user profiles, and audit the success or failure of access to selected keys.

Now that you know what the Registry is, how it works, and what it contains, you might want to know how to manipulate its entries. *Be forewarned.* The Registry Editor is a tool that should have a skull and crossbones for an icon. Like a ship on the high seas flying the pirate's flag, the Registry Editor should be avoided.

If all you need is to examine information stored in the Registry, use the Windows NT Diagnostics tool (WINMSD.EXE), shown in Figure 7-4. Windows NT Diagnostics installs in your SystemRoot\SYSTEM32 directory when you set up Windows NT. You run this program like any program in Windows NT. It's a handy tool and a whole lot safer than mucking about with the Registry Editor.

With Windows NT Diagnostics, you can display specific data from the Registry in an easily readable format. You cannot edit value entries using Windows NT Diagnostics, so the Registry contents are protected while you browse for information. However, you can select and copy any value if you want to paste information in a Registry Editor edit box or in a text editor. It's a good idea to place a program-item icon for Windows NT Diagnostics under Administrative Tools on the Programs menu.

Before going on to perform what could very well amount to open heart surgery on your system, you should acquaint yourself with two very important tools used for Registry management:

- **Backup.** Backs up Registry hives as part of a tape backup routine.

- **Emergency Repair disk.** Restores default hives to the system.

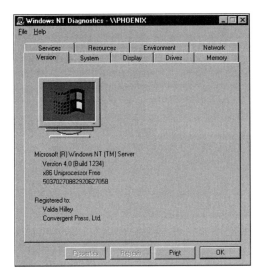

Figure 7-4: The Windows NT Diagnostics program.

As a precautionary measure, back up your Registry and critical system files. Also make sure that you have an emergency repair disk on hand to rescue your system from any Registry-tweaking mishaps. If you have a good set of backup files, you can restore damaged or missing Registry hives.

Running the Registry Editor program

The Registry Editor program does not appear in a Program Manager group after installing Windows NT, but it is installed automatically.

To run Registry Editor

Run the REGEDT32.EXE file from File Manager or Program Manager. Or type **start regedt32** at the command prompt and press Enter. As shown in Figure 7-5, the four local Registry Editor windows appear, each of which bears the name of a predefined key:

- **HKEY_CURRENT_USER.** The HKEY_CURRENT_USER window is the root of the configuration information for the user who is currently logged on. Information such as the user's program groups, screen colors, and Control Panel settings are stored here. This information is referred to as a user's *profile*.

- **HKEY_USERS.** The HKEY_USERS window is the root of all user profiles on the computer. HKEY_CURRENT_USER is a subkey of HKEY_USERS.

- **HKEY_LOCAL_MACHINE.** The HKEY_LOCAL_MACHINE window contains configuration information particular to the computer (for any user).

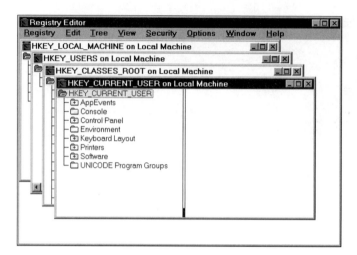

Figure 7-5: The Registry Editor.

- **HKEY_CLASSES_ROOT.** The HKEY_CLASSES_ROOT window is a subkey of HKEY_LOCAL_MACHINE\ SOFTWARE. The information stored here is used to perform such operations as opening the right application when a file is opened from File Manager (file association) and for Object Linking and Embedding (OLE).

Each subtree contains multiple keys, and each key contains a plus sign if it can be expanded with a double-click of the mouse. The display is normally divided into two, where keys appear on the left, and values, if any, appear on the right. You can display keys (tree) only, values only (data), or both (tree and data) by making the appropriate selection from the View menu.

If the currently highlighted key has a value or series of values, these appear to the right of the key in the data portion of the window. Some keys have a single value; others have 20 or more, depending on how the Registry entry is used. A value consists of three parts separated by colons: a field name, data type, and the actual data. There are six standard data types: REG_BINARY, REG_DWORD, REG_EXPAND_SZ, REG_MULTI_SZ, and REG_SZ. Many Registry entries are written in one of the three string formats — REG_SZ, REG_EXPAND, REG_MULTI_SZ — which represent a single string, a string that contains variables such as %systemroot% as well as text, and a string consisting of multiple strings, respectively.

Tip

Your ability to make changes to the Registry using Registry Editor depends on your access privileges. In general, you can make the same kinds of changes in Registry Editor as your privileges allow for Control Panel or other administrative tools. From the Options menu, choose the Read Only Mode command. This command protects the Registry contents while you explore its structure and become familiar with the entries.

Altering Registry data

Within the Registry, you can alter the value entries for a selected key or assign new value entries to keys. This section describes how to find keys and edit, add, or delete keys and value entries.

Warning

When possible, use the administrative tools such as Control Panel and User Manager to make configuration changes, rather than using Registry Editor. Using the administrative tools is safer because these applications know how to store values properly in the Registry. If you make errors while changing values with Registry Editor, there is no warning, because Registry Editor does not understand or recognize errors in syntax or other semantics.

The location of a Registry key in the tree structure may be different from what is described here, depending on whether a computer is running Windows NT as a workstation or a server, and other factors. You can search for a specific key name in the Registry tree. Key names appear in the left pane of the Registry Editor windows. The search begins from the currently selected key and includes all its descendant keys.

Each search is local to the tree where the search begins — that is, if you are searching in the windows for HKEY_LOCAL_MACHINE, the search does not include keys found under HKEY_CURRENT_USER.

To search for a key in Registry Editor

1. From the View menu, choose the Find Key command.

2. In the Find What box of the Find Key dialog box, type the name of the key that you want to find.

   - If you want to restrict the scope of the search or define the search direction, select the Match Whole Word Only box, the Match Case option, or Up or Down in the Direction box.

   - To see the next occurrence of the key name you specified, choose the Find Next button.

3. Choose the Find button.

Because key names are not unique, it's a good idea to search for additional occurrences of a specific key name, to be sure that you find the key you want.

Tip

Some key names include spaces (such as Session Manager); others use underscores (such as Ntfs_rec) or a continuous string (such as EventLog). To ensure that you find the key that you want, search for a portion of the name and make sure that the Match Whole Word Only check box is cleared in the Find dialog box.

To edit any value

1. In the right pane of the Registry Editor window, double-click the value entry.

Or

From the Edit menu, choose the String, Binary, DWord, or Multi String command as appropriate for the selected value.

2. Edit the value that appears in the related Editor dialog box and then choose the OK button.

The Binary and DWord editors give you the flexibility to select the base of a number system in which you want to edit your data. In the Binary editor, you can edit your data as binary (base 2) or hex (base 16). In the DWord editor, you can edit your data in binary, hex or decimal (base 10). Hex is the default base for both editors. The Registry Editor always displays these types of data in hex format in the right pane.

Tip

To view numbers in decimal format, double-click the value entry and select the Decimal format option. Cancel the dialog box when you finish checking the value.

Information stored in a nonvolatile key remains in the Registry until you delete it. Information stored in a volatile key is discarded when you shut down the system. Everything under a volatile key is also volatile. Everything stored under the HKEY_LOCAL_MACHINE\HARDWARE key is volatile.

You can add a key to store data in the Registry. For example, you might add a subkey under CurrentControlSet\Services to start a service process that you have written or to install a device driver that doesn't have an installation program.

To do this, you must have Create Subkey access permission for the key under which you are adding a subkey, as described in *Assigning access rights to Registry keys*, later in this chapter.

To add a key to the Registry

1. Select the key or subkey under which you want the new key to appear and then choose the Add Key command from the Edit menu or press the INS key.

2. In the Key Name box of the Add Key dialog box, type the name that you want to assign your key.

   The key name cannot contain a backslash (\). It must be unique in relation to other subkeys at the same level in the hierarchy — that is, Key1 and Key2 can each have a subkey named Key3, but Key1 cannot have two subkeys named Key3.

3. Leave the Class box blank, as this entry is reserved for future uses.

4. Choose the OK button to display the new key in the Registry Editor window.

Saving Registry data

The Save Key command lets you save the information in a key and all its subkeys in a hive file. This hive file can then be used by the Restore and Load Key commands.

Changes in the Registry are saved automatically, whether you make changes by using Registry Editor or by changing settings in applications. The Save Key command is used specifically to save portions of the Registry as a file on disk. To use the Save Key command, you need Backup privileges, which you have if you are logged on as a member of the Administrators group.

You can use the Save Key command on any key. However, this command does not save volatile keys, which are destroyed when you shut down the system. For example, the HKEY_LOCAL_MACHINE\HARDWARE key is volatile, so it is not saved as a hive file. If you want to view the Hardware hive for debugging, you can save it in a text file by choosing the Save Subtree As command from the Registry menu, as described at the end of this chapter.

To save a Registry key

1. Select the key you want to save as a hive file on a disk.

2. From the Registry menu, choose the Save Key command and then complete the filename information in the Save Key dialog box. Under the FAT file system, this filename cannot have an extension. If the key you are saving is in the Registry of a remote computer, the drive and path that you specify for the filename is relative to the remote computer.

The selected key is now saved as a file. When you use the Load Hive command, you can select the filename for any files saved using the Save Key command. For example, as part of system maintenance, you might use the Save Key command to save a key as a file. When the key that you saved is ready to be returned to the system, you use the Restore command.

You can use the Restore or Restore Volatile command to make a hive file a part of the system configuration. The Restore and Restore Volatile commands let you copy information in a hive file over a specified key. This copied information overwrites the contents of the specified key, except for the key name.

To use the Restore or Restore Volatile commands, you need Restore privileges, which you have if you are logged on as a member of the Administrators group.

To restore a key

1. Select the key where you want to restore the hive.

2. From the Registry menu, choose the Restore command and then complete the filename information in the Restore Key dialog box to specify the hive that you want to restore. If you're running the FAT file system,

this filename cannot have an extension. Also, if you are restoring a key on a remote computer, the drive and path of the filename is relative to the remote computer.

Note

If you want to add a key temporarily to a system, use the Restore Volatile command. If you use this command, the Registry makes a volatile copy, which disappears when the system is restarted.

You cannot restore keys or subkeys that have opened handles. This is why you cannot restore the SAM or SECURITY subtrees (Windows NT always has handles open in these keys). The Restore command is used only for special conditions, such as restoration of user profiles on a damaged system.

Remote Administration

In the same way that you can use Event Viewer or User Manager to view details on another computer, you can use Registry Editor to view and change the contents of another computer's Registry if the server services on the remote computer are running.

This capacity to view a computer's configuration remotely allows you, as a system administrator, to examine a user's startup parameters, desktop configuration, and other parameters. Therefore, you can provide trouble-shooting or other support assistance over the telephone while you view settings on the other computer from your own workstation.

Note

Auto Refresh is not available when you are viewing the Registry from a remote computer. If Auto Refresh is on, manual refresh is disabled. Therefore, when you open a remote Registry, Registry Editor checks to see if Auto Refresh mode is on. If it is, Registry Editor displays the message, "Auto Refresh is not available for remote registries; Registry Editor disables Auto Refresh mode."

To view the Registry for a remote computer

From the Registry menu, choose the Select Computer command and then select or type the name of the computer whose Registry you want to access.

Or

Double-click the name of a computer in the Select Computer list. Under a Windows NT Server, the first name in this list represents the name of a domain. If no computer name appears after this domain name, double-click the domain name to view a list of the computers in that domain.

Two Registry windows appear for the remote computer: one for HKEY_USERS and one for HKEY_LOCAL_MACHINE. You can view or modify the information on keys for the remote computer if the access controls defined for the keys allow you to perform such operations. If you are logged on as a member of the Administrators group, you can perform actions on all keys.

You can use the Load Hive and Unload Hive commands in Registry Editor to display and maintain another computer's Registry without viewing it remotely. You might want to do this to view specific values or to repair certain entries for a computer that is not configured properly or cannot connect to the network.

The hives that make up your computer's Registry are loaded automatically when you start the computer, and you can view the contents of these hives in Registry Editor. If you want to view or change the contents of other hive files, you must use the Load Hive command to display its contents in Registry Editor.

The Load Hive and Unload Hive commands affect only the Registry windows that display HKEY_USERS and HKEY_LOCAL_MACHINE. To use these commands, you must have Restore and Backup privileges, which you have if you are logged on as a member of the Administrators group. The Load Hive command is available only when HKEY_USERS or HKEY_LOCAL_MACHINE is selected. The Unload Hive command is available only when a subkey of one of these handles is selected.

To load a hive into the Registry Editor

1. Select the HKEY_LOCAL_MACHINE or HKEY_USERS root.

2. From the Registry menu, choose the Load Hive command.

3. Use the File Name, Drives, and Directories boxes and the Network button of the Load Hive dialog box to select the file containing the hive that you want to load and then choose the OK button. (If you are loading a hive on a remote computer, the drive and path in the filename is relative to the remote computer.)

Tip

You can find the directory location and names of hives on a computer in HKEY_LOCAL_MACHINE\SYSTEM\CurrentControlSet\Control\Hivelist.

This file must have been created with the Save Key command (as described in *Saving Registry data*, earlier in this chapter), or it must be one of the default hives. Under the FAT file system, the filename cannot have an extension.

If you are unable to connect to another computer over the network, you can load a hive file that you copied to a floppy disk.

4. In the second Load Hive dialog box, type the name that you want to use for the key where the hive is loaded and then choose the OK button.

This name creates a new subkey in the Registry. You can specify any name using any characters and including blank spaces. You cannot load to an existing key.

Data from the loaded hive appears as a new subkey under HKEY_USERS or HKEY_LOCAL_MACHINE (whichever handle you selected before loading the hive). A loaded hive remains in the system until it is unloaded.

The Load Hive command creates a new hive in the memory space of the
Registry and uses the specified file as the backup hive file (filename.LOG)
for the hive. The specified file is held open, but nothing is copied to the file
unless the information in a key or value entry is changed. Likewise, the
Unload Hive command does not copy or create anything; it merely unloads a
loaded hive.

To unload a hive from the Registry Editor

Select the key that represents a hive that you previously loaded and
then choose the Unload Hive command from the Registry menu.

The selected key is removed from the window and is no longer actively
available to the system or for editing in Registry Editor.

You cannot unload a hive that was loaded by the system. Also, you won't be
able to unload a hive that contains an open key.

Backing Up

Earmark this section, because you'll no doubt want to come back to it when
you need to perform maintenance on the Registry. For example, you might
find it necessary to restore backed-up versions of Registry hives if you
replace your current Windows NT computer, a disk controller or hard disk
goes bad, or an electrical failure zaps large parts of a disk.

Backing up Registry hives

You can back up Registry hives using one of four methods:

- Using a tape drive and the Windows NT Backup program, select the
  Backup Local Registry option in the Backup Information dialog box to
  include automatically a copy of the local Registry files in the backup set.

- If you don't have a tape drive, run the REGBACK.EXE or REPAIR.EXE
  program from the Windows NT Resource Tool Kit or use another tool
  that uses the same techniques to back up Registry files.

- Start the computer under a different operating system. Then copy all
  files in the SystemRoot\SYSTEM32\CONFIG directory to a safe backup
  location.

- Use the Save Key command in Registry Editor, which essentially performs the RegBack procedure manually.

  For each direct subkey of HKEY_LOCAL_MACHINE and HKEY_USERS,
  you must choose the Save Key command from the Registry menu,
  specifying filenames that match the key names. For example, save the
  SYSTEM key to \BACKDIR\SYSTEM. On the FAT file system, the filename
  should not have an extension.

Don't use Save Key with the Hardware hive, which is volatile. You won't get any data, because Save Key cannot save volatile keys to disk.

Restoring hives from backup files

To restore a damaged Windows NT system, you must first restore the basic operating system installation. You have two options for restoring the operating system:

■ You can use the Emergency Repair disk to restore your system to the same state it was in just after installation.

■ You can run Windows NT Setup again. You end up with a system that starts the computer but lacks changes made since you first set it up. You can recover most of those changes by copying files from backups by using the Windows NT Backup program for tape backups or by copying from disk backups.

Restoring the basic operating system is only half the battle. Registry hive files are protected while Windows NT is running, so you cannot simply copy those files back onto your system. So, after the system and all of the additional files such as device drivers are restored, you must restore the Registry. Just how you restore the Registry depends on which backup mechanism you used:

■ For tape backups, you can use the Windows NT Restore program to restore the Registry. Then restart the computer.

■ Start the computer using an alternate instance of the operating system (or using MS-DOS if the system files are on a FAT partition). Copy back the files to the SystemRoot\SYSTEM32\CONFIG directory. Then restart the computer using the regular operating system.

■ Use the REPAIR.EXE program from the Windows NT Resource Tool Kit.

■ Use the REGREST.EXE program from the Windows NT Resource Tool Kit. The RegRest program performs a ReplaceKey operation, which swaps backup files for the default files that the Emergency Repair or Windows NT Setup programs installed, and saves the default files under other filenames. Restart the computer after running the RegRest program to see the restored Registry.

Protecting the Registry

By now you understand how the Registry affects your Windows NT system and how important it is to keep the Registry intact. As you begin to set up more Windows NT installations in your enterprise, you need to plan strategies for protecting the Registry for each of those new installations. Following are some suggestions for protecting Registry files under most conditions:

- Do not allow users to log on as members of the Administrators group unless a specific individual has administrative duties.

- Because you can administrate any workstation from a remote computer, you can remove REGEDT32.EXE from workstations. If for some reason you need the ability to administrate each workstation locally, you can place access controls in File Manager on REGEDT32.EXE, thereby limiting the rights of users to start this program.

Note

Windows NT enforces access control on Registry files, so it is difficult for users accidentally or intentionally to damage or delete hives on a running system. While the system is running, it keeps hive files open for exclusive access on all file systems. If the Windows NT SystemRoot is not on an NTFS volume, the Registry files can be tampered with — specifically, users can remove hives for user profiles that aren't currently loaded. With NTFS, such tampering can be prevented.

One of the most common Registry mishaps is when a user inadvertently deletes the Registry. You can protect the Registry from accidental deletions in these ways:

- **Read-only mode.** Choose the Read Only command from the Options menu. When this command is checked, Registry Editor does not save any changes.

- **Confirmation.** Choose the Confirm On Delete command from the Options menu. When this command is checked, the Registry Editor asks you to confirm deletion of any key or value.

Protecting Registry files for user profiles

You can protect the Registry hive files for user profiles in the same way that you protect other files in Windows NT — by restricting access through File Manager. If the files are stored on an NTFS volume, you can use the commands on the Security menu in File Manager to assign permissions. You should change permissions only for user profile hives. The permissions for other hives are maintained automatically by the system and should not be changed.

Assigning access rights to Registry keys

You can assign access rights to Registry keys regardless of the type of file system on the partition where the Windows NT files are stored. To determine which users and groups have access to specific Registry data, set permissions on the Registry keys. This is sometimes called changing ACLs, in reference to the Access Control Lists that govern who has access to data. You can also add or remove names from the list of users or groups authorized to access the Registry keys.

Caution

Changing the permissions to limit access to a Registry key can have severe consequences. Be careful not to set No Access permissions on a key that the Network Control Panel application needs for configuration; doing so causes the application to fail.

At a minimum, ensure that Administrators and the System have full access to the key so that the system starts and the Registry key can be repaired by an administrator.

Because assigning permissions on specific keys can have drastic consequences, you should reserve this action for keys that you add to accommodate custom applications or other custom settings. After you change permissions on a Registry key, be sure to turn on auditing in User Manager and then test the system extensively through a variety of activities while logged on under different user and administrative accounts. You should also audit the key for failed access attempts.

In the Registry Editor, the commands on the Security menu for assigning permission and ownership of keys work the same as similar commands in File Manager for assigning access rights for files and directories.

To assign permission on a key

1. Make a backup copy of the Registry key before making changes.

2. Select the key for which you want to assign access permission. From the Security menu, choose the Permissions command.

3. In the Registry Key Permissions dialog box, assign an access level to the selected key by selecting an option in the Type of Access box as described in Table 7-3 and then choose the OK button.

4. Turn on auditing in User Manager, and then test the system extensively to ensure that the new access control does not interfere with system or application operations.

Table 7-3	Registry Key Permissions
Type of access	*Meaning*
Read	Allows users on the Permissions list to read the key's contents but prevents changes from being saved.
Full Control	Allows users on the Permissions list to access, edit, or take ownership of the selected key.
Special Access	Allows users on the Permissions list some custom combination of access and edit rights for the selected key.

Taking ownership

As a system administrator, you may need to take ownership of a key to protect access to it. You take ownership of a Registry key by choosing the Owner command from the Security menu in Registry Editor and then completing the Ownership dialog box. You can also add users or groups to the Permissions list by following the procedure for managing lists of users and groups that appears throughout Windows NT.

You (or any user) can take ownership of any Registry key if you log on to the computer as a member of the Administrator group. However, if an Administrator takes ownership of a key without being assigned full control by its owner, the key cannot be given back to its original owner, and the event is audited.

Compacting Registry Data

The memory used for the Registry is approximately equal to the size of a hive when it is loaded into memory. Hives vary in size on disk from 20 K to over 500 K. The amount of space used depends chiefly on how many local user profiles are retained and how much information is stored in each profile.

You should remove unused or out-of-date user profiles from a computer by choosing the Delete User Profiles command in Windows NT Setup. (The Setup program protects you from deleting the profile for the currently logged on user.)

You can use the Save Key command to save a user hive and then use the Restore command so that you can use this smaller hive. How much space you gain depends on how much was stored in various user profiles. This procedure is useful only for user profiles, not for the SAM, Security, Software, or System hives.

You might want to examine the contents of a Registry key as text for troubleshooting. You can save a key as a text file, and you can print data from Registry Editor, including a key, its subkeys, and all the value entries of all its subkeys.

The Save Subtree As command also works for the HKEY_LOCAL_MACHINE\HARDWARE subtree, which you cannot otherwise save as a hive file.

To save a Registry key as a text file

In a Registry window, select the key you want to save as a text file. Then choose the Save Subtree As command from the Registry menu and specify a filename.

To print a Registry key

In a Registry window, select the key you want and then choose the Print Subtree command from the Registry menu.

Limiting Registry Size

The total amount of Registry space that can be consumed by Registry data (the hives) is restricted by the Registry size limit, which prevents an application from filling the paged pool with Registry data. Registry size limits affect both the amount of paged pool that the Registry can use and the amount of disk space.

You can view or set the value for RegistrySizeLimit under the following subkey:

```
HKEY_LOCAL_MACHINE\SYSTEM\CurrentControlSet\Control
```

RegistrySizeLimit must have a type of REG_DWORD and a data length of 4 bytes, or it will be ignored. By default, the Registry size limit is 25 percent of the size of the paged pool, which is 32 MB, so the default RegistrySizeLimit is 8 MB (which is enough to support about 5000 user accounts). Setting the PagedPoolSize value under the CurrentControlSet\Control\Session Manager\Memory Management subkey also affects the Registry size limit. The system ensures that the value for RegistrySizeLimit is at least 4 MB and no greater than about 80 percent of the size of PagedPoolSize.

The RegistrySizeLimit limitations are approximate. The PagedPoolSize can be set to a maximum of 128 MB, so RegistrySizeLimit can be no larger than about 102 MB, which supports about 80,000 users (although other limits prevent a Registry this large from being very useful). Also, RegistrySizeLimit sets a maximum, not an allocation (unlike some similar limits in the system). Setting a large value for RegistrySizeLimit does not cause the system to use that much space unless it is actually needed by the Registry. A large value also does not guarantee that the maximum space is actually available for use by the Registry.

The space controlled by RegistrySizeLimit includes the hive space, as well as some of the Registry's run-time structures. Other Registry run-time structures are protected by their own size limits or other means.

To ensure that a user can always at least start the system and edit the Registry if the RegistrySizeLimit is set wrong, quota checking is not turned on until after the first successful loading of a hive (that is, the loading of a user profile).

By convention, if similar data exists under both HKEY_CURRENT_USER and HKEY_LOCAL_MACHINE, the data in HKEY_CURRENT_USER takes precedence. However, values in this key may also extend (rather than replace) data in HKEY_LOCAL_MACHINE. Also, some items (such as device driver loading entries) are meaningless if they occur outside of HKEY_LOCAL_MACHINE.

Summary

The Registry is a convenient and powerful component of the Windows NT operating system. Exercise caution when working with the Registry. This chapter covered

▶ Basic Registry anatomy

▶ Using the Registry Editor

▶ Backing up

▶ Remote administration

▶ Saving and compacting Registry data

▶ Altering Registry data

▶ Protecting the Registry

Part III

Windows NT Server Administration

Chapter 8

Managing User and Group Accounts

In This Chapter

▶ Creating and managing user accounts

▶ Assigning user account properties

▶ Administrating groups

▶ Assigning user rights and permissions

▶ Managing user account security policies

The network administrator's job is never ending. There's always one more person who needs access to the network, so adding new computers and users or modifying existing user accounts is an ongoing task. Whenever you add a user to the network, you install the network client software on the user's computer and create a new user account on the server. This chapter describes techniques and strategies for creating and managing user accounts and groups within a Windows NT network.

User and Group Accounts

As far as Windows NT is concerned, the network is a collection of users and computers. A user is anyone who accesses the network, and every user must have a *user account*. A Windows NT user account contains all the information that defines a particular user to the system. This small database includes the username and password, the groups to which a user belongs, and the rights and permissions the user has for using the system and accessing its resources.

When installed, Windows NT creates three default accounts, each with specific privileges on the system. The Administrator, Initial User, and Guest accounts are described in the following list:

■ **Administrator**. The Administrator has complete control over the entire system operation and security. The Administrator even has control over files owned by other users. Anyone who knows the Administrator account's username and password has complete power over the administration of the entire system.

Rights and Permissions

Many people often confuse the term *rights* with the term *permissions* as used in the Windows NT environment. In fact, these terms have very different and specific meanings.

■ **Right.** A right authorizes a user to perform certain actions on the system and applies to the system as a whole. The actions governed by rights include the ability to log on locally at the computer, shut it down, set its time, back up and restore the server's files, and perform other tasks.

On computers running Windows NT Server in a domain environment, rights are granted and restricted on the domain level; if a group has a right in a domain, its members have that right on all servers in the domain (but not on Windows NT workstations participating in the domain). On each Windows NT workstation, rights granted apply only to that single computer.

■ **Permission.** A permission is a rule associated with an object (a directory, file, or printer) to regulate which users can access the object and in what manner. For example, one user can permit another user to access a directory on his or her computer with the restriction that this other user can only read files in the directory, and not write files to the directory.

Tip

If the password is forgotten or unknown, the administrative account can only be restored by reinstalling Windows NT or using the Emergency Repair disk created during setup. To prevent the administrative account from becoming unusable or inactive, additional users can be assigned administrative privileges.

■ **Initial User.** During installation Windows NT creates an initial user account for the person installing Windows NT. This account is also given the same rights and privileges as the Administrator. The name of this account is established during the installation process.

■ **Guest.** The Guest account is used by default for anyone using the system who does not have an Administrator or User account. Guest privileges give very limited access to the computer's resources.

The administrator is responsible for setting up the directory and file security to restrict guest users from accessing private directories and files. If guest privileges are allowed on a system, the administrator should set up a public directory to store files that are made accessible to guests.

Caution

In some cases, the server may need to be restricted so that only specific users can access it. To restrict guest users from even limited resource usage you can either disable the guest account or assign a password to the guest account.

To simplify administration of user accounts that have similar resource needs, you can categorize the user accounts into groups. A *group* is a name, similar to the username of a user account, that can be used to refer to multiple users. Groups provide a convenient way to give and control access to multiple users who perform similar tasks. Without groups, you would have to modify each user's account so that it had the same abilities and/or restrictions as another user's account. By placing users within a group, you give all of the users in that group the same abilities and/or restrictions in a single action. If you need to change the permissions or rights assigned to the users within the group, you only have to modify one account — the group account.

User groups can be local or global. The terms *local group* and *global group* do not refer to the contents of the group, but to the scope of the group's accessibility. Local groups are local to the security system they are created in. With a Windows NT workgroup workstation, this means the group will only be used on the workstation itself. With a Server domain group, this means the group will only be used on the Servers in the domain. A local group is available only on the domain controllers within the domain in which you create the group, while a global group is available within its own domain and in any trusting domain. Thus global groups extend the network without increasing the administrative burden. A trusting domain can use a global group to control rights and permissions given members of a trusted domain.

Local group characteristics

Local groups define permissions to resources only within the domain in which the local group exists. Hence, the term *local* defines the scope of the resource permissions granted to users within the group.

Not only are local groups an effective way of collectively assigning user rights and permissions for a set of users within the home domain, but they can also be used to gather together numerous global groups and users from other domains. This allows an administrator to change access to domain resources globally with a single modification to the local group permissions.

A local group is a good way to import a group of users and global groups from other domains into a single unit for use in the local domain. A local group can contain user accounts or global groups from one or more domains. The group can be assigned privileges and rights only within its own domain. Local groups created on a Windows NT Workstation computer or a Windows NT Server computer in a workgroup are available only on that computer.

Local groups may contain users and global groups from the local domain (but not other local groups), as well as users and global groups from trusted domains. However, a local group can only be assigned permissions and rights in its home domain. Table 8-1 lists the possible contents of local and global groups.

Table 8-1	Possible Contents of Local and Global Groups	
Local groups	*Global groups*
Can contain local users, global groups, and other domain accounts (trusted)	Can contain local users
Cannot contain other local groups	Cannot contain local groups

Built-in Local Groups

Windows NT automatically creates default user groups during installation. Table 8-2 lists the built-in local groups on both Windows NT Server computers and Windows NT Workstation computers.

Table 8-2	Built-in Local Groups on Windows NT Server and Windows NT Workstation Computers
Name	*Description*
Administrators	Members of this group can fully administer the local computer and any domain resources.
Account Operators	Members of this group can administer domain user and group accounts.
Backup Operators	Members of this group can bypass the security restrictions on directories and files in order to back them up.
Guests	Members of this group have limited access to the domain. In effect, these users can sign on, if they know a guest account and password, but they cannot change any settings on the local computer.
Print Operators	Members of this group can administer the domain printers.
Power Users	Members of this group can share directories on the network; install, share, and manage printers; create common program groups; and set the computer's internal clock.
Replicator	Members of this group are granted the appropriate privileges to replicate files in the domain. This group is only used to support the Directory Replication service.
Server Operators	Members of this group can administer the servers in the domain. This includes logging on locally, restarting the server, or shutting down the server.
Users	Members of this group are normal users of the domain and have limited access to the domain and their own computer. They can make some configuration changes to their environment but have limited functionality. For instance, they cannot create new shared directories or stop and start services.

Account Operators, Print Operators, and Server Operators local groups are available only on Windows NT Server computers acting as primary or backup domain controllers. Power Users is available only on Windows NT Workstation computers or on Windows NT Server computers that are not acting as domain controllers.

Special Groups

Besides the default groups for assigning privilege levels, there is a second type of default group which contains no members. These special groups do not refer to the privilege level of a user but rather to accessing computer resources. The groups have no members because they apply to any account that is using the computer in a specified way. You will not see these groups listed in the User Manager for Domains window; however they may appear when assigning permissions to directories, files, shared directories, or printers.

Windows NT uses special groups to organize users according to how they access different resources. You cannot assign users as members of a special group; users are either members of these groups by default or they become members by virtue of their network activity. Table 8-3 lists the special groups created under Windows NT Server.

Table 8-3	**Windows NT Server Default Special Groups**
Group	*Description*
Interactive users	Users who only log on to the computer locally. Interactive users access resources on the machine at which they are sitting.
Network users	Users who connect to the computer over the network using their own account or an enabled guest account.
Everyone	Every user who accesses the computer, whether locally or remotely. This group includes both interactive and network users.
Creator/Owner	A user who created or took ownership of a resource.
System	The operating system.

The system account and the administrator account (Administrators group) have the same file privileges, but they have different functions under Windows NT. The system account is used by the operating system and by services that run under Windows NT. There are many services and processes within Windows NT that need the capability to log on internally (for example during a Windows NT installation). It is an internal account, does not show up in User Manager, cannot be added to any groups, and cannot have user rights assigned to it. However, the system account does show up on an NTFS volume in File Manager in the Permissions portion of the Security menu. By default, the system account is granted full control to all files on an NTFS volume.

The difference between the Network and Interactive groups is an important concept to grasp because it affects permissions. Consider this: A user A logs on to machine 1 and accesses only the resource physically attached to machine 1. That user is a local or interactive user and Windows NT assigns the user to the Interactive group. Now, if user A moves to another machine and uses the network to access those same resources on machine 1, user A is now working with permissions assigned to the Network group and becomes a member of that group. The permissions assigned to the Interactive group are no longer valid for user A.

Which users can do what

Each user account is, most likely, a member of one or more built-in local groups. As a member of one of the built-in local groups of a domain, a user has rights to perform various tasks on servers in the domain. Similarly, being a member of a built-in group on a Windows NT workstation gives the user rights on that workstation. Some rights are inherent to each built-in local group, and you cannot change them. Other rights (those granted to the local group via user rights) can be altered.

Account Operators Group

Accounts in the Account Operators local group on a server can manage the server's user and group accounts. An account operator can create, delete, and modify almost all users, global groups, and local groups. The exceptions are that account operators cannot modify the user accounts of Administrators, nor can they modify the Administrators, Server Operators, Account Operators, Print Operators, or Backup Operators local groups. They also cannot assign user rights.

Administrators Group

Accounts in the Administrators local group have the right to do almost anything on computers running Windows NT. This includes creating, deleting, and managing user accounts and local groups; sharing directories and printers; granting resource permissions and rights to users; and installing operating system files and programs.

A user logged on to the Administrator account (or an account belonging to the Administrator group) can perform the following tasks:

- Create, modify, or delete user accounts and groups
- Add or remove users from groups
- Assign special rights to groups
- Modify operating system software
- Install or upgrade application software and device drivers
- Format a fixed disk
- Set up the computer for remote administration on a network

Note

Unlike the security in traditional operating systems such as NetWare or LAN Manager 2.x, administrators (equivalent to the Supervisor in NetWare) do not automatically have access to every file on a server. File permissions must specifically grant access to an administrator, or the administrator cannot access the file. Every file on an NTFS volume has an owner who can set permissions on the file. When a user creates a file, that user becomes its owner. This means that any user can protect files from the computer or network administrator.

Administrator Logons

As an administrator, you often have two roles; you are an administrator and a user. Sometimes, you perform administrative tasks; other times, you perform the same tasks as other users.

For this reason, it is a good idea for you to have two user accounts. Create one account in the Administrators group and use it when performing management tasks. Create the other account in the Users group and use it whenever you are not performing management or administrative tasks.

Having two accounts makes the network and computer more secure. While logged on as a regular user, you cannot accidentally change aspects of the network that only administrators can change. For example, if you should happen to introduce a virus or Trojan horse while running under an ordinary user account, the system has more protection. While running under an ordinary user account, that program does not have the rights of an administrator and therefore cannot modify operating system software.

Running under two accounts is extra work because you have to log off and then log on again before you can administer the network. However, the peace of mind you get from knowing that you have a more secure environment is worth it.

Backup Operators Group

Accounts in the Backup Operators local group on Windows NT Server or Windows NT Workstation can back up and restore the computer's files, log on locally at the computer, and shut down the computer.

Guests Group

On a Windows NT Server, members of Guests have the same rights as Users; both groups have only the right to access the server over the network and cannot log on locally at the server.

Guests have fewer rights than Users while working at Windows NT Workstation computers. Users can keep a local profile on the computer, lock the computer, and create, delete, and modify local groups. Guests can do none of these.

Power Users Group

A member of the Power Users local group can do everything that a member of Users can. He or she can also create user accounts; modify the user accounts that he or she has created; put any user accounts on the computer into the Power Users, Users, and Guests built-in groups; and share and stop sharing files and printers located at the computer.

Tip

Because the Power Users group exists on Windows NT Workstations but not on Windows NT Servers, you should put the domain account of each user into the Power Users group on the user's computer. For example, put the user's domain account in the Power Users group on his or her computer; that user automatically becomes a member of the Users group on the domain's servers. This allows the user to have more control over his or her own computer and to share files with other users. However, on the domain's servers, that user is a typical user with no extra abilities.

In general, the account of every average user will automatically be in the Users group on the domain itself. On each user's workstation, administrators can decide whether to put the user's domain account in the Power Users group (for more computer control) or Users group (for less control). This decision depends on how much central control of the computer you want. If you do not want users creating shares on the computers, you should not add the user's domain accounts to the Power Users group.

Print Operators Group

Accounts in the Print Operators local group can share printers, stop sharing printers, and manage printers shared at servers running Windows NT Server. They can also log on locally at servers and shut them down.

Tip

If you want a domain's print operators to administer printers managed by Windows NT Workstation computers in the domain, as well as printers managed by the domain's servers, perform the following steps:

1. Create a Domain PrintOps global group in the domain. Make this global group a member of the domain's Print Operators local group.

2. Add the user account of each print operator to the Domain PrintOps global group.

3. On each computer that manages printers, put the Domain PrintOps global group in the Power Users local group.

Server Operators Group

The basic mission of server operators is to keep network servers running. Accounts in the Server Operators local group have many of the same powers as administrators, except that they cannot manage security on the server. Specifically, server operators can

- Share and stop sharing a server's files and printers
- Lock or override the lock of a server

■ Format the server's disks

■ Log on at servers, back up and restore servers' files, and shut down servers

Users Group

Most user accounts that you create as an administrator exist in the Users local group and represent typical users of the computer or network. These users can only access servers in the domain over the network. They cannot log on to the servers directly and work at them. User accounts also have other characteristics (such as time restrictions) that limit how a user can use the account.

A member of the Users local group of a Windows NT Workstation computer can do the following tasks:

■ Log on at the computer and use it to access the network

■ Lock and shut down the computer

■ Keep a profile at the computer

■ Run applications

■ Manage files

■ Create and delete local groups on the computer

■ Modify the membership of the local groups that he or she has created (but cannot modify built-in local groups or local groups created by anyone else)

Using global groups

A global group, available only on Windows NT Server domains, contains only individual user accounts (no groups) from the domain in which it is created. Once created, a global group can be assigned permissions and rights, either in its own domain or in any trusting domain. In fact, because they have no user rights associated with them, global groups are powerless until they are assigned to a local group or to a user right.

A global group is a good way to export a group of users as a single unit to another domain. For example, in a trusting domain you can grant identical permissions to a particular file to a global group, which then pertain to all individual members of that group. Also global groups defined in a domain can be "exported" to Windows NT workstations because domain Windows NT workstations support local groups and can, therefore, make use of global groups defined in either the workstation's own domain or from other domains.

By using trust relationships, users within a global group can access resources outside of their locally defined domain. Therefore, global groups are
quite suitable for large, multi-domain networks. Global groups can provide
an inclusive list of all user accounts within a domain that require a particular type of access to resources that exist within another domain.

Note

A local group and a global group sharing the same name are two separate
entities each with their own distinct security identifier. Permissions assigned to one group do not apply to the other group sharing the same name.

When Windows NT Server is installed on a computer, it is configured with
three predefined global groups as shown in Table 8-4.

Table 8-4	Default Global Groups on Windows NT Server
Group	**Description**
Domain Admins	Members of this group can fully administer domain resources. These members are automatically added to the local Administrators group.
Domain Guests	Members of this group are automatically added to the Guests group.
Domain Users	Members of this group are automatically added to the local Users group.

User Manager for Domains

You can use User Manager for Domains (User Manager on Windows NT
Workstation) to manage security for domains, servers, and workstations.
With User Manager for Domains you can

- Create and manage user accounts
- Create and manage groups
- Manage security policies
- Establish trust relationships

Creating user accounts

User accounts are unique resources. Each user account has a security
identifier (SID) assigned to it when it is created. Windows NT Server uses
this security identifier for assigning permissions to directories, files, and
shared network resources. This same identifier is used in the auditing
process as well. If you delete a user account and then recreate it, any shared

network resources that were owned by this user become inaccessible to the user. The only way that the user can obtain access to the resource is if an administrator takes ownership, assigns the user the ability to take ownership, and then the user takes ownership. Table 8-5 describes the information contained in a user account.

Table 8-5	Information Contained in a User Account
Item	*Description*
Username	A unique name the user enters when logging on
Password	A user's code word used to log on to his or her user account
Full name	The user's full name
Logon hours	The period of time in which a user is allowed to log on and access network resources
Logon on workstations	The computer names of Windows NT workstations to which a user is allowed to log on and access the network; by default, users can log on and access the network from any workstation
Expiration date	A future date when the system disables the user account
Home directory	A directory on the server that is private to a user; the user controls access to the directory
Logon script	A batch file that runs automatically when the user logs on
Profile	A file containing the settings that define a user's desktop environment on Windows NT workstations
Account type	The particular type of account that defines the scope of a user account

To create a new user account

1. Start User Manager for Domains, which is located in the Administrative tools submenu. The User Manager for Domains window appears as shown in Figure 8-1.

   In most cases, when User Manager for Domains first starts, it displays your logon domain. The title bar shows the domain name, and the body of the User Manager for Domains window displays two lists. The upper list contains user accounts; the lower list contains groups. One or more user accounts, or one group, can be selected and then managed using commands from the User menu. Windows NT Workstation does not display a domain name in the User Manager title bar.

2. From the User menu, choose New User. The New User dialog box appears as shown in Figure 8-2.

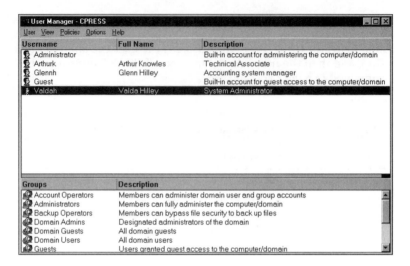

Figure 8-1: The User Manager for Domains window.

Figure 8-2: The New User dialog box.

3. Enter a name, up to 20 characters, for the new user account in the Username field. A user name cannot be identical to any other user or group name of the domain or computer being administered. It can contain any uppercase or lowercase characters except the following:

" / \ [ ] : ; | = , + * ? < >

4. Enter the user's complete name in the Full Name field.

5. Enter a comment for the user in the Description field.

6. Enter and confirm the user's password, up to 14 characters, in the Password and Confirm Password fields. Remember, passwords are case sensitive. (Windows NT distinguishes between uppercase and lowercase characters in passwords.)

   For security, the password is represented by a row of asterisks, with the number of displayed asterisks different from the actual number of characters used in the password.

7. There are four options in the New User dialog box. To specify additional user properties, enable the appropriate check box for the options as shown in Table 8-6.

Table 8-6		User Account Options
Option	*Default*	*Description*
User Must Change Password at Next Logon	On	This option requires that the user change the password immediately after logging on the first time.
User Cannot Change Password	Off	This option prevents the user from ever changing the password. This is a good choice for users who forget their passwords continually. Do not enable this option for any user who has access to sensitive data.
Password Never Expires	Off	Use this option to bypass the Maximum Password account policy.
Account Disabled	Off	Enable this option to create an account in an inactive state.

Tip Also use Account Disabled to temporarily disable an account prior to deleting it. As mentioned before, user accounts have unique security identifiers. If you delete the account, you orphan all of the user data files. This requires you (an administrator) to take ownership of the files in order to access them.

8. Choose the Add button. The user account is added, and the New User dialog box reverts to its default settings. To add another user account, repeat Steps 2 through 8. When you finish creating new user accounts, choose the Close button.

Tip In many situations, it may be quicker and more convenient to copy an existing user account than to create an entirely new one. One major benefit of copying a user account is that group memberships are copied to the new account. To copy a user account, select a user account and choose Copy from the User menu. Complete Steps 3 through 8 in the section on creating a user account. To add another user account, repeat those steps. When you finish creating copies of the selected account, choose the Close button.

Managing User Account Properties

You can modify or customize properties associated with a user account by using the buttons at the bottom of the New User dialog box, shown in Figure 8-2, or by using the User Properties dialog box, which you access by choosing Properties from the User Manager for Domains File menu. You can set these parameters when creating a new account, or you can modify these parameters for an existing account. See the upcoming section *Modifying user account properties* for information on modifying an existing account. Table 8-7 describes each of the buttons in the New User dialog box.

Table 8-7	New User Dialog Box Buttons
Button	*Description*
Groups	Specifies the groups in which the account will be a member.
Profiles	Specifies a user profile, logon script, or home directory to user accounts.
Hours	Restricts the days and hours during which a user can connect to a server.
Logon To	Restricts the computers from which users can log on to domain accounts.
Account	Defines an account expiration date (if any) and the account type for the selected user accounts.

When administering a domain, there are five buttons: Groups, Profile, Hours, Logon To, and Account. When administering a Windows NT Workstation computer, only the Groups and Profile buttons appear.

Assigning profiles

One of the most powerful methods open to administrators for managing user environments is through user profiles for users of Windows NT computers. A profile defines the Program Manager groups and program items in those groups, printer connections, window size and positioning, and screen colors.

Refer to Chapter 9, *Controlling User Environments*, for in-depth information on creating and maintaining user profiles.

To configure the user environment profile

1. Choose the Profile button from the New User, Copy Of, or User Properties dialog box. The User Environment Profile dialog box appears as shown in Figure 8-3.

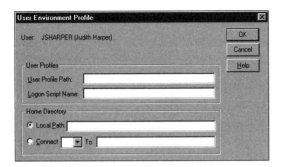

Figure 8-3: The User Environment Profile dialog box.

2. To assign a user profile, type its full pathname in the User Profile Path box. The path should be a network path. The filename can be that of a personal user profile (.USR filename extension) or a mandatory user profile (.MAN filename extension). You might type, for example, \\secrets\profiles\guru.man.

3. To assign a logon script, type the filename in the Logon Script Name box. If the logon script is stored in a subdirectory of the logon script path, precede the filename with that relative path.

4. To specify a home directory, select the Connect box, specify a drive letter, select the To box, and type a network path. Or, select the Local Path box and type a local path (including the drive letter). For example, you might specify drive F and type a network path of \\discover\users\agent. Or, you might type a local path of c:\users\cpress. When administering domain user accounts, specify a network path.

Tip

Optionally, substitute %username% for the last subdirectory in the path. For example, you might specify drive Z and then type a network path of \\discover\accounts\%username%.

If no home directory is assigned here, the system assigns the user account the default local home directory (\USERS\DEFAULT on the user's local drive where Windows NT is installed).

5. Choose the OK button.

Restricting logon hours

You may have situations in which you need to control the time period in which a user can be logged on to the network. Use the Logon Hours dialog box to restrict the days and hours during which a user can connect to a Windows NT Server computer. The default is to allow a user to connect during all hours of all days of the week, but you can optionally restrict a user to certain days and hours. This does not affect a user's ability to use a local computer.

To manage logon hours

1. Choose the Hours button from the New User, Copy Of, or User Properties dialog box. The Logon Hours dialog box appears as shown in Figure 8-4.

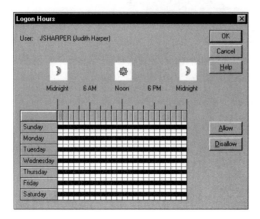

Figure 8-4: The Logon Hours dialog box.

2. In the Logon Hours dialog box, select the hours to be administered.

   To select one hour, click the box for that hour. To select a block of hours, click the beginning of the block and drag through the rows and columns to the end of the block. To select one entire day, click that day in the left column. To select one hour for all seven days, click the top box of that column. To select the entire week, click the top left box (above Sunday).

3. To allow connections during the selected hours, choose the Allow button. To deny connections during the selected hours, choose the Disallow button.

4. Repeat Steps 2 and 3 as necessary.

5. Choose the OK button.

What happens when a user's logon hours expire? Depending on the options set under the Account Policy, a user is either forcefully disconnected from all server resources at the specified time, or is allowed to stay connected without being able to make new connections.

Controlling logon locations

This option is used to control which workstation a particular user can use to log on to the domain servers. The default is to allow a user to log on from any computer, but you can optionally allow a user to log on only from specified computers.

To manage logon workstations

1. Choose the Logon To button from the New User, Copy Of, or User Properties dialog box. The Logon Workstations dialog box appears as shown in Figure 8-5.

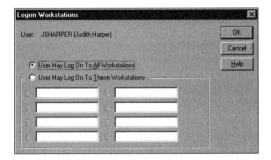

Figure 8-5: The Logon Workstations dialog box.

2. Select either User May Log On To All Workstations or User May Log On To These Workstations.

3. If you select User May Log On To These Workstations, type a computer name in at least one and up to eight of the numbered boxes.

4. Choose the OK button.

Account duration and type

Often there are special considerations you need to take into account when creating or managing a user account. For example, you can set an account to expire after a certain amount of time and you can specify the type of account.

To manage user account information

1. Choose the Account button from the New User, Copy Of, or User Properties dialog box to bring up the Account Information dialog box as shown in Figure 8-6.

Figure 8-6: The Account Information dialog box.

2. Under Account Expires, select either Never or End Of.

3. If you select End Of, specify an expiration date in the End Of box.

4. Under Account Type, select either Global Account or Local Account.

   Most accounts are global accounts. Assign local accounts only when a trust relationship does not exist with the user's home domain.

5. Choose the OK button.

Administrating User Accounts

Creating accounts is only part of your duty as an administrator. Existing accounts always require some sort of administration, whether it is modifying account properties, disabling accounts, or deleting accounts, for example.

Modifying user account properties

You can modify one account or you can make the same change simultaneously to several accounts.

To modify one user account

In the User Manager for Domains window, double-click a user account, or select a user account and then choose Properties from the User menu. Make any desired changes. Then choose the OK button.

To modify two or more user accounts in the same way

1. In the User Manager for Domains window, select two or more user accounts.

2. From the User menu, choose Properties. The User Properties dialog box appears as shown in Figure 8-7. Make any desired modifications.

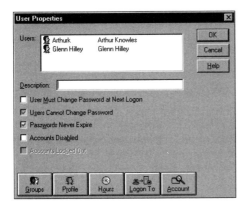

Figure 8-7: The User Properties dialog box for modifying multiple accounts.

 When administering multiple user accounts, do not assign one personal profile to all the accounts. Either assign a mandatory profile, or substitute %USERNAME%.USR for the filename.

Deleting user accounts

Be certain that you want to delete a user account before you do so, because a deleted user account cannot be recovered. The built-in Administrator and Guest accounts cannot be deleted. Internally, Windows NT knows every user account by its SID, a unique number that identifies it. If you delete a user account and then create another user account with the same user name, the new user account will not have any of the rights or permissions that were previously granted to the old account because the user accounts have different SID numbers.

Because of this, it is a good idea to disable a user account first and then periodically delete the disabled accounts. This is a low-risk way to remove users from the account database.

To delete one or more user accounts

1. In the User Manager window, select one or more user accounts.

2. From the User menu, choose Delete.

3. If a confirmation message is displayed, choose the OK button.

4. When the delete message is displayed, choose the Yes button. If multiple user accounts are selected, choose the Yes To All button.

Disabling user accounts

When you disable an account, the disabled user account still exists and is listed in the User Manager for Domains window, but logons to that account are not permitted. Disabled accounts can be restored to enabled status at any time.

To disable or enable a user account

1. In the User Manager window, select one or more user accounts. (Note that the built-in Administrator account cannot be disabled.)

2. From the User menu, choose Properties.

3. To prevent logons to the selected user accounts, select the Accounts Disabled check box. To permit logons to the selected user accounts, clear the Accounts Disabled check box.

4. Choose the OK button.

Renaming user accounts

There may be some instances in which you want to rename a user account, for example, when a user has changed his or her name or you want to get rid of cryptic user names.

1. In the User Manager window, select one user account.

2. From the User menu, choose Rename.

3. In the Change To box, type a user name of up to 20 characters. A user name cannot be identical to any other user or group name of the domain or computer being administered. It can contain any uppercase or lowercase characters except for the following:

   " / \ [ ] : ; | = , + * ? < >

4. Choose the OK button.

Managing user accounts from the command line

If you do not want to use User Manager for Domains, you can use the NET USER command line option instead. With this you can add, modify, or delete a user account from the domain database. The syntax follows:

To modify an existing account

```
NET USER UserName [Password *] [Options] [/DOMAIN]
```

To add a new user account

```
NET USER UserName [Password *] [/ADD] [Options] [/DOMAIN]
```

To delete an existing account

```
NET USER UserName [Password *] [/DELETE] [/DOMAIN]
```

where

> **UserName.** Is the name of the new user account.
>
> **Password.** Is the password for the user. Or you can specify an asterisk (*), which is used to prompt you for the password and then mask the characters you type.
>
> **/DOMAIN.** Specifies that the action is to occur on the primary domain controller. This only applies when executing the command from either a Windows NT Workstation or a Windows NT Server operating in server mode.
>
> **Options.** Specifies one or more of the options shown in Table 8-8 (each option must be separated by at least one space).

Table 8-8	NET USE Command Options
Option	*Description*
/ACTIVE:{NO YES}	Enables or disables the user account. The default is to enable the account.
/COMMENT:"User Description"	Provides a descriptive comment about the user. The maximum length is 48 characters.
/COUNTRYCODE:NNN	Specifies the user account country code. A value of 0 specifies the default system country code.
/EXPIRES:{Date NEVER}	Specifies that the user account expires on the date set. The date is in the form of MM/DD/YY or DD/MM/YY depending on the country code.
/FULLNAME:"User Name"	Specifies the user's complete name.
/HOMEDIR:"PathName"	Specifies a path for the user's home directory. The specified path must exist, or an error message is generated.
/HOMEDIRREQ:{YES NO}	Selects whether a home directory is required.
/PASSWORDCHG:{YES NO}	Enables or disables the user's ability to change the password.

(continued)

Table 8-8 *(Continued)*

Option	Description
/PASSWORDREQ:{YES NO}	Specifies whether the user account must have a password. The default is to require a user password.
/PROFILEPATH:[PathName]	Specifies the pathname for the user profile.
/SCRIPTPATH:PathName	Specifies the pathname for the logon script. The pathname specified is relative to the logon server's logon script path. Generally you need only specify the script filename and extension.
/TIMES:{Times ALL}	Specifies the valid logon times for the user in the format *Day [-Day],Time [-Time],* where the day can be spelled out or abbreviated and the time can be in either 12- or 24-hour notation — for example, M, 6 AM-6 PM, T, 0600-1800 (specifies only Monday and Tuesday from 6 AM to 6 PM) or M-F, 6 AM-6 PM (specifies from Monday to Friday from 6 AM to 6 PM).
/USERCOMMENT: "User Description"	Lets an administrator change the user comment field.
/WORKSTATION: {ComputerName *}	Lists up to eight workstations, separated by commas, from which the user can log on to the network. The * specifies that there are no restrictions.

Creating Groups

Rather than assign individual users to a resource, you can use a group. A group is a named resource that includes one or more users. You can use these groups with any application that can assign permissions or auditing. The same principle applies to managing user rights. By assigning user rights to a group and then adding users to the group, all users of the group obtain the same user rights.

Tip

You can use a global group from a foreign domain to assign user rights and permissions to a shared resource on a local domain without creating a trust relationship. This method has less overhead and does not use as much network bandwidth as a trust relationship between two domains.

There are several built-in groups included in User Manager for Domains. Each of these groups includes different user rights and can be divided into either the local or global groups. Table 8-9 summarizes the user rights for these groups.

Table 8-9	User Rights for Built-in Groups		
User rights	Comments	On Windows NT Server, group granted to	On Windows NT Workstation, group granted to
Manage auditing and security log	Specify what types of events and files are to be audited. View and clear the security log.	Administrators	Administrators
Back up files and directories		Administrators, Server Operators Backup Operators	Administrators, Backup Operators
Restore files and directories	Note that this right supersedes file permissions; when performing a restore, a user with the Restore right can overwrite files for which he or she has no permissions.	Administrators, Server Operators, Backup Operators	Administrators, Backup Operators
Change system time		Administrators, Server Operators	Administrators, Power Users
Access this computer from network	Access the computer from another computer on the network.	Administrators, Everyone	Administrators, Power Users, Everyone
Log on locally	Ability to log on at the computer itself, on the computer's keyboard.	Administrators, Server Operators Account Operators, Print Operators, Backup Operators	Administrators, Backup Operators, Power Users, Users, Guests
Shut down the system		Administrators, Server Operators, Account Operators, Print Operators, Backup Operators	Administrators, Backup Operators, Power Users, Users, Guests
Take ownership of files and other objects	Take ownership of files and directories on the computer.	Administrators	Administrators
Force shutdown from a remote system	This right gives a user no abilities in this version of Windows NT but will be supported in future upgrades of the operating system.	Administrators, Server Operators	Administrators, Power Users

Creating a new local group

1. In the User Manager for Domains dialog box, choose User New Local Group. The New Local Group dialog box displayed in Figure 8-8 appears.

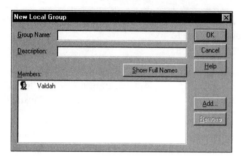

Figure 8-8: The New Local Group dialog box.

2. Enter a name for the group in the Group Name field.

3. Enter a description for the group in the Description field.

4. To add a user to the group, select the Add button. This displays the Add Users and Groups dialog box shown in Figure 8-9.

Tip

If you have cryptic user names, the Show Full Names button displays the account name and the full user name in the Members field.

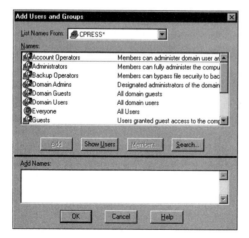

Figure 8-9: The Add Users and Groups dialog box.

5. By default, the domain to which you logged on is displayed in the List Names From drop down list box. However, you can use the domain user database from any domain with which you have established a trust relationship. You can also use the local database for a Windows NT Workstation or a Windows NT Server computer operating in server mode.

6. Only groups are listed in the Names field by default. If you want to include user accounts, click the Show Users button. This adds all of your user accounts to the end of the list. To add an existing group or user, double-click the group or user name displayed in the Names field or select a group or name and click the Add button. This copies the user account or group to the Add Names field.

Tip

If you have a large user domain list it may be easier to select the Search button, which displays the Find Account dialog box. In this dialog box, you can specify the local, global, or user account to locate. You can also specify the domains or computers to include in the search list by enabling the Search Only In radio button and selecting the domains and computers in the list. The default selection has the Search All radio button enabled and includes all domains and computers. Once the account has been entered, select the Search button. Any accounts that have been found are listed in the Search Results field. To add an account, highlight the account and choose the Add button. The accounts that you have added appear in the Add Names field of the Add Users and Groups dialog box.

Tip

To display individual user accounts, select a group name in the Names field and choose the Members button. If you select a local group and choose the Members button, the Local Group Membership dialog box appears; it includes local user accounts and global groups defined in the local group. If you then select a global group and choose the Members button, the Global Group Membership dialog box appears; it includes a list of users defined in the global group. In either of these dialog boxes, you can select individual user accounts (or global groups in the Local Group Membership dialog box) and choose the Add button to add users or global groups to the Add Names field of the Add Users and Groups dialog box.

Tip

If you mistakenly add a name to the Add Names field, you can highlight the name with the mouse and then click the Delete key to remove it.

7. Choose the OK button to return to the New Local Group dialog box. All of the user and group accounts are now displayed in the Members field of the dialog box. Select the OK button to assign the users that you selected to the group and return to the main window of User Manager for Domains.

Tip

If you highlight the users prior to choosing the menu option, these users are added automatically to the Members field. To choose a contiguous range of users, select the first user, and then while holding the Shift key, select the last user. To choose a noncontiguous series of users, hold the Ctrl key while you select each user.

Note

To remove a member from a group, highlight the account in the Members field and click the Remove button.

Copying a local group

The main advantage of copying a group is that the new group will have the same members as the original group. However, the permissions, rights, and built-in abilities of the original group are not copied to the new group.

To make a copy of an existing local group

1. Select a local group in the User Manager for Domains window and choose Copy from the User menu.

2. Enter a new name for the group and change any information.

3. Choose the OK button.

Creating a new global group

1. In the User Manager for Domains window, either select the user accounts that you want as the initial members of the new group or select any group to ensure that no user accounts are initially selected.

2. From the User menu, choose New Global Group. The New Global Group dialog box appears as shown in Figure 8-10.

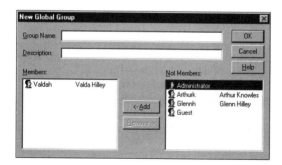

Figure 8-10: The New Global Group dialog box.

If you selected one or more user accounts in Step 1, the selected users are the initial members of the new group.

3. In the Group Name box, type a group name of up to 20 characters. A group name cannot be identical to any other group or user name of the domain or computer being administered. It can contain any uppercase or lowercase characters except the following:

    " / \ [ ] : ; | = , + * ? < >

4. In the Description box, type a description.

5. To add members to the global group, select one or more user accounts from the Not Members box and then choose the Add button. Or, select one or more user accounts from the Not Members box and then drag one of the selected icons to the Members box.

6. To remove members from the global group, select one or more user accounts from the Members box and then choose the Remove button. Or, select one or more user accounts from the Members box and then drag one of the selected icons to the Not Members box.

   When the membership of the global group is defined, choose the OK button.

When Low Speed Connection is selected or when you are administering a Windows NT Workstation computer or a Windows NT Server computer that is not a domain controller, the New Global Group command is unavailable.

Copying a global group

The main advantage of copying a group is that the new group will have the same members as does the original group. However, the permissions and rights of the original group are not copied to the new group.

When Low Speed Connection is selected or when you are administering a Windows NT Workstation computer or a Windows NT Server computer that is not a domain controller, global groups cannot be managed.

To make a copy of an existing global group

1. In the User Manager for Domains window, select one global group.

2. From the User menu, choose Copy.

3. In the Group Name box, type a group name of up to 20 characters. A group name cannot be identical to any other group or user name of the domain or computer being administered. It can contain any uppercase or lowercase characters except the following:

   " / \ [ ] : ; | = , + * ? < >

4. To change the description, type new text in the Description box.

5. To add members to the global group, select one or more user accounts from the Not Members box and then choose the Add button. Or, select one or more user accounts from the Not Members box and then drag one of the selected icons into the Members box.

6. To remove members from the global group, select one or more user accounts from the Members box and then choose the Remove button. Or, select one or more user accounts from the Members box and then drag one of the selected icons to the Not Members box.

7. When the membership of the global group is defined, choose the OK button.

Administrating Groups

Creating groups is only part of your job as an administrator. As time goes by, you will have to alter group memberships, change group properties, and delete groups. The following sections discuss the commands you use to do these tasks.

Managing group memberships for one user account

Use the Group Memberships dialog box to manage the group memberships that the selected user account has in the domain or computer being administered.

To manage group memberships when only one user account is selected

1. Choose the Groups button from the New User, Copy Of, or User Properties dialog box. The Group Memberships dialog box appears as shown in Figure 8-11.

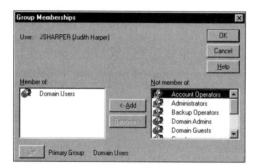

Figure 8-11: The Group Memberships dialog box.

2. To add the user account to one or more groups, select one or more groups in the Not member of box and then choose the Add button. Or, select one or more groups in the Not member of box and then drag one of the selected group icons into the Member of box.

3. To remove the user account from one or more groups, select one or more groups in the Member of box and then choose the Remove button. Or, select one or more groups in the Member of box and then drag one of the selected group icons into the Not member of box.

   You cannot remove the primary group.

4. To change the user account's primary group, select one global group from the Member of box and then choose the Set button.

5. Choose the OK button.

Managing group memberships for multiple user accounts

When two or more user accounts are selected, you can use the Group Memberships dialog box to add all of the selected user accounts to one or more groups of this domain or workstation, or to remove all of the selected user accounts from one or more groups of this domain or workstation.

To manage common group memberships for two or more user accounts

1. In the User Manager window, select two or more user accounts and then choose Properties from the User menu.

2. In the User Properties dialog box, choose the Groups button.

3. To add all of the user accounts to one or more groups, select one or more groups in the Not All Are Members Of box and then choose the Add button. Or, select one or more groups in the Not All Are Members Of box and then drag one of the selected group icons into the All Are Members Of box.

4. To remove all of the user accounts from one or more groups, select one or more groups in the All Are Members Of box and then choose the Remove button. Or, select one or more groups in the All Are Members Of box and then drag one of the selected group icons into the Not All Are Members Of box.

   If even one of the selected user accounts is not a member of a particular group, that group is listed in the Not All Are Members Of box.

   You cannot remove a primary group.

5. To change the primary group for all of the selected user accounts, select one global group from the All Are Members Of box and then choose the Set button.

6. Choose the OK button.

Managing global group properties

If desired, you can modify the membership and description of an existing group.

Note

When Low Speed Connection is selected, or when you are administering a Windows NT Workstation computer or a Windows NT Server computer that is not a domain controller, you cannot manage global groups.

To modify an existing global group

1. In the User Manager for Domains window, double-click one global group. Or, select the global group and then choose Properties from the User menu.

2. To change the description, type new text in the Description box.

3. To add members to the global group, select one or more user accounts from the Not Members box and then choose the Add button. Or, select one or more user accounts from the Not Members box and then drag one of the selected icons into the Members box.

4. To remove members from the global group, select one or more user accounts from the Members box and then choose the Remove button. Or, select one or more user accounts from the Members box and then drag one of the selected icons to the Not Members box.

5. Choose the OK button.

Managing local group properties

The membership and description of an existing local group can be modified.

To modify a local group

1. In the User Manager for Domains window, double-click one local group. Or, select the local group and then choose Properties from the User menu.

2. To view the Full Names of the listed user accounts, choose the Show Full Names button. This can be a lengthy operation when the local group contains numerous users from other domains.

3. To change the description, type new text in the Description box.

4. To add members to the local group, choose the Add button and complete the Add Users And Groups dialog box that appears. You can add user accounts and global groups from this domain and from trusted domains.

5. To remove members from the local group, select one or more names from the Members box and then choose the Remove button.

6. Choose the OK button.

Deleting a group

Be certain that you want to delete a group before you do so, because a deleted group cannot be recovered. Internally, Windows NT knows every group by its security identifier (SID). If you delete a group and then create another group with the same group name, the new group will not have any of the rights or permissions that were previously granted to the old group, because the groups have different SID numbers.

Deleting a local or global group removes only that group; it does not delete the user accounts that were members of the deleted global group.

To delete a group

1. In the User Manager for Domains window, select one group. Do not select one of the built-in groups. They cannot be deleted.

2. From the User menu, choose Delete.

3. If a confirmation message appears, choose the OK button.

4. When the delete message appears, choose the Yes button.

Modifying and creating groups from the command line

You can modify and create both local and global groups from the command line by using the NET command. The syntax for modifying and creating a local group follows:

To modify an existing group

```
NET LOCALGROUP GroupName /COMMENT:"Text Description" /DOMAIN
```

To create a new group

```
NET LOCALGROUP GroupName /ADD /COMMENT:"Text Description" /DOMAIN
```

To modify an existing group or create a new group and add users to the group

```
NET LOCALGROUP GroupName UserName [...] /ADD /COMMENT:"Text Descrip-
tion" /DELETE /DOMAIN
```

The syntax for creating a global group follows:

To modify an existing group

```
NET GROUP GroupName /COMMENT:"Text Description" /DOMAIN
```

To create a new group

```
NET GROUP GroupName /ADD /COMMENT:"Text Description" /DELETE /DOMAIN
```

To create or modify a global group

```
NET GROUP GroupName /ADD /COMMENT:"Text Description" /DELETE /DOMAIN
```

To modify an existing group or create a new group and add users to the group

```
NET GROUP GroupName UserName [...] /ADD /COMMENT:"Text Description"
/DELETE /DOMAIN
```

where

> **GroupName.** Is the name of the group that you want to create or modify.

UserName. Is the name of a user or users (specify multiple users with spaces between the user names) to add to a group.

/ADD. Creates a new group.

/COMMENT. Includes a description for the group.

/DELETE. Deletes a group or removes a user from an existing group.

/DOMAIN. Specifies that the action is to take place on the domain controller. Otherwise the action occurs on the local computer.

Maintaining User Account Security

Every network has certain rules for user accounts that can be used to provide additional security for the network. Windows NT Server is no exception. To establish these rules, choose Policies Account from the User Manager for Domains dialog box.

The Account Policy dialog box shown in Figure 8-12 appears. In this dialog box, you can set the following options:

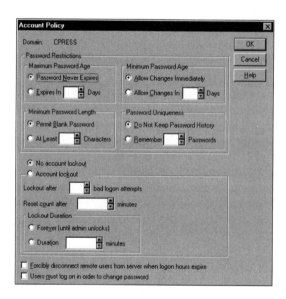

Figure 8-12: The Account Policy dialog box.

■ **Maximum Password Age.** You can require that a user change his or her password every so often by specifying a number in the Expires in Days field. This helps to prevent a potential breach of network security.

Tip A good balance between ease of user management and prevention of potential security breaches is to specify a value of 45 to 60 days.

- **Minimum Password Age.** By specifying a number in the Allow Changes In Days field, you can establish a minimum length of time before the user can change his or her password. This can provide two benefits. First, it can provide some administrative relief by requiring that a user use a specific password for a minimum period of time. Second, if you have the Password Uniqueness option enabled, it provides some network security by preventing a user from setting his or her password back to the password used immediately before the one that just expired.

- **Minimum Password Length.** This particular option has a tradeoff, which you need to consider before implementing. The shorter the password, the easier it is for the user to remember. However, it also makes it easier for a network hacker to gain access to a network by repeated guessing. Longer passwords offer increased network security, but probably require more intervention from you because network users sometimes forget their passwords. To specify the minimum length of a password, enter a number in the At Least Characters field.

 I recommend a minimum password length of eight characters.

Tip

- **Password Uniqueness.** The number entered in the Remember Passwords field specifies the number of passwords that should be recorded in the history list. The history list is a record of the user passwords. Any password included in this record cannot be used by the user when it is time to choose a new password.

- **Account lockout.** This is your best defense against system hackers because it limits the number of times that a user account can be used with the wrong password before the user account is disabled. On the downside, it can also lock out users who forget their passwords during a logon sequence. You specify the number of logon attempts before an account lockout occurs in the Lockout after bad logon attempts field. This number is based on the Reset count after minutes field, which specifies the time frame for determining the number of bad logon attempts. If the number of attempts occurs within the time frame that you specify here, the account is locked out. In the Lockout Duration section, you can specify whether the account is locked out for a specific period of time by entering a number in the Duration field, or you can specify that the account is locked out until an administrator reactivates it by selecting the Forever field.

The final two options in the Account Policies dialog box allow you forcibly to log users off the network when their permissions to use the network (as specified in their user accounts) expire. These options can also be used to force any connected user off the network and close any shared network files (such as an SQL Server database) so that you can make system backups. The last option requires that the user log on first before changing a password. This can prevent a user from using an expired password to gain access to the network for an idle account.

Configuring account policies from the command line

Just as you can create local or global groups from the command line with the NET command, you can also specify the domain account policies. The syntax follows:

```
NET ACCOUNTS [/FORCELOGOFF{Minutes NO}] [/MINPWLEN:Length]
[/MAXPWAGE:{Days UNLIMITED}] [/MINPWAGE:Days] [/UNIQUEPW:Number]
[/DOMAIN]
```

where

- **/FORCELOGOFF.** Specifies that a warning message is to be issued x minutes before a user is forcibly logged off the system. If No is selected, users are not forced off the system.

- **/MINPWLEN.** Specifies the minimum password length. The default is 6; valid ranges are from 0 to 14.

- **/MAXPWAGE.** Specifies the maximum time that a user's password is valid. The default is 90 days; valid ranges are from 1 to 49,710 (same as unlimited if set at 49,710).

- **/MINPWAGE.** Specifies the minimum time before a user can change a password. The default is 0; the valid range is 0 to 49,710.

- **/UNIQUEPW.** Specifies that a user cannot reuse the same password for the number of changes defined. The default is 5; the valid range is 0 to 8.

- **/DOMAIN.** Specifies that the operation should be performed on the primary domain controller when the command is executed on a Windows NT Server operating in server mode or from a Windows NT Workstation.

Assigning user rights

User rights allow a user account to perform a specific action on a computer. User rights are divided into basic and advanced user rights, as summarized in Table 8-10.

Table 8-10		Summary of User Rights		
User right	*Type*	*Description*	*Domain controllers*	*Workstations*
Access this computer from network	Basic	Allows a user to access this computer from a remote computer	X	X

User right	Type	Description	Domain controllers	Workstations
Add work-stations to domain	Basic	Allows a user to create computer accounts and add workstations to the domain. Members of the Administrators and Server Operators can always add workstations to the domain, even if they are not explicitly granted this right.	X	
Back up files and directories	Basic	Allows a user to back up directories and files on a computer regardless of the permissions that have been applied to them.	X	X
Change the system time	Basic	Allows the user to change the system date and time.	X	X
Force shut-down from a remote system	Basic	Allows a user to shut down a computer from another networked computer.	X	X
Load and unload device drivers	Basic	Allows a user to load or un-load device drivers dynamically on the computer.	X	X
Log on locally	Basic	Allows a user to log on to the computer interactively.		
Manage auditing and security log	Basic	Allows a user to manage the auditing of objects in a system. It does not affect the right of an administrator to use the Audit command in User Manager.	X	X
Restore files and directories	Basic	Allows a user to restore directories and files on a computer regardless of the permissions that have been applied to them.	X	X
Shut down the system	Basic	Allows a user to shut down the computer when logged on inter-actively.	X	X

(continued)

Table 8-10 *(Continued)*

User right	Type	Description	Domain controllers	Workstations
Take ownership of files or other objects	Basic	Allows a user to take ownership of directories, files, and other objects on the computer.	X	X
Create a page file	Advanced	Allows a user to create or modify the file used as a backing store for virtual memory.	X	X
Debug programs	Advanced	Allows a user to debug a locally executing application.	X	X
Profile single process	Advanced	Allows a user to profile an application. Generally this is used by developers during the development phase of an application.	X	X
Profile system performance	Advanced	Allows a user to monitor the performance of the operating system.	X	X
Bypass traverse checking	Advanced	Allows a user to scan through a directory tree even if the user does not normally have permission to view the directories.	X	X
Log on as a service	Advanced	Allows an application to log on to the system as a service.	X	X

To give user rights to a user or group

1. Choose Policies User Rights. The User Rights Policy dialog box appears as shown in Figure 8-13.

2. In the drop down list box, select the right you want to assign. This displays a list of users who have this right in the Grant To field.

To display advanced rights in the Right list box, enable the Show Advanced User Rights check box in the lower left corner of the dialog box.

Tip

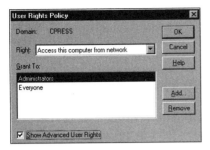

Figure 8-13: The User Rights Policy dialog box.

3. To add a user or group to the list, select the Add button. This displays the Add Users and Groups dialog box where you can select additional users or groups. Users and groups that you select are added to the Grant To field.

4. To remove a user or group, select the user or group in the Grant To field and click the Remove button.

5. Repeat the preceding steps for each user right that you want to assign to specific users or groups. When completed, choose the OK button.

Enabling event auditing

If you want to be able to determine who may be using shared network resources or abusing their privileges on the network, you need to enable the auditing features provided in Windows NT Server. Auditing is divided into several categories and is not enabled in a single application. To audit system events related to account usage or modification and the programs running on the server, choose Policies Audit in the Server Manager for Domains dialog box. The Audit Policy dialog box shown in Figure 8-14 appears.

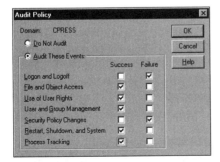

Figure 8-14: The Audit Policy dialog box.

Note

When you select an event to be audited, it is entered in the security log, which can be viewed with the Event Viewer. You can select to audit either the successful use of a privilege, failure to obtain access — which indicates a security violation attempt — or both. The following events can be audited:

- **Logon and Logoff.** Use this option to determine who has logged on or off the network.

Tip

I recommend that you enable this option both for success and failure to determine who may be using the network.

- **File and Object Access.** This option works in conjunction with other applications that have been used to specify auditing. For example, you can use File Manager to enable auditing of a directory and then enable auditing of the success or failure events for the File and Object Access to record access to the audited directory.

- **Use of User Rights.** This selection allows you to audit any use of a user right, other than logon and logoff, such as the ability to log on as a service.

- **User and Group Management.** This option allows you to track any user account or group. For example, it records if a new user is added, an existing user password is enabled, or a new user is added to a group.

Tip

If you have constant problems with a particular user account or group being modified and you cannot determine who is making these changes, I suggest that you enable the previous option for both success and failure. This can help you determine who may be making the changes. For example, I've seen a few problems caused by personnel who have been granted administrative privileges but have not been trained in their use. By using this option, you can determine who needs additional training or who should have their administrative privileges revoked.

- **Security Policy Changes.** Use this option to help you determine who may be making changes to system audit policies, user right policies, or trust relationships.

Tip

I recommend that you enable the previous option both for success and failure to determine who may be modifying network policies — particularly if you have several administrators and find that things have been changing without anyone admitting responsibility.

- **Restart, Shutdown, and System.** This option enables you to determine who may be shutting down servers or creating any event that affects system security or the security log.

- **Process Tracking.** Use this option to determine what applications are executing on your system.

Caution

Auditing the success events for Process Tracking can fill up the security log in a matter of minutes. Enable the previous event for success only when absolutely necessary.

Trusted Domains

Chapter 2, *Redefining the Enterprise Network,* introduced the concept of domains as they apply to a Microsoft network model. This section introduces the concept of trust relationships which are used to simplify the administration of multi-domain networks.

When used in a domain, Windows NT Server extends your administrative authority beyond a single computer to an entire domain. In a domain, you manage one account for each user, and each user needs only one account. Looking back to Chapter 2, you see that a Windows NT network can encompass several domain models. For example, a company could divide its network into separate domains corresponding to department or corporate structure, that is, domains for engineering, marketing, accounting, management, and so on. Having read this chapter, you might have concluded that users can access resources only in the domain in which they are a member. So now the question becomes how do you allow a user from Domain A to access resources in Domain B without it becoming an administrative nightmare? The answer: It's a matter of trust.

A trust relationship is a link between two domains where one domain honors requests from users of another domain. A trust relationship lets you use the domain database on a foreign domain or on a different domain. The foreign domain is referred to as the *trusted domain*, and the domain that contains the database is called the *trusting domain*. The way it works in principle is that the domain database on the trusted domain is applied on the trusting domain for any user who does not have a local account on the trusting domain. This allows you to create an administrative domain (the trusted domain) that contains all of your administrative user accounts and still be able to administer all of your resource domains (the trusting domains). These resource domains contain shared network resources and local user accounts, but they can be administered by users who have accounts in the trusted domain.

Setting up trust relationships

Before you actually create a trust relationship, decide which domain should serve as the account domain — the domain where accounts reside. You should set up the account domain as a trusted domain, permitting all other domains to trust it.

Creating a trust relationship is a two-fold process. First, you have to specify which domain is permitted to trust your domain. Second, in the other domain, you have to establish a trust relationship with the domain that has permitted the trust relationship. You can initiate trust from either domain, but the trust relationship will not be in effect until both domains have established the trust connection. Once the trust relationship is complete, a trusting server will pass through a logon request to a trusted server for validation if the trusting server is not able to validate the user locally.

To initiate a trust relationship

1. Select Trust Relationships from User Manager's Policies menu. The Trust Relationships dialog box appears as shown in Figure 8-15.

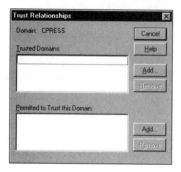

Figure 8-15: The Trust Relationships dialog box.

To permit another domain to trust this domain

From the domain controller that is to be the trusted domain:

2. Click the Add button located next to the Permitted to Trust this Domain list box. The Permit Domain to Trust dialog box appears as shown in Figure 8-16.

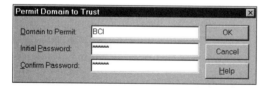

Figure 8-16: The Permit Domain to Trust dialog box.

3. Enter the name of the trusting domain with which you want to establish a trust relationship. Enter a password and confirm it. Then choose the OK button.

From the domain controller that is to be the trusting domain:

4. Select the Add button next to the Trusted Domains list box. The Add Trusted Domain dialog box appears as shown in Figure 8-17.

5. Enter the name of the domain that you want this domain to trust. Enter the same password that you set for the trusting domain.

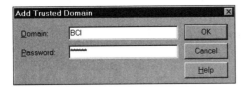

Figure 8-17: The Add Trusted Domain dialog box.

Note

Once a trust relationship is established, the system changes this password. Because of this, you cannot remove one side of an established trust relationship, and then later reestablish that trust using the original password. You must always remove both sides of a trust relationship, and then completely reestablish it.

6. In the Add Trusted Domain dialog box, choose the OK button to return to the Trust Relationships dialog box. The name of the domain you just added is displayed in the Trusted Domains list.

7. In the Trust Relationships dialog box, choose the Close button.

Caution

The password that you set in the preceding steps is used only to create the initial trust relationship. Immediately after the trust relationship has been established, the two domains create their own passwords. If, for any reason, a trust relationship fails, you must remove the trust relationship from both domains and recreate it.

Secret

If you have an administrative account on both domains, you can use this privilege to establish a trust relationship between two domains from a single computer. To do this, you need to cheat a bit. First, use File Manager to connect to the non-local domain (the one of which you are not a member) and use the Connect As option in the Network Connection dialog box to specify an administrative user account (in the form of DomainName\UserName). Once you have connected to the sharepoint, you have administrative privileges on the non-local domain. You may now bring up another copy of User Manager for Domains, choose User Select Domain, and pick the non-local domain. Then you can launch another copy of User Manager for Domains and use the local domain. In both copies of User Manager for Domains, bring up the Trust Relationship dialog box and follow the preceding steps to create the trust relationship.

Summary

This chapter covered many of the basic administrative duties that you carry out on a day-to-day basis as a Windows NT network administrator. After reading this chapter you should be prepared to set up and manage a workgroup or domain network. This chapter covered

▶ The difference in roles, permissions, and responsibilities between a user and an administrator

▶ The different types of account policies — what they are used for and how to use them

▶ The different types of user rights — what they are used for and how to use them

▶ Setting up and managing user accounts

▶ Setting up and managing groups

Chapter 9

Controlling User Environments

In This Chapter

▶ Creating and configuring profiles

▶ Configuring profiles for different hardware and software configurations

▶ Using profiles on Windows NT Workstation and Windows NT Server

▶ Creating home directories and logon scripts

E very user who logs on to a Windows NT network works in a unique environment. Windows NT defines a user environment by available resources such as file and print resources, the configuration of Program Manager icons, wallpaper or backgrounds, automatic network connections, and applications that run on startup. As an administrator, you can customize the user's environment through a file called a *user profile,* which you can create and maintain on a Windows NT Server computer using the User Profile Editor administrative tool.

You can control some elements of the user environment more easily by creating a script that executes whenever the user logs on to a Windows NT Workstation computer or a Windows NT Server computer. Such a script is called a *logon script.* Another important element of the user environment is a directory assigned to a user or to a defined user group on either a workstation or a server where the user can store files. This directory is called a *home directory.*

This chapter explains how to create user profiles, logon scripts, and home directories. It also describes special parameters that you can use in logon scripts so the same script runs in different user environments with the expected result for each individual user.

About User Profiles

In Windows NT, user profiles contain configuration preferences and options for each user. They are particularly useful when you allow users to customize their computing environment, while sharing computers with others who also customize their environments. User profiles also benefit network administrators who typically roam around, accessing the network from a variety of locations. User profiles allow administrators and support technicians to work anywhere as if they were sitting at their own desks.

The user profiles in Windows NT Server enable you to make working with the computer easier for users and/or to restrict users' abilities at their workstations. Whenever a user logs on at a workstation, Windows NT uses the profile to set the computing environment for that user. You also can store the profile on a server (in a domain model) so that it can be used at any workstation to which the user logs on. User profiles also help create a more secure environment by allowing you to add restrictions — such as preventing the user from changing program groups and items that the administrator sets up. This feature can be useful in highly secure environments.

You should use profiles under the following circumstances:

- For "roving" users who log on to different computers at different times. User profiles stored on a domain network server ensure that users have the same work environment at every logon location.

- For multiple users of the same computer. Because user profiles determine the desktop environment and the associated privileges for each user, they help maintain a secure and consistent environment.

Before implementing user profiles, you should consider the following issues:

- Do you want user profiles to work across the network so that they are available to roving users? If so, you must make sure that each user has a home directory on the network and a logon account on the local domain.

- What types of restrictions and settings would you like to define and manage centrally? For example, do you want to limit access to the MS-DOS prompt and other applications or to Control Panel options, or do you want to implement a standard desktop for all users?

- Do you want to use one set of standard settings for all users and computers, or do you want to customize settings by groups of users? Also, do you want to maintain individual settings for users and computers? Typically, you customize settings by groups, where the majority of users are in groups and a small group of individuals (such as administrators) have special privileges.

- Should you use mandatory user profiles? If so, you should copy the necessary files to each user's home directory.

Inside a User Profile

Each Windows NT computer maintains a profile for each user who has logged on to the computer using any account other than a Guest account. The profile contains information about a particular user's Windows NT configuration. Much of this information is about things the user can set, such as color scheme, screen savers, and mouse and keyboard layout. The profile also contains access information, such as whether the user has rights to common program groups or network printers. Only a Windows NT administrator can set these.

Windows NT saves the following environment settings when a user logs off:

■ **Program Manager.** All user-definable settings for Program Manager, including personal program groups and their properties, program items and their properties, and all settings saved by the Save Settings On Exit and Save Settings Now commands.

■ **File Manager.** All user-definable settings for File Manager, including network connections and everything saved by the Save Settings On Exit command.

■ **Command prompt.** All user-definable settings for the command prompt, including fonts, colors, settings for the screen size buffer, and window position.

■ **Print Manager.** Network printer connections and all settings saved by the Save Settings On Exit command.

■ **Control Panel.** All settings for Color, Mouse, Desktop, Cursor, Keyboard, International, and Sound options. For the System option, only the entries in the User Environment Variables box. The other Control Panel options do not contain user-specific settings.

■ **Accessories.** All user-specific application settings affecting the user's Windows NT configuration. These accessory applications include Calculator, Calendar, Cardfile, Clock, Notepad, Paintbrush, and Terminal.

■ **Third-party applications.** Programmers can design any application written specifically for Windows NT so that it tracks application settings on a per-user basis. If this user-specific information exists, Windows NT saves it in the user profile.

■ **Online Help.** Any bookmarks placed in the Windows NT Help bookmark system.

Types of profiles

Windows NT workstations automatically create *local profiles*. When a user logs off, the system stores the profile information in the Registry. When the same user logs on again, the workstation recognizes the user and loads the appropriate profile. Local profiles are computer dependent: Settings made at one workstation are not available when the user logs on at another workstation.

With Windows Server domain accounts, an administrator can also create *server profiles*. This extends the usefulness of profiles in three ways:

■ A user can use the same profile at multiple workstations.

■ A group of users can share the same profile.

■ An administrator can create a custom profile to restrict the user's access to certain aspects of a user's machine.

You accomplish this functionality by using either *personal* or *mandatory* server profiles. A personal profile must have the extension .USR and can be changed by the profile user. A mandatory profile must have the extension .MAN and cannot be changed by the profile user. With a mandatory profile, a user may change the desktop configuration while using the workstation, but the system does not save the changes when the user logs out. A mandatory profile also enables the administrator to restrict users from doing one or more of the following:

■ Creating program items

■ Creating program groups

■ Changing the contents of program groups

■ Changing program item properties

■ Running programs from the File Menu in Program Manager

■ Connecting to network directories or printers (other than those to which the profile itself connects)

If a user's mandatory profile is unavailable during logon, the user cannot log on to the system.

System default and user default profiles

If you power up or reboot a Windows NT machine without actually logging on, Windows NT uses the *system default* profile until a user logs on. The default profile controls only the wallpaper and background color settings.

Windows NT stores the *user default* profile on a per-workstation basis and loads it when a user logs on with one of the following conditions:

■ The user account does not have a profile assigned to it. This occurs the first time that a user logs on; after this initial logon, the user keeps his or her own profile settings.

■ The user's server profile cannot be accessed (the server may be down).

■ The user account is the Guest account.

How Do User Profiles Work?

Windows NT saves profile information when a user logs off and automatically restores the profile when the user logs back on to the workstation. Each time that the user logs on to a computer, Windows NT searches the Registry under the following key to determine whether the user has a local profile:

```
Hkey_Local_Machine\Software\Microsoft\Windows\Current
Version\Profile List
```

Windows NT checks for the user profile in the Registry and in the user's home directory on the server. If the most current profile is on the server, Windows NT copies it to the local computer for use during the current session, and then it loads the settings in this local copy into the Registry. If no local user profile exists, Windows NT copies the server version to the local computer. If no profile is found on the server or on the local computer, Windows NT creates a new user profile on the local computer using default settings.

Both the local and network copies of the user profile automatically update with current settings when the user logs off.

If a user logs on at more than one computer during the same period of time, any changes made to the profile on the computer where the user first logs off are overwritten when the user logs off the other computer. In other words, Window NT saves profile information from the last logoff, and no merging of changes occurs.

Loading and Saving Profiles

Windows NT uses a simple algorithm for determining what profile information to use when a user logs on. If the user logs on from a local account, the system checks to see if the user has logged on to this machine before. If so, Windows NT loads the local profile or a locally cached profile. If not, the system attempts to load the default profile. If it cannot load the default profile, the user cannot log on.

Windows NT also checks whether the user logs on from a domain. If the user logs on from a domain, the system checks for a server profile. If it finds one, the system attempts to load the server profile. If it cannot find a server profile, the system checks to see if the user has logged on to the machine before. If so, Windows NT loads the local profile or a locally cached profile. If not, the system attempts to load the default profile. Here again, if Windows NT cannot load the default profile, the user cannot log on.

If the user has a mandatory profile, Windows NT saves the current settings as the user's locally cached profile. If the user does not have a mandatory profile, Windows NT checks to see if the user has a personal profile. If it finds a personal profile, Windows NT updates the user's personal profile. If no personal profile exists, it creates a personal profile and saves the current settings as the user's locally cached profile.

Note

If the user has the ability to make changes to his or her profile, Windows NT saves the profile as either a local profile or as a server profile whenever the user logs off. If the profile is a server profile, Windows NT saves the user settings to the file and also saves a locally cached copy of the file. This allows the user to log on with the same settings even if the server that stores the profile is down at logon time.

Configuring Server Profiles

User Profile Editor is a Windows NT administrative tool for creating a customized user profile. A customized user profile differs from the user profiles that Windows NT automatically creates and maintains in these ways:

- A user can access a single user profile from any computer on the network.

- A group of users can share a single user profile.

- A custom user profile can limit a user's ability to change the user profile and to gain access to some commands in Program Manager.

Profile considerations

Most of the time, you will use server profiles across multiple machines. There are a couple of issues that you should consider in this case:

- Multiple machines often have different hardware. You should set up a profile to handle the lowest video resolution of the workstations being used.

- Multiple machines often have different software. If icons in a profile point to specific programs, these programs need to exist either in the same directory on each machine or in a central location on a server.

The User Profile Editor

The User Profile Editor, shown in Figure 9-1, is included in the Administrative Tools group on every domain controller. With this tool, you can create the initial user profile for a user (by selecting File, and then Save As File), set the system default profile used by the operating system (by selecting File, and then Save As System Default), and create the default user profile for all new users who log on to the computer (by selecting File, and then Save As User Default).

You can also specify the following options:

- **Disable Run in File Menu.** Enable this check box to prevent a user from running programs from the run line in the Program Manager or File Manager. This option does not prevent a user from running programs from an MS-DOS command prompt or from within any other application that has the ability to launch another application.

- **Disable Save Settings Menu Item and Never Save Settings.** Enable this check box to prevent users from saving any changes they make to the view and placement of Program Manager, File Manager, and Print Manager.

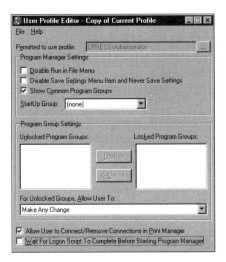

Figure 9-1: The User Profile Editor dialog box.

■ **Show Common Program Groups.** Disable this check box to display only personal program groups in Program Manager. This allows you to further control access to configuration files and system utilities.

■ **StartUp Group.** This option specifies the applications that execute automatically at logon time. To use it, select the Program Manager group from the drop-down list in the StartUp Group field. You can disable it completely by specifying (none).

■ **Locked Program Groups** or **Unlocked Program Groups.** Lock or unlock a group by selecting it and clicking the Lock or Unlock button to move it into the appropriate field.

For unlocked groups, you can specify whether the user can make any changes, such as adding new program groups or program items, deleting existing program items, or changing the description, command line, working directory, shortcut keys, run minimized setting, run in separate address space setting, or icon of a program item.

Only personal Program Manager groups appear in the StartUp Group and Lock/Unlock Program Groups fields.

■ **Allow User to Connect/Remove Connections in Print Manager.** Disable this check box to prevent a user from connecting to or disconnecting from printers in Print Manager.

■ **Wait For Logon Script To Complete Before Starting Program Manager.** Enable this check box to force users to wait until the logon script has completed before they can run any other applications.

You can specify which user or group of users may use each profile by pressing the Browse button next to the Permitted to use profile box. The User Browser dialog box appears, as shown in Figure 9-2.

Figure 9-2: The User Browser dialog box.

Note

Except for the Startup Group, settings in the User Profile Editor window do not affect administrator accounts.

Creating a new user profile

As mentioned earlier in this chapter, you can create two types of user profiles: personal or mandatory. Administrators refer to the mandatory profile as a shared profile because more than one user can use the profile. A personal, or user, profile allows the user to customize the environment. You can assign mandatory user profiles to any number of user accounts, but you should assign each personal user profile to only one user account.

Tip

When you create or edit a user profile, the changes that you make also affect the account under which you are working. To keep your own user profile intact, create a special Profile Administrator's account and log on under that account when you manage user profiles. Make sure to create the Profile Administrator's account as a member of the Domain Admins global group or the Administrators local group.

To create a new user profile

1. Configure the Windows NT environment of your own computer until it is exactly as you want it for the intended users of the profile. Be sure to allow for different hardware and software configurations. In particular, allow for different video displays and maintain consistent program paths.

2. In the User Profile Editor window, configure the options as you want them. If you are not editing the user or system default profile, be sure to complete the Permitted to use profile box.

3. From the File menu, choose how you want to save the profile. If you are creating an initial user profile, choose Save As File. To set the system default profile used by the operating system, choose Save As System Default. To create the default user profile used by all new users who log on to the computer, choose Save As User Default.

Note

The profile that you save is the current profile of the user who is logged on. This profile includes the placement of the Program Manager groups as well as their current state (opened, closed, and so on) so make sure that the default settings for all of the applications (Program Manager, File Manager, Print Manager, and so on) as well as the custom settings for the screen saver, background, color scheme, and other options are what you want before saving the profile.

Copying a user profile

There may be situations in which you want to assign the same personal user profile to a number of users. The easiest way to do this is to make copies of the profile and assign each copy to a different individual.

To copy a user profile

1. From the File Menu, choose Open, select the user profile that you want to copy, and click the OK button.

2. Choose the Browse button next to the Permitted to use profile box. In the User Browser dialog box that appears, add the name of the user or group to which you want to assign the copy of the profile.

3. From the File menu, choose Save As File. Save the profile under a unique filename. Mandatory user profiles must have a file extension of .MAN; personal user profiles must have a file extension of .USR.

Editing existing profiles

You can edit a profile in two ways depending on what parameters or options you need to modify:

■ To make any possible change, assign the profile to an account and log in with that account. Make changes to the user settings and then log off.

■ Use the User Profile Editor to make changes; however, you cannot edit items such as program groups, screen colors, and screen saver.

Creating User Profiles in Windows NT Domains

You can assign user profiles to user accounts in User Manager for Domains as described in the following section.

The first step is to create a working User Profile on the server. You will use this profile as a template for all user accounts.

1. Create an Administrator account (for example, ProfileAdmin) under which to create an initial profile template.

2. Create and share a directory where you want to save the user profiles. For example, create D:\PROFILES and share it as Profiles. The examples in this section use a server called MasterServer in a domain called MajorDomain.

3. Next, log on as ProfileAdmin on MasterServer.

4. Configure the Windows NT environment of your workstation exactly as you want it for the user profile you are creating.

Note

For common items (such as .BMP wallpaper files), point to a central server share so everyone can access them.

5. Open Program Manager, choose Options, and then choose Save Settings Now.

6. Run User Profile Editor and select the desired options.

7. From the User Profile Editor File menu, choose Save As File. Save the profile with a generic name (for example, USERPROF.USR) in the shared profiles directory. If you want to use the profile as a mandatory profile, give it a name such as USERPROF.MAN.

Now that you have a working User Profile template, you can create the second template: a User Account template. Then you will assign the User Profile template to the User Account template.

1. Log on to MasterServer with your regular Administrator account.

2. Run User Manager for Domains and create a new user account (for example, AnyUser). Press the Profile button in the New User dialog box to assign the user the following profile:

```
\\masterserver\profiles\%username%.usr
```

Use %username%.man if you created a mandatory profile as a template.

3. In User Profile Editor, open the following template user profile (the one that you created in the preceding step): d:\profiles\userprof.usr (or .man)

4. Choose the Browse button next to the Permitted to use profile box. Permit the new user to use the profile. For example, permit MajorDomain\AnyUser to use the profile. If you want everyone to use the same profile, you can permit Domain Users to use the profile.

Note

If you do this with share or NTFS permissions, ensure that the users won't be able to save any modifications to the profile. If users save changes to the profile, the next person to log on gets the previous user's modified profile.

5. From the User Profile Editor File menu, choose Save As File. Save the file with a new name that matches the name of the user to whom you just gave permissions. For example, if you just gave permissions to AnyUser, save the file as d:\profiles\AnyUser.usr (or .man).

If you permitted a group of users to use the profile, such as Domain Users, give it a name such as domusr.usr (or .man).

To create profiles for individual users

1. In User Manager for Domains, copy the template user to the new user name. For example, copy AnyUser to ValdaH.

2. Repeat Steps 3 through 5 as just shown to assign the proper user profile for each user that you create. If you permitted Domain Users to use the profile, you must make sure that the users have that profile specified.

Making local profiles available to the domain

To save the default user profiles of a local system and make them available to the domain, use the User Profile Editor. If you have a Windows NT Workstation, you can save your default user profiles from a domain server.

To save a workstation's local default user profile and make it available as a domain user profile from a domain controller, use the following procedure:

1. From a Windows NT server, create a domain user account for the Windows NT workstation and register the computer name on the domain.

2. From a Windows NT workstation, join the domain. When you have successfully joined the domain, log off the computer.

3. From the Windows NT server, run the User Profile Editor and use a domain administrator account name and password to connect to the system root directory (C$) of the Windows NT workstation.

4. Make the workstation's default user profile available to the domain by saving the profile with a .USR extension on the domain controller. Default user profiles are located in the %systemroot%\CONFIG (where

%systemroot% is the root directory for Windows NT, usually WINNT) subdirectory, usually with the following format:

```
<First 5 characters of user name>000
```

Using Profiles with Windows 95 Clients

If you want to make user profiles available on the network (rather than on individual computers), you must perform the following preliminary steps:

- Install and run a 32-bit, protected mode networking client (such as Client for NetWare Networks or Client for Microsoft Networks) on the computers.

- Ensure that a network home directory exists for each user because this is where user profiles are placed.

Setting Home Directories

A home directory is a private storage space assigned to a user or group of users. Users typically store their private data in their home directory, and they can normally restrict or grant access to other users. When a user opens a command prompt window, the default directory is the user's home directory. You can also specify the home directory as the default working directory for applications.

If your network's client workstations have limited hard disk space, you might want to assign each user a home directory on a Windows NT Server computer. Or, if you want to limit a user's access to the files and directories on a workstation, you can create a home directory on the workstation and give the user only List permission on all other directories.

On a Windows NT Server and Workstation computer, you assign home directories assigned in User Manager for Domains and User Manager, respectively. The home directory that Windows NT uses depends on whether the user logs on to the workstation account or the domain account.

There are several options for specifying the home directory. You can use a local pathname, such as C:\USERS\SIDNEY, or by a universal naming convention (UNC) name, such as \\BEAMER\USERS\SIDNEY. The UNC name is the better option for large networks, because it's easier to see where users' home directories reside.

By default, the home directory is the \USERS\DEFAULT directory that Windows NT creates during installation. The most common way to assign a home directory is to specify it using the following syntax:

```
\USERS\accountname
```

Or

```
\USERS\groupname
```

where *accountname* is the user name given to the account and *groupname* is the name of a local or global group whose members all share the same home directory.

To assign a home directory

1. Start User Manager or User Manager for Domains, depending on whether you are using a Windows NT Workstation computer or Windows NT Server computer.

2. Select the name of the user or group whose home directory you want to assign. The User Properties dialog box appears.

3. Press the Profile button to display the User Environment Profile dialog box.

4. Enter the full path specification of the home directory in the Local Path box of the Home Directory group box.

   If you are specifying a remote home directory, specify a disk drive letter and provide the full path (not just the sharename) to the directory. For instance, if the home directory is \GLENNHO on share \\BEAMER\USERS, enter the path

   ```
   \\BEAMER\USERS\GLENNHO
   ```

Note

To allow the user to control access to the home directory, give the user Full Control permission for the directory. Give members of the Administrator or Domain Admins group Full Control permission and give all other users No Access or List permission only.

If you specify a nonexistent directory when you define or modify a user account, Windows NT automatically creates the directory.

When a user logs on to a domain, Windows NT uses the following rules to try to connect automatically to the home directory defined in the user's domain account:

- If the computer where the home directory resides is not available, Windows NT uses the user's home directory on the local computer (if there is one).

- If the home directory specified does not exist or the user does not have a home directory, Windows NT connects the user to the \USERS\DEFAULT directory of the computer that processes the logon.

- If the \USERS\DEFAULT directory does not exist, Windows NT connects the user to the \USERS directory.

Note

Windows NT Server connects the user to the home directory specified in the domain user account only when a user logs on from a Windows NT or Windows for Workgroups 3.11 client. LAN Manager 2.x clients can connect to the home directory by typing the following command at the command prompt:

```
net use <drive>: /home
```

Windows NT provides three environment parameters (see Table 9-1) that you can use in a logon script or other batch file to specify the location of the home directory. You can also use these parameters in Program Manager to specify the working directory of an application.

Table 9-1	Environment Parameters	
Parameter name	**Definition**	**Default value**
%homedrive%	Drive where the home directory is located	Drive where the Windows NT system files are installed
%homepath%	Pathname of the home directory	\USERS\DEFAULT
%homeshare%	UNC name of the shared directory containing the home directory, or a local or redirected drive letter	No default value

If the \USERS\DEFAULT directory does not exist on the drive specified by the %homedrive% parameter, Windows NT sets the value of the %homepath% parameter to the \USERS directory on that drive. If the \USERS directory does not exist, NT sets the %homepath% parameter to the root directory specified by the %homedrive% parameter.

When the user opens a command prompt window, the default directory is the equivalent of %homedrive%%homepath%. If a user's specified home directory points to an unavailable remote computer, Windows NT Workstation Command Prompt uses the user's home directory on the local workstation as its default directory.

You might also want to specify the working directory of each application as %homedrive%%homepath%. That way, all File Open and Save As dialog boxes default to the user's home directory.

The home directory contains many or all files and programs for a specific user. By default, Windows NT accesses the home directory whenever a user evokes a File Open or Save As command.

For Windows NT workstations, you normally store home directories locally. However, you could specify that the home directory be located on a server.

- If storing a home directory locally for a user named VALDAHIL, specify an absolute path such as C:\PROFILES\VALDAHIL.

- If storing a home directory on a server called PUBS for a user named VALDAHIL, specify the complete server name with path, for example, \\PUBS\USERS\VALDAHIL.

Tip

If you want the home directory to equal the user name for the account, specify %USERNAME% for the last directory in the path.

In most cases, User Manager automatically creates the home directory that you specify in the User Environment Profile dialog box. If it cannot (usually because you have specified an invalid 8.3 filename for a home directory that exists on a FAT partition), a message appears instructing you to create the directory manually.

Creating User Logon Scripts

At the beginning of this chapter, I described User Profiles as a function that provides flexibility and control over a user's environment. User profiles, which are modifiable, give users the most flexibility, whereas logon scripts and mandatory profiles give the system administrator the most control.

User logon scripts are nothing more than batch files that the system runs when a user logs on to the domain. User profiles can do everything that logon scripts can do, and more. However, there are several reasons to use logon scripts in addition to user profiles or to replace them:

- You have users who work on MS-DOS and/or OS/2 workstations. User profiles work only on Windows NT workstations.

- You want to manage part of the user's environment, such as network connections, without managing or dictating the entire environment.

- You use only personal profiles, and you want to create common network connections for multiple users.

- You already have LAN Manager 2.x running on your network, and you want to continue to use the logon scripts you created for that system.

- Logon scripts are easier to create and maintain than user profiles.

When specifying the logon script name, you do not need to specify a path. Windows NT automatically combines the name that you specify with the logon script path specified in the workstation's Control Panel Servers option. Logon scripts should be placed in either the directory specified in the Control Panel Servers option or in one of the following directories:

- \WINNT (for Windows NT systems)

- \WINNT\SYSTEM32\REPL\IMPORT\SCRIPTS (for Windows NT Servers)

Logon scripts must exist at the computer where the user logs on. In a domain where a user may log on to multiple servers, you can use the directory replicator service to keep the logon scripts synchronized among the servers. This is why the directory for Server logon scripts is under the default replicator directory (\WINNT\SYSTEM32\REPL).

You can assign a different logon script to each user or create logon scripts for use by multiple users. Whenever a user logs on, the logon script downloads and runs. To assign a logon script to a user, designate the name of the logon script file in the user environment profile, which is defined in User Manager on a Windows NT Workstation computer or User Manager for Domains on a Windows NT Server computer.

Note

Specify only the filename, not the full pathname. By default, logon scripts are located in the *systemroot*\SYSTEM32\REPL\IMPORT\SCRIPTS subdirectory of the primary domain controller and any backup domain controllers.

A logon script is a .BAT, .CMD, or .EXE file that runs automatically when a user logs on at a Windows NT network client running either Windows NT Workstation or MS-DOS. A logon script can automatically configure the user's environment to perform such tasks as making network connections, running applications, and setting environment variables upon startup.

The default file extension for logon scripts is .CMD for client workstations running OS/2 2.1 and .BAT for all other client computers. You can define a different file type as the logon script by specifying the file extension. If the same logon script must run at both Intel-based and RISC-based workstations, you should use a .BAT file that runs the appropriate .EXE file or files on the workstation.

Note

If the network client is a Windows NT or OS/2 LAN Manager client, the file extension can be .CMD or .BAT. However, if the client is an MS-DOS client, the file extension must be .BAT, otherwise the file cannot execute. For compatibility, you should always use a .BAT file extension.

You specify the path to the logon script using the Server option of Control Panel. By default, Windows NT looks for logon scripts on the primary domain controller in the directory *systemroot*\SYSTEM32\REPL\IMPORT\SCRIPTS, where *systemroot* is the disk drive and directory in which Windows NT Server was installed.

The anatomy of a logon script

The batch file for a logon script can contain any Windows NT or MS-DOS command as well as any executable program. This means that you can run another batch file, an MS-DOS application, a Windows application, or any other supported application. Here's what a minimum logon script should contain:

```
NET TIME \\BEAMER /SET /YES
NET USE LPT1: \\BEAMER\HPLJ5 /PERSISTENT:NO
NET USE D: \\BEAMER\C /PERSISTENT:NO
NET USE H: \\BEAMER\VALDA /PERSISTENT:NO
```

The first line synchronizes the client workstation clock with the clock on the server. The second line connects to a HP Laser Jet 5 printer and assigns it to the client's LPT1: parallel port. The third and fourth lines assign shares to local drive letters. All shares are nonpersistent shares to prevent an error from being reported during the logon process. If the share were a persistent share, there would be a device conflict the next time the user logged on to the network because the share would already exist.

If the logon script is to be executed on a Windows for Workgroups or Windows 95 client computer, you may want to create a network share to the client computer's local hard disk drives by including the following line in its logon script:

```
NET SHARE DriveC=C:\ /REMARK:"Administrative share for backups" /
SAVESHARE:NO /FULL:ShareAccessPassword /YES
```

I often include a disk-checking program, such as SCANDISK, and a virus-checking program, such as SCAN, on MS-DOS based computers to check for disk errors and viruses that may be present on the client computer. You could make this a part of your overall security plan, especially on machines that have bootable floppy drives.

Tip

If you want to use the same logon script for various users, you can use the environment parameters shown in Table 9-2 to reduce development and maintenance time.

Table 9-2	Environment Parameters for Logon Scripts
Parameter	*Description*
%homedir%	Redirected drive letter on user's computer that refers to the share point for the user's home directory
%homedrive%	Local or redirected drive where the home directory is located
%homepath%	Path name of the home directory
%homeshare%	UNC name of the shared directory containing the home directory, or a local or redirected drive letter
%os%	The operating system of the user's workstation (do not use if the user has more than one operating system on the workstation)
%processor_architecture%	The processor architecture (such as Intel) of the user's workstation
%processor_level%	The type of processor (such as 486) of the user's workstation
%userdomain%	The domain containing the user's account
%username%	The user name of the user

Note

Use the %processor% parameter in the logon script to run the appropriate .EXE file no matter which processor is being used.

You can set the environment variables shown in Table 9-3 in the logon script.

Table 9-3	Environment Variables for Logon Scripts
Variable	*Description*
ComSpec	Directory for CMD.EXE
LibPath	Directories to search for dynamic link libraries (DLLs)
OS2LibPath	Directories to search for dynamic link libraries (DLLs) under OS/2 subsystem
Path	Directories to search for executable program files
WinDir	Directory in which Windows NT is installed

Replicating logon scripts

If you use logon scripts in a domain with more than one domain controller, you should replicate the logon scripts to all of the backup domain controllers. All servers in a domain can authorize logon requests, but the logon script must reside on the server that approves the user's logon request for the user to log on from any workstation and use the same logon script every time. The validating server has to be able to load the logon script. When using replicated logon scripts, you should designate one of the domain controllers as the export server and all others as import servers. Depending on the amount of network traffic, you can have the primary domain controller (PDC) function as the export server for the logon scripts. By replicating logon scripts, you can maintain a set of identical logon scripts on servers that process logon requests in a domain. This way, logon scripts are always available to users, yet you only have to maintain one copy of each script.

Note

The filename for each user's logon script is defined with other user account information in User Manager for Domains. If you change the path to the logon scripts, this change is not replicated to the client workstations. You must update the path manually in the Server option of Control Panel for each client computer.

To simplify the replication of logon scripts, Windows NT Server creates a \SCRIPTS subdirectory under both the default import and export directories used for replication. If you replicate logon scripts, be sure to use the Server option of Control Panel or Server Manager to change the logon script path to *systemroot*\SYSTEM32\REPL\IMPORT\SCRIPTS or *systemroot*\SYSTEM32\REPL\EXPORT\ SCRIPTS, as appropriate.

If you use logon scripts, LAN Manager assumes that the server that is processing the logon request has a copy of the script on its hard disk. In a network with logon security, there may be multiple servers processing logon requests. If so, each server needs a local copy of logon scripts for every user in the domain. Replication allows you to maintain one set of scripts, copying it periodically to the other servers that process logon requests.

Using logon scripts with Windows 95

You can use user profiles with Windows 95 on a Windows NT network if you configure the Windows 95 computer to use Client for Microsoft Networks.

Note

Windows 95 does not use the PROFILES directory on a Windows NT server; that directory is used only for Windows NT profiles.

To set up user profiles on a Windows NT network

For each computer, be sure to enable user profiles as follows:

1. Start the Passwords applet in Control Panel to bring up the Password Properties dialog box, and then select the User Profiles tab.

2. Choose the option named Users Can Customize Their Preferences And Desktop Settings.

3. Choose the options that you want under User Profile Settings. These options describe what should be included as part of the user profile.

4. Press OK when finished, and then shut down and restart the computer.

Tip

You can enable user profiles after Windows 95 is installed, either locally on a single computer or for multiple computers. You can avoid having to go to each computer to enable user profiles by creating a system policy that can be downloaded automatically when the initial Windows 95 installation is complete.

5. In the Network option in Control Panel, make sure Client for Microsoft Networks is the Primary Network Logon client.

6. On the Windows NT server, ensure that each user is properly set up and has an assigned home directory on a Windows NT network server. (You can use the Windows NT User Manager tool to create this directory.)

When the user logs off, Windows 95 automatically places an updated copy of the user profile in the following path in the user's assigned home directory on the Windows NT network: \\logon_server\user's home directory.

Using logon scripts with Windows for Workgroups

By default, Windows for Workgroups does not run a logon script when a user logs on to a Windows NT Server computer. To run a logon script from Windows for Workgroups, you must configure Windows for Workgroups to log on to the Windows NT domain on startup.

To log on to the Windows NT domain on startup from a Windows for Workgroups computer

1. From Control Panel, launch the Network applet.

2. In the Microsoft Windows Network dialog box, click the Startup button to display the Startup Settings dialog box.

3. In the Options for Enterprise Networking box, select the Log On To Windows NT or LAN Manager Domain check box.

4. In the Domain box, type the name of the Windows NT domain where you want to log on.

5. In the Startup Settings dialog box, click OK.

6. In the Microsoft Windows Network dialog box, click OK to complete the process.

Note Windows for Workgroups does not recognize logon script parameters, and application programming interface (API) calls made from a logon script return an error.

Troubleshooting Logon Scripts

Use the following guidelines to troubleshoot the most common problems with logon scripts:

- Make sure that the logon script is in the directory specified in the Server option of Control Panel. When Windows NT is installed, the logon script directory is as follows:

  systemroot\SYSTEM32\REPL\IMPORT\SCRIPTS

- The only valid path option is a subdirectory of the default logon script directory. If the path is any other directory or it uses the environment variable %homepath%, the logon script fails.

- If the logon script is on an NTFS partition, make sure that the user has Read permission for the logon script directory. If you do not assign explicit permissions, the logon script might fail without providing an error message.

■ Make sure that the logon script has a filename extension of either .CMD or .BAT. The .EXE extension is also supported, but only for genuine executable programs. If you use a nondefault file extension for your processor, be sure to specify it with the filename of the logon script.

■ Attempting to use the .EXE extension for a script file results in the following error message:

```
NTVDM CPU has encountered an illegal instruction.
```

If this error message appears, close the window in which the logon script is running.

If the logon script is to run on a Windows for Workgroups computer, make sure that the Windows NT domain name is specified as a startup option in the Network option of Control Panel.

■ Make sure that any new or modified logon scripts have been replicated to all domain controllers. Replication of logon scripts happens periodically, not immediately. To force replication manually, use Server Manager as described in Chapter 10, *Creating and Administering Domains*.

Summary

User profiles, logon scripts, and home directories are an important part of Windows NT administration. These features provide flexibility and consistency across user desktops, while arming you with several ways to tighten up your network security. This chapter discussed

▶ Assigning home directories

▶ Replicating logon scripts

▶ Using logon scripts with Windows 95 and Windows for Workgroups

▶ Troubleshooting logon scripts

Chapter 10

Creating and Administering Domains

In This Chapter

- ▶ Domain administration
- ▶ Establishing primary domain controllers
- ▶ Synchronizing domains
- ▶ Configuring replication service
- ▶ Establishing trust relationships

Chapter 2, *Redefining the Enterprise Network,* introduced the concept of groups, user accounts, and domains as they pertain to a Windows NT network. Having chosen a domain model and created user accounts for your staff, your job as the administrator focuses on administering and maintaining the entire domain. This can sometimes be an unwieldy task, but the good news is that Windows NT Server facilitates this task by enabling you to perform it from your workstation. You do not have to go to each workstation. This chapter discusses the tasks and methods that you should use to keep your domain functioning.

General Domain Administration

Server Manager is the primary tool used in setting up domains and establishing trust relationships between domains. As the network administrator, you use Server Manager to administer computers and domains either locally or remotely. You can also use this tool to create computer accounts, synchronize primary domain controller databases, and back up domain controllers. In addition, Server Manager allows you to

- View the member computers of a domain
- Select a specific computer for administration
- Manage server properties and services

- Send messages to connected users

- Promote a server to domain controller

Server Manager can perform the tasks just listed in the following types of domains:

- Windows NT Server

- Windows NT Server and LAN Manager 2.x

- LAN Manager 2.x

Who can use Server Manager

To use Server Manager to administer a domain and its servers, you must be logged on to a user account that is a member of the Administrators, Domain Admins, or Server Operators group for that domain. Members of the Account Operators group can also use Server Manager, but only for the purpose of adding computers to the domain.

To administer a Windows NT Workstation computer or a server that is not a domain controller, you must be logged on to a user account that is a member of the Administrators or Power Users group for that computer.

Note

A few Server Manager functions are only allowed for Administrators or Domain Admins. When Server Operators, Account Operators, or Power Users attempt to perform these functions, a message is displayed indicating that access is denied.

To use a Windows NT Workstation or a Windows client to perform administrative tasks, you must first install the appropriate software, which is located in the \CLIENTS\SRVTOOLS directory on the Windows NT Server CD-ROM. See Chapter 12, *Connecting Clients,* for more information.

Understanding Computer Accounts

One of Server Manager's most important functions is the creation of computer accounts. A client can be a Windows NT Server backup domain controller, a Windows NT Server operating in server mode, or a Windows NT Workstation. The computer account is used to establish the trusted connection between a domain controller and a client. The trusted connection is the beginning of the network authentication process for domain members.

Computer accounts have several defining characteristics; for example, a computer account must have the same name as the client computer. Computer accounts have unique security identifiers. When you manage and manipulate these accounts, you should consider the following:

- If you delete an account and then recreate it, the user must rejoin the domain.

- If a user changes from one domain to another domain and then attempts to rejoin the original domain using the original computer account, the attempt fails.

- If a user changes from a domain to a workgroup and then attempts to rejoin the domain using the original computer account, the attempt fails.

- If a user changes the computer name and then attempts to log on, the attempt fails. If the user then changes the name back to the original name, the attempt also fails.

Warning

On a network with two-way trust relationships, if you do not have a computer account, you cannot access the domain controller — even if you have a user account on the domain controller. Without a computer account, the domain controller cannot authenticate you at the user level. If the domain controller cannot authenticate you, you cannot access network resources. On a network with no trust relationships or with a one-way trust relationship, a user account can be mapped for workgroup computers and authenticate the user, thereby providing limited access to network resources.

Creating computer accounts

Whenever you add a user to the domain, you must create a new computer account for the client machine. One benefit to creating computer accounts in Server Manager is that you can specify the computer name of the client computer. This allows you to enforce a naming convention for client workstations on the network. So rather than have names like Underdog, Superwoman, and Fast Eddie, you can have descriptive names like Sidney Cherie, Engineering, or Manufacturing. You also do not have to give out an administrative password (which you would have to change later) to a user or go to the location of the client computer to enter your administrative account and password.

To add a computer to the domain

1. Log on to a user account that is a member of the Administrators, Domain Admins, or Account Operators group of that domain. Then start Server Manager, which is located in the Admin Tools program group. The Server Manager window appears as shown in Figure 10-1.

   In most cases, when Server Manager first starts, it displays your logon domain. The title bar shows the domain name, and the body of the Server Manager window displays a list of computers that are members of the domain.

2. From the Computer menu, choose Add To Domain. The Add Computer To Domain dialog box appears as shown in Figure 10-2.

3. In the Add Computer To Domain dialog box, select either the Windows NT Workstation or Server option or the Windows NT Backup Domain Controller option.

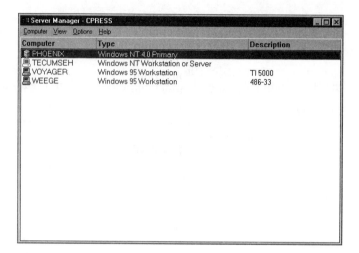

Figure 10-1: The Server Manager window.

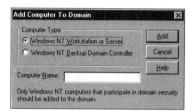

Figure 10-2: The Add Computer To Domain dialog box.

4. Type the computer name in the Computer Name box and then choose the Add button. Server Manager adds an account for that computer name in the domain's security database.

5. Choose the Close button. The computer is added to Server Manager's list. However, until the computer joins the domain (as described in Step 6), the computer's icon in Server Manager's list is dimmed, and its version number and description are absent.

6. After a computer has been added, the user of that computer must join the domain. Workstations and servers can join a domain during installation of Windows NT or after installation using the Network option of that computer's Control Panel. However, domain controllers can join a domain only during installation.

Secret

Treat an added computer name as a security element. Until the intended computer joins the domain, it is possible for a user to give a different computer that computer name and then use the computer account that you have created to have the unauthorized computer join the domain. If the added computer is a server, it receives a copy of the domain's security database when it joins.

Tip

You may need to change a computer name after setting up a computer account. Choose Add To Domain and complete the Add Computer to Domain dialog box, specifying the new computer name. Then instruct the user of that computer to change the computer name in the Network option in Control Panel. Finally, select the old computer name from the list in the Server Manager window and then choose Remove From Domain from the Computer menu.

Removing a computer from the domain

After a computer is removed from a domain, it can no longer participate in domain security. The computer's account is deleted from the domain's security database.

To remove a computer from the domain

1. Select a computer from the list in the Server Manager window. Do not select the primary domain controller. It cannot be removed.

2. From the Computer menu, choose Remove From Domain.

3. Instruct the user of that computer to remove this domain name from the Network option in Control Panel and to enter (as appropriate) another domain name or workgroup name.

Using the command line

You can add or delete computer accounts from the command line using the NET command with the following syntax:

```
NET COMPUTER \\ComputerName /ADD /DEL
```

where *ComputerName* is the name of the computer account that you want to create or delete.

/ADD specifies that you want to create the computer account and add the computer to the domain. /DEL specifies that you want to delete the computer account and remove the computer from the domain.

Managing the Domain

Ensuring that the primary and backup domain controllers remain available to the network at all times is the most important aspect of operating a domain. Think of the consequences if the domain controllers go off-line or if user account databases become unreadable. As a precautionary measure, you must know how to manipulate domain components and be able to recover from disaster.

Promoting a backup domain controller

Because all computer and user accounts are created on the primary domain controller's database, you cannot make any account modifications if the primary domain controller fails and goes off-line. However, you can promote a backup domain controller to a primary domain controller temporarily to make account modifications. Once you have corrected the problem, you can bring the primary domain controller back online.

Caution

When you promote a backup domain controller to a primary domain controller, the process terminates all client connections on both domain controllers. This could cause loss of data for network users. Before promoting a backup domain controller, warn users to save their work and log off of the system.

To promote a backup domain controller to a primary domain controller

1. Select the backup domain controller in the main window.

2. Choose Promote to Primary Domain Controller from the Computer menu. When you do this, you receive a confirmation message that the process may take several minutes to complete. Select the OK button to proceed.

3. After the account synchronization is complete, the backup domain controller appears as a primary domain controller, and the old primary domain controller appears as a backup domain controller in the main window.

Using a RAS-connected BDC as a PDC

Because the promotion process terminates all clients and because a RAS connection will terminate before the role change has been completed, you have to take special steps to use a RAS connection on either the current primary domain controller or on the backup domain controller that you want to promote.

To promote a RAS-connected backup domain controller (BDC) to primary domain controller (PDC) while it is remotely connected to the domain, you must set up the BDC as a dial-out-only RAS client (that is, RAS is not running on this computer). If you promote the RAS-connected client without doing this step, NetLogon stops, changes roles, and restarts. RAS is dependent on NetLogon, so when NetLogon stops, you lose your connection. By having the dial-out services on this remote BDC, the RAS client can function as a PDC because that functionality does not depend on NetLogon running continuously. If neither the RAS Server (which could also be a BDC) nor the RAS-connected BDC are expected to ever serve as a PDC, this is not an issue. A RAS-connected BDC that has been promoted to PDC functions as it should, but possibly with slower response time, depending on line speed.

Partial Synchronization with a RAS-connected BDC

If a remote site has a RAS-connected BDC that dials in nightly to synchronize partially any changes, and on some days more than 2,000 changes are made to the SAM/LSA (Security Account Manager/Local Security Authority) database, the ChangeLogSize default should be increased. (The default ChangeLogSize is 64K, which is approximately 2,000 changes.) This may be necessary if any BDC has been off-line while a lot of changes have occurred. If you do not change the default, this BDC may be forced to do a full synchronization of the database. If minimal changes (for example, fewer than 2,000) occur during the time that the RAS BDC or any BDC does not have a physical connection to the PDC, the default size is sufficient. If an administrator begins to notice any BDCs doing full synchronizations, it could be that many changes are occurring, and the ChangeLogSize needs to be increased.

Demoting a primary domain controller to backup domain controller

Usually, when a server is promoted to primary domain controller, no special action needs to be taken to demote the former primary domain controller to backup domain controller status, because the system does this automatically.

However, if a server is promoted to primary domain controller while the existing primary domain controller is unavailable (for example, if it is being repaired) and if the former primary domain controller later returns to service, you must demote it.

To demote a primary domain controller to backup domain controller

1. Select the former primary domain controller from the list of computers in the Server Manager window. On the Computer menu, the Promote To Primary Domain Controller command changes, becoming the Demote To Backup Domain Controller command.

2. From the Computer menu, choose Demote to Backup Domain Controller.

Bringing a failed primary controller back online

When you bring a failed primary domain controller back online, it usually detects that a new primary domain controller is functioning and defaults to a backup domain controller. If you want to restore it to its role as a primary domain controller, you must manually promote it to a primary domain controller. Before you bring a failed primary domain controller back online, there are a few considerations to keep in mind.

- Never use a domain controller that has stale data. This could occur, for instance, if you bring a failed primary domain controller online before you bring a temporary domain controller online. This situation would cause the temporary domain controller to default to a backup domain controller.

- Make sure the temporary domain controller is functioning properly with the network. Then power up the failed primary domain controller. As in the preceding item, if you have a poor network connection when you bring a failed primary domain controller online, you can cause the temporary domain controller to default to a backup domain controller.

- After you have checked the preceding items, synchronize the user database from the temporary primary domain controller to the failed domain controller. Even though synchronization should occur automatically when you promote the failed primary domain controller back to a primary domain controller, it may not be successful.

  Synchronizing the database ensures that the account database is successfully backed up (because you can check the event logs to make sure) and that any changes you made are maintained. If you do not synchronize the database prior to promoting the failed server, you may overwrite user databases on the backup controllers with an older copy (the one on the failed server) and lose any account modifications the next time that you synchronize the domain.

Synchronizing the domain database

The domain database, which includes computer and user accounts, physically resides on the primary domain controller (PDC). The PDC replicates any changes to this database to backup domain controllers every time that you add a new computer or user account or modify existing accounts. This synchronization is usually done automatically by the system, but sometimes the replication process fails because of a poor network connection or other problem. If the security database on a Windows NT Server computer becomes unsynchronized or if a LAN Manager 2.x Server is unable to establish network connections, you can use Server Manager to replicate this database manually to all controllers in the domain or to a specific controller in the domain.

Note

You can synchronize a LAN Manager 2.x server only with a LAN Manager 2.x primary domain controller; you cannot synchronize a LAN Manager 2.x Server with a Windows NT Server primary domain controller.

Synchronizing an account database can chew up network bandwidth and affect network performance. Therefore, you should use this command during non-peak hours, particularly if you have a large number of accounts and users to replicate to the backup domain controller.

To synchronize all of the backup domain controllers with the primary domain controller

1. Select the primary domain controller in Server Manager's main window.

2. From the Computer menu, choose Synchronize Entire Domain. The program responds with a confirmation message stating that the process may take several minutes to complete. Select the OK button to proceed.

3. After completing the replication process, a message appears prompting you to check the event logs of the primary and backup domain controllers to make sure that the replication process succeeded.

Note

Check the Security event logs to verify that the primary domain controller and backup domain controller sent and received the same number of accounts.

To synchronize a specific backup domain controller with the primary domain controller, use the same procedure as in the preceding, except

1. Select the backup domain controller in Server Manager's main window.

2. From the Computer menu, choose Synchronize with Primary Domain Controller.

Using the Command Line

You can synchronize the entire domain account database by running the following command from a command prompt:

```
NET ACCOUNTS /SYNC /DOMAIN
```

where /SYNC — if used without the /DOMAIN switch — synchronizes the entire domain if executed on a primary domain controller or synchronizes just the backup domain controller with the primary domain controller if run on a backup domain controller.

/DOMAIN synchronizes the entire domain regardless of where the application is executed. Normally, this switch is only used when the command is executed on a Windows NT Workstation or Windows NT Server operating in server mode.

Managing Server Resources

You can use Server Manager to manage a local computer's resources or a remote computer's resources. You also can

■ Stop, start, pause, continue, or configure system services on a remote computer

■ Create new shares or delete existing shares

■ Determine which users are connected to the remote computer

■ Determine what shares are available or in use on a remote computer

■ Configure the Replication and Alert services on a remote computer

Managing services

The normal method to access a Windows NT computer's service control manager database is to use the local computer's Control Panel Services applet. However, you can also use Server Manager to perform the same tasks.

To configure service startup

1. Log on to a user account that has membership in the Administrators local group.

2. Select a computer from the list in the Server Manager window and then choose Services from the Computer menu. The dialog box shown in Figure 10-3 appears.

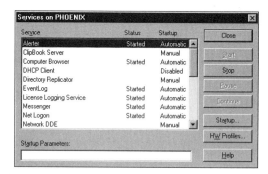

Figure 10-3: The Services dialog box.

Notice that this is the same dialog box that you see when accessing the Services applet under Control Panel. The reason for controlling service options through Server Manager is that you can control the services for any computer in a domain from your workstation.

3. In the Services dialog box, select the desired service and choose the Startup button.

4. In the Service Startup dialog box, select a startup type of Automatic, Manual, or Disabled.

5. To specify the user account that the service will use to log on, select System Account or This Account.

6. If you select This Account, also choose the Browse button and specify a user account by completing the Add User dialog box that appears. After closing the Add User dialog box, type the password for the user account in both the Password and Confirm Password boxes.

7. Choose the OK button, and then in the Services dialog box, choose the Close button.

Starting and Stopping Services

Use the Services dialog box to start, stop, pause, or continue each of the services available on the selected computer, and to pass startup parameters to the service.

Note

Because stopping the Server service disconnects all connected remote users, warn users before stopping that service. Also, once the Server service is stopped, that computer can no longer be remotely administered, and its Server service can only be restarted locally.

To start, stop, pause, or continue a service

1. Select a computer from the list in the Server Manager window and then choose Services from the Computer menu.

2. In the Services dialog box, select the service.

3. Choose the Start, Stop, Pause, or Continue button.

4. In the Services dialog box, choose the Close button.

If you want to pass startup parameters to a service, type the parameters in the Startup Parameters box before choosing the Start button. Backslashes are treated as an escape character. You must type two backslashes for each backslash in a parameter.

Secret

If you intend to use the AT command to schedule commands and programs to run on a computer at a specified time and date, the Schedule service requires special attention. The Schedule service must be running for the AT command to operate.

By default, the Schedule service is configured to log on under the system account, which is the same account used by most services. However, when the Schedule service logs on under the system account, the AT command can only be used to access those network resources that permit Guest access.

In many cases, if you want the AT command to access certain network resources, you must create a special user account and then configure the Schedule service to log on using that user account.

To assign a logon account to the Schedule service

1. Create a user account for the service using User Manager or User Manager for Domains. (Refer to Chapter 8, *Managing User and Group Accounts,* for information on using User Manager.) When creating the account, select the Password Never Expires option.

2. Make the account a member of the appropriate groups so that it is empowered to conduct operations that must be accomplished remotely. For example, to use the AT command to perform regularly scheduled backups of the hard disk of a remote server in a Windows NT Server domain, you should create a user account for the Schedule service as a member of the domain's Backup Operators local group.

3. Assign the user account to the Schedule service using Server Manager or the Services option in Control Panel as follows:

Select Schedule in the Services dialog box and click the Startup button. The Service on *Computer name* dialog box appears as shown in Figure 10-4.

Figure 10-4: The Service on PHOENIX dialog box.

Specify that the Schedule service should use a specific account by enabling the This Account option in the Log On As section of the dialog box. Enter the account information exactly as you created it in User Manager. Choose Close to complete the operation.

Creating and administering shares

The primary reason for stringing together a network is to make resources on the network available across the boundaries of time and space. A resource can be a file, a directory, a printer, a CD-ROM, a modem, or an executable program, depending on the network's purpose. This section covers creating and administering files and directories, which are fundamental resources on all networks.

Sharing a Directory

You share directories to make it easier for users to upgrade software, to have access to data files, or perhaps to serve as a central repository for departmental files. Sharing a directory is as easy as designating the directory to be shared. However, for the administrator of a secure Windows NT domain, sharing a directory involves much more than the click of a mouse. You're concerned with limiting users or simultaneous connections, assigning permission levels, and deciding which groups should have access to which shared directories.

To share a directory

1. Select a computer from the list in the Server Manager window and then choose Shared Directories from the Computer menu. The Shared Directories dialog box appears as shown in Figure 10-5.

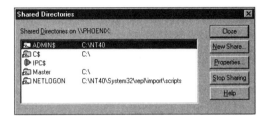

Figure 10-5: The Shared Directories dialog box.

2. In the Shared Directories dialog box, choose the New Share button.

3. Type a Share Name, Path, and Comment in corresponding fields of the New Share dialog box as shown in Figure 10-6.

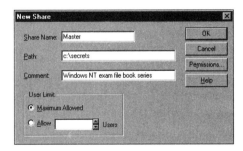

Figure 10-6: The New Share dialog box.

4. If you want to limit the number of users who can connect to the shared directory at one time, select either Maximum Allowed or Allow. If you select Allow, specify a maximum number in the Users box.

5. You should also specify the permission level granted to groups and user accounts. Choose the Permissions button and complete the Access Through Share Permissions dialog box shown in Figure 10-7. Choose OK when finished.

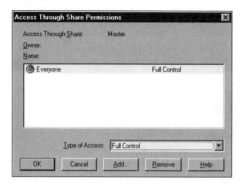

Figure 10-7: The Access Through Share Permissions dialog box.

Note

Unless you change the default setting, a new shared directory provides Full Control to Everyone. When assigning permissions, it is usually better to assign permissions to groups rather than to individual user accounts.

6. To add a group or user account to the list of those granted permissions for this shared directory, choose the Add button and complete the Add Users And Groups dialog box that appears.

7. To remove a group or user account from the list of those granted permissions for this shared directory, select a group or user account from the Name list and then choose the Remove button.

8. Complete the process by choosing the OK button in the New Share dialog box and then choosing the Close button in the Shared Directories dialog box.

Special Shares

If you look in the Shared Directories dialog box (refer to Figure 10-5), you will notice some unusual directory names. A computer's shared resources include those resources (such as directories) that have been shared by a user or an administrator, plus any *special shares* that the system may have created.

Depending on the configuration of the computer being administered, some or all of the special shares listed in Table 10-1 may appear when Windows NT presents a list of the computer's shared resources. As a general rule, do not modify or delete these special shares.

Table 10-1	Special Shares
Sharename	**Description**
driveletter$	Default share
ADMIN$	Remote administration
IPC$	Remote IPC
NETLOGON	Logon server share
PRINT$	Print share
REPL$	Replication share

Setting Permissions for a Shared Directory

Share permissions specify which users can access a shared directory and the type of access those users can have. These permissions control network access to the shared directory, its subdirectories, and their files. Share permissions are effective only when the shared directory is accessed over the network.

Note

Permissions set on a share that is on an NTFS volume operate in addition to NTFS permissions set on the directory itself. On NTFS volumes, share permissions specify the maximum access possible, whereas directory and file permissions specify the maximum access allowed. For NTFS volumes, it is usually better to restrict access by managing the permissions set on directories and files rather than the permissions set on shares.

Stopping Directory Sharing

To stop sharing a directory

1. Select a computer from the list in the Server Manager window and then choose Shared Directories from the Computer menu.

2. In the Shared Directories dialog box, select a share name from the list.

3. Choose the Stop Sharing button.

    The directory itself is not removed, but it is no longer shared and can no longer be accessed by network users.

4. To exit, choose the Close button.

Warning

Using this option immediately stops sharing of the directory. There is no confirmation message. Before you do this, check to see who may be using the share.

In most cases, you should not select one of the special shares which, if it appears in the list, was created by the system (for example, A$, B$, C$, ADMIN$, IPC$, NETLOGON, PRINT$, or REPL$).

Resource accounting

One of your responsibilities as the administrator of a Windows NT domain is to manage and account for resources in the domain. This is a very important task because it affects network security and performance. At any given time, you need to be able to identify which users are on the system, which resources a user is accessing, and how long a user has been connected to your system.

If you want to determine which users are connected to which computer, what network shares are available on a computer, or which shares are in use on a computer, you can have Server Manager display an accounting of these properties for any computer in the domain. In Server Manager language, this kind of statistical information is referred to as *computer properties*. I prefer to look at it as a form of resource accounting. Server Manager will display the following information for any computer:

- A description of the computer
- Connected users
- Shared resources
- Open resources

To review resources

Select a computer listed in the Server Manager's main window and then choose Properties from the Computer menu. The Properties dialog box, as shown in Figure 10-8, appears. Read the information and close the box when you've finished looking at it.

Figure 10-8: The Properties dialog box.

This is the same dialog box that the Control Panel Server applet displays. The difference between using the Control Panel applet and using Server Manager's Properties command is that you can view the properties for any computer in the domain via Server Manager as opposed to seeing just the local machine via the Control Panel Server applet.

Table 10-2 describes the Usage Summary information shown in the Properties dialog box.

Table 10-2	Usage Summary Information
Item	**Description**
Sessions	The number of remote users connected to the computer
Open Files	The number of shared resources opened on the computer
File Locks	The number of file locks by open resources on the computer
Open Named Pipes	The number of named pipes opened on the computer

The Properties dialog box has five buttons along the bottom. Each of these buttons allows you to examine specific properties corresponding to the selected computer as described below.

User Sessions

The User Sessions dialog box allows you to determine the following:

- All of the users connected over the network to the computer

- The resources opened by any one of those users

To access the User Sessions dialog box, shown in Figure 10-9, choose the Users button in the Properties dialog box.

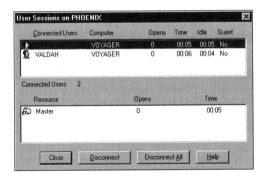

Figure 10-9: The User Sessions dialog box.

By examining the User Sessions dialog box, you have quick answers to questions such as

- How many users are connected?

- Which shares are in use?

- How long has the user been connected to a specific share?

This information can be very useful in helping you monitor and evaluate network performance. For example, you can disconnect one or all of the connected users if you need to stop the Server service or shut down Windows NT. (See the earlier section, *Starting and Stopping Services,* for information on shutting down a service.)

Caution

If you disconnect a user, any files that have been opened by the user cannot close properly, and the user may lose data.

The Connected Users box lists the connected users, the connection to a specific computer, the number of open files, the total connection time, the total idle time, and whether users have connected with guest privileges. The Resource box lists the resource, number of open files, and total connection time in use by a specific user. Table 10-3 lists the information displayed in the Connected Users box.

Table 10-3	User Session Information
Item	*Description*
Connected Users	The user name of the connected user
Computer	The computer name of the computer where the user is logged on
Opens	The number of resources opened on this computer by the user
Time	The elapsed time since the user established the session
Idle	The elapsed time since the user initiated an action
Guest	Whether this user has Guest status on the computer
Resource	The name of the shared resource (shared directory, printer queue, or named pipe) to which the selected user is connected
Opens	The number of opens against this resource by this user
Time	The time elapsed since this resource was first opened

Note that your user account is listed as a user connected to the IPC$ resource while you are remotely administering another computer. It cannot be disconnected.

Caution

If you disconnect users from a network resource, any files that are open cannot be closed properly, and the files may be corrupted. If you disconnect users from a named pipe, the network client application may fail. You might even cause the network server application to fail, which in some cases can bring down the server. Use this option only if necessary.

Shared Resources

The Shared Resources dialog box, shown in Figure 10-10, appears when you select the Shares button from the Properties dialog box. It displays the following information:

- The shared resources on the computer
- The users connected over the network to each shared resource

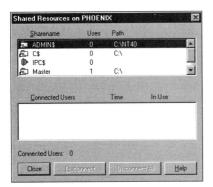

Figure 10-10: The Shared Resources dialog box.

As the system administrator, you can use this dialog box to disconnect one or all of the connected users. For example, you may have limited the number of users who can simultaneously connect to a shared directory, and you then find that another user needs access to that directory. If the directory has reached its user limit, you can disconnect another user. As always, you should send a warning message before you disconnect the user.

Note

When you disconnect a user, the user is disconnected from all shared resources on the computer (not just the resource selected in the Sharename box).

Use the Shared Resources dialog box to view the shared resources available on the computer and the users connected over the network to a selected shared resource. Table 10-4 describes the information provided for each resource in the Shared Resources dialog box.

Note that your user account will be listed as a connected user for the IPC$ share while you are remotely administering another computer. It cannot be disconnected.

Open Resources

You can use the Open Resources dialog box (accessed by choosing the In Use button in the Properties dialog box) to view and manage a computer's open shared resources. The Open Resources dialog box is shown in Figure 10-11.

Table 10-5 lists the information available in the Open Resources dialog box.

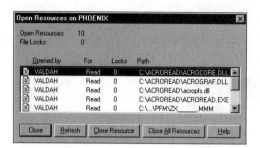

Figure 10-11: The Open Resources dialog box.

Table 10-4	Shared Resources Information
Item	*Description*
Sharename	The name of the shared resource; this could be a shared directory, a printer queue, or a named pipe
Uses	The number of connections to the shared resource
Path	The path of the shared resource
Connected Users	The user name of the user connected to this resource
Time	The time elapsed since the user first connected to this resource
In Use	Whether the user currently has a file open from this shared resource.

Table 10-5	Open Resources Information
Item	*Description*
Open Resources	The total number of open resources (files, printers, or named pipes) on the computer
File Locks	The total number of file locks by open resources
Opened by	The user name of the user who opened the resource
For	The permissions granted when the resource was opened
Locks	The number of locks on the resource
Path	The path of the open resource

Optionally, you can close an open resource by selecting that resource from the list and then choosing the Close Resource button. To close all open resources, choose the Close All Resources button.

Note that your connection will be displayed here as an open named pipe while you are remotely administering another computer. It cannot be closed.

Directory Replication

The directory replication feature allows you to create and maintain identical directory trees and files on multiple computers. You can use this powerful tool as part of a file maintenance regime or for load balancing. It reduces file maintenance because updated files can be derived from a single source, and it relieves server loading by making files available on several servers or workstations.

You need at least two computers in a replication process: the export server and the import or target computer. The export computer is the machine that contains all of the source files to be replicated to the import computer. You must run Windows NT Server on the export server because Windows NT Workstation can only act as an import computer. In addition, a Windows NT Server, a Windows NT Client, or a LAN Manager Server can function as an import computer that receives the replicated directories and files from the export server.

Import and export directories

To perform replication, the export server must store export directories and files in an export directory, and the import computer must store directories and files in an import directory. The default export directory is

```
<WINNT_ROOT>\SYSTEM32\REPL\EXPORT
```

The export server is limited to a single directory tree and a maximum of 32 nested subdirectories.

The default import directory is

```
<WINNT_ROOT>\SYSTEM32\REPL\IMPORT
```

You can replicate logon scripts as long as you set up special directories. The default export directory for logon scripts is

```
<WINNT_ROOT>\SYSTEM32\REPL\EXPORT\SCRIPTS
```

The default import directory for logon scripts on all import computers is

```
<WINNT_ROOT>\SYSTEM32\REPL\IMPORT\SCRIPTS
```

Configuring import and export computers

Most aspects of directory replication are managed for a particular computer by using either the Server Manager Properties command or the Server option in Control Panel.

However, before a computer can participate in replication, you must create a special user account and then, for each computer in a domain that will participate in replication, configure its Directory Replicator service to log on using that special account.

1. To assign a logon account to the Directory Replicator service use User Manager for Domains to create a domain user account with the following characteristics:

   ■ The Password Never Expires option is selected.

   ■ All logon hours are allowed.

   ■ The User Must Change Password At Next Logon option is cleared.

   ■ The domain's Replicator group has the Log On As A Service user right in User Manager for Domains.

   ■ The user account has memberships in the domain's Backup Operators group, Domain Users, and Replicator groups.

Cross Reference

For specific information on how to add user accounts to groups, refer to Chapter 8, *Managing User and Group Accounts.*

2. For each computer that participates in replication, use Server Manager or the Services option in Control Panel to configure the computer's Directory Replicator service to start up automatically and to log on using the user account that you created for the service.

Note

When you configure the replication service to start, it creates a special share called REPL$, which is based on the directory that you specify as the logon script path. Generally this directory is SystemRoot\System32\REPL\Export.

To set up an export computer

1. Use Explorer to create the subdirectories for exporting. These must be subdirectories of the Replication From Path.

   Optionally, add the files that will be exported to these subdirectories. However, it is not necessary to add files at this time. Once you set up replication, any files added later to these subdirectories will be exported automatically. You can also later add additional subdirectories to the Replication From Path.

2. In the Server Manager window, double-click the computer name of the replication export server.

3. In the Properties dialog box, choose the Replication button. The Directory Replication dialog box appears as shown in Figure 10-12.

4. In the Directory Replication dialog box, select the Export Directories option.

   Optionally, to change the path from which subdirectories will be exported, type a local path in the From Path box.

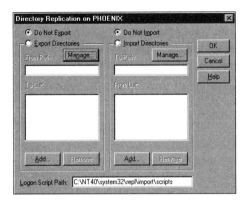

Figure 10-12: The Directory Replication dialog box.

5. To export subdirectories to a domain or computer, choose the Add button under Export Directories and then complete the Select Domain dialog box that appears. The domain name or computer name is added to the To List in the Directory Replication dialog box.

By default, the To List contains a blank entry, which allows a computer to automatically export to the local domain. If any entries are added to the To List, the local domain is no longer exported to it. If necessary, the domain name must be explicitly added to the To List.

To set up an import computer

For Windows NT Workstations in trusted domains, assign the export server's Replicator group membership in the local Replicator group, and add the local Replicator group to the user right Log On As a Service.

Note

Make sure that an appropriate logon account has been assigned to the Directory Replicator service before performing the following procedure:

1. In the Server Manager window, double-click the appropriate computer name.

2. In the Properties dialog box, choose the Replication button.

3. In the Directory Replication dialog box, select Import Directories.

   Optionally, to change the path in which imported subdirectories will be stored, type a local path in the To Path box.

4. To import subdirectories from a domain or export server, choose the Add button under Import Directories and then complete the Select Domain dialog box that appears. The domain name or computer name is added to the From List.

Note

By default, the From List contains a blank entry that allows a computer to automatically import from the local domain. If any entries are added to the From List, the local domain is no longer imported from it. If necessary, the domain name must be explicitly added to the From List.

5. To stop importing subdirectories from an export server or domain, select the domain name or computer name in the From List and then choose the Remove button.

6. To view a list of the subdirectories that have been imported to this computer or to manage locks on those imported subdirectories, choose the Manage button under Import Directories; the Manage Imported Directories dialog box appears as shown in Figure 10-13.

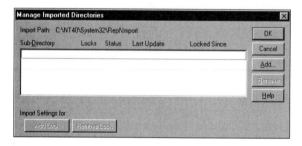

Figure 10-13: The Manage Imported Directories dialog box.

7. To exit, choose the OK button in the Directory Replication dialog box. If it is not already running, the system starts the Directory Replicator service.

8. In the Properties dialog box, choose the OK button.

Caution

If you are importing directories from a domain or server located on the other side of a WAN connection, the import from the local domain may fail. To ensure that this does not occur, manually add the domain or computer name in the From Field.

Note

A Windows NT Workstation cannot act as a replication export server. It can only be used to import a directory tree from an export server. Nor can a Windows NT Workstation change the default replication path from SystemRoot\System32\Repl\Import\Scripts.

Managing Exported Directories

Replication can cause a security breach if it is not managed properly. You must be careful not to replicate sensitive files out onto the network where they might be accessed by any user. Windows NT provides features that let you control the replication process securely. Use the Directory Replication dialog box on the export server to

- Specify the export path.

- Lock a directory to prevent exportation.

- Prevent the exportation of a subdirectory within a specific directory.

- Monitor the date and time that a lock was placed on a directory.

To manage locks, stabilization, and subtree replication for the subdirectories exported from this computer

1. Choose the Manage button in the Directory Replication dialog box. The Manage Exported Directories dialog box appears as shown in Figure 10-14.

Figure 10-14: The Manage Exported Directories dialog box.

2. Make changes as required and choose the OK button in the Directory Replication dialog box to complete the process. If it does not already exist, the system creates the special REPL$ share, required for export replication. If it is not already running, the system starts the Directory Replicator service.

The Manage Exported Directories dialog box displays status information for each subdirectory listed. Table 10-6 describes the available information, and Table 10-7 lists commands and options.

Tip

If you plan to make a lot of changes to a subdirectory marked for export, use the Add Lock button to lock the directory. This prevents the directory from being replicated until you release all of the locks.

Table 10-6	Subdirectory Information
Item	*Description*
Subdirectory	Lists the subdirectories that will be exported from this computer. Any subdirectory created along the export path is included in this list.

(continued)

Table 10-6 *(Continued)*	
Item	*Description*
Locks	Indicates the number of locks applied on the subdirectory. A lock prevents subdirectory export. Export occurs only if the value in this column is zero.
Stabilize	Indicates whether all files and subdirectories in the selected subdirectory must be idle for two minutes before replication can occur (this can prevent partial replication changes if the files are very active). The default is No. Enable the Wait Until Stabilized option to change the status.
Subtree	Indicates whether the entire subdirectory will be exported. Yes is the default setting. If this option is set to No, only the first level of the subdirectory will be replicated. Use the Entire Subtree option to change the setting.
Locked Since	Indicates the date and time that the oldest lock was placed on a subdirectory.

Table 10-7	**Manage Exported Directories Commands and Options**
Item	*Description*
Add Lock	Adds a lock to the selected subdirectory.
Remove Lock	Removes a lock from the selected subdirectory.
Add	Displays the Add Subdirectory dialog box through which you can add new subdirectories to the export list.
Remove	Removes selected subdirectories from the list of exported subdirectories. This only removes the entry from the list. If the subdirectory still exists along the export path, it will be replicated and placed back into the list.
Wait Until Stabilized	Forces the Replicator service to wait until the subdirectory has been idle for two minutes or more before replication can occur.
Entire Subtree	Forces the entire subdirectory to be exported.

Configuring Alerts

Alerts are used to notify a domain administrator of a serious problem that has occurred on a Windows NT computer. You can send an alert to a particular domain user or a specific computer that is monitored by several administrators or support personnel. You can determine which users and compu-ters are notified when administrative alerts occur at a selected computer. Administrative alerts are generated by the system and relate to server and resource use. They warn about security and access problems, user session problems, server shutdown because of power loss when the UPS service is available, and printer problems.

Tip

If you want to guarantee that the alerts are sent, you should also modify the client workstation to start the Alert and Messenger services at system startup. This makes sure that the services are functioning and available to send administrative alerts. If the services are left in their default startup setting of manual, the services attempt to send the alert but may fail due to unforeseen circumstances. If the services fail, the alert cannot be sent. Also, in order to receive an administrative alert, the Messenger service must be running. (A Windows NT Server computer has a default startup setting of automatic and does not have to be reconfigured.)

To configure the Alert service

1. Select the Alert button in the Server dialog box. The Alerts dialog box, shown in Figure 10-15, appears.

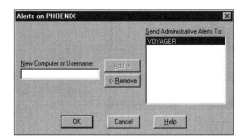

Figure 10-15: The Alerts dialog box.

2. To add a new computer or user to be notified, enter the computer or user name in the New Computer or Username field and then press the Add button. The computer or user name is then moved to the Send Administrative Alerts To field.

3. To remove a computer or user, select the computer or user name in the Send Administrative Alerts To field and press the remove button. This moves the computer or user name to the New Computer or Username field.

Note

You do not have to include the double backslashes (\\) for a computer name as you do for just about every other usage involving a computer name. If you do, the double backslashes are dropped when the name is moved.

4. To add or remove additional computers or users, repeat Step 2 or 3.

5. When you have finished entering or removing computer and user names, press the OK button to return to the Server dialog box.

Sending a message to connected users

Use the Send Message command to send a message to all users who are connected to a computer. You may want to do this before you administer the computer with Server Manager, particularly if you will be disconnecting one or more users or if you will be stopping the Server service on that computer.

To send a message to connected users

1. Select a computer from the list in the Server Manager Window.

2. From the Computer menu, choose Send Message.

3. Type your message in the Message box.

4. Choose the OK button.

Managing Macintosh Clients

Just as you can use the Properties dialog box to manage the Microsoft clients who are connected to your computer, you can use the MacFile Properties dialog box to manage Macintosh clients. To access the MacFile Properties dialog box, shown in Figure 10-16, choose MacFile Properties. This dialog box includes the following options:

Figure 10-16: The MacFile Properties dialog box.

- **Usage Summary.** This group lists the active AppleTalk sessions (the total number of connected Macintosh users), open file forks (combined data and resource forks), and the number of locks on open file forks. It's a quick indication of resource usage on the selected computer.

- **Users.** This option works just like the User Sessions dialog box used for Microsoft clients, except that it displays connected Macintosh users. To display the Macintosh Users dialog box, select the Users button. To disconnect an individual user from all connected resources, select the user in the upper edit field and then press the Disconnect button. To disconnect all connected users, press the Disconnect All button.

Caution

If you disconnect a user, any files that have been opened by the user cannot be closed properly, and the user may lose data. Before you take such an action, send a message warning of the impending disconnection so that the user can save data. You can do this by selecting the user's name in the upper entry and pressing the Send Message button. This displays a dialog box where you can specify the message to send.

■ **Volumes.** This option performs the same action as the Shares button for Microsoft clients, except it displays the Macintosh Accessible Volumes dialog box. This box displays Macintosh users who are connected to a shared resource. The upper entry lists the Macintosh volumes by name, the total number of connected users, and the system path to the shared resource. To disconnect a user, select the volume in the upper entry; the lower entry then lists the individual users, the total time they have been connected to the resource, and whether the resource is currently in use. Select a user and press the Disconnect button. To disconnect all users from the resource, press the Disconnect All button.

Caution

Disconnecting a user should be a last resort if there are any open files, which can be determined by examining the In Use entry. If any data files are open, you run the risk of corrupting the data files by prematurely disconnecting the user.

■ **Files.** This option performs the same basic function as the In Use button located in the Properties dialog box for Microsoft clients. The only real difference is that the Files Opened by Macintosh Users dialog box is displayed instead. Rather than displaying files, this displays entries for file forks. To close an individual file, select the user's name and press the Close Fork button. To close all forks, press the Close All Forks button. If the dialog box has been on-screen for a while, you can press the Refresh button to update the display.

■ **Attributes.** This option allows you to modify the behavior of the Macintosh service. Within the MacFile Attributes dialog box, you can specify the name Macintosh clients see when they browse for resources on this computer. You do so by selecting the Change button in the Server Name for AppleTalk Workstations field. You can specify a message, which Macintosh users see when they log on to the server, in the Logon Message field. This text field can contain up to four lines of text. The Security field allows you to specify whether guests can log on to the server, whether Macintosh workstations can save their passwords locally, and whether the Microsoft User Authentication Module (UAM) must be used to encrypt the user password at logon time. In the Sessions field, you can determine the maximum number of simultaneous Macintosh clients that can connect to this server.

Cross Reference

For more details on the Microsoft UAM and how to install it on Macintosh clients refer to the section on Services for Macintosh in Chapter 12, *Connecting Clients.*

Tip

If you limit the number of simultaneous Macintosh connections to a single server, you can improve the performance of that server. An unlimited connection setting is only limited by the network bandwidth. However, as with any server, the more connections you have, the poorer the performance of that server. If you have multiple Windows NT Server computers, I suggest that you distribute the load evenly for best performance.

You can manage Macintosh volumes by using MacFile Volumes, which displays the Macintosh-Accessible Volumes dialog box, as shown in Figure 10-17. This dialog box can be used to create a new volume, change the properties of an existing volume, or delete a volume.

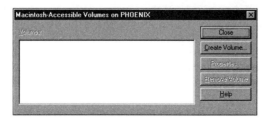

Figure 10-17: The Macintosh-Accessible Volumes dialog box.

To create a new Macintosh volume, select the Create Volume button in the Macintosh-Accessible Volumes dialog box. The Create Macintosh-Accessible Volume dialog box appears, as shown in Figure 10-18. To share any other resource, you need to supply a name for the share, a physical path name, and a password (and confirm it, too). If you want to further restrict access to the shared volume, you can specify that the volume is read-only by enabling the This volume is read-only check box. You can also restrict guests from accessing the volume by disabling the Guest can use this volume check box in the Volume Security field. You can specify the number of simultaneous connections in the User Limit field.

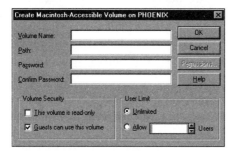

Figure 10-18: The Create Macintosh-Accessible Volume dialog box.

Tip

To further restrict the usage of the shared volume, select the Permissions button. This displays the Properties of Macintosh-Accessible Volumes dialog box where you can specify additional permission settings by group. This includes the ability to See files (same as the List Files permission in Microsoft), See Folders (same as the List Directories permission), or Make Changes (same as the Change permission). You can further specify that all permissions on all subdirectories of the parent directory are replaced (when you make a change to the permission settings) and that the user cannot move, rename, or delete existing files.

Deleting a volume is as simple as selecting the volume and pressing the Remove Volume button in the Macintosh-Accessible Volumes dialog box. This displays a message box that lets you confirm your selection before the volume is deleted.

To change the settings of an existing volume, select the Properties button in the Macintosh-Accessible Volumes dialog box. This displays a Macintosh-Accessible Volumes dialog box specifically for that volume name and physical path. You can then alter properties for that volume.

Summary

Domain administration comprises a large part of an administrator's duties. This chapter covered the following:

▶ Creating computer accounts

▶ Promoting a backup domain controller

▶ Using a RAS-connected BDC as a PDC

▶ Bringing a failed primary controller back online

▶ Synchronizing the domain database

▶ Creating and administering shares

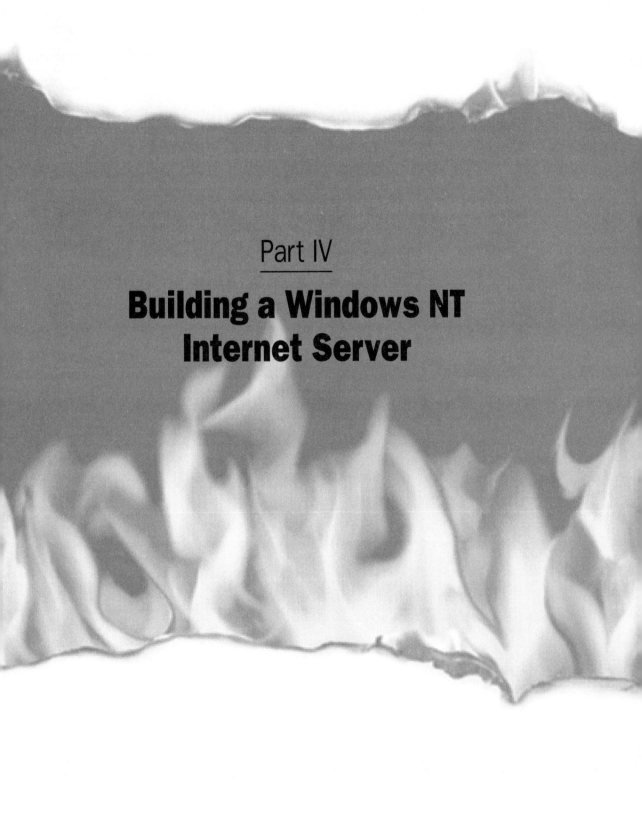

Part IV

Building a Windows NT
Internet Server

Chapter 11

Securing Your Network

The first time you attempt to log on to a Windows NT machine, you can't help noticing Windows NT's first line of defense — the Welcome Box. Before you can gain access to any Windows NT resource, you must first be validated by Windows NT's security subsystem. The logon process only scratches the surface of Windows NT's security features. This chapter shows you how to set up and configure your Windows NT system to take advantage of Windows NT's sophisticated security architecture.

Computer Security Defined

Mention computer security to a group of people, and you'll probably hear advice ranging from how to lock your system in an airtight underground vault to how to deploy high-tech hardware to sniff out would-be hackers before they crack your system. Security may be as simple as placing a computer in a locked room or as intricate as using a logon ID with an associated password or using permissions on files to protect against unauthorized access or accidental damage. On another level, security may involve data encryption for network communications or electromagnetic shields to prevent against electronic eavesdropping. The point is that computer security is a very broad subject encompassing a wide range of issues and solutions.

You employ computer security to ensure that your system functions in the manner intended and that it continues to function correctly even if users do not do what they are supposed to do. It should protect against data loss or damage — either malicious or accidental — and prevent data access by unauthorized users. Simply put, computer system security enables you to manage the integrity, confidentiality, and availability of information systems data and resources.

Security Planning Issues

As the system administrator, you should answer a series of questions to help you make decisions about how to secure a Windows NT environment. Use Table 11-1 to get you going.

Table 11-1	Guidelines for Planning Security	
Question	*Response*	*Plan of action*
Will more than one local user use this computer?	Yes	You may need to create separate protected areas for each user and possibly a common area where each user can exchange information easily.
	No	If local security is the issue, you must secure the floppy drive and configuration data.
Do the policies of the default local groups meet your needs?	Yes	Just add users to the built-in local groups.
	No	Create administrator-defined local groups and grant them rights that satisfy your special needs. Alternatively, you could set permissions on files that effectively modify the abilities of the built-in groups.
Do the default directory permissions on the system files meet the needs of your organization?	Yes	For added security, you should place data and system files on different physical drives so that if a drive fails, you restore only the system drive or the data drive.
	No	Decide what permissions need to change and then add or remove permissions on a group level.
Do you need to restrict what users can do with their personal profiles?	Yes	Apply permission to profiles.
	No	Ensure that users have the appropriate permissions to modify their profiles.
Do you need to prevent users from accessing the command prompt?	Yes	Put the appropriate restrictions on CMD.EXE.
	No	None.
Do you need to prevent users from accessing the floppy drive?	Yes	Use a physical lock on the floppy or a software lock, such as the Windows NT Floppy Lock utility, from the Windows NT Resource Kit.

Question	Response	Plan of action
	No	None. However, do not forget to separate and secure the system files from the user files.
Do you need to prevent users from altering various aspects of the system's configuration?	Yes	Decide what those are and use techniques described later in this chapter.
	No	None.
Are there any standard executables that you do not want users to run, for example, Backup? (NTBACKUP.EXE)	Yes	Identify them and use File Manager to apply restrictions as appropriate.
	No	None.
Do you need auditing enabled?	Yes	Auditing can generate a lot of information. Identify the events that you need audited and only apply auditing as necessary.
	No	None.
Do you have a password policy?	Yes	Double-check it and make sure that it satisfies your current needs.
	No	Identify the level of password protection required. Then create a password policy and implement it using User Manager.
Will users have access to the system unit?	Yes	You should consider physically securing the floppy drive, the power switch, and the system unit. Train users in the use of Windows NT software workstation lock.
	No	Train users in the use of Windows NT software workstation lock.
Will you install the Remote Access Service?	Yes	Use the appropriate RAS security options and any third-party hardware options that could provide additional security.
	No	None.
Is it imperative that you have data encryption?	Yes	Administrators should look for a third-party solution.
	No	None.
Do you want to control Windows NT workstations that are in the domain?	Yes	Make sure that the domain administrators global group is part of the workstations' administrators local group.
	No	None.

Windows NT has several security options that you can apply to software and physical security. This chapter discusses many of these security options. The following list can serve as a guide to point you in the right direction when considering security options:

Windows NT Software Security

Logon Authentication

Workstation Lock

Program Manager Restrictions

User Profiles

Privileges

File and Directory Permissions

Built-in Local Groups

Account and Password Policy

Legal Notice

Domains and Trusted Domains

NTFS Local Security

RAS Callback

Encryption Software (third-party)

Physical Security

Floppy, Keyboard, and Power Switch Lock

Electromagnetic Emission Shield

Information Encryption Device

Use of a Data Center

Secure Cabling

Security Host

The Windows NT Security Model

Before you can gain access to any of the resources on a Windows NT computer, you must log on and be authenticated by the system. Authentication is required even if the computer is a stand-alone Windows NT computer that is not connected to a file server or host computer. Windows NT is able to provide this local security because each computer has an Account and a Security Policy database.

To understand how Windows NT protects objects, it is useful to see all of the major security data structures at work.

When a user logs on to Windows NT, the system creates a special data structure called a *token object* to represent that user. Windows NT associates this token — or a copy of it — with each process that the user runs. This process-token combination is called a *subject*. Subjects operate on Windows NT objects by calling system services. When accessing protected objects such as files and directories, the system compares the contents of the subject's token with the Access Control List (ACL) using a standard access validation routine. The access validation routine determines whether to grant the subject the right to perform the requested operation. The access validation routine may also generate audit messages as a result of the access attempt.

In order to implement Windows NT's security options, you need to understand the security model that forms the foundation of Windows NT's security subsystem. The following list outlines the major security components of Windows NT:

■ The Security Subsystem, or Local Security Authority (LSA), is the center of the Windows NT security system. We refer to the LSA as an integral subsystem rather than an environmental subsystem because it affects the entire Windows NT operating system. It manages the local security policy and provides interactive user authentication services. The LSA also controls the generation of audit messages and enters audit messages into the audit log file.

■ The Security Account Manager (SAM) maintains user and group accounts and provides the user authentication services used by LSA.

■ The Security Reference Monitor (SRM) is responsible for enforcing the access validation and audit generation policy held by the local security authority subsystem. It provides services for validating access to objects (files, directories, and so on), testing subjects (user accounts) for privileges, and generating the necessary audit messages. The reference monitor contains the only copy of the access validation code in the system. This ensures that object protection is provided uniformly throughout Windows NT, regardless of what type of object is being accessed.

■ The User Interface (UI) utilities that are a part of the operating system also play an important role in the security model of Windows NT. The UI is the only hint to most users of the underlying security mechanisms. As the system administrator, you typically use the UI to perform administrative functions such as adding or removing users from the system and looking at the audit log.

Guidelines for Securing Windows NT

For each Windows NT computer in your organization, you can choose whether to have it participate in a domain or a workgroup. In most cases, you want each Windows NT computer to participate in a domain. This way, you have more control over what a user can and cannot do at the computer in the configuration.

A Windows NT workstation that participates in a domain does not actually get a copy of the domain's user account database. However, the workstation still receives all of the benefits of the domain's user and group database.

A Windows NT computer participating in a workgroup has its own database of users and processes logon requests by itself. Computers in a workgroup do not share account information. On a workgroup computer, Windows NT logs on or gives rights only to those user accounts created at that computer.

A review of domains

In a Windows NT Server environment, a domain is the basic unit of security and centralized administration. A domain consists of one or more servers running Windows NT Server, and all of the servers in a domain function as a single system. Optionally, a domain can also include LAN Manager 2.x servers, Windows NT workstations, and other workstations such as those running Windows for Workgroups and MS-DOS.

Domains and trusts

Trusts are administration and communication links between two domains. A trust relationship between two domains enables user accounts and global groups to be used in a domain other than the domain where these accounts are located.

There are two major benefits of trusted domains. First, users only need one user name and password to access resources across multiple domains. Second, you can administer multiple domains from a central location.

To support a tiered administration model such as a trusted domain, Windows NT uses three forms of security accounts:

■ **User accounts.** Each user of the system has a user account for his or her personal use. User accounts have passwords that prevent other users from using them.

You can define user accounts on a local computer level and on a domain. Accounts defined on a local computer can only be used on that computer. Accounts defined on a domain level can be used at any computer in that domain.

- **Global group accounts.** Global groups are defined at domain level (this implies that there is at least one Windows NT server in the collection of computers). A global group may have user accounts from the same domain as members of the global group.

- **Local group accounts.** Local groups are defined on each computer. Local groups may have both user accounts *and* global groups as members. Furthermore, the user accounts and global groups may exist as domain level accounts.

From a security standpoint, user accounts are the basic unit (identifying one individual) for which it is possible to grant or revoke permissions. You can use global groups as a convenient way of setting group-wide access permissions across multiple domains. You can also use local groups as a convenient way of setting group-wide access permissions on resources on the local domain.

Security in a stand-alone configuration

As noted earlier, a stand-alone Windows NT workstation is a special case of a workgroup consisting of one computer. This is not the most popular way of running Windows NT, but it is a requirement for some organizations because they only have to contend with securing individual workstations. Remember, unlike older desktop operating systems such as MS-DOS and OS/2, Windows NT provides local security. Even on a stand-alone computer, Windows NT has built-in logon and access control.

Security in a workgroup configuration

A *workgroup* is simply an organizational unit — a way to group workstations that do not belong to a domain. For Windows NT computers, each workstation that participates in a workgroup maintains its own security policy and security account databases.

For a computer running Windows NT and participating in a workgroup, the system compares the logon information with the local user accounts database. When a user logs on to Windows NT, the From box in the logon dialog box lists only the name of the local computer. The user cannot specify another workgroup or domain for logon.

After successful validation, the user name and password are cached by the computer's redirector for use when connecting to remote resources.

A Windows NT computer not participating in a domain does not interact with domains at all. You create user accounts and local groups on the workstation itself, but these are the only users and groups that the workstation can use. Simply put, the computer cannot use user accounts or global groups from any domain, and a user logged on through a local computer account cannot access any server running Windows NT domain server, except as a guest.

Security in a domain configuration

An important aspect of running Windows NT Server in a domain configuration is that you can perform security administration for Windows NT Servers and Windows NT workstations. This is the recommended solution unless you have only a handful of Windows NT workstations.

At a Windows NT workstation participating in a domain, users can log on to user accounts located in the workstation's domain (or in any domain that the workstation's domain trusts). Furthermore, you can place users and global groups from the domain (and domains trusted by the workstation's domain) in local groups on the workstation, and assign permissions and rights on the workstation to users and global groups from the domain (and domains trusted by the workstation's domain).

Even though a computer participating in a domain can use accounts located in that domain, you can still create user accounts on that computer. Any accounts created on that computer are local to that computer and cannot be used on any other computer. One valid use of this might be when you want to make resources belonging to a workgroup computer available to someone who does not need access to domain resources. For example, you may want to share files on the workstation with users who do not have a domain account.

By default, when a Windows NT Workstation computer joins a domain, the system adds the domain's Domain Admins global group to the workstation's Administrators local group. This allows you, the domain administrator, to manage the Windows NT workstations in the domain.

Domain Administration

Where possible, use the built-in local groups and divide the network administration responsibility. The fewer accounts in the Administrators or Domain Admins group, the better.

A user account consists of all the information that defines a user to Windows NT. Table 11-2 shows the properties of each user account.

Managing user profiles

One of the most powerful tools that you can use to manage user environments is *user profiles*. A profile is a file that serves as a snapshot of a user's desktop environment, defining the Program Manager groups and program items in those groups, printer connections, window size and positioning, and screen colors. With profiles, you can also restrict users' ability to change these settings on their own workstations.

Table 11-2	Domain Account User Properties
Account element	***Comment***
User name	The unique name that the user types when logging on; often a combination of parts of the user's first and last names.
Password	The user's secret password.
Full name	The user's full name.
Logon hours	The hours during which the user can log on. This affects a user's ability to log on to the network and to access servers. You can force users to log off when their logon hours expire by setting parameters in the domain's security policy.
Logon workstations	The computer names of the workstations from which a user can work. By default, the user can use any workstation, but administrators can limit this if they want.
Expiration date	A future date when the account automatically becomes disabled; it is useful to ensure that accounts for temporary employees or students are not kept active unnecessarily.
Home directory	A directory on the server that is private to the user; the user controls access to this directory.
Logon script	A batch file or executable file that runs automatically when the user logs on.
Profile	A file containing a record of the user's desktop environment, such as program groups, network connections, screen colors, and settings determining what aspects of the environment the user can change.
Account type	The account type is either global or local. Most accounts that administrators create are global accounts. This option is available only on Windows NT Server domains.

Cross
Reference

For more information about user profiles, refer to Chapter 9, *Controlling User Environments*.

Using Profiles to Restrict Access

Using personal or mandatory profiles, you can prevent the user from doing one or more of the following:

■ Creating program items

■ Creating program groups

■ Changing the contents of program groups

■ Changing program item properties (such as the application that a program item starts)

■ Running programs from the File menu in Program Manager

■ Making connections to network printers (other than those printers to which the profile itself makes connections)

Tip

Imposing some or all of these restrictions on users is very useful in an environment where you want a high level of security. In a high security environment, you should create a single mandatory profile for each type of job and then assign that profile to all users who fit the job description.

Logon Scripts

Another way that you can enhance user environments is by assigning *logon scripts* to users. If a user has a logon script, that script runs whenever a user logs on at any type of workstation on the network. A script is simply a batch file containing operating system commands (such as commands to make network connections or start applications) or an executable program.

Home Directories

You may also choose to give each user a *home directory* on a server or workstation. A user's home directory gives that user private storage space. Each user has control over the contents of and access to his or her home directory.

Security Accounts

In most situations where you are the system administrator of a particular computer, you are also the primary user of that computer. Yet, in an organization, there is an overall need to centralize administration of user and group accounts. To support this dichotomy of administrative authority, Windows NT uses a tiered approach to account management. The computer administrator may define user accounts and group accounts for use only at that computer. As the central administrator or domain administrator, you can define users and groups for use on any computer in the domain.

How global groups and local groups differ

Although global and local groups serve similar functions, different rules apply to their creation and use. For example,

If you create a global group in Domain A, it can contain only users from Domain A, and any domain that trusts Domain A can use that global group.

If you create a local group in Domain A, it can contain users and global groups from Domain A and any domain that Domain A trusts. However, only servers residing in Domain A can use the local group created on Domain A.

In addition, the account database of a Windows NT computer can have only local groups — global groups do not exist on Windows NT computers. Consequently, a Windows NT computer's local groups can have rights and permissions only on that workstation.

 The names *global group* and *local group* denote where the group can have rights and permissions (the group's *scope*), not the contents of the group. Local groups can contain global groups, but global groups cannot contain either local groups or other global groups.

Using Global and Local Groups

To make the network simpler to administer and easier to maintain, you should employ some strategies for using global groups and local groups.

If you divide domains so that each one represents a division or department within your company, you can think of a global group as being a group of users from the same department. Using this division of domains, you can assign permissions and rights in other domains to groups of users. Furthermore, you can export this group as a single unit to other domains (and to Windows NT computers). Another benefit to creating domains that correspond to departments is that the domain name precedes the group name when it appears in management tools and applications. This way, you know the type of people that group represents (by the group name) and the origin or location of that group (by the domain name).

A local group can include users and global groups from other domains, providing a way to import users and global groups into a single unit for use in the local domain. As an example, suppose that the domain Publishing has a server with a shared directory containing documents that explain new titles that the company is investigating. Managers in other departments (domains) in the company are interested in seeing these documents. As the network administrator, you can arrange this by doing the following:

- Creating global groups in the other domains (such as Marketing\Managers and Sales\Managers)

- Putting the Marketing\Managers and Sales\Managers global groups in the All Managers local group

- In the Publishing domain, creating a local group called All Managers

- Granting permission to read the files in the directory to All Managers

In this example, you could just give permission to read the files to each of the Managers global groups from the other domains and bypass the step of creating the local group. However, in many cases, creating the local group saves time later. For example, suppose that you later add two new directories containing files interesting to managers. If the All Managers local group does not exist, you would have to grant access for the new directories to all of the Managers global groups, instead of just the single local group. This would take a lot of time if the All Managers local group contains many global groups, instead of just the two in this example.

As this example shows, a local group is a way of assembling global groups and assigning all permissions to them in one step. This way, if another global group later needs the same permissions as some existing global groups, you can just add the new global group to the appropriate local group, and it has all of the permissions that it needs. Table 11-3 provides guidelines on which type of group to use and when to use it.

Table 11-3	Local and Global Group Strategies	
Group type	*Purpose of group*	*Comments*
Local	Contain other groups, including users from multiple domains	The local group can contain only global groups (and users); however, no group can contain other local groups. If it is necessary to be able to grant permissions in multiple domains to this local group, you must create manually the local group in every domain in which it is needed. Need permissions and rights in only one domain.
Global	Group users of this domain into a single unit for use in other domains	The global group can be put into local groups or given permissions and rights directly in other domains. A domain's global groups can be given permissions on Windows NT workstations, but a domain's local groups cannot. Need permissions on Windows NT workstations.

Built-in accounts

When you install Windows NT Server or Windows NT Workstation, several default user, global group, and local group accounts are installed into the computer's account database. The following sections explain each of these built-in accounts and how to use them in the administration of a Windows NT network.

Built-in User Accounts

Two default user accounts exist initially on every Windows NT Server and Windows NT computer: Administrator and Guest.

The Administrator account is one that you use when you administer a new server or workstation for the first time. You cannot delete or disable the Administrator account, which ensures that you can never lock yourself out of the computer.

The Guest account allows for *guest logons* by people who do not have an account on the computer, in the computer's domain, or in any of the domains trusted by the computer's domain.

Managing Guest Logons

The Guest account has no password. You use it for two types of guest logons: local guest logons and network guest logon. You can configure each workstation and domain so that it allows both types of guest logons, only one type, or no guest logon at all.

By default, Windows NT disables the Guest account on a Windows NT Server domain. If you want to allow both local and remote guest logons, use User Manager For Domains to enable the Guest account. To allow local guest logons but not network guest logons, enable the Guest account but revoke its Access This Computer From Network right. And to allow network guest logons but not local guest logons, enable the Guest account and revoke its Log On Locally right.

Managing guest logons on a Windows NT workstation works the same way, except that the Guest account is enabled by default. If you want to allow guest logons on the workstation, you need do nothing. If you want to prevent guest logons, you must disable the Guest account.

Built-in Global Groups

Windows NT Server has two permanent built-in global groups: Domain Admins and Domain Users.

Domain Admins initially contains the Administrator account. When creating accounts for individuals to act as administrators of the domain, you should add these accounts to the Domain Admins global group, instead of just putting them into the Administrators local group. This provides a global group that represents all administrators in the domain. You can then put this global group in the Administrators local group of any other domain or any Windows NT workstation that this domain's administrators need to administer.

Domain Users initially contains the Administrator and Guest accounts. Every user account that you subsequently add to a domain automatically becomes a part of the Domain Users global group.

Built-in Local Groups

Windows NT Server and Windows NT Workstation create several default local groups during installation. Membership in these local groups gives a user certain powers, as discussed in *What different types of users can do*, later in this chapter.

In addition to these local groups, there is an identity called *Everyone*. This identity represents all people on the network, including administrators, all types of operators, users, users from other domains, and guests. Administrators cannot change the membership of Everyone— it always automatically contains all users.

Note

Everyone is not actually a local group and does not appear in the User Manager list of groups, but you can assign file permissions to Everyone (in File Manager). You can also assign rights to Everyone (in the Rights dialog box in User Manager for Domains).

Using the Built-in Global and Local Groups

The general strategies discussed so far for using global and local groups also apply to the built-in global and local group. The Administrators local group and Domain Admins global group serve as an example of how these strategies can apply locally or globally.

Being a member of the Administrators local group is what actually makes an account an administrator on a domain or Windows NT workgroup. However, when you create an account on a Windows NT domain, there are two ways to make that account an administrator:

1. Place the account directly into the Administrators local group

2. Put the account in the Domain Admins global group, which is, in turn, a member of the Administrators local group.

Tip

I strongly recommend that you always use the second method: Put the account in the Domain Admins global group. This way, you have a global group that represents all administrators in the domain. You can then put this global group in the Administrators local group of any other domain or any Windows NT workstation that this domain's administrators need to administer.

Every domain also has a Domain Users global group. When you create user accounts in the domain, they are placed in the Domain Users group by default. The Domain Users global group is automatically a member of the Users local group in the same domain and also is a member of the Users local group on all Windows NT workstations participating in the domain.

Domain Admins and Domain Users are the only built-in global groups that correspond to built-in local groups. You can create other global groups that correspond to local groups, if you want to use the same strategies for those types of users. For example, you may want to create a Domain BackupOps global group for the domain's backup operators. Then, if this domain's backup operators need to back up files on a Windows NT workstation or in another domain, you can add the BackupOps global group to the workstation's or domain's Backup Operators local group.

What different types of users can do

Each user account is, most likely, a member of one or more built-in local groups. As a member of one of the built-in local groups of a domain, a user has rights to perform various tasks on servers in the domain. Similarly, being a member of a built-in group on a workstation gives the user rights on that workstation.

For each built-in local group, some rights are inherent to the local group and you cannot change them, whereas you can alter other powers (those granted to the local group via *user rights*). The tables in this section give an overview of the rights of all of the built-in local groups, on both Windows NT Server domains and Windows NT workstations. The sections following these tables provide more details about the most popular local groups.

As an administrator, you can add a user to more than one built-in group. In this case, the user has all of the abilities granted to all of the groups. For example, a user in both the Print Operators and Backup Operators groups has all of the rights granted to print operators and all of the rights granted to backup operators.

Note that not all of the built-in local groups exist on both Windows NT Server domains and Windows NT workstations. Table 11-4 shows which built-in local groups exist on domains and which exist on Windows NT workstations.

Table 11-4	Built-in Local Groups
Windows NT Server domains	*Windows NT workstations*
Administrator	Administrators
Backup Operators	Backup Operators
Server Operators	Power Users
Account Operators	Users
Print Operators	Guests
Users	Replication
Guests	
Replicator	

Table 11-5 shows which rights and built-in abilities are held by each built-in local group on Windows NT Servers and Windows NT workstations.

Administrators

Accounts in the Administrators local group have the right to do almost anything on computers running Windows NT. This includes creating, deleting, and managing user accounts and local groups; sharing directories and printers; granting resource permissions and rights to users; and installing operating system files and programs.

Table 11-5	**Abilities of Built-in Local Groups on Windows NT Servers and Windows NT Workstations**		
User rights	**Comments**	**Group granted to (on Windows NT Servers)**	**Group granted to (on Windows NT workstations)**
Manage auditing and security log	Specify what types of events and file access are to be audited; view and clear the security log	Administrators	Administrators
Back up files and directories		Administrators, Server Operators, Backup Operators	Administrators, Backup Operators
Restore files and directories	Note that this right supersedes file permissions; a user with the Restore right can overwrite files for which he or she has no permissions, when performing a restore	Administrators, Server Operators, Backup Operators	Administrators, Backup Operators
Change system time		Administrators, Server Operators	Administrators, Power Users
Access this computer from network	Access the computer from another workstation on the network	Administrators, Everyone	Administrators, Power Users, Everyone
Log on locally	Ability to log on at the computer itself using the computer's keyboard	Administrators, Server Operators, Account Operators, Print Operators, Backup Operators	Administrators, Backup Operators, Power Users, Users, Guests
Shut down the system		Administrators, Server Operators, Account Operators, Print Operators, Backup Operators	Administrators, Backup Operators, Power Users, Users, Guests
Take ownership of files and other objects	Take ownership of files and directories on the computer	Administrators	Administrators
Force shutdown from a remote system	This right gives a user no abilities in this version of Windows NT, but will be supported in future upgrades of the operating system	Administrators, Server Operators	Administrators, Power Users

Note

Unlike the security in traditional operating systems such as NetWare or LAN Manager 2.x, administrators (equivalent to the Supervisor in NetWare) do not automatically have access to every file on a server. File permissions must specifically grant access to an administrator, or the administrator cannot access the file. Every file on an NTFS volume has an *owner*, who can set permissions on the file. When a user creates a file, that user becomes its owner. This means that any user can protect files from the computer or network administrator.

Administrator Logons

As an administrator, you often have two roles — you are an administrator and a user. Sometimes, you perform administrative tasks; other times, you perform the same tasks as other users.

For this reason, it is a good idea for you to have two user accounts. Create one account in the Administrators group and use it when performing management tasks. Create the other account in the Users group and use it whenever you are not performing management or administrative tasks.

Having two accounts as an administrator makes the network and computer more secure. While logged on as a regular user, you cannot accidentally change aspects of the network that only administrators can change. For example, if you should happen to introduce a virus or Trojan horse while running under an ordinary user account, the system has more protection. While running under an ordinary users account, that program does not have the rights of an administrator and, therefore, cannot modify operating system software.

Running under two accounts is extra work because you have to log off and then log on again before you can administer the network. However, the peace of mind you get from knowing that you have a more secure environment is worth it.

Users

Most user accounts that you create as an administrator exist in the Users local group and represent typical users of the computer or network. Most user accounts that you create as an administrator are of this type. As such, these users can only access servers in the domain over the network. They cannot log directly on to the servers and work at them. User accounts also have other characteristics (such as time restrictions) that limit how a user can use the account.

A member of the Users local group of a Windows NT Workstation computer can do the following:

- Log on at the computer and use it to access the network
- Lock and shut down the computer
- Keep a profile at the computer

- Create and delete local groups on the computer

- Modify the membership of the local groups that he or she has created (but cannot modify built-in local groups or local groups created by anyone else)

Server Operators

The Server Operators local group exists only on servers running Windows NT Server computers, not on Windows NT Workstation computers. The basic mission of server operators is to keep network servers running.

Accounts in the Server Operators local group have many of the same powers as administrators, except that they cannot manage security on the server. Specifically, server operators can do the following:

- Share and stop sharing a server's files and printers

- Lock or override the lock of a server

- Format the server's disks

- Log on at servers, back up and restore servers' files, and shut down servers

Account Operators

The Account Operators local group exists only on servers running Windows NT Server, not on Windows NT Workstation computers.

Accounts in the Account Operators local group on a server can manage the server's user and group accounts. An account operator can create, delete, and modify almost all users, global groups, and local groups. However, account operators cannot modify the user accounts of Administrators, nor can they modify the Administrators, Server Operators, Account Operators, Print Operators, or Backup Operators local groups. They also cannot assign user rights.

Print Operators

The Print Operators local group exists only on servers running Windows NT Server, not on Windows NT Workstation computers.

Accounts in the Print Operators local group can share printers, stop sharing printers, and manage printers shared at servers running Windows NT Server. They can also log on locally at servers and shut them down.

If you want a domain's print operators to administer printers managed by Windows NT Workstation computers in the domain, as well as printers managed by the domain's servers, perform the following steps:

1. Create a Domain PrintOps global group in the domain. Make this global group a member of the domain's Print Operators local group.

2. Add the user account of each print operator to the Domain PrintOps global group.

3. On each workstation that manages printers, put the Domain PrintOps global group in the workstation's Power Users local group.

Backup Operators

Accounts in the Backup Operators local group on a server or workstation can back up and restore the computer's files, log on locally at the computer, and shut down the computer.

Power Users

The Power Users local group exists only on Windows NT workstations, not on servers running Windows NT Server.

A member of the Power Users local group can do everything that a member of Users can. In addition, a Power Users member can create user accounts; modify the user accounts he or she has created; put any user accounts on the workstation into the Power Users, Users, and Guests built-in groups; and share and stop sharing files and printers located at the workstation.

Tip

Because the Power Users group exists on Windows NT workstations but not on Windows NT Servers, you should put the domain account of each user into the Power Users group on the user's workstation. For example, by putting the domain account in the Power Users group on the user's workstation and on the domain's servers, that user automatically becomes a member of the Users group. This allows the user to have more control over their own workstation and to share files with other users, but on the domain's servers, that user is a typical user with no extra abilities.

In general, the account of every average user will automatically be in the Users group on the domain itself. On each user's workstation, administrators can decide whether to put the user's domain account in the Power Users group (for more workstation control) or Users group (for less control). This decision depends on how much central control of the workstation you want to have. If administrators do not want users creating shares on the workstations, they should not add their domain accounts to the Power Users group.

Note that because the Power Users group exists only on Windows NT workstations and not on Windows NT Server domains, the concept of Power Users has no meaning for users who have MS-DOS workstations.

Guests

On a Windows NT Server, members of Guests have the same rights as Users; both groups have only the right to access the server over the network and cannot log on locally at the server.

On Windows NT workstations guests have fewer rights than users. Users can keep a local profile on the workstation; lock the workstation; and create, delete, and modify local groups. Guests can do none of these.

Account policies

The day-to-day activity of a user is influenced by the security policy implemented at that site. The following guidelines should help administrators keep their environment/site operating with a high degree of security.

Granting and Revoking System Access

Assigning a user initial access to Windows NT resources involves the creation of a user account. As a part of your company's security policy, you should create accounts only for users authorized by management. When a user terminates employment or transfers, you should modify or revoke access privileges. The primary goal of timely revocation of system access rights is to prevent abuse of access rights by the departed employee or others.

Note

Windows NT provides the capability to disable a user account without destroying it. This is very useful if an organization needs some administration time before the account is deleted properly.

Passwords

A good password policy helps users protect their passwords from other individuals. This helps to reduce the probability of someone logging on with another's password and gaining unauthorized access to data.

The following tips are all pretty obvious but worth noting for the record. You can provide them in printed form to all new users.

- Do not write down passwords.

- Do not divulge passwords to anyone else.

- Do not use obvious passwords such as your own name, spouse's name, or the names of your children, dogs, cats, and so on.

- Do not distribute user accounts and passwords in the same communication. For example, if administrators are sending a new user's account name and password in writing, send the user name and password at different times.

Enforcing password policies

There are a number of ways you can enforce a password policy and thus provide better protection for unauthorized use of passwords:

- When you create a new account, force the user to change his or her password at the first logon. This ensures that the administrator/supervisor does not know the user's password.

- Enforce a reasonable minimum password length, which thereby increases the number of permutations needed to guess someone's password randomly or programmatically.

- Enforce a maximum and minimum password age to make sure that users do not keep a password for too long. This policy protects against someone looking over a person's shoulder over a period of time and learning the password by remembering the keystrokes. Minimum password age prevents a user from immediately reverting back to a previous password.

- Enforce password uniqueness and history. This prevents users from toggling between their favorite passwords. Administrators can specify the number of unique passwords that users must have before reusing a password.

User Rights

It would be ideal to have only one form of access control to worry about within Windows NT. However, there are many cases where a purely discretionary access control system would be very cumbersome. In all practicality, another means of access control is needed to build a truly usable system.

User Rights protect activities that do not neatly fit within the discretionary access control model. For example, there is a right that allows the administrator to take ownership of other people's files. An administrator of the system has the authority to assign individual User Rights to users or groups of users and can grant someone the Take Ownership Of Files And Objects Right. It allows a user to take ownership of a departed employee's files. The administrator could also take ownership of the files and then grant other users permission to access the files. In either case, this registers a Take Ownership event in the audit log.

What are user rights?

Administrators can directly manipulate *user rights* (also called *rights* or *privileges*), which specify what actions local groups, global groups, and users can perform. However, I recommend that administrators do this rarely, if ever. Instead, use the predefined local groups and their predetermined sets of rights—these groups should serve most needs.

User rights control who can perform specific types of actions on servers running Windows NT Server and Windows NT workstations. These actions include logging on locally at the computer, shutting it down, setting its time, backing up and restoring the server's files, and performing other tasks.

On Windows NT Server, you grant and restrict on the domain level; if a group has a right in a domain, its members have that right on all servers in the domain (but not on Windows NT workgroup computers participating in the domain). On each Windows NT computer, rights granted apply only to that single computer. Table 11-6 describes the default user rights on Windows NT computers.

Table 11-6 Default Granted Rights on Windows NT Computers

User rights	Comments	Granted to (on Windows NT Servers)	Granted to (on Windows NT Workstations)
Manage auditing and security log	Specify what types of events and file access are to be audited; view and clear the security log	Administrators	Administrators
Back up files and directories		Administrators, Server Operators, Backup Operators	Administrators, Backup Operators
Restore files and directories	Note that this right supersedes file permissions; a user with the Restore right can overwrite files for which he or she has no permissions, when performing a restore	Administrators, Server Operators, Backup Operators	Administrators, Backup Operators
Change system time		Administrators, Server Operators	Administrators, Power Users
Access this computer from the network	Access the computer from another work-station on the network	Administrators, Everyone	Administrators, Power Users, Everyone
Log on locally	Ability to log on at the computer itself, on the computer's keyboard	Administrators, Server Operators, Account Operators, Print Operators, Backup Operators	Administrators, Backup Operators, Power Users, Users, Guests
Shut down the system		Administrators, Server Operators, Account Operators, Print Operators, Backup Operators	Administrators, Backup Operators, Power Users, Users, Guests
Take ownership of files and other objects	Take ownership of files and directories on the computer	Administrators	Administrators
Force shutdown from a remote system	This right gives a user no abilities in this version of Windows NT, but will be supported in future upgrades of the operating system	Administrators, Server Operators	Administrators, Power Users

As a member of the Administrators group, you can grant or revoke rights to and from users and global groups. Some user groups have abilities that you cannot control directly — Windows NT grants these abilities to some built-in local groups during installation. The only way for you to grant a user one of these built-in abilities is to make that user a member of the appropriate local group. For example, the only way to allow a person to create user accounts on a Windows NT Server is to make that person a member of either the Administrators or Account Operators local groups on the server.

Granting user rights

All accounts have some form of built-in rights. However, depending on the size of your installation you might find it necessary and, in some cases, desirable to delegate some administrative tasks to other people in your organization. Some commonly delegated tasks are backing up and restoring files, adding new user accounts to the system, and starting and stopping resource sharing. Certain of these administrative tasks require users to have special privileges.

The principle of "least privileges" is based on the idea that the users and the processes in the system should have only the privileges needed to do their work — and for the shortest amount of time possible. An administrator might, for example, grant a user the right to take ownership of a group of files. You can audit when and of which files the user takes ownership to ensure that the user only takes ownership of the files specified by the administrator. You should revoke the take ownership right when the user has finished the task.

Customizing rights

Even though you cannot change the built-in abilities of the default local groups, you can use other methods to control them. For example, if you do not want anyone in the Power Users group to add user accounts to a Windows NT computer's local account database, you should secure the User Manager program file (MUSMGR.EXE) with permissions that do not allow Power Users to execute this application.

Protecting Windows NT Configuration

One of the major costs of supporting a large installation of PCs is maintenance of the configuration of the computers. However, with traditional operating systems such as MS-DOS and OS/2, the organization has very few options for making sure that the known working configuration is not altered by the users. Alterations in a PC's configuration might require a technician to fix the configuration problem. Hence, many organizations are not only concerned with securing confidential data but also with securing configuration data on workstations and servers.

File systems and security

Windows NT supports three file systems: the Windows NT File System (NTFS), the file allocation table (FAT) file system, and the high-performance file system (HPFS). A computer running Windows NT can use one or more of these file systems on its disks and partitions. Administrators must choose which file system(s) to use on each Windows NT computer.

When choosing file systems for a Windows NT computer, use the following guidelines:

- If you require maximum security (local and remote) and the computer does not need to boot MS-DOS or OS/2 in addition to Windows NT, use only NTFS on the computer.

- If the computer does need to boot MS-DOS or OS/2, maintain the current file system (either MS-DOS or HPFS) on drive C. You may optionally put NTFS on additional partitions on the computer, as long as those users do not need to read those partitions under MS-DOS or OS/2 operating systems. Of course, MS-DOS and OS/2 applications can still read and write files created on an NTFS partition.

When choosing file system(s) for servers, use the following guidelines:

- For an x86-based computer, Windows NT looks for certain files in the root directory of drive C at startup, so format this partition with the NTFS, HPFS, or FAT file system. Make sure the partition is large enough to accommodate all of the files users need to access under that file system.

- For a RISC-based computer, format the system partition for the FAT file system. (However, on an ARC system, there is local security on this FAT partition.) If you require NTFS, create a second partition large enough to contain everything you want to protect with Windows NT security.

Table 11-7 describes the advantages and disadvantages of each of the three file systems as they relate to security.

Table 11-7   File System Advantages and Disadvantages

File system	Advantages	Disadvantages
Windows NT File System (NTFS)	Supports complete Windows NT security, so you can specify who has various kinds of access to a file or directory. This "discretionary access control" is available for files on NTFS partitions.	

File system	Advantages	Disadvantages
	Keeps a log of activities to restore the disk in event of power failure or other problems.	
	Supports the fault-tolerance capabilities of Windows NT.	
	Supports file and directory names of up to 256 characters and supports extended file attributes. Automatically generates correct MS-DOS filenames so that files can be shared with MS-DOS users.	
	A program designed to run under other operating systems such as MS-DOS can access NTFS files when running under Windows NT.	
		Recognized only by Windows NT. When the computer is running another operating system (such as MS-DOS or OS/2), that operating system cannot access files on an NTFS partition.
		If you format drive C for NTFS, you cannot run MS-DOS from your hard disk (but you can still run MS-DOS-based applications).
File allocation table (FAT)	The most widely-used file system for PCs, files can be accessed when your computer is running another operating system, such as MS-DOS or OS/2.	
		You must use FAT on the partition for drive C if you want to run MS-DOS from the hard disk. Floppy disks or removable hard disks for sharing data between computers must use FAT. Remote security is available only at a share level.

(continued)

Table 11-7 *(Continued)*

File system	Advantages	Disadvantages
		Files on a FAT partition are not protected by the local security features of Windows NT.
		Files on a FAT partition are restricted to 8-character file-names with 3-character file-name extensions. Cannot support large files.
		Less robust than NTFS; for example, no automatic disk restore features.
High-performance file system (HPFS)	Created for and used by the OS/2 operating system, version 1.2 and higher.	
	Supports long filenames.	
	Provides better error correction than does the FAT file system.	Remote security is available only at a share level. Has not been widely adopted.
		Files on an HPFS partition are not protected by Windows NT local security.
		On HPFS volumes, MS-DOS and Windows 3.1-based applications cannot access files with long filenames or with long directory names in their paths.

Default Directory Permissions

When you create a new subdirectory or file on an NTFS volume, you can set permissions at the file level. If you do not specify permissions, the new subdirectory or file inherits the permissions of the directory containing it. Table 11-8 lists the default directory permissions for an NTFS partition on both Windows NT Server and a Windows NT workstation. A thorough understanding of the default permission serves as a good springboard to running your system with a high degree of integrity.

Table 11-8	Default Directory Permissions						
Enables use	**Full access**	**Change**	**RWXD**	**Read**	**RWX**	**List**	**No access**
\(Root directories of all NTFS volumes)							
Administrators	X						
Server Operators		X					
Everyone		X					
CREATOR OWNER	X						
\SYSTEM32							
Administrators	X						
Server Operators		X					
Everyone		X					
CREATOR OWNER	X						
\SYSTEM32\CONFIG							
Administrators	X						
Everyone						X	
CREATOR OWNER	X						
\SYSTEM32\DRIVERS							
Administrators	X						
Server Operators	X						
Everyone				X			
CREATOR OWNER	X						
\SYSTEM32\SPOOL							
Administrators	X						
Server Operators	X						
Print Operators	X						
Everyone				X			
CREATOR OWNER	X						
\SYSTEM32\REPL							
Administrators	X						
Server Operators	X						
Everyone				X			

(continued)

Table 11-8 *(Continued)*

Enables use	Full access	Change	RWXD	Read	RWX	List	No access
CREATOR OWNER	X						
\SYSTEM32\REPL\EXPORT							
Administrators	X						
Server Operators		X					
CREATOR OWNER	X						
Replicator				X			
\SYSTEM32\REPL\IMPORT							
Administrators	X						
Server Operators		X					
Everyone				X			
CREATOR OWNER	X						
Replicator		X					
NETWORK							X
\USERS							
Administrators			X				
Account Operators			X				
Everyone						X	
\USERS\DEFAULT							
Everyone					X		
CREATOR OWNER	X						
\WIN32APP							
Administrators	X						
Server Operators		X					
CREATOR OWNER	X						
Everyone		X					

LEGEND: R=Read; W=Write; X=Execute; D=Delete; Change=Same as Read, but includes running the file, displaying the file's owner and permissions, and changing the file's attributes; Read=Display the file's data and attributes; List=View the directory; No Access=Does not allow any access; Full Access=All of the preceding, as well as changing data in a file and appending data to a file

In addition to these permissions, the special identity SYSTEM, which represents the operating system, has Full Control permission for all of these directories.

Caution

As an administrator of Windows NT Workstation or Windows NT Server, you should not revoke any of these default permissions. If you revoke the permissions, parts of the operating system may not work. Furthermore, you should not use File Manager to examine the permissions on the SYSTEM32\REPL\IMPORT directory or you could lose the special permissions initially set. These initial permissions enable directory replication to work, and you do not need to change them.

Configuration management and Windows NT applications

Windows NT automatically applies security to certain applications that change the system configuration. Most of these applications require that a user have administrative privileges before he or she can run them. However, there are some cases where it's necessary to apply additional security to satisfy special needs.

The following section discusses applications that you may need to secure with extra permissions above and beyond the default settings. The discussion focuses on applications that modify configuration data that affect the system regardless of who is logged on locally.

Registry Database and Security

The Registry database and the Registry Editor deserve special attention. The Registry database is the single location in Windows NT that stores configuration information for the entire Windows NT operating system. For the most part, the default security in the Registry is more than adequate to protect important configuration data from malicious or accidental damage. However, it is important to understand which applications alter configuration data and how to customize Windows NT to guard against such events.

The Registry Editor application, REGEDT32.EXE, does not appear in any default program groups in Program Manager, although it installs automatically when you install Windows NT.

Users can seriously impair or disable Windows NT with incorrect changes or accidental deletions if they use the Registry Editor to change the system's configuration. Do not allow users to log on as members of the administrative group unless a specific individual has administrative duties.

Tip

Never keep REGEDT32.EXE on workstations, since you can easily administer any workstation from a remote computer. Alternatively, you can use File Manager to place access controls on REGEDT32.EXE, limiting the rights of users to start this application.

Program Manager

One of the first decisions you should make is what restrictions to place on users' desktops (Program Manager). You may want to prevent users from creating, deleting, or renaming program groups. Ordinarily, you would use the User Profile Editor. However, you might have to use the Registry Editor to accomplish the same task or to troubleshoot problems for users. The following section describes the Registry entries that govern Program Manager restrictions.

Restrictions entries for Program Manager

The Restrictions subkey defines restrictions for activities in Program Manager. The subkey is under this Registry path:

```
Software\Microsoft\Windows NT\CurrentVersion\Program
Manager\Restrictions
```

EditLevel REG_DWORD *Number* sets restrictions for what users can modify in Program Manager. Administrators can specify one of the values in Table 11-9.

Table 11-9	Program Manager Edit Level Restrictions
Value	*Meaning*
0	Allows the user to make any change. This is the default value.
1	Prevents the user from creating, deleting, or renaming groups. If this value is specified, the New, Move, Copy, and Delete commands on the File menu are not available when a group is selected.
2	Sets all restrictions in EditLevel=1 and prevents the user from creating or deleting program items. If this value is specified, the New, Move, Copy, and Delete commands on the File menu are not available at all.
3	Sets all restrictions in EditLevel=2 and prevents the user from changing command lines for program items. If this value is specified, the text in the Command Line box in the Properties dialog box cannot be changed.
4	Sets all restrictions in EditLevel=3 and prevents the user from changing any program item information. If this value is specified, none of the areas in the Properties dialog box can be modified. The user can view the dialog box, but all of the areas are dimmed.
NoClose REG_DWORD	Disables the Exit Windows command on the File menu if this value is 1. Users cannot quit Program Manager through the File or Control menu (the Exit Windows and Close commands appear dimmed), or by using Alt+F4. The default is 0.

Value	Meaning
NoFileMenu REG_DWORD	Removes the File menu from Program Manager if this value is 1. All of the commands on that menu are unavailable. Users can start the applications in groups by selecting them and pressing Enter or by double-clicking the icon. Unless you also disable the Exit Windows command, users can still quit Windows by using the Control menu or Alt+F4. The default is 0.
NoRun REG_DWORD	Disables the Run command on the File menu if this value is 1. The Run command appears dimmed on the File menu, and the user cannot run applications from Program Manager unless the application's icon shows in a group. The default is 0.
NoSaveSettings REG_DWORD	Disables the Save Settings on Exit command on the Options menu if this value is 1. The Save Settings command appears dimmed on the Options menu, and any changes the user makes to the arrangement of windows and icons are not saved when Windows NT is restarted. This setting overrides the SaveSettings value in the Program Manager subkey. The default is 0.
Restrictions REG_DWORD	Turns restrictions on or off. If the value is 1, restrictions are turned off. The default is 0.
ShowCommonGroups REG_DWORD	Controls whether Program Manager shows common program groups. If the value is 1, Program Manager shows restrictions. The default is 0.

The Main group

You can impose further restrictions on applications that can be run from built-in tools such as the Control Panel.

Control Panel

There are a number of applications in the Control Panel that can alter the system's configuration. Some options in the Control Panel require users to log on as a member of a specific group. If a user is not a member of the necessary group, an access denied message appears. Even so, administrators may not want users to have access to all of the applications in the Control Panel. The only applications that a user with no administrative duties should ever need to access are the ones that allow customization of personal profiles. These are the Desktop, Color, International, and Cursors applications.

As the administrator, you can customize a desktop to create a program group that contains only the Control Panel applications that you want to allow users to access. Users have access to the applications shown, but they do not have any access to run the other Control Panel applications. Used in conjunction with Program Manager restriction techniques, you can prevent users from modifying these groups. However, users still have permission to run CONTROL.EXE (the Control Panel). Therefore, to further secure CONTROL.EXE, administrators must remove the Control Panel from Program Manager and place execute restrictions on File Manager and Command Prompt. This prevents users from double-clicking on the Control Panel icon or running CONTROL.EXE from the command line.

You can create a new program group by adding program items that pass parameters to CONTROL.EXE, the Control Panel application. For example, to have the Desktop application invoked when a user double-clicks on the Desktop icon, the command line in the Program Item Properties dialog box should be CONTROL.EXE MAIN.CPL desktop. MAIN.CPL is the Control Panel application that has code for the color, fonts, ports, mouse, desktop, keyboard, printer, international, system, and date/time applications.

After creating the new program item, the default icon is the icon for the Control Panel. To have the appropriate desktop icon displayed, choose the Change Icon from the Program Item Properties dialog box. In the Change Icon dialog box, specify the path to MAIN.CPL so that the correct icon for the desktop application can be extracted.

Similarly, to add additional Control Panel program items, repeat this process for each item listed in Table 11-10.

Table 11-10	Control Panel Applets for Restriction
Applet	*Description*
Ports	Set parameters for serial communications port. Users can change settings on COM1 and COM2. If this is an issue, administrators can use techniques described before to hide or secure this application. Administrative rights are required to change settings on COM3 through COM256.
Print Manager	To create a printer (queue) on a Windows NT Server, a user must be logged on as a member of the Administrators, Server Operators or Print Operators group. To create a printer on a Windows NT workstation, a user must be logged on as a member of the Administrators or Power Users group for that workstation. By default, Administrators, Print Operators, and Server Operators have Full Control rights on an Advanced Server; Administrators and Power Users have Full Control rights on a Windows NT computer. All users can manage their own documents.
Network Control Panel Application (NCPA)	To make changes to the network settings through the NCPA, a user must be logged on as a member of the Administrators group. This is true for both Windows NT Server and Windows NT.

Applet	Description
System	To make changes to the size of the virtual memory paging file or to create additional paging files on other local hard drives, a user must be logged on as a member of the Administrators group. This is true for both Windows NT Server and Windows NT. By default, any user can change the priority given to applications running in the foreground and background. If this is an issue, administrators can hide or secure this application.
Date and Time	To make changes to the system's date and time, a user must have the Change the system time option set correctly. By default, this is only granted to members of the Administrators, Server Operators, and Power Users groups.
Drivers	To install or remove kernel drivers (drivers that access the hardware), a user must be logged on as a member of the Administrators group.
Services	To start, stop, pause, continue, or configure the startup for a service, a user must be logged on as a member of the Administrators group.
Devices	To start, stop, or configure the startup for a device, a user must be logged on as a member of the Administrators group.
Server	To manage server properties, a user must be logged on as a member of the Administrators, Server Operators, or Power Users group.
Uninterruptible Power Supply (UPS)	To set up the UPS, a user must be logged on as a member of the Administrators or Server Operators group.
Fonts	The Fonts application controls fonts for the entire system. By default, any user can add or delete fonts. There are some special considerations that should be taken into account when working with fonts. To delete a font, a user needs delete permission on the font files that are stored in <SYSTEMROOT>\SYSTEM32. Administrators can hide or secure the Fonts application.

The remaining applications in the Control Panel (Cursors, Color, Mouse, Desktop, Keyboard, International, Sound, and MIDI mapper) affect only the personal profile of the currently logged on user and hence do not affect the system configuration.

Table 11-11 lists other applications on which you may want to place restrictions.

Table 11-11	Other Applications for Restriction
Application	*Description*
Command Prompt	By default, all users have access to the Command Prompt. Administrators may find it desirable to prevent a specific user or group of users from accessing the Windows NT command prompt. An administrator can prevent users from gaining access to the Command Prompt by using File Manager to deny access to CMD.EXE in the <SYSTEMROOT>\SYSTEM32 directory.
Windows NT Setup	All critical maintenance changes to a Windows NT system require a user to be logged on as a member of the Administrators group.
Change System Settings	To make system settings changes, a user must be logged on as a member of the Administrators group.
Setup Applications	To set up applications on the hard disk for use with Windows NT, a user must be logged on as a member of the Administrators group.
Add/Remove Windows Components	These Windows NT components, such as applications in the Games or Accessories group are not required to have a functioning system. However, administrators may want to prevent users from removing or adding components by securing Windows NT Setup. An administrator can use File Manager to restrict permission for SETUP.EXE in the <SYSTEMROOT>\SYSTEM32 directory.
Add/Remove SCSI Adapters	To install or remove kernel drivers (drivers that access the hardware), a user must be logged on as a member of the Administrators group.
Add/Remove Tape Devices	To install or remove kernel drivers (drivers that access the hardware), a user must be logged on as a member of the Administrators group.
Delete User Profiles	To delete profiles, a user must be a member of the Administrators group.
File Manager	With the exception of File Associations, all File Manager configuration (share and stop sharing directories) tasks require a user to be logged on as a member of the Administrators, Server Operators, or Power Users group.
ClipBook Viewer	By default, all users have access to the ClipBook Viewer. They can share, stop sharing, and delete ClipBook Viewer pages. An administrator can prevent any user or group from using ClipBook Viewer by using File Manager to deny access to CLIPBRD.EXE in <SYSTEMROOT>\SYSTEM32.

The Accessories group

Two applications in this group that do not change system configuration but may be considered potential security problems are Chat and Terminal: Chat, because it allows users to have real-time, two-way conversation across the network; Terminal, because it allows users to use modems to transmit data.

Chat is an application that lets users have a two-way conversation over network Dynamic Data Exchange (DDE). Administrators can prevent users from having this facility by using File Manager to deny access to WINCHAT.EXE in the <SYSTEMROOT>\SYSTEM32 directory.

Terminal can be secured by using File Manager to place restrictions on TERMINAL.EXE in the <SYSTEMROOT>\SYSTEM32 directory.

The Administrative Tools group

You should also be aware of the capabilities of the Windows NT's administrative tools as well as the users and/or groups that have the rights to access them. These tools are listed in Table 11-12.

Table 11-12	Windows NT Administrative Tools
Tool name	**Description**
Disk Administrator	Only a user who is logged on as a member of the Administrators group can log on to Disk Administrator.
Event Log	All users can run the Event Viewer application, but only users logged on as members of the Administrators group can clear logs and view the Security log.
Backup	Users can only back up files on a disk drive to which they normally have access. Otherwise, a user needs to be logged on as a member of the Administrators or Backup Operators group. Notice that backup rights enable users to bypass the protection provided by normal file permissions. Also, use caution in granting restore rights because they enable a user to ignore normal file-permissions conflicts during restoration and to overwrite existing files. If administrators want to make sure that only members of the Administrators or Backup Operators group can use the Backup application, they can use File Manager to secure NTBACKUP.EXE.
User Manager and User Manager for Domains	Members of the Users and Power Users groups have a built-in ability to create and manage local groups. Because there is no way to revoke this right, the only way to prevent these users from having this ability is to use File Manager to deny access to MUSRMGR.EXE ("mini User Manager") in the <SYSTEMROOT>\SYSTEM32 directory.

(continued)

Table 11-12 *(Continued)*

Tool name	Description
User Manager for Domains	This application is shipped only with Windows NT Server; therefore, to use this application, a user must be able to log on locally at a server and have access to USRMGR.EXE. Otherwise, only members of the Administrators and Account Operators group can use User Manager for Domains.
Server Manager	To use Server Manager to administer a domain and its servers, it is necessary to be logged on to a user account that is a member of the Administrators, Domain Admins, or Server Operators groups for that domain. Members of the Account Operators group can also use Server Manager but only to add computer accounts to the domain. To use Server Manager to administer a Windows NT workstation, it is necessary to be logged on to a user account that is a member of the Administrators or Power Users group for that workstation. A few Server Manager functions are allowed only for members of the Administrators or Domain Admins group. When Server Operators, Account Operators, or Power Users attempt to perform these functions, a message is displayed indicating that access is denied.

To perform any administrative tasks, you must log on as a member of specific groups.

Summary

This chapter described the Windows NT security model and the security controls provided by the base operating system. It also discussed practical guidelines for taking full advantage of the security features of Windows NT. It covered

▶ Securing the configuration of Windows NT computers

▶ Guidelines for using local and global groups

▶ Windows NT security planning issues

▶ Using Windows NT file systems in security

Chapter 12

Connecting Clients

In This Chapter

▶ Connecting MS-DOS

▶ Connecting Windows and Windows for Workgroups

▶ Connecting Windows 95

▶ Connecting Windows NT

▶ Connecting Macintosh clients

Windows NT is designed to connect to just about anything. Right out of the box, Windows NT provides connectivity to a variety of operating systems and hardware platforms through its native support for NetBEUI, TCP/IP, SPX/IPX, and NWLink transport drivers. This chapter discusses client connectivity and the problems that you may experience. It also shows you how to connect various clients to Windows NT and keep them connected.

Solving Network Problems

Network problems can be the toughest to troubleshoot because there are so many different components, and the path causing the problem may not be active when you begin the troubleshooting process.

When troubleshooting network problems, start by verifying the network's operating status prior to and during the error condition. To evaluate the network problem, check these factors:

- **Loose adapter cable.** Have you added or moved any network cables? Check cables, connections, and terminators. Rule 1 of troubleshooting network problems is to make sure that the network cable is plugged into the network adapter card. Sounds silly, but it is always worth the check.

- **Network adapter failure.** Have you added or removed any network adapters? Check the adapter connection and any other working adapter. Check the event log for system errors related to the network adapter, the workstation, and the server components. Use PING and/or NBPING to determine if the machine is getting out on the wire and how far. If PING is unable to talk to its closest neighbor, you may want to enlist the help of a LAN protocol analyzer to determine if packets are getting onto the net. If the machine is getting to the wire but not its nearest neighbor, use the analyzer to look for congestion, jitters (Token Ring), and broadcast storm.

- **IRQ conflict with new adapter.** Are the network adapter settings correct? Consult the documentation for the correct network adapter settings and reset the values if necessary. Restart the computer and try again. If you suspect an IRQ conflict, disable the mouse in the Registry by setting the start value to 0x4. You may also want to disable the serial ports.

- **Protocol mismatch.** Have you added or removed any protocols? Check protocol settings, protocol bindings, and the compatibility of the protocol with the network. If two machines are active on the same network but still cannot communicate, they may be using different protocols. For successful communication, both must be using the same protocol. If machine A is only speaking NetBEUI and machine B is only speaking TCP/IP, the two machines are not able to establish a successful connection. Use the network control panel to determine which protocols are supported.

There are two important things to remember about Windows NT and protocols. First, Windows NT does not use the Data Link Control protocol to establish workstation or server sessions. It only uses DLC for mainframe and network printer traffic. Second, NetBEUI is not routable. If the network uses TCP/IP, IPX, or XNS routers, machines on different sides of the router will not be able to establish communication.

- **External network problems.** Are the network connections live? Look at the status lights on the back of the network adapter or on the media attachment unit. If the status lights show activity, the connection is live. If the status lights show no activity, disconnect and reconnect the network cable and check for activity. If the lights on the adapter are off, try a different network outlet.

If the hardware on the local machine checks out, there may be an external network error. Try using PING or NBPING to isolate the problem. Attempt to PING the farthest neighbor in increasing distances until you encounter a problem. Also use a LAN protocol analyzer to help locate jitters (Token Ring only), congestion, and broadcast storms.

Supporting Windows NT Clients

Connecting a Windows NT workstation to another computer running Windows NT Server or Windows NT Workstation is the easiest connection you can make. Most of the problems you might experience with Windows NT clients have to do with authentication, provided that the hardware is functioning properly.

Troubleshooting authentication problems

You can attribute many network troubles to a failing or improperly configured network card or incorrect network transport drivers. The symptoms
caused by a bad network card or an incorrect driver manifest themselves in
one of two ways:

- **Authentication problem.** The client workstation cannot find the domain
  controller and, therefore, cannot gain access to the network.

- **Connectivity problem.** Users on a client workstation cannot access a
  particular shared resource.

The first indication that you have a hardware-related network problem is a
message stating that the initial authentication process failed and that
Windows NT has used cached information for authentication and to log you
on to the system. Note that you can log on using cached information only if
you have logged on successfully at least once before the failure occurs. If
Windows NT cannot complete authentication, you cannot log on to the system to solve the problem. On a Windows NT Server domain controller, the
inability to be authenticated is a serious problem. If you encounter an authentication problem just after system installation during the initial logon,
it's difficult — if not impossible — to correct the problem.

Authentication problems fall into two basic groups. The domain controller
may fail to authenticate you during the logon sequence or while attempting
to access a shared resource on the domain.

Authentication failures that are not caused by a failed network adapter, as
discussed in the preceding section, are often caused by one of the following
problems:

- **No computer account.** If a Windows NT client is a member of the domain
  but has no computer account on the domain controller, there is no
  trusted connection between the Windows NT client and the domain controller. This means that the domain controller cannot authenticate you
  or log you on to the system. A similar problem can occur if a Windows
  NT client changes from a domain to a workgroup and then attempts to
  join the domain again. Even though a computer account still exists on the
  domain controller, the client cannot reuse the account. Instead, you
  must create a new computer account, although it can have the same
  name. This is because computer accounts are like user or group
  accounts in that they have an assigned security identifier (SID). The
  system stores the SID in the computer account on the domain controller
  and in the Registry of the Windows NT client. However, when a user
  changes from a domain to a workgroup or from one domain to another,
  the system reassigns the SID based on the new configuration.

- **No user account.** Generally this problem occurs when the user attempting to log on does not have a user account on the domain controller or
  the user misspells his or her user account name or password. You can

experience similar problems if you have set up the user account so that the user must enter a new password at the next logon, or if the account has been locked out due to repeated attempts to log on to the system with an invalid password.

- **A trust relationship.** If a Windows NT client is a member of a workgroup, make sure that you *do not* have any two-way trust relationships established on the domain to which that client needs access. In this situation, a Windows NT client cannot establish a trusted connection to the domain, even though the user has a valid user account. It is quite similar to the no-computer-account situation mentioned before. In a domain without trust relationships or a one-way trust relationship, a workgroup computer can access the domain resources by mapping its local user account to a user account on the domain. When two-way trust relationships exist, user account mapping does not take place.

Authentication problems related to accessing shared resources usually have to do with a user's specified permissions or rights. The same problem can occur for printer access or named pipe access. To solve these kinds of problems, check the client permissions in the following order:

- **Group membership.** Make sure that the user account is a member of the group that has permission to access the shared resource.

- **Share permissions.** Check the shared resource to be sure that the group has the appropriate permission to access the sharepoint. Also make sure that the user is not a member of any group to which you have assigned the No Access permission. The No Access permission assignment overrides any other group permission level for the user. For example, if you have a printer called HP_Laser, you assign a user to the LaserPrinter group that has Print permission for that printer, and you also assign the user to the ColorPrinter group that has the No Access permission assigned for the printer, the user cannot print to the HP_Laser print queue.

- **Directory and file permissions.** If the user can access the sharepoint but cannot access directories and files, the user account probably is not a member of the appropriate group. The user may also be a member of a group that has the No Access permission assigned.

- **Cached account information.** Windows NT also caches group account information when accessing a shared resource. If you add a logged-on user to a group that has the appropriate permissions to access the shared resource, the user still cannot access the shared resource. The user must log off and then log back on again to flush the cache. When the user attempts to access the resource again, the system permits access.

Tip

To flush an internal cache, sometimes you may have to shut down and restart the computer instead of just logging off and then back on again.

Isolating hardware problems

Isolating configuration errors from hardware errors is often the easiest way to pinpoint the source of a problem. Hardware problems may originate from a defective network adapter or an incompatible network adapter driver. This is why you should always install the MS Loopback adapter when you install Windows NT Server. This way you can log on to the system, even if the network adapter completely fails.

On a Windows NT Workstation or a Windows NT Server operating in server mode, you always have the capability to log on using the local (that is, Workgroup) account database. You log on locally by selecting the computer name instead of the domain name in the logon dialog box's From field. You can then use the Administrator account that you created when you installed Windows NT Workstation — that is, if you remember the Administrator password. If you do not know the password and you have no cached authentication information to use, the only recourse is to solve the problem in a blind fashion as follows:

1. Replace the network card.

2. Try the repair process.

3. Copy the system event log to a diskette if the file system is a FAT partition.

4. Read the log on another Windows NT computer to try to discover the cause of the failure.

If this does not work, you have to delete and reinstall Windows NT.

Isolating resource conflicts

Resource conflicts generally fall into four categories: an interrupt conflict, an I/O (input/output) port conflict, a DMA (Direct Memory Access) conflict, or a memory conflict. Following are some ways to isolate the conflict.

Interrupt conflicts are the most common problems, particularly because there are only 16 interrupts and not all of these are available for use. If the network adapter is using one of the reserved interrupts or one that is rarely available, that may be the problem. If this is not the case, you may have an I/O conflict, which is generally more difficult to diagnose. If your Windows NT computer is still working, you can try to use WINMSD.EXE (Windows NT Diagnostics located in the Administrators Tools Program Manager group) to help you solve the problem.

Start WINMSD and select the IRQ/Port Status button. The Resources dialog box as shown in Figure 12-1 appears.

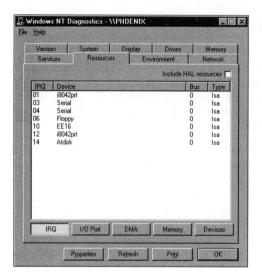

Figure 12-1: The Windows NT Diagnostics Resources dialog box.

However, WINMSD does not list every interrupt or I/O port used by the system — only those in use by installable device drivers. Just keep in mind that most manufacturers' I/O port summaries only include a starting I/O address; they rarely include the complete I/O range. It is possible to have an I/O overlap, where one I/O port range starts inside an existing I/O range.

Tip

If you have a Plug and Play BIOS, such as those commonly used in computers on a PCI expansion bus, take a look at the BIOS settings. Some PCI components can have their interrupt assigned by the BIOS. This can override the Plug and Play capability to assign an interrupt dynamically. It can also cause problems with Windows NT's capability to detect or change an interrupt assignment for a network adapter.

Tip

When looking for a memory buffer problem, start with the BIOS settings. The BIOS can be used to shadow (copy from RAM to ROM) a memory location. If this address range is shadowed, the network adapter cannot use it. You might experience similar problems caused by shadowing a SCSI or network adapter's ROM.

Another item — not directly related to any of the preceding — that can cause a network adapter failure is the speed of the machine's expansion bus. The ISA standard bus speed is a maximum of 8 MHz, but many users push this speed to 10 MHz, 12 MHz, or even higher. This can cause some peripherals to fail or to operate in an unpredictable manner. Although this configuration may work under MS-DOS, Windows, or Windows for Workgroups, it may not work under Windows NT.

Windows 95 Clients

Windows 95 supports a variety of network operating systems right out of the box. This includes Microsoft Windows NT-based networks in either a workgroup (peer-to-peer) or domain. You can even mix the two if desired. You can also install network software to connect to a Novell NetWare file server as a network client and share client resources with any other Novell NetWare server or client. You can even install both the Microsoft network support and the Novell network support simultaneously. However, you cannot have both of these network clients configured to share files and printers simultaneously. Only one of these client drivers can support file or print sharing to other network clients.

Tip

Windows 95 includes a file describing some of the specific network-related problems and solutions that you may encounter in upgrading Windows 3.x installations to Windows 95. This file is called NETWORK.TXT and is located in the root installation folder (generally C:\WINDOWS).

Problems can also occur when you mix network transport protocols. The initial version of Windows 95 includes support for the Microsoft NetBEUI, IPX/SPX-compatible, TCP/IP, and DLC protocols. It also includes support for the Novell NetWare IPX ODI protocol, IBM's DLC protocol, Digital Equipment Corporation (DEC) Pathworks, Banyan Vines Ethernet or Token Ring protocols, and SunSoft's PC-NFS protocol. Some of these protocols are 32-bit, such as the NDIS 3.0 drivers, whereas others are 16-bit, such as the NDIS 2.0 and ODI drivers. Although mixing these different protocols can provide simultaneous access to different networks, it can also cause problems. For example, if you use multiple network drivers, clients may be able to connect to one network but fail to connect to the other. Or, if you add an additional network transport protocol to a current network driver, you may suddenly find that the server cannot authenticate you or that you cannot connect to a resource.

Isolating hardware resource conflicts

The first step to take in isolating a hardware failure is to use the Control Panel System applet.

Start Control Panel and select the Device Manager tab to display the Device Manager page as shown in Figure 12-2. This page displays all of the installed hardware that Windows 95 recognizes and for which it has a driver installed.

Select the device and choose the Properties button to display the device properties in the General page as shown in Figure 12-3. This page displays a message in the Device status field indicating the current operating status. If the message "This device is working properly" appears, the cause is generally a software-related problem, such as an incorrectly configured network protocol driver. If a device is not working properly, the device tree displays a small icon (a circle with a line crossing through it) next to it.

Figure 12-2: The Windows 95 System Properties Device Manager dialog box.

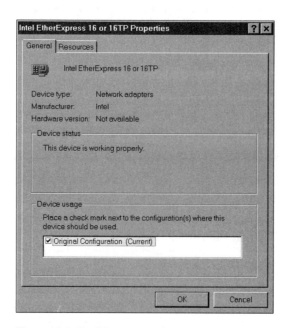

Figure 12-3: The Windows 95 Device Manager's General Properties dialog box.

If there isn't a software-related problem as described before, there may be a hardware-related error, in which case an error message appears in the Device status field. To reconfigure the device, select the Resources tab to display the Resources dialog box, as shown in Figure 12-4.

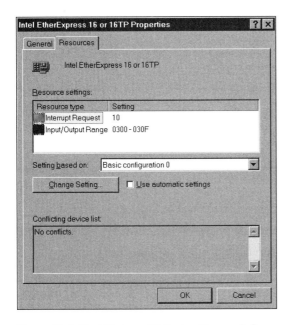

Figure 12-4: The Windows 95 Device Manager's Resources Properties dialog box.

If you have a resource conflict, such as an I/O, an interrupt, a DMA, or a memory conflict, it is displayed in the Conflicting device list field — if Windows 95 has recognized the conflict. Windows 95 displays a resource conflict only for MS-DOS and Windows device drivers that registered a resource usage in a manner that Windows 95 was able to detect. If Windows 95 cannot detect a resource that is in use, it may configure another device to use it and cause a device failure.

Before you reserve any system resources, determine what resources are already in use.

Select the Properties button for the Computer Device in the System Properties dialog box to display the Computer Properties dialog box as shown in Figure 12-5.

Click the View Resources tab, and then select the Interrupt request (IRQ), Input/output (I/O), Direct memory access (DMA), or Memory buttons to display the resources that are in use.

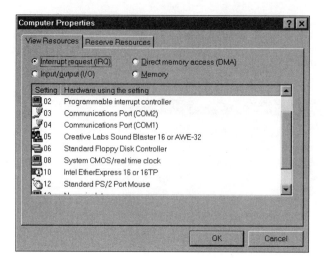

Figure 12-5: The Windows 95 Computer Properties View Resources dialog box.

Warning

Do not reserve a resource that is in use by a system device, such as the interrupt for the hard disk, or the device may not be operable under Windows 95. If you reserve such a device by mistake, immediately reboot the system and press the F5 key when you see the "Starting Windows 95" message on the screen to start Windows 95 in safe mode. In safe mode, you can reconfigure the system and undo the change that you made.

To change a resource from the setting assigned to it by Windows 95

1. Launch the Control Panel System applet to display the System Properties dialog box and then select the Device Manager tab.

2. Expand the tree for the device type that you want to change. For example, to change a network card's allocated resource, expand the Network Adapter tree.

3. Select the device and click the Properties button. This displays the device properties General page as shown earlier in Figure 12-3.

4. Select the Properties tab to display the Resources page as shown earlier in Figure 12-4.

5. Clear the Use automatic settings check box. This allows you to change a resource setting from what Windows 95 assigned for a Plug and Play device to a setting for a device of your own choosing.

6. Select a resource under the Resource type column in the Resource settings field and click the Change Setting button. This displays a resource edit dialog box where you can change the resource assignment. Repeat this step for each resource that you want to modify.

7. Choose the OK button in each dialog box to return to the System Properties dialog box.

Isolating software resource conflicts

You may experience additional problems with Plug and Play, PCMCIA, or parallel port network adapters that seem to be hardware-related but are really software configuration problems. You may also experience software-related problems with network client drivers and/or network transport protocols.

Look at your network adapter configuration first if you have either a software-configurable or Plug and Play network adapter. In a software-configurable network adapter, such as those from Intel, run the Softset utility from MS-DOS (when you see the "Starting Windows 95" prompt, press F8 and selectÁommand Prompt Only). Verify that the I/O port is the same as the one selected for the network adapter configuration, the interrupt is not used by any other device, and if you also use a DMA channel or upper memory address, that these are free. Then make sure that you have excluded the memory address, if it is used on the network adapter, from the EMM386.EXE device driver line in the CONFIG.SYS file. For example, if you have a network adapter that uses the D000-D3FF address, the EMM386.EXE entry should look like this:

```
DEVICE=C:\WINDOWS\COMMAND\EMM386.EXE X=D000-D3FF
```

If this area is not excluded, a memory conflict occurs when the network driver attempts to access the network adapter. If you are using an NDIS driver, Windows 95 generally makes the appropriate exclusion internally. However, if you use a 16-bit network driver — particularly those that bind to the network adapter before the 32-bit components load — you must include the memory exclusion on your expanded memory manager device line or the network device driver fails to bind to the adapter. If the exclusion does not include the entire network adapter buffer, the network driver may bind to the adapter but cause unexpected results. For example, with a partially excluded buffer, authentication failures can occur with a Windows NT Server, but you may have normal authentication on a LAN Manager for UNIX.

Plug and Play

You can also encounter a resource conflict using a Plug and Play network adapter when you load a 16-bit network driver. Troubleshooting is even more confusing when you load a 16-bit network driver successfully but then find that you cannot successfully use a 32-bit NDIS 3.1 transport protocol on the same Plug and Play network adapter. This is because when a 16-bit network driver is loaded, it binds to the Plug and Play network adapter and generally disables the Plug and Play functionality. When Windows 95 attempts to load the 32-bit Plug and Play network adapter driver, the driver fails to load because the network adapter can no longer be found or configured. This causes the 32-bit network transport drivers to fail to bind to the adapter. The solution to this problem is to use the software configuration disk that shipped with the adapter to configure it to function in non-Plug and Play mode. Then remove the network adapter from the Device Manager page of the Control Panel System applet. Once you have done these steps, run the Add New Hardware Control Panel wizard to find your adapter and install an appropriate device driver. You should then be able to add and use a 32-bit network transport protocol in addition to your existing 16-bit network driver.

Not all 16-bit network drivers support multiple network transport protocols being bound to the same physical adapter. The Microsoft NDIS and Novell ODI drivers generally support multiple network transport protocols. If your network driver supports one of these specifications, you should use it to bind 16-bit and 32-bit transport protocols successfully.

PCMCIA Cards

Windows 95 includes 32-bit PCMCIA drivers for PCMCIA chipsets from Cirrus Logic, Compaq, Databook, Intel, Maxtor, SCM Swapbox, Vandem, VLSI, and a generic PCIC or compatible PCMCIA chipset. If you have one of these chipsets and supported 32-bit PCMCIA drivers for PCMCIA cards, things should be in good shape. However, *all* of your PCMCIA cards must have 32-bit drivers. This is because you cannot simultaneously install the 16-bit (real-mode) and 32-bit (protected-mode) PCMCIA drivers. If you do, neither will work, and Windows 95 will fail to load. This makes sense when you consider that there is only one PCMCIA controller and both of these drivers want full control of it.

Connecting Windows for MS-DOS Clients

Even though Windows NT and Windows 95 are available for use as network clients, not everyone can use them. In some cases, the network client hardware platforms do not have enough horsepower to support Windows NT or enough memory to support Windows 95 effectively. In other cases, the company is being conservative by limiting the migration path or does not have enough money in the budget to upgrade all users to Windows NT or Windows 95.

When looking for a reason that an MS-DOS, Windows 3.x, or Windows for Workgroups network client cannot connect to the network, look for a resource conflict. Most of the time, this resource conflict is caused by a memory manager. The rest of the time a true hardware resource conflict probably exists, or there is a software configuration problem.

Windows 3.1 connectivity

If you are still using Windows 3.x as a client operating system, most problems that occur are related to MS-DOS configuration. Begin by booting just MS-DOS and the network drivers, and then log on to the network. If that is successful, you should look for problems related specifically to Windows 3.x. If it fails, you must resolve the MS-DOS problems before you can continue.

Note

If you are installing Windows 3.x for the first time and you have already installed the MS-DOS Connection, you should specify the network type as LAN Manager 2.1. This installs the appropriate Windows 3.x drivers for connecting to network resources.

Tip

If you want to set up a shared copy of Windows 3.x for all network clients, connect to the network with an MS-DOS Connection boot disk. Connect to a sharepoint where you want the shared copy to be installed. To copy all of the files to the shared directory on the server, use the Windows Setup program in administrative mode (setup/a) on a client workstation. Network clients can then connect to this shared directory and run the network installation (setup/n) to install the configuration and required boot files on their local computers.

As with the other operating systems I've discussed, the first network configuration item to troubleshoot when running Windows 3.x in enhanced mode is — you guessed it — an upper memory conflict. Most often, this conflict is with the network adapter's memory buffer. Depending on the expanded memory manager you use, it may automatically exclude the memory addresses you specified on the memory manager's command line in the CONFIG.SYS file. To find out if you really have a memory conflict, try commenting out the memory manager in the CONFIG.SYS file and rebooting the system. Then start Windows. If the problem still exists, you have a different problem. It could be a driver problem, a corrupted file, a hardware conflict, or something similar.

If commenting out the memory manager solved the problem, just remove the comments from the memory manager and reboot the system. Then check to see if you have a memory conflict only with Windows in enhanced mode by starting Windows 3.x in standard mode. Do this by using the command line switch /s or /2 (for example, win/s). If everything works in standard mode but fails when you start Windows in enhanced mode (WIN or WIN/3), you probably have an upper memory conflict. If so, do the following:

1. Begin testing by adding the line EMMExclude=A000-FFFF to the SYSTEM.INI file in the [386Enh] section. Then try to run Windows in enhanced mode once again.

2. If this works, start subdividing the exclusion. Change A000-FFFF to D000-FFFF and try again. If that works, break it up again to D000-E7FF and try it again.

3. If adding the exclusion failed, try the A000-CFFF range. If that works, break it up again to A000-B7FF and try it again.

4. Once you find the half of the memory range that solves the problem, keep lowering the exclusion range by half until the problem recurs. Then start adding increments of 4 KB until the problem no longer occurs. At this point, you can be assured that you have found the problem area and excluded it from use by Windows.

If you do not have a memory conflict, you may have a problem caused by one of the Windows 3.x internal network configuration settings. In this case, you can modify the defaults by adding or changing the entries in the SYSTEM.INI file in the [386Enh] section. These entries include the following:

- **NetDMASize.** Specifies DMA size. If the network adapter uses a DMA channel to transfer data, you may have to increase the size of the buffer that Windows allocates. The value entered here should be a multiple of four for best performance. The default is 0 for ISA (standard AT or compatible) computers and 32 for MCA (Microchannel). You rarely would need a DMA buffer over 64 KB.

- **NetHeapSize.** Specifies the size of the internal data buffer used for network transfers. The default is 12 KB, and modifications should be made in increments of four. For example, if you want to increase the buffer to 32 KB, change this value to 20.

Tip

This parameter can also be used in standard mode. Just place the key word under the [standard] section. The default buffer size is 8 KB for standard mode operation.

- **NetAsyncFallback.** Specifies that Windows should attempt to save a failing asynchronous NetBIOS request. Generally, if the allocated buffer is too small, Windows fails the request. If this value is set to On, Windows attempts to save the request by allocating a buffer in local memory and preventing any other applications from running until the request has been received or the timeout specified in NetAsyncTimeout has been reached. Values can be On or Off. The default is Off.

- **NetAsyncTimeout.** Specifies the time, in seconds, for Windows to enter a critical section and wait for an asynchronous NetBIOS request to be received. The default is 5.0 seconds; you may enter any value and include a decimal if desired.

- **NoWaitNetIO.** Specifies that synchronous NetBIOS requests be converted to asynchronous NetBIOS requests. This can improve performance but may cause compatibility problems. Values can be On or Off. The default is On.

- **TimerCriticalSection.** Specifies the length of time, in milliseconds, for Windows to enter a critical section and wait when an application uses a timer interrupt. Some network software fails if this setting is not used. The default is 0 for a LAN Manager and 10000 for a Windows NT Server network.

- **InDOSPolling.** Prevents Windows from running other applications when a memory resident application (TSR or network driver, usually) has the InDOS flag set. This flag is used by applications that have to be in a critical section when performing an INT21h (most of the MS-DOS functionality is an INT21h API) operation. Values can be On or Off. The default is Off.

- **Int28Critical.** Specifies that Windows maintains a critical section for software that uses the INT28h interface. Some network virtual device drivers perform internal task switching on this software interrupt and may hang the real-mode network software. Values can be On or Off. The default is On — make sure it stays that way.

■ **UniqueDOSPSP.** Specifies that all MS-DOS virtual machines (VMs) use a unique program segment prefix (PSP). Many network drivers use the PSP to identify the VM that requested the network data. The values can be On or Off. The default is On for a LAN Manager or MS-Net-compatible network and Off for all others.

■ **PSPIncrement.** Specifies the offset (in increments of 16 bytes) to ensure that the PSP for each VM is unique. The range is from 2 to 64, with a default of 2. For LAN Manager networks, the default is 5.

Windows for Workgroups connectivity

This section discusses some of the problems you might experience when using Windows for Workgroups computers within a Windows NT network.

Authentication Problems

The most common failure in Windows for Workgroups is an authentication failure. In this situation, you cannot access the domain controller to be authenticated during a logon sequence, which means that you have no access to the domain's shared resources. This usually happens only with protected-mode protocols when more than one protocol is installed. The solution is to install the NWLink (IPX/SPX-compatible) protocol and the NetBEUI protocol with NWLink being the default. This can be good or bad depending on which version of Windows NT Server you are using or even which service pack you have installed.

The good part is that NWLink is routable, whereas NetBEUI is only bridge-able. Routers are usually more efficient than bridges. The bad part is that the default setting for Windows NT Server is to use automatic detection of the Ethernet packet types — this can cause you more problems than it solves. If you leave this setting as is and use NWLink on a WFW client, you may see authentication failures on Windows NT Server. The solution is to change the packet type to 802.3 with the Windows NT Control Panel Network applet. You should also set the WFW clients to use the 802.3 packet in the Network Setup applet.

Note

Authentication failures can be further complicated by networks that have mixed Windows NT Workstations, Windows for Workgroups computers, and Novell NetWare servers. To avoid potential problems, make sure that you select a single packet type to use.

Tip

In a mixed Novell and Microsoft network, you should also configure the NWLink settings to assign a unique network number to each Windows NT Server. This can prevent additional connection-related problems.

Troubleshooting Connectivity Problems

When looking at Windows for Workgroups 3.1 (WFW) network problems, things can become a little tricky. This is because WFW can use both real-mode (NDIS 2.0) network drivers and protected-mode (NDIS 3.0) network drivers. It can also support multiple 16-bit network transport protocol stacks, multiple 32-bit network transport protocol stacks, or both simultaneously.

Troubleshooting network connectivity on a Windows for Workgroups computer consists of two separate strategies. You either troubleshoot real-mode or protected-mode drivers, but not both simultaneously. Usually, you are concerned with protected-mode drivers because these offer the greatest performance. However, not every transport protocol is available in a protected-mode version. For example, the Data Link Control (DLC) protocol is only available in a real-mode driver, and it is used to access IBM mainframes or to control a network-capable HP printer.

If you are using both NDIS 2.0 and NDIS 3.0 drivers and are experiencing connectivity problems, you should first determine which component is having the problem. Start with these steps:

1. Boot the system but do not start Windows for Workgroups. Instead, issue a NET LOGON command to log on to the network. If you can successfully log on and access resources on the network, the problem is probably related to protected-mode drivers.

2. To verify that the problem is related to protected-mode drivers, start Windows for Workgroups. It displays a message stating that the real-mode drivers were already started, which prevents protected-mode drivers from being loaded. Ignore this message for now. Just check the network connectivity. If it is working properly and you can access shared resources, you have a problem with NDIS 3.0 (protected-mode) drivers.

3. Next, determine which driver is causing the problem. The best way to do this is by removing the NDIS 2.0 support with the Network Setup applet. After you have removed all of the real-mode drivers, restart the computer. If the problem goes away, you have an interaction problem with real-mode and protected-mode drivers. The simple solution is to use only the protected-mode (NDIS 3.0) drivers. However, this may not be viable if you have to use a real-mode protocol and drivers. In this case, you may have to use only the real-mode drivers.

Tip

Sometimes, the interaction problem is caused by loading the NDIS 2.0 drivers into upper memory blocks. You can add the LoadHigh switch to the SYSTEM.INI file to disable loading of the NDIS 2.0 drivers into upper memory and force them to load into conventional memory. This switch and others are discussed later in this section.

4. Next, look at the NDIS 3.0 protocol settings. Select a single protocol to use, such as NetBEUI if the network supports it. After restarting the computer, see if network connectivity is working properly. Perform this same step for each protocol you use to verify that each works properly.

5. Then start mixing protocols. Add an additional protocol, such as the IPX/SPX-compatible protocol, and restart the computer. Confirm that the network works properly. Repeat this for each additional protocol you have installed, but use only two protocols (maximum) at a time. The idea here is to find the two protocols that conflict with each other.

6. Once you have identified the conflicting pair, you can mix all protocols. At this point, it is a matter of isolating the conflict and attempting to solve it via configuration settings in the [Network] section of the SYSTEM.INI file. For example, you may need to disable DirectHosting support.

7. To resolve the problem and continue to provide support for all of the required protocols, you may have to install another network adapter and bind the conflicting protocol to use only that network adapter.

Windows for Workgroups includes several .INI settings that are used to control the behavior of the network components. The primary entries are in the SYSTEM.INI file under the [Network] section and include the entries shown in Table 12-1.

Table 12-1	.INI Settings for Windows for Workgroups
.INI setting	*Description*
AutoLogon	Specifies whether to prompt you automatically to log on when WFW starts. Values can be Yes or No. The default is Yes. If you have a blank password, there is no logon prompt.
ComputerName	Establishes the name of your computer, which is used for all NetBIOS name resolution and is specified during the installation.
UserName	Specifies the default user name to be supplied during a logon attempt.
Workgroup	Specifies the name of your workgroup. Although this name can be different from your domain name, for simplicity, it should be the same. The only time that you would want to use different names is if you want to segment shared resources during browsing. For example, if you have a lot of computers on a single domain, all of the computers are listed under this domain when you browse it; but if you also have WFW computers using different workgroup names, they appear under their workgroup names. To browse a workgroup, you have to select it separately.
Reconnect	Specifies whether to restore previous network connections after a successful logon. Values can be Yes or No. The default is Yes.
Reshare	Specifies whether to restore previous shared resources when the operating system is restarted. You do not have to be logged on to the system for the resources to be shared. Values can be Yes or No. The default is Yes.

(continued)

Table 12-1 *(Continued)*

.INI setting	Description
LMLogon	Specifies whether to prompt you for a domain logon when you log on. Values can be 1 (enabled) or 0 (disabled). The default is 0. This setting is changed in the Control Panel Network applet. Press the Logon button to display a dialog box where you can enable domain logon via a check box.
LMAnnounce	Specifies whether the WFW computer is made visible to LAN Manager computers in the browse lists. Values can be Yes or No. The default is No.
LogonDomain	Specifies the name of the Windows NT Server or LAN Manager domain where you log on. This setting is changed in the Control Panel Network applet. Click the Logon button to display a dialog box where you can specify the name of the domain and enable the Logon To Domain check box.
AutoStart	Determines the redirector the real-mode (NDIS 2.0) network components use when you start the network before booting WFW (for example, if you issue a NET LOGON command). Values can be Basic, Full, Netbind, Popup, NetBEUI, or Workstation. The default is Full. Netbind only binds the protocol and network drivers; Popup loads the popup interface; NetBEUI loads theNetBEUI protocol; and Workstation loads the Workstation service andprompts you to log on.
LoadHigh	This item is only installed if you also have real-mode (NDIS 2.0) drivers installed on the system. When specified, this setting is used to load NDIS 2.0 drivers into upper memory blocks. Values can be Yes or No. The default is Yes.
EnableSharing	Specifies whether local resources are shared on the network. Values can be either Yes or No. The default is selected by the Network Setup applet in the Network group.
NoSharingControl	Disables the user's ability to change the EnableSharing entry via the Network Setup applet. Values can be 0 (disables user control) or 1 (enables user control). There is no default because this entry must be manually added to the SYSTEM.INI file.
FileSharing	Specifies whether to share directories on the local computer. Values can be Yes or No. The default is selected by the Network Setup applet in the File and Print Sharing dialog box.
LogonDisconnected	Specifies whether to connect to a previously connected resource so that it is immediately available for use or just to identify the resource connection and actually connect to it when a user attempts to access the resource. This is referred to as a *ghosted connection.* Values can be Yes or No. The default is No to enable ghosted connections. This setting can be changed in the Control Panel Network applet via the Logon button.

.INI setting	Description
PrintSharing	Specifies whether to share directories on the local computer. Values can be Yes or No. The default is selected by the Network Setup applet in the File and Print Sharing dialog box.
Comment	Specifies a description to be displayed in the browse list. It can be changed in the Network Control Panel applet.
LogonValidated	Used internally to verify that a user was logged on to the domain. When the user logs off, this setting is used again to make sure that the connections are properly disconnected so that the next user cannot use any of the previous connections. Values can be Yes or No. The default is Yes if validated by a domain server or No if not validated by a domain server.
StartMessaging	Specifies whether to load the messenger service (provided by WinPopUp). Values can be Yes or No. The default is No. This setting can be changed in the Control Panel Network applet via the Logon button.
LoadNetDDE	Specifies whether to load Network DDE support at system startup. Values can be Yes or No. The default is Yes.
DomainLogonMessage	Specifies whether a message is displayed after a successful logon to the domain. Values can be Yes or No. The default is Yes. This setting can be changed in the Control Panel Network applet via the Logon button.
CacheThisPassword	Determines whether to cache passwords in the local user's password file. Values can be Yes or No. The default is specified by the last user who logged on and changed the Save This Password in the Password File check box.
DirectHosting	Specifies that direct hosting over IPX be enabled first and, if that fails, hosting over NetBIOS. Some monolithic drivers (such as Novell's NETX driver) require that this setting be disabled. Values can be On or Off. The default is On.
MaintainServerList	Specifies the possibility of your computer becoming a master or backup browse master. Values can be Auto, Yes, or No. If set to Auto, the computer queries the network for a master browser. If no master browser is available, this computer becomes the master browser. If set to Yes, this computer always maintains a browse list and becomes the master browser if the original master browser goes off-line. If set to No, this computer never becomes a master browser. Note that a browse master is determined by an election (query) process. A Windows NT Server computer has the highest priority, followed by LAN Manager Servers, Windows NT Workstations, and, finally, a Windows for Workgroups computer.
DeferBrowsing	Disables the automatic expansion of the browse list in the Browse dialog box for directories or printers. Values can be Yes or No. The default is No unless Remote Access is installed. It can be changed in any Browse dialog box by setting or clearing the Always Browse check box.

Using the Administration Configuration Program

Windows for Workgroups includes the ADMINCFG.EXE program, which is not installed by default. To install it, you must manually expand it from the distribution media, or you can copy it from the \CLIENTS\WFW\NETSETUP program. It can only be run on a computer that has WFW installed. When run, it prompts you for the location of the WFWCFG.SYS file to be opened. Once you select the file, you may be prompted for a password. After that has been entered, the main dialog box shown in Figure 12-6 appears. This dialog box is used to disable the client workstation's capability to share directories, printers, and clipboard pages.

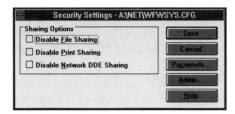

Figure 12-6: The Windows for Workgroups Security Settings dialog box.

If you select the Passwords button, the dialog box shown in Figure 12-7 appears. This dialog box is used to provide the following options:

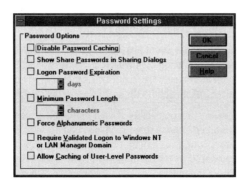

Figure 12-7: The Windows for Workgroups Password Settings dialog box.

- **Disable Password Caching.** Disables caching of passwords in the password file that the user has supplied during a successful connection attempt. This option requires a user to specify a password every time that an attempt is made to connect to a shared resource.

- **Show Share Passwords in Sharing Dialogs.** Determines if an asterisk is to be displayed in the password box for each character the user enters (the default) or if the actual password in normal text is displayed.

- **Logon Password Expiration.** Specifies a password expiration date so the user is forced to change a password.

- **Minimum Password Length.** Specifies a minimum password length.

Note

The two settings just mentioned are only useful for a workgroup. If the user is a member of a domain, it is better to set the account policies with User Manager, which applies to all users of the domain.

- **Force Alphanumeric Passwords.** Specifies that the user must use an alphanumeric password rather than all alphabetic characters. This means there must be at least one digit in the user's password.

- **Require Validated Logon to Windows NT or LAN Manager Domain.** Specifies that only authenticated users of the domain be allowed to access shared resources on the computer. Normally, a workgroup computer allows anyone who knows the password to access a shared resource. Enabling this check box prevents any non-domain members from accessing the shared resources.

- **Allow Caching of User-Level Passwords.** Specifies that the password file also contain passwords for user-level (domain access) shared resources and the default share level (workgroup-only access). This password file can be used to store all of the passwords needed by a user to access a shared resource, which can be useful for users who can't remember passwords without writing them down and violating security. The only password that the user needs to know is the password to open the password file, and this is the same password he or she uses to log on to the system.

If you choose the Admin button in the Security Settings dialog box, the Administrator Settings dialog box, as shown in Figure 12-8, appears. In this dialog box, you can specify the following settings:

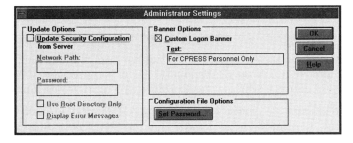

Figure 12-8: The Windows for Workgroups Administrator Settings dialog box.

- **Update Security Configuration.** If this check box is enabled, you can specify a UNC pathname to the location of the WFWSYS.CFG file. You specify the pathname in the Network Path field, which is used to update all connected users of a shared WFW installation. If a password is required to access the file, enter it in the Password field.

■ **Use Root Directory Only.** Specifies whether the user uses the settings stored in the WFWCFG.SYS file in the root directory of the shared installation or the WFWCFG.SYS file in a subdirectory that has the same computer name as the workstation. If no subdirectory is found, the WFWCFG.SYS file located in the root directory is used.

■ **Display Error Messages.** Displays security-related error messages on the client workstation if enabled.

■ **Custom Logon Banner.** Displays a custom sign-on banner when the user logs on to the network. To display the banner, enter the text in the Text field.

■ **Set Password.** Displays a Password dialog box where you can specify a password that is required to open the WFWCFG.SYS file to make any modifications. This can prevent a user from changing any settings that you specify.

Supporting MS-DOS Clients

If you encounter MS-DOS connectivity problems, look for a memory management conflict again, particularly if the network adapter was working but has now failed. However, it doesn't have to be a network buffer memory address conflict. The memory management conflict can also be caused by loading a driver into upper memory, when the driver makes certain assumptions about its operating characteristics and thereby fails. The conflict can also be caused by loading an operating system component (such as a file, buffer, or file control block) into upper memory.

First, determine if the initial cause is actually memory manager related. The easiest way to do this is to comment out the memory manager in the CONFIG.SYS file and reboot the computer. If the problem disappears, you have a memory manager problem. You then need to determine the type of problem.

To determine if you have an upper memory area conflict

1. First, exclude the entire A000-FFFF memory range in the memory manager and reboot. If the problem goes away, you probably have a simple memory conflict, which is easily solved, if a bit time consuming.

2. Next, change the memory exclusion from A000-FFFF to A000-CFFF and reboot. If the problem goes away, you have a memory address conflict in the A000-CFFF range.

3. If it does not go away, change the memory exclusion to D000-FFFF and reboot. If the problem goes away, you have a memory address conflict in the D000-FFFF range.

If the problem was solved in either Step 2 or 3, the next step is to subdivide the exclusion once more. As an example, exclude A000-B7FF instead of A000-CFFF. If that fails, try B800-CFFF. If that works, continue the process of halving the memory exclusion until you reach a multiple of 4 KB that continues to work properly. For example, this is *x*000-*x*1FF for a 4-KB exclusion, *x*000-*x*7FF for a 32-KB exclusion, and *x*000-*x*FFF for a 64-KB exclusion, where *x* is either A, B, C, D, E, or F for the appropriate 64-KB page in the upper memory area.

Tip

One odd memory address conflict that you might encounter is a conflict with a network adapter's reserved boot ROM address. A network boot ROM is used to boot a workstation from a network drive, rather than from a local hard disk. Some network adapters, such as some of the Intel models, reserve an address range for the network boot ROM even if no ROM is installed. If you do not exclude this area, the network connectivity can be a bit spurious. For example, you may be able to connect to a LAN Manager Server and access resources without problems but fail to be authenticated by a Windows NT Server or access resources on a Windows NT domain. You can locate this reserved address by using the Softset utility that shipped with the network adapter.

If excluding a memory address does not solve the problem but commenting out the memory manager does, you probably have either an operating system component or a driver loading into upper memory that is causing a network driver to fail. To determine if the problem is caused by loading a driver into upper memory, just remove the statements preceding the device drivers that load the driver into upper memory. For example, for MS-DOS, change the DEVICEHIGH=DeviceDriver to DEVICE=DeviceDriver; for QEMM, change the *QemmRootPath*\LOADHI.SYS DEVICE=DeviceDriver to DEVICE=DeviceDriver, where *QemmRootPath* is the QEMM installation directory. Do the same for the AUTOEXEC.BAT file by removing the LOADHIGH or LH (for MS-DOS upper memory support) statements preceding any of the drivers.

If you are using QEMM, comment out the following drivers if they are installed in the CONFIG.SYS:

- **DOSDATA.SYS.** Loads MS-DOS components (files, buffers, and so on) into upper memory.

- **DOS-UP.SYS.** Loads additional MS-DOS system components into upper memory.

- **ST-DBL.SYS.** Stealths the MS-DOS DoubleSpace compression driver by swapping it in and out of the EMS page frame.

- **ST-DSPC.SYS.** Stealths the MS-DOS DriveSpace compression driver by swapping it in and out of the EMS page frame.

Note

Other memory managers have similar functionality provided by different drivers. Refer to the documentation to find the exact driver names to comment out.

Problems with shadowing and stealth features

If you are using QEMM or another third-party memory manager, you should also consider upper memory problems that can occur from shadowing a ROM or using stealth. *Shadowing* a ROM is the process of copying the memory contained in the ROM to system RAM and remapping the address to the new location to increase performance. *Stealthing* is a process of mapping RAM into the same location as a system ROM so that the RAM can be used as an upper memory area for loading device drivers.

You can also stealth the MS-DOS compression drivers which creates an additional set of mappings: one for software to access the EMS page frame, and one for MS-DOS to access the stealth compression driver that shares the same address as the EMS page frame. Since any of these items can cause problems, remove them one at a time to see if you can find the cause.

Tip

There is a little problem that can throw you off track when removing these configuration switches from the memory manager. Removing a switch affects the amount of upper memory that is available, which means that a device driver may fail to load high. If the driver that fails to load into upper memory is the cause of the problem, it seems as if the configuration switch that you removed solved the problem. However, it may not have, because the next time you maximize the upper memory area, the same driver may be loaded into upper memory again, and the problem may recur.

If you do not have an upper memory conflict, the problem generally falls into a resource conflict category. This could be an interrupt, I/O, or DMA conflict.

Tip

The PROTOCOL.INI file contains the resources currently allocated for use by the network adapter driver. If you change the network adapter configuration, you also have to change the resource assignments in this file.

The final item to consider is the network driver configuration. If you are using a LAN Manager client driver to connect to a Windows NT domain, try removing it unless you absolutely must continue to use it.

Note

Windows NT Server includes the Network Client Administrator in the Network Tools Program Manager group that you can use to create installation diskettes to install the MS-DOS 3.0 Connection client drivers. The MS-DOS Connection can work with any existing NDIS 2.0 network adapter driver and includes support for the NetBEUI, NWLink, and TCP/IP protocols. The TCP/IP protocol supports DHCP and WINS, which can make your life as an administrator quite a bit easier.

Check the network transport bindings if you are using multiple network transports. For example, the default installation includes both the NetBEUI and NWLink transports with IPX/SPX being the default transport. However, these multiple transports can sometimes cause problems. If you have bridges installed on the network to create a single logical network, try using only the NetBEUI protocol to see if you can connect with it. If you have routers instead of bridges, try the NWLink protocol.

If your network is TCP/IP based, forget about NetBEUI and the NWLink protocols and use just the TCP/IP protocol. Try pinging yourself (PING ComputerName) to see if the software is installed and working. When you get a return (if it is working correctly), check the IP address. If it is in the 127.0.0.x range, the software is not configured properly. Either a DHCP server cannot be found on the network, or the routers may not support DHCP and are filtering out the relevant packets. In the first case, check the Windows NT Server domain controllers to verify that the DHCP service is running; in the second case, check the documentation for the router to determine what packet types it may be filtering. You can also take a look at Chapter 18, *Configuring DHCP Servers*, and Chapter 19, *Setting Up WINS Servers,* which are concerned with only DHCP and WINS and might offer some additional insight. As a temporary measure, you can assign a permanent IP address for the computer by running the setup program located in the MS-DOS Connection directory (usually, C:\NET).

Tip

The MS-DOS Connection includes a built-in diagnostics capability. The first time you execute the command NET DIAG, MS-DOS looks for another computer that is acting as the diagnostic server. If a diagnostic server cannot be found, it prompts you to become the diagnostic server. The syntax for executing the command follows:

```
NET DIAG /NAMES /STATUS
```

where */NAMES* can be used to specify the name of another diagnostic server so you avoid potential collisions with other diagnostic servers and clients, and */STATUS* can be used to obtain configuration information from another computer.

MS-DOS connection pointers

The Microsoft MS-DOS Connection version 3.0 ships with Windows NT Server and is located in the \CLIENTS\MSCLIENT subdirectory of the CD-ROM. You can use the Network Client Administrator tool, located in the Network Tools Program Manager group, to create installation diskettes. You can use these diskettes to install the MS-DOS Connection on client computers. If you have a network adapter that is not included in the supported network adapter list, check the \CLIENTS\WDL\NETWORK subdirectory on the CD-ROM to see if your network adapter is listed there. If so, just copy the entire set of files to an additional floppy diskette and specify Other when you are prompted for a network adapter in the MS-DOS Connection setup program. The program prompts you to insert the Original Equipment Manufacturer (OEM) diskette to copy the appropriate network drivers. You can use this same strategy with any OEM driver, even one that is not included on the Windows NT Server CD-ROM, as long as the driver includes an NDIS 2.0 (real-mode) network driver.

Before you install the MS-DOS Connection on all of your MS-DOS clients, you should be aware of a few limitations:

- **Intel 8088 processors.** If you have an older IBM XT or compatible computer with an Intel 8088 processor, you cannot use the full redirector. During the setup, you have to change from the default full redirector setting to the basic redirector setting. The setup program may pause for up to five minutes on a computer with an 8088 processor; if this occurs, do not restart the machine, just wait for the setup program to continue.

- **Minimum free memory.** The MS-DOS Connection setup program requires a minimum of 429 KB of free conventional memory. If you have too many terminate and stay resident (TSR) programs loaded or too many existing network drivers that leave you with less than 429 KB free, you have to remove the drivers before you run the setup program.

- **NWLink protocol.** The NWLink protocol that is included in the MS-DOS Connection does not support SPX. It only supports IPX. If you have software that uses Novell's SPX protocol, it will not work with the MS-DOS Connection. You should use your existing Novell network drivers instead.

- **DLC protocol.** If you install the DLC protocol, you have to edit the AUTOEXEC.BAT file manually. Make sure that the first network line (before the drivers) is NET INITIALIZE /dynamic and the last network line (after all the drivers, but before the NET START command) is NETBIND.

- **Browsing.** The MS-DOS Connection does not include a browse master. Therefore, in order to browse for network resources, you must have a Windows for Workgroups, Windows NT Workstation, or Windows NT Server computer that is accessible from the client and is operating as a browse master.

 Note
Even without a browse master accessible from the client, you can still connect to shared network resources. You just need to know the resource name and its location. For example, to connect to a shared CD-ROM drive (with the sharename *CD-ROM*) on a server (called *SRV*), use the command NET USE *DriveLetter*: \\SRV\CD-ROM where *DriveLetter* is an MS-DOS drive letter (F:, for example).

- **Remote Access Software.** Windows NT Server also includes the Remote Access Software 1.1a client, which you can use to connect to a Windows NT Server, Windows NT Workstation, Windows 95, or Windows for Workgroup computer that is running the RAS Server. However, you cannot use the RAS setup program to install the software if you have also installed the MS-DOS Connection. Instead, use the MS-DOS Connection setup program and select the Microsoft Remote Network Access Driver from the list of supported adapters. Then check that the Listed Options are correct and follow the prompts. After exiting the setup program, run the RASCOPY.BAT program to copy the RAS support files. Once the software has been installed, change to the RAS subdirectory (generally, C:\NET\RAS) and run the setup program there to configure modem settings. If you decide to remove RAS, use the MS-DOS Connection setup program to remove the Microsoft Remote Network Access Driver. Do not use the setup program in the RAS subdirectory.

- **TCP/IP.** There are a few quirks with the TCP/IP protocol for the MS-DOS Connection. For example, the MS-DOS Connection does not support DNS resolution using WINS or WINS resolution using DNS, perform as a WINS proxy agent, or register its computer name with the WINS server. You may experience other minor differences.

- **Domain authentication.** To be authenticated by a Windows NT Server computer, the MS-DOS Connection client must be using the full redirector.

Note

If you are using TCP/IP and have a router between the server and the client, you need to add an entry in the client LMHOST file. The format is *999.999.999.999 ComputerName* #DOM:*DomainName* where *999.999.999.999* is the server's TCP/IP IP address, *ComputerName* is the name of the server, and *DomainName* is the name of the domain. For example, for a MS-DOS Connection client to be authenticated by my server (called *SRV*) in the WORK domain, the entry would be *128.0.0.1 SRV #DOM:WORK.* You also have to add the MS-DOS Connection client's IP address to the server's LMHOST file or manually register the client's computer name with a WINS server that has WINS Manager.

The MS-DOS Connection uses some components that were migrated from the Windows for Workgroups drivers. As a result, along with the common entries in the PROTOCOL.INI file, such as adapter configuration settings, you will also find a copy of WFWSYS.CFG and entries in a SYSTEM.INI file. The WFWSYS.CFG file is unique to each installation, but you can use the ADMINCFG program (located on the Windows for Workgroups installation diskettes or in the \CLIENTS\WFW\NETSETUP subdirectory on the Windows NT Server CD-ROM) to configure some of the security-related settings (such as password caching, validated logons, and so on).

Note

ADMINCFG is a Windows program, not an MS-DOS program, so you must have a copy of Windows for Workgroups on the client installation to change the WFWSYS.CFG file. You can also copy it to a diskette and modify it from another machine running Windows for Workgroups and having access to the ADMINCFG.EXE program.

The specific entries in the SYSTEM.INI file that apply to the MS-DOS Connection are under the [Network] section and include those in Table 12-2.

Table 12-2	.INI Settings for MS-DOS Connection
Setting	**Description**
autologon	Specifies whether the MS-DOS Connection client automatically prompts you to log on when it starts. Values can be Yes or No. The default is Yes.
computername	The name of your computer, which is used for all NetBIOS name resolution.
lanroot	The installation directory of the MS-DOS Connection client.

(continued)

Table 12-2 *(Continued)*

Setting	Description
username	The default user name to be supplied during a logon attempt.
workgroup	The name of your workgroup. Although this name can be different from your domain name, for simplicity, it should be the same.
reconnect	Specifies whether to restore previous network connections after a successful logon. Values can be Yes or No. The default is Yes.
dospophotkey	Specifies the key to press (including the Ctrl+Alt keys) to launch the popup interface. The default key is N, meaning that you press Ctrl+Alt+N to launch the popup interface.
domainlogon	Specifies whether MS-DOS Connection prompts you for a domain logon when you log on. Values can be 1 (enables) or 0. The default is determined during software installation; if you make no changes, it is disabled (0).
logondomain	Specifies the name of the Windows NT Server or LAN Manager do main where you log on.
preferredredir	Specifies which redirector to use when you load the network drivers with the NET START command. Values can be Basic, Full, Netbind, Popup, NetBEUI, or Workstation. The default is Full, unless it is changed during the software installation. Normally, the values are Full or Basic as determined by the setup program. However, you can specify any of the alternatives. Netbind only binds the protocol and network drivers, Popup loads the popup interface, NetBEUI loads the NetBEUI protocol, and Workstation loads the Workstation service and prompts you to log on.
autostart	Determines the redirector that is in use. If you installed a network adapter during setup and specified Run Network Client Logon, the autostart entry lists the redirector (Basic, Full, Netbind, Popup, NetBEUI, or Workstation). If you have not installed a network adapter or choose Do Not Run Network Client, the autostart entry has no value, but the NET START command still appears in the AUTOEXEC.BAT file.

There are two additional sections in the SYSTEM.INI file. They are the [network drivers] and [Password Lists] sections, which include the NDIS network adapter and protocol drivers to load and the user password list files respectively.

Connecting Macintosh Clients

One of the biggest advantages of Windows NT Server is its interoperability with other operating systems. You can integrate Windows NT Server with any MS-NET compatible networks, which is to be expected, but you can also integrate Novell networks. With the Gateway Service for NetWare, you can use a Windows NT Server to provide access to NetWare shared directories or print queues even if your network clients do not support the IPX/SPX protocols. If you add the optional software packages, such as the File and Print Services for NetWare, Windows NT Server can emulate a Novell NetWare Server. If you also include the Directory Services for NetWare, you can use a single logon to access not only Microsoft network domain resources, but also Netware network resources.

Support for Macintosh networks is quite similar, except Windows NT Server includes all of the tools that you need to support Macintosh clients instantly. This support is provided by the Services for Macintosh program. You can even support UNIX-based clients — although UNIX integration in the base package is not nearly as full featured as other network integration options.

Macintosh client connectivity

Macintosh problems generally fall into three different categories: authentication-related problems, directory- or file-related problems, and printer-related problems. Most of these authentication problems are correctable by installing the Microsoft UAM (Universal Authentication Module) on the client computer or removing the requirement for the Microsoft UAM in the Services for Macintosh program on Windows NT Server. Some directory- and file-related problems require a bit more drastic action for correction on the server or, in some cases, cannot be corrected at all. Noncorrectable problems are generally caused by limitations in the Macintosh operating system or Windows NT file system. When the problem is printer related, there is generally a workaround that can be implemented on either the Windows NT Server computer or the Macintosh computer depending on how the printer is accessed.

Authentication-related issues

Before you can determine exactly what type of authentication problem is occurring on the network — and how to solve it — you need to look at the three different types of network logons: The Services for Macintosh program can use a Macintosh guest account, the Windows NT Server domain Guest account, or a Windows NT domain user account.

The primary difference between the Macintosh guest account and the Windows NT domain Guest account is that any Macintosh user can connect to a Windows NT Server Macintosh Volume using the Macintosh guest account if you have enabled the Guests Can Use This Volume check box (the default) for a volume. When a user connects using the guest account, no password is required. This means that there is no restriction on who can access the volume. If you disable the Guests Can Use This Volume check box, you can still allow users to connect, but only if they have the Microsoft UAM installed and use the domain Guest account (if you have enabled it in User Manager for Domains) or a specific domain user account.

Tip

Always disable the Guests Can Use This Volume check box on any Macintosh volume that you create. You can still allow all users to connect using the domain Guest account by publishing the Guest password if desired. However, by using the domain Guest account, you can further restrict access to shared files, which prevents network disruptions and eases administrative duties.

Caution

Never disable the Guests Can Use This Volume check box on the Microsoft UAM Volume; if you do, new Macintosh clients cannot connect to install the Microsoft UAM on their computers. If you disable this property, you must distribute the Microsoft UAM on a floppy or other media before new clients can access domain resources.

The Microsoft UAM is used to encrypt a password that is sent out over the network so that a hacker, or just a curious user, cannot capture a user account and password for unauthorized use. When network clients use the Microsoft UAM to connect to domain resources, they can be authenticated using the Macintosh guest account or any domain account simply by choosing the Guest or Registered User option, which is generally in the UAM. To use the domain Guest account, use the Registered User option, and then specify Guest in the name field and a password in the password field if one is required.

This process may vary a bit depending on the version of the operating system used on the Macintosh client and the settings that you have enabled for the Services for Macintosh program. If the Macintosh client is using a version of the operating system older than version 7.1, the option to use the Macintosh guest account and clear text password encryption (that is, no encryption) is still available to the user via the Apple standard UAM. This is the case even if the Require Microsoft Authentication check box has been enabled in the MacFile Attributes dialog box on the Windows NT Server computer. However, if the version of the operating system is 7.1 or later and the Require Microsoft Authentication check box has been enabled, the Macintosh guest option is unavailable, and only the Microsoft encrypted password option is available.

Given this information, you can see that figuring out why a client cannot connect can be a troublesome process. It depends on how you configured the Services for Macintosh, how Macintosh clients are configured, and what version of the Macintosh operating system they have installed. To make things simple, you should require every user to have System 7.1 or later, the Microsoft UAM installed in their AppleShare folder, and a domain user account. On servers running the Services for Macintosh, make sure that the Require Microsoft Authentication check box is enabled, the domain Guest account is disabled in User Manager for Domains, and the Guests Can Use This Volume check box is disabled for every Macintosh volume on the server aside from the Macintosh UAM Volume. This strategy provides you with consistent user access to shared resources by allowing any Macintosh user to obtain the Microsoft UAM from the Microsoft UAM Volume, but the user requires a Windows NT domain user account with an encrypted password to access any shared resources.

Installing the Microsoft UAM

For Macintosh clients to install the Microsoft UAM and abide by your network security policy, they must follow these steps:

1. On the Macintosh client, select the Chooser from the Macintosh Apple menu to display the Chooser dialog box.

2. Select the AppleShare icon and the zone in which the Windows NT Server running the Service for Macintosh server resides to update the list of file servers.

3. Select the Windows NT Server from the file server list and click the OK button.

4. In the Logon dialog box, select the Guest option and click the OK button. This displays the Server dialog box.

5. In the Server dialog box, select the Microsoft UAM Volume, disable the Checked Items Are Opened At System Startup Time check box, and click the OK button.

6. Close the Chooser dialog box.

7. On the Macintosh Desktop, open the Microsoft UAM Volume folder.

8. Open the AppleShare folder.

9. Open the local computer's System folder.

10. Drag the Microsoft UAM into the System folder.

11. Close the System, AppleShare, and Microsoft UAM folders.

Now you're ready to connect to Windows NT Server computers using your domain account. You can connect shared volumes or shared printers on the network.

Directory- and file-related issues

Once you have eliminated authentication problems by establishing a common user access policy, as described in the preceding section, access problems generally fall into one of two categories. Either the file in a shared environment has been renamed due to name translation, or the permissions have been set or modified so that they prevent user access.

Filename Translation

When you start mixing network client access to a shared directory, you also start running into name translation problems as users with different systems save various files in the directory. Filenames change (are translated) as the files are saved, depending on the system in which the user is operating; for all intents and purposes, the files disappear. Understanding how name translation occurs can help you find these files. The basic rules are as follows:

■ All Macintosh volumes must be created on an NTFS partition.

A valid NTFS directory or file can contain a maximum of 255 characters if it is created by a Windows NT or Windows 95 client. The name can contain any character except

```
?, \, *, ", <, >, |, /, : (colon).
```

- A valid Macintosh directory or file can contain a maximum of 31 characters and can include any characters except a : (colon).

- A valid MS-DOS directory or file can contain a maximum of eight characters followed by a three-character extension separated by a single period (8 dot 3). The name can contain any character except a space and

  `, /, [', '], ;, =, ", \, :, |, , (comma), *.`

If a name is longer than the MS-DOS convention, the name is shortened according to these basic steps:

1. All spaces are removed.

2. The characters are raised to uppercase.

3. All illegal characters are dropped from the name.

4. The first six characters of the filename are used, followed by a tilde (~) and a single digit. The file extension (the first three characters of the last part of the name separated by a period) is appended to the name.

5. If the name is not unique, the single digit is incremented. If a valid name cannot be generated with a single digit, the name is truncated to five characters, followed by a tilde and two digits, followed by a three-character extension.

- If the NTFS name is more than 31 characters, the Macintosh client can view only the MS-DOS 8-dot-3-compatible filename.

If a Win32 application saves a data file or renames a directory of more than 31 characters, both MS-DOS and Macintosh clients see a shortened version of the filename. This name can be fairly cryptic. For example, a file named "Development Project File for August 1, 1995.DOC" becomes "DEVELO~1.DOC" for MS-DOS and Macintosh clients. If the original were "Project File 8-1-95.DOC," the name would remain the same for Macintosh clients but would become "PROJEC~1.DOC" for MS-DOS clients.

Permission Problems

Permissions on files are set with the File Manager MacFile menu option. These permissions only apply to Macintosh users. However, if you share a directory on a Windows NT Server as both a Macintosh volume for Macintosh clients to access and as a regular sharepoint for other network clients, you have to maintain the corresponding permissions. If you don't, unpredictable results can occur.

Macintosh clients assign permissions based on three distinct sources: the owner, user/group, or everyone. For each of these sources, three permission levels can be applied. These permission levels include the capability to See Folders, See Files, and Make Changes. However, Windows NT includes permissions based on groups or users and can include more levels than those defined for Macintosh clients. To maintain the appropriate permissions, use the permission settings defined in Table 12-3 and stick to the Windows NT Server subset when assigning permissions for other network clients.

Table 12-3	Macintosh to Windows NT Permission Levels
Macintosh permission	*Corresponding Windows NT permission*
See Folders	Read
See Files	Read
Make Changes	Write and Delete

Summary

Windows NT is well suited as a heterogeneous network operating system. You can connect virtually any kind of client to a Windows NT server. This chapter discussed the following:

▶ Solving network problems

▶ Supporting Windows NT clients

▶ Connecting Windows 95 clients

▶ Connecting Windows for MS-DOS clients

▶ Supporting MS-DOS clients

▶ Connecting Macintosh clients

Chapter 13

Coexisting with NetWare

In This Chapter

▶ Installing Microsoft Client Service for NetWare

▶ Forging a migratory path from NetWare to Windows NT

▶ Installing Microsoft Gateway Service for NetWare

▶ Managing network connections

Although Windows has become the predominant operating system on PC desktops, Novell's NetWare has grown into the predominant network operating system. To fulfill the requirements of today's enterprise computing environment, these two systems must work together. This chapter explains what the connectivity services for Novell's NetWare are. It also describes procedures for installing and configuring those services (which include Client Service for NetWare and Gateway Service for NetWare in Windows NT Server) and for configuring the NWLink IPX/SPX Compatible Protocol (NWLink).

Windows NT in a NetWare Environment

For two computers to share resources, they have to share a common protocol. The marriage between Windows NT and NetWare is no exception. Microsoft and NetWare networks use different communications protocols for passing requests from clients to servers. Microsoft networking clients use the Server Message Block (SMB) Protocol to perform remote requests to Microsoft networking servers, whereas NetWare clients use the NetWare Core Protocol (NCP) to communicate with NetWare networking servers. This section describes in detail the two options for marrying NetWare to Windows NT. One option is provided by Novell and the other by Microsoft.

Novell's NetWare Client for Windows NT

NetWare Services for Windows NT allows you to connect Windows NT to NetWare Servers, map drive letters to NetWare volumes, and redirect printed output to NetWare print queues. NetWare Services also allows you to execute DOS- and Windows-based NetWare network management utilities, as well as access shared applications on NetWare Servers.

NetWare Services uses Windows NT's modular architecture to integrate the Windows NT low-level networking functions with a NetWare network. Consisting of an IPX protocol stack that is compliant with the Transport Driver Interface (TDI) layer and providing a complete Novell Open Datalink Interface (ODI) environment, NetWare Services integrates seamlessly with the normal Windows NT networking components.

For example, if you have a single network interface card (NIC), NetWare Services allows you to install ODI-compliant support for NetBEUI packets so that you can maintain connectivity to Microsoft network resources. If you have two or more NICs, you can install NetWare Services to operate over one NIC, while maintaining a "pure" Microsoft environment over the other.

Although NetWare Services for Windows NT provides the necessary client functionality, it falls short as a solution for application servers. This is because as a client option, it is geared toward connectivity with NetWare Servers.

Microsoft's NWLink

To enhance Windows NT's viability as an application server, Microsoft developed its own application server solution. NWLink, an implementation of the Novell IPX/SPX protocol suite, has been designed to be integrated with Windows NT native networking components.

NWLink provides all of the peer-to-peer connectivity capabilities of a true IPX/SPX server and allows network clients running Novell's IPX/SPX protocol stack to communicate directly with a Windows NT system. This, in turn, allows network applications running on the Windows NT system to process packets from, and thus service requests from, client workstations running over IPX/SPX.

NWLink supports both the Novell NetBIOS and the Microsoft Windows Sockets APIs. In the case of NetBIOS, NWLink provides its own enhanced version that improves performance by reducing the number of acknowledgment packets required when communicating with other NWLink-based Windows NT systems. When dealing with systems that are not NWLink-based, it adheres to the normal 1:1 packet-acknowledgment ratio found in a true NetWare environment.

NWLink relies on Windows NT support of the Streams Protocol environment to implement a true IPX protocol stack. This implementation is almost identical to the way in which Windows NT integrates Transmission Control Protocol/Internet Protocol (TCP/IP), which is also a Streams-based protocol.

Windows NT connectivity to NetWare

Windows NT includes an implementation of the Internetwork Packet Exchange (IPX) and Sequenced Packet Exchange (SPX) transport protocols used by NetWare networks. However, a Windows NT computer must also be able to send NetWare Core Protocol (NCP) packets to request and receive file and print services. The connectivity services for NetWare include Client Service for NetWare in Windows NT and Gateway Service for NetWare in Windows NT Server. These services translate the Server Message Block (SMB) packets used for Microsoft networking requests into the NCPs used by NetWare.

Note

The Microsoft implementations of the IPX, SPX, and Novell NetBIOS protocols can seamlessly coexist with other protocols on the same network adapter card. For example, a single network card on a Windows NT computer can receive IPX/SPX, TCP/IP, Microsoft NetBEUI, and AppleTalk packets.

With these connectivity services, your Windows NT workstation can access files, directories, and printers on Novell NetWare Servers. You can run NetWare utilities and NetWare-aware applications from your Windows NT computer. In addition, with the Gateway Service for NetWare on your Windows NT Server computer, you can configure a gateway so that Microsoft networking clients — computers running Windows NT, Windows 95, Windows for Workgroups, or LAN Manager 2.x — do not need NetWare Client software to access files and printers on NetWare Servers.

You can use Windows NT with NetWare networks as a client and as a server.

- As a client, Windows NT can access NetWare file and print resources while concurrently accessing Windows-based systems and other services on heterogeneous systems.

- As a server, client systems running the MS-DOS, Windows, or Windows NT operating systems can access NetWare and Windows NT-based Servers concurrently.

How a gateway works

A gateway enables two different networks to communicate. On a Windows NT Server computer, Gateway Service for NetWare acts as a translator between the Server Message Block (SMB) protocol used by the Windows NT network and the NetWare Core Protocol (NCP) used by the NetWare network. With a file gateway, for example, clients of a Windows NT Server computer can access files on NetWare Servers without having to load additional NetWare connectivity components.

All file access over the gateway is done by sharing drives that are redirected to NetWare volumes or directories. The file gateway uses a NetWare account on the Windows NT Server computer to create a validated connection to the NetWare Server. This connection appears on the Windows NT Server computer as a redirected drive. When you share the redirected drive, it becomes like any other shared resource on the Microsoft network.

For example, you can connect the Windows NT Server computer to a NetWare directory called \\NW4\SYS\DATA, which becomes drive Z on the Windows NT Server computer. If the name of the Windows NT Server computer is THOR and you give drive Z the sharename DATA_USERS, a Microsoft networking client can access the NetWare directory by connecting to \\THOR\DATA_USERS. The Microsoft networking client is unaware that this shared resource is part of the NetWare network.

Note

A gateway enabled on a Windows NT Server computer seamlessly integrates the Microsoft network with file and print resources on the NetWare network. Because requests from Microsoft networking clients are processed through the Windows NT Server, access over the gateway is slower than direct access from the client to the NetWare network. For Microsoft networking clients that require frequent access to NetWare resources, Windows NT with Client Service for NetWare or Windows for Workgroups with the client software supplied by Novell is a better solution. On a Windows for Workgroups computer, loading the necessary network protocols in high memory preserves valuable conventional memory for application software.

Note

When you create the gateway, Windows NT uses two accounts to log on at the NetWare Server. From that point forward, NetWare maps its resources to Windows NT users just as if these services were native on the Windows NT Server. Every user on the Windows NT domain has access to these resources, assuming the user has sufficient rights. However, every user has to go through Gateway Service and the Gateway Service logon at NetWare to accomplish this. If you have hordes of Windows NT users trying to get at these NetWare resources, count on some slow response times.

Also, because of the architecture of the gateway, 100 Windows NT users can access the NetWare Server at the same time regardless of the kind of NetWare Server installed. For instance, a five-user NetWare v3.12 LAN could be connected to a Microsoft Windows NT Server via the gateway, and 100 Windows NT users could get to the NetWare resources. The two NetWare logons would be used, leaving the NetWare user count at three, but with 100 Windows NT users accessing the NetWare Server.

This characteristic of the gateway is an easy way to circumvent NetWare's expensive licenses. There's nothing illegal — to my knowledge — about this setup, but it will bury you with slow response times and NT Server overhead.

Preparing to Install Connectivity Services

Gateway Service for NetWare is a Microsoft Windows NT Server service that logs on to the NetWare Server in order to connect to it. You need to create at least one account on the NetWare Server so that the Windows NT Server can log on as an administratively empowered user. Create a second NetWare account for the gateway. Windows NT uses the first logon to make the connection, and the gateway service makes the second.

Here's a list of things to do before installing Gateway Service:

1. Create two NetWare user accounts with rights to your administrator group or supervisor rights, or the equivalent.

2. Make a list of the names of your servers and volumes that you want to map back to Windows NT users.

3. Make a list of the printers that you want to make available to Windows NT users.

4. Decide which Windows NT users are to have access to the NetWare resources.

5. Install an additional network I/O card in both the NetWare and NT Servers.

6. Obtain the name of your preferred NetWare Server.

7. Log on as a member of the Administrators group for the local computer.

8. Remove any existing NetWare redirectors, such as NetWare Services for Windows NT from Novell, and then restart your computer.

To remove existing NetWare redirector installations

1. Launch the Network applet from the Control Panel.

2. In the Network Settings dialog box, select the existing NetWare redirector software in the Installed Network Software box.

3. Choose the Remove button. When Windows NT asks you to confirm your choice, choose the Yes button.

4. In the Network Settings dialog box, choose the OK button.

5. Restart your computer for the changes to take effect.

Installing connectivity services

When you install the Gateway and Client Service on your Windows NT Server computer, Setup automatically installs the NWLink Transport Protocol if it is not already on your computer.

To install connectivity services

1. From the Control Panel, launch the Network applet.

2. When the Network Settings dialog box appears, choose the Services tab and then click the Add button.

3. In the Select Network Service dialog box, select Gateway (and Client) Service for NetWare if you are using Windows NT Server

   or

   Client Service for NetWare if you are using Windows NT Workstation, and then choose the Continue button.

4. In the Windows NT Setup dialog box, enter the path where the connectivity service files are located and then choose the OK button.

5. In the Network Settings dialog box, choose OK.

6. When the NWLink IPX/SPX Protocol Configuration dialog box appears, specify the network adapter card you want to use to communicate with the NetWare network. By default, the frame type is 802.3.

   You can always change the settings later, as described in the next section, *Configuring the NWLink IPX/SPX Compatible Transport Protocol*.

7. To restart Windows NT so that the changes take effect, choose Yes.

Note

The NetWare network is added to the first place in the network search order.

An icon labeled GSNW is added to the Control Panel when Gateway Service for NetWare is installed. When Client Service for NetWare is installed, the icon is labeled CSNW. The icon looks like the Network icon, except that one of the cable connectors is red.

Configuring the NWLink IPX/SPX Compatible Transport Protocol

After installing the NWLink software, you can specify the network adapter card that it will use and the frame type of your network. The default settings are optimized for most environments, but you can modify protocol parameters after installation if, for example, you want to bind the protocol to a different network adapter card.

To configure the IPX protocol

1. In the Control Panel, launch the Network applet.

2. Click the Protocols tab, select NWLink IPX/SPX Compatible Transport and then click the Properties button.

3. In the Adapter box of the NWLink IPX/SPX Protocol Configuration dialog box, select the name of the adapter card to which you want to bind the transport.

4. In the Frame Type box, specify the frame format for IPX/SPX packets on your network and then choose OK. By default, the frame type is 802.3. If the network traffic on the specified adapter card uses a different frame type, click the down arrow in the Frame Type box and select the appropriate frame type.

5. In the Network Settings dialog box, choose OK.

6. Windows NT prompts you to restart the computer so that the changes take effect. Choose the Yes button to restart the computer.

   If you choose the No button, you can continue to work, but your configuration changes do not take effect until the computer is restarted.

If your computer is on a Token Ring network, you can use the ipxroute command line utility to further configure your computer. This utility is installed with the NWLink IPX/SPX Compatible Transport Protocol.

Specifying a preferred NetWare Server

1. The first time you log on after the connectivity service is installed, you should specify to which NetWare Server you want your Windows NT computer to connect by default when you log on. This server, which is referred to as the *preferred server,* validates your user credentials when you log on to the NetWare network. You also use it to request information about resources available on the NetWare network.

2. Although you do not have to specify a preferred server, it is a good idea, especially if you need to avoid logging on to NetWare Servers that are limited to a small number of user connections.

To specify a preferred server when the connectivity service is first installed

1. In the Select Preferred Server for NetWare dialog box, select the name of a server on the NetWare network or select <None> from the list provided, and then choose OK.

   Or

   Type a server name directly in the Server box and then choose OK.

2. If you choose <None>, the connectivity service attempts to connect to the nearest available server each time you log on.

The preferred server setting affects only the account under which you are logged on when you make the setting. When other users log on, they are also prompted for a preferred server. If you later change your preferred server, other users are unaffected.

Selecting a Preferred Server after Installation

When you install your connectivity service, you can specify a preferred NetWare Server or you can specify no preferred server. You can change your preferred NetWare Server at any time.

To specify a preferred NetWare Server after installation

1. From the Control Panel, choose the GSNW or CSNW option.

2. When the Gateway Service for NetWare or Client Service for NetWare dialog box appears as shown in Figure 13-1, select a server from the list provided in the Select Preferred Server box, or type the name of a NetWare Server directly into the box, and then choose OK.

3. If your password on the NetWare Server is different from that on the Windows NT computer, enter your NetWare password at the prompt, and then choose OK.

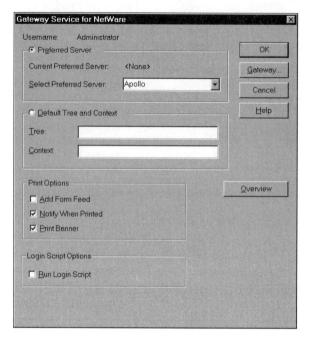

Figure 13-1: The Gateway Service for NetWare dialog box.

The next time you log on, the connectivity service connects to the NetWare Server you specify as the preferred one.

File and Print Gateways

You use file and print gateways in the following situations:

- For clients of the Microsoft network that need access to NetWare resources but cannot use multiple protocols

- For Microsoft networking clients that are using Microsoft Remote Access Service

- On networks on which you want to limit IPX/SPX traffic or on which you are migrating to TCP/IP; a gateway on a Windows NT Server computer can connect to NetWare resources and share them with clients of the Microsoft network.

Enabling a gateway

Before you can enable a gateway on a Windows NT Server computer:

- You must have a user account on the NetWare network with the necessary rights for the resources that you want to access.

- The NetWare Server must have a group named NTGATEWAY with the necessary rights for the resources that you want to access.

- The NetWare user account must be a member of the NTGATEWAY group.

After the gateway connection is established, it is not disconnected unless the computer is turned off or the Windows NT administrator disconnects the shared resource or disables the gateway. Logging off the Windows NT Server computer does not, by itself, disconnect the gateway.

By controlling membership in the NTGATEWAY group, the NetWare administrator can control which Windows NT Server computers can be gateways to the NetWare Server, and what kind of access to what files each user account has.

The NetWare administrator has total control over whether the gateway allows access to files and print queues on the NetWare Server. The network administrator can control access to NetWare network resources either over the gateway or directly on the NetWare network:

- On the Windows NT Server computer acting as a gateway, the administrator can use multiple share restrictions to limit which network users or groups have access to gateway shares and files.

- Using NTGATEWAY, the administrator can set trustee rights on the directories and files to which users and groups are allowed access through the gateway. There is no auditing of gateway access.

To make a NetWare Server available to a gateway account

1. Use the NetWare syscon utility to create the NTGATEWAY group account on the NetWare file server.

2. Use syscon to create a NetWare user account with the name and password that you will use to log on from the Windows NT Server computer.

3. Add the gateway account to the NTGATEWAY group.

4. Establish trustee rights for the NTGATEWAY group.

To activate the file gateway on the Windows NT Server computer, specify the NetWare volume or directory. Volumes, directories, and print queues are represented in Windows NT by their Universal Naming Convention (UNC) names. However, NetWare syntax is also supported.

UNC names begin with two backslashes (\\) followed by the remote (in this case, NetWare) server name, and then the names of the volume or directory points on the server separated by single backslashes.

For example, if the file server named NW4 contains the THOR volume on which there is a directory WINAPPS\WORD, the UNC name for the directory is \\NW4\THOR\WINAPPS\WORD.

To enable a gateway

1. In the Control Panel on the Windows NT Server computer that is to be the gateway, choose the GSNW option.

2. In the Gateway Service for NetWare dialog box, choose the Gateway button. The Configure Gateway dialog box appears as shown in Figure 13-2.

3. In the Configure Gateway dialog box, select the Enable Gateway check box.

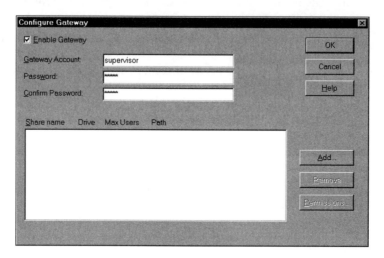

Figure 13-2: The Configure Gateway dialog box.

4. In the Gateway Account box, type the name of your gateway account on the NetWare file server. Type the password for the gateway account in both the Password and Confirm Password boxes.

Activating a file gateway

To activate a file gateway, you must have previously enabled a gateway on your Windows NT Server computer, as described in the preceding section.

To activate a file gateway

1. In the Control Panel on the Windows NT Server computer that is to be the gateway, choose the GSNW option.

2. In the Gateway Service for NetWare dialog box, choose the Gateway button.

3. In the Configure Gateway dialog box, choose the Add button to create a NetWare share for Microsoft networking clients.

4. In the New Share dialog box shown in Figure 13-3, type the information about the redirected share and then choose OK.

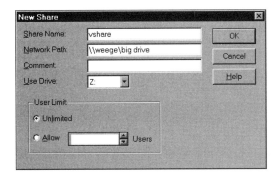

Figure 13-3: The New Share dialog box.

Windows NT Server creates a connection to the NetWare resource that you specify in the Network Path box, assigns it the redirected disk drive that you specify in the Use Drive box, and creates a share on the Microsoft network using the sharename that you specify in the Share Name box.

If the connection fails with an Access Denied message from the NetWare Server, be sure that you entered your account name and password correctly in the Configure Gateway dialog box. If you did, you may not have a valid account on the NetWare Server, or your account may not be a member of the NTGATEWAY group. It is also possible that your account or the NTGATEWAY group has insufficient trustee rights to access the specified NetWare volume or directory.

Setting permissions for a gateway share

If you want to control user access, you can set permissions for the share when you create it or you can do it later if your needs change. You can set permissions on a gateway share using either File Manager or the Gateway Service. For information on setting permissions with File Manager, see File Manager in the *Windows NT Server System Guide*.

To set permissions for a gateway share using the Gateway Service

1. In the Control Panel, choose the GSNW option.

2. In the Gateway Service for NetWare dialog box, choose the Gateway button.

3. From the list of gateway shares provided in the Configure Gateway dialog box, select the share for which you want to set permissions, and then choose the Permissions button.

   If the Permissions button is dimmed, the gateway may be disabled. If the Enable Gateway check box is cleared, enable the gateway as described earlier in this chapter.

   In the Access Through Share Permissions dialog box, you can add groups and users, change the permissions for the listed groups and users, and remove a group or user from the permissions list.

4. To add a user to the list of authorized share users, choose the Add button in the Access Through Share Permissions dialog box.

   The Add Users And Groups dialog box displays the groups on the computer or in the domain in the List Names From box. You can display users, find the users in a group, or find the domain to which a group or user belongs.

   Local groups are shown for the computer or domain whose name is followed by an asterisk (*). You can select another domain from the List Names From box. Domains are listed only if your computer is a member of a domain on a Windows NT network. The domains shown have a trust relationship with your computer's domain.

5. To display the names of users on the selected computer or domain, choose the Show Users button.

6. To view the members of a group, select the group and choose the Members button.

   The Local Group Membership dialog box appears, listing the group's members. For Windows NT Server domains, global groups that are members of a local group appear in the list.

   To see a global group's users list, select the group name from the list and choose the Members button in the Local Group Membership dialog box. To add the group to the list in the Add Users And Groups dialog box, choose the Add button in the Local Group Membership dialog box.

7. To add a group or user, you must know the domain to which the group's or user's account belongs. For Windows NT Server domains, choose the Search button to find the domain of a group or user. When the Find Account dialog box appears, type the name of the group or user in the Find User Or Group box, and specify the domains you want to search. Then choose the Search button. To include the groups or users in the Add Users and Groups dialog box, select them in the Search Results box and choose the Add button.

8. To add groups or users to the list, select them in the Names box and choose the Add button, or double-click the name of the group or user. Or you can type the names of groups and users in the Add Names box. Separate names with a semicolon.

If the account of the group or user is not located on the computer or domain shown by the List Names From box, you must specify the location. Type the computer or domain name followed by the group or user name and separate the names with a backslash, for example, sales\anniep. You can type the name without waiting for Windows NT to list groups in the Names box.

9. If you are adding users or groups to a permissions list, select the permission from the Type Of Access box for the groups or users shown in the Add Names box.

10. Choose the OK button.

11. In the Configure Gateway dialog box, choose the OK button.

12. In the Gateway Service for NetWare dialog box, choose the OK button.

Activating a print gateway

A print gateway functions much like the file gateway just described: After you have enabled the Gateway Service on a Windows NT Server computer, the NetWare printer appears on the Windows NT network like any other shared printer. Print jobs sent to the print gateway are redirected to the corresponding NetWare print queue. You configure a NetWare print gateway through Print Manager.

To configure a print gateway, a gateway must be enabled. All access to NetWare printers is through the user account used to enable the gateway.

To configure a NetWare print gateway

1. From the Windows NT Server computer that is to serve as a gateway, use Print Manager to connect to a NetWare print queue. In Print Manager, select the printer icon or window for the print queue.

2. From the Printer menu, choose Properties, or choose the Properties button on the toolbar.

3. In the Printer Properties dialog box, select the Share This Printer On The Network check box.

   Print Manager creates a sharename in the Share Name box for the printer, using MS-DOS naming conventions. This allows MS-DOS-based computers to connect to the printer. If you edit the sharename and the Windows NT network has clients that are running MS-DOS, be sure to follow MS-DOS naming conventions.

4. In the Location box, type a description of the printer's location to let network users know where their documents will be printed.

5. Choose the OK button.

Once the queue is shared, networking clients can access the print queue. Microsoft networking clients can connect to the shared NetWare print queue as they would to any Windows NT printer.

Connecting to a NetWare Print Queue

If your Windows NT computer has Gateway Service for NetWare or Client Service for NetWare, you can establish a connection to a NetWare print queue through Print Manager or from the command prompt.

You can connect to a NetWare print queue using Print Manager.

1. From the Printer menu, choose Connect To Printer, or choose the Connect Printer button on the toolbar.

2. In the Connect To Printer dialog box, select a printer from the Shared Printers box, or type the name of a computer and print queue in the Printer box.

    For NetWare networks, the Shared Printers box shows servers and print queues. If the NetWare network is first in the network search order for print providers (the default), the list of servers on the NetWare network is displayed automatically in the Shared Printers box. Double-click a server name to display or hide its print queues. When you select a print queue in the Shared Printers box, Print Manager fills in the Printer box.

    When you type the name of a print queue directly in the Shared Printers box, precede the computer name with two backslashes (\\) and separate the computer name from the print queues name with a single backslash (\). For example, type **\\win_nt\hp4si.**

    NetWare syntax cannot be used because there is no syntax for print queues.

3. Choose the OK button.

4. If a printer driver is not available locally for a NetWare print queue, Print Manager prompts you to install a printer driver. Choose the OK button to continue.

5. In the Select Driver dialog box, select the appropriate driver for the printer in the Driver box.

6. In the Windows NT Setup dialog box, type the directory and path where Windows NT printer drivers are stored, and then choose the Continue button.

    Windows NT installs the driver and displays a printer window for the connected print queue.

Be sure to set the correct printer options after the appropriate driver has been loaded. You can now print to the NetWare print queue just as you would to a Windows NT printer.

Setting printing options

Printing options are already set for the user logged on to Windows NT, and these same options can be set for NetWare print queues. The printing defaults are to suppress form feed, to print a banner (blank page) between documents, and to notify you when your document is finished printing. You can change these options by changing the configuration of your connectivity service.

Note

Settings in the connectivity service affect all NetWare print queues you are using from your Windows NT computer. The options are equivalent to settings available through the NetWare capture utility.

To set printing options

1. In the Control Panel, choose the GSNW or CSNW option.

2. In the Print Options box of Client Service for NetWare or Gateway Service for NetWare dialog box:

    Clear the Add Form Feed check box to instruct the printer not to eject a page after printing a document.

    Clear the Notify When Printed check box to stop notification when your document has been printed.

    Clear the Print Banner check box to stop printing a banner page before your document prints,

3. Choose the OK button when the printing options are as you want them.

Connecting to a NetWare Volume or Directory

When Gateway Service for NetWare or Client Service for NetWare is installed on your Windows NT computer, you can connect to volumes and directories on NetWare file servers using File Manager or the net command at the command prompt.

File Manager

With File Manager, you can browse and connect to resources on both the Windows NT and NetWare networks. Once you are connected to a NetWare volume, you can drag and drop directories and files to move and copy them between your Windows NT computer and NetWare Servers.

The list of servers on the NetWare network is displayed automatically in the Shared Directories box. The servers, volumes, and directories are displayed in a tree structure. Both volumes and directories are represented by the shared directory icon. Choose an item to expand the list; for example, choose a directory to display its subdirectories.

The NetWare Server validates you before it allows you to see directories in a NetWare volume. Windows NT displays the Enter Network Credential dialog box so that you can provide a user name and a password for the server if the server cannot validate you.

On a NetWare network, you can type the server name in the Path box and choose the OK button if you know the name of a server and need to see the names of its volumes. Precede the server name with two backslashes (\\). Windows NT adds the name of the server's first volume directory to the Path box and displays all of the server's volumes in the Shared Directories box.

You can type a network path in the Path box. On NetWare networks, you can type the name using either Universal Naming Convention (UNC) or NetWare syntax.

To connect to a NetWare drive using File Manager

1. From the Disk menu, choose Connect Network Drive, or choose the Connect Drive button on the toolbar.

2. File Manager displays the first free drive letter in the Drive box. You can accept the displayed drive letter for the connection or choose another in the Drive box.

3. In the Path box, select or type a network path.

   If you have connected to the volume or directory previously, select the path from the list displayed by the Path box. The Path box displays the previous 10 paths.

   Or

   You can use the Shared Directories box to select a network path.

4. You are connected by default under the user name and password that you used to log on. If you want to connect under a different user name, type it in the Connect As box.

5. Choose the OK button. If a password is required, Windows NT displays the Enter Network Password dialog box where you can type the password.

Managing Network Connections

When the connectivity service is running, you can manage connections to the NetWare network just as you manage connections on the Microsoft network. You can view and manage active connections and define persistent connections with the net use command.

Managing NetWare file attributes

NetWare file attributes are not exactly the same as those on Windows NT. The file rights mappings in Table 13-1 are applied when a NetWare file is opened by Gateway Service.

Table 13-1	File Rights Mappings
Windows NT file attributes	*NetWare file attributes*
R (Read Only)	RO, DI (Delete Inhibit), RI (Rename Inhibit)
A (Archive)	A
S (System)	Sy
H (Hidden)	H

Gateway Service does not support mapping to the following NetWare file attributes:

RW (Read/Write), S (Shareable), T (Transactional), P (Purge), RA (Read Audit), WA (Write Audit), and CI (Copy Inhibit).

When you copy a file from a Microsoft networking client to the NetWare file server via Gateway Service, the RO, A, Sy, and H file attributes are preserved.

You can use the NetWare utilities, such as filer and rights, from a Windows NT Server computer with an activated gateway to set attributes that are not supported by the Windows NT-to-NetWare file rights mapping.

Administrating NetWare Clients

On Windows NT Server computers that have File and Print Services for NetWare (FPNW) installed, creating and managing user accounts for users of NetWare clients is similar to creating and managing Windows NT user accounts. This section provides information about creating NetWare client accounts and how to set account policies.

Creating a NetWare-compatible client user account

The procedure for creating a user account for a NetWare client user is basically the same as you would follow to create a regular user account for a Microsoft client user. However, you provide additional information when creating a NetWare client user account.

To create a NetWare-compatible client user account

1. Start User Manager for Domains.

2. From the User menu, select New User.

3. Fill in the New User dialog box as follows:

   - In the Username box, type a user name of up to 20 characters.

   - In the Full Name box, type the user's complete name. This entry is optional but recommended.

   - In the Description box, type a description of the user or of the user account. This entry is optional but recommended.

   - In both the Password and Confirm Password boxes, type a password of up to 14 characters. You must type the same password in both boxes.

   Select or clear the following options:

   - User Must Change Password At Next Logon forces the user to change the password.

   - User Cannot Change Password prevents the user from changing the password.

   - Password Never Expires prevents the password from expiring.

   - Account Disabled prevents use of this account.

   - Maintain NetWare Compatible Login enables the account to log on from a NetWare client computer. If the domain has Directory Services Extensions for NetWare installed, this also enables the account to be propagated to NetWare Servers in the domain.

4. Choose the NW Compat button and fill in the NetWare Compatible Properties dialog box as follows:

   - Select or clear the NetWare Compatible Password Expired box. When the box is marked, the user must change the password the next time that he or she logs on from a NetWare client computer. Be sure that the user has at least one grace logon if this box is marked so that he or she can log on and change the password.

   - To allow the user an unlimited number of grace logons, select Unlimited Grace Logins. To limit the number, select Limit Grace Logins and type the maximum number to allow the user in the Allow box (or use the up or down arrows to select a number). Grace logons are the extra number of times that a user can log on with an expired password.

   - In the Concurrent Connections group box, select Unlimited to allow unlimited simultaneous connections to the server. To limit the number of concurrent connections, choose Allow and type a number in the Allow box.

5. Choose the OK button.

6. To set other account options, choose one or more of the other buttons at the bottom of the User Properties dialog box.

7. When finished, choose the Add button to add the new account.

Note

When you create a NetWare-enabled account (either by creating a new account or enabling an existing account for NetWare), the account's Windows NT Server password and NetWare password are synchronized. If you are creating a new account (as NetWare-enabled), the password that you supply for the Windows NT account will be the same for the NetWare client. If you are enabling an existing Windows NT Server account to be used from a NetWare client, you are prompted to provide a new password for that user.

Enabling a user account for NetWare

You can enable an existing Windows NT Server user account to log on from NetWare client computers by using the User Properties dialog box.

If you have Directory Services Extensions for NetWare installed, the following procedure is necessary for the account to be propagated to NetWare Servers in the domain.

To enable an existing user account to log on from NetWare client computers

1. Start User Manager for Domains.

2. From the list of users, select the user account that you want to enable for NetWare. Then choose Properties from the User menu.

3. In the User Properties dialog box, select the Maintain NetWare Compatible Login box.

4. Choose the NW Compat button and fill in the NetWare Compatible Properties dialog box as follows:

   ■ Select or clear the NetWare Compatible Password Expired box. When the box is marked, the user must change the password the next time that he or she logs on from a NetWare client computer. If you mark this box, be sure that the user has at least one grace logon.

   ■ To allow the user an unlimited number of grace logons, select Unlimited Grace Logins. To limit the number, select Limit Grace Logins and type the maximum number to allow the user in the Allow box (or use the up or down arrows to select a number). Grace logons are the extra number of times a user can log on with an expired password.

- In the Concurrent Connections group box, select Unlimited to allow unlimited simultaneous connections to the server. To limit the number of concurrent connections, choose Allow and type a number in the Allow box.

5. Choose OK.

6. In the User Properties dialog box, choose OK.

Setting NetWare-compatible account properties

The NetWare-compatible properties are the additional user account properties that you can set for users who are NetWare-enabled.

To set the NetWare-compatible properties for a user account

1. Start User Manager for Domains.

2. Select the user whose NetWare-compatible properties you want to set and then choose Properties from the User menu.

3. Choose the NW Compat button.

4. Select or clear the NetWare Compatible Password Expired box. When the box is marked, the user must change the password the next time that he or she logs on from a NetWare client computer. If you mark this box, be sure that the user has at least one grace logon.

5. To allow the user an unlimited number of grace logons, select Unlimited Grace Logins. To limit the number, select Limit Grace Logins and type the maximum number to allow the user in the Allow box (or use the up or down arrows to select a number). Grace logons are the extra number of times that a user can log on with an expired password.

6. In the Concurrent Connections group box, select Unlimited to allow unlimited simultaneous connections to the server. To limit the number of concurrent connections, choose Allow and type a number in the Allow box.

7. Choose the OK button.

Creating a NetWare-compatible home directory

There are two parts to creating home directories for users. The first is setting the root path for all home directories on the FPNW Server. The second is creating and assigning the user's home directory within the home directory root path.

To set the home directory path for a user

1. Choose the FPNW icon in the Control Panel or choose the Properties command in the FPNW menu in Server Manager. The File and Print Services for NetWare On dialog box appears.

2. In the Home Directory Root Path box, type a directory or path. This path is relative to where the NetWare volume (drive:\SYSVOL) has been installed. This will be the root location for users' individual home directories. Choose the OK button.

3. In File Manager, create home directories for each user. Be sure to create these as subdirectories of the directory that you specified in Step 2.

4. In User Manager for Domains, select the user whose NetWare-compatible home directory path you want to set and then choose Properties from the User menu.

5. In the User Properties dialog box, choose the Profile button.

6. In the User Environment Profile dialog box, type the relative path of the user's home directory in the NetWare Compatible Home Directory Relative Path box. The path that you type here is relative to the home directory root path specified in Step 2. This must be the same directory that you created in Step 3.

7. Choose the OK button.

Setting NetWare workstation restrictions

To specify the NetWare client computers where a NetWare user can log on

1. Start User Manager for Domains.

2. Select the user for which you want to set workstation restrictions. Then choose Properties from the User menu.

3. Choose the Logon To button.

4. To allow the user to log on from all NetWare client computers, select User May Log On To All NetWare Compatible Workstations. To allow the user to log on from only certain NetWare client computers, select User May Log On To These NetWare Compatible Workstations.

5. If you selected User May Log On To These NetWare Compatible Workstations, you must specify the allowed computers. To add a NetWare client computer to the user's allowed list, do the following:

   ■ Choose the Add button.

   ■ In the Add NetWare Compatible Workstation dialog box, type the network address and node number of the workstation from which you want to allow the user to log on.

■ Choose the OK button to enter the workstation(s) address, and then choose the OK button to add the workstation(s) to those where the user can log on.

6. To remove a NetWare client computer from the user's list, select the computer and choose the Remove button.

7. When finished, choose the OK button.

Summary

This chapter covered

▶ Installing connectivity sevices

▶ Enabling and activating gateways

▶ Managing network connections

Chapter 14

Using Remote Access Service

Today, the network is our company. An organization is no longer defined by where we work. Instead our companies are defined by those colleagues whose company we keep. Software technology such as that provided in Windows NT Remote Access Service is largely responsible for this newly defined corporate structure known as the *mobile workspace*. This chapter shows you how to install, configure, and administrate Remote Access servers and clients to create a flexible wide area network.

Understanding RAS

Microsoft Remote Access Service (RAS) for Windows NT lets you connect to your office network from remote sites such as your home, a hotel, or anywhere there is an outlet for your computer and a phone jack for your modem. Once you have connected to a remote site, Remote Access lets you work with all of your applications as though you were physically in the office, directly connected to the network or local database. For example, you can

■ Access remote databases through the Windows NT Explorer

■ Send and receive electronic mail

■ Print files on the office printer

After connecting to your office network, the telephone link is transparent. That is, you can access and view network resources in the same way as your office colleagues who are working on computers physically connected to the LAN.

Remote node versus remote control

In order to understand how RAS works, it is important to distinguish between remote node and remote control access solutions. Remote control solutions, such as CloseUP and pcAnywhere, connect using modems over standard phone lines, but the only data they pass over the wire is screen shots from the host machine. All the processing takes place at the host. Remote node, on the other hand, usually uses the same hardware (a modem and a standard phone line) but instead of passing screen shots over the wire, the user is logged on to the network as though she or he were just another network user — albeit one on a very slow LAN! Remote node allows the user to connect directly to the network and act as a full peer on the local LAN.

RAS takes full advantage of the processing power of the remote user's PC. It enables the remote user to connect directly to the network and act as a full LAN peer member. It is as though one had extended the network wire to the remote user; the only difference is that the wire is not Ethernet but rather the slower asynchronous line. In remote node, packets from the corporate LAN are sent across the asynchronous line to the remote PC, where the application executes locally. It is ideal for applications that are truly client/ server, such as e-mail, or groupware applications, such as Lotus Notes. It is also appropriate for quickly copying a file to your home office.

In a remote control solution, users share a CPU or multiple CPUs on the server, whereas the RAS Server's CPU is dedicated to communications, not to running applications. With remote control, the user dials into an access server to take over control of a PC or host connected to the network. Processing takes place on the corporate network while screen updates are sent to the remote laptop or desktop. Therefore, remote control is ideal for obtaining information from large databases — keeping the processing local to the LAN, rather than attempting to send the entire database over an asynchronous line. When the database search is completed, all that is sent to the remote user are the results.

Although remote node is appealing to users and offers a great deal of flexibility, there are drawbacks. For instance, performance depends on a number of factors beyond simply the raw line or port speed of the server. In addition, security and accounting are issues that must be considered.

Remote control also holds additional value specifically for the network manager. Using remote control, help desk personnel can log on to a user's PC and perform diagnostics directly, often resolving problems on the spot. In addition, security and management are easier because databases and systems being accessed still reside physically on the LAN.

Remote control, however, still has its limitations. For instance, if the remote user is not using the same version of software as the gateway PC or host, problems may arise. If the remote user needs a specific application, it must be on the local PC in the appropriate version; otherwise, the remote user will be unable to perform his or her task.

Remote Access has a number of advantages and disadvantages. Because the remote workstation is logically connected to the network, you can achieve true client/server computing. On the other hand, because data transfer rates are dependent on the limitations of the serial devices being used, large amounts of data may take a long time to move over the connection.

In software applications architecture, the RAS client normally executes applications from the remote workstation. Contrast this with the remote control client, which runs applications from the host-side CPU. The RAS arrangement is better suited to graphical, client/server-based applications. Because network traffic is reduced in RAS, the user achieves higher performance. Remote control, however, can be useful in non-client-server environments.

Making Remote Connections

Remote Access Service can be as simple as two modems and a single analog phone line or as elaborate as a pool of modems allowing up to 256 simultaneous connections to the RAS Server. RAS adds a great deal of flexibility to your network plans in terms of hardware and software. You can even use RAS in place of a network card in your workstation!

In addition to the more traditional methods of remote communication (modems and serial cables), which are relatively limited in their transfer rate capabilities, Remote Access Service also supports ISDN and X.25 communication adapters. Both of these communication methods are fully digital — unlike modems, which must convert the computers' digital signals into analog tones and back because the telephone system carries only analog signals.

Modems for RAS

Remote Access Servers most often connect clients via modem. This is the most simple RAS implementation when connecting distant sites. To use RAS over a modem connection, you need the following:

■ Two modems, one on the server side of the connection and one on the client side

■ An analog telephone line

Compatibility between the server and client modems is of paramount importance for a trouble-free connection. Ideally, the same brand of modem should be used for the client and the connection to the Remote Access Server. When setting up the modems, select the same initial speed and enable the same features. If the same brand of modems is not available, at least choose a modem for the client with the same CCITT standard as the server's modem.

Computer to computer

A RAS can be easily implemented between two computers with a serial connection. Using a null-modem cable, you can connect the server and client directly via their serial ports. To use RAS over a serial connection, you need

- A client and a server machine

- A null-modem cable (9 pin or 25 pin, depending on your serial port connector)

Cross Reference

Appendix A, *Remote Access Technical Notes*, contains detailed information on constructing a RAS-ready null-modem cable.

ISDN

ISDN, which stands for Integrated Services Digital Network, evolved from the telephony network. This network provides end-to-end digital connectivity to support a wide range of services, including voice and non-voice, to which users have a limited set of multiple-use user interfaces. ISDN provides a single standard interface to access all network services, allowing voice, data, fax, video, and graphics to use the same line, with all of the error-free performance associated with digital technology.

ISDN Basics

ISDN carries voice and data by bearer channels (B channel) occupying a bandwidth of 64 Kbps each. A delta channel (D channel) handles signaling at 16 Kbps or 64 Kbps. H channels are provided for user information at higher bit rates.

There are three types of ISDN service: Basic Rate ISDN (BRI), Primary Rate ISDN (PRI), and Broadband ISDN (B-ISDN).

BRI consists of two 64 Kbps bearer channels (B channels) and one 16 Kbps signaling channel (D channel) for a total of 144 Kbps. You may hear this referred to as *2B+D*. The basic service is intended to meet the needs of most individual users.

Depending on the type of equipment you buy, you may use the bandwidth in a variety of ways:

- Simultaneous voice and data, allocating one B channel for each.

- B channels aggregated for more bandwidth. A single ISDN line can provide up to 128 Kbps bandwidth, to be used for circuit-switched data or video, and the B channels of multiple ISDN lines can be combined (inverse multiplexing).

Because signaling doesn't use the entire bandwidth of the D channel, it can also be used for packet-switched data, up to 9.6 Kbps.

PRI is intended for users with greater capacity requirements. Typically, the channel structure is 23 B channels (each one is 64 Kbps) plus one 64 Kbps D channel for a total of 1.544 Mbps. You may hear this referred to as *23B+D*.

B-ISDN is still in development and will support as much as 150 Mbps but will be dependent on a complete optical fiber network. This could be a medium for future high-definition television (HDTV) projects.

Getting ISDN

More than 56 percent (115 million lines) of the regional Bell operating companies have ISDN network access. Most of the Ameritech service region and major U.S. cities are wired for ISDN.

If you need information about ISDN in your area, contact the local telephone company. Table 14-1 lists companies offering ISDN as of the writing of this book.

Table 14-1 **Companies Offering ISDN**

Company	Service area
Ameritech (800) TEAMDATA	Illinois, Indiana, Michigan, Ohio, Wisconsin
Bell Atlantic (800) 570-ISDN	Delaware, Maryland, New Jersey, Pennsylvania, Virginia, Washington, DC, West Virginia
Bell South (800) 428-ISDN	Alabama, Florida, Georgia, Kentucky, Louisiana, Mississippi, North Carolina, South Carolina, Tennessee
GTE (800) GTE-4WCN, **Cincinnati Bell** (513) 566-DATA	Ohio, Kentucky
Nevada Bell (702) 333-4811 (small businesses), (702) 688-7100 (large businesses)	Nevada
Nynex (800) GET-ISDN	New York, Massachusetts, Rhode Island, Vermont, Maine, New Hampshire
Pacific Bell (800) 4PB-ISDN (ISDN service center), (800) 995-0346 (24 hr. automated ISDN)	California
Rochester Telephone (716) 777-1234	New York
Southern New England Telephone (SNET) (800) 430-ISDN	Connecticut
Southwestern Bell (800) SWB-ISDN	Missouri, Texas
Stentor (800) 578-ISDN	Canada
US West (800) 236-5226	Arizona, Colorado, Minnesota, Nebraska, Oregon, South Dakota, Washington

ISDN Hardware Requirements

In addition to the ISDN line, you'll need some of the following components, depending on how you intend to use your ISDN line:

- **Network Terminating device (NT1).** An NT1 serves as the network interface, providing line testing and diagnostic capability, as well as two-to-four wire conversion. You generally need to buy one device for each ISDN line that you install. Check with your ISDN vendor because some vendors integrate the NT1 into their other ISDN components.

- **Terminal Adapter (TA).** This protocol converter adapts non-ISDN equipment (for example, your computer, fax machine, telephone, and so on) to the ISDN network. TAs can be external boxes or internal PC cards. TAs can also be integrated into other devices, such as ISDN telephones.

Note

Some TAs aggregate the B channels, providing up to 128 Kbps of bandwidth. Inverse multiplexing Terminal Adapters are available to aggregate the bandwidth of more than one ISDN line.

- **Digital modems.** A digital modem is an ISDN Terminal Adapter that can emulate an analog fax/modem in order to interoperate with an analog modem or fax. Don't expect ISDN transfer speeds while in emulation mode; the capabilities of the analog device at the other end of the connection control performance. Several ISDN equipment vendors are offering these flexible devices, which allow you to continue to connect to analog devices and network services while ensuring that as much of your connection as possible is digital.

- **ISDN bridges.** Some Terminal Adapters also function as Ethernet bridges to support connection to a LAN. Many support compression, so that you can get the best performance from your ISDN line.

- **ISDN telephones.** ISDN telephones have an internal Terminal Adapter, and most also have an RS232 interface for your computer. Thus, an ISDN telephone can be used to support simultaneous voice and data transmission over an ISDN line. These telephones are typically used in a business environment, because many of their features involve working with other ISDN telephone stations on the same telephone system.

- **Inverse multiplexers.** If more than 112 Kbps of bandwidth is required, Terminal Adapters that perform inverse multiplexing are available. In LAN-to-LAN connections when 112 Kbps won't provide the desired performance or when broadcast quality video is required, an inverse multiplexer can aggregate multiple ISDN lines to provide the necessary bandwidth.

- **Wiring requirements.** ISDN was designed to work on standard copper twisted-pair wiring. If you have enough unused wires in your home or office to add a regular analog telephone line, you have enough for an ISDN line. If you decide to run your own wiring from the telephone company demarcation point, use 22- or 24-gauge wire containing four twisted-pair copper conductors.

X.25

X.25 is an international protocol used for wide area networks (WANs). Online services, such as CompuServe or Delphi, may use an X.25 network to connect the computer that a caller accesses to the service's main computers.

An X.25 network transmits data with a packet-switching protocol. This protocol relies on an elaborate worldwide network of packet-forwarding nodes that can participate in delivering an X.25 packet to its designated address.

To use RAS with X.25, you need the following:

■ A modem for dial-up connections

■ A smart X.25 direct interface card for direct connections

■ A leased line for direct connections

Point-to-Point Tunneling Protocol

Windows NT 4.0 Server and Workstation added support for Point-to-Point Tunneling Protocol. The Point-to-Point Tunneling Protocol (PPTP) is an extension to the standard Point-to-Point Protocol (PPP) that is used to create multi-protocol Virtual Private Networks (VPNs) via the Internet. VPNs connect both branch offices and telecommuters into an enterprise-wide corporate network and can eliminate all long- distance charges, along with the management and security responsibilities of maintaining private networks.

Interoperability

Making a connection via RAS is just part of the overall remote access solution. Once a connection is successfully made, usefulness and productivity are determined by whether you're able to interoperate with the network just as if your computer were physically attached to it. Interoperability means being able to connect to any resource on the network no matter what kind of "box" it may be. For example, you may have NetWare, UNIX, or Macintosh machines and resources on the network, and they all need to be accessible to you over that remote network connection. Coexisting and interoperating in an enterprise-wide network is a matter of protocol.

There are two schools of thought on how to coexist and interoperate in a heterogeneous environment. One strategy runs networks in parallel using a *gateway,* a hardware and software device that connects to dissimilar systems, between the networks. Another strategy suggests implementing a common transport, in which one or two protocols form the backbone of the transport, and using other protocols that are compatible with the backbone.

Beginning with Windows NT 3.51 RAS, Microsoft improved and increased the functionality of RAS in multi-protocol environments by implementing Point-to-Point Protocol (PPP).

Point-to-Point Protocol (PPP) is a data link protocol that provides a standard method of sending network packets, or datagrams, over a point-to-point link. The PPP standard allows support for many protocols, including AppleTalk, DECnet, OSI, IP, IPX, and NetBEUI, which enables remote access solutions such as RAS to interoperate in a multi-vendor network.

Cross Reference

For a thorough discussion of networking principles and protocols, refer to Chapter 2, *Redefining the Enterprise Network*, and Chapter 3, *Designing the Windows NT Network*.

How important is PPP?

Previous versions of RAS functioned as NetBIOS gateways. You would make a connection using NetBEUI/NetBIOS and then inherit other protocols from the server. Although you could share network resources in a multi-vendor LAN environment, you could not run applications that relied on a protocol other than NetBEUI on the client side.

On the server side, support for PPP enables the Windows NT RAS Server to receive calls from, and provide network access to, other vendors' remote access workstation software. RAS Setup automatically binds any installed, supported protocols to the RAS drivers.

Serial Line Internet Protocol for compatibility

SLIP, the Serial Line Internet Protocol, is an older communications standard found in UNIX environments. SLIP does not provide automatic negotiation of network configuration; it requires user intervention. Although SLIP is an older standard that is not recommended now that PPP is available, older UNIX systems may be configured as SLIP servers and attached to the Internet. By providing SLIP support in the RAS Client, Microsoft has made it possible for Windows NT users to access these servers and, thus, the Internet.

Installing Remote Access Software

Installing Remote Access Services software is not complex. The installation process is fairly straightforward if you've planned how you're going to use RAS — including the network protocols that you'll need. Evaluate your goals for using Remote Access and answer the following:

- Do you want access to the machine to which you're dialing or to the entire network?

- What network protocols are used throughout the network that you want to access?

- What kinds of software will you use over the RAS connection?

- Who will be allowed to dial into your network?

- Will your remote access server be used as a gateway to the Internet?

- Will you use PPP or SLIP to establish a workstation Internet connection?

Resolving these types of questions will assist in planning your RAS implementation and in choosing setup options and features.

Installing Remote Access Services

You install Remote Access Service for Windows NT Workstation and Windows NT Server by using the Network option in the Control Panel (if you did not install RAS during Windows NT installation).

1. Go to the Control Panel and choose the Network option. The Network dialog box, shown in Figure 14-1, appears.

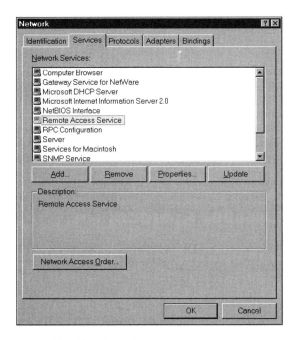

Figure 14-1: The Network dialog box.

2. In the Network dialog box, select the Services tab and click the Add button. Select Remote Access Service from the Select Network Service dialog box. Then click OK.

The installation program prompts you for the path to the distribution files. Usually, it expects to use the same path from which you installed Windows NT. If the path to your installation media is different from the path presented, type the correct path and click the OK button. The RAS files will be copied to your computer.

3. After the installation program copies the RAS files to your computer, you're prompted to select a COM port to which your modem or other communications device is attached. The Add Port dialog box, shown in Figure 14-2, lists all of the ports available to Windows NT for RAS. This includes multi-port adapters, ISDN cards, X.25 cards, or other devices that you have successfully installed. Select the port you will use for Remote Access and click the OK button.

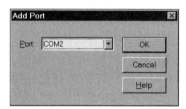

Figure 14-2: The Add Port dialog box.

4. Once you tell Remote Access Setup on which port to find a communications device, it offers to automatically detect the modem type connected to the selected port. You can avoid the detection process and manually select a modem by clicking the Cancel button or click the OK button to detect the modem automatically.

Note

If the modem is external, make sure the modem is turned on and hooked up to the system before using modem detection.

5. If you allowed RAS Setup to go through the autodetection process, it displays a dialog box showing the detected modem. Click the OK button to accept the modem.

6. If RAS did not detect your modem or if you chose to select the modem manually, select the device attached to the port from the list. Only supported modems are listed. If you are adding a port after initial RAS installation, you can use the Detect button to automatically detect the modem connected to the new port.

Smart Modem Detection

Allowing the RAS Setup program to detect your modem might sound like a sure thing but pay attention to the selection that it makes. It is possible that the Modem Detection phase may present you with more than one modem from which to choose and your modem might not be listed as one of the choices. The RAS Setup program tries to detect the modem type based on the response that it receives when it queries the attached device. The trouble is that some modems return the same response string, and RAS cannot detect the difference between them. Also, because aliased modems have the same DETECT_RESPONSE string, modem detection will always list all modems that are aliased to the same modem.

Windows NT RAS supports over 200 modems. The MODEM.INF file (located in the \WINNT\SYSTEM32\RAS directory) lists all of the modems supported by RAS, along with the command and response strings that each modem needs for correct operation. Modems that are not listed in the MODEM.INF file can be added manually.

In the MODEM.INF file, individual modems will have separate command sections. Modems with identical command sequences can now be aliased. For example, if modem 2 has the same command sequence as modem 1, modem 2's section might be as follows:

```
[modem 2]
alias=modem 1
```

Aliases to aliased sections are not allowed. In other words, in the previous example, if you have modem 3, which has an identical command sequence to modem 1 and modem 2, you can alias modem 3 to modem 1, but you cannot alias modem 3 to modem 2.

Configuring the modem and port

After selecting the modem type, RAS requests information about how to configure the device's port. RAS needs to know whether the port should operate in a two-way mode, sending and receiving calls, or whether it should send only or receive only. You also must indicate whether you want to use modem features such as error control and modem compression. You configure the modem and port via the Configure Port dialog box, shown in Figure 14-3, which lists supported modems with the detected modem highlighted.

1. In the Port Usage box, specify how RAS should use the port by choosing one of these options:

   ■ The Dial out only option means the computer acts as a RAS client only. Choose this setting if you do not want other computers to be able to dial directly into your computer.

   ■ The Receive calls only option means the computer acts as a RAS Server only. Choose this setting if you want to allow other computers to dial into your computer and you do not plan to dial out from your computer.

   ■ The Dial out and Receive calls option means the computer can act as a client or server, so you get the best of both worlds.

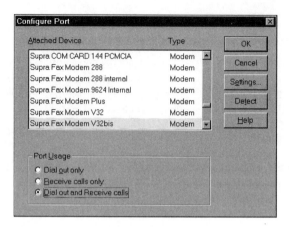

Figure 14-3: The Configure Port dialog box.

2. Next, you have to provide information specific to the type of device attached to the port. Select the device from the list and choose the Settings button to specify the following options:

   ■ The Enable Modem Speaker option sets the modem speaker so that you can hear the modem during operation.

   ■ The Enable Hardware Flow Control (RTS/CTS) option allows the modem to tell Remote Access software when the line is congested or clear so that the Remote Access software can temporarily stop transmitting data when necessary. *Handshaking* streamlines data transmission, prevents overrun errors, and improves overall data throughput.

   ■ The Enable Modem Error Control option checks errors on blocks of data through cyclic redundancy checks (CRCs). Modem error control causes the modem to retransmit garbled data, ensuring that only error-free data passes through the modem.

   ■ The Enable Modem Compression option compresses the modem-to-modem data stream, reducing the number of bytes transmitted and therefore reducing the transmission time. The reduction achieved depends on the amount of redundancy in the transmitted data.

If you're in doubt about any of these settings, stick with the default. Click the OK button to accept the settings.

Note

You can make changes to any of the settings after completing setup by selecting the Configure button in the Network Settings dialog box.

Completing RAS Setup

Now that you have told RAS Setup what kind of modem to use, how to use the port, and what modem features to use, RAS Setup displays the Remote Access Setup screen (shown in Figure 14-4) so that you can tell the Remote Access software how to operate.

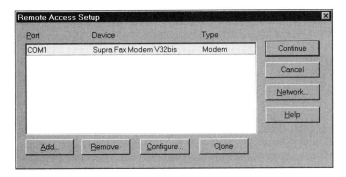

Figure 14-4: The Remote Access Setup screen.

You use the Remote Access Setup screen to configure RAS network settings and to configure or reconfigure the ports:

- Use the Add button to make a port available to RAS.

- Use the Remove button to disable a port, making it unavailable to RAS.

- Use the Configure button to change the Remote Access settings for the port, such as the attached device or the intended usage (dialing out only, receiving calls only, or both).

- Select the Clone button to copy the same modem setup from one port to another.

- Select the Network button to configure RAS network settings.

Because your primary concern at this point is with configuring RAS network settings, press the Network button to display the Network Configuration dialog box, shown in Figure 14-5.

The Network Configuration dialog box enables you to configure RAS client and server-wide settings that define the following:

- **Network access.** Allows access to the entire network or restricts access to the RAS Server only.

- **Network protocols.** Specify and configure network protocols for the dial-in connections (server) and for dial-out connections (client).

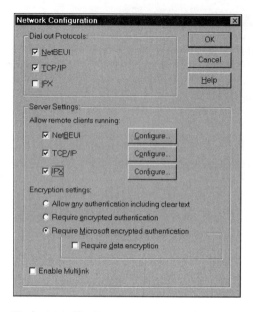

Figure 14-5: The Network Configuration dialog box.

- **Security features.** Set authentication and data encryption options.

- **Enable Multilink**. Enables Multilink functionality when you select the Enable Multilink check box. Applies to Windows NT Server computers only.

Note

Dial-Up Networking Multilink combines multiple physical links into a logical bundle. This aggregate link increases your bandwidth. The most common use is bundling ISDN channels, but you can also bundle two or more modems or a modem and an ISDN line. To use Multilink, both the clients and servers must have Multilink enabled. For more information, see *Configuring ISDN parameters* later in this chapter.

Configuring RAS Servers to Use LAN Protocols

Because RAS provides access to a LAN, your next step is to specify and configure the protocols to use on the LAN. A RAS computer may access a LAN as a client or as a server, so you must also configure LAN protocols for RAS for use in each role.

How do you know whether you're a client or a server?

You determined your RAS computer's role when you specified how the computer uses RAS-enabled ports. If you set a port to the Dial out only option, the computer acts as a RAS client only. If you set a port to the Receive calls only option, the computer acts as a RAS Server only. Finally, if you set a port to the Dial out and receive calls option, the computer acts as a client or a server.

Note

You should install the network protocols either when you initially set up Windows NT or — if you plan to use TCP/IP protocol with RAS — before you install RAS (see Chapter 17, *Installing and Configuring TCP/IP*). If you have not already installed TCP/IP and you select it as a protocol during RAS Setup, the setup program installs TCP/IP after installing the Remote Access software. However, I recommend that you install TCP/IP first to make sure that it is set up and functioning properly — many problems with RAS and TCP/IP can be traced back to incorrect settings in the TCP/IP configuration.

LAN protocol configuration details vary depending on the protocols already installed on your system and the ones that you select during RAS Setup. However, you follow the same basic sequence to set up any of the protocols. The following text outlines this sequence.

Note

Network LAN protocol settings apply to all RAS operations for all RAS-enabled ports.

Protocols on the RAS Server

RAS enables NetBEUI, TCP/IP, and IPX protocols on the RAS Server by default, but you can adjust these bindings to allow RAS to use only certain protocols. Enabling all three protocols allows RAS clients to use any combination of protocols to access remote resources. It is the easiest way to configure a Windows NT RAS Server, but you should evaluate the pros and cons of each protocol.

NetBEUI. RAS clients that run NetBIOS applications or need access to NetBIOS resources, such as file servers, on the remote network should always use NetBEUI. The NetBEUI protocol is the fastest and most efficient transport to access NetBIOS resources. With the RAS NetBIOS gateway enabled, clients have access to all remote NetBIOS resources even if they are not running NetBEUI.

TCP/IP. RAS clients that run Windows Sockets applications need to use the TCP/IP protocol if the applications run over the TCP/IP protocol. It is possible for these clients to access a NetBIOS resource if the NetBIOS name can be resolved via the LMHOSTS file. However, it is much easier and more efficient to use the NetBEUI protocol to access NetBIOS resources.

IPX. Clients that run Windows Sockets applications will need to use the IPX protocol if the applications run over the IPX protocol. An example of this would be the Client Service for NetWare that comes with Windows NT.

Selecting Protocols for Dialing Out

In the Network Configuration dialog box, select the protocols for dialing out in the Dial out Protocols box. Note that if no ports are configured for dial out, the Dial out Protocols box will be dimmed. The Dial out Protocols box sets the protocols used when this computer dials out as a RAS Client to another computer. If you do not select a protocol in the Dial out Protocols box, you will be unable to select that protocol later when you configure a phone book entry for dialing out.

Selecting Protocols for Receiving Calls

Select the protocols for receiving calls in the Server Settings box. Note that if no ports are configured to receive calls, the Server Settings box will not appear in the Network Configuration dialog box. The Server Settings box sets the LAN protocols that the RAS computer can use for servicing remote clients. You must also configure parameters for each protocol that you want the RAS Server to support; this procedure is described in the upcoming section, *Completing LAN protocol configuration.*

Selecting an Encryption Option

As part of RAS security, all authentication and logon information is encrypted when it is transmitted over the phone lines. You can select one of the following encryption options when setting up a RAS entry:

- The Allow any authentication including clear text option permits connection using any authentication requested by the client (MS-CHAP, MD5-CHAP, SPAP, and PAP). This option is useful if you have different RAS Clients.

- The Require encrypted authentication option permits connection using any authentication requested by the client except PAP.

- The Require Microsoft encrypted authentication option permits connection using MS-CHAP authentication only.

- The Require data encryption option means all data sent over the wire is encrypted.

Completing LAN protocol configuration

If you have interrupted the RAS Setup process, you can complete the LAN protocol configuration by doing the following:

1. Choose the Network option in the Control Panel.

2. In the Network dialog box, select the Services tab, and then select Remote Access Service and click the Configure button.

3. In the Remote Access Setup dialog box, click the Network button to display the Network Configuration dialog box (see Figure 14-5).

Windows NT RAS Authentication

Windows NT RAS supports several different authentication methods that allow it to interoperate better within a multi-vendor network. They are as follows:

RSA MD5-CHAP (RAS client only). The RSA MD5-CHAP algorithm produces a 128-bit hash code, or message digest, of an input file. This algorithm was designed for speed, simplicity, and compactness on a 32-bit architecture. The algorithm processes the input in 512-bit blocks. RSA MD5-CHAP is the standard message digest algorithm used with PPP CHAP. Windows NT 3.5x and 4.0 support RAS MD5-CHAP for dial-out, allowing Windows NT 3.5 clients to connect with virtually all third-party PPP servers. Because RSA MD5-CHAP requires the availability of the clear text password at the server, Windows NT 3.5 does not support MD5 for dial-in.

RSA MD4 (MS-CHAP). RSA MD4 (also called MS-CHAP) is a one-way hash function, a computation that takes a variable-size input and returns a fixed-size (128-bit) string, or hash value. One-way hash functions produce a message digest algorithm, which creates a very secure checksum for a message. It is secure in the sense that given a pre-existing checksum, it is nearly impossible to figure out how to alter the message without altering the checksum. If you know the checksum for a message and can verify that it is correct, you can be confident that the message was not altered.

A Microsoft version of RSA MD4 is enabled on the Windows NT 4.0 RAS Server by default and is the most secure encryption algorithm that Windows NT 4.0 RAS Server supports. Administrators and users can also implement data encryption when using Microsoft encrypted authentication. This option uses the RC4 algorithm to encrypt RAS session user data transmitted on the wire,

if encryption is negotiated between the client and the server at RAS connection setup time. Either the client or the server can require data encryption to be negotiated.

DES (Data Encryption Standard). DES is an algorithm for encrypting data designed by the National Bureau of Standards, so it is impossible for anyone without the decryption key to get the data back in unscrambled form. DES encrypts and decrypts data using a 64-bit key specified in the Federal Information Processing Standard Publication 46, dated January 15, 1977. It uses a binary number as an encryption key with 72 quadrillion possible combinations. The key, randomly chosen for each session, is used to create the encryption pattern for transmission. DES is supported for backward compatibility with LAN Manager-based systems.

Password Authentication Protocol (PAP). Windows NT 4.0 RAS supports clear text authentication via PPP PAP. RAS supports both domain-user name and user name formats for the PAP Peer-ID. Clear text authentication is the least sophisticated authentication method. It should be used only when dialing into SLIP servers or PPP servers that do not support encrypted authentication. Note that Windows NT RAS Server has an option that prevents clear text passwords from being negotiated. This enables system administrators to enforce a high level of security.

SPAP (Shiva Password Authentication Protocol) (RAS Server only). SPAP is a version of PAP implemented by Shiva in their remote client software. Windows NT 4.0 RAS Server supports SPAP to allow interoperability with Shiva clients. Shiva's SPAP, unlike standard PAP, does not send the clear text password on the wire.

(continued)

(continued)

The authentication method that the Windows NT 4.0 RAS uses depends on what type of client and server make the RAS connection.

The following table lists the types of authentication methods used between RAS clients and Servers.

Client	Server	Method
Windows NT 4.0 RAS Client	NT 4.0 RAS Server	MS-CHAP (1)
Windows NT 3.5 RAS Client	NT 3.5 RAS Server	MS-CHAP (1)
Windows NT 3.5 RAS Client	Windows NT 3.1 RAS Server	MS-CHAP (1)
Third-party RAS Client	Windows NT 3.5 RAS Server	MD5-CHAP, SPAP, or SAP (2)
Windows NT 3.5 RAS Client	Windows NT 3.1 RAS Server	MS-CHAP (1)
Windows NT 3.5 RAS Client	Third-party RAS PPP Server	MD5-CHAP, SPAP, or Clear Text (2)
Windows NT 3.5 RAS Client	Third-party RAS SLIP Server	Clear Text
MS RAS Client 1.1a	Windows NT 3.x or 4.0 RAS Server	DES

Complete the protocol configuration for TCP/IP, NetBEUI, and IPX on the RAS Server as described in the following sections.

Configuring a RAS Server to Use TCP/IP

Configuring the RAS Server for TCP/IP involves two different configuration aspects:

1. RAS requires its own basic configuration and IP address.

2. RAS must be configured to supply IP addresses to RAS clients.

Before you start, be sure that TCP/IP is installed. (If you have not installed TCP/IP, refer to Chapter 17, *Installing and Configuring TCP/IP.*)

To configure RAS to use TCP/IP

1. In the Network Configuration dialog box, enable the TCP/IP check box and click the Configure button to bring up the RAS Server TCP/IP Configuration dialog box as shown in Figure 14-6.

   The RAS Server TCP/IP configuration options are as follows:

   ■ **Allow remote TCP/IP clients to access**. Select whether to allow TCP/IP clients to access the entire network or this (the RAS Server) computer only.

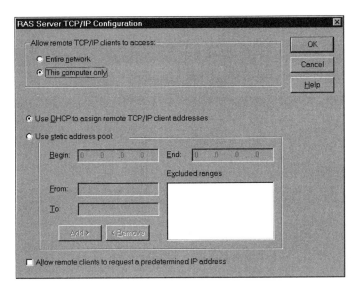

Figure 14-6: The RAS Server TCP/IP Configuration dialog box.

- **Use DHCP to assign remote TCP/IP client addresses**. If your network uses Dynamic Host Configuration Protocol (DHCP), you should check this option to allow the DHCP Server to provide IP addresses to clients.

- **Use static address pool**. Type the Begin and End IP addresses from the range allocated for RAS clients. These numbers should be assigned by the network administrator and should be entered in dotted decimal notation (for example, 110.11.0.0). To define excluded addresses within the IP address pool range, use the Excluded ranges controls, as follows: Type the first IP address that is part of the excluded range in the From box, and type the last number in the To box. Then choose the Add button. Continue to define any other excluded ranges in the same way. To exclude a single IP address, type the number in the From and To box and then choose the Add button. To remove an IP address range from the excluded range, select the range in the Excluded ranges box, and then choose the Remove button.

- **Allow remote clients to request a predetermined IP address.** RAS Servers can allow clients to request a specific address. Clients specify the address by entering it in Remote Access.

2. After selecting the appropriate options, choose the OK button to return to the Network Configuration dialog box. At this point, you can either click OK to end the protocol configuration process or select another protocol to configure.

Configuring a RAS Server to Use IPX

Before you configure RAS Server to use IPX, confirm that IPX is installed. (In the Network Configuration dialog box, the IPX check box is selected if IPX is installed.) Then follow these steps:

1. Choose the IPX Configure button in the Network Configuration dialog box. The RAS Server IPX Configuration dialog box appears as shown in Figure 14-7.

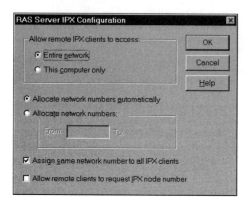

Figure 14-7: The RAS Server IPX Configuration dialog box.

2. In the RAS Server IPX Configuration dialog box, select whether to allow IPX clients to access the entire network or the RAS Server only, and then select a method for allocating IPX network numbers:

   - **Allocate network numbers automatically.** The Windows NT RAS software uses the NetWare Router Information Protocol (RIP) to determine an IPX network number that is not being used on the IPX network. The RAS Server assigns that number to the remote client.

   - **Allocate network numbers (manual override).** Manual assignments can be useful if you want more control of network number assignments for security or monitoring purposes. If you choose to allocate network numbers manually, type the first network number in the From box. RAS automatically determines the number of available ports and inserts the ending network number for you.

   - **Assign same network number to all IPX clients.** Select this check box to assign the same network number to all IPX clients by using either the automatic or the standard allocation method.

   - **Allow remote clients to request an IPX node number.** Select this box to allow the remote client to request its own IPX node number rather than using the node number provided by the RAS Server.

Allowing a remote client to choose the node number is a potential security threat to your network. It allows a client to impersonate a previously connected client and access network resources accessed by the other client.

2. After selecting the appropriate options, choose the OK button to return to the Network Configuration dialog box. At this point, you can either click OK to end the protocol configuration process or select another protocol to configure.

Configuring a RAS Server to Use NetBEUI

Remote Access Setup enables NetBEUI and the NetBIOS gateway by default. The only configuration option you need to consider is whether NetBEUI clients can access the entire network or the RAS computer only. Choose one of these options in the RAS Server NetBEUI Configuration dialog box. Restart your computer after making any changes.

Configuring RAS Clients

With the Remote Access Server software successfully installed and configured, you're ready to set up the client software and grant Remote Access permissions for users to dial into your server.

RAS clients use Dial-Up Networking, the client version of Windows NT Remote Access Service (RAS), to enter and maintain names and telephone numbers of remote networks, as well as to select the network protocols to use for a specific Phonebook entry. Clients connect to and disconnect from these networks using the Dial-Up Networking program.

Specifying remote network information

To specify remote network information

1. Start Dial-Up Networking by selecting it from the Accessories menu located under Programs on the Start menu. The Dial-Up Networking window appears as shown in Figure 14-8.

2. Assuming that you're setting up the RAS client for the first time, press the New button to bring up the New Phonebook Entry dialog box, as shown in Figure 14-9.

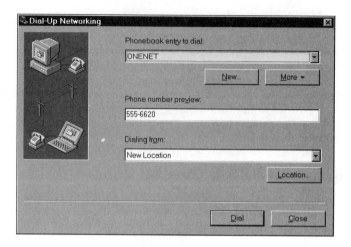

Figure 14-8: The Dial-Up Networking window.

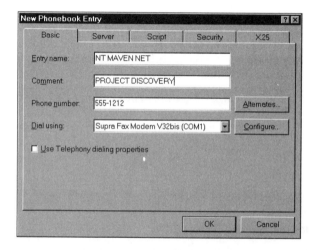

Figure 14-9: The New Phonebook Entry dialog box.

3. Click the Basic tab, if it is not displayed already, and enter the name, an optional description, and phone number of the remote network that you want to dial. You can assign alternate phone numbers for the entry by clicking the Alternates button and filling in additional phone numbers.

4. Use the drop-down list box in the Dial using field to indicate the modem or device to use when dialing this server.

Next, you must configure network protocol settings. Network protocols are the protocols that you use to communicate with computers on the LAN once you are connected to a RAS (Dial-Up) Server. PPP is the primary WAN protocol for RAS. You can run native TCP/IP, IPX, and NetBEUI applications using the PPP protocol. SLIP is an older standard and is provided on RAS clients to permit them to connect to the installed base of SLIP servers.

To configure Network Protocol Settings

1. In the New Phonebook Entry dialog box, choose the Server tab. In the Dial-Up server type drop-down list box, choose the type of server for this entry.

The three most common remote connections are the following:

- Microsoft RAS Servers. These include LAN Manager 2.1, Windows for Workgroups 3.11 with server extension, Windows NT 3.1 or later, and Windows 95.

Configuring the Client for Point-to-Point Protocol (PPP)

PPP supports four protocols that you can use for each specific phonebook entry. Which protocol(s) you select depends on the applications you plan to run and the type of RAS Server you use.

NetBEUI over RAS. If you select PPP without selecting a protocol, RAS uses the same NetBEUI implementation that was used in Windows NT 3.1 RAS. Users dialing into Windows NT 3.1 RAS or WFWG 3.11 RAS Servers need to use this protocol unless the server is going to be upgraded to Windows NT 3.5x or 4.0. If the user does not select a protocol and tries to connect to a Windows 3.1 RAS Server, the RAS client will give the user a choice to "Back Down" to standard NetBEUI.

NetBEUI over PPP. NetBEUI is the fastest protocol supported over RAS and should be used whenever the user needs to access NetBIOS resources such as file servers or printers on the remote Windows NT network.

IPX over PPP. Client Service for NetWare users has to use IPX over RAS to access NetWare resources while using NetBEUI on the remote Windows NT network. Other applications written to the Windows Sockets specification can also be used over IPX/PPP. If you need NetBIOS support, you should use NetBEUI in addition to IPX for greatest efficiency.

TCP/IP over PPP. If you need TCP/IP sockets support, you must select TCP/IP. You can use the TCP/IP protocol to access NetBIOS resources, but it is not as efficient as the NetBEUI protocol. RAS clients dialing into a third-party PPP Server may have to use TCP/IP to access NetBIOS resources on the remote LAN. Because standard broadcast name resolution is not supported over TCP/IP RAS, you need to use some other name resolution method such as the LMHOSTS file.

- Non-Microsoft Point-to-Point Protocol (PPP) Servers.
- Serial Line Internet Protocol (SLIP) Servers.

The Dial-Up server type list box shows the following choices:

- PPP: Windows NT, Windows 95 Plus, Internet.
- SLIP: Internet. TCP/IP is the only supported network protocol. There is no software compression.
- Windows NT 3.1, Windows for Workgroups 3.11. NetBEUI is the only supported network protocol.

2. Select a network protocol to use: TCP/IP, IPX/SPX, or NetBEUI. You can select more than one. Protocols already installed on the computer will be checked by default. If you selected a SLIP Server as the Dial-Up server type, you must use TCP/IP as the network protocol.

3. The Enable PPP LCP extensions (RFC 1570) check box enables newer PPP features. These extensions may cause problems when calling servers with older PPP software. Clear the Enable PPP LCP extensions (RFC 1570) check box only if consistent problems occur. Clearing the check box prevents LCP from sending Time-Remaining and Identification packets and requesting callback during the LCP negotiation of PPP.

4. Check the Enable software compression check box to compress information before sending it.

5. After setting the protocol options, press OK to return to the New Phonebook Entry dialog box.

Configuring Dial-Up Networking for TCP/IP over PPP

If TCP/IP is installed, the Phonebook will automatically select TCP/IP using PPP.

To configure TCP/IP parameters

1. In the New Phonebook Entry dialog box, choose the Server tab.

2. In the Network Protocol Settings section, choose the TCP/IP Settings button to bring up the PPP TCP/IP Settings dialog box, shown in Figure 14-10.

3. In the PPP TCP/IP Settings dialog box, select the Server assigned IP address option or the Specifiy an IP address option and provide the IP address that you want to use when connecting to the RAS Server. You can also select the Use default gateway on remote network option, if you require access to resources available through the default gateway. Choose the OK button to return to the Edit Phonebook Entry dialog box.

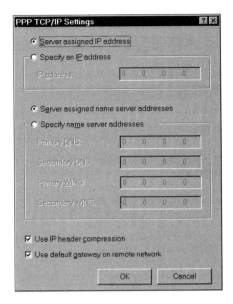

Figure 14-10: The PPP TCP/IP Settings dialog box.

Note

The Use default gateway on remote network option is only used if the Dial-Up Networking Client is using a network card to simultaneously connect to a LAN. When checked, packets that cannot be routed on the local network are forwarded to the default gateway on the remote network. In addition, address conflicts between the remote and local networks will be resolved in favor of the remote network. When this option is enabled, the user can access systems on the local subnet and any subnet on the remote network.

4. In the Network Protocol Settings dialog box, choose the OK button. In the Edit Phonebook Entry dialog box, complete any remaining configuration tasks, and then choose the OK button. The TCP/IP settings for RAS are available the next time you dial.

Configuring a RAS Phonebook entry for SLIP

SLIP support permits Windows NT RAS clients to connect to a SLIP Server. You configure SLIP from the Network Protocol Settings dialog box following the same steps shown previously in the section, *Configuring Dial-Up Networking for TCP/IP over PPP.*

1. In the New Phonebook Entry dialog box, choose the Server tab. In the Dial-Up server type drop-down list box, choose SLIP:Internet. Then click the TCP/IP Settings button to bring up the SLIP TCP/IP Settings dialog box as shown in Figure 14-11.

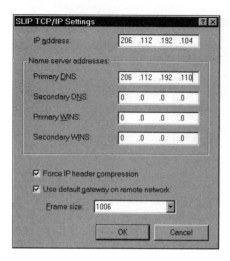

Figure 14-11: The SLIP TCP/IP Settings dialog box.

2. Assign an appropriate IP address to the client computer, and enter Name server addresses corresponding to the Primary and Secondary DNS and/ or WINS Servers on the remote server's network.

3. Enable the Force IP header compression and the Use default gateway on remote network options as described below.

   ■ **Force IP header compression**. RAS SLIP supports Van Jacobson (VJ) TCP/IP packet header compression. VJ is a protocol optimization supported in most SLIP implementations. When the Force IP header compression check box is cleared (the default), RAS SLIP attempts to detect compressed packets and, if found, automatically shifts into VJ mode. This gives the best chance of a successful connection and, in most cases, the best performance available.

   In cases where both ends are attempting to detect compression, compression may not be activated. If you are certain that the remote server supports VJ compression, you can check the Force IP header compression check box to activate compression and improve performance. You can verify that compression is occurring by monitoring the compression information on the Port Status screen.

   If the Force IP header compression check box is selected and the remote server does not support VJ compression, inbound traffic continues normally, but outbound traffic cannot succeed. Because most applications require communication in both directions, the session usually appears to stop in this case.

   ■ **Use default gateway on remote network**. The Use default gateway on remote network check box applies only to RAS clients that are simultaneously connected to a LAN using a network card. When checked, packets that cannot be routed on the local network are forwarded to the default gateway on the remote network. In addition, address conflicts between the remote and local networks are resolved in favor of the remote network.

■ **Frame size**. If you select SLIP, you must also choose an outgoing frame size. The default setting is 1006; 1500 is also available if your Remote Access Server accepts 1500-byte packets.

Automatic logon

When you use RAS to connect to a remote computer, the remote computer expects a specific series of commands and responses to log you on successfully. The sequence is identical each time you log on to the remote system.

If both the remote server and client are Windows NT 3.5x or 4.0 computers, connection and logon can be completely automated using Windows NT built-in security. If you log on to the Windows NT RAS client using a user name and password that is valid on the remote network and select the Authenticate Using Current User Name and Password check box in the Edit Phonebook Entry dialog box, Windows NT RAS automatically connects to the remote Windows NT RAS Server.

If you log on to a remote computer that is not a Windows NT 3.5x or 4.0 computer, you must configure the security settings for each RAS entry to handle the logon requirements for the remote device to which you are connecting. The remote logon will be either manual — using a Terminal screen that allows you to interact with the remote computer — or you can automate the remote logon using scripts that are stored in SWITCH.INF or PAD.INF (for X.25 networks).

Cross Reference

Appendix A, *Remote Access Technical Notes*, contains detailed information on creating and editing MODEM.INF, SWITCH.INF, and PAD.INF files.

If you dial into a remote computer that requires a logon procedure, you must configure the security settings for that RAS entry to use a RAS Terminal logon, as described in the following procedure. After RAS connects to the remote system, a character-based window appears and displays the logon sequence from the remote computer. You use this screen to log on to the remote computer.

To configure a RAS entry to use a RAS Terminal logon after dialing

1. In Remote Access, select the entry to which you want to connect and press the Edit button. If the Security button is not visible, press the Advanced button.

2. Choose the Security button. Next, select Terminal in the After Dialing box, and then click the OK button until you return to the Remote Access main screen.

3. After you dial and connect to this entry, the After Dial Terminal screen appears with prompts from the remote computer. Log on to the remote computer and use the After Dial Terminal dialog box to respond to the prompts.

4. After you have completed all interaction with the remote computer, choose the Done button to close the After Dial Terminal dialog box.

Performing Special Configurations

This section contains information about configuring RAS in special situations and using specialized hardware.

Configuring ISDN parameters

You need an ISDN card on the server and on each client to use ISDN. Remote Access expects to find an ISDN card installed in the computer before it allows you to set ISDN parameters. If you haven't already installed the necessary hardware, read through this section first to get an overview of the setup process.

Note

If you install more than one ISDN card, you must restart your computer after you have installed the ISDN drivers. Otherwise, all of the available ISDN ports may not show up when you configure Remote Access for ISDN.

Note

If you remove and then reinstall RAS on a computer that was previously configured with RAS and ISDN, you will not be able to add the ISDN ports in RAS Setup. You must reconfigure the ISDN driver before reinstalling and reconfiguring RAS with ISDN ports.

To specify ISDN parameters for each Phonebook entry that requires an ISDN connection

1. Access the RAS Phonebook by double-clicking on the Remote Access icon. Select the appropriate entry or use the Add button to enter a new entry. With the Phonebook Entry dialog box open, locate the ISDN button. (If the ISDN button does not appear, make sure you have set the dialog box to show advanced options.)

2. In the Port field of the Advanced Settings dialog box, select Any ISDN port, and then select the ISDN button. The ISDN Settings dialog box appears showing the following options:

   ■ **Line Negotiation**. You can select a line type and disable line negotiation, depending on your ISDN tariff rates and the capability of the ISDN line between your computer and the Remote Access Server.

   For example, if you have only Voice grade lines in your area, you can select a line type of 56K Voice and disable line negotiation. This configuration speeds up the connection. If 64K Digital connections are affordable in your area, you can select 64K Digital and disable line negotiation. This configuration saves you from incurring higher costs without your knowledge by preventing your ISDN card from occasionally negotiating a 56K Voice line type.

■ **Channel Negotiation**. Channel negotiation takes place only if the ISDN card supports it and if you enable Negotiate line type. For example, if you choose to connect with two channels and enable Negotiate line type, ISDN tries to connect with two channels. If that fails, it tries to connect with one channel. If you do not enable channel negotiation or if your card does not support negotiation, ISDN does not connect at all if it fails to connect with two channels.

3. After you have made your selections, click OK to return to the Remote Access screen.

Some options such as channel negotiation capabilities are specific to the ISDN card. Check with the manufacturer of your card to determine which options the card supports.

ISDN Phone Numbers

To connect through ISDN when requesting more than two channels, you must specify a phone number for each channel. For example, if you request three channels, you must specify three phone numbers (separated by colons, no spaces). Insert the phone numbers in the Phone Number field of the Phonebook Entry dialog box, as you would when adding, editing, or cloning any other entry. For example,

555-1234:555-1234:555-5678

If you request four channels, specify four phone numbers. For example,

555-1234:555-1234:555-5678:555-5678

If there are more channels specified than phone numbers given, the extra channels will attempt to use the last number. For this reason, you can use one number for a two-channel call because ISDN lines normally support two channels each. However, some ISDN phone companies require a unique number for each channel. Check with your ISDN provider.

Optimizing RAS on ISDN

Because RAS can use one or more B channels per connection, you can optimize RAS for the maximum number of connections or the best throughput.

To maximize the number of connections

1. If you have a lot of people calling in to the Remote Access Server, configure each channel to operate as a port. This configuration allows the greatest number of people to call in.

   Or

2. Use one B channel per incoming call. This transfers data at a rate of 64 KB per second. The 16-KB D channel control is shared between the two B channels, and control information is passed over the D channel so that the adapter knows which B channel is being referenced.

To maximize throughput

1. If you have just a few people calling in but need more data transmission speed, configure both channels to act as a single port. With this configuration, line speed increases to 128 kilobits per second. If you have installed more than one card, you can combine the channels on each card and get even faster transmission speed. (This will reduce the number of possible connections.)

   On a one ISDN port Windows NT RAS client, you can transfer data using two B channels, giving you an effective rate of 128 Kbps.

If you have more ISDN ports available, you can increase the throughput even further:

(No. of ISDN ports) x (No. of B channels) x (Channel data transfer rate) = Throughput BPS

To do this, you need hardware support on both the client and server side. The incoming call determines how many channels are used. If there are not enough channels available, the call fails. (Currently you cannot instruct the server to limit the number of B channels used per connection.)

Configuring X.25 parameters

You configure X.25 parameters much as you do ISDN — by setting options for each Phonebook entry that uses an X.25 connection. Make sure that you have an X.25 PAD or smart card installed in your computer.

To configure X.25 parameters

1. Bring up the Dial-Up Networking applet. Select the appropriate entry or use the New button to enter a new entry. With the Phonebook Entry dialog box open, locate the X.25 button.

Quick Answers: ISDN

My ISDN connection fails to connect, and I get the error message "No answer." What does this message mean?

This message means one of several things may be wrong:

■ The Remote Access Server did not answer because it is turned off, the modem isn't connected, or something similar. Contact your system administrator.

■ The line is busy.

■ There's a problem with your hardware. Make sure that your ISDN cards have been installed and configured correctly.

■ A poor line condition, such as too much static, interrupted your connection. Wait a few minutes and try dialing again.

■ You did not enable line-type negotiation in the ISDN Settings dialog box, and a connection could not be made with the line type you chose in the ISDN Settings dialog box.

■ Your ISDN switching facility is busy.

2. In the Port field of the Advanced Settings dialog box, select Any X.25 port, and then click the X.25 button. The X.25 Settings dialog box appears showing the following options:

- **PAD Type**. Select the type of X.25 packet assembler/disassembler (PAD). For dial-up PADs, select the name of the X.25 provider.

- **X.121 Address**. Enter the X.121 address (the X.25 equivalent of a phone number) for the Remote Access Server you want to call.

- **User Data**. Enter additional connection information required by the X.25 host computer. Typically, you leave this field blank unless the host system administrator advises otherwise.

- **Facilities**. Enter any additional facility parameters you want to request from your X.25 provider. For example, some providers support /R to specify reverse charging. For details, consult your X.25 documentation or provider.

3. After you have selected the appropriate options, click OK.

Quick Answers: X.25

Why does the server consistently fail to authenticate the client when connecting through a dial-up PAD?

Congestion on the Remote Access Server's leased line may be the cause. The administrator should make sure that the speed of the leased line can support all of the COM ports at all of the speeds that clients use to dial in.

For example, four clients connecting at 9600 bps (through dial-up PADs) require a 38,400-bps (4 x 9600) leased line on the server end. If the leased line does not have adequate bandwidth, it can cause timeouts and degrade performance for connected clients. This example assumes the Remote Access Service is using all of the bandwidth. If it is sharing the bandwidth, fewer connections can be made.

I can establish a connection, but why do the network drives keep disconnecting? Or, I'm dropping sessions or getting network errors.

This problem arises when X.25 parameters, such as the size of the send and receive window, are set differently for the server, the network, and the client X.25 software. Change the Negotiate network parameters option in the X.25 settings to Yes.

When transferring files, I often get error messages such as "Network drive disconnected" or "Network drive no longer exists." Why?

By enabling the Negotiate network parameters option on the client's (if using the direct X.25 connection) and the server's X.25 software, you let the server, the network, and the client use commonly negotiated X.25 network parameters.

What's happening to the new entries that I create in MODEM.INF and PAD.INF? They don't seem to work.

In MODEM.INF, check other entries for direct connections and external PADs and see the comments that go with them. You may need a line analyzer or a terminal program to see the response for the PAD. For dial-up PAD entries, use the same entry in the sample PAD.INF file that comes with Windows NT, paying attention to the comments that go with it.

Introduction to Remote Access Security

Remote access means that networks are becoming more open. Mobile employees are staying in touch while traveling, customers are calling into corporate bulletin boards, vendors are coordinating deliveries with master production schedules, and, of course, users are accessing the wide-open Internet. But "open" does not mean a remote access network needs to be vulnerable to a security breach. Remote access security provisions should meet the following three objectives:

- **Provide adequate security.** A security system should validate users with passwords to protect network-attached resources from unauthorized access. Added security measures can grant users access only to certain resources and protect the network communications link itself from eavesdropping. The more levels of security provided, the more secure the network resources and information become.

- **Provide ease of administration.** The security system should be easy to both set up initially and maintain over time. The security system's administrative functions must also be secure from tampering by users.

- **Be transparent to users.** Users may attempt to circumvent security methods that are difficult to use, so the security system should, to the extent possible, make logging on from a home office as easy as logging on from a workstation attached to the corporate LAN.

Security standards

After setting up the RAS Server and client software, you should begin to consider security. On the surface, the connection between a RAS Server and client appears to be as simple as a handshake. On the contrary, when a client dials a Remote Access Server, the server responds by sending a challenge to the client. In response to the challenge, the client sends back an encrypted message. Next, the server compares the client's response to a user database to determine if the client has a valid account. If the account is valid, the server checks it to see if Remote Access permission has been granted. Upon determining that permission exists, the server connects the client. As you can see, the door to the RAS Server, and possibly the rest of your network, is secure.

RAS authentication is similar to, yet separate from, logging on to a Windows NT Server. Remote users must be authenticated by a Remote Access Server before they can access or become part of the network. To connect to the network through Remote Access, a user must have a valid Windows NT Server user account that has been given Remote Access permission. You can grant or revoke Remote Access permissions and set security options as needed using the Remote Access Administrator program.

There are two popular standards for password-based authorization: PAP and CHAP.

PAP (Password Authorization Protocol)

PAP is a simple, standards-based password protocol. A user's ID and password are transmitted at the beginning of an incoming call and then validated by the receiving equipment using a central PAP database. The PAP password database is encrypted, but PAP does not encrypt the user ID or password on the transmission line.

PAP is a standards-based solution that provides interoperability in a multi-vendor network, it is inexpensive to install and operate, and the database is encrypted to prevent password snooping. Its disadvantage is that the password is transmitted in the clear, making it easy to snoop by tapping the line.

CHAP (Challenge Handshake Authorization Protocol)

CHAP is a standards-based authentication service for periodically validating users with a sophisticated challenge-handshake protocol. The initial CHAP authentication is performed during the logon attempt; the network administrator can specify the rate of subsequent authentications. The use of repeated challenges is intended to limit the time of exposure to any single attack. CHAP transmissions are encrypted to afford greater protection.

CHAP provides greater security than PAP while maintaining multi-vendor interoperability, it is inexpensive to install and operate, and it is secure against eavesdropping because CHAP encrypts the password during transmission in the WAN. However, because CHAP's standard password database is in plain text form, it is vulnerable to snooping.

Network access permission

After passing Remote Access authentication and connecting to the LAN, users can access any resource on the application server for which they have permission.

Remote users are subject to Windows NT security, just as they are at the office. In other words, they cannot do anything for which they lack sufficient privilege, nor can they access resources for which they do not have permission.

Remote Access authentication does not negate security restrictions on a file or application server.

Note
When using RAS in a Windows NT Server domain environment, changes in Remote Access permission do not take effect immediately on all servers. It can take up to 15 minutes for replication of the change to other servers in the domain. If necessary, you can resynchronize the domain to ensure that a user with revoked permissions cannot gain access to the network before the change is automatically replicated.

Remote Access Servers participating in the same Windows NT Server domain have identical copies of the user account database, ensuring easy administration and identical security restrictions for all access points to the network.

Granting access rights

You must give users specific permission before they can successfully connect through Remote Access Client software. You use the Remote Access Administration utility located in the Remote Access program group to set permissions and restrictions. The following procedure assumes that the user has an account for the domain or server in question.

To grant or revoke dial-in permission

1. Double-click the Remote Access Admin icon to start the Administrator's utility.

2. If you have more than one server or domain, select the server or domain for which you want to set permissions.

3. Choose Permissions from the Users menu. The Remote Access Permissions dialog box appears as shown in Figure 14-12. If the focus is on a domain or a group of servers, you are setting domain-wide permission. If the focus is on a workstation, you are setting privileges for that workstation only.

4. Select a user for whom you want to allow access to the network, and then check the Grant dialin permission to user check box. If you want to use the Call Back security feature, select the call back mode, and then click OK to return to the Remote Access Admin window.

Note

Do not assign callback permission to users who are connecting to the network through a switchboard.

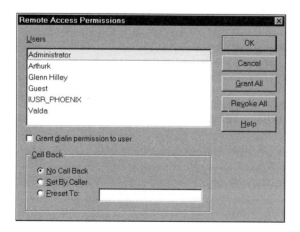

Figure 14-12: The Remote Access Permissions dialog box.

Notice that there is a guest account already listed in the users information. I recommend that you do not grant guest accounts dial-in permission. However, if you decide to do so, be sure to assign a password to the guest account.

Do not assign callback permission to users who are connecting to the network through a switchboard.

Because browsing for users and their permissions over a remote connection takes a long time, it's often more convenient to turn browsing off by default.

To turn off browsing

From the Options menu, select Low Speed Connection, unless it is already activated.

Configuring Client Security

Security settings on the Windows NT RAS client can be configured in the Security section of the Remote Access Phonebook. You can adjust each RAS Phonebook entry to require the type of authentication and encryption you need.

In the Phonebook Entry dialog box, press Advanced, and then press Security. The Security Settings dialog box appears.

To configure your computer for authentication, you may choose from four authentication options. Each option applies to PPP connections only. SLIP connections always use clear text authentication, which is accomplished through a Terminal mode session that occurs automatically after device connection has been completed. Connections to down-level RAS Servers use a down-level authentication protocol that is the security equivalent of the Microsoft encrypted authentication selection. To use data encryption, you must be connected to a Windows NT version 3.5 (or later) RAS computer, and you must use encrypted authentication. (These options were discussed in detail earlier in the chapter in the sidebar, *Windows NT RAS Authentication*.)

Setting Callback Permission

With callback, users dialing into a Remote Access Server must identify themselves with passwords or identification numbers. The server then automatically terminates the connection and calls the user back at a predetermined telephone number.

This is reliable for verifying a call from a particular site, such as a telecommuter's home or a branch office. However, it has several disadvantages: It does not address the issue of mobile workers calling in from locations such as client sites or hotel rooms, it adds a delay to establishing a network connection, it can be bypassed using call forwarding, and it may not protect against unauthorized use from authorized locations.

You can assign one of two types of callback permission:

- **Set By Caller.** The server asks the user to type in a number at which to be called back.

- **Preset To.** The server calls the user back at a predetermined number specified by the system administrator. This type of callback provides additional security by ensuring that the user is calling from a known location.

To set up callback permission

1. From the Users menu, choose Permissions.

2. In the Call Back box, select the type of callback permission you want to grant: No Call Back, Set By Caller, or Preset To.

3. If you select Preset To callback, type the user's telephone number in the Preset To text box.

Do not assign callback permission to users connecting to the network through switchboards.

Getting the Most from Remote Access

This section presents tips that can help your company save money on remote access, whether your remote access network links two buildings across town or connects thousands of users throughout the world. The tips address all of the different areas of your network, including wide area network services, network management, and remote and central site equipment.

The careful selection of network services and the management of network resources can benefit you substantially. Long after your equipment invoices are paid off, the savings in ongoing line charges and labor costs will continue. Also shop carefully for remote site and central site access equipment, where selecting the right equipment can mean substantially reduced network service charges, fewer administrative expenses, and happier, more productive users.

Utilize ISDN to consolidate lines

ISDN Primary Rate Interface (PRI) is a digital service that combines 23 distinct 64-Kbps channels into a single high-speed link. Each high-speed link is less expensive than the equivalent bandwidth achieved with multiple low-speed links. In addition, the higher throughput of digital communications reduces connect times, resulting in shorter, less expensive sessions, and the pooling of lines permits up to 25 percent better utilization, allowing the 23 consolidated channels to replace about 30 individual modem lines.

One of the most powerful capabilities of PRI is its ability to integrate onto one line the traffic from a number of different network services, including analog, switched 56, frame relay, and ISDN Basic Rate Interface (BRI). To use this capability, make sure your central site equipment can identify and process these services on a per-channel basis.

If your network handles a large amount of traffic, you can use multiple ISDN PRIs to handle any number of concurrent circuits.

Implement advanced bandwidth management techniques

Bandwidth on demand, which offers advantages at both ends of the connection, must be supported by both remote site and central site equipment. To take full advantage of bandwidth on demand technology, make sure the equipment you use supports Multichannel Protocol Plus (MP+), a standard that allows equipment to add and drop channels in real time to accommodate increases and reductions in traffic flow.

At the users' end, the advantage of bandwidth on demand is readily apparent. Users can "demand" the amount of bandwidth they need for whatever application they are running, becoming more productive as a result.

At the central site, bandwidth on demand allows channels to be released for use by others. For example, a user downloading a large file would be granted additional bandwidth automatically during the download in the form of an additional channel. When the download is complete, the channel would be released automatically, freeing it up for use by others.

Use ISDN BRI to increase productivity and lower phone bills

With increasing use of graphics and the proliferation of very large files, even 28.8 Kbps analog modems with compression can seem painfully slow. An ISDN Basic Rate Interface line, which consists of two 64-Kbps channels, can nearly quadruple the top end of analog modem performance. In addition, ISDN's digital nature provides error-free transmission and can set up connections with the network five to ten times faster than analog modems.

Evaluate equipment carefully, though. Some ISDN equipment such as Terminal Adapters and internal PC card solutions do not offer compression or support multilink protocols (either MP or MP+). ISDN equipment with advanced multilink capabilities can combine both BRI channels into a 128-Kbps data stream and compress it by as much as 4-to-1 for a total throughput of 512 Kbps. At rates like this, users get the effect of being connected directly to the LAN, and phone bills can decrease by 75 percent or more. For example, downloading a 2-MB file at 28.8 Kbps takes over nine minutes; at 512 Kbps the same file downloads in just 30 seconds. The savings on download times will quickly add up, and shorter connect times allow existing access lines to serve more users.

Use dial-up bandwidth on demand for backup and overflow needs

Whether you use leased lines or frame relay as the primary method of connecting your major facilities, dial-up bandwidth on demand provides a cost-effective solution for backup and overflow. When your primary network is down or saturated, a parallel bandwidth-on-demand network will take over automatically. The main advantage of bandwidth on demand is that you are charged for it only when you use it — so you no longer pay for reserve bandwidth that sits idle most of the time.

Make your entire remote access network centrally manageable

An obvious but often overlooked method of simplifying remote access network management is to make sure that both remote and central site equipment can be managed from a central location.

Is each board, box, or rack-mounted device at your central site manageable from a central console? Can an off-site expert dial in to isolate, diagnose, and fix a problem? If the answer to either question is "no" for any component of your network, that component should be upgraded or replaced.

Can your remote users' equipment be managed from a central site? Can configuration and software upgrades be performed remotely? If not, replace your remote equipment with something that can.

When evaluating remote site equipment, avoid the temptation to make price the determining factor. When you consider the real costs of support personnel and user down time, it takes only a few hard-to-solve problems — like a user inadvertently changing a configuration file — to wipe out the "savings" of inexpensive equipment. In the long run, you will save money by getting "intelligent" equipment that can be managed remotely, but not tampered with locally, even when the workstation is powered off.

Beef up remote access security

Sooner or later it will happen. A hacker will plant a destructive virus or wipe out a disk drive before its scheduled backup. A disgruntled employee will sabotage a database or publish a list of executive salaries. Or a competitor will steal your customer list or the design to your next generation product. Whatever the damage, you can be sure it will be expensive to fix and will disrupt your business operations and productivity.

To make sure your remote access network is tamper-proof, install equipment that has sophisticated passwords, callback, caller ID, restricted access, and other protections. To make security provisions easier to administer and to minimize the chances of someone altering your security mechanisms, consider using a RADIUS management database server. RADIUS (Remote Authentication Dial-In User Service), the most robust security database standard in the industry, is being supported increasingly by equipment vendors.

Consolidate remote access equipment

It used to take quite a collection of different equipment to construct a remote access network: modem banks, terminal servers, bridges, routers, gateways, inverse multiplexers, data compression units, line adapters, and so forth. The collective cost of buying this equipment is bad enough, but the bill for managing it all is even worse.

State-of-the-art equipment can consolidate the many functions performed by these individual components and eliminate the need for entire racks of equipment. Consolidation also heads off the long-term problem of running out of space in your equipment room. Too many pieces of equipment can overwhelm available power, air conditioning, or physical limitations, and force costly upgrades that do nothing to enhance the network itself.

Eliminate modem banks

Thanks to new digital modem technology, modem banks are no longer a necessary evil. Central site devices equipped with digital modems offer traditional analog modem users compatibility with digital access lines and equipment.

Digital modem technology is transparent, so analog modem users can continue to dial the same phone numbers and perceive absolutely no differences — except for better performance. The enhanced performance results from fewer analog-to-digital conversions, the error-free nature of digital transmissions, and the lessened chance that a high-speed modem will need to throttle back to 9.6 Kbps because of line noise.

Install integrated access devices

The typical home office has two lines: one for personal calls and one for business calls. Now, more home office users need more lines for data traffic. Otherwise, they must choose between missing either voice calls or incoming faxes if they run a remote session.

Many users order an additional phone line — only to learn that the telephone company must install expensive new wiring from the telephone pole on their street all the way into their house. To avoid this expense, install ISDN BRI on one of the lines and an ISDN integrated access device (IAD), instead. An ISDN IAD allows a single BRI line to behave like three separate lines. Multiplex both ISDN channels to set up a remote access session at 128 Kbps/s and you still can receive incoming voice or fax calls on the same twisted pair wire. Or simultaneously hold a voice call on one BRI channel and a data call on the other. The IAD you select must be able to handle voice, data, and fax video interchangeably and allow the two BRI channels to operate separately or in combination.

Integrate data, voice, and video

You can realize substantial savings by integrating all of the data, voice, and video traffic from your branch offices onto a single access line. There are two options for this traffic: a multiplexer with a leased-line connection or an integrated access device (IAD) that supports bandwidth on demand. If your branches are in your local calling area and your local carrier charges low leased-line rates, a multiplexer solution is most economical. For branch offices out of your local calling area, an IAD is best. Make sure the IAD is compatible with your remote access, videoconferencing, and PBX equipment; incorporates drop-and-insert capabilities; and supports MP+ and AIM.

Use bandwidth on demand for Internet

The Internet has become an essential business tool. If your company already has an Internet gateway, you are probably using a high-speed leased line with adequate capacity for peak loads. But during non-peak periods, that line probably sits idle and wastes money. A more economical approach is to install a lower-speed dedicated line and supplement it with additional channels for times of peak traffic. The dedicated connection to your Internet Service Provider (ISP) will give your employees access to the Internet and let outsiders access your Web Server. As your incoming or outgoing traffic needs increase, dial-up bandwidth is added automatically in 64-Kbps chunks. When the extra bandwidth is no longer needed, the dial-up circuits are dropped, so you pay only for the bandwidth you need, when you need it. Make sure your ISP supports MP+ so you can take full advantage of bandwidth on demand.

Summary

This chapter showed you how to install and implement RAS and Dial-Up Networking under a variety of scenarios and configurations. If you want to get to the nuts and bolts of RAS, I suggest you read Appendix A, *Remote Access Technical Notes*, which includes all of the technical details. This chapter covered

▶ Installing and configuring RAS and Dial-Up Networking for its supported protocols, including PPP

▶ Configuring RAS for ISDN and X.25 connections

▶ Implementing RAS security options

Chapter 15

Tuning and Optimizing Windows NT Server

In This Chapter

▶ Identifying bottlenecks

▶ Windows NT memory management

▶ Disk subsystem performance issues

▶ Solving physical network problems

Windows NT is a highly configurable network operating system. As a system administrator responsible for optimizing performance, you should be familiar with the tunable parameters for the various subsystems and how they affect system performance. This chapter is for technical administrators who want to know how to get the most from their Windows NT installation. It also explains how to optimize performance and identify bottlenecks that drain system performance.

Identifying Bottlenecks

Generally speaking, a *bottleneck* is a device with the smallest *max.throughput* for an interaction in the system. This device determines the maximum throughput the system can achieve. To understand how and where bottlenecks occur, take a look at Figure 15-1 which shows a block diagram of a 486 personal computer.

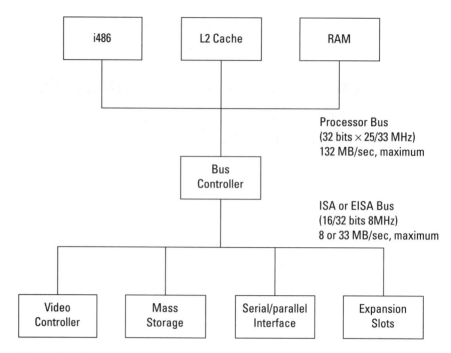

Figure 15-1: Block diagram of a 486 IBM-compatible personal computer.

To carry the analysis a bit further, take a look at how Windows NT executes a program:

1. To execute a program, Windows NT loads the program into RAM using a process called *demand paging.* Because Windows NT loads the program in pages, the entire program does not have to reside in memory at one time.

2. Once the program is in memory, Windows NT transfers control to the instructions in the program. Instructions move from RAM into the processor to tell the processor what to do next. For example, if the program instructs Windows NT to read or write data to a disk or to the network, data passes from memory to the appropriate adapter, which then transfers data to or from the media (disk or network, in this case).

As Figure 15-1 shows, data moves from the processor, along the I/O-memory bus, to the appropriate adapter or device. Unfortunately, the circuitry controlling the bus access and routing slows things down quite a bit. In the design in Figure 15-1, the processor and the I/O-memory bus run at the same rate: 8 MHz.

An alternative is to partition the system hardware into two separate buses, so slower I/O traffic does not interfere with the high-speed processor memory traffic of today's systems. These buses are fast enough that they seldom cause a computer system bottleneck.

The two memory caches form a memory hierarchy, which speeds system operation considerably while also reducing bus traffic. The cache built into the 486 processor is 8K and holds recently used code and data. By keeping these bytes near the processor in high-speed (expensive) memory, access to them is much more rapid. Usually it takes one processor cycle to fetch something from the first-level cache. The second-level cache, often referred to as an L2 cache, is larger, slightly cheaper memory that is not in the processor chip itself. The second-level cache can usually be accessed in two processor cycles. It is not unusual for a main memory access to take around 10 processor cycles, so the caches provide a huge performance boost when the data is present there.

The main difference between Figure 15-2 and Figure 15-1 is the addition of multiple processors. This permits multiple programs (or parts of programs, called *threads*) to execute simultaneously. Because these programs all use the same memory, cache design is very important to reduce memory traffic and the potential for memory to be a bottleneck in such systems. The common memory usually limits the amount of useful concurrence (ability of the multiple processors to work together), and the limits are very application-dependent.

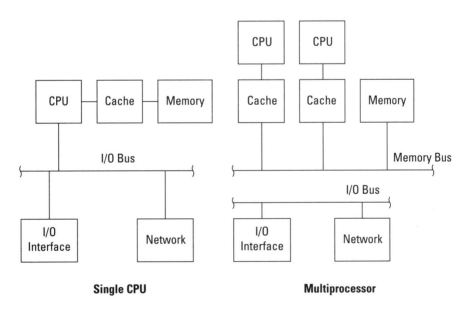

Figure 15-2: Block diagram of a multiprocessor computer.

Four components have the greatest effect on Windows NT Server performance. They are, in order of importance:

1. **I/O system.** Disk intensive processes take more time if the I/O system is slow.

2. **Memory.** The more memory you have in the Windows NT Server computer, the less often the paging file is used. Because reading RAM is much faster than accessing the paging files, increasing the memory can improve performance. (This assumes that the services are not up against an I/O bottleneck. Extra memory that is never needed does not improve performance.)

3. **Processor.** If your I/O system is fast enough and not a bottleneck, and you have enough memory to handle all the services of the server and additional services, your next improvement should be a fast processor. Windows NT processes are multi-threaded and can make good use of additional processors, assuming all of the other bottlenecks have been eliminated.

4. **Network adapters.** Network adapters come in a variety of flavors, from 4 Mbps ArcNet to 155 Mbps ATM. At the high end, the card tends to do most of its own processing, whereas at the lower end, the card may require significant processor cycles. The speed of the card may also be an issue, although even the slowest cards move faster than most PC hardware buses.

Disk Subsystem Performance Issues

Optimizing disk I/O is the most important aspect of a Windows NT Server installation. The disk subsystem configuration consists of at least one disk controller device and one or more hard disks, as well as disk configuration, type of disk, size, volume configuration, and associated file systems. The goal is to select a combination of these components and technologies to enhance the performance characteristics of the Windows NT Server. Disk subsystem I/O as it relates to reads, writes, and caching defines the performance characteristics that are most important to Windows NT Server.

Look for the following disk subsystem components and features:

- Intelligent, fast SCSI-2 disk controller or disk array controller
- Controller memory cache
- Bus master card; a processor onboard results in fewer interrupts to the system CPU(s)
- Asynchronous read and write support
- 32-bit EISA or MCA architecture
- RAID support at the hardware level
- Fast SCSI-2 drives
- Read ahead caching (at least one track)

Ordinarily, SCSI controllers have a greater effect on system performance than drives do. The differences in the controllers include technical specifications; features; functions, such as base board controller adapters for MCA, EISA, and PCI; and RAID adapters (with and without cache) for MCA, EISA, and PCI. Some of these controllers may not be fully SCSI-2 compliant and may not interact with Windows NT in the expected manner.

Because there is such a variety, specific performance guidelines are difficult to determine. A good approach is to use controllers located on the base board first, and then add bus adapter controllers for specific needs. Wide SCSI uses a 16-bit disk data path instead of a normal 8-bit path, and may be helpful for large sequential data transfers that may occur in applications such as CAD/CAM, print servers, and so on.

SCSI Basics

SCSI is the Small Computer System Interface. It is an I/O bus that is widely used in the computer industry to attach peripheral devices such as hard drives, tape drives, and CD-ROM drives to the computer's central processor.

Standardization work for SCSI has been ongoing in the industry for several years. In 1986, the American National Standards Institute (ANSI) officially approved the SCSI specification as a standard defining the mechanical, electrical, and functional requirements for attachment of SCSI peripheral devices.

Performance improvements in both processors and peripheral devices over the years have pushed the original SCSI specification to its limit. Consequently, new and improved versions of the specification have been developed to increase performance and improve functionality of the interface in an industry standard manner. SCSI-2 refers to a revision of the standard that defines Fast-SCSI-2, Fast-Wide SCSI-2, and some advanced command and control features.

Fast-SCSI-2 and Fast-Wide SCSI-2

When SCSI was first introduced, it was an 8-bit parallel bus that transferred a single byte of data with each bus cycle. When operating in synchronous mode (the fastest mode possible), data phase transfers could run at a maximum rate of 5 Mbps. With the introduction of Fast-SCSI-2, the bus speed doubled, and the data transfer rate increased to 10 Mbps.

Fast-Wide SCSI-2 was developed to double the transfer rate one more time. This is accomplished by "widening" the parallel bus to 16 bits and using the same bus speed as Fast-SCSI-2. The result is that Fast-Wide SCSI-2 has a maximum transfer rate of 20 Mbps.

These data rates only apply to the Data Transfer phase. All other bus phases used for Command Setup and Command Complete transfer control bytes at 2 to 4 Mbps in asynchronous mode. This is an initiator/target handshaking protocol that uses the 8-bit parallel path to guarantee compatibility of all SCSI devices (Fast-SCSI-2 or Fast-Wide SCSI-2).

The decision to operate in Fast-Wide mode during the Data Transfer phase is made on a drive-by-drive basis during *negotiation* between the controller and drive in the Command Setup phases. The controller and drive negotiate individually for the highest data transfer speed that they can handle between themselves. This means that it is possible for a Fast-SCSI-2 controller to communicate with both Fast-SCSI-2 hard drives and the new Fast-Wide SCSI-2 hard drives. The reverse is also true — a new

(continued)

(continued)

Fast-Wide SCSI-2 controller can be used with either type of hard drive.

Performance

Fast-Wide SCSI-2 provides higher bandwidth between the hard drives and the SCSI controller. Because many environments today are not constrained by the bandwidth of Fast-SCSI-2, they will not exhibit an immediate performance improvement with Fast-Wide SCSI-2 technology. Most file/print servers and application servers access the storage subsystem in a random pattern. In those cases, there are other factors, such as the mechanical limitations of the disk drives, that are more important to performance than bus bandwidth. If applications access data on the drives in mostly a random manner with small block sizes, then little, if any, performance improvement will be seen. This is because the mechanical latencies of the disk drive — that is, the wait times incurred as the head seeks the designated tracks and waits for the appropriate sectors to rotate under the head — are far greater than the data transfer times.

There are several key concepts and guidelines to help you select appropriate disk subsystem components.

- Optimize access to randomly accessed data and indexes by distributing the database over several physical disks, in a single striped volume (RAID 0 or RAID 5). This results in multiple heads being able to access the data and indexes.

- Optimize access to sequentially accessed data by isolating it from the randomly accessed data and index volume(s), on separate physical disks which may be RAID configured (usually RAID 1, mirrored for logs). Sequential access is faster via a single head that is able to move in one direction.

- Duplexing intelligent disk controllers (SCSI or Array) usually yields greater performance. This is especially true of systems that must sustain high transaction throughputs, systems with small data (buffer) caches, and systems with large data volumes. In addition, if the number of physical disks exceeds a controller's capacity, another controller is necessary.

- A good method for determining the number of disks required for an optimal disk subsystem is to multiply the number of I/Os per application transaction by the total number of application transactions per second, as generated by the users or the applications. This yields the total number of user- or application-generated I/Os per second. Take this value and divide it by the average sustainable I/Os per second of the physical disks that you may use (an average range is between 30 and 50 I/Os per second, which includes system overhead and latency). The result is a recommended number of disks for this particular SQL Server solution.

Disk load balancing

If your system uses multiple hard disks, it is important that you balance the total I/O load across those multiple disks. Otherwise, a disk may end up servicing a disproportionate percentage of the I/O load and consequently degrade performance.

Here are some tips for balancing disk load:

■ If you have a large number of executable application program files, place them on a disk that does not have the Windows NT operating system files on it.

■ If you can separate files into similar types (based on size or function, for example), try to locate similar types in the same file system. Then you can select configuration options that improve the performance of the I/O with that file system (for example, a file system with many similar large files might achieve better performance using a larger page size).

■ Use as few file systems per disk as possible (one file system per disk is recommended for performance reasons).

■ Put the user files/file system on a disk that does not contain operating system files.

For optimum performance on systems with multiple disks, distribute paging and swapping activity evenly across the entire disk subsystem. Place swap files on as many different disks as possible. If your system mixes high- and low speed disks, use the fastest disk available for swapping. Always avoid placing swap areas on slow disks; it affects system performance. If your system uses high-speed disk controllers, limit yourself to one swapping area for each independent channel of each high-speed controller. For daisy-chained controllers, stick to one swap area per daisy chain unless you are confident that the controller and device driver can support overlapped seeks (manage concurrent operations on different disks).

How to determine disk bottleneck

To use Performance Monitor to find a disk bottleneck, look for Disk object counters that indicate that the demand on disk resources is larger than demand on any other single resource in the system. Table 15-1 lists Performance Monitor counters for Disk objects.

Table 15-1	Disk Object Counters
Counter	*Description*
% Disk Read Time	Percentage of elapsed time the selected disk drive is busy servicing read requests.
% Disk Time	Percentage of elapsed time the selected disk drive is busy servicing read or write requests.
% Disk Write Time	Percentage of elapsed time the selected disk drive is busy servicing write requests.
Avg. Disk Bytes/Read	Average number of bytes transferred from the disk during read operations.
Avg. Disk Bytes/Transfer	Average number of bytes transferred to or from the disk during write or read operations.
Avg. Disk Bytes/Write	Average number of bytes transferred to the disk during write operations.
Avg. Disk sec/Read	Average time in seconds of a read of data from the disk.
Avg. Disk sec/Transfer	Time in seconds of the average disk transfer.
Avg. Disk sec/Write	Average time in seconds of a write of data to the disk.
Disk Bytes/sec	Rate at which bytes are transferred to or from the disk during write or read operations.
Disk Queue Length	Number of outstanding requests on the disk at the time the performance data is collected. It includes requests in service at the time of the snapshot. This is an instantaneous length, not an average over the time interval. Multi-spindle disk devices can have multiple requests active at one time, while other concurrent requests await service. This counter may reflect a transitory high or low queue length, but if there is a sustained load on the disk drive, it is likely that this counter will be consistently high. Requests experience delays proportional to the length of this queue minus the number of spindles on the disks. This difference should average less than 2 for good performance.
Disk Read Bytes/sec	Rate at which bytes are transferred from the disk during read operations.
Disk Reads/sec	Rate of read operations on the disk.
Disk Transfers/sec	Rate of read and write operations on the disk.
Disk Writes/sec	Rate of write operations on the disk.
Disk Write Bytes/sec	Rate at which bytes are transferred to the disk during write operations.

Counters to Watch

To check disk subsystem performance, pay particular attention to the following counters:

- **LogicalDisk: Disk Queue Length.** Check LogicalDisk: Disk Queue Length to see how many system requests are waiting for disk access. The number of waiting I/O requests should be sustained at no more than 1.5 to 2 times the number of spindles making up the logical disk. Most disks have one spindle, although RAID disks usually have more. A RAID device appears as one physical disk in Performance Monitor.

- **LogicalDisk: % Disk Time.** LogicalDisk: % Disk Time is the percentage of time the disk is busy servicing read or write requests. For servers it would not be unusual for the account disks to be constantly busy up to 100 percent. The system performance would still be satisfactory as long as the Disk Queue Length was within the aforementioned limits.

If both LogicalDisk: Disk Queue Length and LogicalDisk: % Disk Time values are consistently high, consider adding more controllers and drives.

Note

Physical Disk: Counters only show counter data for the first physical disk in a logical disk subsystem. If, for example, you have a logical disk system "g:\" as a striped file system comprised of five drives, you will be able to monitor Logical Disk: Counter information for g:\ and Physical Disk: Counter information for only the first of the five drives. Physical Disk: Counter information for the remaining four drives will be zero.

Optimizing Hardware for Disk Bottleneck

When a disk bottleneck has been identified in the system, be sure that it isn't really more memory that is needed. When the system is running short of memory, it starts paging to and from the disk, which often is the reason for the observed disk bottleneck. If this is the case, adding more memory to the system should increase performance dramatically.

Optimizing Software for Disk Bottleneck

If you have access to the application's source code, you can try optimizing the application itself; otherwise try the following:

- **Optimize the application.** If the average disk byte transfer is low and much smaller than the expected maximum throughput, you can optimize throughput from a disk even when the disk utilization is 100 percent. If the system load is reading and writing many small files, you can obtain a much higher throughput by increasing the size of the files.

- **Ensure that diskperf is turned off.** Microsoft claims that when diskperf is turned on it degrades performance by only 1.5 percent for 386 20-MHz computers, less for 486 systems, and almost nothing for Pentium systems. However, we have observed several cases of measurable degradation of disk performance with multi-processor Pentium systems; therefore, I recommend that you always turn off diskperf when performing customer benchmarks.

■ **Use the FAT file system instead of NTFS.** Using the FAT file system instead of NTFS is faster in some cases. It may be because the FAT file system is handling only 8 bytes instead of 16 bytes and no security checking is provided.

Application-Specific Tuning

The most critical performance aspect of an application is the type and frequency of disk I/O. The number of drives and controllers needed by an application is determined by the type of I/O that it generates and the frequency of that I/O. Write I/Os take up to four times longer than read I/Os in non-cached RAID5. Also, some applications generate many small random accesses, whereas other applications may do large sequential transfers. Many small random I/Os typically need more drives than large sequential transfers, even though the data transferred may be less for the small random I/Os. For example, for a 20-GB database that would be accessed by many small random I/Os, it would be better to have twenty 1-GB drives than five 4-GB drives.

Mail and client servers typically generate small random I/Os, whereas CAD/CAM applications use very large files and generate large sequential disk I/Os.

Isolating I/O

One sound approach to improving performance is to isolate an application's I/O on dedicated controllers and drives. For example, in a situation where you are planning a mail server, use two drives connected to one controller for system files and then use a second controller connected to a number of drives for the mail server's data files. As the application grows, another controller with drives may be added.

If a system has two (or more) dissimilar applications that are disk I/O intensive, use separate controllers and drives for each application.

Windows NT Memory Management

To understand Windows NT's memory management techniques, you need to understand certain aspects of Windows NT's memory management process.

Physical memory

Physical memory is the actual RAM storage installed on the computer system. *Virtual memory* is logical memory space from an application or operating system. A page of virtual memory may not have physical memory associated with it, but when the page is referenced, the operating system allocates and associates a page of physical memory. As applications reference virtual memory, the operating system applies, or maps, physical memory to the virtual memory transparently. With virtual memory capability, Windows NT gives applications 32 bits of virtual address space (4 GB) without requiring 4 GB of physical memory in the system.

Page faults

A *page fault* occurs when an application (or the system itself) references a location in its virtual memory address space that is not currently mapped to a physical page frame. The processor notifies the operating system that a page needs to be mapped by raising a page fault condition. The operating system then maps the virtual reference to a physical page frame by using a page from one of the lists of free pages to satisfy the page fault. If there are not enough pages on the free lists, the operating system reclaims pages that are used to map other locations. If these pages were previously modified, the operating system schedules the modified data to be written to the page file prior to reclamation. The latter operation is referred to as a *page write*. Once a new page has been mapped following a page fault, the contents of that page usually must be read from disk; this operation is referred to as a *page read*. Page reads and page writes are collectively referred to as *paging I/O* operations.

Thrashing

The term *thrashing* refers to excessive contention for physical memory. During the thrashing condition, application processes are contending for physical memory to map virtual memory references. If the system doesn't have sufficient physical memory to satisfy the minimal working sets of all of the active processes plus the system I/O cache, the active memory consumers will contend for the physical memory. Each time a page is demanded, it must be reclaimed from somewhere (usually from the same process that is demanding it). If the reclaimed page is modified, it must be written to disk, into the pagefile. When pages are being passed around at a rapid rate among the active memory consumers, it is known as thrashing. In the thrashing condition, the system is spending an inordinate amount of system resources passing pages around and performing paging I/O, rather than performing application activities.

Working sets

In Windows NT, the term *working set* refers to the amount of physical memory (in bytes) currently allocated by the system to a process (or to the system itself). Note that the Windows NT term "working set" is different from the classic definition, which refers to memory that is currently in active use by a process (whether or not it is actually allocated to the process). The working set of a Windows NT process may be a subset or superset of the memory that is actually in active use by the process. Performance Monitor reports process working sets in the process object Working Set. Note that process working sets include shared data (for example, pages in DLLs), so the sum of process working sets may be greater than the physical memory in the system. This is because each process includes a shared page in its working set count, even though only one physical page is involved.

Working Set Management

Windows NT uses a modified local FIFO (First In First Out) memory management strategy. Processes have minimum and maximum working set sizes. When the system has abundant memory, working sets may grow beyond the maximum working set size; this is called *working set expansion*. When a process takes a page fault, the page is ordinarily obtained from one of the free lists (the list of zeroed pages, free pages, or standby pages). *Standby pages* are unmodified pages that have been reclaimed from processes recently but still contain valid process data. If available memory becomes scarce, the Memory Manager builds up the free lists again by trimming process working sets. Trimming involves removing pages from a process, writing them to the pagefile if they're modified, and placing them on the appropriate free list. If the process faults a page that was recently trimmed but is still on the standby or modified list (with the process's valid data), the fault is resolved by simply moving the page back into the process's working set without any disk I/O. This is referred to as a *transition fault*.

Memory contention

A popular axiom in the computer industry is "If the system is paging, it needs more memory." This rule is sometimes true, but there are degrees of paging activity; some level of paging may be tolerable on a Windows NT system. In fact, some high-end applications use huge in-memory arrays or databases; for these applications, paging is essential.

Paging can be viewed as contention for a resource — physical memory. As with most resources, some contention is tolerable. However, as the contention increases, the system eventually reaches a point where system resources (CPU time, bus bandwidth, and disk time) are spending too much time passing pages back and forth between the various threads that are contending for memory. If we were to graph memory contention versus average response times, we would see a fairly smooth line from zero contention up to a point where response times start to increase dramatically. This point is the place where thrashing starts to occur. As memory contention increases past the point of thrashing, response times typically increase exponentially. System managers usually try to prevent systems from thrashing for active, business-critical activities. Short periods of thrashing activity may be acceptable for some environments.

In looking at the Memory object in Performance Monitor, it is important to keep in mind that not all page faults result in actual disk I/O. There are two major classes of faults: soft faults and hard faults. Soft faults do not require disk I/O. Hard faults require I/O. Examples of soft faults are demand zero faults and transition faults. A *demand zero fault* occurs when a process references a page in memory for the first time; the page must be cleared (zeroed) before the process can use it. Windows NT clears the page and then clears the indication that it is modified so that it won't consume space in the pagefile until it actually contains program data.

Hard faults are reported in the Memory: Pages/sec object. This object counts both page reads and page writes. Memory: Pages Input/sec reports read faults; Memory: Pages Output/sec reports pages written to the pagefile. Memory: Page Reads/sec and Memory: Page Writes/sec report the number of I/O calls to read or write pages; each call may operate on one or more pages at a time.

By comparing Memory: Page Reads/sec to Memory: Pages Input/sec, you can determine how much page clustering the system is performing — how many pages are being read per read I/O. Similarly, you can compare Memory: Page Writes/sec to Memory: Pages Output/sec to determine page write clustering.

No single Windows NT Performance Monitor object indicates that the system is thrashing or paging excessively. Excessive paging activity is generally characterized by a combination of *all* of the following:

- Memory: Page Faults/sec is high (roughly greater than 200 per second for a low-end server; greater than 600 per second for a high-end server). Remember that Page Faults/sec alone doesn't indicate excessive paging, because it includes both soft faults and hard faults.

- Memory: Pages/sec is high (roughly greater than 60 pages per second for a low-end server; roughly 60 pages per second per disk for a mid-range to high-end server). Memory: Pages/sec reports hard page faults per second.

- Memory: Available Bytes is less than or equal to about 4 MB, the system's goal for free memory.

- LogicalDisk: %Disk Time is high (roughly greater than 50 to 60 percent) for the disks that contain pagefiles.

- LogicalDisk: Queue Length is high (roughly greater than or equal to 2).

In addition, excessive paging is often accompanied by only moderate CPU utilization, because the CPU is waiting for disk I/O much of the time. This isn't always the case, however, since it is possible to have a computer-bound workload combined with a workload that is generating heavy paging traffic.

 Note Pagefile: % Utilization does not indicate the degree of paging on the system. A high pagefile utilization simply indicates that the Memory Manager has trimmed some process's working sets. This does not necessarily mean that paging has been excessive, just that trimming has been performed.

Adjusting I/O caching

Windows NT caches most I/O in a large system-wide cache, which is in its system virtual memory. The Windows NT system treats this cache similarly to a process's working set. When memory is in demand on the system, the I/O cache will be trimmed just like a process working set. When memory is abundant, memory will be applied to I/O caching as the I/O is performed. This design allows the I/O cache to function as a self-tuning entity. The I/O cache competes for memory, along with processes, when memory is in short supply; the I/O cache grows when memory is abundant.

There is one Windows NT setting that affects the I/O cache. The Control Panel Networks applet has a dialog box to configure the Server function. This setting is only applicable for Windows NT Server systems. (To find the dialog box, open the Main program group in Program Manager, open Control Panel, and choose Networks. Scroll down the list box, choose Server, and then click Configure.) The Maximize throughput for file sharing option allows the I/O cache to grow to its maximum working set size. This allows the I/O cache's working set to grow to almost the full size of physical memory on a system under heavy I/O load. This does not mean the I/O cache will always be that large, because the I/O cache will still compete for memory with other processes' working sets. Conversely, choosing the Maximize throughput for network applications option will cause the I/O cache to be given a default maximum working set value, based on the amount of physical memory in the system. Note that Microsoft SQL Server's installation procedure changes this setting to Maximize throughput for network applications, which may not be appropriate for servers that have an SQL Server installed and also run other I/O intensive applications.

Isolating memory and cache bottlenecks

When Windows NT first opens a file, the cache maps the file into its address space and then can read the file as if it were an array of records in memory. When an application requests file data, the file system first looks in the cache to see if the data is there, and then the cache subsystem tries to copy the record to the application's buffer. If the page is not in the working set of the cache, a page fault occurs, as shown in Figure 15-3.

If the page is in memory, it is mapped (not copied) into the cache's working set. This means a page table entry is validated to point to the correct page frame in memory. If the page is not in memory, the Memory Manager gets the page from the correct file on the peripheral system. This means that the cache is treated much like the working set of a process. It grows and shrinks as demand dictates. This also means that the cache will grow when copying files, while the available memory will shrink.

To find a memory bottleneck, use the Performance Monitor to identify situations where the system is running low on memory and starts paging. Look at %Usage and %Usage Peak in the Pagefile object to see if they are consistently high, which indicates that the system contains too little memory.

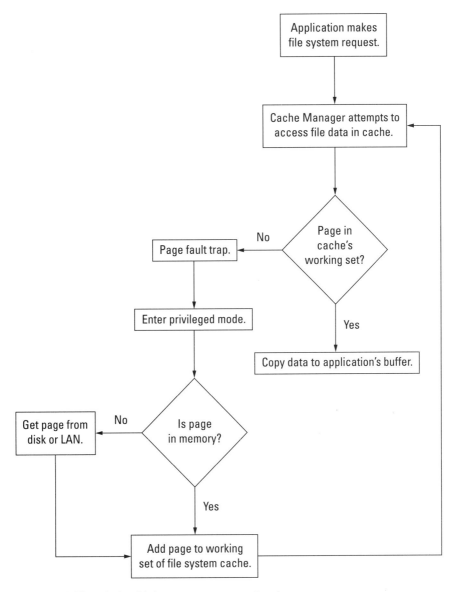

Figure 15-3: The relationship between memory and cache.

The following counters normally provide enough information to determine memory and cache bottlenecks:

- Processor Time% (Total Processor Time% if there is more than one processor)
- Pagefile: %Usage and %Usage Peak
- Cache: Copy Read Hits%, Data Map Hits%

- Memory: Pages/sec
- Percent disk time
- TCP: Segments/sec

The following items also indicate memory bottlenecks:

- Available Bytes counter (from the Memory object) is consistently low. When Available Bytes drops below 4 MB, the Memory Manager starts trimming working sets on the off-chance that some pages are not in active use. This activity degrades performance.

- %Disk or TCP: Segments/sec is high, because lack of memory causes the disk and/or LAN to suffer due to the paging.

In general, it is important to be aware of the system load nature to find cache bottlenecks. If there are no repetitive tasks, you can expect the cache hit rates to be low. However, if the system load is a repetition of a few minor files, the Cache object counter's Copy Read Hits% and Data Map Hits% should be high. If you expect high cache hit rates due to a specific system load but actual investigation indicates a lower value, a cache bottleneck may be revealed. To investigate the actual amount of cache being used, look at the Memory object counters: Cache Bytes and Cache Bytes Peak.

Identifying memory hogs

Windows NT maintains two *pools* of system memory: the *nonpaged pool* and the *paged pool*. The nonpaged pool is memory that the operating system guarantees will not be paged out. This memory is guaranteed to be resident at all times, so it is a limited resource. Device drivers and the kernel (the heart of the operating system) require nonpaged memory for various data to prevent page faults when processing core functions that require exclusive access to operating system data. The paged pool is system memory (in the system address space) that is pageable. The paged pool is allocated and used by the operating system and device drivers; only activities (at low IRQ levels) that can sustain page faults use paged pool memory. Windows NT usually requires more paged pool than nonpaged pool memory.

A *memory leak* occurs when a section of software (an application, driver, or the operating system) allocates memory and fails to return the memory back to the system when it is no longer in use. Memory leaks are characterized by steadily increasing memory consumption. If a driver or the operating system has a memory leak, Performance Monitor will show either nonpaged pool or paged pool bytes and the number of allocations will increase steadily. These counters are found in the Performance Monitor Memory objects: Pool Nonpaged Allocs, Pool Nonpaged Bytes, Pool Paged Allocs, and Pool Paged Bytes. If an application has a memory leak, it shows up as a steadily increasing process virtual memory size while the process is running. The relevant counters are Process, Virtual Bytes, and Working Set.

Pagefile layouts

When deploying a system for a workload that generates paging I/O (such as a large database), you can take steps to optimize the pagefile layout. The Windows NT Memory Manager can take advantage of additional pagefiles to distribute paged I/O traffic across multiple pagefiles. You should configure systems that require more than a moderate amount of paging I/O traffic as follows:

■ Use several pagefiles, each on a separate disk.

■ Place the disks on separate SCSI adapters.

■ Create pagefiles of equal size on each of the paging disks. This spreads the pagefile load evenly among the pagefiles, even when the pagefiles approach full capacity.

Do not place pagefiles on disks that contain database or transaction processing log files and other performance-critical files, because the latency of updating these files has a direct impact on end-user response times.

Pagefile Size

It is difficult if not impossible to predetermine the size of a pagefile required to support a given workload. I recommend using a two-phase approach to determine the optimum pagefile size:

1. To get started, make a reasonable estimate (see sidebar, *Sizing Pagefiles*) of the pagefile size required, configure the pagefile, and run the workload. You may find it useful to start up Performance Monitor and set an alert on Pagefile: % Utilization (perhaps at 60 percent). If pagefile consumption becomes high, you can create an additional pagefile.

2. Set up a Performance Monitor log for the first month or so, to capture Pagefile: % Utilization (every 10 minutes is probably adequate) and log it to disk. After a month, you may decide to add or remove pagefile space.

Windows NT supports dynamic creation of pagefiles. If a system requires more pagefile space, you can add pagefiles without rebooting the system.

Memory objects

The Memory object type includes counters that describe the behavior of both real and virtual memory on the computer. Real memory is allocated in units of pages. Virtual memory may exceed real memory in size, causing page traffic as virtual pages are moved between disk and real memory. Table 15-2 lists Memory object counters in Performance Monitor.

Sizing Pagefiles

Without historical data on which to base a decision on sizing the pagefile, the administrator must either make a guess or use the initial Windows NT configuration values, which are based on the Windows NT installation routine's guess. Windows NT sizes the pagefile using the following formula:

Size of physical memory +12 megabytes

For large systems with varied, memory-intensive workloads, this may not be adequate. Perhaps a better initial estimate for a large system would be as follows:

Two to three times the size of physical memory

After running the system for a while, the administrator may decide to raise or lower the pagefile sizes.

Table 15-2	Memory Object Counters
Counter	**Description**
Available Bytes	Displays the size of the virtual memory currently on the Zeroed, Free, and Standby lists. Zeroed and Free memory is ready for use, with Zeroed memory cleared to zeros. Standby memory is memory that has been removed from a process's working set but is still available. Note that this is an instantaneous count, not an average over the time interval.
Cache Bytes	Measures the number of bytes currently in use by the system cache. The system cache is used to buffer data retrieved from a disk or LAN. The system cache uses memory not in use by active processes in the computer.
Cache Bytes Peak	Measures the maximum number of bytes used by the system cache. The system cache is used to buffer data retrieved from a disk or LAN. The system cache uses memory not in use by active processes in the computer.
Cache Faults/sec	Cache faults occur whenever the cache manager does not find a file's page in the immediate cache and must ask the Memory Manager to locate the page elsewhere in memory or on the disk so that it can be loaded into the immediate cache.
Commit Limit	Size (in bytes) of virtual memory that can be committed without having to extend the paging file(s). If the paging file(s) can be extended, this is a soft limit.
Committed Bytes	Displays the size of virtual memory (in bytes) that has been committed (as opposed to simply reserved). Committed memory must have backing (that is, disk) storage available or must be assured never to need disk storage (because main memory is large enough to hold it). Note that this is an instantaneous count, not an average over the time interval.

Counter	Description
Demand Zero Faults/sec	Number of page faults for pages that must be filled with zeros before the fault is satisfied. If the Zeroed list is not empty, the fault can be resolved by removing a page from the Zeroed list.
Free System Page Table Entries	The number of page table entries not currently in use by the system.
Page Faults/sec	A count of the page faults in the processor. A page fault occurs when a process refers to a virtual memory page that is not in its working set in main memory. A page fault will not cause the page to be fetched from disk if that page is on the standby list, and hence already in main memory, or if it is in use by another process with which the page is shared.
Page Reads/sec	Number of times that the disk was read to retrieve pages of virtual memory necessary to resolve page faults. Multiple pages can be read during a disk read operation.
Page Writes/sec	Number of times that pages have been written to the disk because they were changed since last retrieved. Each such write operation may transfer a number of pages.
Pages Input/sec	Number of pages read from the disk to resolve memory references to pages that were not in memory at the time of the reference. This counter includes paging traffic on behalf of the system cache to access file data for applications. This is an important counter to observe if you are concerned about excessive memory pressure (that is, thrashing) and the excessive paging that may result.
Pages Output/sec	A count of the number of pages that are written to disk because the pages have been modified in main memory.
Pages/sec	Number of pages read from the disk or written to the disk to resolve memory references to pages that were not in memory at the time of the reference. This is the sum of Pages Input/sec and Pages Output/sec. This counter includes paging traffic on behalf of the system cache to access file data for applications. This is the primary counter to observe if you are concerned about excessive memory pressure (that is, thrashing) and the excessive paging that may result.
Pool Nonpaged Allocs	Number of calls to allocate space in the system nonpaged pool. Nonpaged pool is a system memory area where space is acquired by operating system components as they accomplish their appointed tasks. Nonpaged pool pages cannot be paged out to the paging file but instead remain in main memory as long as they are allocated.

(continued)

Table 15-2 *(Continued)*

Counter	Description
Pool Nonpaged Bytes	Number of bytes in the nonpaged pool, a system memory area where space is acquired by operating system components as they accomplish their appointed tasks. Nonpaged pool pages cannot be paged out to the paging file but instead remain in main memory as long as they are allocated.
Pool Paged Allocs	Number of calls to allocate space in the system paged pool. Paged pool is a system memory area where space is acquired by operating system components as they accomplish their appointed tasks. Paged pool pages can be paged out to the paging file when not accessed by the system for sustained periods of time.
Pool Paged Bytes	Number of bytes in the paged pool, a system memory area where space is acquired by operating system components as they accomplish their appointed tasks. Paged pool pages can be paged out to the paging file when not accessed by the system for sustained periods of time.
Pool Paged Resident Bytes	Size of paged pool resident in core memory. This is the actual cost of the paged pool allocation, since this is actively in use and using real physical memory.
System Cache Resident Bytes	Number of bytes currently resident in the global disk cache.
System Code Resident Bytes	Number of bytes of System Code Total Bytes that currently reside in core memory. This is the code working set of the pageable executive. In addition to this, there is another ~300-K bytes of non-paged kernel code.
System Code Total Bytes	Number of bytes of pageable pages in NTOSKRNL.EXE, HAL.DLL, and the boot drivers and file systems loaded by NTLDR/OSLOADER.
System Driver Resident Bytes	Number of bytes of System Driver Total Bytes that currently reside in core memory. This number is the code working set of the pageable drivers. In addition to this, there is another ~700-K bytes of non-paged driver code.
System Driver Total Bytes	Number of bytes of pageable pages in all other loaded device drivers.
Transition Faults/sec	Number of page faults resolved by recovering pages that were in transition, that is, being written to disk at the time of the page fault. The pages were recovered without additional disk activity.
Write Copies/sec	Number of page faults that have been satisfied by making a copy of a page when an attempt to write to the page is made. This is an economical way of sharing data because the copy of the page is only made on an attempt to write to the page; otherwise, the page is shared.

Memory Indicators

Performance Monitor provides Available Bytes of memory. Remember that Windows NT will utilize excess memory for I/O caching and for process working set expansion. So, given a moderate amount of activity, even systems with huge amounts of memory may show low Memory: Available Bytes. Memory: Available Bytes merely shows how much memory is currently on the free lists; there may be a lot of relatively unused memory — in processes and the I/O cache — which will be reclaimed by the virtual Memory Manager as soon as memory becomes in demand.

The Windows NT Memory Manager attempts to keep about 4 MB of memory available for miscellaneous activities like process creation. If Memory: Available Bytes is persistently below 4 MB and there is significant paging activity, the system may need more memory.

Finally, if you have done everything that you can to manage memory efficiently (for example, analyzed and possibly modified the pagefile layout, removed extraneous applications or services from the system, and tuned the application working set size — if source code is available), and you still have memory contention or unacceptable paging, you have no choice but to add more memory.

Optimizing hardware for memory and cache bottlenecks

When you have determined there is a memory bottleneck in the system, the most obvious solutions are to add more memory and cache or to use as many two-way interleaves as possible (number of processors that can access memory at the same time).

Adding memory and cache

Adding more memory should be done with care because of how Windows NT (and possibly later versions) utilizes its memory, in particular the file system cache. If the file system cache uses all free memory when random file I/O is performed, the system must search the file system cache prior to performing physical I/O. If the requested block is not in the cache, this activity degrades performance, especially if the file system cache is large (which it can be in a system with a lot of memory). Therefore, too much memory can decrease performance, in particular during random file I/O system load.

Adding more memory without upgrading the secondary cache may degrade the performance. This is because the secondary cache now has to map the larger memory space, usually resulting in lowered hit rates in the cache. This slows down processor-bound programs because they are scattered more widely in memory after memory has been added. Our experience with increasing the amount of first, second, and third level cache has resulted only in performance improvements, independent of the memory size!

A clumsy but efficient way to optimize the system is to slowly increase the amount of memory in the system and re-test until system performance decreases. This can be done by either physically adding memory or by slowly increasing the values of /MAXMEM at the end of your Windows NT version line in BOOT.INI.

Adding Interleaves

Going from one-way to two-way interleave improves performance significantly; going from two-way to four-way interleave does not. Therefore, I recommend that you always use two-way or more interleave when using two or more processors. This often requires that memory banks are fully populated.

Optimizing software for memory and cache bottlenecks

If you have access to the application's source code, you can try to optimize the application itself; otherwise, try to configure Windows NT and/or the application to make the best use of the available memory and cache.

Configuring Windows NT

Windows NT has one kernel parameter, LargeSystemCache, which is related to how Windows NT divides memory into file system cache and available memory. It specifies, for a nonzero value, that the system favor the system-cache working set rather than the processes working set. Setting this parameter to a high value will force the system to keep more in cache, thereby reducing the amount of available memory.

This is useful during a system load where a few small files are utilized frequently. It degrades performance during a system load where many different small and larger files are utilized, because the time required to search the cache when the item is not in the cache slows down throughput.

CPU/clock speed

The type and number of CPUs in each computer will dictate the performance potential for many client/server environments. Computers based on the Pentium CPU offer better performance potential than those based on earlier 486 CPUs. When computers have the same CPU, performance potential increases with clock speed. A Pentium CPU with a 133-MHz clock will offer better performance potential than a Pentium with a 100-MHz clock. Computers with multiple CPUs will offer performance potential that exceeds computers with single CPUs, although the performance increase may not be linear — a computer with two CPUs will not typically provide twice the performance of a computer with a single CPU.

How to determine a processor bottleneck

To use Performance Monitor to find a processor bottleneck, look for situations that indicate that the demand on processor resources is larger than demand on any other single resource in the system. The following counters are normally enough to help you compare the two types of demand:

- Processor Time% (Total Processor Time% if more than one processor)
- Processor Queue Length
- Memory: Pages/sec
- Percent disk time
- TCP: Segments/sec

A processor bottleneck has occurred when the processor utilization is close to 100 percent and all the other demands are much lower.

Processor Objects

The Processor object type includes as instances all processors on the computer. A processor is the part in the computer that performs arithmetic and logical computations and initiates operations on peripherals. It executes (runs) programs on the computer. Table 15-3 lists Processor object counters.

Table 15-3	Processor Object Counters
Counter	*Description*
% Privileged Time	Percentage of processor time spent in privileged mode in non-idle threads. The Windows NT service layer, the executive routines, and the Windows NT kernel execute in privileged mode. Device drivers for most devices other than graphics adapters and printers also execute in privileged mode. Unlike some early operating systems, Windows NT uses process boundaries for subsystem protection in addition to the traditional protection of user and privileged modes. Therefore, some work done by Windows NT on behalf of your application may appear in other subsystem processes in addition to the privileged time in your process.
% Processor Time	Percentage of the elapsed time that a processor is busy executing a non-idle thread. It can be viewed as the fraction of time spent doing useful work. Each processor is assigned an idle thread in the idle process, which consumes unproductive processor cycles not used by any other threads.

(continued)

Table 15-3 *(Continued)*

Counter	Description
% User Time	Percentage of processor time spent in user mode in non-idle threads. All application and subsystem code executes in user mode. The graphics engine, graphics device drivers, printer device drivers, and the Window Manager also execute in user mode. Code executing in user mode cannot damage the integrity of the Windows NT executive, kernel, and device drivers. Unlike some early operating systems, Windows NT uses process boundaries for subsystem protection in addition to the traditional protection of user and privileged modes. Therefore, some work done by Windows NT on behalf of your application may appear in other subsystem processes in addition to the privileged time in your process.
Interrupts/sec	Number of device interrupts that the processor is experiencing. A device interrupts the processor when it has completed a task or when it otherwise requires attention. Normal thread execution is suspended during interrupts. An interrupt may cause the processor to switch to another, higher-priority thread. Clock interrupts are frequent and periodic and create a background of interrupt activity.

Complex Processor Bottlenecks

It is possible to have processor bottlenecks at lower utilization, where the % Processor Time counter does not show the bottleneck. One reason is that some of the processes might be so quick that they do not register any processor usage. However, most likely it will be due to threads with a random arrival and service pattern. According to queuing theory, the length of the queue is 2 when the device utilization is 66 percent. Actually, queues can form at even lower processor utilization. The most commonly occurring situation is a bi-modal distribution of service, when most requests are very short or long with few that are medium length. This situation is called a *hyper-exponential service distribution*.

Use the Processor Queue Length counter, which tracks the threads in the Ready State, to understand the actual number of threads waiting in line. A steady growth or continuing high value of this number indicates processor bottlenecks even when Processor Time is much lower than 90 percent.

Optimizing Hardware for Processor Bottlenecks

Depending on the platform, the most obvious ways to optimize a processor bottleneck are as follows:

■ Change the priorities of the processes.

■ Increase processor speed.

- Add more processors.

- Increase amount of cache.

Increasing processor speed

Increasing the processor speed from Intel 486 33 MHz to 66/100 MHz and from Pentium 60/66 MHz to 90 MHz only increases the processor speed on-chip; that is, there is no increase in the speed to the cache controller or to the memory. This means that going from Pentium 66 MHz to 90 MHz, for example, does not improve system performance by 50 percent.

If an application is single-threaded (and therefore, not scalable) and only one thread is executed at a time, increasing processor speed will improve performance.

Adding processors

If an executed application is scalable, adding processors will often improve performance more than increasing the processor speed. Table 15-4 shows the performance gains that you achieve by adding processors to a system.

Table 15-4	Multi-Processor Performance	
From processor	*To processor*	*Performance improvement*
1	2	95%
2	3	System load dependent
2	4	30%
2	6	50%

Network Performance Issues

Network bottlenecks manifest themselves in a number of ways. Usually, the culprit is the physical LAN infrastructure, the workstation, or software application demands.

There are three forms of network performance problems; each causes the network protocol to have to transmit each block of data many times (or to time out):

- **A server overload.** The server is being asked to do more than it can, possibly because of another inadequate resource such as memory.

- **A network overload.** The amount of data that needs to be transferred is greater than the capacity of the physical medium.

- **A data integrity loss.** The network is faulty and intermittently transfers data incorrectly.

For optimal network performance, pay attention to the ramifications of the components that you select. This means knowing the ramifications of both hardware and software components: the network media (10Base-2, 10Base-T, AUI, and so on), the adapter type, the NIC driver, the topology (Ethernet, Token Ring, ATM, switching, and so on), the frame type, and the network speed. Careful selection of hardware and software can make a network operate both faster and more reliably.

You should take the following basic steps prior to changing performance parameters:

- Install a high-performance network adapter card in the server.
- Disable protocols and network cards not used in the environment.
- Use multiple network adapter cards, if appropriate
- Segment the LAN, if appropriate.

Network adapters can provide widely varying levels of performance. An adapter's bus type, bus width, and amount of onboard memory affect performance the most.

Bus types include ISA, EISA, MCA, and PCI bus architectures. Currently, PCI bus slots on the system board provide the best performance.

Bus width translates into the number of pins that connect from the adapter to the bus of the computer in which it is installed. When the bus width of the adapter matches (or closely matches) the bus width of the computer, performance tends to be better. Always try to use adapters that match the bus width.

How to determine a network bottleneck

To use Performance Monitor to find a network bottleneck, look for situations that indicate that the demand on network resources is larger than demand on any other single resource in the system.

Network Counters

The Network Interface object type includes those counters that describe the rates that bytes and packets are sent and received over a network TCP/IP connection. It also describes various error counts for the same connection. Table 15-5 lists the Network object counters.

Table 15-5	Network Object Counters
Counter	*Description*
Bytes Received/sec	Rate at which bytes are received on the interface, including framing characters.

Counter	Description
Bytes Sent/sec	Rate at which bytes are sent on the interface, including framing characters.
Bytes Total/sec	Rate at which bytes are sent and received on the interface, including framing characters.
Current Bandwidth	Estimate of the interface's current bandwidth in bits per second (bps). For interfaces that do not vary in bandwidth or for those where no accurate estimate can be made, this value is the nominal bandwidth.
Output Queue Length	Length of the output packet queue (in packets). If this is longer than 2, delays are being experienced, and the bottleneck should be found and eliminated if possible. Since the requests are queued by NDIS in this implementation of Windows NT, this will always be 0.
Packets Outbound Discarded	Number of outbound packets that were discarded — even though no errors had been detected — to prevent their being transmitted. One possible reason for discarding such a packet could be to free up buffer space.
Packets Outbound Errors	Number of outbound packets that could not be transmitted because of errors.
Packets Received Discarded	Number of inbound packets that were discarded (even though no errors had been detected) to prevent their being delivered to a higher-layer protocol. One possible reason for discarding such a packet could be to free up buffer space.
Packets Received Errors	Number of inbound packets that contained errors, preventing them from being delivered to a higher-layer protocol.
Packets Received Non-Unicast/sec	Rate at which non-unicast (that is, subnet broadcast or subnet multicast) packets are delivered to a higher-layer protocol.
Packets Received Unicast/sec	Rate at which (subnet) unicast packets are delivered to a higher-layer protocol.
Packets Received Unknown	Number of packets received via the interface that were discarded because of an unknown or unsupported protocol.
Packets Received/sec	Rate at which packets are received on the network interface.
Packets Sent/sec	Rate at which packets are sent on the network interface.
Packets Sent Unicast/sec	Rate at which packets are requested to be transmitted Non-to non-unicast (that is, subnet broadcast or subnet multicast) addresses by higher-level protocols. The rate includes the packets that were discarded or not sent.
Packets Sent Unicast/sec	Rate at which packets are requested to be transmitted to (subnet) unicast addresses by higher-level protocols. The rate includes the packets that were discarded or not sent.
Packets/sec	Rate at which packets are sent and received on the network interface.

Counters to watch

Windows NT has a Network Interface object that includes the following counters:

- **Bytes Total/sec.** The rate at which bytes are sent and received on the interface, including framing characters (not the case for Bytes Total/sec found in the NetBEUI and TCP objects)

- **Current Bandwidth.** Estimates an interface's current bandwidth

- **Output Queue Length.** The length of the output packet queue. If this is more than 2, delays are being experienced, and the bottleneck should be removed, if possible.

- **Packets/sec.** The number of packets sent and received

Because a network utilization counter is not available, use some of the preceding counters to determine network utilization; that is, compare the total bytes sent and received with the network bandwidth. Find out if there is data waiting on the output queue to the network from the client to the server and from the server to the client.

Compare also the expected network capacity (for Ethernet, 1.25 Mbps) with the actual (Bytes Total/sec) and Windows NT's estimate of bandwidth. It is most likely that it will be revealed that Windows NT's estimate of the bandwidth will be considerably lower than the expected network capacity. This is due to collisions on the wire that cause the adapter to retry the transmission after a random delay. Lore has it that Ethernet networks start to have significant collision at about 67 percent utilization, or 833,375 bytes per second under random load. To obtain higher network throughput, provide a regular traffic pattern on the network, if possible.

Use the following counters in conjunction with the counters just mentioned to determine if the network really is the bottleneck and not the processor, disk, or something else.:

- Processor Time% (Total Processor Time% if more than one processor)
- Pagefile: %Usage
- Memory: Available Bytes
- Memory: Cached Bytes
- Disk: Bytes Total
- Interrupt rate

Optimizing Software for Network Bottlenecks

If you have access to the application's source code, you can try to optimize the application itself; otherwise, try optimizing the network parameters as described in the following sections.

Optimizing Windows NT network parameters

In Windows NT, it is possible to configure a variety of network parameters for different network transport mechanisms, such as NetBEUI and TCP/IP. Many of these parameters do not appear in the Registry by default, and the system therefore uses a default value. To change the default value, add an entry in the Registry (if it does not appear) and specify a new value. For a complete description of parameters, see *Optimizing Windows NT,* Volume 3 of Resource Kit Appendix B *Registry Value Entries.*

The NetBEUI parameters are found in the path:

```
HKEY_LOCAL_MACHINE\SYSTEM\CurrentControlSet\Services\NBF\Parameters
```

Table 15-6 describes the parameters used in the preceding syntax.

Table 15-6	NetBEUI Parameters
Parameter	*Description*
EnableOplocks	Specifies whether the server allows clients to use oplocks on files. Oplocks are a significant performance enhancement but have the potential to cause lost cached data on some networks, particularly wide area networks.
MaxWorkItems	Specifies the maximum number of receive buffers, or work items, the server can allocate. If this limit is reached, the transport must initiate flow control at a significant performance cost.
RawWorkItems	Specifies the number of special work items for raw I/O that the server uses. A larger value can increase performance but costs more memory.

The TCP/IP parameter is found in this path:

```
HKEY_LOCAL_MACHINE\SYSTEM\CurrentControlSet\Services\Tcpip\Parameters
```

Optimizing network traffic

There are two ways to increase the network throughput:

- Provide regular network traffic by submitting load on the network in a periodic pattern; try to avoid output queues. This will decrease the number of collisions on the wire and therefore increase the overall network throughput.

- Submit a few large files rather than many small ones. The optimum is a file size just lower than the expected network media capacity (1.25 MB for Ethernet).

General tips for configuring application software

Whenever you install application software on your Windows NT network, you should think carefully about the implications of the various installation options. Pay particular attention to network traffic, network response time, and resource usage.

Network Traffic

When you install network-aware application software, you are typically asked to decide where to store the application's executable data files. You usually have three options:

1. Place a single, read-only version of the executable files on a share area on the server (where all client users can share them).

2. Place individual copies of all of the executable files on the client's local hard disk.

3. Use some combination of options 1 and 2 (some executables on the server and some on the client's hard disk).

The primary difference between each approach involves the amount of network traffic that each configuration will generate, the response time, and the reliability/error recovery implications.

Option 1 will generate the most network traffic. When you store all executables on the server, the entire executable must be copied over the network in order to load into client memory. A problem often arises with this option when all of the clients load some application programs as part of the boot process. This can result in large spikes of network activity in the morning when all of the PCs are being booted up at the same time. In such situations, with very large networks, demand may exceed network bandwidth. This will cause performance to suffer. In such situations, it makes better sense to use option 3 (a combination of executables stored locally and on the server) if possible.

Another application program issue to consider is the use of overlays. Certain application programs (word processors, in particular) make extensive use of overlays. These overlays are called into memory when needed and then returned to disk when not needed. In a network configuration, these overlays might reside on the server (by default); when they are called, they are loaded over the network. This can cause heavy, unanticipated network traffic which, if not planned for, can affect overall network performance. It is worthwhile to determine if any of your applications operate in this manner, and if so, evaluate how to configure the application to minimize this type of traffic.

Network Response Time

Response time over a network configuration is a highly variable issue — one that can be affected by any number of factors. In general, the goal is to try to achieve response times that approximate local resource response times (meaning, for example, that you can load a program over the network in about the same time it takes to load from your local disk). If you experience response time problems, check to see if they are related to throughput. One simple way to check this is to use the Windows NT Performance Monitor tool. This tool provides throughput (Kbps read and write) for network drives.

Network Resources

Finally, your application software configuration should make efficient use of network resources. A good rule of thumb is to use only the network resources necessary for the task currently at hand. Often, clients are configured to create nine links to five different servers at boot time when, in reality, only two or three of those links are active at any given time. A good solution to such a situation is to use an application launcher product. These products can be configured to create the links for an application package when that package is invoked.

Solving physical network problems

The most effective way to monitor the status of your physical network is via the ongoing use of intelligent network hardware. These devices collect and store status information that can be used to evaluate the health of your physical network.

If your network does not use such devices, use a network protocol analyzer (such as the SMS Network Monitor tool) to assess the health of your network. These analyzers can be used to capture samples of network traffic and then analyze the captured data for any of the indicators of physical network problems. If you have the opportunity to analyze network traffic, it is usually worthwhile to identify the longest (in terms of bit delay, not necessarily in terms of physical distance) client-to-server path through the network and use that path to generate network traffic for your data capture (for example, copy large files to and from the server over this path).

Network Utilities

If you do not have access to network analyzers or SmartHUBs, there are some software-only network statistics programs provided with Windows NT that can be used to gauge the relative health of the network. They are the NETSTAT, NBTSTAT, and NETMON utilities.

NETSTAT

The NETSTAT tool gathers statistics from the network adapter of the local computer or a specified remote computer, as well as some transport protocol driver data. The statistics can be used to determine the relative health of that machine's network connection based on the incidence of errors recorded. Table 15-7 lists the statistics provided by the NETSTAT utility.

Table 15-7	NETSTAT Statistics
Statistic	*Purpose*
Foreign Address	The IP address and port number of the remote computer to which the socket is connected. The name corresponding to the IP address is shown instead of the number if the HOSTS file contains an entry for the IP address. In cases where the port is not yet established, the port number is shown as an asterisk (*).
Local Address	The IP address of the local computer, as well as the port number that the connection is using. The name corresponding to the IP address is shown instead of the number if the HOSTS file contains an entry for the IP address. In cases where the port is not yet established, the port number is shown as an asterisk (*).
Proto	The name of the protocol used by the connection.
(state)	Indicates the state of TCP connections only.

To use NETSTAT to display protocol statistics and current TCP/IP network connections, use the following syntax:

```
netstat [-a] [-e][n][s] [-p protocol] [-r] [interval]
```

Table 15-8 describes the parameters used in the preceding syntax.

Table 15-8	Parameters for NETSTAT Syntax
Parameter	*Description*
-a	Displays all connections and listening ports; server connections are usually not shown.
-e	Displays Ethernet statistics. This can be combined with the -s option.
-n	Displays addresses and port numbers in numerical form (rather than attempting name lookups).
-p *protocol*	Shows connections for the protocol specified by *protocol*; *protocol* can be tcp or udp. If used with the -s option to display per-protocol statistics, *protocol* can be tcp, udp, or ip.

Parameter	Description
-r	Displays the contents of the routing table.
-s	Displays per-protocol statistics. By default, statistics are shown for TCP, UDP, and IP. The -p option can be used to specify a subset of the default.
interval	Redisplays selected statistics, pausing interval seconds between each display. Press Ctrl+C to stop redisplaying statistics. If this parameter is omitted, NETSTAT prints the current configuration information once.

NBTSTAT

The NBTSTAT tool provides network statistics for active and pending NetBIOS connections. This diagnostic command displays protocol statistics and current TCP/IP connections using NetBIOS over TCP/IP. Use the following syntax:

```
nbtstat [-a remotename] [-A IPaddress] [-c] [-n] [-R] [-r] [-S] [-s]
[interval]
```

Table 15-9 describes the parameters used in the preceding syntax.

Table 15-9	Parameters for NBTSTAT Syntax
Parameters	**Description**
-a remotename	Lists the remote computer's name table using the computer's name.
-A Ipaddress	Lists the remote computer's name table using the computer's IP address.
-c	Lists the contents of the NetBIOS name cache, giving the IP address of each name.
-n	Lists local NetBIOS names.
-R	Reloads the LMHOSTS file after purging all names from the NetBIOS name cache.
-r	Lists name resolution statistics for Windows networking. On a Windows NT computer configured to use WINS, this option returns the number of names resolved and registered via broadcast or via WINS.
-S	Displays both workstation and server sessions, listing the remote hosts by IP address only.
-s	Displays both workstation and server sessions. It attempts to convert the remote host IP address to a name using the HOSTS file.
interval	Redisplays selected statistics, pausing interval seconds between each display. Press Ctrl+C to stop redisplaying statistics. If this parameter is omitted, NBTSTAT prints the current configuration information once.

The column headings generated by the NBTSTAT utility have the following meanings:

In	Number of bytes received.
Out	Number of bytes sent.
In/Out	Whether the connection is from the computer (outbound) or from another system to the local computer (inbound).
Life	The remaining time that a name table cache entry will live before it is purged.
Local Name	The local NetBIOS name associated with the connection.
Remote Host	The name or IP address associated with the remote host.
Type	The type of name. A name can either be a unique name or a group name.
<03>	Each NetBIOS name is 16 characters long. The last byte often has special significance, because the same name can be present several times on a computer. This notation is simply the last byte converted to hexadecimal. For example, <20> is a space in ASCII.
State	The state of NetBIOS connections. The possible states are shown in Table 15-10.

Table 15-10   Possible States for NetBIOS Connections

State	Meaning
Connected	The session has been established.
Associated	A connection endpoint has been created and associated with an IP address.
Listening	This endpoint is available for an inbound connection.
Idle	This endpoint has been opened but cannot receive connections.
Connecting	The session is in the connecting phase where the name-to-IP address mapping of the destination is being resolved.
Accepting	An inbound session is currently being accepted and will be connected shortly.
Reconnecting	A session is trying to reconnect if it failed to connect on the first attempt.
Outbound	A session is in the connecting phase where the TCP connection is currently being created.

State	Meaning
Inbound	An inbound session is in the connecting phase.
Disconnecting	A session is in the process of disconnecting.
Disconnected	The local computer has issued a disconnect, and it is waiting for confirmation from the remote system.

NETMON

NETMON, for Network Monitor, is a network diagnostic tool that monitors local area networks and provides a graphical display of network statistics. Network administrators can use these statistics to perform routine trouble-shooting tasks, such as locating a server that is down or that is receiving a disproportionate number of work requests. NETMON is available as a part of Microsoft's Systems Management Server product.

Multiple Adapters

One of the characteristics of Windows NT Server is its ability to support multiple adapters in the server computer. In the server computer, multiple adapters can be used to connect the server to multiple network segments. This, in effect, increases the total network bandwidth available for accessing the server, because traffic from a given segment does not have to share the network media with traffic from another segment. Also, multiple adapters can be used to connect different network topologies (Ethernet and Token Ring, for example).

Transport protocol software

Windows NT supports multiple transport protocols either individually or simultaneously. Microsoft provides several protocols for use with Windows NT:

- NetBEUI (NetBIOS Extended User Interface), which is a small, efficient, and fast protocol tuned for small LANs

- TCP/IP (Transmission Control Protocol/Internet Protocol), which provides communication across wide area networks (WANs) and routers

- NWLink (NetWare Link), which provides a protocol compatible with the Novell NetWare IPX/SPX protocol, so that Windows NT computers can interoperate with Novell NetWare servers

- One additional protocol covered in this section is DLC (Data Link Control). DLC is traditionally used to provide connectivity between an IBM mainframe and an MS-DOS-based PC. DLC is a transport protocol defined by IBM. It is mainly used to communicate with IBM mainframes and minicomputers, typically model 3270 or AS/400 machines. In addition, Windows NT also uses DLC to communicate with network printers such as the Hewlett- Packard (HP) LaserJet 4 Si. Such printers have a network interface card (NIC) that contains a MAC and a DLC protocol stack.

If there are no WAN links in the network, NetBEUI and NWLink are installed automatically during Windows NT Setup.

Always view transport protocol tuning as a two-part process, since both ends of the connection (client and server) are tuned independently. Transport tuning performed at the server computer affects all connections involving that server computer. Transport tuning performed at the client computer affects only those connections involving that client.

Tuning NBF Server Transport Protocol

NetBEUI Frame (NBF) is the implementation of the NetBIOS Extended User Interface (NetBEUI) protocol driver. It is a small, fast, and efficient protocol that is supplied with all Microsoft networking products.

NetBEUI advantages include its small stack size (important for MS-DOS computers), its speed of data transfer on the network, and its compatibility with all Microsoft-based networks. On a Windows NT Server, NetBEUI is the fastest protocol.

The major disadvantage of NetBEUI is that it is a LAN transport and therefore does not support routing. In small installations where all workstations and servers are on a single LAN and no routing is required, NetBEUI is the protocol of choice.

NetBEUI Frame (NBF) has many tunable parameters but, in general, NetBEUI Frame is a self-tuning protocol on Windows NT. By default, NBF uses all of the resources necessary to handle client requests, and when it is not actively working, it doesn't use many resources.

There are several situations where you would change NetBEUI Frame parameters:

- Your network is slow, or the computers on the network are slow. You can increase the parameters to wait longer for replies from your slow network or slow computers.

- Server resources are limited, and you would like to allocate a limited amount of networking resources. By setting a ceiling on your networking resources, you are setting the maximum amount of resources that Windows NT will allocate for networking.

- You know the network traffic to and from the server will be high, so you can allocate resources at startup and not wait for the demand. This will improve performance because on-demand requires overhead to allocate more resources as needed.

Out of the preceding items, only the last reason could improve overall network performance. By understanding your environment and the resources it requires, you can allocate needed resources at startup. This removes the operating system from allocating resources as requests increase. The process of allocating more resources on demand takes time and can limit performance as resources are allocated and demand increases.

NBF tuning parameters

Modify the following NBF parameters as necessary. The NBF parameters are found in the path:

`HKEY_LOCAL_MACHINE\SYSTEM\CurrentControlSet\Services\NBF\Parameters`

The NBF module supports some configurable parameters that control various operational aspects of the protocol. Changing the initial startup settings for large networks will improve performance; after that, two other parameters can have a major impact on performance:

- **AddNameQueryTimeout.** Specifies the length of time that NBF waits for a response to a private query on the network (such as an add name query). The default is 5,000,000 milliseconds (1/2 second). The maximum possible setting should not exceed 10 seconds. You might need to raise this on extremely busy or large networks in order to allow additional time for the response to arrive.

- **AddNameQueryRetries.** Specifies the maximum number of times that NBF will retry sending a private network query (such as an add name query). The default is 3, and the minimum is 1. Lowering this value on very small or lightly used networks can reduce the time spent waiting by the server.

NBF Timer Parameters (T1, T2, and Ti)

There are three timer parameters that NetBEUI uses to regulate network traffic. These timers are T1 (response timer), T2 (acknowledgment timer), and Ti (inactivity timer). You should change these timers when you run over slow networks or communicate with slow computers. The values assigned to these timers must always maintain the following relationship:

$T2 < = T1 < = Ti$

The response timer T1 (DefaultT1Timeout) indicates how long the sender should wait before assuming the I-frame(s) were lost and need to be resent. The default value of 600 milliseconds is good for many networks, but the optimum value depends greatly on your network configuration. Decreasing this value to 250 milliseconds may improve performance, but if set too low, the network will get bogged down with unnecessary frame retransmissions and performance will degrade. Trial and error may be the best approach for setting this timer.

When return traffic does not allow the receiver to send an I-frame within a legitimate time period, the acknowledgment timer will fire, and the ACK will be sent. The value for this timer is set via the T2 parameter. The default T2 (DefaultT2Timeout) setting is 150 milliseconds. If the sender has to wait until the T2 timer fires in order to receive a response, the link will be underutilized while the sender waits for the ACK. This might occur over slow links. If the timer is too low, it will fire off and send unnecessary ACKS, generating excess traffic. NBF is optimized so that the last frame the sender wants to send is sent with the POLL bit turned on. This will force the receiver to immediately send an ACK.

The inactivity timer Ti (DefaultTiTimeout) is used to determine if the link has gone down. By default, it is set to 30 seconds. If Ti goes by without activity on the link, NetBEUI sends an I-frame containing an NBF SESSION-ALIVE frame. This is ACKed, and the link is maintained. On slow links, you may want to set Ti higher in order to minimize generation of SESSION-ALIVE frames.

Tuning TCP/IP Server Transport Protocol

The Windows NT Server uses Microsoft's TCP/IP software regardless of the type of TCP/IP software used on the client workstations (FTP's TCP/IP software or Wollongong Pathway Access's TCP/IP software).

The TCP/IP parameters that most affect network performance follow:

- **TCP/IP Window Size.** The TcpWindowSize parameter determines the maximum amount of data (in bytes) that can be sent or received by the system. By default, it will use 32 KB (32,768 bytes) as its window size. Because the default is set for the maximum, increasing your client's window size can often improve the performance of large data transfers. If your typical network client/server operations involve the transfer of large, contiguous files, increasing the default window size on the client to 16 KB may improve file transfers.

- **TCP/IP Segment Size.** The TcpRecvSegmentSize and TcpSendSegmentSize parameters control the minimum amount of data (in bytes) that can be sent or received as a single unit. The two parameters control the maximum amount of data (in bytes) that can be sent or received as a single unit. The default setting for both is 1460 bytes. It is difficult to suggest how to change these values without knowing the specific traffic patterns for a given network. Setting the segment size very small will underutilize network bandwidth. Setting the segment size larger than the maximum packet size of the network will require the IP engine to fragment the data and then reassemble it at the other end.

- **TCP Keep Alive Timer(s).** The TcpKeepCnt and TcpKeepTries parameters control the time that a TCP connection will remain active without network activity. In certain cases — typically when users don't log off but power off their workstation — this timer must be reduced so that sessions will be properly terminated at the transport protocol level. By default, the TCP/IP transport protocol will keep a non-responsive client connection alive for 40 minutes. The default setting is calculated as TcpKeepCnt (120 seconds) x TcpKeepTries 20 = 40 minutes.

Tuning NWLINK Server Transport Protocol

IPX/SPX (NWLINK) is a protocol stack that is used in Novell networks. Like NetBEUI, it is a relatively small and fast protocol on a LAN. But, unlike NetBEUI, it does support routing.

The major disadvantage of NWLINK is that it is a Novell proprietary protocol, so it is normally used to connect to and operate with Novell NetWare.

Tuning the DLC Protocol

There are three timer parameters that DLC uses to regulate network traffic. These timers are T1 (response timer), T2 (acknowledgment timer), and Ti (inactivity timer). These timers are changed when you run over slow networks or communicate with slow computers. The values assigned to these timers must always maintain the following relationship:

T2 < = T1 < = Ti

Summary

The goal in tuning Windows NT is to determine what hardware resource is experiencing the greatest demand (bottleneck) and then adjusting the operation to relieve that demand and maximize total throughput. A system should be structured so that its resources are used efficiently and distributed fairly among the users. The concepts presented in this chapter should be used as guidelines and not as absolutes. Each Windows NT Server environment is unique and requires experimentation and tuning appropriate to its conditions and requirements. This chapter covered

▶ Determining a disk bottleneck

▶ Isolating memory and cache bottlenecks

▶ Determining a processor bottleneck

▶ Determining a network bottleneck

Part V

TCP/IP on Windows NT

Chapter 16

Understanding TCP/IP

In This Chapter

▶ TCP/IP standards and RFCs (Request For Comments)

▶ Microsoft TCP/IP protocols and utilities

▶ Microsoft TCP/IP architecture

▶ Implementing Microsoft TCP/IP

▶ NetBIOS over TCP/IP

Although TCP/IP was the brainchild of the military, it has become the de facto protocol for general-purpose intersystem communication. In fact, statistics from major trade publications show that while TCP/IP and IPX/SPX run neck-in-neck for LAN protocol dominance, TCP/IP is clearly favored as the protocol of choice on the corporate backbone. Companies may find TCP/IP a better protocol solution because it includes a routable, internetworking protocol for scalable networks; establishes a basis for connectivity to foreign systems such as UNIX, VMS, and mainframes; and provides a foundation for scalable client-server application development, namely, via Windows Sockets and DCE-compatible Remote Procedure Calls.

Introduction to TCP/IP

The Transmission Control Protocol/Internet Protocol (TCP/IP) is an industry-standard suite of protocols designed for wide area network environments. TCP/IP was developed in 1969 by the U.S. Department of Defense Advanced Research Projects Agency, as a resource-sharing experiment called ARPANET. Its purpose was to provide high-speed communication links using packet switched networks. Since 1969, ARPANET has grown into a worldwide community of networks known as the Internet.

TCP/IP standards

The standards for TCP/IP are published by the Internet Engineering Task Force (IETF) and other working groups in a series of documents called RFCs (Request For Comments). RFCs describe the internal workings of the

Internet. Some RFCs describe network services or protocols and their implementations, whereas others summarize policies. TCP/IP standards are always published as RFCs, although not all RFCs specify standards.

Note

TCP/IP standards are developed by consensus. Anyone can submit a document for publication as an RFC. Documents are reviewed by a technical expert, a task force, or the RFC editor. When a document is published, it is assigned an RFC number. The original RFC is never updated. If changes are required, a new RFC is published with a new number. Therefore, it's important to verify that you have the most recent RFC on a particular topic.

A member organization requiring a specific service that is not yet supported must submit an RFC to other members of the IETF. Once all members agree on the proposal and there is a shipping product that supports it, it becomes part of the TCP/IP standard. The key RFCs supported in Microsoft TCP/IP (and for Microsoft Remote Access Service) are described in Table 16-1. An exhaustive, up-to-date list of all RFCs can be found on the Internet via ds.internic.net.

Table 16-1	Key Requests for Comments (RFCs) Supported by Microsoft TCP/IP
RFC	**Title**
768	User Datagram Protocol (UDP)
783	Trivial File Transfer Protocol (TFTP)
791	Internet Protocol (IP)
792	Internet Control Message Protocol (ICMP)
793	Transmission Control Protocol (TCP)
826	Address Resolution Protocol (ARP)
854	Telnet Protocol (TELNET)
862	Echo Protocol (ECHO)
863	Discard Protocol (DISCARD)
864	Character Generator Protocol (CHARGEN)
865	Quote of the Day Protocol (QUOTE)
867	Daytime Protocol (DAYTIME)
894	IP over Ethernet
919, 922	IP Broadcast Datagrams (broadcasting with subnets)
959	File Transfer Protocol (FTP)
1001, 1002	NetBIOS Service Protocols
1034, 1035	Domain Name System (DOMAIN)

RFC	Title
1042	IP over Token Ring
1055	Transmission of IP over Serial Lines (IP-SLIP)
1112	Internet Gateway Multicast Protocol (IGMP)
1122, 1123	Host Requirements (communications and applications)
1134	Point-to-Point Protocol (PPP)
1144	Compressing TCP/IP Headers for Low-speed Serial Links
1157	Simple Network Management Protocol (SNMP)
1179	Line Printer Daemon Protocol
1188	IP over FDDI
1191	Path MTU Discovery
1201	IP over ArcNet
1231	IEEE 802.5 Token Ring MIB (MIB-II)
1332	PPP Internet Protocol Control Protocol (IPCP)
1334	PPP Authentication Protocols
1533	DHCP Options and BOOTP Vendor Extensions
1534	Inter-operation Between DHCP and BOOTP
1541	Dynamic Host Configuration Protocol (DHCP)
1542	Clarifications and Extensions for the Bootstrap Protocol
1547	Requirements for Point-to-Point Protocol (PPP)
1548	Point-to-Point Protocol (PPP)
1549	PPP in High-level Data Link Control (HDLC) Framing
1552	PPP Internetwork Packet Exchange Control Protocol (IPXCP)
1553	IPX Header Compression
1570	Link Control Protocol (LCP) Extensions
Draft RFCs	NetBIOS Frame Control Protocol (NBFCP); PPP over ISDN; PPP over X.25; Compression Control Protocol

Note

The Internet Activities Board (IAB) is responsible for setting Internet standards and for managing the process of publishing RFCs. The IAB governs two groups: the Internet Research Task Force (IRTF) and the Internet Engineering Task Force (IETF). The IRTF is responsible for coordinating all TCP/IP-related research projects. The IETF focuses on Internet problem solutions. The IAB publishes the *IAB Official Protocol Standard*, a quarterly memo that is useful in determining the current RFC for each protocol.

A suite of protocols

In reality, TCP/IP is a suite of protocols which, when used together, make up two defining standards:

- **Transmission Control Protocol (TCP).** This protocol specifies how two nodes on a single network communicate.

- **Internet Protocol (IP).** This protocol dictates how a node on one network inter-operates with a node on another.

TCP/IP includes a range of protocols that provide distinct services and capabilities necessary for communication between and control of otherwise incompatible computers and networks. The transport protocol suite can be broken down into its smaller components, which include the User Datagram Protocol (UDP), Address Resolution Protocol (ARP), and Internet Control Message Protocol (ICMP).

In addition to the Transmission Control Protocol (TCP) and Internet Protocol (IP), there are the File Transfer Protocol (FTP), the Simple Mail Transfer Protocol (SMTP), the Telnet Protocol, and the Simple Network Management Protocol (SNMP).

Other protocols within the TCP/IP family are the Reverse Address Resolution Protocol (RARP), and the Exterior Gateway Protocol (EGP).

TCP/IP protocol details

Each TCP/IP protocol provides a specific service or set of services to move data from one computer or network to another. The services that some of these provide — the File Transfer Protocol (FTP), for instance — are self-explanatory. Others aren't so obvious.

In the lexicon of the TCP/IP world, an interconnected set of networks is called an Internet. The Internet Protocol (IP) is responsible for accepting segmented data (in the form of a Protocol Data Unit, or PDU) from a host computer and sending it across the Internet through the required gateways until the data reaches its destination.

The IP delivery process provides what is known as an unreliable connectionless service; that is, some PDUs aren't delivered properly. Even PDUs that are delivered may arrive at their destinations out of sequence. TCP takes care of this problem by providing transport mechanisms that ensure that data is delivered error-free, in the order it was sent, and without loss or duplication.

TCP's basic role is providing reliable end-to-end data transfer between two processes, called transport users (these include FTP, SMTP, and Telnet). In specific terms, the TCP standard describes five levels of service: multiplexing (the ability to support multiple users), connection management, data transport, error reporting, and a variety of special capabilities.

In the basic data transfer process, a transport user such as FTP passes data to TCP, which encapsulates the data into a segment that contains user data and control information (for example, the destination address). TCP ensures reliable data delivery by numbering outgoing segments sequentially and then having the destination TCP module acknowledge arrival by number. If segments arrive out of order, they can be reordered via sequence number. If a segment fails to arrive, the destination TCP module will not acknowledge its receipt, and the sending TCP module resends it.

TCP allows the transport user to specify the quality of transmission service that it requires, permits special urgent data transmissions, and provides security classifications that can be used in routing segments to data-encryption devices. In trying to provide high-quality transmission services, TCP attempts to optimize the underlying IP and network resources. Available parameters include timeout delays and message-delivery precedence. Interrupt-driven urgent transmissions include terminal-generated break characters and alarm conditions.

The services provided by TCP and IP are defined by primitives and parameters. A primitive is a mechanism for specifying the function to be performed, whereas parameters are used to pass data and control information.

Only two primitives — SEND and DELIVER — are used to define the IP services. Parameters available with these primitives include source and destination host addresses, the recipient protocol (usually TCP), an identifier that distinguishes one user's data from another's, and user data.

TCP offers two primitives and associated parameters: service request and service response primitives. A TCP user sends service request primitives to TCP; TCP issues the service response primitives to the user. Many of these primitives set off an exchange of TCP segments between host processes or computers, and TCP passes the segments to IP in a SEND primitive and receives them from IP in a DELIVER primitive.

FTP options allow the transfer of ASCII and EBCDIC character sets and the use of transparent bit streams that permit exchanging any sort of data or text file. FTP also provides data-compression options and has password/identifier mechanisms for controlling user access.

SMTP provides the underlying capabilities for a network electronic mail facility. It does not, however, provide the user interface. Primarily, it provides mechanisms for transferring messages between separate systems. SMTP accepts e-mail messages prepared by a native mail facility (such as cc:Mail) and delivers them using TCP to send and receive messages across the network. With SMTP, users can send mail to users anywhere in the local network as well as those on the Internet.

Another protocol, Telnet, outlines a network terminal-emulation standard. It allows terminals to connect to and control applications running in a remote host just as if it were a local user of the host. In implementation, Telnet takes two forms: user and server modules. The user module interacts with the terminal I/O module, providing translation of terminal characteristics into the network-specific codes and vice versa. The server module interacts with processes and applications, serving as a terminal handler to make remote terminals look as if they are local.

SNMP

Among the other TCP/IP protocols, the most widely applied is the SNMP, or Simple Network Management Protocol. SNMP is an application that supports the exchange of network management messages among hosts, including a central host that is often called a network management center.

SNMP was designed to operate over UDP, the User Datagram Protocol. UDP operates at the same level as TCP, providing a connectionless service for the exchange of messages while avoiding the overhead of TCP's reliability facilities. It is useful in transaction-oriented applications.

ARP and RARP provide mechanisms for hosts to learn Internet addresses. ARP allows a host to discover another host's address, and RARP permits a host to find out its own address, an important capability for diskless PCs without permanent ways to store their Internet addresses.

Transmission Control Protocol (TCP)

The Transmission Control Protocol (TCP) is one of two primary protocols in the TCP/IP protocol suite. It provides a reliable, connection-oriented delivery service. TCP views data as a stream of bytes, rather than frames. The data is transmitted in segments.

Connection-oriented means that for each segment sent, the receiving host must return an acknowledgment (ACK) within a specified period for bytes received. If an ACK is not received, the data is retransmitted. If the received segment is damaged, the receiving host will discard it; because an ACK is not sent, the sender retransmits the segment. Reliability is achieved by assigning a sequence number to each byte transmitted and a checksum to each segment. Bytes received out of sequence signal that other bytes are on their way. The receiving host waits until it has received all bytes before sending an acknowledgment. Checksum tells the receiving host what it should have received.

User Datagram Protocol (UDP)

The User Datagram Protocol (UDP) provides a connectionless datagram service that offers unreliable, "best effort" delivery. This means that the arrival of datagrams and the correct sequencing of packets is not guaranteed.

UDP is used by applications that don't require an acknowledgment of receipt of data. The Domain Name Resolver (DNR), the NetBIOS over TCP/IP (NBT) driver, Simple Network Management Protocol (SNMP), and other sockets-based applications use UDP.

Internet Protocol (IP)

The Internet Protocol (IP) is the second of the two primary TCP/IP protocols. Unlike the reliable, connection-oriented delivery provided by the TCP Protocol, the Internet Protocol is an unreliable, "best effort," connectionless delivery service. IP is unreliable in that delivery is not guaranteed. A packet might be lost, delivered out of sequence, duplicated, or delayed. Connectionless means that

- IP packets are independent from other packets.

- An acknowledgment is not required when data is received.

- The sender or receiver are not informed when a packet is lost or sent out of sequence.

- IP assumes that delivery might be difficult. It will always make a "best effort" attempt to deliver a packet.

The IP Protocol

- Provides routing of information from one host to another. Routing is its primary function.

- Provides a mechanism for fragmentation and reassembly of packets, by setting rules that tell routers what to do with packets. If a router is unable to transfer the entire datagram, the router can fragment the packet into smaller pieces before continuing.

- Defines how data is transferred throughout the internetwork.

The implementation of IP in Microsoft TCP/IP does not fragment packets. However, because a router could fragment the IP packet, Microsoft TCP/IP does handle reassembly.

Internet Control Message Protocol (ICMP)

The Internet Control Message Protocol (ICMP) is a mechanism for reporting errors due to delivery problems. In a connectionless system, datagrams are delivered without any coordination between the originating and destination workstations. If the time-to-live counter expires due to network congestion or the unavailability of the destination workstation, IP fails to deliver the datagram. In order to receive a message reporting this error, ICMP must be implemented in all TCP/IP implementations.

The most common ICMP messages are echo request, echo reply, redirect, source quench, and destination unreachable. ICMP messages are contained within IP datagrams. This ensures that the ICMP message will be able to find its way to the appropriate host within the Internet. The Internet Control Message Protocol (ICMP) is defined in RFC 792.

Address Resolution Protocol (ARP)

For computers to communicate on a network, they must ultimately know each other's physical address. The Address Resolution Protocol (ARP) is used to obtain the physical address of a TCP/IP host and map it to the host's logical IP address. The IP address is used by TCP/IP to identify a host as part of a TCP/IP Internet. The process of obtaining the physical address is known as address resolution.

Address resolution is accomplished when the requesting host sends a request broadcast on the local network with the target host's destination IP address. The target host responds to the request by sending a broadcast reply with its physical address and adds the physical address to the sender's hardware address field.

When the requesting host receives the physical address, both the IP and physical address are stored locally as an entry in the ARP cache. All hosts maintain an ARP cache that includes their own IP-physical address mapping. The ARP cache is always checked for an IP-physical address mapping before initiating a broadcast. For Windows NT, the ARP cache entries expire after ten minutes.

Other Protocols

Two common protocols in which users are interested are SLIP (Serial Link Internetwork Protocol) and PPP (Point-to-Point Protocol). These protocols are used for communication between two TCP/IP-based host machines via asynchronous or synchronous modems and telephone lines. The base Windows NT product does not currently support these protocols, but they are under study for a future release.

Table 16-2 lists the TCP/IP protocols provided with Windows NT.

Table 16-2   TCP/IP Protocols Built In to Windows NT

Protocol	Primary function
Address Resolution Protocol (ARP)	Resolution of IP-physical address
Internet Protocol (IP)	Routing functions
Internet Control Message Protocol (ICMP)	Reporting errors
Transmission Control Protocol (TCP)	Connection-oriented delivery service
User Datagram Protocol (UDP)	Connectionless datagram service
RFC NetBIOS over TCP/IP	Interface to Windows NT resources
Sockets Interface	Interface between applications and TCP/IP protocols
PING	Verifies configurations and tests connections
Simple Network Management Protocol (SNMP)	Monitors host activity. Windows NT is an SNMP agent. MIB-1 (Management Information Blocks-1) and the Windows NT extension MIBs are fully supported.

TCP/IP Utilities

Microsoft TCP/IP utilities work with Microsoft TCP/IP to provide workstation access to UNIX host computers and the TCP/IP Internet. Table 16-3 provides an overview of Microsoft TCP/IP utilities.

Table 16-3	TCP/IP Utilities Built In to Windows NT
TCP/IP utility	**Function**
FTP	Provides bidirectional file transfers between a Windows NT workstation and any TCP/IP host running FTP server software. Windows NT does not provide the server software, so without this utility, a UNIX workstation cannot use FTP to transfer files with a Windows NT Server.
TFTP	In addition to FTP, Windows NT also provides TFTP (Trivial File Transfer Protocol) which copies files but does not perform access control checking. It uses UDP rather than TCP as the underlying protocol.
Telnet (Kermit/TTY)	Telnet provides a virtual terminal service for remote interactive sessions. Basic terminal emulation of TTY (scrolling), VT-100 (ANSI), and VT-52 terminals are supported. The Telnet service executes as a component within the LMSVRCS process. The Windows NT Terminal accessory supports and can use this Telnet service. This allows a user to make remote connections with UNIX systems that are running the Telnet server component. Windows NT does not supply a Telnet server component. Note: You must first start the Telnet service and then use the Windows Terminal program as the terminal emulation window.
RCP (remote copy)	Copies files between a Windows NT workstation and a UNIX host.
RSH (remote shell)	Allows execution of commands on a remote computer.
Domain Name	Works with a Domain Name Server (DNS) to resolve UNIX environment domain names.

TCP/IP Tools

Windows NT provides a number of tools to help manage and control the TCP/IP environment. Table 16-4 lists the TCP/IP tools that ship with Windows NT.

The TCP/IP stack

The body of standards making up the TCP/IP suite fits within a five-layer communications framework, or stack, shown in Figure 16-1. Before examining these layers individually, it's important to understand several other concepts.

Table 16-4	TCP/IP Tools Built In to Windows NT
TCP/IP tool	**Function**
Hostname	Hostname displays the computer name as configured in the Registry.
Netstat	Netstat displays the network status, including protocols in use, connections, data in process, IP address, and state. The command line for netstat may include a numeric value, which sets the number of seconds between interactions. For example, netstat 4 produces the report every four seconds.
PING	PING uses the ICMP Echo command to attempt to locate a particular host. This tool is most useful for troubleshooting network problems. Determining which hosts are visible to a workstation can help to isolate network failures.
Route	Route displays and allows dynamic modification of routine data. You can use Route to instruct the ARP to which gateway to send for a particular destination IP address.

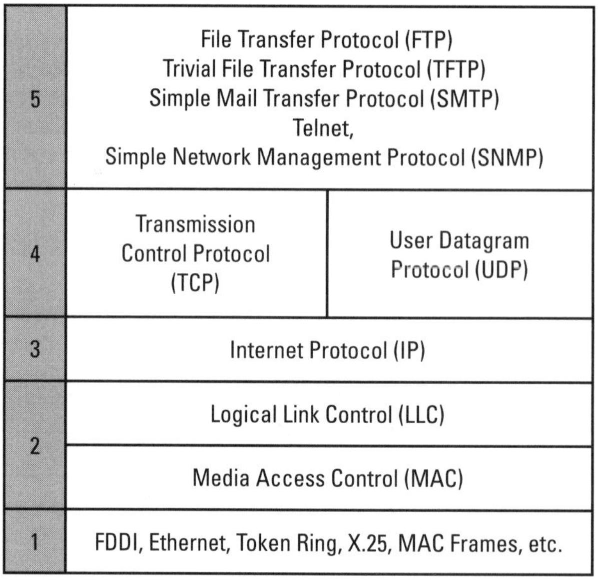

5	File Transfer Protocol (FTP) Trivial File Transfer Protocol (TFTP) Simple Mail Transfer Protocol (SMTP) Telnet, Simple Network Management Protocol (SNMP)
4	Transmission Control Protocol (TCP) / User Datagram Protocol (UDP)
3	Internet Protocol (IP)
2	Logical Link Control (LLC) Media Access Control (MAC)
1	FDDI, Ethernet, Token Ring, X.25, MAC Frames, etc.

Figure 16-1: The TCP/IP protocol stack.

The Department of Defense based its model of data communication on three agents: processes, hosts, and networks. Processes are the fundamental communications entities and are executed on hosts, which are internetworked computers that can support multiple processes. Hosts, in turn, communicate with each other via a network. Successful completion of an operation on the Internet requires action by all three agents.

For data to be transferred from one process to another, the data must first get to the host in which the process resides and then to the process within the host. In this model, a communications facility is concerned only with routing data between hosts, which direct data to processes.

The network access layer handles the exchange of data among a host, the network to which that host is attached, and a host within the same network. The sending host provides the network with the network address of the receiving host to ensure that the network routes the data properly. The TCP/IP network access layer services correspond to those provided by the physical layer, data link layer, and parts of the network layers in the OSI reference model as shown in Figure 16-2.

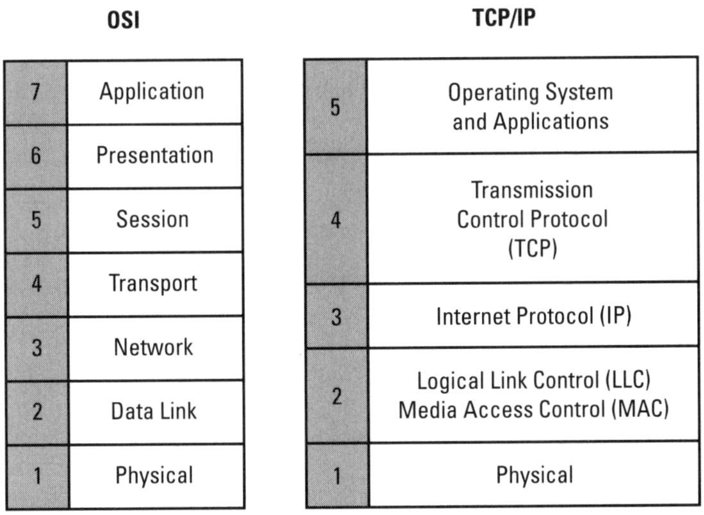

OSI		TCP/IP	
7	Application	5	Operating System and Applications
6	Presentation		
5	Session	4	Transmission Control Protocol (TCP)
4	Transport		
3	Network	3	Internet Protocol (IP)
2	Data Link	2	Logical Link Control (LLC) Media Access Control (MAC)
1	Physical	1	Physical

Figure 16-2: Comparison of the OSI model to the TCP/IP protocol stack.

The specific physical, or media-access, protocol used to put TCP/IP data on the wire is independent of TCP/IP's top three layers. This means that TCP/IP can operate over virtually any media-access protocol, including Ethernet, Token Ring, or ArcNet.

The separation of the physical layer functions from the higher layers also means that the services provided by the Internet, host-to-host, and process layers are not affected by the specifics of the underlying network protocol used. The same high-level software can function properly regardless of the type of network to which a host is connected.

The Internet layer provides services that permit data to traverse hosts residing on multiple networks. The Internet routing protocol runs not only on local hosts, but also on gateways that connect two networks. A gateway's primary responsibility is to relay data from one network to the other, making sure it gets to the appropriate destination host.

The host-to-host layer ensures the reliability of the data sent between two TCP/IP hosts. The process layer provides protocols needed to support various end-user applications, such as file transfer or electronic mail.

TCP/IP Naming Schemes

IP addressing is a scheme for identifying TCP/IP hosts. The term *hosts* can refer to workstations, servers, and routers. UNIX environments — where TCP/IP is the preferred protocol stack — use a scheme different from Windows NT. Both have three levels of addressing as shown in Table 16-5.

Table 16-5	Address Levels
Windows NT	**UNIX environments**
RFC NetBIOS names	Domain names
IP addresses	IP addresses
Physical addresses	Physical addresses

Domain names

Domain names are used in UNIX environments with a domain name server (DNS). Domain names provide a hierarchical naming scheme for TCP/IP hosts. This scheme allows organizations to divide their network logically, similar to the way they divide their organization, and also delegate authority to network administrators in each area. These areas are commonly referred to as zones of authority. Table 16-6 lists the top-level domain names used on the Internet.

Domain names have the following characteristics:

- Labels are separated by periods.
- Labels can be up to 63 bytes long.
- Domain names are limited to 256 bytes.
- Labels are read from right to left, beginning at the root.

Table 16-6	Internet Top-level Domain Names
Domain name	**Meaning**
com	Commercial organizations
edu	Educational institutions
gov	Government institutions
mil	Military groups
net	Major network support centers
org	Organizations other than those above
arpa	Temporary ARPANET domain (obsolete)
int	International organization
<country code>	Each country (geographic scheme)

NetBIOS over TCP/IP name resolution methods

NetBIOS over TCP/IP (NETBT.SYS) is the network component that performs computer-name-to-IP-address-mapping name resolution. RFC 1001 and 1002 define three methods for implementing NetBIOS over TCP/IP (NBT): b-node (broadcast node), p-node (point-to-point node), m-node (mixed node), and h-node (a combination of b-node and p-node that uses broadcasts as a last effort).

B-Node

When using b-node, broadcasts are used for both name registration and name resolution. Figure 16-3 illustrates b-node resolution.

Looking at Figure 16-3, you can see that all three workstations and Server 4 broadcast to their respective subnets to register their names, using a name registration request broadcast. To prevent another computer from registering the same name, each computer guards its registered name by issuing negative name registration broadcasts if another computer tries to register the same name.

For the workstations to locate Server 4, each workstation broadcasts a name query request; Workstation 1 broadcasts to the local subnet while the broadcast from Workstations 2 and 3 must go through the IP router. You must configure — by enabling ports 137 and 138 — to forward or pass the name registration and name query broadcasts.

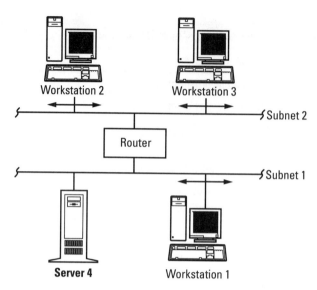

Figure 16-3: Example of b-node name registration and resolution.

If the IP router does not forward the name registration and name query broadcasts, computers on different subnets will not receive the broadcasts so they cannot see each other. For example, Workstations 2 and 3 will not be able to connect to Server 4 or Workstation 1 if the router does not forward the broadcasts.

Microsoft enhancements to NBT

Microsoft enhances the normal b-node implementation of broadcasting to the local subnet to resolve the NetBIOS name. The NBT name resolution process also includes consulting LMHOSTS, an ASCII file that contains a list of NetBIOS names and their corresponding IP addresses.

When NBT attempts to resolve a name, the following procedure is followed:

■ The NBT cache is checked to see if it is aware of a mapping for the specified name. If the name is found, the corresponding IP address is used. (This name cache is originally created from the LMHOSTS file when the NBT service starts.)

■ If the NBT cache does not contain an entry for the specified name, it uses the b-node mechanism to locate it. If the name is resolved, the result is stored in the cache for future use.

■ If both of the preceding procedures fail, the nonpreloaded entries in LMHOSTS are searched for a mapping. If the mapping is found, it is stored in the cache as well.

Note The LMHOSTS file is located in \WINNT\SYSTEM32\DRIVERS\ETC and can be of any length. However, it is searched linearly, which means search time will be a limiting factor. Some operations will start timing out if this takes too long.

The NetBIOS name cache is updated whenever a new name is resolved through subnet broadcasting or by finding a name in the LMHOSTS file. It can also be refreshed with the NBTStat -r command. This will cause NBT to reparse the LMHOSTS file and reload the cache. (Note that there is no addname command as with Windows NT 2.1 TCP/IP.)

P-Node (or Point to Point Node)

With p-node name resolution, broadcasts are *not* used for name registration or name resolution. Instead, all systems register themselves with a NetBIOS Name Server (NBNS) upon startup. The NBNS is responsible for mapping computer names to IP addresses and making sure that no duplicate names are registered on the network. All computers must know the IP address of the NBNS, which is equivalent to a WINS Server. If the computers are not configured with the correct IP address for the NBNS, p-node name resolution will not work.

The p-node name resolution method uses directed User Datagram Protocol (UDP) datagrams and TCP sessions for its communication to and from the NBNS. Figure 16-4 illustrates b-node resolution.

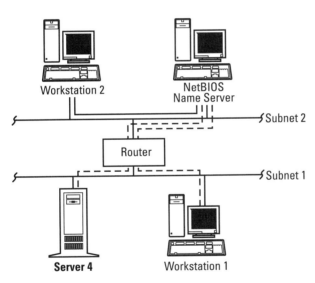

Figure 16-4: Example of p-node name registration and resolution.

In Figure 16-4, the workstations and server know the IP address of the NetBIOS Name Server (NBNS) computer. Therefore, on startup, they can directly contact the NBNS to register their names with a name registration request. The NBNS protects registered names by sending negative name registration messages if another computer tries to register with a name that is already registered.

Workstation 1 or 2 locates Server 4 by sending a name query request to the NBNS which returns the appropriate IP address for Server 4.

P-node name resolution has one huge drawback. If the NBNS is inaccessible, there is no way to resolve names and thus no way to access other computers on the network.

M-Node (or Mixed Node)

M-node uses a combination of b-node and p-node for name registration and resolution. This method first uses b-node and then p-node, which in theory should increase LAN performance. Figure 16-5 illustrates m-node resolution.

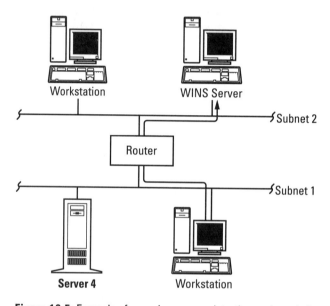

Figure 16-5: Example of m-node name registration and resolution.

- **Name Registration.** On startup, a system first attempts to register its name using b-node. If it is successful, the system then tries to register its name using p-node. P-node must succeed for the system to successfully initialize TCP/IP. If the b-node registration fails, p-node registration is not attempted, and the system simply fails to initialize TCP/IP.

- **Name Resolution.** When trying to resolve a name, the system will first try b-node name resolution. If b-node succeeds, the request will return the appropriate IP address without trying p-node. P-node resolution is attempted only if b-node fails to resolve the name.

M-node has the advantage over p-node in that if the NBNS is unavailable, computers on the local subnet can still be accessed via b-node resolution. Therefore, in Figure 16-5, if the NBNS is unavailable, Workstation 1 can still access Server 4.

M-node is typically not the best choice for larger networks because it uses b-node and thus results in broadcasts.

H-Node

H-node name resolution also uses both p-node and b-node; however, it only uses b-node as a last resort. When configured to use h-node, a system will always first try to use p-node and then use b-node *only* if p-node fails. In addition, a system can be configured to use the LMHOSTS file after p-node fails and before trying b-node. H-node resolution does not require successful p-node registration for a system to initialize; however, the system will use only b-node until p-node registration succeeds.

If the NBNS is unavailable and the system resorts to using b-node resolution, it will continue to attempt to contact the NBNS so that it can return to using p-node if the NBNS becomes available.

This method provides an advantage over both b-node and m-node because, as long as the NBNS is available, broadcasts will not be used.

The Internet Address

In an IP network, there are only two types of nodes: hosts and routers. A host is a source, or target, of information on an IP network and may be a PC or a workstation. Routers look at the target IP addresses and select a route that will lead to that location. Each host, router, or accessible device on a TCP/IP network must have a unique IP address. The IP address identifies a computer's location on the network, similar to the way that a street address identifies a house on a city block. Just as a street address must identify a unique residence, an IP address must be globally unique and have a uniform format. If a device, such as a router, supports multiple channels (for example, two WAN ports, two Ethernet ports, and one Token Ring port), each channel or port must be issued a unique address.

An IP address is 32 bits long and is composed of four 8-bit fields. The fields are separated by periods. Each field can represent a decimal number from zero through 255. This format is called dotted decimal notation. For example,

Machine Language Code (Binary)	Dotted-decimal Notation
10000011 01101011 00000011 00011011	131.107.3.27

There are three distinct parts of an IP address, each separated by a dot or decimal. The first part is called the class. Next comes the network address, which helps the IP program determine where the packet originated. The network address identifies the network as a whole and must be unique to the Internet. All computers on a given network must have the same network address.

Finally, there is the host address, which specifies the host that created the address. The host address identifies a workstation, server, or router within a network and must be unique to the network address. Each portion has its own name, class bits, network bits, and host bits.

A host can be any device that runs an application. Most hosts are computers; traditionally the term *host* has been reserved for multi-user mainframes and minicomputers, but PCs and workstations are hosts in the Internet sense of the term, as are intelligent hubs, RMON monitors, and other devices.

Hosts whose addresses share a network number can send local broadcasts to one another and communicate without a router. Hosts with differing network numbers can communicate only via an IP router.

Address classes

The Internet community has defined five classes of addresses to accommodate networks of varying sizes. Windows NT supports Class A, B, and C networks. The class of address defines the fields used for the network address and host address. It also determines the number of networks and the number of hosts per network.

Table 16-7 shows the network address and host address fields for Class A, B, and C IP addressing.

Table 16-7	Network and Host Address Fields		
Class	*IP address*	*Network address*	*Host address*
A	w.x.y.z	w	x.y.z
B	w.x.y.z	w.x	y.z
C	w.x.y.z	w.x.y	z

- **Class A addresses.** Class A addresses are assigned to networks with a very large number of hosts. The high-order bit in a Class A address is always set to zero. The next seven bits (first field) represent the network address. The remaining 24 bits (last three fields) represent the host address. This allows for 126 networks and approximately 17 million hosts per network.

- **Class B addresses.** Class B addresses are assigned to medium-sized networks. The high-order bits in a Class B address are always set to 1 – 0. The next 14 bits (first two fields) represent the network address. The remaining 24 bits (last two fields) represent the host address. This allows for 16,384 networks and approximately 65,000 hosts per network.

- **Class C addresses.** Class C addresses are usually used for small LANs. The high-order bits in a Class C address are always set to 1 – 1 – 0. The next 21 bits (first three fields) represent the network address. The remaining eight bits (last field) represent the host address. This allows for approximately 2 million networks and 254 hosts per network.

- **Class D addresses.** Class D addresses are used for multicasting to a number of hosts. Packets are passed to a selected subset of users on a network. Only those hosts registered for the multicast address will receive the packet. The high-order bits in a Class D address are always set to $1 - 1 - 1 - 0$. The remaining bits are for the address that interested hosts will recognize.

- **Class E addresses.** Class E is an experimental address that is reserved for future use. The high-order bits in a Class E address are set to $1 - 1 - 1 - 1$.

Note

If you plan on using Internet resources, you must obtain one or more unique network addresses from the Network Information Center (NIC). Currently, only Class C network addresses are available.

IP addressing guidelines

The following guidelines apply to the network address:

- **The network address must be unique.** If you are on the Internet, the network address must be unique to the Internet. If you are not on the Internet, the network address must be unique to your internetwork. Table 16-8 shows valid network address ranges for private Internets.

- **The network address cannot begin with the number 127.** The number 127 in a Class A address is reserved for internal loopback functions.

- **The first field in a network address cannot be zero (all bits set to 0).** Zero indicates that the address is a local host and will not be routed.

- **The first field in a network address cannot be 255 (all bits set to 1).** The number 255 acts as a broadcast.

Table 16-8   Valid Private Internet Network Address Ranges

Class	Beginning	Ending
Class A	001.x.y.z	126.x.y.z
Class B	128.0.y.z	191.255.y.z
Class C	192.0.0.z	223.255.255.z

The following guidelines apply to the host address:

- **The host address must be unique to the network address.** Table 16-9 shows valid host address ranges for private Internets.

■ **All 1 bits cannot be used as the host address.** If all bits are set to 1, the address is interpreted as a broadcast rather than a host address.

■ **All 0 bits cannot be used as the host address.** If all bits are set to 0, the address is interpreted to mean "this network only."

Table 16-9	Valid Private Internet Host Address Ranges	
Class	*Beginning*	*Ending*
Class A	w.0.0.1	w.255.255.254
Class B	w.x.0.1	w.x.255.254
Class C	w.x.y.1	w.x.y.254

Dividing the Network

Without more information than the network and host address, IP software believes that all hosts within an IP network are reachable on the same segment or circuit. If you had a Class A network, by default you would have more than 16 million users all on one Ethernet. Network response time could be measured with a sun dial. The subnet mask lets you subdivide the network into logical units. In your address, the subnet mask defines how many of your network's host bits will be reserved as subnetwork bits — in other words, what the routing instructions for your LAN should be. These instructions are used only for information transmitted from one location in your LAN to another location in your LAN.

How can you tell one IP network from another? The tedious approach is to translate each IP address to its binary equivalent, check to see which class of network this IP address describes, and then check the values of the next 7 bits for a Class A, 14 bits for a Class B, and 24 bits for a Class C. However, there are some shortcuts with dotted-decimal addresses, the most common form of IP address.

As described earlier, in dotted-decimal addresses, the 32 bits of the IP address are separated into four 8-bit bytes with each byte separated by a period and each byte's binary value converted to decimal. So instead of seeing an IP address as

00010010.01010001.00110010.11000001

You see

18.81.50.193

Now you can use the decimal value found in the first position to tell what class of IP network you are working with. A value below 128 in the first byte indicates that this is a Class A IP address; if the value is between 128 and 191, it is Class B; and if the value is between 192 and 223, it is Class C.

Once you know the network class for an IP address, you can determine to which network it belongs. To determine the unique network value, you need to add the class bits to the number of network bits. Class A addresses have one class bit and seven network bits, or eight bits — one byte — so the first dotted-decimal byte refers to this network.

Why use subnets?

A network with 16,777,214 host addresses (Class A), or even one with 65,534 (Class B), is likely to be unwieldy. A Class C network with 254 addresses may even be undesirably large for many organizations. As a result of traffic patterns and congestion, upper limits on the number of allowable nodes in a network, distance limitations on LANs, and other reasons, many organizations divide their networks into subnets. Other benefits to using subnets are that they

- Allow you to mix different technologies, such as Ethernet and Token Ring

- Overcome limitations of current technologies

- Reduce network congestion by redirecting traffic

- Allow point-to-point links

In effect, some number of the leftmost (or most significant) bits of the host addresses are expropriated and used to designate subnets. The subnet is part of the network identified by the network number, but only hosts that are on the same subnet can communicate without a router. Members of different subnets will not see each other's local broadcasts. They will need to go through a router to communicate, even though they may be on the same network.

Wherever a 1 appears in the binary representation of the subnet mask, the corresponding binary digit in the IP address is allocated to the network number and the subnet number. The class of the address determines whether the network number consists of 7, 14, or 21 bits; the remaining masked digits make up the subnet number. The zeros in the subnet mask correspond to the residual host number.

If the subnet mask stops at an octet boundary, it may be the same as the default mask, which is no mask at all. In other words, if you perform a bitwise logical AND with a Class B address and the Class B default mask, you get precisely the same network number that you would get by simply looking at the first two octets. There is no subnet number carved out of the Class B host octets. The so-called default subnet masks simply ratify the separation of IP addresses into network ID and host ID on one of the octet boundaries. With one of these default masks, there are no subnets defined.

It is considered good practice to use contiguous bits, starting from the left, for subnet mask values, although it is not always an absolute requirement. Following this rule, decimal representations of subnet mask values follow the sequence 128, 192, 224, 240, 248, 252, 254, 255.

Note

Typically, an organization acquires just one network address from the NIC. Dividing the network into subnets requires each subnet to use a different network address. A unique subnet address can be created by partitioning the host portion into two parts. One part can be used to identify the subnet as a unique network. This is referred to as *subnetting*.

A network address from the NIC is only required if you plan on accessing Internet resources. If your internetwork is private, you can assign any valid network address to a network as long as it is unique within your internetwork. If this is the case, subnetting is not required.

Subnet Addressing

The first step in implementing subnet addressing is to define your current needs, keeping in mind future needs. This includes

- **Determining the total number of subnets within your internetwork.** You'll need a unique subnet number for each subnet wide area network connection (required for most routers).

- **Calculating the total number of hosts you'll have on each subnet.** All TCP/IP hosts require at least one IP address. For example, routers require a minimum of two IP addresses, one for each connection to a network.

To implement subnet addressing you must define

- A unique network address for each subnet

- A range of valid IP addresses for each subnet

- A subnet mask for your internetwork

Subnet Masks

To implement subnet addressing, some bits from the host address are used for the network address of the subnet. The purpose of the subnet mask is to inform TCP/IP hosts which bits of the 32-bit IP address correspond to the network address and which bits correspond to the host address. This is accomplished by masking the network address. Bits corresponding to the network address are set to 1. Bits corresponding to the host address are set to 0.

Note

If you do not use subnets, Windows NT requires that you use a default subnet mask. The default subnet mask has all bits corresponding to the network address set to 1. The decimal value is 255.

Table 16-10 shows the default subnet masks used by Windows NT.

Table 16-10   Default Subnet Masks Used by Windows NT

Address class	Bits used for subnet mask	Dotted-decimal notation
Class A	11111111 00000000 00000000 00000000	255.0.0.0
Class B	11111111 11111111 00000000 00000000	255.255.0.0
Class C	11111111 11111111 11111111 00000000	255.255.255.0

Defining a Subnet Mask

The number of bits used for the subnet mask determines the possible number of subnets and hosts per subnet. To implement subnet addressing, you must define a subnet mask for your internetwork. The number of host bits that are set to 1 will vary, depending on the total number of subnets. Table 16-11 is an example of a Class A and Class B subnet mask using four bits from the host address.

Table 16-11   Class A and B Subnet Masks Example

Address class	Bits used for subnet mask	Dotted-decimal notation
Class A	11111111 11110000 00000000 00000000	255.240.0.0
Class B	11111111 11111111 11110000 00000000	255.255.240.0

Before you define a subnet mask, you should have a good idea of the number of subnets and hosts you'll have in the future. Using more bits for the subnet mask than required will save you from reassigning IP addresses in the future.

Tables 16-12 and 16-13 display subnet masks for Class A and Class B networks.

To define a subnet mask

1. Determine the number of bits in the host address required for the subnet mask, based on the number of subnets.

2. Evaluate the possible number of hosts per subnet.

3. Use additional bits for the subnet mask if

   You'll never require as many hosts per subnet as allowed by the remaining bits.

   The number of subnets will increase in the future, requiring additional bits from the host address.

Table 16-12	Subnet Masks for Class A Networks		
Number of subnets	**Number of hosts per subnet**	**Required number of bits**	**Subnet mask**
0	Invalid	1	Invalid
2	4,194,302	2	255.192.0.0
6	2,097,150	3	255.224.0.0
14	1,048,574	4	255.240.0.0
30	524,286	5	255.248.0.0
62	262,142	6	255.252.0.0
126	131,070	7	255.254.0.0
254	65,534	8	255.255.0.0

Table 16-13	Subnet Masks for Class B Networks		
Number of subnets	**Number of hosts per subnet**	**Required number of bits**	**Subnet mask**
0	Invalid	1	Invalid
2	16,382	2	255.255.192.0
6	8,190	3	255.255.224.0
14	4,094	4	255.255.240.0
30	2,046	5	255.255.248.0
62	1,022	6	255.255.252.0
126	510	7	255.255.254.0
254	254	8	255.255.255.0

Note

You can use more than eight bits for the subnet mask. Remember, the more bits used for the subnet mask, the fewer hosts per subnet.

Defining a Network Address Range

The range of network addresses is defined using the same number of host bits as the subnet mask. Possible bit combinations are evaluated and then converted to a decimal format.

To define the network address range

1. Using the same bits as the subnet mask, list all possible bit combinations.

2. Cross out values that use all 0s or 1s.

3. Calculating the bits from left to right, convert the bits to decimal format to determine the range of network addresses.

Table 16-14 is an example of a Class B network, using three bits from the host address.

Table 16-14 Example of a Class B Network Using Three Bits

Bit values	Decimal value	Minimum values for network and host address	Maximum values for network and host address
00000000	0	Invalid	Invalid
00100000	32	x.y.32.1	x.y.63.254
01000000	64	x.y.64.1	x.y.95.254
01100000	96	x.y.96.1	x.y.127.254
10000000	128	x.y.128.1	x.y.159.254
10100000	160	x.y.160.1	x.y.191.254
11000000	192	x.y.192.1	x.y.223.254
11100000	224	Invalid	Invalid

Implementing TCP/IP on Windows NT

Windows NT requires that all workstations are configured with the following items:

- **An IP address.** The host address must be unique to the network address. The network address must be unique to the Internet.

- **The IP address of the default gateway (if routing).** The default gateway parameter tells IP the address of the router connection for the datagram. If you do not specify a default gateway, communications will be limited to the local network unless a route is specified with the route command.

Windows NT requires that you always use a subnet mask. If you are not using subnets, you must use one of the default subnet masks shown in Table 16-15.

Table 16-15   Default Subnet Masks Used by Windows NT

Address class	Default subnet mask
Class A	255.0.0.0
Class B	255.255.0.0
Class C	255.255.255.0

A successful network starts on paper

As you have read through this book, you may have noticed a dominating theme concerning Windows NT overall — that is, don't rush to install and configure any aspect of Windows NT. Take plenty of time to plan. Designing a successful TCP/IP network is no different. Implementing TCP/IP under Windows NT should follow a few key steps:

1. **Planning.** Do as much as possible on paper before starting any task. It's easier to erase a bad decision on paper than to reinstall system components or Windows NT entirely. You also don't want to have to pull wiring out of the wall to correct your internetwork.

2. **Preparation.** Be sure to have the components and tools needed to perform the installation. You don't want to do any last-minute jury rigging while management stands waiting to throw the power switch.

3. **Installation.** The installation should be straightforward and orderly if the proper planning and preparation were done.

4. **Checkout.** Once installed, the installation should be checked to ensure that it was successful and the system functions as it should.

Determining the scope of your TCP/IP network

The scope of your TCP/IP network depends on your goals. Evaluate your company's needs as they pertain to TCP/IP and internetworking. Formulate a series of questions that help paint a clear picture of your networking goals. For example,

- What is the main reason you need to use TCP/IP?

- Do you use it for e-mail or terminal emulation?

- Do you have UNIX workstations that need to communicate with your Windows NT network?

During the planning phase, you will need to do the following:

- **Identify the physical relationships between TCP/IP hosts and clients.** Often, this involves analysis of the geographical (and logical) relationships between your users as well as a review of your bridging and routing components.

- **Establish ground rules.** For example, will any of your host machines ever be connected to the Internet? Will any of the client machines ever need access to the Internet?

■ **Determine which hosts the clients need to access.** Where are the hosts located? Map out the physical route between client and hosts, identifying all bridges, routers, hubs, and so on.

The goal is to develop a complete set of routes that your traffic is likely to take. Before too long, you will likely identify a few dozen hosts and many more clients. Next, categorize these hosts and clients along physical lines. Group together all hosts and clients that reside on the same Token Ring or Ethernet segments.

Tip

Assemble this information using a spreadsheet to organize the data into columns with the following headings: device name, host or client ID, segment type, segment number, proposed TCP/IP address, proposed TCP/IP routing address, and notes. Having the information in tabular form makes it easier to review the TCP/IP addressing for each host or client. You can also use the table to help you lay out the routing IP address information.

Once you have the projected number of hosts, clients, and network segments, you can begin to establish permanent TCP/IP addresses. The next section provides guidelines for establishing an addressing scheme for your TCP/IP network.

Identifying a Network Connection

Connections within a TCP/IP network are usually identified in one of three ways, all of which identify the same network connection, but at different levels of TCP/IP:

■ By name, as in the fully qualified host and domain name, such as phoenix.cpress.com

■ As an IP or network address used by the IP layer of TCP/IP, such as 198.26.1.5

■ By the network card address [the 48-bit Medium Access Control (MAC) address] also known as the physical address, such as 01 50 7D 10 34 46

Having three addressing levels allows for some degree of flexibility and inevitable change within a network. For example,

■ The host and domain name usually remains unchanged for the longest period of time. These items are under the control of the system designer and, therefore, are not subject to outside influences.

■ IP addresses, however, may change due to network growth and reconfiguration, such as when you move a machine from one location to another, especially if you support a lot of mobile computer users.

■ A machine's MAC address may change due to growth or performance reasons (you may want to pop in one of those superfast PCI Ethernet cards) or if a card is replaced for failure. The MAC address probably has the shortest lifespan of the three address levels.

Planning the IP Address Space

To plan an IP addressing scheme, you need to collect certain information:

- The maximum number of hosts you want to interconnect. Be sure to consider your entire organization and not just a single department. Take inventory. How many computers do you have at each location within your building or site? Figure on one address for each staff member and then add a 15 to 20 percent margin for safety.

- A breakdown of departments, site locations, and whether they need to communicate.

- If you already have TCP/IP internetworks installed, you need their operating parameters.

If your company is small, you should have no problem assembling this information. A large organization may have to spend more time and energy gathering this data, but the large organization really needs to have accurate data and standards.

What about MAC addresses?

When you connect TCP/IP systems to a shared cable such as an Ethernet or Token Ring LAN, communication between stations must take place using Medium Access Control (MAC) addresses; these addresses are normally built into the network adapter card. Since the IP address is configured independently of the MAC address, the IP address can remain unchanged even if the network card fails or is replaced.

Every Ethernet or Token Ring card comes with a preconfigured 48-bit MAC address. LAN standards also allow locally managed addresses; network cards can be loaded with a 48-bit address chosen by the network manager. Locally managed addresses are not normally used in TCP/IP networks. There's no point in adding a second layer of address management to the headache.

MAC addresses are important because some TCP/IP facilities such as BOOTP (Boot Protocol) use MAC addresses as fixed reference points for obtaining other information. In order to use these features, you must record the MAC address of each computer that will use the facility. The addresses show up as reference points in look-up tables in information servers.

Registering your site

Getting network numbers is easy. Send e-mail to info@internic.com (the Network Information Center). Ask for an Internet Number Template, fill out their form, and you'll receive a TCP/IP network number. Your best bet is to ask for one or two Class C networks. Even though each Class C network can only support up to 254 hosts, the information center will be happy to give you more than one.

Registering Your Domain

Next, you should register your domain and get an e-mail channel to the outside world. Your domain is used as part of every host address in your TCP/IP network. Registering your domain is important mainly because it lets e-mail flow in and out of your organization easily. Registering a domain name is a little more complex than getting addresses, because someone on the Internet must act as the domain name server for your network. Fortunately, many business and educational institutions provide this service for free.

Autonomous Systems

You can bypass routing your internetwork through the core Internet by building an autonomous system. This is a collection of LANs and WANS managed by a single body. It is ideal for a corporate body that wants to remain closed to the net world.

Choosing Your Network Number

The best advice I can give you here is, don't do it. Having said that, and with a clear conscience, I'm going to give you some ground rules for choosing your own network number. I can think of several situations in which you might not need a proper address, for example, if you are testing a system or never want to be bothered with the outside world.

The first thing that you need to consider is the size of your network, which plays into the decision about IP address class.

Second, don't think that because you're not connecting to an outside network — that is, the Internet — you can haphazardly assign IP addresses to your machine. You must ensure that you have unique IP addresses in your internetwork for TCP/IP. Again, let me point out that as your network grows and the momentum of TCP/IP brings on a new wave of communication scenarios, it will be extremely difficult for you to move your organization into the fold of the Internet if you do not have a unique address. The best way to be sure that your address is indeed unique is to apply for a regist-ered address.

If after reading the first couple of paragraphs you decide that your organization's network is never going public, never going on the Internet, and never going to communicate with another company's computers via TCP/IP, here are some guidelines for choosing your own network number:

- Class A addresses are allocated to super large networks, so do not use a Class A address.

- It's really easy to pick up IP addresses these days. They're plastered throughout company literature and software manuals, and if you're paying close attention to this book, you'll see several more. The rule here is, don't use them.

- If you cruise the Internet and collect a lot of FAQs, RFCs, and the like, you'll discover some of the more publicized addresses. Don't use these either.

So far all I've said is "don't", and you're probably saying, "Well, what do I do?"

- **Look at Class B addresses.** Choose a limited number of addresses toward the higher part of the address range. Odds are that these addresses won't be allocated for quite some time — you'll probably have an official address by then anyway.

- **If Class B doesn't suit your organization's needs, use Class C.** Choose Class C addresses in the same manner described for Class B.

Once you set up these numbers, you are not locked in. If you later decide you want to open a communications channel to another organization or two and discover that your IP addresses walk all over each other, you can set up a router to translate the addresses between the networks. The router then has to isolate the address space between the two networks so that it can map unused addresses from one network to the other.

Microsoft TCP/IP Client and Server Applications

This section presents an overview of the client and server components that are critical to the configuration and operation of the protocol suite.

Dynamic Host Configuration Protocol (DHCP)

The DHCP client and server are Windows Sockets applications that are used to provide automatic configuration of various TCP/IP protocol components. The server is configured with *scopes*, which are ranges of IP addresses to hand out, along with additional configuration parameters that go along with those addresses. For instance, a scope might be set up for a range of IP addresses, and it might also include a default gateway, DNS server, NetBIOS Name Server (WINS), and so on.

Windows Internet Name Service (WINS)

WINS is a NetBIOS name service as described in RFC1001/RFC1002. When a Windows NT system is configured as an h-node (default for WINS clients), it attempts to use a WINS server for name registration and resolution first and, if that fails, it resorts to subnet broadcasts.

WINS in a DHCP Environment

WINS is especially helpful on DHCP-enabled networks. One of the DHCP-provided parameters can be the address of a WINS server, so as soon as the client is configured by DHCP, it registers its name(s) and address with the WINS server and can then be easily located by the other computers on the network. This combination of DHCP and WINS is ideal for dynamic situations.

Microsoft Remote Access Server PPP/SLIP support

Windows NT Remote Access Server (RAS) includes client and server support for Point-to-Point Protocol (PPP) and client-only support for Serial Line IP (SLIP). Microsoft recommends that you use PPP because of its flexi-bility and its role as an industry standard and for future flexibility with client and server hardware and software. In addition, Microsoft RAS servers can act as NetBIOS gateways for clients that dial in using the proprietary RAS protocol and NetBEUI, providing access to NetBIOS resources over NetBEUI, IPX, or TCP/IP. Windows NT Server RAS supports up to 256 simultaneous remote clients, and Windows NT Workstation RAS supports only one remote client at a time.

RAS Servers

RAS Servers act as proxies for their remote TCP/IP clients on the network to which they are attached. They use proxy ARP to respond to ARP requests for their clients and set up host routes to each of their clients from the network. RAS Servers can obtain configuration parameters for their clients from a DHCP Server and then use PPP IPCP (Internet Protocol Control Protocol) as defined in RFC1332 to configure their clients with these parameters dynamically over the RAS link.

RAS Clients

RAS Clients using TCP/IP can be configured to use the default gateway on the remote network while they are connected to a PPP server. If so, this default gateway overrides any default gateway that is configured for local networks while the RAS connection is established. The override is accomplished by manipulating the IP route table. Any local routes, including the default gateway, get their metric (hop count) incremented by one, and a default route with a metric of one hop is dynamically added for the duration of the connection. One-hop routes are also added for the IP multicast address (224.0.0.0), for the local WAN interface, and for the network to which the PPP server is attached. This can present a problem with connecting to resources via the local network default gateway, unless static routes are added at the client.

Using RAS To Route Between Networks

RAS was primarily designed to allow individual network clients to gain access to services on a remote network, not to link networks together. However, in some applications, it is possible to use a RAS Server to link a small network to a larger one, such as the Internet.

Summary

If you plan to put your Windows NT Server on the Internet, you had better understand TCP/IP. This chapter provides a solid introduction to TCP/IP and how it is implemented on Windows NT. It covered

▶ TCP/IP standards

▶ TCP/IP protocol details

▶ TCP/IP naming schemes

▶ The Internet address

▶ Dividing the network

Chapter 17

Installing and Configuring TCP/IP

In This Chapter

▶ Installing TCP/IP

▶ Configuring TCP/IP

▶ Configuring TCP/IP to use DNS

▶ Configuring SNMP

▶ Troubleshooting TCP/IP

This chapter explains how to install TCP/IP and the SNMP service for Windows NT and how to configure the protocols on your computer.

Preparing to Install TCP/IP

Installing TCP/IP is a tedious process. The majority of failed installations can be attributed to either a lack of information or improper information. To manually configure TCP/IP, you must do the following:

■ Decide whether you want this computer to function as a Dynamic Host Configuration Protocol (DHCP) Server (this applies to Windows NT Server only). If you already have a DHCP Server on your network, you can use the DHCP option to configure TCP/IP for this new installation. Obviously you cannot set up this new installation as a DHCP Server in hopes of using the DHCP option to configure itself. Do not choose this option if you want this computer to act as a DHCP Server.

■ Decide whether you want this computer to function as a Windows Internet Name Service (WINS) Server.

Note

The preceding option is available only for Windows NT Server.

■ Decide whether you want this computer to function as a WINS proxy agent.

If this computer serves as a DHCP Server, you cannot use DHCP for automatic configuration, and you have to configure TCP/IP manually. Have the following information on hand before beginning the installation process:

■ The IP address and subnet mask for each network adapter card installed on the computer

Cross Reference

Refer to Chapter 16, *Understanding TCP/IP,* for more information on setting up IP addresses and subnets.

- The IP address for the default local gateways (IP routers)

- The IP addresses and DNS domain name of the DNS Servers on the internetwork [only if you plan to use Domain Name Service (DNS)]

- The IP addresses for WINS Servers, if WINS Servers are available on your network

To install and configure Simple Network Management Protocol (SNMP) service on your computer, you need the following information:

- Community names in your network. A community is a group of hosts to which a Windows NT computer running the SNMP service belongs. You can specify one or more communities to which the Windows NT computer using SNMP sends traps. The community name is placed in the SNMP packet when the trap is sent.

- Trap destination for each community. Trap destinations are the names or IP addresses of hosts to which you want the SNMP service to send traps with the selected community name.

- IP addresses or computer names for SNMP management hosts.

Installing TCP/IP

You can install TCP/IP as part of Custom Setup when you first install Windows NT. If you're upgrading from a previous release of Windows NT, Windows NT 4.0's Setup program automatically installs the new TCP/IP protocol while preserving your previous TCP/IP settings.

To install Microsoft TCP/IP

1. Log on as a member of the Administrators group on the local computer where you want to install and configure TCP/IP. Start the Network applet in the Control Panel.

2. In the Network dialog box, shown in Figure 17-1, choose the Protocols tab to display the Network Protocols dialog box. Then click the Add button.

3. In the Select Network Protocol dialog box, shown in Figure 17-2, select TCP/IP Protocol from the protocols list, and then click the OK button.

4. The TCP/IP Setup message box appears allowing you to indicate whether TCP/IP configuration will be dynamic using DHCP or manual. Click Yes if you already have a DHCP Server operating on your network and want to have DHCP configure TCP/IP dynamically when your system restarts. Otherwise click No to indicate that you will configure TCP/IP manually.

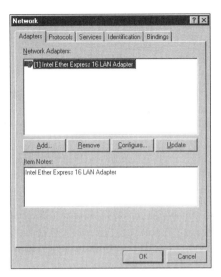

Figure 17-1: The Network dialog box.

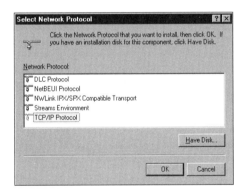

Figure 17-2: The Select Network Protocol dialog box.

5. Next, Windows NT Setup displays a message asking for the full path to the Windows NT distribution files. Type the path and click Continue. Setup copies the necessary files to your hard disk and returns you to the Network dialog box. Click Close to complete the operation.

   You can specify a drive letter for floppy disks, a CD-ROM drive, or a shared network directory, or you can specify the Universal Naming Convention (UNC) path name for a network resource, such as \\BEAMER\MASTER. The installation program copies all necessary files to your hard disk.

If you are installing from floppy disks, Windows NT Setup may request disks more than once. This is normal and is not an error condition.

6. Depending on how you answered the question about configuration in the TCP/IP Setup message box, Windows NT Setup displays a message offering two options to complete TCP/IP setup:

If you indicated that you want to configure TCP/IP dynamically using DHCP, Windows NT automatically completes all configuration settings for TCP/IP.

If you answered No to DHCP configuration in the TCP/IP Setup message box, you must configure TCP/IP manually. Click the button to continue.

Windows NT includes several other TCP/IP utilities and services, which are described in Table 17-1. You install these services by following Steps 1 through 3 that were given earlier for installing TCP/IP, and choosing the appropriate option in the protocols list. Detailed installation information for most of these options is covered in this book.

Universal Naming Convention

The Universal Naming Convention (UNC) for gaining access to a shared resource as used by Windows NT is defined as follows:

```
\\servername\sharename\path\filename
```

The *servername* identifies the name of the computer where the information resides, and the *sharename* identifies the name of the shared file resource under which the information has been shared. If you know the name of a specific file that you want to open, you can append the path and filename of the file to the end of the UNC name. A UNC name may be used with the File Open, File Save As, and Printer Setup common dialog boxes to access a shared resource without first connecting to that shared resource in File Manager, Print Manager, or by using the Network button.

If the resource to which you are connecting is password protected, Windows NT does not prompt you for the password, nor does it look up the password in your password-list file, if you are using UNC names. So, if the remote resource is password protected, you cannot access the resource using a UNC name unless you are already connected to that resource (for example, using File Manager or Print Manager).

For example, if you want to open a document titled SECRETS.DOC, which is located on a computer named VALDAHIL in a directory that is shared as MYEYES, then you can type \\VALDAHIL\MYEYES\SECRETS.DOC when prompted for the name of a file. The File Open and File Save As dialog box routines pass the provided filename to the application that displayed the dialog box, and the application can either open the file or save the file depending on the requested action.

Table 17-1	TCP/IP Installation Options
Option	*Description*
TCP/IP Internetworking	Includes the TCP/IP protocol, NetBIOS over TCP/IP and Windows Sockets interfaces, and the TCP/IP diagnostic utilities. These elements are installed automatically.
Connectivity Utilities	Installs the TCP/IP utilities. Select this option to install the connectivity utilities.
SNMP Service (Simple Network Management Protocol)	Installs the SNMP service. Select this option to allow this computer to be administered remotely using management tools such as Sun Net Manager or HP Open View. This option also allows you to use Performance Monitor to monitor statistics for the TCP/IP services and WINS Servers.
TCP/IP Network Printing Support	Allows this computer to print directly over the network using TCP/IP. Select this option if you want to print to UNIX print queues or TCP/IP printers that are connected directly to the network. This option must be installed if you want to use the Lpdsvr service so that UNIX computers can print to Windows NT printers.
FTP Server Service	Allows files to be shared over the network with remote computers that support FTP and TCP/IP (especially non-Microsoft network computers). Select this option if you want to use TCP/IP to share files with other computers.
Simple TCP/IP Services	Provides the client software for the Character Generator, Daytime, Discard, Echo, and Quote of the Day services. Select this option to allow this computer to respond to requests from other systems that support these protocols.
DHCP Server Service	Installs the server software to support automatic configuration and addressing for computers using TCP/IP on your internetwork. This option is available only for Windows NT Server. Select this option if this computer is to be a DHCP Server. (If you select this option, you must manually configure the IP address, subnet mask, and default gateway for this computer.)
WINS Server Service	Installs the server software to support WINS, a dynamic name resolution service for computers on a Windows internetwork. This option is available only for Windows NT Server. Select it if this computer is to be installed as a primary or secondary WINS Server. Do not select this option if you intend for this computer to serve as a WINS proxy agent.

(continued)

Table 17-1 *(Continued)*

Option	Description
Domain Name System (DNS) Service	Installs the server software to support DNS, a distributed name resolution service for computers on TCP/IP intenetworks. DNS is the name resolution service used by the Internet. Select this option if this computer is to be installed as a primary or secondary DNS Server. This option is available only for Windows NT Server computers.
Enable Automatic DHCP Configuration	Turns on automatic configuration of TCP/IP parameters for this computer. Select this option if there is a DHCP Server on your internetwork to support dynamic host configuration. This option is not available if the DHCP Server Service or WINS Server Service option is selected.

Note

After installing TCP/IP, Windows NT Setup deposits several files into the \systemroot\SYSTEM32\DRIVERS\ETC directory, including default HOSTS, NETWORKS, PROTOCOLS, QUOTES, and SERVICES files plus a sample LMHOSTS.SAM file.

Using DHCP to configure TCP/IP

To successfully run TCP/IP on your computer, you must configure it with the IP addresses, subnet mask, and default gateway for each network adapter on the computer to which TCP/IP is bound. As indicated earlier in this chapter, you can manually configure TCP/IP or use a DHCP Server.

The best method for ensuring easy and accurate installation of TCP/IP is to use automatic DHCP configuration. (If you plan to set up a DHCP Server, read Chapter 18, *Configuring DHCP Servers*.)

If you already have a DHCP Server on your network, TCP/IP configuration is just a mouse-click away:

1. If you're setting up TCP/IP as part of the initial Windows NT installation process, enable the Obtain an IP Address from a DHCP Server option in the IP Address tab of the Microsoft TCP/IP Properties dialog box.

   Or

   If Windows NT is already installed and you're installing or reconfiguring TCP/IP, launch the Network applet, select the Protocols tab, select TCP/IP and click the configure button. Then enable the Obtain an IP Address from a DHCP Server option in the IP Address tab of the Microsoft TCP/IP Properties dialog box.

2. Click OK when done and then restart the computer. Upon restart, the computer uses the address you specified to seek out the DHCP Server and automatically retrieves the correct configuration information for your computer.

Note

If you attempt to configure TCP/IP via the Network applet after enabling the DHCP option, the system warns you that any manual settings override the automatic settings provided by DHCP. As a general rule, you should not change the automatic settings unless you specifically want to override a setting provided by DHCP.

Configuring TCP/IP manually

After installing Microsoft TCP/IP protocol software, you must manually provide valid addressing information if you are installing TCP/IP on a DHCP Server or if you are not using DHCP to configure a computer dynamically.

Caution

To avoid duplicate addresses, be sure to use the valid values for IP addresses and subnet masks. If duplicate addresses do occur, some computers on the network may function unpredictably.

To configure the TCP/IP protocol manually, you must be logged on as a member of the Administrators group for the local computer you are trying to configure.

1. When you are installing TCP/IP for the first time, the Microsoft TCP/IP Properties dialog box appears automatically after you install TCP/IP protocol. Choose the OK button in the Network dialog box.

   Or

   If you are reconfiguring TCP/IP, start the Network option in the Control Panel to display the Network dialog box. In the Network Protocols list, select TCP/IP Protocol and click the Configure button.

2. In the Adapter list of the IP Address dialog box, shown in Figure 17-3, select the network adapter for which you want to set IP addresses. The Adapter list contains all network adapters to which IP is bound on this computer.

   You must set specific IP addressing information with correct values for each bound adapter. The bindings for a network adapter determine how network protocols and other layers of network software work together. Windows NT automatically binds network protocols to each network adapter during the installation process. If you have two network adapters in your system and you choose to install all available protocols, Windows NT binds each protocol to each adapter installed in your computer.

3. For each bound network adapter, type values in the IP Address and Subnet Mask boxes.

   The value in the IP Address box identifies the IP address for your local computer or, if more than one network card is installed in the computer, for the network adapter card selected in the Adapter box.

   The value in the Subnet Mask box identifies the network membership for the selected network adapter and its host ID. This value allows the computer to separate the IP address into host and network IDs. The subnet mask defaults to an appropriate value, as shown in the following list:

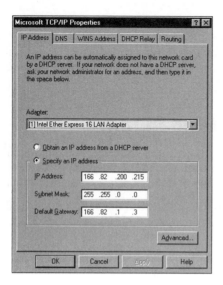

Figure 17-3: The IP Address dialog box.

Address	Class	Subnet mask
Class A	1-126	255.0.0.0
Class B	128-191	255.255.0.0
Class C	192-223	255.255.255.0

4. For each network adapter on the computer, type the correct IP address value in the Default Gateway box.

   This value specifies the IP address of the default gateway (or IP router) used to forward packets to other networks or subnets. It should be the IP address of your local gateway and is required only for systems on internetworks. If this value is not provided, IP functionality is limited to the local subnet unless a route is specified with the TCP/IP route utility.

   If your computer has multiple network cards, you can specify additional default gateways using the Advanced IP Addressing dialog box, as described later in this chapter.

Configuring TCP/IP to use Windows Internet Name Services

If there are WINS Servers installed on your network and you want to use WINS in combination with broadcast name queries to resolve computer names, you should configure WINS options as described in this section.

To configure or reconfigure TCP/IP to use WINS

1. Start the Network applet if it is not already running. When the Network dialog box appears click the Protocols tab, select TCP/IP Protocol, and then click the Configure button. The Microsoft TCP/IP Properties dialog box appears.

2. Click the WINS Address tab. The WINS Address dialog box appears as shown in Figure 17-4, displaying a list of all the network adapters to which IP is bound on this computer.

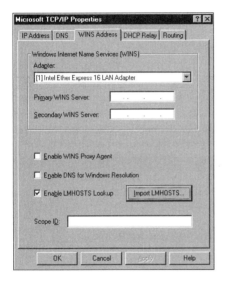

Figure 17-4: The WINS Address dialog box.

3. In the Adapter list, make sure the network adapter for which you want to set WINS addresses is selected and then type IP addresses in the Primary WINS Server box, and, optionally, the Secondary WINS Server box.

Note If you do not provide addresses for WINS Servers, Windows NT uses name query broadcasts (the b-node mode for NetBIOS over TCP/IP) plus the local LMHOSTS file to resolve computer names to IP addresses. Furthermore, Windows NT cannot broadcast beyond the local network.

There are several other options in the WINS Address dialog box that affect the WINS functionality on the local computer.

You can have the local computer serve as a WINS proxy agent by using a WINS Server database to resolve names. This option extends the network beyond the local subnet by allowing other computers configured for broadcast name resolution to use the proxy computer to deliver name resolution services provided by a WINS Server. As a general rule, you should have no more than three WINS proxy agents on a subnet.

To configure the local computer as a WINS proxy agent

Specify an IP address for a WINS Server as described earlier. Then select the Enable WINS Proxy Agent check box. Note that you cannot configure a computer that acts as a WINS Server to also serve as a proxy agent.

Cross Reference

Refer to Chapter 19, *Setting UP WINS Servers*, for more information on Windows proxy agents.

With Windows NT 4.0, Microsoft has implemented DHCP, WINS, and DNS so that they complement each other when used on the same network. Consider the following:

- DHCP allows you to allocate dynamic IP addresses automatically to clients that move between subnets.

- Using WINS, clients register their computer name and IP address automatically, every time they start up their computer. If the computer moves between subnets, this information is updated automatically as well.

- Using DNS, clients can locate non-WINS supporting resources through the static mappings maintained in the configuration files. In addition, any non-WINS aware client that uses DNS to resolve names and has a static mapping to the DNS service can locate a WINS client, provided you configure the Microsoft DNS Server to use a WINS Server for additional names resolution.

To use DNS for name resolution on your network

Select the Enable DNS for Windows Name Resolution check box. Windows NT finds the DNS Server by using the IP address specified in the DNS dialog box. If you have not configured DNS options for TCP/IP, be sure to do so as described in the following section, *Configuring TCP/IP to use DNS*.

The final option for NetBIOS name resolution via WINS is to use an LMHOSTS file.

To use an LMHOSTS Lookup file

Select the Enable LMHOSTS Lookup check box. Then click Import LMHOSTS and specify the directory path for the LMHOSTS file you want to use. By default, Windows NT uses the LMHOSTS file found in \systemroot\SYSTEM32\DRIVERS\ETC.

Finally, your internetwork might use NetBIOS over TCP/IP. Refer to Chapter 16, *Understanding TCP/IP*, for more information on NetBIOS over TCP/IP (NBT). If you have set up your network with its own scope identifier, you should enter the scope identifier in the Scope ID box. The Scope ID defines a group of computers that communicate only with each other as they all have identical Scope IDs. If you did not define a scope for your internetwork, leave this field blank.

When you finish setting WINS options, click OK. When the Microsoft TCP/IP Properties dialog box reappears, click OK. When the Network dialog box reappears, click Close. Then restart your computer to have the settings take effect.

Configuring TCP/IP to use DNS

As mentioned earlier in this chapter, DNS offers added benefits to a Windows network. You should use DNS to extend network interoperability to non-Windows network computers such as UNIX computers. DNS configuration is global for all network adapters installed on a computer.

To configure TCP/IP DNS connectivity

1. Start the Network option in the Control Panel to display the Network dialog box if it is not already running. Click the Protocols tab and select TCP/IP Protocol, and then choose the Configure button.

2. In the Microsoft TCP/IP Properties dialog box, choose the DNS tab. The DNS dialog box appears, as shown in Figure 17-5.

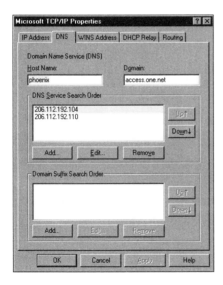

Figure 17-5: The DNS configuration dialog box.

3. In the DNS dialog box, you can, optionally, type a name in the Host Name box (usually the computer name).

The name can be any combination of A-Z letters, 0-9 numerals, and the hyphen (-) plus the period (.) character used as a separator. (Some characters that can be used in Windows NT computer names, particularly the underscore, cannot be used in host names.) By default, Windows NT uses the computer name, but you can assign any host name you want without affecting the computer name.

Although supplying a host name is optional, several utilities use it to identify the local computer by name for authentication. For example, REXEC can use this value to learn the name of the local computer. Also, DNS Servers store host names in a table that maps names to IP addresses for use by DNS.

4. Optionally, type a name in the Domain box. The domain name is usually an organization name followed by a period and an extension that indicates the type of organization, such as cpress.com. You can use any combination of A-Z letters, 0-9 numerals, and the hyphen (-) plus the period (.) character used as a separator. Chapter 16, *Understanding TCP/IP,* describes the Domain Name System and address format in detail.

Note that a DNS domain is not the same as a Windows NT or LAN Manager domain.

5. To enter the IP addresses of DNS Servers in the DNS Service Search Order box, choose the Add button. The TCP/IP DNS Server dialog box appears. Type the IP address of the DNS Server that will provide name resolution, and then click Add. The DNS Server IP address appears in the DNS Service Search Order box.

You can add up to three IP addresses for DNS Servers. The servers running DNS are queried in the order listed. To change the order of the IP addresses, select an IP address to move, and then use the up- or down-arrow buttons. To remove an IP address, select it and choose the Remove button.

6. To enter domain suffixes in the Domain Suffix Search Order box, choose the Add button. The TCP/IP Domain Suffix dialog box appears. Type the DNS domain suffix to append to host names during name resolution, and then click Add. The suffix appears in the Domain Suffix Search Order box.

You can add up to six domain suffixes. To change the search order of the domain suffixes, select a domain name to move and use the up- or down-arrow buttons. To remove a domain name, select it and choose the Remove button.

7. When you are done setting DNS options, choose the OK button.

8. When the Microsoft TCP/IP Properties dialog box reappears, click OK. When the Network dialog box reappears, choose the Close button. Restart your computer to have the settings take effect.

Configuring Advanced TCP/IP Options

If your computer has multiple network adapters connected to different networks using TCP/IP, you can choose the Advanced button in the IP Addressing dialog box to configure options for the adapters or to configure alternate default gateways.

To configure or reconfigure advanced TCP/IP options

1. Start the Network option in the Control Panel to display the Network dialog box. Choose the Protocols tab, select TCP/IP Protocol, and click the Configure button.

2. In the IP Addressing dialog box, choose the Advanced button. The Advanced IP Addressing dialog box appears, as shown in Figure 17-6.

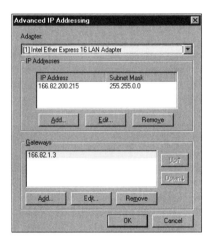

Figure 17-6: The Advanced IP Addressing dialog box.

3. In the Adapter list, select the network adapter for which you want to specify additional configuration values. The IP address and default gateway settings in this dialog box are defined only for the selected network adapter.

4. In the IP Addresses box, choose the Add button and enter an additional IP address and subnet mask for the selected adapter. Then click Add to set the IP address.

Secret

Optionally, if your network card uses multiple IP addresses, repeat this process for each additional IP address. You can specify up to five additional IP addresses and subnet masks for identifying the selected network adapter. This can be useful for a computer connected to one physical network that contains multiple logical IP networks. You can configure up to 255 IP addresses (theoretically) on a single network card by making changes to the Registry. (I have configured and tested as many as 30 IP addresses on a single NIC in my test station.)

5. In the Gateways box, choose the Add button and type the IP address for an additional gateway that the selected adapter can use. Then click Add to set the IP address. Repeat this process for each additional gateway.

You can specify up to five additional default gateways for the selected network adapter. To change the priority order for the gateways, select an address to move and use the up- or down-arrow buttons. To remove a gateway, select it and choose the Remove button.

6. When you are done setting advanced options, choose the OK button. When the Microsoft TCP/IP Properties dialog box reappears, choose the OK button. When the Network dialog box reappears, choose the OK button to complete advanced TCP/IP configuration. Restart your computer to have the changes take effect.

Routing and IP Gateways

To connect discrete TCP/IP networks you need a device called a *router* positioned between the networks. Routers are also referred to as gateways in the Internet world. This is why you see dialog boxes that refer to gateways when configuring Microsoft TCP/IP options. A router contains information about the networks connected to it in the internetwork. Although each IP host can maintain static routes for specific destinations, usually the router is used to find remote destinations. (The default gateway is needed only for computers that are part of an internetwork.)

When IP prepares to send a packet, it inserts the local (source) IP address and the destination address of the packet in the IP header and checks whether the network ID of the destination matches the network ID of the source. If they match, the packet is sent directly to the destination computer on the local network. If the network IDs do not match, the routing table is examined for static routes. If none are found, the packet is forwarded to the default gateway for delivery.

The default gateway is a computer connected to the local subnet and other networks that knows the network IDs for other networks in the internetwork and how to reach them; therefore, it can forward the packet to other gateways until the packet is eventually delivered to a gateway that is connected to the specified destination. This process is known as *routing*.

Internetwork routing through gateways

When TCP/IP is configured on a computer, the IP address for a default gateway is specified. Users can add static routes by using the route utility to specify a route for a particular system. Static routes always override the use of default gateways.

IP gateways are not required on networks that are not part of an internetwork. If a network is part of an internetwork and a system does not specify a default gateway (or if the gateway computer is not operating properly), only communication beyond the local subnet is impaired. If the default gateway becomes unavailable, the computer cannot communicate outside its own subnet. Multiple default gateways can be assigned to prevent such a problem. However, when a computer is configured with multiple default gateways, retransmission problems can result in the system trying the other routers in the configuration.

To configure multiple default gateways in Windows NT, you must provide an IP address for each gateway in the Advanced Microsoft TCP/IP Configuration dialog box.

Configuring a multihomed system for IP routing

IP forwarding (routing) allows a multihomed computer running Windows NT to participate with other static routers on a network. You should check this option if you have two or more network cards and your network uses static routing, which also requires the addition of static routing tables.

Note

You cannot use this option if your computer has only one network adapter and one IP address. Also, this option does not support routers running the Routing Information Protocol (RIP).

To configure or reconfigure IP routing

1. In Control Panel, double-click the Network icon. The Network dialog box appears. Click the Protocols tab, select TCP/IP Protocol, and then click Configure. The Microsoft TCP/IP Properties dialog box appears.

2. Click the Routing tab. The Routing dialog box appears.

3. To turn on static routing, select the Enable IP Forwarding check box.

4. When you are done setting routing options, click OK. When the Microsoft TCP/IP Properties dialog box reappears, click OK again. When the Network dialog box reappears, click Close. Restart your computer to have the settings take effect.

Using DHCP across routers

Although Windows NT provides dynamic host configuration protocol (DHCP) services, and DHCP is based on the Bootstrap protocol (BOOTP), Windows NT does not provide BOOTP services. BOOTP, originally created for loading diskless computers, is both a service and a protocol (used to implement the service). However, BOOTP is not just for diskless workstations, it also provides centralized control of IP addresses by allowing IP addresses to be managed from a single database. In this case, a Windows NT DHCP Server database.

Generally speaking, a Windows NT DHCP Server can provide IP addresses to clients spanning multiple subnets if the router that separates them can act as an RFC 1542 (BOOTP) relay agent. If the router cannot function as a relay agent, each subnet that has DHCP clients requires a DHCP Server. Router functionality depends on the router itself and not on Windows NT.

Although Windows NT does not support configuring routers for DHCP/ BOOTP relay, you can configure a Windows NT Server computer to serve as a DHCP relay agent. A DHCP relay agent sits on a client's subnet and intercepts DHCP (and BOOTP) broadcast messages and sends the packets directly to the DHCP Server. These directed messages can cross IP routers. In this way, a DHCP relay agent acts as a local proxy for the remote DHCP Servers.

To configure or reconfigure a DHCP relay agent

1. In Control Panel, double-click the Network icon. The Network dialog box appears. Click the Protocols tab, select TCP/IP Protocol, and then click Configure. The Microsoft TCP/IP Properties dialog box appears.

2. Click the DHCP Relay tab. The DHCP Relay dialog box appears as shown in Figure 17-7.

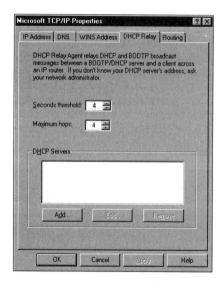

Figure 17-7: The DHCP Relay dialog box.

The configurable parameters for a DHCP relay agent are:

- **Seconds Threshold.** When the relay agent receives a client message, the relay agent compares the value of the seconds field in the message with the value of the seconds threshold to determine whether or not to relay the message. If the seconds field is greater than or equal to the seconds threshold, the relay agent relays the message.

- **Maximum Hops.** When the relay agent receives a client message, the relay agent compares the value of the hops field in the message with the value of the maximum hops to determine whether or not to relay the message. If the hops field is less than or equal to the maximum hops, the relay agent relays the message. By definition, a relay agent is not allowed to relay a message whose hops field exceeds a value of 16.

■ **DHCP Servers.** This parameter identifies the server or servers to which you want to relay DHCP/BOOTP messages.

3. To change the value in the Seconds threshold box, select it and type in a new value or click the arrows to select a new value. The default value is 4.

4. To change the value in the Maximum hops box, select it and type in a new value or click the arrows to select a new value. The default value is 4.

5. Click Add under DHCP Servers. The DHCP Relay Agent dialog box appears. In the Domain Server box, type the IP address of a server to which you want to relay DHCP/BOOTP messages. Click Add to move the address to the DHCP Servers list. Repeat the process for any additional server addresses.

6. When you are done setting DHCP relay options, click OK. If you have not already installed the BOOTP (DHCP) Relay Agent service, you will be prompted to do so now. Otherwise when the Network dialog box reappears, click Close. If you are installing and configuring a DHCP relay agent, restart your computer to have the settings take effect. If you are just reconfiguring a DHCP relay agent, the changes take effect immediately without restarting the computer.

Simple Network Management Protocol

Simple Network Management Protocol (SNMP) has become the de facto mechanism for the distributed management of computer networks. The most significant aspect of SNMP is the power and flexibility it provides to monitor and control networks.

Installing SNMP

You install SNMP in the same way you install other TCP/IP utilities and services: using the Control Panel Network applet. To install and/or configure SNMP, you must log on as a member of the Administrators group for the local computer where you want to install and configure TCP/IP.

To install SNMP

1. Start the Network applet in the Control Panel.

2. In the Network dialog box, choose the Services tab to display the Select Network Service dialog box. Select SNMP Service, and then click OK.

3. Next, Windows NT Setup displays a message asking for the full path to the Windows NT distribution files. Type the path and click Continue. Setup copies the necessary files to your hard disk and displays the Microsoft SNMP Properties dialog box.

Configuring SNMP agent information

SNMP agent information allows you to comment about the user and the physical location of the computer and to indicate the types of service to report. The types of service that can be reported are based on the computer's configuration.

The SNMP configuration information identifies communities and trap destinations.

- A community is a group of hosts to which a Windows NT computer running the SNMP service belongs. You can specify one or more communities to which the Windows NT computer using SNMP sends network-management information in traps (discrete blocks of data). The community name is placed in the SNMP packet when the trap is sent.

- When the SNMP service receives a request for information that does not contain the correct community name and does not match an accepted host name for the service, the SNMP service can send a trap to the trap destination(s), indicating that the request failed authentication.

- Trap destinations are the names or IP addresses of hosts to which you want the SNMP service to send traps with the selected community name.

You might want to use SNMP for statistics but may not care about identifying communities or traps. In this case, you can specify the "public" community name when you configure the SNMP service.

To configure SNMP agent information

1. In the Microsoft SNMP Properties dialog box, choose the Agent tab. The Agent dialog box appears, as shown in Figure 17-8.

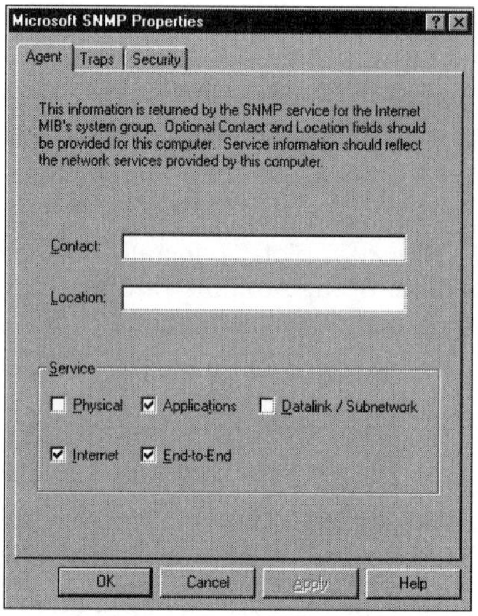

Figure 17-8: The Agent dialog box.

2. In the SNMP Agent dialog box, type the computer user's name in the Contact box and the computer's physical location in the Location box. These comments are used as text and cannot include embedded control characters.

3. Set the services options as described in Table 17-2. Check all boxes that indicate network capabilities provided by your Windows NT computer. SNMP must have this information to manage the enabled services.

If you have installed additional TCP/IP network devices, such as a bridge or router, you should consult RFC 1213 for additional information.

4. Go on to configure SNMP Traps and Security information and after you complete all procedures, choose the OK button. When the Network dialog box reappears, choose the OK button. SNMP service and SNMP security are ready to start without rebooting the computer.

Table 17-2	SNMP Services
Option	*Meaning*
Physical	Select this option if this Windows NT computer manages any physical TCP/IP device, such as a repeater.
Applications	Select this option if this Windows NT computer includes any applications that use TCP/IP, such as electronic mail. This option should be selected for all Windows NT installations.
Datalink/Subnetwork	Select this option if this Windows NT computer manages a TCP/IP subnetwork or datalink, such as a bridge.
Internet	Select this option if this Windows NT computer acts as an IP gateway.
End-to-end	Select this option if this Windows NT computer acts as an IP host. This option should be selected for all Windows NT installations.

Configuring SNMP traps

1. In the Microsoft SNMP Properties dialog box, choose the Traps tab. The Traps dialog box appears, as shown in Figure 17-9.

2. To identify each community to which you want this computer to send traps, enter the name in the Community Names box. After typing each name, choose the Add button to move the name to the Send Trap with Community Names list.

Typically, all hosts belong to *public*, which is the standard name for the common community of all hosts. To delete an entry in the list, select it and choose the Remove button.

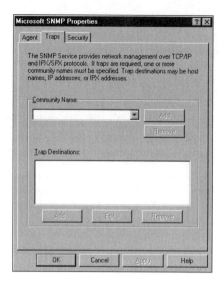

Figure 17-9: The Traps dialog box.

Note

Community names are case sensitive.

3. To specify hosts for each community to which you send traps, after you have added the community and while it is still highlighted, click Add under the Trap Destinations box. The Service Configuration dialog box appears. Enter a host name, its IP address, or its IPX address in the IP Host/Address or IPX Address box. Then choose the Add button to move the host name or IP address to the Trap Destination for the selected community list.

4. To enable additional security for the SNMP service, choose the Security button. Continue with the configuration procedure, as described in the next section, *Configuring SNMP security*.

5. To specify Agent information (comments about the user, location, and services), choose the Agent button. Continue with the configuration procedure, as described in *Configuring SNMP agent information* earlier in this chapter.

6. When you have completed all procedures, choose the OK button. When the Network Settings dialog box reappears, choose the OK button. The Microsoft SNMP service is ready to start without rebooting the computer.

Configuring SNMP security

SNMP security allows you to specify the communities and hosts from which a computer accepts requests and to specify whether to send an authentication trap when an unauthorized community or host requests information.

To configure SNMP security

1. In the Microsoft SNMP Properties dialog box, choose the Security tab. The SNMP Security dialog box appears as shown in Figure 17-10.

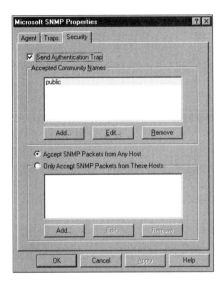

Figure 17-10: The Security dialog box.

2. If you want to send a trap for failed authentications, select the Send Authentication Trap check box.

3. In the Accepted Community Names box, click the Add button. The Security Configuration dialog box appears. Type the community name you want to accept requests from. Click Add to move the name to the Accepted Community Names list.

   A host must belong to a community that appears on this list for the SNMP service to accept its requests. Typically, all hosts belong to *public*, which is the standard name for the common community of all hosts. To delete an entry in the list, select it and choose the Remove button.

5. Specify whether to accept SNMP packets from any host or from only specified hosts.

   ■ If the Accept SNMP Packets from Any Host option is selected, no SNMP packets are rejected on the basis of source host ID. The list of hosts under Only Accept SNMP Packets from These Hosts has no effect.

   ■ If the Only Accept SNMP Packets from These Hosts option is selected, SNMP packets are accepted only from the hosts listed. Click Add to display the IP Host/Address or IPX Address dialog box. Then type the host names, IP addresses, or IPX addresses of the hosts from which you want to accept requests. Next choose the Add button to move each host name or IP address to the list box. To delete an entry in the list, select it and choose the Remove button.

6. Choose the OK button. The Microsoft SNMP Properties dialog box reappears.

7. After you complete all procedures, choose the OK button. When the Network dialog box reappears, choose the OK button. SNMP service and SNMP security are ready to start without rebooting the computer.

TCP/IP Troubleshooting Tools and Strategies

Your approach to troubleshooting TCP/IP should be no different from troubleshooting any other computer problem. Ask yourself the following questions:

■ What works? What doesn't work?

■ Is there any relationship between the things that do and don't work?

■ Did the component or service ever work on this computer/network?

■ If so, what has changed since it last worked?

With those questions answered, you're ready to proceed with the troubleshooting process. The following section describes the tools you'll use to troubleshoot TCP/IP problems.

IPConfig

IPConfig is a command-line utility that prints out the TCP/IP-related configuration of a host. When used with the /all switch, it produces a detailed configuration report for all interfaces, including any configured serial ports (RAS). Output from this report may be redirected to a file and pasted into other documents as follows:

```
Windows NT IP Configuration
  Host Name . . . . . . . . . : valmac1.cpress.com
  DNS Servers . . . . . . . . :
  Node Type . . . . . . . . . : Hybrid
  NetBIOS Scope ID. . . . . . :
  IP Routing Enabled. . . . . : No
  WINS Proxy Enabled. . . . . : No
  NetBIOS Resolution Uses DNS : No
Ethernet adapter Elnk31:
  Description . . . . . . . . : ELNK3 Ethernet Adapter
  Physical Address. . . . . . : 00-17-AF-1D-2B-91
  DHCP Enabled. . . . . . . . : Yes
```

```
IP Address. . . . . . . . . : 10.57.9.138
Subnet Mask . . . . . . . . : 255.255.248.0
Default Gateway . . . . . . : 10.57.8.1
DHCP Server . . . . . . . . : 10.54.16.157
Primary WINS Server . . . . : 10.54.16.157
Secondary WINS Server . . . : 10.54.16.159
Lease Obtained. . . . . . . : Sunday, June 25, 1995 11:43:01
PM
Lease Expires . . . . . . . : Wednesday, June 28, 1995
11:43:01 PM
Ethernet adapter NdisWan5:
Description . . . . . . . . :
Physical Address. . . . . . : 00-00-00-00-00-00
DHCP Enabled. . . . . . . . : No
IP Address. . . . . . . . . : 0.0.0.0
Subnet Mask . . . . . . . . : 0.0.0.0
Default Gateway . . . . . . :
```

Ping

Ping is a tool that helps to verify IP-level connectivity. When troubleshooting, the ping command is used to send an ICMP echo request to a target name or IP address. First try pinging the IP address of the target host to see if it responds, as this is the simplest case. If that succeeds, then try pinging the name. Ping uses Windows Sockets-style name resolution to resolve the name to an address, so if pinging by address succeeds but pinging by name fails, the problem lies in address resolution, not network connectivity. Type **ping -?** to see what command-line options are available. For example, ping allows you to specify the size of packets to use, how many to send, whether to record the route used, what TTL value to use, and whether to set the "don't fragment" flag.

The following example illustrates how to send two pings, each 1450 bytes in size, to address 10.57.13.152:

```
C:\>ping -n 2 -l 1450 10.57.13.152
Pinging 10.57.13.152 with 1450 bytes of data:
Reply from 10.57.13.152: bytes=1450 time=10ms TTL=32
Reply from 10.57.13.152: bytes=1450 time=10ms TTL=32
```

By default, ping only waits 750 ms for each response to be returned before timing out. If the remote system being pinged is across a high-delay link such as a satellite link, responses could take longer to be returned. The -w (wait) switch can be used to specify a longer timeout.

ARP

The ARP command is useful for viewing the ARP cache. If two hosts on the same subnet cannot ping each other successfully, try running the arp -a command on each computer to see if they have the correct MAC addresses listed for each other. You can determine a host's MAC address using

IPConfig. If another host with a duplicate IP address exists on the network, the ARP cache may have had the MAC address for the other computer placed in it. You can use arp -d to delete an entry that may be incorrect. You can add an entry by using arp -s.

Tracert

Tracert is a route-tracing utility. Tracert uses the IP TTL field and ICMP error messages to determine the route from one host to another through a network.

Route

Use route to view or modify the route table. Route print displays a list of current routes known by IP for the host. Sample output is shown in the *IPConfig* section of this chapter. Use route add to add routes to the table, and use route delete to delete routes from the table. Note that routes added to the table are not made permanent unless the -p switch is specified. Non-persistent routes only last until the computer is rebooted.

In order for two hosts to exchange IP datagrams, they must both have a route to each other or use default gateways that know of a route. Normally, routers exchange information with each other using a protocol such as Routing Information Protocol (RIP) or Open Shortest Path First (OSPF). Windows NT did not include support for either of these routing protocols; therefore, when these computers are used as routers, it is often neces-sary to manually add routes. Microsoft is working on RIP and OSPF support for Windows NT.

Netstat

Netstat displays protocol statistics and current TCP/IP connections. Netstat -a displays all connections, and netstat -r displays the route table, plus active connections. The -n switch tells netstat not to convert addresses and port numbers to names. Sample output follows:

```
C:\>netstat -e
Interface Statistics
Received Sent
Bytes 3995837940 47224622
Unicast packets 120099 131015
Non-unicast packets 7579544 3823
Discards 0 0
Errors 0 0
Unknown protocols 363054211
C:\>netstat -a
Active Connections
Proto      Local Address  Foreign Address      State
```

```
TCP valmac1:1572     10.57.13.152:nbsession    ESTABLISHED
TCP valmac1:1589     10.57.9.147:nbsession     ESTABLISHED
TCP valmac1:1606     11.1.105.245:nbsession    ESTABLISHED
TCP valmac1:1632     10.57.9.213:nbsession     ESTABLISHED
TCP valmac1:1659     10.55.86.169:nbsession    ESTABLISHED
TCP valmac1:1714     10.55.80.203:nbsession    ESTABLISHED
TCP valmac1:1719     10.54.67.36:nbsession     ESTABLISHED
TCP valmac1:1241     10.57.9.101:nbsession     ESTABLISHED
UDP valmac1:1025     *:*
UDP valmac1:snmp     *:*
UDP valmac1:nbname   *:*
UDP valmac1:nbdatagram *:*
UDP valmac1:nbname   *:*
UDP valmac1:nbdatagram *:*
C:\>netstat -s
IP Statistics
Packets Received = 5378528
 Received Header Errors = 738854
 Received Address Errors = 23150
 Datagrams Forwarded = 0
 Unknown Protocols Received = 0
 Received Packets Discarded = 0
 Received Packets Delivered = 4616524
 Output Requests = 132702
 Routing Discards = 157
 Discarded Output Packets = 0
 Output Packet No Route = 0
 Reassembly Required = 0
 Reassembly Successful = 0
 Reassembly Failures = 0
 Datagrams Successfully Fragmented = 0
 Datagrams Failing Fragmentation = 0
 Fragments Created = 0
ICMP Statistics
 Received Sent
 Messages 693 4
 Errors 0 0
 Destination Unreachable 685 0
 Time Exceeded 0 0
 Parameter Problems 0 0
 Source Quenchs 0 0
 Redirects 0 0
 Echos 4 0
 Echo Replies 0 4
 Timestamps 0 0
 Timestamp Replies 0 0
 Address Masks 0 0
 Address Mask Replies 0 0
TCP Statistics
Active Opens = 597
 Passive Opens = 135
 Failed Connection Attempts = 107
 Reset Connections = 91
 Current Connections = 8
```

```
Segments Received = 106770
Segments Sent = 118431
Segments Retransmitted = 461
UDP Statistics
Datagrams Received = 4157136
No Ports = 351928
Receive Errors = 2
Datagrams Sent = 13809
```

NBTStat

NBTStat is a useful tool for troubleshooting NetBIOS name resolution problems. NBTStat -n displays the names that were registered locally on the system by applications, such as the server and redirector. NBTStat -c shows the NetBIOS name cache, which contains name-to-address mappings for other computers. NBTStat -r purges the name cache and reloads it from the LMHOSTS file. NBTStat -a *<name>* performs a NetBIOS adapter status command against the computer specified by name. The adapter status command returns the local NetBIOS name table for that computer plus the MAC address of the adapter card. NBTStat -s lists the current NetBIOS sessions and their status, including statistics, as follows:

```
NetBIOS Connection Table
Local Name State In/Out Remote Host Input Output
_____

VALMAC1 <00> Connected Out CNSSUP1<20> 6MB 5MB
VALMAC1 <00> Connected Out CNSPRINT<20> 108KB 116KB
VALMAC1 <00> Connected Out CNSSRC1<20> 299KB 19KB
VALMAC1 <00> Connected Out STH2NT<20> 324KB 19KB
VALMAC1 <03> Listening
```

You've seen how the arp, ping, netstat, and NBTStat utilities can provide useful information when you are trying to determine the cause of TCP/IP networking problems. Recommendations follow for using these utilities to assess and diagnose specific situations.

How can you determine whether TCP/IP is installed correctly on a Windows NT system?

Try using ping on the local system by typing the IP loopback address 127.0.0.1 from the command line: **ping 127.0.0.1**. The system should respond immediately. If ping is not found or the command fails, check the event log with Event Viewer and look for problems reported by Setup or the TCP/IP service. You should also attempt to ping the IP addresses of your local interface(s) to determine whether you configured IP properly. Successful use of ping indicates that the IP layer on the target system is probably functional.

How can you determine if the FTP Server service is installed correctly on a Windows NT system?

Try using ftp on the local system by typing the IP loopback address from the command line: **ftp 127.0.0.1**. The interaction with the server locally is identical to the interaction expected for other Windows NT (and most UNIX) clients. This utility can also be used to determine whether the directories, permissions, and so on, of the FTP Server service are configured properly.

What causes Error 53 when connecting to a Windows NT, Windows for Workgroups, or LAN Manager server?

Error 53 is returned when the specified computer name cannot be resolved. If the computer is on the local subnet, confirm that the name is spelled correctly and that the target system is running TCP/IP as well. If the computer is not on the local subnet, be sure that its name and IP address mapping is available in the LMHOSTS file. If things appear to be installed properly, try using ping with the remote system to be sure that its TCP/IP software is functional.

After adding a new mapping to the LMHOSTS file, what if it takes an unusually long time to connect to the server?

A large LMHOSTS file with an entry at the end of the file, possibly following some #INCLUDEs, could cause this behavior. Two things can be done to speed things up. Mark the entry as a preloaded entry by following the mapping with the #PRE tag, and use the NBTStat -r command to update the local name cache immediately. The alternative is to place the mapping higher in the LMHOSTS file. As discussed in Chapter 16, *Understanding TCP/IP*, the LMHOSTS file is parsed sequentially to locate non-#PREloaded entries. Therefore, it is advisable to place frequently used entries near the top of the file and the #PRE entries near the bottom.

What if users are having difficulty connecting to a particular server, even when specifying the same name?

Use the NBTStat -n command to determine (authoritatively) under what name the server is registered on the network. The output of this command lists several names the system has registered using NetBIOS over TCP/IP. One resembling the system's computer name should be present. If not, try one of the other unique names displayed. The NBTStat command can also display the cached entries for remote systems — either names #PREloaded from LMHOSTS or names recently resolved due to current net-work activity. If the name the remote users are using is the same and the other systems are on a remote subnet, be sure that they have the sys-tem's mapping in their LMHOSTS file.

What do you do when you can only connect using IP addresses and cannot connect to foreign systems with host names using Telnet, FTP, and so on?

Check the host name resolution configuration using the Network icon in the Control Panel (found under the TCP/IP Connectivity option) to be sure that the appropriate hosts and DNS setup have been configured for the system. If you are using the HOSTS file, be sure that the remote system is spelled the same way in the file as it is being used by the application. If you are using DNS, be sure that the IP addresses of the DNS Servers are correct and in the proper order. Try using ping with the remote system by typing both the host name and IP address to determine whether the host name is being resolved properly.

When using Telnet with a particular computer, the banner identifies a computer other than the one that was intended, even though I specified the correct IP address. How can this be?

Situations like this usually arise when two systems on the same network are configured (mistakenly) with the same IP address. The Ethernet and IP address mapping is done by the ARP (Address Resolution Protocol) module, which believes the first response it receives. The impostor computer's reply sometimes comes back before the intended computer's reply. These problems are difficult to isolate and track down. The command arp -g displays the mappings in the ARP cache. If you know the Ethernet address for the intended remote system, you can easily determine if the two match. If not, try using arp -d to delete the entry, then ping the same address (forcing an ARP) and check the Ethernet address in the cache again using arp -g. Chances are that if both systems are on the same network, you will eventually get a different response. If not, it may be necessary to filter the traffic from the impostor host to determine the owner or location of the system.

What do I do when a TCP/IP connection to a remote system appears to be hung?

The netstat -a command shows the status of all activity on TCP and UDP ports on the local system. The state of a good TCP connection is usually established with 0 bytes in the send and receive queues. If data is blocked in either queue or if the state is irregular, there is probably a problem with the connection. If not, you are probably experiencing network or application delay.

What do I do when the TCP/IP configuration dialog reports: "Your default gateway does not belong to one of the configured interfaces. Do you want to change it?"

This error indicates that the default gateway is not located on the same logical network as any of the installed interface(s) on the system. This problem is determined by comparing the net ID portion of the default gateway (by computing a bitwise AND operation between the subnet mask and the default gateway) and the net ID(s) of any of the installed interfaces. For example, a system with a single interface configured with an IP address of 102.54.0.1 and a subnet mask of 255.255.0.0 would require that the default gateway be of the form 102.54.a.b because the net ID portion of the IP interface is 102.54.

Removing TCP/IP Components

If you want to remove the TCP/IP protocols or any of the services installed on a computer, use the Network option in the Control Panel.

When you remove any network software, Windows NT warns you that the action permanently removes that component. You cannot reinstall a component that has been removed until after you restart the computer.

To remove any TCP/IP component

1. In the Control Panel, choose the Network option.

2. In the Installed Network Software list in the Network Settings dialog box, select the component you want to remove.

3. Choose the Remove button. Press OK when finished.

Summary

This chapter showed you how to install and configure Microsoft TCP/IP. It also covered

▶ Configuring SNMP

▶ Removing TCP/IP components

▶ Troubleshooting TCP/IP

Chapter 18

Configuring DHCP Servers

In This Chapter

▶ Implementing DHCP

▶ Defining DHCP scopes

▶ Configuring DHCP options

▶ Administering DHCP Clients

▶ Managing the DHCP database files

▶ Setting local policies

▶ Troubleshooting problems involving DHCP Clients

Every computer running TCP/IP must have specific information to identify itself uniquely, the network of which it is a member, and the location for packets not bound for computers on the local network. This information is referred to as the TCP/IP address, subnet mask, and default gateway, respectively.

TCP/IP parameters are difficult to manage properly, easily misconfigured, and require a great deal of administrative overhead. Dynamic Host Configuration Protocol (DHCP) was designed to configure dynamically workstations with IP addresses and related TCP/IP information. This chapter describes how to install DHCP Servers and how to use DHCP Manager to manage these servers.

DHCP Overview

The Dynamic Host Configuration Protocol (DHCP) was designed by the Internet Engineering Task Force (IETF) to reduce the amount of configuration required when using TCP/IP. DHCP is defined in RFCs (Request For Comments) 1533, 1534, 1541, and 1542.

DHCP centralizes TCP/IP configuration and lets you manage the allocation of TCP/IP configuration information by automatically assigning IP addresses to systems configured to use DHCP. Two types of systems use DHCP:

■ **DHCP Clients**. When installing TCP/IP on a DHCP Client system, you do not have to supply TCP/IP configuration information. Instead, simply select the Enable Automatic DHCP Configuration check box, which makes the system a DHCP Client. With this box checked, each time the DHCP Client reboots, it sends out a message requesting an IP address lease from a DHCP Server.

As long as a DHCP Server responds with an IP address to lease, the DHCP can fully load TCP/IP and use TCP/IP to communicate on the network without having to supply any configuration information.

■ **DHCP Servers**. To use DHCP on a given network, you need at least one DHCP Server on that network. After installing the DHCP Server service on a system, you then define and create a DHCP scope on the DHCP Server. A DHCP scope consists of a pool or range of IP addresses that the DHCP Server can lease to DHCP Clients.

When a DHCP Server receives a request from a DHCP Client for an IP address lease, it selects an available (unleased) IP address from its pool of IP addresses and offers it to the DHCP Client. In most cases, the DHCP Server also returns an additional TCP/IP configuration.

Configuring DHCP Servers for a network provides these benefits:

■ The administrator can centrally define global and subnet TCP/IP parameters for the entire internetwork and define parameters for reserved clients.

■ Client computers do not require manual TCP/IP configuration. When a client computer moves between subnets, it is reconfigured for TCP/IP automatically at system startup time.

DHCP components

Under Windows NT, DHCP consists of two services: a DHCP Client service and a DHCP Server service. You cannot stop the DHCP Client service dynamically through Control Panel Services. You must first disable the service and then shut down and restart the workstation. However, you can use Control Panel Services to stop and start the DHCP Server service dynamically without having to shut down and restart the system.

How DHCP works

DHCP was designed as an extension to the Bootstrap Protocol (BOOTP), which is used to boot and configure diskless workstations across the network.

Note The Bootstrap Protocol (BOOTP) was originally defined in RFC 951. The latest BOOTP RFC is RFC 1542, which includes support for DHCP. (Both RFCs are included on the *Windows NT Secrets* companion CD-ROM.) The major advantage of using the same message format as BOOTP is that an existing router can act as an RFC 1542 (BOOTP) relay agent to relay DHCP messages between subnets. Therefore, with a router acting as an RFC 1542 (BOOTP) relay agent between two subnets, it is possible to have a single DHCP Server providing IP addresses and configuration information for systems on both subnets.

Leasing an IP Address

To obtain an IP address from a DHCP Server, DHCP Clients pass through a series of states as shown in Figure 18-1.

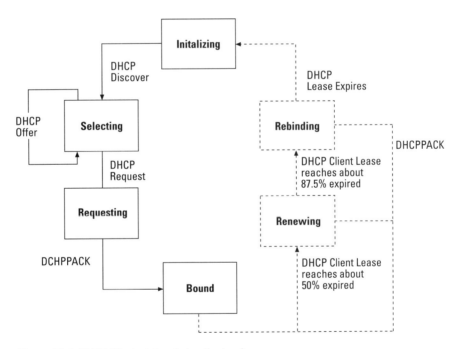

Figure 18-1: DHCP Client states during the leasing process.

- **Initializing State.** When a DHCP Client boots, TCP/IP initially loads and initializes with a NULL IP address so that it can communicate with the DHCP Servers on the network via TCP/IP. The DHCP Client then broadcasts a DHCPDISCOVER message to its subnet. The DHCPDISCOVER message contains the DHCP Client's media access control (MAC) address and computer name. In addition, if this DHCP Client has successfully received an IP address from a DHCP Server previously, the client includes the previous IP address in the DHCPDISCOVER message to try to lease the same IP address.

Note

Windows NT DHCP Clients store their leased IP address in the Registry. Each time the system boots and sends out a DHCPDISCOVER message, it requests the IP address that was stored in the Registry.

Because the DHCP Client does not yet have an IP address and does not know the IP address of any DHCP Servers, the source IP address for the DHCPDISCOVER broadcast is 0.0.0.0, and the destination is 255.255.255.255.

- **Selecting State.** Any DHCP Servers that receive the DHCPDISCOVER message and have a valid configuration for the DHCP Client respond with a DHCPOFFER message. The DHCP Servers send their DHCPOFFER messages via broadcast because the DHCP Client does not yet have an IP address. This message contains the following components:

  - The DHCP Client's MAC address

  - An offered IP address

  - An appropriate subnet mask

  - A server identifier (the IP address of the offering DHCP Server)

  - Length of the lease

  When a DHCP Server sends a DHCPOFFER message offering an IP address, the DHCP Server reserves the IP address so that it cannot offer that same address to another DHCP Client. This is important in networks that have several DHCP Clients; it prevents more than one DHCP Client from accepting the same configuration information.

  If a DHCP Client does not receive a DHCPOFFER message from a DHCP Server on startup, it retries the request four times every five minutes at four-, six-, eight-, and sixteen-second intervals.

  The DHCP Client accepts the DHCPOFFER under the following conditions:

  - The client receives the requested IP address.

  - The client is willing to accept any IP address.

  - The client has tried to accept an IP address two or more times unsuccessfully.

- **Requesting State.** The DHCP Client collects all of the DHCPOFFER messages, selects an offer — usually the first offer received — and sends a DHCPREQUEST message to the DHCP Server. The DHCPREQUEST message indicates that the DHCP Client accepts the offered IP address. It includes at a minimum the server identifier from the accepted

DHCPOFFER and may also include a request for any additional configuration information that the DHCP Client requires, such as a default gateway and the IP address of a WINS Server.

Note that even at this stage, the TCP/IP protocol is still not fully initialized on the DHCP Client, so the DHCPREQUEST message is sent via broadcast. Broadcasting the message ensures that the same DHCP Servers that received the initial DHCPDISCOVER message also receive this message. Because the server identifier is included in the DHCPREQUEST, any other DHCP Servers that offered the DHCP Client an IP address return the offered IP address to their pool of available IP addresses.

■ **Bound State.** The DHCP Server responds to the DHCPREQUEST message with a DHCPACK (DHCP acknowledgment) message that contains a valid lease for the negotiated IP address as well as any configuration parameters. Here again, the DHCP Server sends the DHCPACK message via broadcast because the DHCP Client does not yet have an IP address. When the DHCP Client receives the DHCPACK message, it completes initialization of TCP/IP and becomes a bound DHCP Client and can use TCP/IP to communicate on the network.

Renewing IP address leases

DHCP Clients lease their IP address from a DHCP Server. When the lease expires, they can no longer use the IP address. For this reason, DHCP Clients must renew their lease on the IP address, preferably before the lease has expired or is about to expire. Once again, during the process of renewing its lease, a DHCP Client passes through a series of states as shown in Figure 18-2.

■ **Renewing State.** By default, a DHCP Client first tries to renew its lease when 50 percent of the lease time has expired. To renew its lease, a DHCP Client sends a *directed* DHCPREQUEST message to the DHCP Server from which it obtained the lease.

If permitted, the DHCP Server automatically renews the lease by responding with a DHCPACK message. This DHCPACK message contains the new lease as well as any configuration parameters so that the DHCP Client can update its settings in case the administrator updated any settings on the DHCP Server. Once the DHCP Client has renewed its lease, it returns to the *bound* state.

■ **Rebinding State.** If a DHCP Client attempts to renew its lease on an IP address and for some reason is unable to contact a DHCP Server, the DHCP Client displays a message similar to the following message:

```
The DHCP Client could not renew the lease for the IP Address
198.166.205.10. Your lease is valid until Sun January 21 05:50:55
1996. DHCP will try to renew the lease before it expires. If you
want to see DHCP messages in the future, choose YES. Otherwise
choose NO.
```

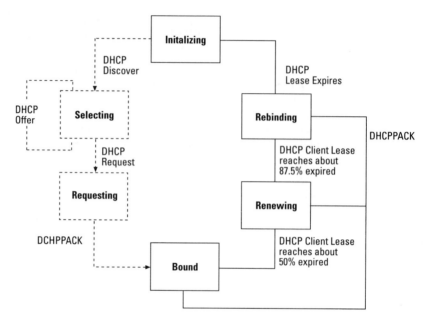

Figure 18-2: DHCP Client states during the lease renewal process.

If, for some reason, the DHCP Client is unable to communicate with the DHCP Server from which it obtained its lease, it attempts to contact any available DHCP Server when 87.5 percent of the lease time has expired. The DHCP Client broadcasts DHCPREQUEST messages so that any DHCP Server can renew the lease. Any DHCP Server can respond with a DHCPACK message renewing the lease or a DHCPNACK message that forces the DHCP Client to re-initialize (begin the leasing process anew) and obtain an IP address lease for a new IP address.

If the lease expires or the DHCP Client receives a DHCPNACK message, it must immediately stop using the expired IP address. However, the DHCP Client can return to the initializing stage and attempt to obtain another IP address lease.

Additional DHCP messages

There are seven possible DHCP messages that may pass between a DHCP Client and a DHCP Server as listed in Table 18-1.

Table 18-1	DHCP Messages
Sent by DHCP Clients	*Sent by DHCP Servers*
DHCPDECLINE	DHCPACK
DHCPREQUEST	DHCPNAK
DHCPDISCOVER	DHCPOFFER
DHCPRELEASE	

DHCPDECLINE. After receiving a DHCPACK message from the DHCP Server, the DHCP Client checks the configuration parameters sent by the DHCP Server. The DHCP Client sends a DHCPDECLINE message to a DHCP Server if the configuration parameter sent by the DHCP Server is invalid. After sending the DHCPDECLINE message, the DHCP Client returns to the initializing state and again attempts to lease an IP address. At this time, the DHCP Client does not have a valid IP address so it broadcasts the DHCPDECLINE message using address 255.255.255.255.

DHCPNAK. A DHCP Server sends a DHCPNAK message to a DHCP Client to inform the DHCP Client that it has incorrect configuration information. This forces the DHCP Client to release its IP address, return to the initializing state, and go through the process of acquiring an IP address lease again.

DHCPRELEASE. A DHCP Client sends a DHCPRELEASE message to a DHCP Server to relinquish its IP address and cancel its lease on the IP address. This message includes the IP address intended for release as well as the DHCP Client's MAC address. When the DHCP Server receives a DHCPRELEASE message, it marks the IP address as being available to lease.

Note

For DHCP to function properly, a DHCP Server does not depend on a DHCP Client to send a DHCPRELEASE message when the client is shutting down without problems. In fact, the DHCP Client does not send a DHCPRELEASE message on shutdown. Not sending the message reduces the load on the DHCP Server and increases the likelihood that, when a DHCP Client system reboots, it can obtain a lease on the same IP address. As a result, DHCP Clients typically obtain a lease on an IP address and retain the same IP address as long as they remain on the same subnet.

If you need a DHCP Client to immediately release its IP address on shutdown, the user shutting down the system should first enter **ipconfig /release** from a command prompt. Otherwise, the DHCP Server maintains the IP address as leased and unavailable for 24 hours after the IP address lease time expires.

Implementing DHCP Servers

Before you actually deploy DHCP Servers, you should take time to plan the installation carefully. This section offers strategies for placing DHCP Servers on small- and large-scale installations. Because WINS is an obvious complement to DHCP, the planning tasks described here also apply for WINS Servers.

The following steps describe the general planning tasks:

1. Compile a list of requirements, including

   ■ The number and kinds of systems you need to support

   ■ Interoperability with existing systems, especially requirements for mission-critical accounting, personnel, and similar information systems

   ■ Hardware support and related software compatibility (including routers, switches, and servers)

   ■ Network monitoring software, including SNMP requirements and other tools

2. Isolate the areas of the network where processes must continue uninterrupted and target these areas for the last stages of implementation.

3. Review the geographic and physical structure of the network to determine the best plan for defining logical subnets as segments of the internetwork.

4. Define the components in the new system that require testing and develop a phase plan for testing and adding these components.

   For example, the plan could define units of the organization to phase into using DHCP and the order for types of computers to phase in (including Windows NT Servers and workstations, Microsoft RAS Servers and Clients, Windows for Workgroups computers, and MS-DOS Clients).

5. Create a pilot project for testing. Make sure the pilot project addresses all of the requirements identified in Step 1.

6. Create a second test phase, which includes tuning the DHCP (and WINS) Server-Client configuration for efficiency. This task can include determining strategies for backup servers and for partitioning the address pool at each server.

7. Document all architecture and administration issues for network administrators.

8. Implement a final phase for getting all organizational units to use DHCP.

The placement of the servers in the physical network is not a major planning issue because you can administrate these servers remotely from any Windows NT Server computer that is DHCP-enabled. DHCP Servers (and

WINS Servers) do not participate in the Windows NT Server domain model, so domain membership is not an issue in planning for server placement. Because most routers can forward DHCP configuration requests, DHCP Servers are not required on every subnet in the internetwork.

Implementing DHCP Servers in a small LAN

If you have a small LAN that does not use routers and subnetting, you can probably use a single DHCP Server to serve the network. In this case, you need to consider the following issues as part of the planning process:

- The hardware and storage requirements for the DHCP Server

- Which computers can immediately become DHCP Clients for dynamic addressing and which computers should keep their static addresses

- The DHCP option types and their values for the DHCP Clients

Implementing DHCP Servers in a large LAN

Large networks usually use IP routers and relay agents, so DHCP Servers on one node of the internetwork can respond to TCP/IP configuration requests from remote nodes. The relay agent forwards requests from local DHCP Clients to the DHCP Server and subsequently relays responses back to the Clients. Besides the issues mentioned regarding a small LAN, additional planning issues for a large enterprise network include

- Compatibility of hardware and software routers with DHCP. Routers must support RFCs 1532, 1533, and 1541. These RFCs deal with the forwarding of packets required by the DHCP service. If the routers do not support these RFCs, they may discard the network packets required for DHCP operation. In this case, you may need a firmware upgrade. Consult your documentation to determine if the routers support these specifications. If the routers do support these RFCs but you have connectivity problems, check the documentation to see if the default configuration passes or drops these packet types.

- Physical subnetting of the network and relative placement of DHCP Servers. This includes planning for placement of DHCP (and WINS) Servers among subnets in a way that reduces b-node broadcasts across routers.

  B-node resolves names using broadcast messages. This option is the worst possible option to use because it can flood the network segment with broadcast messages, lowering the network's ability to carry data over the network and effectively lowering network bandwidth on the segment. Also, broadcasts are not forwarded by routers, so if the requested resource is on the other side of a router, it will not be found. The only reason I would recommend using b-node is for a very small network with a single subnet that does not have a dedicated network administrator to maintain the network (using broadcasts can essentially eliminate the need to maintain an LMHOST file or WINS database. For a small network, very little network bandwidth is eaten by the broadcasts).

Note

Another good reason to use b-node is that computers located on the same segment can still find each other even if the WINS Server or DNS Server is down or unavailable.

- The DHCP option types and their values defined per scope for the DHCP Clients. This may include planning for scopes based on the needs of particular groups of users. For example, for a group that uses portable computers docked at different stations or for a unit that frequently moves computers to different locations, you can define shorter lease durations for the related scopes. This way, frequently changed IP addresses are available for reuse.

As one example, the segmenting of the WAN into logical subnets could match the physical structure of the internetwork. One IP subnet can serve as the backbone. Each physical subnet would maintain a separate IP subnet address off this backbone.

In this example, a single computer running Windows NT Server could serve as both the DHCP and WINS Server for each subnet. Each server would administer a defined number of IP addresses with a specific subnet mask and would also serve as the default gateway. Because the server is also acting as the WINS Server, it can respond to name resolution requests from all systems on its subnet.

These DHCP and WINS Servers can act as backup servers for each other. The administrator can partition the address pool for each server to provide addresses to remote clients.

There is no limit to the maximum number of clients that a single DHCP Server can service. However, a network may have practical constraints based on the IP address class and server configuration issues such as disk capacity and CPU speed.

- Multiple DHCP Servers. If you are planning to implement multiple DHCP Servers (which is a good way to distribute the load on a large network) each DHCP Server must have a statically assigned IP address. You must exclude these IP addresses from the DHCP scope that you create.

Note

You do not necessarily need a DHCP Server on each subnet. An appropriate router can forward DHCP requests across subnets — if the router does not support the RFCs mentioned previously, you should not use DHCP.

- Static IP addresses. You must exclude any static IP addresses, such as those used by other DHCP Servers, non-DHCP computers, routers, and non-Microsoft Remote Access Software (RAS) clients that are using PPP (Point-to-Point Protocol) to connect to the network from the DHCP scope. If you forget to exclude these IP addresses, a name/address conflict is sure to occur, which could prevent clients from communicating or cause the network to crash (in the case of a router).

■ DHCP Server database replication. This feature doesn't exist in the current implementation, so if you install multiple DHCP Servers in order to support a single segment, you also have to split the DHCP scope into distinct IP ranges.

■ DHCP Server database backup. Because the DHCP database contains all of the DHCP scopes for the server and the configuration parameters, it is a good idea to implement a backup policy. Normally the DHCP database is backed up automatically, and this backup is used if the original is corrupted; however, you should not rely on this as your only backup. Instead, back up the database regularly and copy the files from the SYSTEMROOT\SYSTEM32\DHCP\BACKUP\JET directory as described later in this chapter.

Installing DHCP Servers

You install a DHCP Server as part of the process of installing TCP/IP. These instructions assume that you have already installed the Windows NT Server operating system on the computer.

Caution

Before installing a new DHCP Server, check for other DHCP Servers on the network to avoid interfering with them.

You must log on as a member of the Administrators group for the computer that you are installing or administering as a DHCP Server.

To install a DHCP Server

1. Start the Network option in the Control Panel. When the Network dialog box appears, click the Services tab to display the Network Services dialog box as shown in Figure 18-3.

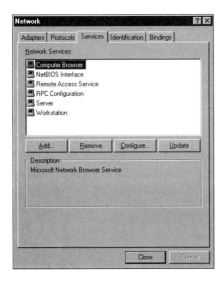

Figure 18-3: The Network Services dialog box.

2. In the Network Services list, select Microsoft DHCP Server, and then click OK.

3. Windows NT Setup displays a message asking for the full path to the Windows NT Server distribution files. Provide the appropriate location and choose the Continue button. All necessary files are copied to your hard disk.

4. Complete all of the required procedures for manually configuring TCP/IP as described in Chapter 17, *Installing and Configuring TCP/IP*. All of the appropriate TCP/IP and DHCP software is ready for use after you reboot the computer.

Cross Reference

If the DHCP Server is multihomed (has multiple network adapters), you must use the Advanced Microsoft TCP/IP Configuration dialog box to specify IP addresses and other information for each network adapter. Refer to Chapter 17, *Installing and Configuring TCP/IP*.

If any adapter on the DHCP Server is connected to a subnet that you do not want this server to support, you must disable the bindings to that subnet for the particular adapter.

To disable bindings

1. Choose the Network option in the Control Panel. Then choose the Bindings button in the Network dialog box. The Network Bindings dialog box appears as shown in Figure 18-4.

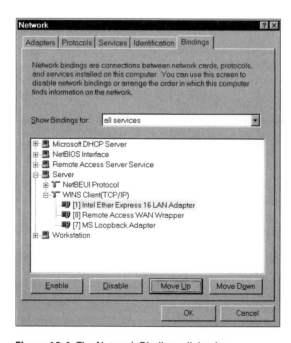

Figure 18-4: The Network Bindings dialog box.

2. Disable the related binding by highlighting it in the Bindings list box.

You cannot use DHCP to automatically configure a new DHCP Server, because a computer cannot act as a DHCP Client and server simultaneously.

Once it's installed, the DHCP Server service starts automatically during system startup. You should pause the service while configuring scopes for the first time.

To pause the DHCP Server service at any Windows NT computer

1. In the Control Panel, choose the Services icon. Or in Server Manager, choose Services from the Computer menu.

2. In the Services dialog box, select the Microsoft DHCP Server service.

3. Choose the Pause button, and then choose the Close button.

You can also start, stop, and pause the DHCP service at the command prompt using the commands net start dhcpserver or net stop dhcpserver or net pause dhcpserver.

Guidelines for Creating DHCP Scopes

A DHCP scope is an administrative grouping of computers running the DHCP Client service. You create a scope for each subnet on the network in order to define parameters for that subnet.

Each scope has the following properties:

- A unique subnet mask used to determine the subnet related to a given IP address

- A scope name assigned by the administrator when the scope is created

- Lease duration values to be assigned to DHCP Clients with dynamic addresses

Unless your network is small, you should have two or more available DHCP Servers on the network that can provide a DHCP Client with a valid IP address and configuration information. If there is only one DHCP Server and it fails, the client can no longer use TCP/IP on the network when the DHCP Client's lease on the IP address expires. In addition, if there are no DHCP Servers available, DHCP Clients cannot initialize TCP/IP and use it to communicate on the network.

Do not overlap scopes

DHCP Servers cannot coordinate the assignment of IP addresses from overlapping IP address pools because the servers do not communicate directly with one another.

Because there is no communication between DHCP Server A and DHCP Server B, if DHCP Server A leases an IP address that overlaps Server B's address pool, there is no way for DHCP Server B to know if this IP address has been leased. As a result, DHCP Server B could provide a different DHCP Client with a lease on the same IP address provided for lease by Server A, thus leading to network communication problems. Therefore, it is imperative that DHCP Servers each have their own unique pool of IP addresses; they cannot share IP addresses with any other IP address pools on any other DHCP Servers.

Allow one DHCP Server per subnet

The best method for implementing DHCP on a network with multiple subnets is to place a DHCP Server on each subnet and connect the subnets via routers that can act as RFC 1542 (BOOTP) relay agents. A router that functions as an RFC 1542 (BOOTP) relay agent does not simply forward the DHCP broadcasts onto the other subnets, but instead modifies the DHCP message to indicate from which subnet the broadcast came. This enables the DHCP Server to determine from which of its DHCP scopes to lease an IP address, provided it has a valid scope for the subnet.

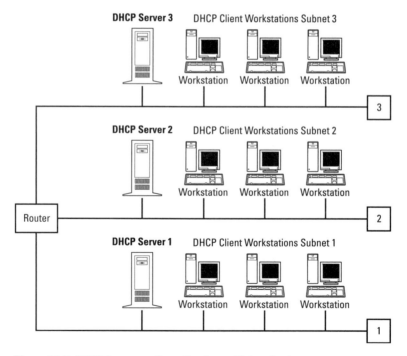

Figure 18-5: DHCP Server configuration for multiple subnets.

Configure each DHCP Server with a large portion of the IP address pool (approximately 75 percent) for its local subnet and the remaining portion (approximately 25 percent) of the IP address pool for another subnet as shown in Figure 18-5.

For example, DHCP Server 1 is on Subnet 1 and has a DHCP scope for its subnet and a DHCP scope for Subnet 2. Therefore, if the DHCP Server on Subnet 2 (DHCP Server 2) is unavailable, there is still a DHCP Server available that can lease some valid IP addresses for Subnet 2. DHCP Server 2 is configured similarly to DHCP Server 1, with a large portion of the IP addresses for its subnet and a small portion of the IP addresses for Subnet 1. DHCP Server 3 is the only server that has a DHCP scope with valid IP addresses for Subnet 3. As a result, if DHCP Server 3 is unavailable, DHCP Clients on Subnet 3 cannot obtain an IP address lease. DHCP Server 1 or DHCP Server 2 could have an additional DHCP scope that would permit them to provide IP address leases for Subnet 3.

If you have a limited number of DHCP Clients on each subnet, you would not typically want to place a DHCP Server on each subnet. In this case, you could use the DHCP Server configuration shown in Figure 18-6.

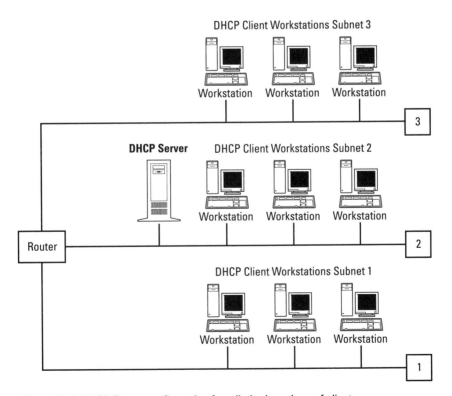

Figure 18-6: DHCP Server configuration for a limited numbers of clients.

Figure 18-6 shows only one DHCP Server that has a DHCP scope for each subnet. Therefore, when the DHCP Server receives a request for an IP address lease from a DHCP Client on any of the three subnets, the DHCP Server can provide an IP address to lease.

Caution

Even though you can use a single DHCP Server in a network, it is not ideal. If that single DHCP Server goes down, the DHCP Clients cannot obtain an IP address lease. As a result, the DHCP Clients cannot use TCP/IP to communicate on the network.

For a DHCP Server to lease an IP address to a DHCP Client that is on the other side of a router, the router must function as an RFC 1542 (BOOTP) relay agent. If the router can not act as an RFC 1542 (BOOTP) relay agent, the preceding implementations will not work.

Tip

Instead of using a router as shown in Figures 18-5 and 18-6, you could configure a multihomed Windows NT Server machine as a DHCP Server, with three network cards and IP routing enabled. The three network cards would use the IP addresses shown for the three connections to the router, and the DHCP Server would have the same three DHCP scopes.

Using DHCP Manager

The DHCP Manager icon is added to the Network Administration Tools group under Programs in the Start menu when you set up a Windows NT Server computer to act as a DHCP Server. You must use DHCP Manager to perform these tasks:

■ Create one or more DHCP scopes to begin providing DHCP services

■ Define properties for the scope, including the lease duration and IP address ranges for distribution to potential DHCP Clients in the scope

■ Define default values for options (such as the default gateway, DNS Server, or WINS Server) to be assigned together with an IP address

■ Add any custom options

To start DHCP Manager

Double-click the DHCP Manager icon in the Network Administration group. Or, at the command prompt, type **start dhcpadmn** and press Enter. The DHCP Manager window appears as shown in Figure 18-7.

The first time that you start DHCP Manager, the DHCP Manager window shows the local computer. Subsequently, the window shows a list of the DHCP Servers to which DHCP Manager has connected, plus their scopes. The status bar reports the current DHCP Manager activities.

Note

When you are working with DHCP Manager, all computer names are DNS host names only, such as *publishing.cpress.com*. The NetBIOS computer names used in Windows networking are not allowed.

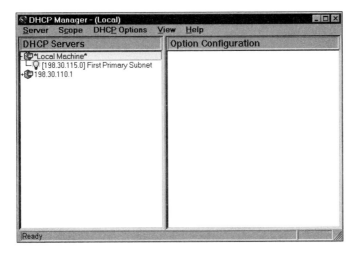

Figure 18-7: The DHCP Manager window.

To connect to a DHCP Server

1. From the Server menu, choose the Add command.

2. In the Add DHCP Server To Server List dialog box, type the IP address for the DHCP Server to which you want to connect, and then choose the OK button.

To disconnect from a selected DHCP Server

From the Server menu, choose Remove, or press Del.

Creating scopes

You must use DHCP Manager to create, manage, or remove scopes.

To create a new DHCP scope

1. In the DHCP Servers list in the DHCP Manager window, select the server for which you want to create a scope.

2. From the Scope menu, choose Create. The Create Scope dialog box appears as shown in Figure 18-8.

3. To define the available range of IP addresses for this scope, type the beginning and ending IP addresses for the range in the Start Address and End Address boxes.

   The IP address range includes the Start and End values.

Note

You must supply this information in order for the system to activate this scope.

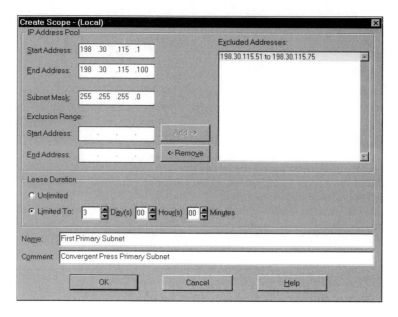

Figure 18-8: The Create Scope dialog box.

4. In the Subnet Mask box, DHCP Manager proposes a subnet mask, based on the IP address of the Start and End addresses. Accept the proposed value, unless you know that a different value is required.

5. To define excluded addresses within the IP address pool range, use the Exclusion Range controls, as follows:

   ■ Type the first IP address that is part of the excluded range in the Start Address box and type the last number in the End Address box. Then choose the Add button. Continue to define any other excluded ranges in the same way.

   ■ To exclude a single IP address, type the number in the Start Address box. Leave the End Address box empty and choose the Add button.

   ■ To remove an IP address or range from the excluded range, select it in the Excluded Addresses box, and then choose the Remove button.

   The excluded ranges should include all IP addresses that you assigned manually to other DHCP Servers, non-DHCP Clients, diskless workstations, or RAS and PPP clients.

6. To specify the lease duration for IP addresses in this scope, select Limited To. Then type values defining the number of days, hours, and seconds for the length of the address lease.

   If you do not want IP address leases in this scope to expire, select the Unlimited option.

7. In the Name box, type a scope name.

   Use any name that describes this subnet. The name can include any combination of letters, numbers, and hyphens. Blank spaces and under-score characters are also allowed. You cannot use Unicode characters.

8. Optionally, in the Comment box, type any string to describe this scope, and then choose the OK button.

Note

When you finish creating a scope, a message reminds you that the scope has not been activated and allows you to choose Yes to activate the scope immediately. However, you should not activate a new scope until you have defined the DHCP options for this scope.

Now you can continue with the procedures described in *Configuring DHCP Options* and *Administrating DHCP Clients* later in this chapter. After you have configured the options for this scope, you must activate it so that DHCP Client computers on the related subnet can begin using DHCP for dynamic TCP/IP configuration.

To activate a DHCP scope

From the Scope menu, choose the Activate command.

The menu command name changes to Deactivate when the selected scope is currently active.

Changing scope properties

The subnet identifiers and address pool make up the properties of scopes. You can change the properties of an existing scope.

To change the properties of a DHCP scope

1. In the DHCP Servers list in the DHCP Manager window, select the scope for which you want to change properties, and from the Scope menu, choose Properties. Or, in the DHCP Servers list, double-click the scope you want to change.

2. In the Scope Properties dialog box, change any values for the IP address pool, lease duration, or name and comment as described before in *Creating scopes*.

3. Choose the OK button to have the changes take effect.

Removing a scope

When you are no longer using a subnet or whenever you want to remove an existing scope, you can use DHCP Manager to remove it. If any IP address in the scope is still leased or in use, you must first deactivate the scope until all client leases expire or all client lease extension requests are denied.

To remove a scope

1. In the DHCP Servers list in the DHCP Manager window, select the scope you want to remove.

2. From the Scope menu, choose Deactivate. (This command name changes to Activate when the scope is not active.) The scope must remain deactivated until you are sure that the scope is not in use.

3. From the Scope menu, choose Delete. (The Delete command is not available for an active scope.)

Configuring DHCP Options

You use DHCP Manager to define the configuration parameters that a DHCP Server assigns to a client as DHCP options. Most options that you want to specify are predefined, based on standard parameters defined in RFC 1542.

When you configure a DHCP scope, you can assign DHCP options to govern all configuration parameters. You can also assign, create, edit, or delete DHCP options. These tasks are described in the following sections.

Assigning DHCP configuration options

Besides the IP addressing information, you must configure other DHCP configuration options pertaining to DHCP Clients for each scope. You can define options globally for all scopes on the current server, specifically for a selected scope, or for individual DHCP Clients with reserved addresses. Active global options always apply unless overridden by scope options or DHCP Client settings. Active options for a scope apply to all computers in that scope, unless overridden for an individual DHCP Client.

To assign DHCP configuration options

1. In the DHCP Servers list in the DHCP Manager window, select the scope you want to configure.

2. From the DHCP Options menu, choose the Global or Scope command, depending on whether you want to define option settings for all scopes on the currently selected server or the scope currently selected in the DHCP Manager window. The DHCP Options: Scope dialog box appears as shown in Figure 18-9.

3. In the Unused Options list in the DHCP Options: Scope dialog box, select the name of the DHCP option that you want to apply, and then choose the Add button to move the name to the Active Options list.

   This list shows predefined options and any custom options that you added. For example, if you want to specify DNS servers for computers, select the option named DNS Servers in the Unused Options list and choose the Add button.

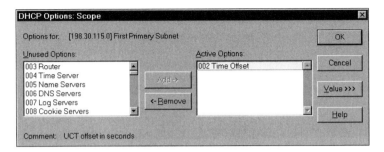

Figure 18-9: The DHCP Options: Scope dialog box.

If you want to remove an active DHCP option, select its name in the Active Options box, and then choose the Remove button.

4. To define the value for an active option, select its name in the Active Options box and choose the Values button. Then choose the Edit button and edit the information in the Current Value box, depending on the data type for the option, as follows:

- For an IP address, type the assigned address for the selected option.

- For a number, type an appropriate decimal or hexadecimal value for the option.

- For a string, type an appropriate ASCII string containing letters and numbers for the option.

  For example, to specify the DNS name servers for use by DHCP Clients, select DNS Servers in the Active Options list. Then choose the Edit button and type a list of IP addresses for DNS servers. The list should appear in the order of preference.

5. When you have completed all of the changes, choose the OK button.

Tip If you are using DHCP to configure WINS Clients, set options #44 WINS Servers and #46 Node Type. These options allow DHCP-configured computers to find and use the WINS Server automatically.

Creating new DHCP options

You can add custom parameters to DHCP Client configuration information. You can also change values or other elements of the predefined DHCP options. The added options appear in the list of available DHCP options in the DHCP Options dialog boxes for defining options globally, per scope, and per individual reserved DHCP Client.

To add new DHCP options

1. From the DHCP Options menu, choose Defaults.

2. In the Option Class list in the DHCP Options: Default Values dialog box, select the class for which you want to add new DHCP options, and then choose the New button. The Add Option Type dialog box appears as shown in Figure 18-10.

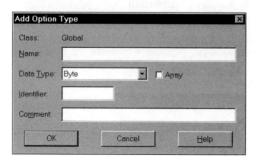

Figure 18-10: The Add Option Type dialog box.

The option class can include the DHCP standard options or any custom option you add.

3. In the Name box of the Add Option Type dialog box, type a new option name.

4. From the Data Type list, select the data type for this option as described in Table 18-2. If this data type represents an array, check the Array box.

Table 18-2	Data Type List
Data type	*Meaning*
Binary	Value expressed as an array of bytes
Byte	An 8-bit, unsigned integer
Encapsulated	An array of unsigned bytes
IP address	An IP address of the form w.x.y.z
Long	A 32-bit, signed integer
Long integer	A 32-bit, unsigned integer
String	An ASCII text string
Word	A 16-bit, unsigned integer

If you select the wrong data type, an error message appears, or the value is truncated or converted to the required type.

5. In the Identifier box, type a unique code number associated with this DHCP option. This number must be between 0 and 255.

6. In the Comment box, type a description of the DHCP option, and then choose the OK button.

7. In the DHCP Options: Default Values dialog box, select the option, choose the Edit button, and type the value to become the default for this DHCP option.

8. Choose the OK button.

You can delete custom DHCP options, but you cannot delete any predefined DHCP options.

To delete a custom DHCP option

1. From the DHCP Options menu, choose Defaults.

2. In the DHCP Options: Default Values dialog box, select the related class in the Option Class list.

3. In the Option Name list, select the option you want to delete, and then choose the Delete button.

Changing DHCP option values

You can change the values for the predefined and custom DHCP options for configuring clients. For example, you could change the default values for these built-in options:

- 3 = Router, to specify the IP addresses for the routers on the subnet. Also the equivalent of the Default Gateway entry in the TCP/IP Configuration dialog box

- 6 = DNS Servers, to specify the IP addresses of the DNS name servers used at your site

- 15 = Domain Name, to specify the DNS domain names used for host name resolution

To change a DHCP option value

1. From the DHCP Options menu, choose Defaults. The DHCP Options: Default Values dialog box appears as shown in Figure 18-11.

2. In the Option Class list in the DHCP Options: Default Values dialog box, select the option class for which you want to change values.

3. If you want to change the default value for an option, select the option you want to change in the Option Name list, choose the Change button, and then type a new value in the Value box.

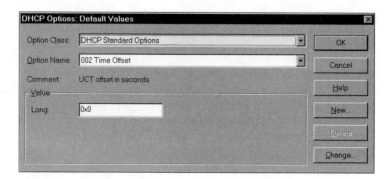

Figure 18-11: The DHCP Options: Default Values dialog box.

Choosing the Change button displays a special dialog box for editing strings, arrays of IP addresses, or binary values.

4. If you want to change basic elements of a custom option, select it in the Option Name list, and then choose the Change button.

   You can change the name, data type, identifier, and comment for a DHCP option by following the procedures described earlier in *Creating new DHCP options.*

5. When you complete all of the changes you want to make, choose the OK button.

Defining options for reservations

You can assign DHCP options and specify custom values for DHCP Clients that use reserved IP addresses.

To change DHCP options for reservations

1. From the Scope menu, choose Active Leases.

2. In the IP Address list of the Active Leases dialog box, select the reserved address whose options you want to change, and then choose the Properties button to display the Client Properties dialog box. (The Properties button is only available for reserved addresses; it is not available for DHCP Clients with dynamic addresses.) Then click the Options button in the Client Properties dialog box. The DHCP Options: Reservation dialog box appears as shown in Figure 18-12.

3. In the DHCP Options: Reservation dialog box, select an option name in the Unused Options list, and then choose the Add button to move the name to the Active Options list.

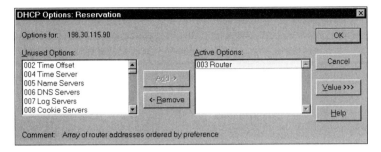

Figure 18-12: The DHCP Options: Reservation dialog box.

If you want to remove a DHCP option that has been assigned to the scope, select its name in the Active Options list, and then choose the Remove button.

4. To change a value for an option selected in the Active Options list, choose the Value button. Then choose the Edit button and enter a new value in the Current Value box.

Predefined DHCP Client configuration options

The tables in this section list the predefined options available for configuration of DHCP Clients. These options are defined in RFC 1533. Table 18-3 describes basic options.

Table 18-3		Basic Options
Code	*Option name*	*Meaning*
0	Pad	Causes subsequent fields to align on word boundaries.
255	End	Indicates end of options in the DHCP packet.
2	Time offset	Specifies the Universal Coordinated Time (UCT) offset in seconds.
3	Router	Specifies a list of IP addresses for routers on the client's subnet.
4	Time server	Specifies a list of IP addresses for time servers available to the client.
5	Name servers	Specifies a list of IP addresses for name servers available to the client.
6	DNS servers	Specifies a list of IP addresses for DNS name servers available to the client.

(continued)

Table 18-3 *(Continued)*

Code	Option name	Meaning
7	Log servers	Specifies a list of IP addresses for MIT_LCS User Datagram Protocol (UDP) log servers available to the client.
8	Cookie servers	Specifies a list of IP addresses for RFC 865 cookie servers available to the client.
9	LPR servers	Specifies a list of IP addresses for RFC 1179 line-printer servers available to the client.
10	Impress servers	Specifies a list of IP addresses for Imagen Impress servers available to the client.
11	Resource location servers	Specifies a list of RFC 887 Resource Location servers available to the client.
12	Host name	Specifies the host name (of up to 63 characters) for the client. The name must start with a letter, end with a letter or digit, and have only letters, numbers, and hyphens as interior characters. The name can be qualified with the local DNS domain name.
13	Boot file size	Specifies the size of the default boot image file for the client, in 512-octet blocks.
14	Merit dump file	Specifies the ASCII pathname of the file where the client's core image is dumped if a crash occurs.
15	Domain name	Specifies the DNS domain name that the client should use for DNS host name resolution.
16	Swap server	Specifies the IP address of the client's swap server.
17	Root path	Specifies the ASCII pathname for the client's root disk.
18	Extensions path	Specifies a file that is retrievable via TFTP and contains information interpreted the same as the vendor-extension field in the BOOTP response, except the file length is unconstrained and references to Tag 18 in the file are ignored.

Table 18-4 shows IP layer parameters on a per-host basis.

Table 18-4	IP Layer Parameters per Host	
Code	*Option name*	*Meaning*
19	IP layer forwarding	Enables or disables forwarding of IP packet for this client. 1 enables forwarding; 0 disables it.
20	Non-local source routing	Enables or disables forwarding of datagrams with non-local source routes. 1 enables forwarding; 0 disables it.
21	Policy filter masks	Specifies policy filters that consist of a list of pairs of IP addresses and masks specifying destination/mask pairs for filtering non-local source routes. Any source routed datagram whose next-hop address does not match a filter is discarded by the client.
22	Max DG reassembly size	Specifies the maximum size datagram the client can reassemble. The minimum value is 576.
23	Default time-to-live	Specifies the default time-to-live (TTL) the client uses on outgoing datagrams. The value for the octet is a number between 1 and 255.
24	Path MTU aging timeout	Specifies the timeout in seconds for aging Path Maximum Transmission Unit (MTU) values (discovered by the mechanism defined in RFC 1191).
25	Path MTU plateau table	Specifies a table of MTU sizes to use when performing Path MTU Discovered as defined in RFC 1191. The table is sorted by size from smallest to largest. The minimum MTU value is 68.

Table 18-5 lists IP parameters that affect the operation of the IP layer on a per-interface basis. A client can issue multiple requests, one per interface, to configure interfaces with their specific parameters.

Table 18-5	IP Parameters per Interface	
Code	*Option name*	*Meaning*
26	MTU option	Specifies the MTU discovery size for this interface. The minimum MTU value is 68.
27	All subnets are local	Specifies whether the client assumes that all subnets of the client's internetwork use the same MTU as the local subnet where the client is connected. 1 indicates that all subnets share the same MTU; 0 indicates that the client should assume some subnets may have smaller MTUs.

(continued)

Table 18-5 *(Continued)*

Code	Option name	Meaning
28	Broadcast address	Specifies the broadcast address used on the client's subnet.
29	Perform mask discovery	Specifies whether the client should use Internet Control Message Protocol (ICMP) for subnet mask discovery. 1 indicates the client should perform mask discovery; 0 indicates the client should not.
30	Mask supplier	Specifies whether the client should respond to subnet mask requests using ICMP. 1 indicates the client should respond; 0 indicates the client should not respond.
31	Perform router discovery	Specifies whether the client should solicit routers using the router discovery method in RFC 1256. 1 indicates the client should perform router discovery; 0 indicates the client should not use it.
32	Router solicitation address	Specifies the IP address to which the client submits router solicitation requests.
33	Static route	Specifies a list of IP address pairs that indicate the static routes the client should install in its routing cache. Any multiple routes to the same destination are listed in descending order of priority. The routes are destination/router address pairs. (The default route of 0.0.0.0 is an illegal destination for a static route.)

Table 18-6 lists link layer parameters per interface. These options affect the operation of the data link layer on a per-interface basis.

Table 18-6   **Link Layer Parameters per Interface**

Code	Option name	Meaning
34	Trailer encapsulation	Specifies whether the client should negotiate use of trailers (RFC 983) when using the ARP protocol. 1 indicates the client should attempt to use trailers; 0 indicates the client should not use trailers.
35	ARP cache timeout	Specifies the timeout in seconds for ARP cache entries.

Code	Option name	Meaning
36	Ethernet encapsulation	Specifies whether the client should use IEEE 802.3 (RFC 1042) or Ethernet v. 2 (RFC 894) encapsulation if the interface is Ethernet. 1 indicates the client should use RFC 1042 encapsulation; 0 indicates the client should use RFC 894 encapsulation.

Table 18-7 shows TCP parameters. These options affect the operation of the TCP layer on a per-interface basis.

Table 18-7		TCP Parameters
Code	Option name	Meaning
37	Default time-to-live	Specifies the default TTL that the client should use when sending TCP segments. The minimum value of the octet is 1.
38	Keepalive interval	Specifies the interval in seconds that the client TCP should wait before sending a keepalive message on a TCP connection. A value of 0 indicates the client should not send keepalive messages on connections unless specifically requested by an application.
39	Keepalive garbage	Specifies whether the client should send TCP keepalive messages with an octet of garbage data for compatibility with older implementations. 1 indicates a garbage octet should be sent; 0 indicates it should not be sent.

Table 18-8 shows application layer parameters. These miscellaneous options are used to configure applications and services.

Table 18-8		Application Layer Parameters
Code	Option name	Meaning
40	NIS domain name	Specifies the name of the Network Information Service (NIS) domain as an ASCII string.
41	NIS servers	Specifies a list of IP addresses for NIS servers available to the client.
42	NTP servers	Specifies a list of IP addresses for Network Time Protocol (NTP) servers available to the client.

Table 18-9 shows options for vendor-specific information.

Table 18-9	Vendor-specific Information	
Code	**Option name**	**Meaning**
43	Vendor specific information	Supplies binary information, which clients and servers use to exchange vendor-specific information. Servers not equipped to interpret the information ignore it. Clients that don't receive the information attempt to operate without it.
44	WINS/NBNS servers	Specifies a list of IP addresses for NetBIOS name servers (NBNS).
45	NetBIOS over TCP/IP NBDD	Specifies a list of IP addresses for NetBIOS datagram distribution servers (NBDD).
46	WINS/NBT node type	Allows configurable NetBIOS over TCP/IP clients to be configured as described in RFC 1001/1002, where 1=b-node, 2=p-node, 4=m-node, and 8=h-node.
47	NetBIOS scope ID	Specifies a string that is the NetBIOS over TCP/IP scope ID for the client, as specified in RFC 1001/1002.
48	X Window system font	Specifies a list of IP addresses for X Window font servers available to the client.
49	X Window system display	Specifies a list of IP addresses for X Window System Display Manager servers available to the client.
58	Renewal (T1) time value	Specifies the time in seconds from address assignment until the client enters the renewing state.
59	Rebinding (T2) time value	Specifies the time in seconds from address assignment until the client enters the rebinding state.

Administrating DHCP Clients

The easiest method for installing and configuring a system to use TCP/IP is to enable automatic DHCP configuration on the system. With this enabled, the DHCP Client contacts a DHCP Server during system boot for its configuration information — IP address, subnet mask, and default gateway.

A Windows NT Server set up as a DHCP Server can service the following DHCP Clients:

- Windows NT Workstation
- Windows NT Server
- Windows for Workgroups 3.11 (WFWG), with the Microsoft 32-bit TCP/IP VxD installed

- Microsoft Network Client for MS-DOS with real mode TCP/IP driver (included on the Windows NT Server CD)

- LAN Manager 2.2c for MS-DOS (included on the Windows NT Server CD)

Tip

You can use the ipconfig utility to troubleshoot the IP configuration on computers that use DHCP, as described in Chapter 17, *Installing and Configuring TCP/IP*. You can also use ipconfig to troubleshoot on TCP/IP-32 clients on Windows for Workgroups 3.11 computers and on computers running Microsoft Network Client version 2.0 for MS-DOS.

Managing client leases

The lease for the IP address assigned by a DHCP Server has an expiration date, which the client must renew if it is going to continue to use that address. You can view the lease duration and other information for specific DHCP Clients, and you can add options and change settings for reserved DHCP Clients.

To view client lease information

1. In the DHCP Servers list in the DHCP Manager window, select the scope for which you want to view or change client information.

2. From the Scope menu, choose Active Leases. The Active Leases dialog box appears as shown in Figure 18-13.

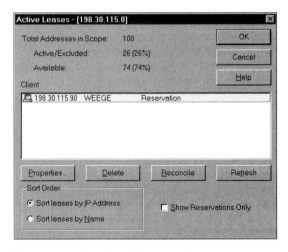

Figure 18-13: The Active Leases dialog box.

3. In the Active Leases dialog box, select the computer whose lease you want to view in the Client list, and then choose the Properties button.

If you want to view only clients that use reserved IP addresses, check the Show Reservations Only box.

4. If you want to view the unique identifier and other client information, including the lease expiration date, select the Properties button to bring up the Client Properties dialog box as shown in Figure 18-14.

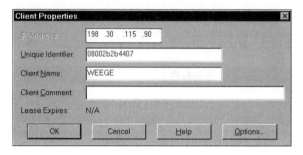

Figure 18-14: The Client Properties dialog box.

Note

You can edit the name, unique identifier, and comment, or choose the Options button in the Client Properties dialog box only for clients with reserved IP addresses.

You can cancel the DHCP configuration information for a DHCP Client that is no longer using an IP address or for all clients in the scope. This has the same effect as if the client's lease expired — the next time that client com-computer starts, it must enter the rebinding state and obtain new TCP/IP configuration information from a DHCP Server.

Note

Delete only entries for clients that are no longer using the assigned DHCP configuration. Deleting an active client could result in duplicate IP addresses on the network, because a DHCP Server might assign deleted addresses to new active clients.

You can use ipconfig /release at the command prompt to get a DHCP Client computer to delete an active client entry and safely free its IP address for reuse.

To cancel a client's DHCP configuration

1. Make sure that the client is not using the assigned IP address.

2. In the IP Client list of the Active Leases dialog box, select the client you want to cancel, and then choose the Delete button.

Managing client reservations

You can reserve a specific IP address for a client. Typically, you need to reserve addresses in the following cases:

■ For domain controllers if the network also uses LMHOSTS files that define IP addresses for domain controllers

■ For clients that use IP addresses that were assigned using another method for TCP/IP configuration

■ For assignment by RAS servers to non-DHCP Clients

■ For DNS servers

If multiple DHCP Servers are distributing addresses in the same scope, the client reservations on each DHCP Server should be identical. Otherwise, the DHCP reserved client receives different IP addresses, depending on the responding server.

Note

The IP address and static name specified in WINS take precedence over the IP address assigned by the DHCP Server. For such clients, create client reservations with the IP address that is defined in the WINS database.

To add a reservation for a client

1. From the Scope menu, choose Add Reservations. The Add Reserved Clients dialog box appears as shown in Figure 18-15.

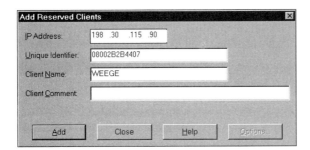

Figure 18-15: The Add Reserved Clients dialog box.

2. In the Add Reserved Clients dialog box, type information to identify the first reserved client:

IP Address specifies an address from the reserved address pool. You can specify any reserved, unused IP address. DHCP Manager warns you if a duplicate or nonreserved address is entered.

Unique Identifier usually specifies the media access control (MAC) address for the client computer's network adapter card. You can determine this address by typing **net config wksta** at the command prompt on the client computer.

Client Name specifies the computer name for this client. This is used for identification purposes only and does not affect the actual computer name for the client. This is not available for MS-DOS-based clients; in this case, only the Unique Identifier appears.

Client Comment is any optional text you enter to describe this client.

3. Choose the Add button to add the reservation to the DHCP database. You can continue to add reservations without dismissing this dialog box.

4. When you have added all reservations, choose the Close button.

After reserving the IP address in DHCP Manager, you should restart the client computer to configure it with the new IP address.

If you want to change a reserved IP address for a client, you have to remove the old reserved address and add a new reservation. You can change any other information about a reserved client while keeping the reserved IP address.

To change the reserved IP address

1. Make sure that the reserved client is not using the old IP address. To do this, shut down the client computer immediately after issuing the ip config/release command on that client computer.

2. In the Active Leases dialog box, select the reserved IP address in the Client list and choose the Delete button. Then choose the OK button.

3. From the Scope menu, choose Add Reservations, and then enter information for a new reservation as described earlier in this section.

To change basic information for a reserved client

1. From the Scope menu, choose Active Leases.

2. In the Client list of the Active Leases dialog box, select the address of the reserved client that you want to change, and then choose the Properties button.

3. In the Client Properties dialog box, change the unique identifier, client name, or comment. Then choose the OK button.

You can change values in the Client Properties dialog box for reserved clients only.

You can also view and change the option types that define configuration parameters for selected reserved clients by choosing the Options button in the Client Properties dialog box. To change options for a reserved client, follow the same procedure as used to originally define options, as described in *Defining options for reservations* earlier in this chapter.

Guidelines for Setting Local Policies

This section provides suggestions for setting lease options, dividing the free address pool among DHCP Servers, and avoiding DNS naming problems.

Manual allocation of IP addresses

DHCP Servers can dynamically or manually allocate IP addresses. Both methods use the same DHCP Client-Server protocol, but the network administrator manages them differently at the DHCP Server.

Manual allocation follows the policy used in most current TCP/IP implementations. With this method, the network administrator defines the IP address and other configuration options that the DHCP Servers provide for a particular computer. The DHCP Servers respond based on the client's unique identifier, which is the network adapter's MAC-layer address. DHCP Servers cannot allocate any IP addresses assigned in this way to other clients using either automatic or dynamic allocation. The address has a permanent lease.

You would use manual allocation, for example, for the range of IP addresses you need to provide through RAS servers. Make sure to exclude these addresses from the range of dynamically allocated addresses.

Lease options

To define appropriate values for lease duration, you should consider the frequency of the following events for your network:

- Changes to DHCP options and default values
- Network interface failures
- Computer removals — for any purpose
- Subnet changes by users because of office moves, laptop computers docked at different workstations, and so on

These types of events cause the client to release IP addresses or cause the leases to expire at the DHCP Server. Consequently, the IP addresses are returned to the free address pool for reuse.

If many changes occur on your internetwork, you should assign short lease times, such as two weeks. This way, the DHCP Server can reassign the addresses to new DHCP Client computers requesting TCP/IP configuration information.

Another important factor is the ratio between connected computers and available IP addresses. For example, the demand for reusing addresses is low in a network where 40 systems share a class C address (with 254 available addresses). A long lease time such as two months would be appropriate in such a situation. However, if 230 computers share the same address pool, demand for available addresses is much greater, so a lease time of a few days or weeks is more appropriate.

Note

When specifying short lease durations, it's imperative that the DHCP Server remains available to accommodate clients seeking to renew leases. Backup servers become particularly important with short lease durations.

Partitioning the address pool

You might decide to install more than one DHCP Server, so that the failure of any individual server does not prevent DHCP Clients from starting. However, DHCP does not provide a way for DHCP Servers to cooperate in ensuring that assigned addresses are unique. Therefore, you must divide the available address pool among the DHCP Servers to prevent duplicate address assignment.

A typical scenario is a local DHCP Server that maintains TCP/IP configuration information for two subnets. For each DHCP Server, the network administrator allocates 70 percent of the IP address pool for local clients and 30 percent for clients from the remote subnet and then configures a relay agent to deliver requests between the subnets.

This scenario allows the local DHCP Server to respond to requests from local DHCP Clients most of the time. The remote DHCP Server assigns addresses to clients on the other subnet only when the local server is not available or is out of addresses. You can use this same partitioning method among subnets in a multiple subnet scenario to ensure the availability of a responding server when a DHCP Client requests configuration information.

Avoiding DNS naming conflicts

Although you can use DNS (Domain Name Service) to provide names for network resources, DNS configuration is static, which can create problems. With DHCP, a host can easily have a different IP address if its lease expires or for other reasons, but there is no standard for updating DNS servers dynamically when IP address information changes. Therefore, DNS naming conflicts can occur if you use DHCP for dynamic allocation of IP addresses.

This problem primarily affects systems that extend internetworking services to local network users. For example, a server acting as an anonymous FTP server or as an e-mail gateway might require users to contact it using DNS names. In such cases, such clients should have reserved leases with an unlimited duration.

Using DHCP with diskless workstations

If your network includes diskless workstations or X terminal BOOTP clients that need configuration information to use TCP/IP, you must build profiles. (BOOTP is the internetworking Bootstrap Protocol used to configure systems across internetworks. DHCP is an extension of BOOTP.) Profiles are discussed in Chapter 9, *Controlling User Environments*.

You might decide to continue to manage these workstations using existing BOOTP servers. If so, you must exclude these addresses from the free address pool maintained by the DHCP Server.

Managing the DHCP Database Files

The following files are stored in the *systemroot*\\SYSTEM32\\DHCP directory that is created when you set up a DHCP Server:

■ DHCP.MDB is the DHCP database file.

■ DHCP.TMP is a temporary file DHCP creates for temporary database information.

■ JET.LOG and the JET*.LOG files contain logs of all transactions done with the database. These files are used by DHCP to recover data if necessary.

■ SYSTEM.MDB is used by DHCP for holding information about the structure of its database.

Caution

Do not remove or tamper with the DHCP.TMP, DHCP.MDB, JET.LOG, and SYSTEM.MDB files.

The DHCP database and related Registry entries are backed up automatically at a specific interval (15 minutes by default), based on the value of Registry parameters. You can also force database backup while working in DHCP Manager.

Backing up the DHCP database onto another computer

You may find a situation where you need to back up a DHCP database to another computer.

To move a DHCP database

Use the Replicator service to copy the contents of the DHCP backup directory to the new computer.

Troubleshooting DHCP Servers

This section describes some of the more common errors that may occur with a DHCP system.

Using routers as RFC 1542 (BOOTP) relay agents

Many routers that are currently available do not function properly as an RFC 1542 (BOOTP) relay agent with DHCP. The DHCP messages include some new fields as well as some fields that are used in a different manner. For instance, the broadcast bit in a DHCP message causes most "normal" (that is, non-RFC 1542) BOOTP relay agents that perform any validity checking on BOOTP requests to discard the DHCP message silently. In addition, the DHCPNACK message also causes BOOTP relay agents to discard the DHCP message, because a DHCPNACK includes all zeros in the IP address field for the client — this was not permitted in the original BOOTP specification.

Before implementing DHCP and expecting a router to function as an RFC 1542 (BOOTP) relay agent for DHCP, first verify with the router manufacturer that the router supports RFC 1541 and RFC 1542.

The following error conditions indicate potential problems with the DHCP Server:

- **The RPC server is unavailable** or **Error 1753: The DHCP Server service is not running on the target system.** When attempting to connect to a DHCP Server, the DHCP Manager utility may return one of these messages. Both of these errors are indications that the Microsoft DHCP Server service is not running on the system to which the DHCP Manager is attempting to connect.

- **The DHCP Client couldn't obtain an IP address** or **The DHCP Client couldn't renew the IP address lease.** On a DHCP Client, one of these popup messages may appear. These errors both indicate that the DHCP Client system was unable to communicate with a DHCP Server. Both of these conditions could result from the DHCP Server service not being started on any DHCP Servers or the DHCP Client's connection to the network not functioning for some reason.

A "The DHCP Client couldn't obtain an IP" address error message may also be generated if the DHCP Servers that received the DHCP Client's request have no more IP addresses available to lease.

If your system develops any of these problems, the first task is to make sure that the DHCP services are running.

To ensure that the DHCP services are running

1. Use the Services option in the Control Panel to verify that the DHCP or WINS services are running.

In the Services dialog box for the client computer, Started should appear in the Status column for the DHCP or WINS Client service. For the DHCP or WINS Server itself, Started should appear in the Status column for the DHCP or Windows Internet Name service.

2. If the necessary service is not started on either computer, start the service.

In rare circumstances, the DHCP Server may not boot or a STOP error may occur. If the DHCP Server is down, follow these steps to restart it.

To restart a DHCP Server that is down

1. Turn off the power to the server and wait one minute.

2. Turn on the power, start Windows NT Server, and log on under an account with Administrator rights.

3. At the command prompt, type **net start dhcpserver** and press Enter.

Restoring the DHCP database

If you ascertain that the DHCP services are running on both the client and server computers but the error conditions described earlier persist, the DHCP database is not available or is corrupt. If a DHCP Server fails for any reason, you can restore the database from the automatic backup files.

To restore a DHCP database

Restart the DHCP Server. If the DHCP database has become corrupted, it is automatically restored from the DHCP backup directory specified in the Registry.

If you have a corrupted primary database file and this is not detected by the DHCP service, you can force the backup copy to be used by editing the Registry.

To force the restoration of a DHCP database

Set the Registry key HKEY_LOCAL_MACHINE\SYSTEM\CurrentControlSet\Services\DHCPServer \Parameters\RestoreFlag to 1. Then restart the DHCP service by entering **net stop dhcpserver** followed by **net start dhcpserver**.

To manually restore a DHCP database

If the two preceding restore methods do not work, manually copy all DHCP database files from the backup directory to the \DHCP working directory. Then restart the DHCP Server service.

Summary

This chapter focused on implementing the DHCP services on your network. It discussed

▶ Basic planning issues and the management options that are available for manipulating DHCP Clients

▶ Preparation for the possibility of a failure with the services database

▶ Basic performance tips

Chapter 19

Setting Up WINS Servers

In This Chapter

▶ Configuring WINS Servers

▶ Managing the WINS database

▶ Troubleshooting WINS

▶ Creating static mappings on a WINS Server

▶ Configuring replication between WINS Servers

▶ Creating a WINS Proxy Server

Maintaining a TCP/IP network can place a huge burden on a system administrator. In addition to the normal responsibilities that go along with administrating a Windows NT network, TCP/IP introduces another facet of administration: managing computer names and addresses. In the past, system administrators manually created and maintained LMHOSTS files to map computer names to IP addresses. Along came DNS (Domain Name Service) and WINS (Windows Internet Name Service), which are distributed databases for registering and querying dynamic computer-name-to-IP-address mappings. This chapter describes WINS operation and how to install and configure WINS Servers.

Name Resolution for TCP/IP on Windows NT

To communicate over a TCP/IP network, the system has to resolve computer names into IP addresses. TCP/IP has no idea how to establish communication with a computer name such as \\CPRESS1, but it does know how to communicate with 166.82.200.215. The process that TCP/IP networks use to discover a computer's IP address from the computer's name is known as *resolution.* It's not enough just to resolve or decode a computer's IP address from its name; each node (computer connection) on a TCP/IP network must have a unique name and address. To ensure that each Windows NT computer on a TCP/IP network has a unique name and address, the computer registers its name and IP address during startup. This process is called *registration.* To resolve the computer name to its IP address, TCP/IP can use a variety of name resolution methods: broadcast name resolution, a static mapping file (LMHOSTS), DNS name resolution, or Windows Internet Name Service (WINS).

Broadcasts

Broadcasting on a computer network is very similar to broadcasting over a police band or citizen band radio. With a radio, a dispatcher's or caller's voice is amplified (broadcast) over a channel so that it can be heard by everyone whose radio is turned on. To contact a particular person, the dispatcher's message includes the name or ID of that person. Every person who receives the broadcast message listens to determine for whom it is intended, and the person whose name was called in the message responds to the dispatcher.

By relying on broadcasts to resolve computer names to IP addresses, the network becomes bogged down with additional network traffic. The more systems that you have on a given network, the more broadcasts on the network, which can lead to heavy network congestion. Each time that a computer tries to make a network connection, it broadcasts one or more times in an effort to resolve the computer name of the system at the other end of the connection to an IP address.

When using broadcasts to resolve computer names to IP addresses, the system must forward the broadcasts throughout the network as shown in Figure 19-1.

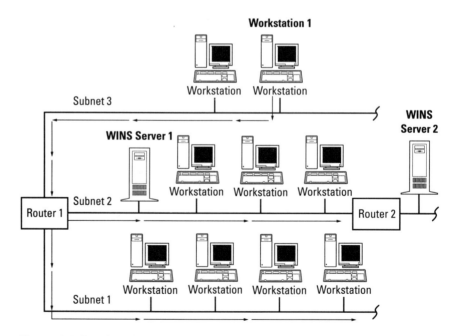

Figure 19-1: Broadcast forwarding (arrows indicate broadcast directions).

In Figure 19-1, a user on Workstation 1 issues the net use \\server2\share command. In order to resolve Server 2's computer name, Workstation 1 broadcasts for Server 2. To make sure that all systems on the network can communicate with each other, all broadcasts are forwarded throughout the network. Depending on the number of name resolutions at any one time, this can cause significant network traffic. In addition, each system on the network must examine each broadcast to determine if the broadcast is meant for that particular system.

LMHOSTS file

An LMHOSTS file contains a list of computer names mapped to IP addresses. When you use an LMHOSTS file to resolve a computer name to an IP address, you have to maintain that file. As the network administrator, you have to keep track of each workstation's computer name and the IP address in use by the workstation. If a workstation changes computer names or IP addresses, you have to update the LMHOSTS file. Because each workstation has its own local copy of the LMHOSTS file, you have to update the file and distribute it to all of the other workstations every time a computer name or IP address changes. To decrease this double-duty maintenance, most systems use LMHOSTS files in conjunction with one of the other two name resolution methods. Typically, most workstations are configured to try broadcasts first and then try the LMHOSTS file.

Note

If you use the LMHOSTS file for name resolution and the Dynamic Host Configuration Protocol (DHCP) for IP address assignment, there is still significant overhead involved in maintaining the IP-address-to-host-name mappings. This is because the LMHOSTS file is a static file that must be manually modified each time that a DHCP Client receives a new IP address from a DHCP Server. Each DHCP Client requires a copy of the modified LMHOSTS file. For example, workstations that frequently move between subnets receive a new IP address every time they change subnets, which requires you to modify the LMHOSTS file on all workstations.

DNS (Domain Name Service) Server

The DNS Server uses a distributed database with a hierarchical naming system for resolving computer names, the root of which is managed by the Internet Network Information Center. The DNS Server naming scheme uses a very structured naming scheme that must be followed closely, such as cpress1.publish.com, where cpress1 is the computer name and publish.com is the domain name.

Cross Reference

Refer to Chapter 16, *Understanding TCP/IP,* for more information about DNS (Domain Name Service).

WINS

The Windows Internet Name Service (WINS) was designed to eliminate the need for broadcasts and provide a dynamic database that maintains computer-names-to-IP-address mappings. There are two types of systems that use WINS:

- **WINS Clients.** WINS Clients are configured with the IP address of one or more WINS Servers. On startup, a WINS Client communicates directly with a WINS Server to register its computer name and corresponding IP address. When a WINS Client needs to resolve a computer name to an IP address, such as when a net use \\cpress\share is performed, the WINS Client sends a request to the WINS Server for the IP address of the computer name being used.

- **WINS Servers.** A WINS Server maintains a database that maps the IP address of a WINS Client to its computer name, also referred to as a NetBIOS name. Therefore, instead of using broadcasts to resolve a computer name to an IP address when trying to establish a network connection, a WINS Client requests the IP address for the desired system from a WINS Server, which retrieves the IP address from its database.

A network typically has one or more WINS Servers that WINS Clients can contact when they need to resolve a computer name to an IP address. You can set up WINS Servers on a given network so that they replicate all computer names to IP address mappings in their WINS databases to each other. In general, you should implement WINS Servers so that you can do the following:

- **Reduce broadcast traffic on the network**. Instead of broadcasting to every computer on a network in an attempt to resolve a computer name to an IP address, the workstation sends a message directly to a WINS Server requesting the IP address for a given computer name. Furthermore, a DHCP Server can provide a DHCP Client with IP addresses for WINS Servers.

- **Eliminate the need for the LMHOSTS file**. Using WINS eliminates the need for network administrators to maintain the LMHOSTS file. Because administrators do not need to keep track of which computer name maps to which IP address, there is less administrative overhead involved in using TCP/IP.

- **Provide dynamic name registration**. WINS complements DHCP on a network. If you use DHCP by itself, you still have to maintain the LMHOSTS file. However, using WINS with DHCP provides dynamic IP addressing and name resolution without broadcasts or static files.

- **Prevent duplicate computer names**. Every time that a WINS Client starts up, it registers its computer name with a WINS Server. If the WINS Server already has a registration for the requested computer name, it rejects the WINS Client's registration attempt, thereby preventing duplicate computer names.

Setting Up WINS Name Resolution

The Windows NT DNS Server service can use the WINS service to resolve the names of computers running Windows or Windows NT. For example, you might want to use a UNIX computer to connect to a computer that has a WINS name and a changing IP address (for example, an address acquired through the DHCP service). In this case, configure the UNIX computer's resolver to use the Windows NT computer running the DNS service and make sure that the computer running the DNS service has a properly configured WINS Server service. Then decide in which domain the WINS names belong. For example, you might decide that the domain cpress.home.dom is the space in which all WINS computers are named. You would then expect WINS lookup to handle queries for secretstation.cpress.home.dom, looking for the SecretStation computer.

Note that Windows NT servers running DNS and also providing WINS lookup must not be configured to use DNS for Windows name resolution. To ensure that you have the proper configuration, choose Network from the Control Panel, go to the advanced configuration settings for the TCP/IP protocol, and clear the Use DNS for Windows Name Resolution check box.

To provide WINS names through the DNS service

1. Use any text editor to open the PLACE.DOM file.

2. Find or create the Start of Authority (SOA) record for the domain in which you want to use WINS names. The SOA record points to the computer that is the best source of information on computer names in the domain. The record can span more than one line if you enclose it in parentheses so that the program reads it as a single line.

3. Create a new line under this line, consisting of the string $WINS. Note that this must be on a line by itself and start in column 1. Do not put the $WINS line in reverse-lookup (IN-ADDR.ARPA.) domains.

4. Save the file.

■ **Eliminate the need for DNS Servers**. Because WINS uses NetBIOS names, it is more flexible than DNS for name resolution. You can gain some advantages by using DNS Servers in conjunction with WINS Servers. See the sidebar, *Setting Up WINS Name Resolution*.

How WINS Works

When you configure a system to use WINS for its name registration, it adheres to h-node. (For name resolution, it also adheres to h-node but with a few differences.)

Cross Reference

The term *h-node* refers to one of the NetBIOS over TCP/IP modes that defines how NBT identifies and accesses network resources. Refer to Chapter 16, *Understanding TCP/IP*, for more information on NetBIOS over TCP/IP.

During name registration, the WINS Client

1. Checks to see if it is the local machine name.

2. Checks its cache of remote names. Any name that is resolved is placed in a cache where it remains for 10 minutes.

3. Tries to contact the WINS Server.

4. Tries broadcasting.

5. Checks the LMHOSTS file, if configured to use the LMHOSTS file.

6. Finally, tries the HOSTS file and then a DNS, if so configured.

Note

If the DHCP Server configures the DHCP Client to use m-node name resolution, the client first attempts to broadcast and then tries the WINS Server.

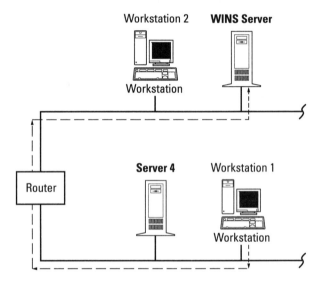

Figure 19-2: Communication between WINS Clients and WINS Server.

In Figure 19-2, Workstations 1 and 2 and Server 4 are all configured with the IP address of the WINS Server (all three computers could also be configured via a DHCP Server). Therefore, they all communicate directly with the WINS Server to register their names with Name Registration Request packets. Workstation 1 or 2 locates Server 4 by directing a name query request to the WINS Server, which responds with the IP address for Server 4.

Registering a computer name

When a WINS Client starts, it sends a Name Registration Request message to the WINS Server in order to register its computer name. A WINS Client sends one Name Registration Request for each of the names that it needs to register with the WINS Server. The Name Registration Request includes the WINS Client's IP address and the name that the client is requesting to register.

Note

The Name Registration Request is sent directly to the IP address that the WINS Client has for its WINS Server.

When the WINS Server receives a Name Registration Request from a WINS Client, it checks the WINS database to ensure that the name being registered is unique. Based on this check, the WINS Server responds with either a positive or negative Name Registration Response as follows:

- If the requested name is unique, the WINS Server responds with a positive Name Registration Response. The response includes a parameter, called a Time To Live (TTL), that indicates when the WINS Client must renew its registration.

- If there is a duplicate name registered in the WINS database, the WINS Server attempts to discover the legitimate owner of the name by sending what is referred to as a *challenge* to the currently registered owner of the name. If the current registered name owner responds successfully to the WINS Server, the WINS Server sends a negative Name Registration Response to the WINS Client that attempted to register the name.

The WINS Server sends the Name Registration Response via a directed send since it knows the IP address of the WINS Client (it is included in the Name Registration Request sent by the WINS Client).

Renewing a computer name

WINS Clients must renew their name registrations before the Time To Live (TTL) value returned by the WINS Server expires.

When a WINS Client renews its name registration, it sends a Name Refresh Request to the WINS Server. The Name Refresh Request includes the WINS Client's IP address and the name that the client is requesting be refreshed. The Name Refresh Request is sent via a directed send to the IP address that the WINS Client has for its WINS Server.

The WINS Server responds to a Name Refresh Request with a Name Refresh Response message that includes a new Time To Live (TTL).

A WINS Client first attempts to refresh its name registrations after one eighth of the TTL has expired. If the WINS Client does not receive a Name Refresh Response, it attempts to refresh its registrations every one eighth of the TTL, until half of the TTL has expired.

At this point, the WINS Client then attempts to refresh its registrations with the secondary WINS Server with whose IP address it has been configured. On switching to the secondary WINS Server, the WINS Client attempts to refresh its registrations every one eighth of the TTL, until it is successful or half of the TTL has expired.

After a WINS Client has successfully refreshed its registrations one time, it refreshes every time half of the TTL has expired.

Releasing a computer name

On shutdown, WINS Clients notify the WINS Server that they are shutting down so that the names they registered can be removed from the WINS database.

When a WINS Client shuts down gracefully, it sends a Name Release Request to the WINS Server for each name that it has registered with the WINS Server. The Name Release Request includes the WINS Client's IP address and the name that should be removed (released) from the WINS Server's WINS database. Because the WINS Client knows the IP address for the WINS Server, the Name Release Request is sent via a directed send.

When the WINS Server receives a Name Release Request, it checks the WINS database for the specified name. Based on the check of the database, the WINS Server sends a positive or negative Name Release Response to the WINS Client and removes the specified name from the WINS database. The Name Release Response contains the released name and a TTL of 0 (zero).

WINS Clients ignore the Name Release Response, so if the WINS Server sends a negative Name Release Response, the WINS Client still releases the name and shuts down.

The WINS Server sends a negative Name Release Response only if it encounters a WINS database error (which should never happen) or if the address of the WINS Client does not match the address stored in the WINS database.

Planning your WINS Installation

For a small Microsoft-based network, install DHCP and WINS services on each domain controller. This allows you to configure your TCP/IP-based network clients so that they fully interoperate with any other server or client on the network. A single WINS Server can accommodate about 1500 name registrations and 760 name query requests. In theory, this means that you can use one WINS Server with a backup WINS Server for every 10,000 clients. However, I recommend that you use one WINS Server per logical grouping to provide additional fault tolerance and load balancing.

As with DHCP Servers, you should have two or more available WINS Servers on the network. If you deploy only one WINS Server and it goes down, the WINS Clients have to fall back to using broadcasts for their name registration and resolution.

By having two WINS Servers, at least one WINS Server remains available to handle any name registrations and resolutions if one WINS Server goes down. An added benefit to having multiple WINS Servers is that you can balance the load of name registration and resolution requests between the servers. To take advantage of this capability, configure WINS Clients with the IP addresses of a primary and a secondary WINS Server. In the event that the primary WINS Server becomes unavailable, the WINS Client can contact the secondary WINS Server for name registration and resolution as shown in Figure 19-3.

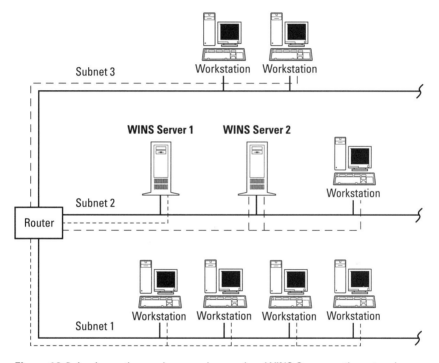

Figure 19-3: Implementing a primary and secondary WINS Server on the network.

Figure 19-3 shows WINS Clients on Subnet 1 with WINS Server 1 as their primary WINS Server and WINS Server 2 as their secondary WINS Server. If WINS Server 1 goes down, the WINS Clients on Subnet 1 automatically begin using WINS Server 2 for all name registrations and resolutions. The WINS Clients on Subnets 2 and 3 behave just the opposite of those on Subnet 1 since they have WINS Server 2 as their primary WINS Server and WINS Server 1 as their secondary WINS Server.

The WINS Clients on Subnets 2 and 3 always use WINS Server 2 for name registration and resolution, unless it goes down. Even though they use WINS Server 2, they can resolve the computer names of the systems on Subnet 1 to their IP addresses because WINS Server 1 and WINS Server 2 replicate their WINS database entries to each other.

Remember that WINS Clients know the IP addresses of their WINS Servers. Because the messages passed between the WINS Server and WINS Clients are all sent to a specific IP address, you do not need a specially configured IP router to enable communication between WINS Servers and WINS Clients on different subnets.

Extending the network with WINS Proxy Agents

WINS Proxy Agents extend the name resolution capabilities of the WINS Server to non-WINS-capable network clients. A WINS Proxy Agent listens for broadcast name registrations and broadcast name resolution requests from non-WINS Clients. When the WINS Proxy Agent detects a name resolution broadcast, it forwards the request of the non-WINS Client to a WINS Server so that the WINS Server can resolve the computer name to an IP address.

In the case of name registration broadcasts by non-WINS Clients, the WINS Proxy Agent forwards the request to ensure that a WINS Client has not registered the same name. WINS Proxy Agents are not responsible for registering non-WINS Client names with the WINS Server.

For a computer to serve as a WINS Proxy Agent, you must configure it as a WINS Client.

To configure a WINS Client as a WINS Proxy Agent

1. Launch Control Panel and start the Networks applet.

2. Select TCP/IP Protocol and press the Configure button.

3. Select the Advanced button to bring up the Advanced TCP/IP configuration dialog box. Then check the Enable WINS Proxy Agent check box to specify this computer as a WINS Proxy Agent.

You need a WINS Proxy Agent on each subnet because broadcast messages are not passed across routers. When a non-WINS Client attempts to find another computer, it uses a broadcast message to obtain the IP address of the requested computer. If this computer is on the same subnet, the request succeeds. However, if the computer is on a different subnet, the request fails (unless you have domain controllers on both sides of the routers).

A WINS Proxy Agent does not store information obtained from a broadcast in the WINS Server's database. This is why you must have a WINS Proxy Agent on each subnet that contains non-WINS Clients. The WINS Proxy Agent responds to name query requests from WINS Clients or WINS Servers and then broadcasts on its local subnet to find the non-WINS Client. Once the WINS Proxy Agent finds the non-WINS Client, it passes the IP address to the WINS Client or server that issued the name query request. Figure 19-4 illustrates the communication process that a WINS Proxy Agent uses when interacting with a non-WINS Client.

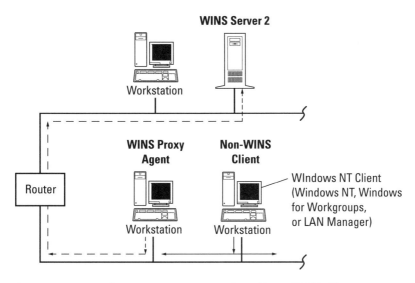

WINS Server 2

Workstation

WINS Proxy
Agent

Non-WINS
Client

WIndows NT Client
(Windows NT, Windows
for Workgroups,
or LAN Manager)

Router

Workstation   Workstation

Figure 19-4: A WINS Proxy Agent interoperating with non-WINS Clients.

When a WINS Client requires access to another computer, it issues a name query request. The system can route this name query request to WINS Servers only if the primary or secondary WINS Server for the WINS Client does not contain a registration for the requested computer. If a WINS Server cannot resolve the routed name query request, the WINS Client issues a broadcast message. Both broadcast messages and routed name query messages consume network bandwidth that could otherwise be used to transfer data. However, if your WINS Servers have a complete listing of the computer names and IP addresses, the primary WINS Server can respond to the name query request, thereby limiting the number of routed name query requests and broadcast messages.

Installing WINS Servers

The Windows Internet Name Service (WINS) is a Windows NT service that runs on a Windows NT computer. The supporting WINS Client software is automatically installed for Windows NT Server and for Windows NT computers when the basic operating system is installed.

You can install a WINS Server at the same time that you install Microsoft TCP/IP in Windows NT Server or after you've already installed TCP/IP. You must log on as a member of the Administrators group to install a WINS Server.

To install a WINS Server

1. Choose the Network option in Control Panel. When the Network Settings dialog box appears, choose the Add Software button.

2. In the Network Software list in the Add Network Software dialog box, select TCP/IP Protocol And Related Components and then choose the Continue button.

3. In the Windows NT TCP/IP Installation Options dialog box, check the appropriate options to install including, at a minimum, WINS Server Service.

Note

If you want to use SNMP to configure the WINS Server service remotely, make sure to install the SNMP Service by enabling the SNMP Service check box.

4. Choose the OK button. Windows NT Setup displays a message asking for the full path to the Windows NT Server distribution files. Type the appropriate location and choose the Continue button. All necessary files are copied to your hard disk.

5. Complete all of the required procedures for manually configuring TCP/IP as described in Chapter 17, *Installing and Configuring TCP/IP*. When the Network Settings dialog box reappears, choose the Close button.

All of the appropriate TCP/IP and WINS Server software is ready for use after you reboot the computer.

To start and stop the WINS service

1. In Control Panel, choose the Services icon. Or in Server Manager, choose Services from the Computer menu.

2. In the Services dialog box, select Windows Internet Name Service and choose the Start or Stop button. Then choose the Close button.

Note

You can also use the command net start wins or net stop wins to start and stop the WINS service at the command prompt.

Configuring WINS Servers

WINS consists of two components: the WINS Server, which responds to name queries and registrations, and client software, which queries the server for computer name resolution. After the WINS Server has been installed on a Windows NT Server version 4.0 system, the WINS Server is ready to receive name registrations and resolve name requests as soon as you restart the computer. Installation is the only step required to get the WINS Server up and running. However, after the initial installation, how you configure the WINS Server greatly affects the performance of the WINS Server and the network.

You use the WINS Manager (WINSADMN.EXE) utility from the Network Administration group in Program Manager to configure local and remote WINS Servers. The first step is to connect to a WINS Server in the WINS Manager dialog box, as shown in Figure 19-5.

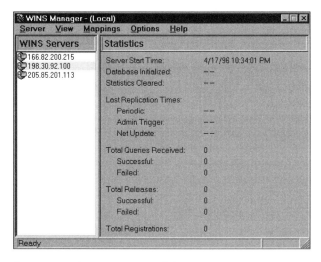

Figure 19-5: Connecting a WINS Server.

Whether a computer name or an IP address is specified in the WINS Manager dialog box determines how WINS Manager establishes the connection to the WINS Server. If a computer name is supplied, WINS Manager establishes the connection to the WINS Server via named pipes. If an IP address is supplied, WINS Manager uses TCP/IP to establish the connection.

To configure a WINS Server

1. From the Server menu, choose the Configuration command. (This command is available only if you are logged on as a member of the Administrators group for the WINS Server that you want to configure.) The WINS Server Configuration dialog box appears as shown in Figure 19-6.

2. To view all of the options in the dialog box, choose the Advanced button.

3. For the configuration options in the WINS Server Configuration dialog box, specify time intervals using the spin buttons, as described in Table 19-1.

4. If you want this WINS Server to pull replicas of new WINS database entries from its partners when the system is initialized or when a replication-related parameter changes, check Initial Replication in the Pull Parameters options and then type a value for Retry Count.

   The retry count is the number of times that the server should attempt to connect (in case of failure) with a partner for pulling replicas. Retries are attempted at the replication interval specified in the Preferences dialog box. If all retries are unsuccessful, WINS waits for a period before starting replication again.

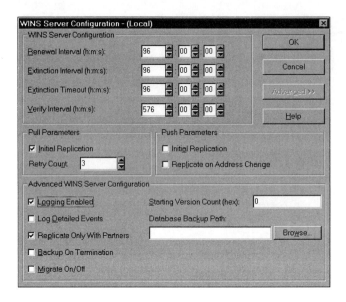

Figure 19-6: The WINS Server Configuration dialog box.

Table 19-1	WINS Server Intervals
Configuration option	*Meaning*
Renewal Interval	Specifies how often a client reregisters its name. The default is five hours.
Extinction Interval	Specifies the interval between when an entry is marked as released and when it is marked as extinct. The default is four times the renewal interval.
Extinction Timeout	Specifies the interval between when an entry is marked extinct and when the entry is finally scavenged from the database. The default is the same as the renewal interval.
Verify Interval	Specifies the interval after which the WINS Server must verify that old names it does not own are still active. The default is 20 times the extinction interval.
Initial Replication (Pull Parameters)	Enables the WINS Server to pull new WINS database entries from its partners (other WINS Servers).
Retry Count	The number of times the WINS Server attempts to contact a partner from which to pull the WINS database entries.
Initial Replication (Push Parameters)	Allows the WINS Server to notify its partners of the status of its WINS database when the system is initialized.
Replicate on Address Change	Allows the WINS Server to notify its partners of its WINS database status when a name registration changes.

5. To inform partners of the database status when the system is initialized, check Initial Replication in the Push Parameters group.

6. To inform partners of the database status when an address changes in a mapping record, check Replicate on Address Change.

As a final step in configuring the WINS Server, you should specify advanced configuration options:

Press the Advanced button to expand the WINS Server Configuration dialog box (if advanced options do not show already). Set any Advanced WINS Server Configuration options, as described in Table 19-2. When you have completed all changes in the WINS Server Configuration dialog box, choose the OK button.

Table 19-2   Advanced WINS Server Configuration Options

Configuration option	Meaning
Logging Enabled	Specifies whether logging of database changes to JET.LOG should be turned on.
Log Detailed Events	Specifies whether logging events are recorded in detail. (This option requires considerable system resources and should be turned off if you are tuning for performance.)
Replicate Only With Partners	Specifies that replication proceeds only with WINS pull or push partners. If this option is not checked, an administrator can ask a WINS Server to pull or push from or to a non-listed WINS Server partner. By default, this option is checked.
Backup On Termination	Specifies that the database backs up automatically when WINS Manager is closed.
Migrate On/Off	Specifies that static unique and multihomed records in the database are treated as dynamic when they conflict with a new registration or replica. This means that if these records are no longer valid, they are overwritten by the new registration or replica. Check this option if you are upgrading non-Windows NT systems to Windows NT. By default, this option is not checked.
Starting Version Count	Specifies the highest version ID number for the database. Usually,you do not need to change this value unless the data-base becomes corrupted and you need to start fresh. In such a case, set this value to a number higher than the version number counter for this WINS Server on all of the remote partners that earlier replicated the local WINS Server's records. This value can be seen in the View Database dialog box in WINS Manager.

(continued)

Table 19-2 *(Continued)*

Configuration option	Meaning
Database Backup Path	Specifies the directory where the computer stores WINS database backups. WINS uses this directory to perform an automatic restoration of the database in the event the database is found to be corrupted when WINS is started. Do not specify a network directory.

Setting up replication partners

WINS Servers communicate among themselves to fully replicate their databases, ensuring that a name registered with one WINS Server is eventually replicated to all other WINS Servers within the internetwork. All mapping changes converge within the *replication period* for the entire WINS system, which is the maximum time for propagating changes to all WINS Servers. All released names are propagated to all WINS Servers after they become extinct, based on the interval specified in WINS Manager.

Replication is carried out among replication partners, rather than each server replicating to all other servers. To configure WINS Servers to replicate their WINS database entries among each other, you must configure each WINS Server as a pull or push partner with at least one other WINS Server:

- **Pull partners**. A pull partner is a WINS Server that "pulls" WINS database entries (replicas) from its push partners, by requesting any new WINS database entries (replicas) that the push partners have. The pull partner requests entries with a higher version number than the last entry it received during the last replication.

- **Push partners**. A push partner is a WINS Server that sends a message to its pull partners notifying them when its WINS database has changed. When the WINS Server's pull partner(s) respond to the message with a replication request, the WINS Server sends a copy ("pushes") of its new WINS database entries (replicas) to its pull partner(s).

Note

The documentation included in the Windows NT Server version 4.0 package refers to some WINS database entries as *replicas*, that is, entries in the WINS database that have been replicated from other WINS Servers.

Configuring WINS Servers to replicate their WINS database entries with each other extends the benefit of WINS across the entire network as shown in Figure 19-7.

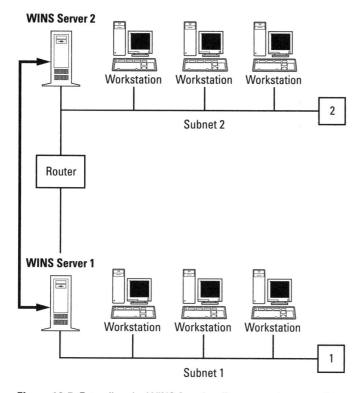

Figure 19-7: Extending the WINS functionality across the network.

In Figure 19-7, WINS Clients on Subnet 1 register their computer name with WINS Server 1, and WINS Clients on Subnet 2 register their computer name with WINS Server 2. When WINS Clients on Subnet 1 need to resolve a computer name to an IP address, they contact WINS Server 1. Because WINS Server 1 and WINS Server 2 replicate their WINS database entries with each other, WINS Server 1 can resolve a computer name from Subnet 2 to its IP address.

If WINS Server 1 and WINS Server 2 did not replicate their WINS database entries with each other, WINS Server 1 would not be able to resolve a computer name from Subnet 2 to its IP address.

Replication Considerations

Replication of the WINS database can be started in one of three ways:

- At system startup and then again at an interval configured by the administrator, the WINS Server can request any new WINS database entries from its pull partners.

- When a WINS Server reaches its threshold for the number of registrations and changes to the WINS database, the WINS Server notifies all of its pull partners, who then request the new entries.

- The administrator can cause replication to occur through WINS Manager.

Note

WINS Servers replicate only new entries in their database; the entire WINS database is *not* replicated each time replication occurs.

Once you decide whether a WINS Server will be a push partner or a pull partner, you have to configure the push or pull settings appropriately. For pull partners, you set an appropriate interval between replication attempts based on the network. Typically, WINS Servers that are located near each other should replicate more frequently than WINS Servers across WAN links. For push partners, you determine an appropriate update count based on the number of registrations that a server handles. Typically, a WINS Server that receives hundreds of name registrations every morning when users first log on should not be configured to replicate a small number of registrations.

For each WINS Server, you must configure threshold intervals for triggering database replication. You can base the intervals on a specific time, a time period, or a certain number of new records. If you designate a specific time, replication occurs one time only. If you specify a time period, replication is repeated at that interval.

To add a replication partner for a WINS Server

1. From the Server menu, choose the Replication Partners command.

   This command is available only if you are logged on as a member of the Administrators group for the local server.

2. In the Replication Partners dialog box, click the Add button. The Add WINS Server dialog box appears as shown in Figure 19-8.

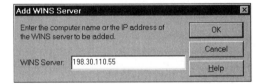

Figure 19-8: The Add WINS Server dialog box.

3. In the Add WINS Server dialog box, type the name or IP address of the WINS Server that you want to add to the list, and then choose the OK button. If WINS Manager finds this server, it adds it to the WINS Server list in the Replication Partners dialog box.

4. From the WINS Server list in the Replication Partners dialog box, select the server that you want to configure and then complete the steps described in *Configuring Replication Partner Properties* later in this chapter.

5. When you finish adding replication partners, choose the OK button.

To delete replication partners

1. From the Server menu, choose the Replication Partners command.

2. In the Replication Partners dialog box, select one or more servers in the WINS Server list and then choose the Delete button or press Del.

   WINS Manager asks you to confirm the deletion if you checked the related confirmation option in the Preference dialog box.

To limit which WINS Servers are displayed in the Replication Partners dialog box

1. Check Push Partners to display push partners for the current WINS Server.

2. Check Pull Partners to display pull partners for the current WINS Server.

3. Check Other to display the WINS Servers that are neither push nor pull partners for the current WINS Server.

Configuring Replication Partner Properties

When you designate replication partners, you need to specify parameters to control the conditions under which replication should begin.

To configure replication partners for a WINS Server

1. In the WINS Server list of the Replication Partners dialog box, select the server that you want to configure.

2. Check either Push Partner or Pull Partner or both to indicate the replication partnership that you want and then choose the related Configure button.

3. Complete the entries in the appropriate Properties dialog box, as described in the following procedures.

To define pull partner properties

1. In the Start Time box of the Pull Partner Properties dialog box, enter a time to indicate when replication should begin.

   You can use any separator for hours, minutes, and seconds. You can type AM or PM only if these designators are part of your time setting (as defined using the International option in Control Panel).

2. In the Replication Interval box, enter a time in hours, minutes, and seconds to indicate how often replications occur or use the spin buttons to set the time you want.

   If you want to return to the values specified in the Preferences dialog box, choose the Set Default Values button.

3. Choose the OK button to return to the Replication Partners dialog box.

To define push partner properties

1. In the Update Count box of the Push Partner Properties dialog box, enter a number for how many additions and updates to database records will result in changes that need replication. (Replications that have been pulled in from partners do not count as insertions or updates in this context.) The minimum value for Update Count is 5.

   If you want to return to the value specified in the Preferences dialog box, choose the Set Default Values button.

2. Choose the OK button to return to the Replication Partners dialog box.

Under Replications Options, as shown in the Replication Partners dialog box in Figure 19-9, you can configure a WINS Server as a push and/or pull partner to the WINS Server that you are currently administering with WINS Manager.

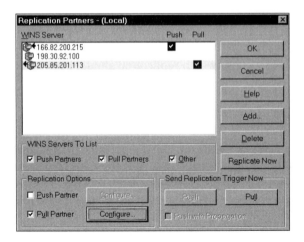

Figure 19-9: Replication options in the Replication Partners dialog box.

■ The Configure button for push partners allows you to set the update count (number of new WINS database entries) that the WINS Server must reach before it sends a push message.

■ The Configure button for pull partners allows the administrator to set the start time and replication interval for the selected partner.

The Send Replication Trigger Now settings affect the push and/or pull operations for a specific WINS Server as follows:

- The Push and Pull buttons permit an administrator to send push or pull messages to only the selected WINS Servers, whereas the Replicate Now button initiates replication with all partners.

- The Push with Propagation box causes the selected WINS Servers to obtain new WINS database entries from the WINS Server that sent the message. When the selected WINS Servers receive new entries, they propagate the push message to all their pull partners. If the selected WINS Servers do not receive any new entries, they do not propagate the push message.

Forcing Replication

You can replicate the database between partners immediately instead of waiting for the start time or replication interval specified in the Preference dialog box. You may want to begin replication immediately after you make a series of changes, such as entering a range of static address mappings.

To send a replication trigger

1. In the Replication Partners dialog box, select the WINS Servers to which you want to send a replication trigger and then choose the Push or Pull button, depending on whether you want to send the trigger to push partners or pull partners.

   Optionally, you can check the Push with Propagation box if you want the selected WINS Server to propagate the trigger to all of its pull partners after it has pulled in the latest information from the source WINS Server. If it has the same or more up-to-date replicas than the source WINS Server, it does not propagate the trigger to its pull partners.

   If Push with Propagation is not checked, the selected WINS Server does not propagate the trigger to its other partners.

To start replication immediately

In the Replication Partners dialog box, choose the Replicate Now button.

Configuring WINS Clients

When TCP/IP is installed on a workstation, you can configure it to use a WINS Server to resolve computer names to IP addresses by supplying the IP addresses of a primary and secondary WINS Server.

A Windows NT Server version 4.0 operating as a WINS Server can support the following operating systems as WINS Clients:

- Windows NT Workstation version 4.0
- Windows NT Server version 4.0

- Windows for Workgroups 3.11 (WFWG), with the Microsoft 32-bit TCP/IP VxD installed

- Microsoft Network Client for MS-DOS with real-mode TCP/IP driver, which is one of the clients included on the Windows NT Server version 4.0 CD

- LAN Manager for MS-DOS 2.2c, which is included on the Windows NT Server version 4.0 CD

Note

If a DHCP Server is used to supply an IP address and other configuration information to DHCP Clients, the DHCP Server can also be configured to supply WINS configuration information. To supply the necessary WINS configuration information to DHCP Clients, the DHCP Server must have the following DHCP Options:

- 044 WINS/NBNS Servers configured with the IP address of one or more WINS Servers

- 046 WINS/NBT Node Type set to 0x1 (b-node), 0x2 (p-node), 0x4 (m-node), or 0x8 (h-node) (for more information on the node types, see the section, *NetBIOS over TCP/IP Name Resolution Methods,* in Chapter 16, *Understanding TCP/IP.*

Using WINS Manager

When you install a WINS Server, Windows NT adds WINS Manager to the Network Administration group in Program Manager. You can use WINS Manager to view and change parameters for any WINS Server on the internetwork. To administer a WINS Server remotely, run WINS Manager on a Windows NT Server computer that is not a WINS Server. You must log on as a member of the Administrators group for a WINS Server to configure that server.

To start WINS Manager

1. Double-click the WINS Manager icon in Program Manager.

Note

At the command prompt, type **start winsadmn** and press Enter. You can include a WINS Server name or IP address with the command.

2. If the Windows Internet Name Service is running on the local computer, that WINS Server opens automatically for administration. If the Windows Internet Name Service is not running when you start WINS, the Add WINS Server dialog box appears, as described in the following procedure.

Note

If you specify an IP address when connecting to a WINS Server, the system connects using TCP/IP. If you specify a computer name, the system connects over NetBIOS.

To connect to a WINS Server for administration

1. In the WINS Manager window, select a server in the WINS Servers list. This list contains all WINS Servers to which you previously connected or have been reported by partners of this WINS Server.

   Or

   If you want to select another server to which you have not previously connected, choose the Add WINS Server command from the Server menu.

2. In the WINS Server box of the Add WINS Server dialog box, type the IP address or computer name of the WINS Server with which you want to work and then choose the OK button. (You do not have to include double backslashes before the name. WINS Manager adds these for you.)

The title bar in the WINS Manager window shows the IP address or computer name for the currently selected server, depending on whether you used the address or name to connect to the server. WINS Manager also shows some basic statistics for the selected server, as described in Table 19-3. You can display additional statistics by choosing the Detailed Information command from the Server menu.

Table 19-3	Statistics in WINS Manager
Statistic	*Meaning*
Database Initialized	The last time static mappings were imported into the WINS database.
Statistics Cleared	The last time statistics for the WINS Server were cleared with the Clear Statistics command from the View menu.
Last Replication Times	The last time the WINS database was replicated.
Periodic	The last time the WINS database was replicated based on the replication interval specified in the Preferences dialog box.
Admin Trigger	The last time the WINS database was replicated because the administrator chose the Replicate Now button in the Replication Partners dialog box.
Net Update	The last time the WINS database was replicated as a result of a network request, which is a push notification message that requests propagation.
Total Queries Received	The number of name query request messages received by this WINS Server. Successful indicates how many names were successfully matched in the database, and Failed indicates how many names this WINS Server could not resolve.

(continued)

Table 19-3 *(Continued)*

Statistic	Meaning
Total Releases	The number of messages received that indicate a NetBIOS application has shut itself down. Successful indicates how many names were successfully released, and Failed indicates how many names this WINS Server could not release.
Total Registrations	The number of messages received that indicate name registrations for clients.

To see detailed information about the current WINS Server

1. From the Server menu, choose the Detailed Information command.

   The Detailed Information dialog box shows information about the selected WINS Server, as described in Table 19-4.

2. To dismiss the Detail Information dialog box, choose the Close button.

Table 19-4 Detailed Information Statistics for WINS Manager

Statistic	Meaning
Last Address Change	Indicates the time at which the last WINS database change was replicated.
Last Scaveng-ing Times	Indicates the last times that the database was cleaned for specific types of entries.
Periodic	Indicates when the database was cleaned based on the renewal interval specified in the WINS Server Configuration dialog box.
Admin Trigger	Indicates when the database was last cleaned because the administrator chose the Initiate Scavenging command.
Extinction	Indicates when the database was last cleaned based on the Extinction interval specified in the WINS Server Configuration dialog box.
Verification	Indicates when the database was last cleaned based on the Verify interval specified in the WINS Server Configuration dialog box.
Unique Registrations	Indicates the number of name registration requests that have been accepted by this WINS Server.
Unique Conflicts	Indicates the number of conflicts encountered during registration of unique names owned by this WINS Server.
Unique Renewals	Indicates the number of renewals received for unique names.

Statistic	Meaning
Group Registrations	Indicates the number of registration requests for groups that have been accepted by this WINS Server.
Group Conflicts	Indicates the number of conflicts encountered during registration of group names.
Group Renewals	Indicates the number of renewals received for group names.

Setting preferences for WINS Manager

You can configure several options for administration of WINS Servers. The commands for controlling preferences are on the Options menu.

To set preferences for WINS Manager

1. From the Options menu, choose the Preferences command.

2. To see all of the available preferences, choose the Partners button in the Preferences dialog box.

3. Select an Address Display option to indicate how you want address information to be displayed throughout WINS Manager — as a computer name, an IP address, or an ordered combination of both.

Note

Remember that the kind of address display affects how a connection is made to the WINS Server — for IP addresses, the connection is made via TCP/IP; for computer names, the connection is made via named pipes.

4. Check Auto Refresh if you want the statistics in the WINS Manager window to be refreshed automatically. Then enter a number in the Interval box to specify the number of seconds between refresh actions.

   WINS Manager also refreshes the statistical display automatically each time an action is initiated while you are working in WINS Manager.

5. Check the LAN Manager-Compatible check box if you want computer names to adhere to the LAN Manager naming convention.

   LAN Manager computer names are limited to 15 characters, as opposed to 16-character NetBIOS names used by some other sources, such as Lotus Notes. In LAN Manager names, the 16th byte is used to indicate whether the device is a server, workstation, messenger, and so on. When this option is checked, WINS adds and imports static mappings with 0, 0x03, and 0x20 as the 16th byte.

   All Windows networking, including Windows NT, follows the LAN Manager convention. So this box should be checked unless your network accepts NetBIOS names from other sources.

6. Check Validate Cache Of Known WINS Servers At Startup Time if you want the system to query the list of servers each time the system starts to find out if each server is available.

7. If you want a warning message to appear each time you delete a static mapping or the cached name of a WINS Server, check the Confirm Deletion Of Static Mappings And Cached WINS Servers option.

8. In the Start Time box, specify the default for replication start time for new pull partners. Then specify values for the Replication Interval to indicate how often data replicas are exchanged between the partners. The minimum value for the Replication Interval is 40 minutes.

9. In the Update Count box, specify a default for how many registrations and changes can occur locally before a replication trigger is sent by this server when it is a push partner. The minimum value is 5.

10. When all options are set for your preferences, choose the OK button.

Managing static mappings

Static mappings are permanent lists of computer-name-to-IP-address mappings that cannot be challenged or removed, except when an administrator removes the specific mapping. You use the Static Mappings command in WINS Manager to add, edit, import, or delete static mappings for clients on the network that are not WINS-enabled.

WINS static mappings are useful when it is important that a specific system, such as an important server, is always able to register its computer name. For example, if a user setting up a system happens to choose a computer name that matches the server's computer name, problems could occur. For example, if the server is down when the user boots the new system, the server cannot register its name when it tries to boot because another computer has already registered with the same name. A WINS static mapping avoids this problem by preventing the user's system from registering the server's computer name as its own.

Caution

If your network also uses DHCP, a reserved (or static) IP address overrides any WINS Server settings. Do not assign static mappings to WINS-enabled computers.

To view static mappings

1. From the Mappings menu, choose the Static Mappings command.

Caution

You cannot cancel changes made to the WINS database while working in the Static Mappings dialog box. You must manually delete any entries that are added in error or manually add back any entries that you mistakenly delete. This is because all changes made to the WINS database in this dialog box take effect immediately.

2. In the Static Mappings dialog box, select a Sort Order option, either by IP address or by computer name. This selection determines the order in which entries appear in the list of static mappings.

3. To edit or add a mapping, follow the procedures described in *Adding static mappings* and *Editing static mappings*.

4. To remove existing static mappings, select the mappings you want to delete from the list and then choose the Delete Mapping button.

5. To limit the range of mappings displayed in the list of static mappings, choose the Set Filter button and follow the procedure in *Filtering the range of mappings* later in this chapter. To turn off filtering, choose the Clear Filter button.

6. When you finish viewing or changing the static mappings, choose the Close button.

Adding static mappings

You can use either of two methods to add static mappings to the WINS database for specific IP addresses:

- Type static mappings in a dialog box

- Import files that contain static mappings

To add static mappings to the WINS database by typing entries

1. In the Static Mappings dialog box, choose the Add Mappings button.

2. In the Name box of the Add Static Mappings dialog box, type the computer name of the system for which you are adding a static mapping. (You do not need to type two backslashes because WINS Manager adds these for you.)

3. In the IP Address box, type the address for the computer.

   If Internet Group or Multihomed is selected as the Type option, the dialog box shows additional controls for adding multiple addresses. Use the down-arrow button to move the address you type into the list of addresses for the group. Use the up-arrow button to change the order of a selected address in the list.

4. Select a Type option to indicate whether this entry is a unique name or a group with a special name, as described in Table 19-5.

5. Choose the Add button.

   The mapping is immediately added to the database for that entry, and the boxes are cleared so that you can add another entry.

6. Repeat this process for each static mapping you want to add to the database and then choose the Close button.

Table 19-5	Type Options for Static Mappings
Type option	*Meaning*
Unique	Unique name in the database, with one address per name.
Group	Normal group, where addresses of individual members are not stored. The client broadcasts name packets to normal groups.
Internet Group	Groups with NetBIOS names that have 0x1C as the 16th byte. An internet group stores a maximum of 25 addresses for members. For registrations after the 25th address, WINS overwrites a replica address, or if none is present, it overwrites the oldest registration.
Multihomed	Unique name that can have more than one address (multihomed computers). The maximum number of addresses is 25. For registrations after the 25th address, WINS overwrites a replica address, or if none is present, it overwrites the oldest registration.

Note

Because each static mapping is added to the database when you choose the Add button, you cannot cancel work in this dialog box. If you make a mistake in entering a name or address for a mapping, you must return to the Static Mappings dialog box and delete the mapping there.

You can use the Import Mappings button to import the contents of an LMHOSTS file into the WINS database as static mappings for unique and group names. Performing an import does not require an actual LMHOSTS file. You can select any file, but it must have the same format as the LMHOSTS file.

When importing from an LMHOSTS file, the WINS database ignores keywords other than #DOM. For entries in the file that include #DOM, an internet group static mapping is created, and the IP addresses from the file are added to the group for that domain.

You can also import entries for static mappings for unique and special group names from any file that has the same format as the LMHOSTS file. The WINS database ignores scope names and keywords other than #DOM. However, you can add normal group and multihomed names only by typing entries in the Add Static Mappings dialog box.

To import a file containing static mapping entries

1. In the Static Mappings dialog box, choose the Import Mappings button.

2. In the Select Static Mapping File dialog box, which is similar to the standard Windows NT Open dialog box, specify a filename for a static mappings file by typing its name in the box or by selecting one or more filenames in the list. Then choose the OK button to import the file.

The specified file is read, and a static mapping is created for each computer name and address. If the #DOM keyword is included for any record, an internet group is created (if it is not already present), and the address is added to that group.

Editing static mappings

You can change the IP addresses in static mappings owned by the WINS Server you are currently administering.

To edit a static mapping entry

1. In the Static Mappings dialog box, select the mapping you want to change and choose the Edit Mapping button, or double-click the mapping entry in the list.

    You can view, but not edit, the Computer Name and Mapping Type option for the mapping in the Edit Static Mappings dialog box.

2. In the IP Address box, type a new address for the computer and then choose the OK button. The change is made in the WINS database immediately.

If you want to change the computer name or group type related to a specific IP address, you must delete the entry and redefine it in the Add Static Mappings dialog box.

Filtering the range of mappings

You may want to limit, or filter, the range of IP addresses or computer names displayed in the Static Mappings or Show Database dialog boxes.

You can specify a portion of the computer name or IP address or both when filtering the list of mappings.

To filter mappings by address or name

1. In the dialog box for Static Mappings or Show Database, choose the Set Filter button.

2. In the Set Filter dialog box, type portions of the computer name, address, or both in the Computer Name or IP Address boxes.

    You can use the asterisk (*) wildcard for portions of the name or address or both. For example, you could type \\acct* to filter all computers with names that begin with acct. However, for the address, a wildcard can be used only for a complete octet. That is, you can type 11.101.*.*, but you cannot enter 11.1*.1.1 in these boxes.

3. Choose the OK button.

The selected range is displayed in the Static Mappings or Show Database dialog box. The filtered range remains until you clear the filter. A message tells you if no mappings match the range you specified, and the list of mappings is empty. If a filter is in effect for the range of mappings, the Clear Filter button is available for restoring the entire list.

To clear the filtered range of mappings

In the Static Mappings or Show Database dialog box, choose the Clear Filter button. The list now shows all mappings found in the database.

Managing the WINS database

Because your WINS Server uses the same database format as the DHCP Server (a modified Access database), it has the same basic issues.

The following files are stored in the *systemroot*\\SYSTEM32\\WINS directory that is created when you set up a WINS Server:

- JET.LOG is a log of all transactions done with the database. This file is used by WINS to recover data if necessary.

- SYSTEM.MDB is used by WINS for holding information about the structure of its database.

- WINS.MDB is the WINS database file.

- WINSTMP.MDB is a temporary file that WINS creates. This file may remain in the \\WINS directory after a crash.

You should back up these files when you back up other files on the WINS Server.

Caution

The JET.LOG, SYSTEM.MDB, WINS.MDB, and WINSTMP.MDB files should not be removed.

As records are added and deleted, the database grows in size. Its growth affects the performance of the WINS Server. Like any database, the WINS database of address mappings needs to be cleaned and backed up periodically. As your WINS.MDB database approaches 25 to 30 megabytes, you should compact it.

To compact the WINS database

1. At the WINS Server, stop the Windows Internet Name Service using the Control Panel Services option or by typing **net stop wins** at the command prompt.

2. Run COMPACT.EXE (which is found in the *systemroot*\\SYSTEM32 directory) with the following syntax:

```
COMPACT DatabaseName TemporaryDatabaseName
```

where *DatabaseName* is the name of the database to compact and can be a fully qualified pathname, and *TemporaryDatabaseName* is a name to use as a temporary database. It, too, can be a fully qualified pathname.

Caution

Do not compact the SYSTEM.MDB file. This can cause WINS Server service not to start. If you compact it inadvertently, restore your configuration from a previous backup.

3. Restart the Windows Internet Name Service on the WINS Server.

Because there is potential for failure caused by the compact utility or by data corruption on your SystemRoot partition, you should back up your WINS databases regularly — and definitely before you compact them. Before you back up or compact the database you should scavenge (clean) the database to delete old records that are no longer needed.

Working with the WINS Database

The WINS database contains all the address mappings for your WINS Clients. Like any database, it requires a certain amount of maintenance and care. The following sections discuss maintenance issues such as purging entries, compacting the database, and backing up the database.

Scavenging the WINS database

The local WINS database should be cleared periodically of released entries and old entries that were registered at another WINS Server but did not get removed from this WINS database for some reason. This process, called *scavenging*, is done automatically over intervals based on the renewal and extinction intervals in the Configuration dialog box. You can also clean the database manually (for example, if you want to verify old replicas immediately instead of waiting for the specified interval).

The WINS Server automatically performs scavenging in the following manner:

1. If a WINS Client does not renew its name registration before the renewal interval expires, its registration is marked as "released."

2. Once the extinction interval expires for a "released" entry, it is marked as "extinct" in the WINS database.

3. Finally, after the extinction timeout has expired, the "extinct" entry is removed from the WINS database.

Using the default times for all of the intervals and timeouts, a name registration that has not been removed remains in the WINS database for about four hours. If any of the intervals or timeouts have been increased, the entry remains in the database even longer. Therefore, it is possible to use WINS Manager to force the WINS database to be scavenged through the Initiate Scavenging option under the Mappings menu.

To scavenge the WINS database

From the Mappings menu, choose the Initiate Scavenging command. WINS Manager cleans the database and displays its results as shown in Table 19-6.

Table 19-6	Scavenging Results
State before scavenging	*State after scavenging*
Owned active names for which the Renewal interval has expired	Marked *released*
Owned released name for which the Extinction interval has expired	Marked *extinct*
Owned extinct names for which the Extinction timeout has expired	Deleted
Replicas of extinct names for which the Extinction timeout has expired	Deleted
Replicas of active names for which the Verify interval has expired	Revalidated
Replicas of extinct or deleted names	Deleted

Backing up the WINS database

WINS Manager provides backup tools so that you can back up the WINS database. After you specify a backup directory for the database, WINS performs complete database backups every 24 hours, using the specified directory. Make sure to perform a full backup by disabling the Perform Incremental Backup option if you plan to use this copy to restore your configuration. You should also periodically back up the Registry entries for the WINS Server.

To back up a WINS database

1. From the Mappings menu, choose the Backup Database command.

2. In the Select Backup Directory dialog box, specify the location for saving the backup files.

   Windows NT proposes a subdirectory of the \WINS directory. You can accept this proposed directory. However, the most secure location is on another hard disk. Do not back up to a network drive, because WINS Manager cannot restore from a network source.

3. If you want to back up only the newest version numbers in the database (that is, changes that have occurred since the last backup), check Perform Incremental Backup. You must have performed a complete backup before this option can be used successfully.

4. Choose the OK button.

To back up the WINS Registry entries

1. Run REGEDT32.EXE.

2. In Registry Editor, select the HKEY_LOCAL_MACHINE window and then select this key:

    ```
    SYSTEM\CurrentControlSet\Services\WINS
    ```

3. From the Registry menu, choose Save Key.

4. In the Save Key dialog box, specify the path where you store backup versions of the WINS database files. Once the key is saved, close RegEdit.

Troubleshooting WINS Servers

The following error conditions indicate potential problems with the DHCP Server or WINS Server:

- The administrator cannot use WINS Manager to connect to a WINS Server. The message that appears might be, "The RPC server is unavailable."

- The WINS Client service or Windows Internet Name Service is down and cannot be restarted.

If your system develops any of these problems, the first task is to make sure the WINS services are running.

To ensure the WINS services are running

1. Use the Services option in Control Panel to verify that the WINS services are running.

    In the Services dialog box for the client computer, Started should appear in the Status column for the WINS Client service. For the WINS Server itself, Started should appear in the Status column for the Windows Internet Name service.

2. If the necessary service is not started on either computer, start the service.

In rare circumstances, the DHCP Server may not boot, or a STOP error may occur. If the DHCP Server is down, follow these steps to restart it.

To restart a DHCP Server that is down

1. Turn off the power to the server and wait one minute.

2. Turn on the power, start Windows NT Server, and log on under an account with Administrator rights.

3. At the command prompt, type **net start dhcpserver** and press Enter.

Tip

Use Event Viewer to find the possible source of problems with DHCP services.

To locate the source of "duplicate name" error messages

Check the WINS database for the name. If there is a static record, remove it from the database of the primary WINS Server.

Or

In the Registry, set the value of MigrateOn to 1, so the static records in the database can be updated by dynamic registrations (after WINS successfully challenges the old address).

To locate the source of "network path not found" error messages on a WINS Client

Check the WINS database for the name. If the name is not present in the database, check whether the computer uses b-node name resolution. If so, add a static mapping for it in the WINS database.

If the computer is configured as a p-node, m-node, or h-node and if its IP address is different from the one in the WINS database, it may be that its address changed recently, and the new address has not yet replicated to the local WINS Server. To get the latest records, ask the WINS Server that registered the address to perform a push replication with propagation to the local WINS Server.

To discover why a WINS Server cannot pull or push replications to another WINS Server

1. Confirm that the router is working.

2. Ensure that each server is correctly configured as either a pull or push partner:

   ■ If Server A needs to perform pull replications with Server B, make sure that it is a push partner of Server B.

   ■ If Server A needs to push replications to Server B, it should be a pull partner of WINS Server B.

To determine why WINS backup is failing consistently

Make sure the path for the WINS backup directory is on a local disk on the WINS Server. WINS cannot back up its database files to a remote drive.

If you have determined that the Windows Internet Name Service is running on the WINS Server but you cannot connect to the server using WINS Manager, the WINS database is not available or has becomes corrupted. If a WINS Server fails for any reason, you can restore the database from a backup copy.

You can use the menu commands to restore the WINS database or restore it manually.

To restore a WINS database using menu commands

1. From the Mappings menu, choose the Restore Database command.

2. In the Select Directory To Restore From dialog box, select the location where the backup files are stored and then choose the OK button.

To restore a WINS database manually

1. In the *systemroot*\SYSTEM32\WINS directory, delete the JET.LOG, JET*.LOG, WINS.TMP, and SYSTEM.MDB files.

2. From the Windows NT Server installation source, copy SYSTEM.MDB onto the WINS Server. The installation source can be the Windows NT Server compact disc, the installation floppy disks, or a network directory that contains the master files for Windows NT Server.

3. Copy an uncorrupted backup version of WINS.MDB to the *systemroot*\SYSTEM32\WINS directory.

4. Restart the Windows Internet Name Service on the WINS Server.

Summary

This chapter focused on implementing the DHCP and WINS services on your network. It covered

▶ Basic planning issues

▶ Management options for manipulating your DHCP and WINS Clients

▶ Issues when utilizing DHCP and WINS in a mixed Windows NT and UNIX environment

▶ How to prepare for a failure with the services database

▶ Basic performance tips

Part VI

Windows NT Services

Chapter 20

Installing a Worldwide Web HTTP Server

In This Chapter

▶ Installing the EMWAC HTTP Server

▶ Configuring the HTTP Server

▶ Working with WAIS

T he HTTP Server for Windows NT, developed by the European Microsoft Windows NT Academic Center (EMWAC), implements the HTTP/1.0 protocol. It runs as a Windows NT service, just like the FTP Server that comes with Windows NT. In comparison to the UNIX HTTP Server daemon, which is called *httpd,* the Windows NT HTTP Server service is called *https.* The HTTP Server service is configured using a Control Panel applet.

Windows NT HTTP Server Installation

The HTTP Server is distributed in three versions — for the Intel, MIPS, and DEC Alpha architectures — which are all included on the CD-ROM that accompanies this book. Select the appropriate distribution ZIP file according to your system's platform or processor.

To install HTTP Server, you must log on to your Windows NT system as a user with administrative privileges.

1. Unzip the appropriate distribution file into a temporary directory. When you unzip the distribution file, you should have the following files:

HTTPS.EXE	The HTTP Server itself
HTTPS.CPL	The Control Panel applet
HTTPS.HLP	The Control Panel applet Help file
HTTPS.DOC	EMWAC manual in Word for Windows format
HTTPS.PS	EMWAC manual in PostScript ready for printing

HTTPS.WRI	EMWAC manual in Windows Write format
EGSCRIPT.ZIP	Sample CGI script programs
COPYRITE.TXT	The copyright statement for the software
READ.ME	Summary of new features

2. Copy HTTPS.EXE, HTTPS.CPL, and HTTPS.HLP into the *\WINNT*\SYSTEM32 directory, where *\WINNT* is the name of your Windows NT directory.

3. Start the Control Panel from the Program Manager. You should see an icon representing the HTTP Server applet in the Control Panel.

4. Determine which version of HTTPS you have. To display the version number, at the Windows NT command prompt, type **HTTPS -VERSION**

   (At the time of this writing, .094 is the latest version of the HTTPS software. However, the CD-ROM that comes with this book may contain a later version. If so, unzip and print the corresponding manual from the CD-ROM.)

5. Next, check the IP address of your machine using the following command: **HTTPS -IPADDRESS.**

   This command displays the name of your machine (for example, valda.cpress.com) and its IP address as reported by the Windows Sockets API. If this information is incorrect, you need to reconfigure the TCP/IP software on your machine. The HTTP Server will not work if this address (or list of addresses, if your machine has more than one network interface) is incorrect.

   Because you start, stop, and pause the HTTP Server through the Services option in the Control Panel, you must install HTTPS into the table of Windows NT Services. Installing HTTPS as a service also registers it with the Event Logger so you can log errors to an Event Log and view them with the Event Viewer.

6. To install HTTPS as a Windows NT Service, type **HTTPS -INSTALL** at the Windows NT command line.

   The program registers itself with the Service Manager and with the Event Logger and then reports success or failure. If the installation fails at this point, refer to the section called *Troubleshooting installation problems* later in this chapter.

Note You must execute this command using the copy of HTTPS.EXE that you placed in the *\WINNT*\SYSTEM32 directory. Do not use any other copy, especially if you plan to delete.

7. To verify that the installation has succeeded, start the Windows NT Control Panel and double-click on the Services icon. The resulting dialog box should list HTTP Server as one of the installed services. If so, see the Configuration section of this manual for further instructions.

Installing over a previous version of HTTPS

If you have an older version of HTTPS installed on your machine, you must remove that version before you install a later version.

To remove an older version of the HTTP Server, type **HTTPS -REMOVE** at the command prompt.

Note

You can use either the version you already have installed or the new version of HTTPS.EXE to perform this Remove operation. *If you are replacing version 0.7 or earlier with version 0.8 or later, read the next section.*

Upgrading from Version 0.7 or Earlier to Version 0.8 or Later

With version 0.8, the "short name" by which the HTTP Service is known to the operating system changed from HTTP Server to HTTPS. This means that the Windows NT Registry stores information about the service in a different place from earlier versions. If you are upgrading from an earlier version of HTTPS, this change has two consequences:

■ The information stored in the Registry by the earlier version of HTTPS must be deleted. This can be done by running the earlier version of HTTPS from the command line with the -REMOVE flag. Alternatively, version 0.8 or later (when you run it with the -REMOVE option) detects whether information relating to version 0.7 or earlier is present in the Registry; if so, it deletes it. Both methods have been observed to cause the Event Log Service to terminate with an access violation occasionally. This is harmless — just restart the Event Log Service from the Services dialog box in the Control Panel.

■ When you replace version 0.7 or earlier with 0.8 or later, any events recorded in the Event Log by the earlier version will be unintelligible. This is because you deleted the information in the Registry that tells the Event Viewer program where to find the HTTPS.EXE file.

Troubleshooting installation problems

Occasionally, installation does not go as smoothly as you would like. Here are some common problems.

The system says that HTTPS is not a Windows NT program.

Check to make sure that you are running the correct executable for your system's processor. If not, unzip the correct distribution ZIP file for your processor type.

The system says that the HTTP Service won't install because of a "duplicate service name."

You must remove a previous version of the HTTP before installing a later version. See the section, *Installing over a previous version of HTTPS*.

HTTPS waits for a while and then terminates with a "usage" message.

You cannot run HTTPS from the command line or from File Manager without a command-line argument. The HTTPS program is a Windows NT "service" and must be started through the Services dialog box in the Control Panel.

Removing the HTTP Server

The following steps describe what to do if you want to remove the HTTP Server from your computer or if you want to move the program to a new location.

1. If the HTTP Server is running, stop it by clicking on the Stop button in the Services dialog box in the Control Panel. (Check to see if anyone is accessing the service before you shut it down.)

2. At the Windows NT command line, type **HTTPS -REMOVE** to remove the HTTP Server from the Service Manager's list of services.

3. If you want to remove the HTTP Server entirely, delete the HTTPS.EXE program, the HTTPS.CPL Control Panel applet, and the HTTPS.HLP files.

4. If you want to move HTTPS.EXE to a new location, first move the file to its target directory, then type **HTTPS - INSTALL.** This command informs the Service Manager and Event Logger of the new location of the program. To use the HTTP Server, you must start it again from the Control Panel.

HTTPS Configuration

You configure the HTTP Server by using the HTTP Server applet in the Control Panel.

Launch the HTTP Server applet to bring up the configuration dialog box, as shown in Figure 20-1.

Note

The dialog box displays the version number of the HTTP Server applet in the lower left-hand corner. The version number reported by the HTTPS -VERSION command must be the same as the version number of the HTTP Server applet. If there is no version number in the lower left-hand corner, you are using version 0.2 of the applet.

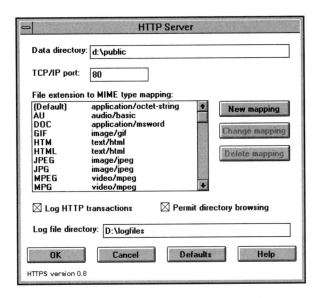

Figure 20-1: The HTTP Server configuration dialog box.

To configure the HTTP Server

- Specify a data directory in the Data directory field. The default directory is D:\HTTP. The Data directory may be located on a disk which uses the FAT, HPFS, or NTFS file systems. If you want to place the Data directory somewhere other than on a local drive, be sure to read the section, *Putting the Data directory on a file server,* later in the chapter.

- Indicate the port that TCP/IP should monitor by inserting a positive integer representing a legal and otherwise unused port in the TCP/IP port field. The default port is 80.

Note

TCP/IP uses port addressing (a 16-bit address) to deliver information to the appropriate layer services. There are a number of defined ports ranging from 0 to 255 that have been allocated for most common application layer services, such as Telnet and FTP. For a complete listing, see the Well-Known Ports List (filename WELLPORT.TXT) on the CD-ROM that accompanies this book.

- Specify the MIME type that corresponds to a given filename extension. Refer to the next section for more detailed information.

- If you want the HTTP Server to record each HTTP request it receives in a log file, check the Log HTTP transactions box.

- Specify the directory that will contain the log file in the Log file directory field. The default directory is the Windows system directory (\WINNT). (This option is disabled unless the Log HTTP transactions box is checked.)

When you have finished making changes to the configuration, click on the OK button. The changes take effect the next time you start the HTTP Server. If the HTTP Server is already running, a dialog box appears reminding you to stop and restart the HTTP Server.

Specifying file extension to MIME type mapping

The HTTP protocol represents the type of each file as a MIME type/subtype pair. The HTTP Server infers the MIME type of file from the filename extension by using a mapping table. You can configure the mapping table by using the list in the Control Panel applet and the buttons to its right, which are labeled New Mapping, Change Mapping and Delete Mapping (see Figure 20-1). The default contents of the mapping table are as follows:

File extension	MIME type
(Default)	application/octet-string
AU	audio/basic
DOC	application/msword
GIF	image/gif
HTM	text/html
HTML	text/html
JPEG	image/jpeg
JPG	image/jpeg
MPEG	video/mpeg
MPG	video/mpeg
PDF	application/pdf
PS	application/postscript
RTF	application/rtf
TIF	image/tiff
TIFF	image/tiff
TXT	text/plain
WAV	audio/wav
XBM	image/x-xbitmap
ZIP	application/zip

To add a new mapping to the table, press the New mapping button in the HTTP Server configuration dialog box. A dialog box like the one in Figure 20-2 appears.

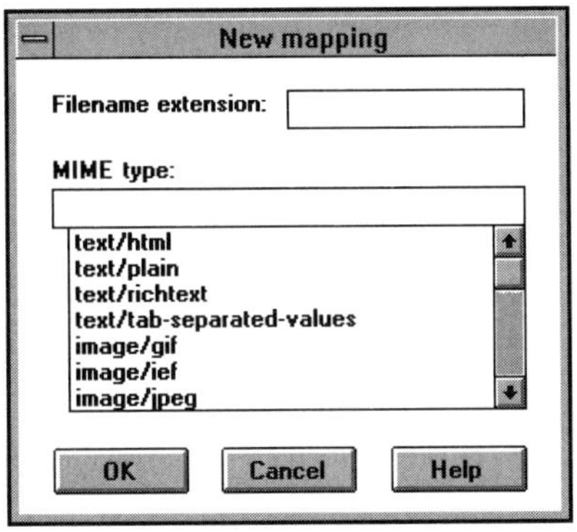

Figure 20-2: The New mapping dialog box.

Type the extension that you want to map into the Filename extension field and select the MIME type to which you want it mapped (or enter the MIME type yourself if it's not in the list). Then press OK to add the new mapping to the main list. Note that you cannot create a new mapping for a filename extension that is already in the mapping list — an extension may only occur once in the list.

To change an existing mapping, select it from the list in the main HTTP Server dialog box, and click on the Change mapping button. A dialog box, similar to the New mapping box shown in Figure 20-2, will appear. You can use this box to change the filename extension or to select a new MIME type (or both).

To delete an existing mapping, select it from the list in the main HTTP Server dialog box, and click on the Delete mapping button.

Putting the Data directory on a file server

If the directory you want to make available to HTTP clients is located on a file server instead of on the local Windows NT machine, you need to take special steps.

Normally, directories on the file server are mapped to a drive letter on the local system. You might expect that simply using the mapped drive letter in the HTTP Server configuration dialog box would have the desired effect, and indeed it does — until you log off the local machine.

Drive mappings are established only when someone logs on to the Windows NT machine. They are specific to a user, not to the machine. The HTTP Server is normally kept running, whether someone is logged on to the machine or not. Often, it is set to start up automatically when the operating system loads, when no one is logged on, and, therefore, no drive mappings are in effect. To make a directory available in these circumstances, you can specify the HTTP Data directory in the HTTP configuration dialog box using a UNC (Universal Naming Convention) form of directory name, for instance,

`\\CLYDE\INFOSERVER`

Here, CLYDE is the name of the server, and INFOSERVER is the sharename of the directory that is to be served using HTTP.

Using the Services dialog box

You use the Services dialog box in the Windows NT Control Panel to manage the HTTPS operation.

After you install HTTPS, you can start it by launching the Services applet in the Control Panel, selecting HTTP from the list of services, and pressing the Start button. Upon successful startup, the HTTP Server appears in the list of services with status "Started," ready to respond to HTTP clients.

If the service fails to start, see the section, *Troubleshooting,* later in this chapter.

Starting HTTPS Automatically

If you want HTTPS to start automatically when the system is started, configure the service startup as follows:

Note

To configure service startup, you must be logged on to a user account that has membership in the Administrators local group.

1. In the Control Panel window, choose the Services icon.

2. In the Services dialog box, select the HTTP Service.

3. Click on the Startup button.

4. In the Service Startup dialog box, select a startup type (Automatic, Manual, or Disabled).

5. To specify the user account for the service to use to log on, select System Account or This Account.

6. If you select This Account, also choose the Browse button and specify a user account by completing the Add User dialog box that appears.

   After closing the Add User dialog box, type the password for the user account in both the Password and Confirm Password boxes.

7. If you want the service to provide a user interface on the desktop that can be used by whoever is logged on when the service is started, mark the Allow Service to Interact with Desktop check box. (This option can be used only if the service is running as a LocalSystem account.)

8. Choose the OK button and then choose the Close button in the Services dialog box.

Pausing the HTTP Server

Choosing the Pause button in the Services dialog box to pause the HTTP Server causes the following behavior:

- Any HTTP transactions currently under way are unaffected. They will run to completion.

- New HTTP connections are queued. When the service is resumed, they are accepted and processed.

- If more than five incoming connections are received while the service is paused, the extra connections are rejected.

Error logging

If an error occurs during server operation, the error is logged in the Application Event Log. You can view this log with the Event Viewer, which is located in the Administrative Tools program group in the Program Manager.

Note

The Event Viewer uses the HTTPS.EXE program to interpret messages associated with events. If you remove the HTTPS.EXE file, the HTTP Server events in your Application Event Log become unintelligible.

The errors logged in the Application Event Log are usually associated with an HTTPS problem (for example, a file I/O error, a system call failure caused by lack of resources, or a problem with the configuration information).

Problems associated with the client (for example, the client sends a URL that points to a file that does not exist) are recorded in the Application Event Log as Warning events.

When the HTTP Server is started or stopped, Information events are recorded in the Application Event Log.

HTTP transaction logging

If you checked the Log HTTP transactions box in the HTTP Server configuration dialog box, it records a line of information in a log file for every HTTP request that the Server receives. The log file is stored in the Log file directory, as specified via the HTTP Server configuration dialog box.

A new log file is created every day. The filename uses the form HS*YYMMDD*.LOG, so that, for instance, the file corresponding to 4 July 1995 would be HS950704.LOG. For performance reasons, the current log file is kept open until the first HTTP transaction of the following day. When this transaction occurs, the preceding day's log file is closed, a new log file is opened, and the transaction is logged to it.

The following information is recorded in the log file:

- The time and date of the request
- The IP address of the server
- The IP address of the client
- The HTTP command
- The URL requested
- The version of the HTTP protocol used (if there is no version, HTTP 0.9 is in use)

The HTTP Directory and URLs

The HTTP Data directory is the directory where you put files that you want to make available to HTTP clients. Directories in the file system above the Data directory or on other disks are not accessible to HTTP clients. The Data directory can be located on a disk that uses the FAT, HPFS, or NTFS file systems.

URLs are relative to the Data directory. Thus, if the HTTP client asks for a URL of the form

```
HTTP://MYMACHINE.MYDOMAIN.AC.UK/MYDIR/MYFILE.HTM
```

the HTTP Server sends a file called MYFILE.HTM in the MYDIR subdirectory of the Data directory.

Files with the hidden or system attributes are ignored (that is, treated as if they don't exist).

The Data directory tree must be accessible by the user ID under which HTTPS runs. Normally, this is the SYSTEM user ID. By default, any file in the Data directory tree for which the SYSTEM user has read permission can be retrieved by any HTTP client. If you want to prevent access to a particular file, use the Security/Permissions menu option in the File Manager to ensure that the SYSTEM user cannot access that file. Remember that the SYSTEM user is in the Administrator's group (even though it does not appear in the User Manager list of members).

Browsing the HTTP directory tree

Suppose that an HTTP client asks for a URL of the form

```
HTTP://MYMACHINE.MYDOMAIN.AC.UK/MYDIR
```

where MYDIR is a directory. The HTTP Server responds in one of three ways, depending on the contents of the directory and how the directory is configured:

1. If a file called DEFAULT.HTM exists in the MYDIR directory, the HTTP Server sends that file to the client.

2. Otherwise, if directory browsing is enabled, the Server sends a list of files and subdirectories within MYDIR to the client.

3. If directory browsing is not enabled, the Server sends an error message to the client.

Thus, directory browsing enables a user to navigate through the Data directory according to its hierarchical structure — rather like Gopher. You can enable directory browsing using the HTTP Server Control Panel configuration applet.

If you don't want to allow browsing of a particular directory, create a file called NOBROWSE and place it in the directory. The file's contents are irrelevant — its presence causes Step 2 to be omitted. Note that the top-level Data directory may also have a DEFAULT.HTM or NOBROWSE file.

WAIS Index Searches

The HTTP Server can search local WAIS (Wide Area Information Server) databases. Before reading this section, you should read the WAIS Toolkit for Windows NT manual. (The manual should be available where you obtained this HTTP Server software.) When the Server receives an HTTP GET command for a URL, which denotes an HTML file and includes a search term, the HTTP Server passes the filename and the search term to the WAISLOOK program. The output from the WAISLOOK program is passed back to the client as an HTML document containing the result of the search. Note that the name of the HTML file must be the same as the name of the WAIS database (apart from the extension). Also, to ensure that the HTTP Server can execute the WAISLOOK program, make sure that the WAISLOOK.EXE file resides in the *WINNT*\SYSTEM32 directory.

There are a number of ways to exploit the search capabilities of the HTTP Server and the WAIS Toolkit (which is on the CD-ROM that accompanies this book). The following example indicates one way of using these capabilities.

Example: A simple index of text files

This example illustrates how to set up an index for a very common situation: You have a large number of text files (for example, an archive of Usenet news messages) that you want to allow HTTP clients to search.

Prepare the Directory Structure

Let's assume that the HTTP Data directory is E:\WEB, where drive E is on an NTFS partition. Within that directory, you've created a subdirectory, NEWS, to hold a number of newsgroup indexes. Under NEWS, you've created a directory ALT.ATHEISM for that newsgroup. Now, you want to create a directory of files under ALT.ATHEISM that is to hold the actual news messages, one to each file.

Here is the directory tree in graphical form:

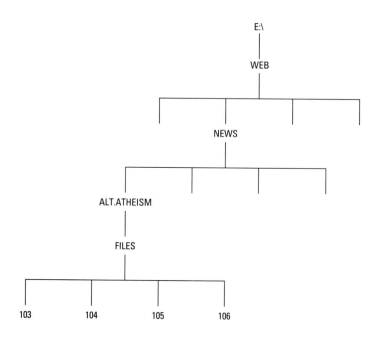

The news messages in this example have filenames that do not include extensions. Normally, such messages are mapped by the mapping table to MIME type application/octet-string, which is not appropriate for these files. Therefore, you should configure the (Default) extension mapping in the HTTP Server configuration dialog box so that these files are returned as text/plain by the HTTP Server.

Index the Messages

Using a Windows NT command prompt, change to the HTTP Data directory (E:\WEB). Now you must run the INDEX command so that the filenames in the filename table created by the indexing program are related to the HTTP Data directory.

To run the INDEX command, enter the following text:

```
WAISINDEX -D NEWS\ALT.ATHEISM\INDEX -T NETNEWS
NEWS\ALT.ATHEISM\FILES\*
```

This command creates the following files: INDEX.SRC, INDEX.INV, and ETC in the E:\WEB\NEWS\ALT.ATHEISM directory.

Test the Index

To verify that the index functions correctly, enter the WAISLOOK command to examine it:

```
WAISLOOK -D NEWS\ALT.ATHEISM\INDEX RELIGION
```

This command should return a list of files and headlines that contain the word *religion*.

Create the HTML File

Now, you need to create an HTML file that invites the user to search the index. In the E:\WEB\NEWS\ALT.ATHEISM directory, create a file named INDEX.HTM that looks something like this:

```
<TITLE>SEARCH THE ALT.ATHEISM NEWS ARCHIVE.</TITLE>
<BODY>
<P>
PLEASE ENTER THE TERM(S) TO SEARCH FOR.
<ISINDEX>
</BODY>
```

Note that the HTML file must have the same name and path as the database, but (of course) it should have an HTM or HTML extension to identify it as an HTML file according to the extension mapping table.

If the HTTP client user retrieves this file, she can enter a search term (because of the <ISINDEX> tag). When she types RETURN (or otherwise initiates a request), the client requests a URL such as

```
HTTP://MYHOST.MYDOMAIN.AC.UK/NEWS/ALT.ATHEISM/INDEX.HTM?SEARCH+WORDS
```

The HTTP Server invokes the WAISLOOK program to search the index and returns an HTML file containing the list of matching messages.

Update the Index

When a new message (say, 107) arrives in the E:\WEB\NEWS\ALT.ATHEISM\FILES directory, you should run the WAISINDEX command to update the index. Change to the E:\WEB directory, and issue the command

```
WAISINDEX -D NEWS\ALT.ATHEISM\INDEX -T NETNEWS -A
NEWS\ALT.ATHEISM\FILES\107
```

This adds the new file to the directory. Normally, of course, you would arrange for this command to be executed automatically in a batch file.

Scripts and Forms

The HTTP Server conforms to the Common Gateway Interface (CGI) 1.1 standard (see HTTP://HOOHOO.NCSA.UIUC.EDU/CGI/). This means that you can write your own programs (known as CGI scripts) that can be invoked by WWW clients and run on the Windows NT machine that is running HTTPS. CGI scripts can, for instance, be used to provide a gateway between WWW and a database package or to process user input read from an HTML form.

Script execution

A script is an executable Windows NT program with an .EXE extension. It must be located within the HTTP Data directory tree, and it must be a Windows NT console application — one which can, in principle, be used from the Windows NT command line. A script cannot be a GUI program or another Windows NT Service. Because of a bug in Windows NT 3.1, a script cannot be a DOS program, either.

Full details of how to write CGI scripts are given in the CGI specification referred to before. Briefly, the script accesses information about how it was invoked through environment variables, reads any information supplied by the client in a POST request via STDIN, and sends output to the client through STDOUT. The file EGSCRIPT.ZIP contains two example scripts (executable and C source) and a corresponding makefile. The makefile assumes you have the Windows NT Software Developer's Kit (SDK) installed. (However, you don't have to have the SDK to write scripts.)

A CGI script executes under the following circumstances:

■ When the HTTP Server receives a POST request for a URL that corresponds to an executable file.

■ When the HTTP Server receives a GET request for a URL that corresponds to an executable file and contains a query string.

If the script is specified in a GET request *without* a query string in the URL, the script is sent to the client as an application/octet-string file (or to whatever the .EXE extension corresponds in the mapping table). If you do not want to allow users to download your script like this, you should use the File Manager to assign execute-only permission to the script, so that it can't be read by the SYSTEM user.

Using forms with HTTPS

HTML lets you create *forms* that allow the user to submit information (such as a complex database query) to an HTTP Server. A description of how to create forms can be found at

`HTTP://HOOHOO.NCSA.UIUC.EDU/SDG/SOFTWARE/MOSAIC/DOCS/FILL-OUT-FORMS/OVERVIEW.HTML`

A client program can submit a form using either the GET or POST method. The query string (in GET) or the body of the request message (in POST) contains the data entered into the form by the user. See the scripts in EGSCRIPT.ZIP for an example of how to decode the data from a form.

Here is an example form defined in HTML:

```
<head><title>A test form</title></head>
<body>
A test form for checking out the POST method in HTTPS. <p>
<form action="http://host.domain.edu/scripts/egscript.exe"
method="POST">
Field 1 (text entry field) <input type="text" name="field1"> <p>
Field 2 (checkbox) <input type="checkbox" name="field2"> <p>
Field 3 (radio buttons)<br>
<input type="radio" name=field3 value="Male" checked> Male<BR>
<input type="radio" name=field3 value="Female"> Female <BR>
<input type="radio" name=field3 value="Neuter"> Neuter<BR>
<p>
Field 4 (select)
<select name="field4">
<option> First
<option> Second
<option> Third
<option> Fourth
</select>
<p>
Field 5 (textarea) <textarea name=field5 rows=4 cols=40>
</textarea>
<p>
Field 6 (submit) <input type="submit" value="Go">
</form>
</body>
```

The action attribute of the form is the URL of the script. In this example, the method attribute is POST.

If the action attribute of the example form is changed to

```
HTTP://HOST.DOMAIN.EDU/SCRIPTS/EGSCRIPT.EXE/FOO/BAR
```

the script program SCRIPTS/EGSCRIPT.EXE still executes. The /FOO/BAR part is passed to the script in the PATH_INFO environment variable. It is not a good idea to create directories with names ending in .EXE — the server can become confused.

Command-line parameters

If a script is invoked with a URL that includes a query string, for instance,

```
HTTP://HOST.DOMAIN.EDU/SCRIPTS/PERL.EXE/FOO/BAR?MYSCRIPT.PL
```

the query string is passed to the script in the command line. Thus, this example would result in the following command being executed:

```
SCRIPTS\PERL.EXE MYSCRIPT.PL
```

This is a useful mechanism for executing scripts in interpreted languages, where the executable program is the interpreter itself.

The query string is decoded before being passed to the command line; any "+" characters are replaced by spaces, and any %*XX* sequences (where *XX* is two hex digits) are replaced by the corresponding ASCII character. (If required, the undecoded query string is available to the script in the QUERY_STRING environment variable.)

Note

If the undecoded query string contains an "=" character, the CGI specification states that the query string shall not be passed to the script in the command line. If you want to pass an "=" in the command line, encode it in the URL as %3D.

Supported environment variables

The CGI standard specifies certain environment variables that are used for conveying information to a CGI script. The following subset of these environment variables is supported by HTTPS:

```
CONTENT_LENGTH
CONTENT_TYPE
GATEWAY_INTERFACE
HTTP_ACCEPT
PATH_INFO
QUERY_STRING
REMOTE_ADDR
REQUEST_METHOD
SCRIPT_NAME
SERVER_NAME
SERVER_PROTOCOL
SERVER_PORT
SERVER_SOFTWARE
```

Other HTTP headers received from the client are available in environment variables of the form HTTP_*. For instance, the User-Agent: header value is available in HTTP_USER_AGENT. Note that "-" in the header name is replaced by "_" in the corresponding environment variable name.

Clickable Images

The HTTP Server supports the use of *clickable images*. In other words, it can return different documents depending on where the user clicks the mouse in an image.

Here is a typical example of a clickable image document in HTML:

```
<html>
<head><title>WWW Servers in UK</title><head>
<body>
<h1>WWW Servers in the UK</h1>
<hr>
```

To have a server added to the map send email to:

```
<a href="http://www.ed.ac.uk/webperson.html">
<address>webperson@ed.ac.uk</address>
</a>
<p>
<hr>
<a href="/ukmap.map">
<img src="/Images/ukmap.gif" ismap>
</a>
<hr>
</body>
```

Note the use of the ISMAP attribute in the IMG tag. This attribute tells the client to append the mouse coordinates to the URL when the client sends the coordinates to the server.

The URL in the enclosing <A> anchor element must refer to a map file on the HTTP Server with the extension .MAP. This file contains information about how to map the coordinates of the mouse click to another URL. The mapped-to URL is the one actually returned to the client.

Map file format

A *map file* is a text file consisting of definitions, comments, and blank lines. Comment lines start with a #. Definition lines have one of the following four forms:

```
default URL
circle x y r URL
rectangle x0 y0 x1 y1 URL
polygon x0 y0 x1 y1 x2 y2 ... URL
```

The keywords may be abbreviated to DEF, CIRC, RECT, and POLY, respectively.

The default keyword defines the URL to be used if the mouse click falls outside any other shape defined in the file. There must always be a default statement in the map file.

The circle statement defines a circle with center *(x,y)* and radius *(r)* and the URL to use if the mouse click lies within the circle.

The rectangle statement defines a rectangle with top left at *(x0,y0)* and bottom right at *(x1,y1)* and the URL to use if the mouse click lies within the rectangle.

The polygon statement defines a polygon with vertices at *(x0,y0)*, *(x1,y1)*, *(x2,y2)*, and so on (up to 100 vertices) and the URL to use if the mouse click lies within the polygon.

The coordinates are measured from the top left-hand corner of the image. The coordinates can be separated within the statement by any combination of blank spaces, tabs, commas, and parentheses, as shown in the following example. (This means that you can use image configuration files in exactly the same format as for the CERN HTTPD Server.)

The *URL* at the end of each line can either point to a local file (in which case, it must start with a forward slash), or it can refer to a document on another server (in which case, it must be a full URL). In the latter instance, the HTTP Server sends a "302 Found" redirection message containing the URL in question to the client. Clients that are capable of understanding the redirection message automatically fetch the document. Other clients display an explanatory message containing a hyperlink to the document.

Here is an example map file. Suppose that your image is 1000 by 1000 pixels in size.

```
# Circle at centre of image
circle (500,500) 100 /local/file.htm

# Rectangle at lower right
rectangle 550 550 850 850 http://some.other.host.uk/some/file.html

# Triangle at lower left
polygon 10,700 200,700 10,900 /another/local/file.htm

# Use this URL if mouse is outside any of above shapes
default /error.htm
```

Note that there is a slight overlap between the circle and the rectangle. If the mouse click occurs in the overlap, the first matching shape in the file determines the URL to be returned — in this case, the circle.

Troubleshooting

This section lists some of the problems that you may have in running the HTTP Server and describes how to overcome them.

Errors starting the HTTP Server

When starting the HTTP Server, you may see one of the following error messages:

Could not start the HTTP Server service on \\yourmachine.
Error 0002: The system cannot find the file specified.

The Service Manager could not locate HTTPS.EXE. This probably means that it has been moved or has not been installed correctly. Remove and reinstall HTTPS according to the instructions given earlier in this chapter.

Could not start the HTTP Server service on \\yourmachine.
Error 0005: Access is denied.

HTTPS.EXE is inaccessible to the SYSTEM user. By default, the Service Manager starts the HTTP Server process under a user ID of SYSTEM. The executable file for the service must be readable by this user.

Could not start the HTTP Server service on \\yourmachine.
Error 2140: An internal Windows NT error occurred.

This message usually indicates a problem with the configuration of the HTTP Server. Further information detailing the precise problem is recorded in the Application Event Log. A description of some of the most common errors is given below.

Errors recorded in the Event Log

This section records some of the error messages that may appear in the Application Event Log. Many of these are self-explanatory.

Windows Sockets library function "bind" failed. The address or port is already in use.

One of the following situations may cause this error:

- The TCP/IP port you have specified in the HTTP Server configuration dialog box is conflicting with another application. Choose a different port number.

- The IP address that the HTTP Server is using is incorrect. Start the Network Control Panel applet and configure the TCP/IP software to use the correct IP address.

Windows Sockets library function "accept" failed. The call was canceled.

This indicates that the HTTP Server terminated abnormally for some reason. Restart the service.

Registry Entries

HTTP Server makes several entries to the Windows NT Registry. A number of other entries are added to the Registry implicitly by the Service Control Manager. The entries in this section are not guaranteed to remain the same between releases of the HTTP Server (for instance, there were significant changes between versions 0.7 and 0.8). The information is intended for advanced users of Windows NT who understand the function and structure of the Registry.

The Service Control Manager creates the following entry in the HKEY_LOCAL_MACHINE database:

```
SYSTEM\CurrentControlSet\Services\HTTPS
```

Under this entry, the HTTP Server itself creates a Parameters key containing the following configuration entries.

Entry name	Entry type	Description
Directory	REG_SZ	HTTP Data directory name
PortNo	REG_DWORD	TCP/IP port number
DefaultMIMEType	REG_SZ	MIME type used for file extensions not listed explicitly
BrowsingEnabled	REG_DWORD	Non-zero if browsing is enabled
LogDirectory	REG_SZ	Directory where log files are stored
LoggingEnabled	REG_DWORD	Non-zero if logging is enabled
ExtensionMapping	See below	

The ExtensionMapping entry holds the mapping table. It contains a key name for each file extension, and the value of the key (type REG_SZ) is the corresponding MIME type.

Formal Command Syntax

The formal description of the HTTPS command options follows:

Syntax: HTTPS [-REMOVE | -INSTALL] [-VERSION] [-IPADDRESS]

Description: The HTTPS command installs or removes the HTTP Server.

Options: The following list contains the options available for use with the HTTP Server command.

-install   Adds the HTTP Server to the list of installed services. Make sure that you are executing a copy of HTTPS.EXE that you aren't planning to delete later.

-remove   Removes the HTTP Server from the list of installed services. This also deletes the HTTP Server configuration information from the Registry.

-version   Reports the version number of the HTTP Server.

-ipaddress   Reports the IP addresses on which the HTTP Server is listening.

Unresolved Problems

The following problems exist on HTTP Server and have not been resolved yet — usually because EMWAC has not been able to duplicate the problem.

Sluggish CGI programs

Some beta testers have reported that CGI scripts return their output to the client with excruciating slowness. This seems to depend somewhat on the client software — Macintosh clients did not experience the problem whereas Windows clients did.

Possibly there is some problem with the TCP/IP implementation in the client or in Windows NT.

Problems retrieving GIF files

Some users have reported that GIF files that appear in-line within an HTML document are not being retrieved correctly. The error message indicates that the file is unavailable. This problem seems to depend on client software.

Problems with multiple network interfaces

Some users have reported that the support for multiple network interfaces does not function and only one interface is listened on.

Chapter 21

Installing a Gopher Server

In This Chapter
▶ Installing GOPHERS

▶ Operating GOPHERS

▶ Working with WAIS databases

The Gopher Server for Windows NT implements the "classic" gopher protocol, as described in RFC 1436. It runs as a Windows NT "service," just like the FTP Server that comes with Windows NT. In comparison to the UNIX gopher server daemon which is called *GOPHERD*, the Windows NT Gopher Server service is called *GOPHERS*, pronounced "gopher-ess."

GOPHERS Installation

The Gopher Server is distributed by the European Microsoft Windows NT Academic Center (EMWAC) in three versions — for the Intel, MIPS, and DEC Alpha architectures — and are all included on the CD-ROM accompanying this book. Select the appropriate distribution ZIP file according to your system's platform or processor.

1. Unzip the distribution file into a temporary directory. When you unzip the distribution file, you should have the following files:

GOPHERS.EXE	The Gopher Server itself
GOPHERS.CPL	The Control Panel applet
GOPHERS.HLP	The Control Panel applet Help file
GOPHERS.DOC	The EMWAC manual in Word for Windows format
GOPHERS.WRI	The EMWAC manual in Windows Write format
GOPHERS.PS	The EMWAC manual in PostScript ready for printing
COPYRITE.TXT	The copyright statement for this product
READ.ME	Summary of new features

2. Log on to your Windows NT system as a user with administrative privileges.

3. Copy GOPHERS.EXE, GOPHERS.CPL, and GOPHERS.HLP into the *WINNT*\SYSTEM32 directory, where *WINNT* is the name of your Windows NT directory.

4. Start the Control Panel from the Program Manager. You should see an icon representing the Gopher Server applet in the Control Panel.

5. Determine which version of GOPHERS you have. To display the version number, at the Windows NT command prompt, type **GOPHERS -VERSION**.

   At the time of this writing, .91 is the latest version of the GOPHERS software. However, the CD-ROM that comes with this book may contain a later version; if so, unzip and print out the corresponding manual from the CD-ROM.

6. Next, check the IP address of your machine using the following command: **GOPHERS -IPADDRESS**.

   This command displays the name of your machine (for example, valda.cpress.com) and its IP address as reported by the Windows Sockets API. If this information is incorrect, you must reconfigure the TCP/IP software on your machine. The GOPHERS Server will not work if this address (or list of addresses, if your machine has more than one network interface) is incorrect.

   Because you start, stop, and pause the GOPHER Server through the Services option in Control Panel, you must install GOPHERS into the table of Windows NT Services. Installing GOPHERS as a service also registers it with the Event Logger so that you can log errors to an Event Log and view them with the Event Viewer.

7. To install GOPHERS as a Windows NT Service, type **GOPHERS -INSTALL** at the Windows NT command line.

   The program registers itself with the Service Manager and with the Event Logger and then reports success or failure. If the installation fails at this point, refer to the section *Troubleshooting installation problems* later in this chapter.

Note You must execute this command using the copy of GOPHERS.EXE that you placed in the *WINNT*\SYSTEM32 directory. Do not use any other copy, especially if you plan to delete it.

8. To verify that the installation has succeeded, start the Windows NT Control Panel and double-click on the Services icon. The resulting dialog box should list GOPHERS Server as one of the installed services. If so, see the Configuration section of this manual for further instructions.

9. If you plan to use the WAIS index searching capabilities of the Gopher Server, you should install the WAIS Toolkit for Windows NT, which is also on the CD-ROM that accompanies this book.

Installing over a previous version of GOPHERS

If you have an older version of GOPHERS installed on your machine, you must remove that version before you install a later version.

To remove a previous version of the Gopher Server, type **GOPHERS -REMOVE** at the command prompt.

Note

You can use either the version you already have installed or the new version of GOPHERS.EXE to perform this remove operation. *If you are replacing version 0.7 or earlier with version 0.8 or later, read the next section.*

Upgrading from Version 0.7 or Earlier to Version 0.8 or Later

With version 0.8, the "short name" by which the Gopher Service is known to the operating system changed from Gopher Server to GOPHERS. This means that the Windows NT Registry stores information about the service in a different place from earlier versions. If you are upgrading from an earlier version of the Gopher Server, this change has two consequences:

- The information stored in the Registry by the earlier version of GOPHERS must be deleted. Do this by running the earlier version of GOPHERS from the command line with the -REMOVE flag. Alternatively, version 0.8 or later (when you run it with the -REMOVE option) will detect whether information relating to version 0.7 or earlier is present in the Registry, and if so it will delete it. However, both methods have been observed to cause the Event Log Service to terminate with an access violation occasionally. This is harmless — just restart the Event Log Service from the Services dialog box in the Control Panel.

- When you replace version 0.7 or earlier with version 0.8 or later, any events recorded in the Event Log by the earlier version will be unintelligible. This is because you deleted the information in the Registry that tells the Event Viewer program where to find the GOPHERS.EXE file.

Troubleshooting installation problems

Occasionally, installation does not go as smoothly as you would like. Here are some common problems:

The system says that GOPHER.EXE is not a Windows NT program.

Check to make sure that you are running the correct executable for your system's processor. If not, unzip the correct distribution ZIP file for your processor type.

The system says that the Gopher Service won't install because of a "dupli-cate service name."

You must remove a previous version of the GOPHERS before installing a later version. See the earlier section, *Installing over a previous version of GOPHERS.*

GOPHERS waits for a while and then terminates with a "usage" message.

You cannot run GOPHERS from the command line or from File Manager, except with a command-line argument. The GOPHERS program is a Windows NT Service and must be started through the Services dialog box in the Control Panel.

"Create Service Failed with error: service already installed."

This error message occurs if you type GOPHERS -INSTALL when the Gopher Server is already installed. You cannot install two Gopher Servers.

Removing GOPHERS Server

The following steps describe how to remove the GOPHERS Server from your computer or move the program to a new location.

1. If the GOPHERS Server is running, stop it by using the Stop button in the Services dialog box in the Control Panel. (Check to see if anyone is accessing the service before you shut it down.)
2. At the Windows NT command line, type **GOPHERS -REMOVE** to remove the GOPHERS Server from the Service Manager's list of services.
3. If you want to remove the GOPHERS Server entirely, delete the GOPHERS.EXE program, the GOPHERS.CPL Control Panel applet, and the GOPHERS.HLP files.
4. If you want to move GOPHERS.EXE to a new location, first move the file to its target directory, and then type **GOPHERS -INSTALL**.

   This command informs the Service Manager and Event Logger of the new location of the program. For this change to take effect, you must start the GOPHERS Server again from the Control Panel.

GOPHERS Configuration

You configure the GOPHERS Server using the GOPHERS Server applet in the Control Panel.

Launch the GOPHERS Server applet to bring up the configuration screen as shown in Figure 21-1.

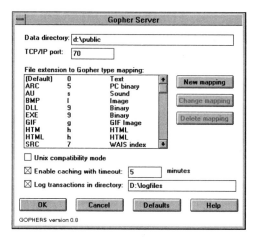

Figure 21-1: The Gopher Server configuration dialog box.

The dialog box displays the version number of the GOPHERS Server applet in the lower left-hand corner. The version number reported by the GOPHERS -VERSION command must be the same as the version number of the GOPHERS Server applet. If there is no version number in the lower left-hand corner, you are using version 0.2 of the applet.

To configure the GOPHERS Server

■ Specify a data directory in the Data directory field. The default directory is D:\GOPHERS. The data directory can be located on a disk that uses the FAT, HPFS, or NTFS file systems. If you want to place the data directory somewhere other than on a local drive, be sure to read the section, *Putting the Gopher directory on a file server,* later in the chapter.

■ Indicate the port that TCP/IP should monitor by inserting a positive integer representing a legal and otherwise unused port in the TCP/IP port field. The default port is 80.

TCP/IP uses port addressing (a 16-bit address) to deliver information to the appropriate layer services. There are a number of defined ports ranging from 0 to 255 that have been allocated for most common application layer services, such as Telnet and FTP. For a complete listing, see the CD-ROM that accompanies this book.

■ If you want to keep a log, check the Log transactions in directory box to instruct the GOPHERS Server to record each GOPHERS request that it receives in a log file. Logging is disabled by default.

Specify the directory to contain the log file in the Log file directory field. The default directory is the Windows system directory (\WINNT). This option is disabled unless the Log transactions box is checked.

■ Specify the GOPHERS type that corresponds to a given filename extension. Refer to the section, *File extension to GOPHERS type mapping,* for more detailed information.

■ Enable or disable caching. The default setting is for caching disabled.

Specify the timeout interval (in minutes) after which Gopher's cache files will be deemed to be out of date. Specify 0 to prevent cache files from being timed out. The default is five minutes.

■ Enable or disable a special UNIX compatibility mode. If this mode is enabled, GOPHERS pays attention to files in the data directory with names starting with a dot. It treats such files (and also the .CAP directory, if any) in the same way as the UNIX GOPHERD program does. Do not enable this option if you set the data directory to point to a FAT volume, because directory and filenames cannot begin with a dot on FAT volumes. The default is disabled.

When you have finished making changes to the configuration, click on the OK button. The configuration will take effect the next time you start the Gopher Server. If the Gopher Server is already running, a dialog box appears reminding you to stop and restart it.

File extension to Gopher type mapping

The Gopher protocol represents the type of each file in a single byte. Several different types are defined in the protocol. The Gopher Server infers the type of file from the filename extension by using a mapping table. You can configure the mapping table by using the list in the Control Panel applet and the buttons on the right-hand side, labeled New mapping, Change mapping, and Delete mapping (see Figure 21-1). The default contents of the mapping table are as follows:

File extension	*Gopher type*	*Meaning*
ARC	5	Binary archive
AU	s	Sound
BMP	I	Windows bitmap
DLL	9	Binary
EXE	9	Binary
GIF	g	GIF image
HTM	h	HTML
HTML	h	HTML
SRC	7	WAIS index
TXT	0	Text file
UUE	6	UUencoded
ZIP	5	Binary archive

To create a new mapping, click on the New mapping button. A dialog box, similar to the Change mapping box shown in Figure 21-2, will appear. You can use this box to specify the filename extension and to select the corresponding Gopher type. Note that you cannot create a new mapping for a filename extension that is already present in the mapping list — an extension may only occur once in the list. To change a mapping that already exists, select it from the list and click the Change mapping button. A dialog box like the one in Figure 21-2 will be displayed.

Figure 21-2: The Change mapping dialog box.

You can alter the extension you want to map by using the Filename extension field and selecting the Gopher type to which you want it mapped (or you can type in the Gopher type character if it's not in the list). Then select OK to confirm your changes.

To delete an existing mapping, select it from the list in the main Gopher Server dialog box and click on the Delete mapping button.

If there is no entry in the mapping table for a particular extension, the Gopher Server will use the default extension mapping. This mapping is shown in the list with (Default) in the File extension column. You can change the default extension mapping in the same way as other mappings, but you cannot delete it.

Putting the Gopher directory on a file server

If the directory tree that you want to make available to Gopher clients is located on a file server instead of on the local Windows NT machine, you will need to take special steps.

Normally, directories on the file server are mapped to a drive letter on the local system. You might expect that simply using the mapped drive letter in the Gopher Server configuration dialog box would have the desired effect, and indeed it does — until you log off the local machine.

Drive mappings are established only when someone logs on to the Windows NT machine. They are specific to a user, not to the machine. The Gopher Server is normally kept running, whether or not someone is logged on to the machine. Often, it is set to start up automatically when the operating system loads, when no one is logged on. Therefore, no drive mappings are in effect.

To make the directory available in these circumstances, you can specify the Gopher data directory to the Gopher configuration dialog box using a UNC form of directory name, for instance,

```
\\CLYDE\INFOSERVER
```

Here, CLYDE is the name of the server, and INFOSERVER is the sharename of the directory that is to be served using Gopher.

Using the Services dialog box

You use the Services dialog box in the Windows NT Control Panel to manage GOPHERS operation.

After you install GOPHERS, you can start it by launching the Services applet in the Control Panel, selecting GOPHERS from the list of services, and then pressing the Start button. Upon successful startup, the GOPHER Server appears in the list of services with status "Started" and is ready to respond to GOPHER clients.

If the service fails to start, see the section, *Troubleshooting,* later in this chapter.

Starting GOPHERS Automatically

If you want GOPHERS to start automatically when the system is started, configure the service startup as follows:

Note

To configure service startup, you must be logged on to a user account that has membership in the Administrators local group.

1. In the Control Panel window, click on the Services icon.

2. In the Services dialog box, select the GOPHERS service.

3. Click on the Startup button.

4. In the Service Startup dialog box, select a startup type (Automatic, Manual, or Disabled).

5. To specify the user account for the service to use to log on, select System Account or This Account.

6. If you select This Account, also choose the Browse button and specify a user account by completing the Add User dialog box that appears.

   After closing the Add User dialog box, type the password for the user account in both the Password and Confirm Password boxes.

7. If you want the service to provide a user interface on the desktop that can be used by whoever is logged on when the service is started, mark the Allow Service to Interact with Desktop check box. (This option can be used only if the service is running as a LocalSystem account.)

8. Choose the OK button, and then in the Services dialog box, choose the Close button.

Pausing the GOPHER Server

Using the Pause button in the Services dialog box causes the following behavior:

- Any GOPHER transactions currently underway are unaffected. They will run to completion.

- New GOPHER connections are queued. When the service is resumed, the new connections are accepted and processed.

- If more than five incoming connections are received while the service is paused, the extra connections are rejected.

Error logging

If an error occurs during server operation, the error is logged in the Application Event Log. You can view this log with the Event Viewer, which is located in the Administrative Tools program group in the Program Manager.

Note

The Event Viewer uses the GOPHERS.EXE program to interpret messages associated with events. If you remove the GOPHERS.EXE file, the GOPHER Server events in your Application Event Log become unintelligible.

The errors logged in the Application Event Log are usually associated with a GOPHERS problem (for example, a file I/O error, a system call failure caused by lack of resources, or a problem with the configuration information).

Problems associated with the client (for example, the client sends an invalid GOPHER selector or a selector that points to a file that does not exist) are recorded in the Application Event Log as Warning events.

When the GOPHER Server is started or stopped, Information events are recorded in the Application Event Log.

Gopher transaction logging

If you check the Log transactions box in the Gopher Server configuration dialog box, the server records a line of information in a log file for every request that it receives. The log file is stored in the Log file directory, which can also be configured in the configuration dialog box.

A new log file is created every day. The filename is of the form GS*YYMMDD*.LOG, for instance, the file corresponding to 4 July 1995 would be GS950704.LOG. For performance reasons, the current log file is kept open until the first transaction of the following day. When this transaction occurs, the preceding day's log file is closed, a new log file is opened, and the transaction is logged to it.

The following information is recorded in the log files:

- The time and date of the request
- The IP address of the server
- The IP address of the client
- The Gopher selector string sent by the client

The Gopher Directory Tree

The Gopher directory (also known as the Data directory) is the root of the directory tree that GOPHERS makes available to Gopher clients. Directories within the tree are treated as Gopher menus, and files are treated as Gopher documents. Points in the file system above the Gopher directory, or on other disks, are not accessible to Gopher clients. The Gopher directory can be located on a disk that uses the FAT, HPFS, or NTFS file systems.

The Gopher directory must be accessible by the user ID under which GOPHERS runs. By default, this is the SYSTEM user ID.

Files with hidden or system attributes are ignored by GOPHERS.

Link files

The Gopher Server treats files ending with .GFR (or, in UNIX compatibility mode, files starting with a dot) in a special way. They are assumed to contain link information, which points to another Gopher server.

The format of such link files is very similar to the equivalent for the UNIX GOPHERD program. The file contains a number of key=value pairs, one to each line. Here is a typical example of a link file:

```
NAME=THE EDINBURGH UNIVERSITY GOPHER SERVER
HOST=GOPHER.ED.AC.UK
PORT=70
NUMB=5
PATH=
TYPE=1
```

The Name gives a user-friendly string, which is displayed instead of the filename in the Gopher menu. The Host is the name of the computer on which the linked-to server resides, and the Port is the TCP/IP port number for the server. (Specifying a + sign for the Host or Port means "use this Gopher server's host name or port number.") The Numb is a number that is used to control the order in which items appear in the Gopher menu (all numbered items appear in order before all unnumbered items). The Path (empty in this example) is the Gopher selector for the linked-to directory or file. The Type is the Gopher type character for the linked-to object, which overrides the type inferred from the filename extension mapping.

The case of the keyword to the left of the equals (=) sign is not significant. The order of the lines in the file are not significant.

Here is another example of a link file. This file contains three links, which must be separated by a line containing a single hash (#) character.

```
NAME=GOPHERS IN THE UK
HOST=PCSERVER2.ED.AC.UK
PORT=70
TYPE=1
PATH=1/GOPHERS/OUR_LINKS
#
NAME=GO STRAIGHT TO MY DATA
HOST=+
PORT=+
TYPE=0
PATH=0\DATA\MINE\MYDATA.TXT
#
NAME=GOPHERS IN EUROPE
HOST=SUNIC.SUNET.SE
PORT=70
TYPE=1
PATH=1/OTHER GOPHER AND INFORMATION SERVERS/EUROPE
```

The first and third links in the file point to other Gopher servers. The second link points to a file in the Gopher directory tree on this server.

Gopher selectors

In general, the format of the Gopher selector for a file or directory depends on the server software. It is entirely opaque to the Gopher client.

The format of the Gopher selector used by GOPHERS is as follows:

- The first character is the Gopher type of the corresponding item.

- The next character is a backslash.

- Subsequent characters are the pathname of the corresponding file, relative to the Gopher data directory.

For example, consider the Gopher selector used in the example in the preceding section:

```
O\DATA\MINE\MYDATA.TXT
```

The first character indicates that the object is a text file. It and the first backslash are removed to obtain the path (relative to the Gopher Data directory) of the indicated object: The file MYDATA.TXT is in the directory MINE which is a subdirectory of DATA which is a subdirectory of the Gopher Data directory.

Forward slashes may also be used in selectors. The Gopher Server will convert them to backslashes before analyzing the selector.

When you write a link file or an alias file (see the next section), it is important that you make the type character in the selector (the Path=field) the same as the type character in the Type=field.

Note that the format for selectors is different from the format used in GOPHERS version 0.2 (which did not use the leading type character and backslash).

Aliases

Unless special action is taken, a Gopher client will simply use file and directory names when constructing a Gopher menu display. The Gopher protocol allows the server to transmit to the client a "user-friendly name" — an alias — instead of a file or directory name.

The alias information is stored in an alias directory ALIAS.GFR (or .CAP if UNIX compatibility mode is enabled). This directory can exist at each level in the Gopher directory tree. When GOPHERS prepares a menu to transmit to the client, for each file in the directory, it will look in the alias directory for a file with a matching name. If it finds such a file, GOPHERS assumes that the file is in the link file format, as just defined. It will construct a menu entry based on the information in the file.

The Name item contains the user-friendly string for display by the client. The Port and Host items are optional, but if present should indicate the current host and port number (for example, using the "+" convention). The Type item can be used to override the type deduced from the file's extension. The Numb item functions as described before. The Path item must be present if the Type is present, and it usually points to the object being aliased.

Here is an example directory tree:

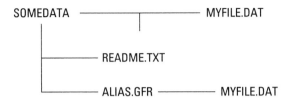

Suppose the file SOMEDATA\ALIAS.GFR\MYFILE.DAT looks like this:

```
NAME=THE DATA FROM MY EXPERIMENT
PATH=9\SOMEDATA\MYFILE.DAT
TYPE=9
```

In this situation, when constructing the menu for the SOMEDATA directory, GOPHERS will arrange for the client to display the string "The data from my experiment" instead of the filename MYFILE.DAT. It will also inform the client that the file is binary (type 9) instead of the default type for extension .DAT (which would be '0' - text — unless GOPHERS has been configured otherwise). Because there is no file called README.TXT in the ALIAS.GFR directory, the client will simply display the name README.TXT in the menu.

If the Name= item is present but empty, the file will not be included in the Gopher menu. This is a good way of "hiding" files so that Gopher clients can't see them.

Caching

To improve performance, the Gopher Server implements a caching strategy. When it creates a menu for a client from a directory, alias files, and link files, it stores the menu in a cache file in the directory called CACHE.GFR (or, in UNIX compatibility mode, .CACHE). The next time it receives a request for a menu from that directory, it uses the cache file. Caching is particularly useful for improving performance when a directory contains a large number of files and aliases.

Because the contents of directories may change, it is important that the cache files are recreated periodically. If the Gopher Server finds a cache file older than a certain timeout period, it recreates it. The cache file timeout period (which is specified in minutes) is configurable in the Gopher Server Control Panel applet. The default is five minutes.

If the cache timeout is set to 0, cache files are never timed out. If you change anything in the Gopher directory, you must delete the cache file for the change to be visible to clients.

Caching may be enabled and disabled using a check box in the Gopher Server configuration dialog box. Note that by default, caching is *disabled*.

UNIX compatibility mode

If you are planning to move a Gopher service from a UNIX platform to Windows NT, you may be interested in the UNIX compatibility mode of GOPHERS.

The UNIX Gopher Server program GOPHERD treats any hidden files (with names starting with a dot) in its directory tree as special cases; they are assumed to contain link information, which points to information on another Gopher server. Files called .CACHE are assumed to contain menu cache information. The GOPHERD program also treats any .CAP directories it finds in a special way: The directory is assumed to contain information about how to display the files in its parent directory.

The Gopher Server for Windows NT offers the same functionality as the GOPHERD program in these respects but uses different filenames. This is because some file systems that Windows NT uses (such as FAT) do not support filenames that begin with a dot.

To cope with a Gopher directory tree that is copied from a UNIX system to a Windows NT system (for example, using the Windows NT RCP command with the -R flag), GOPHERS has a special UNIX compatibility mode. In UNIX compatibility mode, the GOPHERD conventions are employed for GOPHERS: The .CAP directory contains alias information, the .CACHE file is used for cache information, and other files beginning with a dot contain link information. This mode is selected through the Gopher Server configuration dialog box in the Control Panel. It is only available if the Gopher directory is on a volume using a file system that supports filenames starting with a dot.

In Normal mode (the default), GOPHERS will not display files or directories to the client if they have names that start with a dot. This mode is mandatory if the Gopher directory is located on a FAT volume.

WAIS Index Searches

GOPHERS can search local WAIS databases. This section describes how to configure the Gopher Server to do this. Before reading it, you should read the WAIS Toolkit for Windows NT manual. (This manual should be available where you obtained this Gopher Server software.)

By default, files with extension .SRC are treated as type 7 (search files). When a Gopher selector indicating a search file is received from a Gopher client, the Gopher Server passes the filename (and the search term supplied by the user) to the WAISLOOK program. The output from the WAISLOOK program is passed back to the client.

To ensure that the Gopher Server can execute the WAISLOOK program, the WAISLOOK.EXE file should be located in the *WINNT*\SYSTEM32 directory.

There are a number of ways to exploit the search capabilities of the Gopher Server and the WAIS Toolkit. The following example indicates one way of using these capabilities.

Example: A simple index of text files

This example illustrates how to set up an index for a very common situation: You have a large number of text files (for example, an archive of Usenet news messages) that you want to allow Gopher clients to search.

Prepare the Directory Structure

Let's assume that the Gopher Data directory is E:\GOPHER, where drive E is on an NTFS partition. Within that directory, you've created a subdirectory, NEWS, to hold a number of newsgroup indexes. Under NEWS, you've created a directory ALT.ATHEISM for that newsgroup. Now, you're going to create a directory of files under ALT.ATHEISM that is to hold the actual news messages, one to each file. You're also going to create a directory ALIAS.GFR to hold alias files under the NEWS directory.

Here is the directory tree in graphical form:

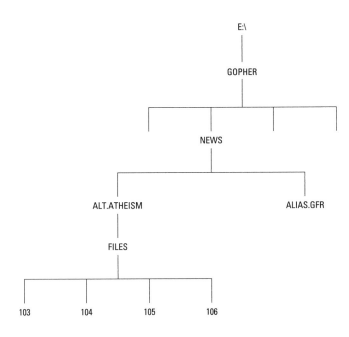

Note that the news messages themselves (in this example) have filenames that are simply numbers.

Index the Messages

Using a Windows NT command prompt, change to the Gopher Data directory (E:\GOPHER). This is so that the filenames in the filename table created by the indexing program will be related to the Gopher Data directory.

Delete the cache file NEWS\ALT.ATHEISM\FILES\CACHE.GFR if it exists and move any link files in NEWS\ALT.ATHEISM\FILES\ out of the way, so that they don't get indexed. Then run the indexing command

```
WAISINDEX -D NEWS\ALT.ATHEISM\INDEX -T NETNEWS
NEWS\ALT.ATHEISM\FILES\*
```

This command will create files called INDEX.SRC, INDEX.INV, and ETC in the E:\GOPHER\NEWS\ALT.ATHEISM directory.

Test the Index

To verify that the index functions correctly, enter the WAISLOOK command to examine it:

```
WAISLOOK -D NEWS\ALT.ATHEISM\INDEX RELIGION
```

This command should return a list of files and headlines that contain the word *religion*.

Create the Alias File

Now, you need to create a menu entry that points to the index. In the E:\GOPHER\NEWS\ALIAS.GFR directory, create a file ALT.ATHEISM that looks like this:

```
NAME=SEARCH THE ALT.ATHEISM NEWS
HOST=+
PORT=+
TYPE=7
PATH=7\NEWS\ALT.ATHEISM\INDEX.SRC
```

If the Gopher client user selects the NEWS directory from the root of the Gopher directory tree, she will see (instead of the ALT.ATHEISM directory) an item in the resulting menu "Search the alt.atheism news." Selecting this menu item will cause the Gopher client to prompt her for a search word. The Gopher Server will invoke the WAISLOOK program to search the index and will return a Gopher menu containing the list of matching messages.

Update the Index

When a new message (say, 107) arrives in the E:\GOPHER\NEWS\ALT.ATHEISM\FILES directory, you should run the WAISINDEX command to update the index. Change to the E:\GOPHER directory, and issue the command

```
WAISINDEX -D NEWS\ALT.ATHEISM\INDEX -T NETNEWS -A
NEWS\ALT.ATHEISM\FILES\107
```

This will add the new file to the directory. Normally, of course, you would arrange for this command to be executed automatically in a batch file.

Troubleshooting

This section lists some of the problems that you may have in running the Gopher Server and describes how to overcome them.

Errors starting the Gopher Server

When starting the Gopher Server, you may see one of the following error messages:

Could not start the Gopher Server service on \\yourmachine.
Error 0002: The system cannot find the file specified.

The Service Manager could not locate GOPHERS.EXE. This probably means that it has been moved or has not been installed correctly. Remove and reinstall GOPHERS according to the instructions earlier in this chapter.

Could not start the Gopher Server service on \\yourmachine.
Error 0005: Access is denied.

GOPHERS.EXE is inaccessible to the SYSTEM user. By default, the Service Manager starts the Gopher Server process under a user ID of SYSTEM. The executable file for the service must be readable by this user.

Could not start the Gopher Server service on \\yourmachine.
Error 2140: An internal Windows NT error occurred.

This usually indicates a problem with the configuration of the Gopher Server. Further information detailing the precise problem will be recorded in the Application Event Log. A description of some of the most common errors follows.

Errors recorded in the Event Log

This section records some of the error messages that may appear in the Application Event Log. Many of these are self-explanatory.

Windows Sockets library function "bind" failed. The address or port is already in use.

One of the following situations may cause this error:

- The TCP/IP port specified in the Gopher Server configuration dialog box conflicts with another application. Choose a different port number.

- The IP address that the Gopher Server is using is incorrect. Start the Network Control Panel applet and configure the TCP/IP software to use the correct IP address.

Windows Sockets library function "accept" failed. The call was canceled.

This message indicates that the Gopher Server terminated abnormally for some reason. Restart the service.

GOPHERS puts the local IP address instead of the host name into menu items that it returns to clients.

GOPHERS.EXE obtains the local host name from the GETHOSTNAME( ) Windows Sockets call. If the name returned by that call is not a fully qualified domain name, the Gopher Server uses the IP address instead of the name.

Registry Entries

Gopher Server makes several entries to the Windows NT Registry. A number of other entries are added to the Registry implicitly by the Service Control Manager. The information in this section is not guaranteed to remain the same between releases of the Gopher Server. It is intended for advanced users of Windows NT who understand the function and structure of the Registry.

The Service Control Manager creates the following entry in the HKEY_LOCAL_MACHINE database:

```
SYSTEM\CurrentControlSet\Services\GOPHERS
```

Under this entry, the Gopher Server itself creates a Parameters key containing the following configuration entries:

Entry name	Entry type	Description
AlternateHostName	REG_SZ	Contains an alternative host name to use when returning Gopher menus
CacheDir	REG_SZ	.CAP or ALIAS.GFR according to UNIX mode setting
CacheFile	REG_SZ	Name of file in which to store cache
CacheTimeout	REG_DWORD	Cache timeout in minutes
CachingEnabled	REG_DWORD	Non-zero if caching is enabled
DefaultFileType	REG_SZ	Gopher-type byte used for files whose extensions are not explicitly mapped
Directory	REG_SZ	Gopher data directory name
ExtensionMapping	See below	
LinkFileExtension	REG_SZ	GFR for normal mode; null string for UNIX mode

Entry name	Entry type	Description
LogDirectory	REG_SZ	Directory where log files are stored
LoggingEnabled	REG_DWORD	Non-zero if logging is enabled
Port	REG_DWORD	TCP/IP port number

The ExtensionMapping entry holds the mapping table. It contains a key name for each file extension, and the value of the key (type REG_SZ) is the corresponding Gopher-type byte.

Note that the AlternateHostName entry is not set by the Control Panel applet. It must be entered manually using a Registry editor — something you should not attempt unless you are very familiar with the Registry.

Formal Command Syntax

The formal description of the GOPHERS command options is as follows.

Syntax: GOPHERS [-REMOVE I -INSTALL] [-VERSION] [-IPADDRESS]

Description: The GOPHERS command installs or removes the Gopher Server.

Options: The following list contains a description of the options that you can use with the GOPHERS command.

-install   Adds the Gopher Server to the list of installed services. (Make sure you are executing a copy of GOPHERS.EXE that you aren't planning to delete later.)

-remove   Removes the Gopher Server from the list of installed services. This will also delete the Gopher Server configuration information from the Registry.

-version   Reports the version number of the Gopher Server.

-ipaddress   Reports the IP addresses on which the Gopher Server is listening.

Chapter 22

Installing a Wide Area Information Server

In This Chapter

▶ Installing the WAIS Server

▶ Operating the WAIS Server

▶ Creating WAIS databases

T he WAIS Server for Windows NT implements a subset of the Z39.50-88 protocol with WAIS-specific extensions. It runs as a Windows NT "service," just like the FTP Server that comes with Windows NT.

WAIS Server Installation

Besides the WAIS Server, you also need to install the WAIS Toolkit files WAISINDEX.EXE and WAISERV.EXE. See Chapter 23, *Installing the WAIS Toolkit,* for details.

To install the WAIS Server

1. Log on to your Windows NT system as a user with administrative privileges.

2. The WAIS Server is distributed in two versions, for the Intel and DEC Alpha architectures. Select the appropriate ZIP file for your processor.

3. Unzip the file. You should have the following files:

WAIS.EXE	The WAIS Server service
WAIS.CPL	The Control Panel applet
WAIS.DOC	This chapter in Word for Windows format
WAIS.WRI	This chapter in Windows Write format
WAIS.PS	This chapter in PostScript ready for printing
COPYRITE.TXT	The copyright statement for this product
READ.ME	Summary of new features

4. Copy WAIS.EXE and WAIS.CPL into the *WINNT*\SYSTEM32 directory, where *WINNT* is the name of your Windows NT directory.

5. Start the Control Panel from the Program Manager. You should see an icon representing the WAIS Server applet in the Control Panel.

6. Determine which version of WAIS you have. To display the version number, at the Windows NT command prompt, type **WAIS -VERSION.**

   At the time of this writing, .094 is the latest version of the WAIS software. However, the CD-ROM that accompanies this book may contain a later version; if so, unzip and print out the corresponding chapter from the CD-ROM.

7. Next, check the IP address of your machine using the following command: **WAIS -IPADDRESS.**

   This command displays the name of your machine (for example, valda.cpress.com) and its IP address as reported by the Windows Sockets API. If this information is incorrect, you need to reconfigure the TCP/IP software on your machine. The WAIS Server cannot work if this address (or list of addresses, if your machine has more than one network interface) is incorrect.

   Because you start, stop, and pause the WAIS Server through the Services option in the Control Panel, you must install WAIS into the table of Windows NT Services. Installing WAIS as a service also registers it with the Event Logger so that you can log errors to an Event Log and view them with the Event Viewer.

8. To install WAIS as a Windows NT Service, type **WAIS -INSTALL** at the Windows NT command line.

   The program registers itself with the Service Manager and with the Event Logger and then reports success or failure. If the installation fails at this point, refer to the section, *Installation problems,* later in this chapter.

Note

You must execute this command using the copy of WAIS.EXE that you placed in the *WINNT*\SYSTEM32 directory. Do not use any other copy, especially if you plan to delete it.

9. To verify that the installation has succeeded, start the Windows NT Control Panel and double-click on the Services icon. The resulting dialog box should list WAIS Server as one of the installed services. If so, see the section, *WAIS Server Configuration,* later in this chapter for further instructions.

Installing over a previous version of WAIS

If you have an older version of WAIS installed on your machine, you must remove that version before you install a later version.

To remove a previous version of the WAIS Server, type **WAIS -REMOVE** at the command prompt.

Upgrading from Version 0.1 to Version 0.2 or Later

With version 0.2, the "short name" by which the WAIS Service is known to the operating system changed from *WAIS Server* to *WAIS*. This means that the Windows NT Registry stores information about the service in a different place from earlier versions. If you are upgrading from version 0.1 of the WAIS Server, this change has two consequences:

■ The information stored in the Registry by the earlier version of WAIS must be deleted. This can be done by running the earlier version of WAIS from the command line with the -REMOVE flag. Alternatively, version 0.2 or later (when you run it with the -REMOVE option) detects whether information relating to version 0.1 is present in the Registry. If so, it deletes it. Both methods occasionally cause the Event Log Service to terminate with an access violation. This is harmless — just restart the Event Log Service from the Services dialog box in the Control Panel.

■ When you replace version 0.1 with 0.2 or later, any events recorded in the Event Log by the earlier version will be unintelligible. This is because you deleted the information in the Registry that tells the Event Viewer program where to find the WAIS.EXE.

Installation problems

Sometimes, installation does not go as smoothly as you would like. Here are some common problems and possible solutions:

The system says that WAIS.EXE is not a Windows NT program.

This is probably because you are trying to run an executable for the wrong sort of processor. Check that you have unpacked the correct ZIP file for your processor type.

WAIS waits for a while and then terminates with a "usage" message.

You must not run WAIS from the command line or from the File Manager, except with the -INSTALL, -REMOVE, -VERSION, or -IPADDRESS options. The WAIS program is a Windows NT Service and must be started through the Services dialog box in the Control Panel.

The system says that the WAIS Service won't install because of a "duplicate service name."

You must remove the previous version of the Gopher Service using the WAIS -REMOVE command before installing with WAIS -INSTALL.

"Create Service Failed with error: service already installed."

This error message occurs if you type WAIS -INSTALL when the WAIS Server is already installed. You cannot install two WAIS Servers.

Removing WAIS Server

The following steps describe how to remove the WAIS Server from your computer or to move the program to a new location.

1. If the WAIS Server is running, stop it by clicking on the Stop button in the Services dialog box in the Control Panel. (Check to see if anyone is accessing the service before you shut it down.)

2. At the Windows NT command line, type **WAIS -REMOVE** to remove the WAIS Server from the Service Manager's list of services.

3. If you want to remove the WAIS Server entirely, delete the WAIS.EXE program, the WAIS.CPL Control Panel applet, and the WAIS.HLP files.

4. If you want to move WAIS.EXE to a new location, first move the file to its target directory, and then type **WAIS -INSTALL.**

   This command informs the Service Manager and Event Logger of the new location of the program. To use the WAIS Server, you must start it again from the Control Panel.

WAIS Server Configuration

You configure the WAIS Server using the WAIS Server applet in the Control Panel.

Launch the WAIS Server applet to bring up the configuration dialog box shown in Figure 22-1.

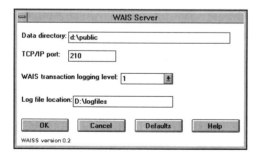

Figure 22-1: The WAIS Server dialog box.

Note

The dialog box displays the version number of the WAIS Server applet in the lower left-hand corner. The version number reported by the WAIS -VERSION command must be the same as the version number of the WAIS Server applet. If there is no version number in the lower left-hand corner, you are using version 0.2 of the applet.

To configure the WAIS Server

■ Specify a data directory in the Data directory field. The default directory is D:\WAIS. The Data directory can be located on a disk that uses the FAT, HPFS, or NTFS file systems. If you want to place the Data directory somewhere other than on a local drive, be sure to read the section, *Putting the Data directory on a file server,* later in this chapter.

■ Indicate the port that TCP/IP should monitor by inserting a positive integer representing a legal and otherwise unused port in the TCP/IP port field. The default port is 210.

Note

TCP/IP uses port addressing (a 16-bit address) to deliver information to the appropriate layer services. A number of defined ports ranging from 0 to 255 have been allocated for most common application layer services, such as Telnet and FTP. For a complete listing, see the CD-ROM that accompanies this book.

■ The WAIS Server records information in a text file about each WAIS request it receives. The list box in the Control Panel lets you select either no logging or a varying amount of logging information up to "full logging" which records everything. The default setting is None.

■ Specify the directory that will contain the log file in the Log file location field. The default directory is the Windows system directory (\WINNT). This option is disabled unless the WAIS transaction logging level is set to 0.

When you have finished making changes to the configuration, click on the OK button. The changes take effect the next time you start the WAIS Server. If the WAIS Server is already running, a dialog box appears reminding you to stop and restart it.

Putting the Data directory on a file server

If the directory tree that you want to make available to WAIS clients is located on a file server instead of on the local Windows NT machine, you need to take special steps.

Normally, directories on the file server are mapped to a drive letter on the local system. You might expect that simply using the mapped drive letter in the WAIS Server configuration dialog box would have the desired effect, and indeed it does — until you log off the local machine.

Drive mappings are established only when someone logs on to the Windows NT machine. They are specific to a user, not to the machine. The WAIS Server is normally kept running, whether someone is logged on to the machine or not. Often, the WAIS Server is set to start up automatically when the operating system loads, when no one is logged on; therefore, no drive mappings are in effect. To make a directory available in these circumstances, you can specify the WAIS Data directory in the WAIS configuration dialog box using a UNC form of directory name, for instance,

\\CLYDE\INFOSERVER

Here, CLYDE is the name of the server, and INFOSERVER is the sharename of the directory that is to be served using WAIS.

Using the Services dialog box

You use the Services dialog box in the Windows NT Control Panel to manage WAIS operation.

After you install WAIS, you can start it by launching the Services applet in the Control Panel, selecting WAIS from the list of services, and then pressing the Start button. Upon successful startup, the WAIS Server appears in the list of services with status "Started" and is ready to respond to WAIS clients.

If the service fails to start, see *Troubleshooting* later in this chapter.

Starting WAIS Automatically

If you want WAIS to start automatically when the system is started, configure the service startup as follows:

Note

To configure service startup, you must be logged on to a user account that has membership in the Administrators local group.

1. In the Control Panel window, choose the Services icon.

2. In the Services dialog box, select the WAIS Service.

3. Click on the Startup button.

4. In the Service Startup dialog box, select a startup type (Automatic, Chapter, or Disabled).

5. To specify the user account for the service to use to log on, select System Account or This Account.

6. If you select This Account, also choose the Browse button and specify a user account by completing the Add User dialog box that appears.

   After closing the Add User dialog box, type the password for the user account in both the Password and Confirm Password boxes.

7. If you want the service to provide a user interface on the desktop that can be used by whoever is logged on when the service is started, mark the Allow Service to Interact with Desktop check box. (This option can be used only if the service is running as a LocalSystem account.)

8. Choose the OK button, and then in the Services dialog box, choose the Close button.

Pausing the WAIS Server

To pause the WAIS Server, select the Pause button in the Services dialog box. This causes the following:

- Any WAIS transactions currently underway are unaffected. They run to completion.

- New WAIS connections are queued. When the service is resumed, these new connections are accepted and processed.

- If more than five incoming connections are received while the service is paused, the extra connections are rejected.

The WAISERV program

When the WAIS Server receives an incoming TCP/IP connection from a WAIS client, WAIS.EXE executes the WAISERV.EXE program. This program reads and writes information to the connection and handles all of the Z39.50 protocol encoding and decoding and the database searching.

WAISERV.EXE is a Windows NT *console* application, meaning that you can execute it from the command line. However, you should only run it from the command line to invoke the -V flag when you want to determine the version of the program. WAISERV.EXE is documented in Chapter 23, *Installing the WAIS Toolkit.*

You should place WAISERV.EXE in *WINNT*\\SYSTEM32 so that WAIS.EXE can find and execute the program.

Error logging

If an error occurs during server operation, the error is logged in the Application Event Log. You can view this log with the Event Viewer, located in the Administrative Tools program group in the Program Manager.

The Event Viewer uses the WAISS.EXE program to interpret messages associated with events. If you remove the WAISS.EXE file, the WAIS Server events in your Application Event Log become unintelligible.

The errors logged in the Application Event Log are usually associated with a system call failure caused by lack of resources or a problem with the configuration information.

When the WAIS Server is started or stopped, Information events are recorded in the Application Event Log.

Problems detected by the WAISERV.EXE program are recorded in the log file rather than in the Event Log.

WAIS transaction logging

If you select anything other than "None" for the WAIS transaction logging level in the WAIS Server configuration dialog box, the WAIS Server records information for every WAIS request it receives.

A new log file is created every day. The filename is of the form WS*YYMMDD*.LOG; therefore, the file corresponding to 4 July 1995 would be WS950704.LOG. You should periodically clear out the log directory.

The WAIS Data directory

The WAIS Data directory is the root of a directory tree within which you must locate files and databases you want to make available to WAIS clients. Points in the file system above the Data directory or on other disks are not accessible to WAIS clients. The Data directory must be located on a disk that uses the HPFS or NTFS file systems, because the indexing process requires long filename support.

The Data directory tree must be accessible by the user ID under which WAIS runs. Normally, this is the SYSTEM user ID.

Creating WAIS databases

You create WAIS databases using the WAISINDEX.EXE program from the WAIS Toolkit for Windows NT. Before reading this section, you should read Chapter 23, *Installing the WAIS Toolkit*.

When the WAISERV.EXE program runs, its current directory is the WAIS Data directory, and all file references are related to that directory. Therefore, when you index a set of files and create a WAIS database (by running the WAISINDEX program), the WAIS Data directory must be the current directory. To run the program, do the following.

Prepare the Directory Structure

Let's assume that the WAIS Data directory is E:\WAIS, where drive E is on an NTFS partition. Within that directory, you've created a subdirectory MyList to hold the database of mail messages from a mailing list. Now, create a directory file under MyList, which is to hold the actual mail messages, one to each file.

The mail messages in this example have filenames that do not include extensions, such as 103.

Here is the directory tree in graphical form:

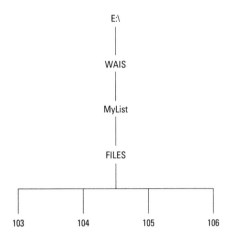

Index the Messages

Using a Windows NT command prompt, change to the WAIS Data directory (E:\WAIS). This way the filenames in the filename table, created by the indexing program, are related to the WAIS Data directory.

Run the indexing command

```
waisindex -d MyList\index -export -t netnews MyList\files\*
```

This command creates the following files: index.src, index.inv, etc, in the E:\WAIS\MyList directory.

Test the Database

To verify that the index functions correctly, use the WAISLOOK program (from the WAIS Toolkit for Windows NT) to examine it:

```
waislook -d MyList\index foobar
```

This program should return a list of files and headlines that contain the word *foobar*.

You should also test the operation of the database with a remote WAIS client by copying the index.src file to the client machine and selecting that database to make a query.

Register the Database

If your database is for public use, you may want to register it with the "database of databases." To do this, first check the information in index.src, making sure that it contains an IP address and a DNS (Domain Name System) name. Also check the TCP/IP port that you are using for the WAIS Server. Then mail the file to the following addresses:

wais-directory-of-servers@cnidr.org

wais-directory-of-servers@quake.think.com

Update the Database

When a new message (say, 107) arrives in the E:\WAIS\MyList\files directory, you should run the WAISINDEX command to update the index. Change to the E:\WAIS directory and issue the command

```
waisindex -d MyList\index -t netnews -a MyList\files\107
```

This command adds the new file to the directory. Normally, of course, you would include this command in a batch file so that it would be executed automatically.

Note that the WAISERV program does *not* automatically reindex the database if a new file is added to the directory. You must do that yourself.

Troubleshooting

This section lists some of the problems that you may have in running the WAIS Server and describes how to overcome them.

Errors starting the WAIS Server

When starting the WAIS Server, you may see one of the following error messages:

Could not start the WAIS Server service on \\yourmachine.
Error 0002: The system cannot find the file specified.

The Service Manager could not locate WAIS.EXE. This probably means that it has been moved or has not been installed correctly. Remove and reinstall the WAIS Server as described earlier in this chapter.

Could not start the WAIS Server service on \\yourmachine.
Error 0005: Access is denied.

WAIS.EXE is inaccessible to the SYSTEM user. By default, the Service Manager starts the WAIS Server process running under a user ID of SYSTEM. The executable file for the service must be readable by this user.

Could not start the WAIS Server service on \\yourmachine.
Error 2140: An internal Windows NT error occurred.

This message usually indicates a problem with the configuration of the WAIS Server. Further information detailing the precise problem is recorded in the Application Event Log.

Errors recorded in the Event Log

This section records some of the error messages that may appear in the Application Event Log. Many of these messages are self-explanatory.

Windows Sockets library function "bind" failed. The address or port is already in use.

One of the following situations may cause this error:

- The TCP/IP port you have specified in the WAIS Server configuration dialog box is conflicting with another application. Choose a different port number.

- The IP address that the WAIS Server is using is incorrect. Start the Network Control Panel applet, and configure the TCP/IP software to use the correct IP address.

Windows Sockets library function "accept" failed. The call was canceled.

This message indicates that the WAIS Server terminated abnormally for some reason. Restart the service.

Registry Entries

WAIS Server makes several entries to the Windows NT Registry. A number of other entries are added to the Registry implicitly by the Service Control Manager. The entries in this section are not guaranteed to remain the same between releases of the WAIS Server. The information is intended for advanced users of Windows NT who understand the function and structure of the Registry.

The Service Control Manager creates the following entry in the HKEY_LOCAL_MACHINE database:

```
SYSTEM\CurrentControlSet\Services\WAIS\Parameters
```

Under this entry, the WAIS Server itself creates the following entries, which are used to hold the configuration information:

Entry name	Entry type	Description
Directory	REG_SZ	WAIS Data directory name
PortNo	REG_DWORD	TCP/IP port number
LogDirectory	REG_SZ	Directory where log files are created
LogLevel	REG_DWORD	Volume of log information: 0 means none, 10 is the maximum

Formal Command Syntax

The formal description of the WAIS command options is as follows:

Syntax: WAIS [-remove | -install] [-version] [-ipaddress]

Description: The WAIS command installs or removes the WAIS Server.

Options: The following list contains the options that you can use with the WAIS command.

-install   Adds the WAIS Server to the list of installed services. Make sure that you are executing a copy of WAIS.EXE that you aren't planning to delete later.

-remove   Removes the WAIS Server from the list of installed services. This also deletes the WAIS Server configuration information from the Registry.

-version   Reports the version number of the WAIS Server.

-ipaddress   Reports the IP addresses on which the WAIS Server is listening.

Chapter 23

Installing the WAIS Toolkit

In This Chapter

▶ Installing the WAIS Toolkit

▶ Working with WAIS databases

Installing the WAIS Toolkit

You should install the WAIS Toolkit if you plan to use its searching capabilities with the GOPHER Server (GOPHERS), the HTTP Server (HTTPS), or the WAIS Server (WAISS) for Windows NT.

Three programs are provided in the Toolkit:

■ WAISINDEX creates a WAIS index of all the words in a set of files. This index is ported directly from the CNIDR program (also called WAISINDEX) in the "freeWAIS" version 0.202 distribution.

■ WAISLOOK takes one or more words and displays the names of files in the index that contain those words, ranked according to frequency of occurrence.

■ WAISSERV accepts WAIS protocol requests through stdin and sends back responses using the same protocol through stdout. It is designed for use with the WAIS Server for Windows NT (WAISS), rather than on its own.

The WAIS Toolkit is distributed in three versions: for the Intel, MIPS, and DEC Alpha architectures, each of which is included on the CD-ROM accompanying this book. Select the appropriate distribution ZIP file according to your system's platform or processor.

To install the WAIS Toolkit, you must log on to your Windows NT system as a user with administrative privileges.

1. Unzip the appropriate distribution file into a temporary directory. When you unzip the distribution file, you should have the following files:

WAISINDX.EXE	The WAISINDEX program
WAISLOOK.EXE	The searching program
WAISSERV.EXE	The Z39.50 searching program
WAISTOOL.DOC	The EMWAC manual in Word for Windows format
WAISTOOL.WRI	The EMWAC manual in Windows Write format
WAISTOOL.PS	The EMWAC manual in PostScript
READ.ME	Summary of new features

2. If you have installed a previous version of the Toolkit, remove it by deleting the old files, or by moving them to another directory (off the PATH) so you can delete them after you have validated that the new version works correctly.

3. Decide in which directory you are going to put the tools and move the .EXE programs there. Ensure that the directory is on the PATH so that the commands can be executed from the command line. If you plan to use the WAIS Toolkit with the WAIS, Gopher, or HTTP Servers, you should put the .EXE programs into the *WINNT*\\SYSTEM32 directory so that the servers can find them.

4. If you are storing the tools on NTFS, rename the WAISINDX.EXE program to WAISINDEX.EXE. (It is not distributed with that name because of problems when extracting the file to a FAT volume.)

5. For each program within WAIS, determine which version of the Toolkit you have. To do this, at the Windows NT command prompt, type the following commands, pressing the Enter key after each command:

```
waisindex - v
waislook - v
waisserv - v
```

(In fact, there are two version numbers for WAISINDEX and WAISSERV — the first number refers to the version of the free WAIS code from which the programs were ported; the second number refers to the Windows NT version.)

To remove the Toolkit, simply delete the files.

Troubleshooting Installation Problems

Occasionally, installation does not go as smoothly as you would like. You may receive the following error message:

```
The system says that WAISINDEX.EXE is not a Windows NT program.
```

If you receive this message, you are probably trying to run an executable for the wrong sort of processor. Check that you have unpacked the correct ZIP file for your processor type.

Creating and Searching a Simple Database

This section describes how to create a simple index using WAISINDEX and how to search it using WAISLOOK.

Preparation

1. Create a directory called C:\TESTWAIS.

2. Create a subdirectory called C:\TESTWAIS\FILES to hold the files that you plan to index.

3. Put some text files into the C:\TESTWAIS\FILES directory. They can be anything you like as long as they are ASCII files.

Creating an index

1. Make C:\TESTWAIS the current directory.

2. Execute WAISINDEX, giving it the following parameters:

```
waisindex -d myindex files\*
```

3. Observe the messages from WAISINDEX to check that there are no errors.

4. Do a DIR command on the C:\TESTWAIS directory to check that WAISINDEX has created seven index files, named MYINDEX.*.

Searching the index

1. Make sure that the current directory is C:\TESTWAIS.

2. Execute WAISLOOK, giving it the following parameters:

```
waislook -d myindex word
```

replacing *word* with a word that occurs in the files that you have indexed.

3. Review the output of WAISLOOK, which shows you the names of the files that contain the word you selected.

The WAISINDEX Program

You use the WAISINDEX program to build and update WAIS databases. The program cannot work with a database on a FAT partition, because the intermediate files that it creates during the indexing process do not conform to the FAT 8.3 filename restriction.

Syntax

Use the following syntax to build and update WAIS databases:

```
waisindex [ -d index_filename ] [ -a ] [ -r ]
[ -mem mbytes ] [ -register ] [ -export ]
[ -e [ file ] ] [ -l log_level ]
[ -pos | -nopos ] [ -nopairs | -pairs ]
[ -nocat ] [ -T type ] [ -t type ]
[ -contents | -nocontents ]
[-v] [-stdin] [-keywords "string"]
[-keyword_file filename] [-M type,type]
[-x filename[,...]]
filename filename ...
```

Description

WAISINDEX creates an index of the words in files so that they can be searched quickly by tools such as WAISLOOK. The index takes about as much disk space as the original text. Its seven files have the following extensions:

.cat	The catalog of the indexed files, with about three lines of information for each indexed file. This is a text file.
.dct	The dictionary of indexed words. This is a binary file.
.doc	The document table. This is a binary file. A file may contain several documents, depending on the type specified in the -t option.
.fn	The filename table. This is a binary file. The filenames stored in this table are supplied as the final parameters to WAISINDEX. Thus, if file names are supplied relative to the current directory (for example, files/*), they are stored in the filename table in that form. The resulting filenames from a database search are related to that directory.

.hl	The headline table. This is a binary file. A *headline* is ideally a line of descriptive text summarizing the contents of a document. The headline is normally taken from the document itself. For instance, it may be the Subject line if the document is a mail message, the first line of the file, or simply the filename itself. The type of the file is determined by which -t option is indicated to WAISINDEX.
.inv	The inverted file index. This is a binary file.
.src	The source description structure. This is a text file.

Options

The following list describes the options you can use with the WAISINDEX program:

-d *index_filename*	This is the base filename for the index files. Therefore, if D:\wais\foo is specified, the index files are called D:\wais\foo.cat, and so on. The default is .\index.
-a	Appends the index to an existing one. It is useful for incremental additions or updates. This option only adds to an index; if a file has changed it is reindexed, but the old entries are not purged. To save space, it is a good idea to reindex the whole set of files periodically. However, if you don't specify this option, the existing index is overwritten.
-v	Displays the version number of the program.
-r	Recursively indexes subdirectories.
-mem *mbytes*	Indicates how much main memory (in megabytes) to use during indexing. The usefulness of this option in the Windows NT environment is unknown.
-register	Causes the program to display instructions about how to register a WAIS database manually, using electronic mail. (The Windows NT version of WAISINDEX cannot automatically register a WAIS database with the directory of servers.)
-export	Causes the source description file created by WAISINDEX to include the host name and the WAIS default TCP port (210) to be used by the clients. Without this option, the source description file contains no connection information and is used only for local searches.

-e [*filename*]	Redirects error output to the named file or suppresses error output if *filename* is omitted. Error output defaults to stderr (usually the console) if -e is not used.
-l *log_level*	Sets logging level. Currently only levels 0, 1, 5, and 10 are meaningful. Level 0 means log nothing (silent). Level 1 logs only errors and warnings (messages of high priority). Level 5 logs messages of medium priority (such as indexing filename information). Level 10 logs everything.
-pos (-nopos)	Includes word position information in the index; don't include is the default. This option increases the index size but allows search engines to do proximity.
-nopairs (-pairs)	Prevents the building of word pairs from consecutive capitalized words. Build is the default.
-nocat	Prevents the creation of a catalog. This option is useful for databases with a large number of documents, because the catalog contains three lines per document.
-contents	Includes (excludes) the contents of the file from the index. The (-nocontents) filename and header is still indexed. The default is type dependent.
-T *type*	The filename table (.fn) and the catalog (.cat) created by WAISINDEX contain a "type" string for each file indexed. This option sets the type string to *type*. The default depends on the type of file being indexed; it is TEXT in most cases. Possible values are TEXT, TEXT-FTP, WSRC (WAIS .src structures), DVI, PS, PICT, GIF, TIFF, and HTML. This type of information is used only by the WAIS Server. The HTTP and WAIS Toolkits have their own mechanisms for determining the type of a file.
-t *type*	Tells WAISINDEX the type of files being indexed. The list of recognized types is given later in the section, *File types*. The default is TEXT. This type of information allows WAISINDEX to derive an appropriate headline, which is stored in the headline table (.hl). It is also used to determine whether the files being indexed consist of multiple documents.
-stdin	Reads the list of filenames to be indexed from standard input (stdin), rather than from the command line.
-keywords "*string*"	Displays keywords to be indexed for each document.
-keyword_file *filename*	Displays a file of keywords to be indexed for each document.
-M *type*	For multi-type documents.

-x *filename*[,...]	Ensures that the filename(s) are not indexed. Two or more filenames are separated by a comma with no space between them.
filename filename...	These are the files that are indexed according to the preceding arguments. The filenames given here are stored in the filename table. Wildcards may be used.

The document table can be no larger than 16 MB, which limits the indexer to databases with headlines that total less than 16 MB (because that is the principal component of the table). This space limitation is typically a problem for database types where a record is essentially a headline (one_line, archie).

Synonym files

A synonym file is used to reduce the size of an index and to facilitate more effective searching. It consists of lines of words. The first word is the *datum* or basic term; subsequent words on the line are synonyms. Lines beginning with a hash (#) are treated as comments.

When indexing a database, the synonym file (if it exists) is read into a table. Each word from a document to be indexed is translated using the table that corresponds to the word's datum value. The translated word (rather than the original word) is then recorded in the database.

When a database search is performed, the search word(s) are similarly translated using the synonym file before the search is performed. The synonym file has the same name as the database but must have the extension .syn. It must be located in the same directory as the rest of the database files. If the WAISINDEX program does not find a synonym file, it issues a warning message.

Here is a sample synonym file:

```
# First word is base term, rest are synonyms
boat ship yacht launch galleon destroyer dinghy
shoe slipper boot sneaker trainer
```

File types

This is the list of file types that the WAISINDEX program parses:

bibtex	BibT$_E$X / LaT$_E$X format.
bio	Biology abstract format.
cmapp	CM applications from Hypercard.
dash	Entries separated by a row of dashes. At least twenty dashes must be present for a line to be recognized as a separator. Each entry is indexed as a separate document.

dvi	DVI format.
emacsinfo	The GNU documentation system.
first_line	The first line of the file is the headline.
filename	Uses only the filename part of the pathname for the title.
ftp	Special type for FTP files. The first line of the file is the headline.
gif	GIF files. Indexes only the filename.
html	Hypertext Markup Language (HTML). The text within the <TITLE> element is the headline.
irg	Internet resource guide.
jargon	Jargon File 2.9.8 format.
listserv_digest	LISTSERV mail digest format.
mail_digest	Standard Internet mail digest format.
mail_or_rmail	Mail, rmail, or both.
medline	Medline format.
mh_bboard	MH bulletin board format.
ms_kbase	MS Knowledge Base format.
netnews	Netnews format.
nhyp	Hypertext format, Polytechnic of Central London.
one_line	Each line in the file is a separate document.
para	Paragraphs separated by blank lines. Each paragraph is a separate document.
pict	Pict files. Indexes only the filename.
ps	PostScript format.
refer	Refer format.
rn	Netnews saved by the [rt]?rn newsreader.
server	Server structures (.src) for the directory of servers.
text	Simple text files. This is the default.
tiff	Tiff files. Indexes only the filename.
URL what-to-trim what-to-add	This type has been superseded by the html type, which is preferred.

The WAISLOOK Program

The WAISLOOK program is used to search WAIS databases. It is executed automatically by the GOPHERS and HTTPS Servers when they need to search WAIS databases, but it may also be executed manually from the console. In the latter case, many of the following options are not relevant.

Syntax

Use the following syntax to execute the WAISLOOK program.

```
waislook [-d dbname] [-h hostname] [-p port]
[-debug] [-v] [-http|-gopher] [-t title]
[-q virtpath] search words ...
```

Description

This program searches an index for documents that contain the search words. It ranks documents according to how often the words occur and whether they appear in the document headline. If more than 40 documents (the default) are found, only the topmost 40 are returned.

The program generates either an HTML document or a Gopher menu containing the result of the search, or it displays the names of the documents and their corresponding headlines on the console.

Options

The following list describes options that you can use with the WAISLOOK program:

-debug	Enables debugging. In this mode, debugging information is sent to stderr.
-v	Displays the version number of WAISLOOK.
-h *hostname*	Specifies the name of the host to quote when generating HTML output or gopher menu output. It is not used in interactive mode and has no default value.
-p *port*	Specifies the number of the TCP/IP port to quote when generating HTML output or gopher menu output. It is not used in interactive mode and has no default value.
-d *dbname*	Specifies the name of the WAIS database to search. The name should not have an extension or a trailing dot. It defaults to .\index. It is almost always necessary to use this option.

-http	Specifies that the program has been invoked from the HTTP Server and should output the results of the search in HTML. This option cannot be combined with -gopher.
-gopher	Specifies that the program has been invoked from the WAIS Toolkit and should output the results of the search as a gopher menu. This option cannot be combined with -http.
-t *title*	Specifies the title to use in the output HTML document if the -http option has been selected. If the title contains spaces, enclose it in double quotes.
-q *virtpath*	Lets you specify a virtual pathname to be inserted in front of the filenames returned by WAISLOOK when the -https option is in effect. This option may be used by some versions of the HTTP Server for Windows NT. Note that the freeware HTTP Server does not support virtual paths.
search words ...	Specifies one or more search words after all the options. The first search word may not begin with a hyphen (to distinguish it from the options). If more than one search word is given, documents that contain any of the search words are returned. Note that Boolean combinations of search words are not yet supported.

The WAISSERV Program

The WAISSERV program is used to search WAIS databases. It is executed automatically by the WAIS Server (WAISS) when it receives an incoming call from a WAIS client. It may also be executed manually from the console but is not particularly useful in this mode.

Syntax

Use the following syntax to execute the WAISSERV program:

```
waisserv [-d directory] [-e file] [-v] [-l level ]
```

Description

This program reads WAIS protocol requests from its standard input (stdin) and writes the response to standard output (stdout). Like WAISLOOK, it ranks the documents that it finds according to how often the words occur and whether they appear in the document headline. If more than 40 documents are found, only the topmost 40 are returned.

Options

The following list describes options that you can use with the WAISSERV program.

-v   Displays the version number of the program.

-d *directory*   Specifies the directory containing the WAIS databases. The name should not have an extension or a trailing dot. Defaults to the current directory.

-e *file*   Specifies that log information should be written to *file*. Defaults to NUL:.

-l *level*   Specifies the amount of logging information to write to the file. The *level* is a number from 0 (no logging information — the default) to 10 (full information).

Chapter 24

Installing Internet Mail Services

In This Chapter

▶ Installing EMWAC Internet Mail Services

▶ How the Internet Mail Services work

▶ Setting up mailing lists

The European Microsoft Windows Academic Center (EMWAC) Internet Mail Services for Windows NT (known as IMS) is a suite of server programs that allow you to use Windows NT as a mail server for Internet mail. With IMS, your Windows NT machine can receive messages from Internet, store them in individual users' mail boxes, accept outgoing mail from users, and relay that mail to its destination anywhere on the Internet. IMS supports mail aliases and can also run (optionally) mailing lists.

The IMS suite is comprised of several components:

- **SMTP Receiver (Windows NT Service).** Listens for incoming mail and stores it for processing by the SMTP Delivery Agent.

- **SMTP Delivery Agent (Windows NT Service).** Delivers mail addressed to local users into their incoming mailbox and sends other mail out onto the Internet. It uses MX records in the DNS for routing mail and supports aliases and mailing lists.

- **POP3 Server (Windows NT Service).** This component allows local users to download mail from their incoming mailbox on Windows NT to their own computer, using POP3 mail clients.

- **IMAP Server (Windows NT Service).** With IMAP, mail is stored permanently on the Windows NT machine, and an IMAP client such as Pine is used to access it. The user can organize her mail into hierarchical folders.

- **A Configuration Program (Windows NT Application).** This program allows you to configure the EMWAC Internet Mail Services.

Protocol Specifications

The following sections cover protocol specifications for SMTP Receiver and POP3 Server.

SMTP Receiver

The SMTP Receiver is a server implementation of the SMTP protocol defined in RFC 821 and RFC 1123. The following SMTP commands are supported by this version:

- HELO
- QUIT
- MAIL
- RCPT
- DATA
- RSET
- NOOP
- VRFY

POP3 Server

The POP3 Server implements the POP3 protocol defined in RFC 1725. The following POP3 commands are supported by this version:

- USER name
- PASS string
- STAT
- LIST [msg]
- RETR msg
- DELE msg
- NOOP
- RSET
- TOP msg n
- QUIT

The following optional POP3 commands are not supported in this version:

- APOP name digest
- UIDL [msg]

Installing Internet Mail Services

The EMWAC Internet Mail Services is distributed in three versions, for the Intel, MIPS, and DEC Alpha architectures, each of which is included on the CD-ROM accompanying this book. Select the appropriate distribution ZIP file according to your system's platform or processor. It will be one of the following:

- IMSi386.ZIP for an Intel platform

- IMSMips.ZIP for a MIPS platform

- IMSAlpha.ZIP for a DEC Alpha platform

To install Internet Mail Services, you must log onto your Windows NT system as a user with administrative privileges.

1. Unzip the appropriate distribution file into a temporary directory. When you unzip the distribution file, you should have the following files:

   SMTPDS.EXE   The SMTP Delivery Agent

   SMTPRS.EXE   The SMTP Receiver

   POP3S.EXE   The POP3 Server

   MCTRL.EXE   The configuration program

   COPYRITE.TXT   The copyright statement for the software

   READ.ME   Summary of new features

Note

All the EXE files with the exception of MCTRL.EXE are Windows NT Services.

2. Copy the .EXE files into the *WINNT*\\SYSTEM32 directory, where *WINNT* is the name of your Windows NT directory.

3. Determine which version of the services you have. To display the version number for each service, at the Windows NT command prompt, type:

```
SMTPDS -VERSION
SMTPRS -VERSION
POP3S -VERSION
```

4. Next, use the following command to check the IP address of your machine:

```
SMTPDS -IPADDRESS
SMTPRS -IPADDRESS
POP3S -IPADDRESS
```

   This command displays the name of your machine (for example, valda.cpress.com) and its IP address as reported by the Windows Sockets API. If this information is incorrect, you need to reconfigure the TCP/IP software on your machine. The services cannot work if this address (or list of addresses, if your machine has more than one network interface) is incorrect.

Because you start, stop, and pause the services through the Services option in the Control Panel, you must install HTTPS into the table of Windows NT Services. Installing HTTPS as a service also registers it with the Event Logger so that you can log errors to an Event Log and view them with the Event Viewer.

5. To install a program as a Windows NT Service, type the following at the Windows NT command line:

```
SMTPRS -INSTALL
SMTPDS -INSTALL
POP3S -INSTALL
```

Each program registers itself with the Service Manager and with the Event Logger, and then reports success or failure. If the installation fails at this point, refer to the upcoming section, *Troubleshooting installation problems*.

Note

You must execute this command using the copy of *.EXE that you placed in the \WINNT\SYSTEM32 directory. Do not use any copy that you plan to delete.

6. To verify that the installation has succeeded, start the Windows NT Control Panel and double-click the Services icon. The resulting dialog box should list EMWAC POP3 Server, EMWAC SMTP Delivery Agent, and EMWAC SMTP Receiver as installed services.

7. Before you run the services, use MCTRL.EXE to configure them. You may want to create an icon in the Program Manager for this program.

Once you have configured the Internet Mail Services, you can use the Start button in the Control Panel to start each service. If you have any difficulty starting the services, see the upcoming section, *Troubleshooting installation problems*.

Installing over a previous version of a service

If you have installed a previous version of any of the services, you should remove it by typing (for each service)

```
servicename -remove
```

where *servicename* is the filename of the Internet Mail Service you want to remove.

Upgrading from Versions 0.1x and 0.2x

The Registry entry location for the EMWAC IMS Version 0.30 or later has changed. Therefore you have to remove any previous versions before you install Version 0.30 or later. This can be done by running the earlier version of POP3S, SMTPDS, and SMTPRS from the command line with the -remove flag.

Troubleshooting installation problems

Occasionally, installation may not go as smoothly as you would like. Here are some common problems and their possible solutions.

The system says that *servicename* is not a Windows NT program.

Check to make sure that you are running the correct executable for your system's processor. If not, unzip the correct distribution ZIP file for your processor type.

The system says that the service won't install because of a "duplicate service name".

You must remove a previous version of the service before installing a later version. See the preceding section, *Installing over a previous version of a service.*

The service waits for a while, and then terminates with a "usage" message.

You cannot run the services from the command line or from File Manager, except with a command-line argument. The Internet Mail Services programs are Windows NT "Services" and must be started through the Services dialog box in the Control Panel.

Removing Internet Mail Services

The following steps describe what to do if you want to remove one or all of the Internet Mail Services from your computer, or if you want to move the program to a new location.

1. If any of the EMWAC services is running, stop the service by clicking the Stop button in the Services dialog box in the Services Control Panel applet. (Check to see if anyone is accessing the service before you shut it down.)

2. To remove the Services from the Service Manager's list of services and the service-specific configuration information from the Registry, type

   ```
   servicename -remove
   ```

   at the Windows NT command line, where *servicename* is the filename of the Internet Mail Service you want to remove.

3. If you want to remove the Services entirely, delete the MCTRL.EXE, SMTPDS.EXE, SMTPRS.EXE, and POP3S.EXE files.

4. If you want to move the Internet Mail Services to a new location, first move the files to the target directory, and then type

   ```
   smtprs -install
   smtpds -install
   pop3s -install
   ```

These commands inform the Service Manager and Event Logger of the new location of the programs. For your changes to take effect, you must start the Services again from the Control Panel.

Configuring Internet Mail Services

You configure the EMWAC Internet Mail Services through the EMWAC Internet Mail Services Configuration Program (MCTRL.EXE). Launch the Services applet to bring up the configuration dialog box.

The dialog box displays several tabbed folders or screens allowing you to configure these options:

- Directories for mailboxes, mail spooling, and postmaster
- Event logging
- Miscellaneous options
- Mailing lists
- Aliases

Directories

The Mailbox directory template defines the location of the incoming mail directory for each local user. Each user must have a different directory, which is formed by substituting the user's name or home directory for keywords in the template. The keywords are:

> %HOME%   The user's home directory
>
> %USERNAME%   The user's login name

Note

If %HOME% is used, it must be at the beginning of the template and if %USERNAME% is used, it must be at the end. The default is %HOME%\INETMAIL\INBOX.

The Mail spool directory is the root of a directory tree that is used as a staging post for messages in transit through the system. The default is %SystemRoot%\EMWAC\MAIL.

The Postmaster field contains the mail address of the postmaster for the system. The default is ADMINISTRATOR.

Event logging

You can enable event logging for different components of the Internet Mail Services:

- **POP3 Log.** If checked, POP3 transactions are logged.

■ **SMTP Inlog.** If checked, incoming SMTP messages are logged.

■ **SMTP Outlog.** If checked, outgoing SMTP messages are logged.

Miscellaneous configuration items

You can use the Services configuration dialog box to configure the following items for the EMWAC Internet Mail Services:

■ **Prohibit Incoming Mail Relay**. If this box is not checked, incoming mail addressed to anywhere on the Internet is accepted for relaying. If it is checked, only mail addressed to local users or mailing lists is accepted. It is not checked by default.

■ **Automatically Create Inbox Enabled.** If this box is checked and an incoming mail message is addressed to a local user who does not have a mail inbox, SMTPDS tries to create one. Or if a POP3 user connects to the POP3S and the user does not have a mail inbox, SMTPDS tries to create one.

If this box is not checked, and an addressee does not have a mail inbox directory, then POP3S or SMTPDS returns a failure message like "No mail inbox."

This feature is enabled by default.

Mailing lists

The Mailing Lists configuration dialog box contains a scrolling list of all the mailing lists known to the SMTP Delivery Agent. In addition to the scrolling list, the following options appear in the dialog box:

■ The **Moderator** field displays a moderator address if a selected list is moderated. The field is empty if the selected list is not moderated.

■ The **Add** button brings up the List Membership dialog box for the selected mailing list, so that you can specify the name of a new mailing list to create.

■ The **Delete** button allows you to delete the selected mailing list.

■ The **Members** button also brings up the List Membership dialog box for the selected list.

Aliases

You can configure IMS to redirect mail using aliases. When IMS processes a message addressed to a local user on the Windows NT system, it checks the recipient's name against an *alias table*. If a matching entry is found, the message is redirected to the replacement address specified in the table.

To set up an alias

1. Select the Aliases tab in the Configuration program. The Aliases screen appears.

2. In the User name field, type the recipient name you want to redirect (foo, for example).

3. In the Map to field, type the address to which messages should be sent (for example, RhodeIslandRed@abc.xyz.com). Then click the Set button.

   Now, any messages to foo@*thismachine.mycompany.com* (assuming your machine is called thismachine.mycompany.com) are sent on to RhodeIslandRed@abc.xyz.com. foo does not need to be a registered user of your machine.

To delete an alias select it in the list box and press Delete.

Wildcard Aliases

To redirect mail for all names matching a pattern, you can specify wildcards in the User name field. For instance, specifying a user name of "T*Y" would match Tony, Tiny, toby, terry, and so on. (Note that matching is not case sensitive.)

You can also specify a single wildcard as the first character of the Map to field. This wildcard is replaced by the actual user name when the table entry is used. For instance, if the user name string is f* and the corresponding Map to string is *-blue@xyz.com, then a message for fargle@thismachine.mycompany.com is redirected to fargle-blue@xyz.com.

This feature can be used to redirect all mail to users at this machine to another machine, by specifying a user name of * and a Map to address of *@thatmachine.mycompany.com.

The order of entries in the map table is significant. It is processed top-to-bottom, and the first matching entry is used. Thus, specific entries should be positioned near the top of the list, and less specific entries (containing wildcards) towards the end of the list. Use the Up and Down buttons to move entries around.

How the Internet Mail Services Work

The following sections explain the components involved in getting the Internet Mail Services to function.

SMTP Receiver

The SMTP Receiver listens for incoming mail messages on TCP/IP port 25 and places them in the incoming mail directory.

A message is stored as two separate files, named *uniquename*.MSG and *uniquename*.RCP. The *uniquename* is a unique identifier by which the message is known while it is in the system.

The .MSG file contains the message itself. The file is byte-stuffed (that is, a redundant dot is inserted at the beginning of lines that start with a dot), and the end of the file is indicated by a single dot on a line by itself.

The .RCP file contains the names of the recipients of the message and the originator of the message (to whom non-delivery reports are sent).

SMTP Delivery Agent

The SMTP Delivery Agent deals with messages that have been received by the SMTP Receiver. It removes messages from the incoming directory and stores them in a holding directory. For each distinct mail domain in the list of message recipients, SMTPDS creates a subdirectory (within the domains directory), where it places information about the recipients in that domain.

For local deliveries, SMTPDS temporarily stores recipient information in a special $local$ subdirectory within the domains directory. It then copies messages into each local recipient's incoming mail directory.

For mail that is destined elsewhere, SMTPDS issues a request to the DNS (Domain Name Service) for an MX record for the corresponding domain. (It determines the DNS server address from the Windows NT Registry ; therefore you must configure Windows NT with a DNS address.) It uses the MX record to determine the IP address(es) to which it should send messages for that domain. SMTPDS attempts to establish contact with that domain and submit the message(s). If unsuccessful, it waits a while before attempting to contact the domain again. It persistently tries to contact the domain for several days.

The message files in the holding directory are of the form *uniquename*.MSG. These files are byte-stuffed, and the end of the files is indicated by a single dot on a line by itself.

The files in the domains directory are of the form *uniquename*.RCP. These files contain the names of the recipients of the message and the originator of the message (to whom non-delivery reports are sent).

The domains directory also contains files that record routing information and details of how many times the Delivery Agent has attempted to contact each domain.

You should not attempt to edit or change any of the above files.

POP3 Server

The POP3 Server listens on TCP/IP port 110 for connections from POP3 mail clients. When a mail client attaches, the server verifies that the password supplied by the client is correct (that is, there is a corresponding user registered on the Windows NT machine). It then transfers messages from a local user's incoming mail directory to the POP3 client mail program.

Directories

This section describes how the EMWAC Internet Mail Services use disk directories.

Mailbox Directory

If a registered user on the Windows NT system wants to receive incoming mail, she must create an incoming mail directory. This mailbox directory must match the mailbox template, which is configured using MCTRL.EXE. Mail is delivered into this directory by the SMTP Delivery Agent and may be removed from the directory by the POP3 Server under control of a POP3 client.

You can use MCTRL.EXE to create a mailbox directory automatically. When an incoming mail directory is created automatically, the POP3S and SMTPDS try to base it on the following rules (for an NTFS partition):

- If your mailbox template has a pattern %HOME%\..., POP3S can create a mailbox directory for a user. The user has "Full Control" of it, and the System user has "Add" permission for it.

- If your mailbox template has a pattern ...\%USERNAME%, both POP3S and SMTPDS can create a mailbox directory for a user. The System user has "Full Control" of it.

Both POP3S and SMTPDS can create incoming mail directories for users on a FAT partition.

If you plan to create users' mailbox directories manually, follow the preceding rules to set permissions on each inbox directory.

I recommend that you run all the IMS Services as the Local System user (the default). Otherwise, you need to set up all the preceding permissions manually, which is difficult to get right.

Tip   If you have a "%HOME%\..." template, SMTPDS tries to create a mailbox directory for a user, and if it is sucessful, the user may not have the correct permissions on the directory. Therefore, I recommend that you do not create mailboxes this way.

Mail Spool Directory

You can use the Mail Spool Directory configuration program to specify the Mail Spool Directory for the Internet Mail Services. The spool directory contains a number of subdirectories that are used as staging posts for messages. Some of these subdirectories and the files within them have names that exceed the DOS 8.3 filename limitation; therefore it is vital that the Mail Spool Directory is placed on a disk partition that supports long filenames (for example, an NTFS partition).

The directory structure under the Mail Spool Directory is as follows. (See the previous section, *How the Internet Mail Services Work,* for detailed information on how messages are passed between directories.)

- **Incoming.** This directory holds messages received by the SMTP receiver. The SMTP Delivery Agent also places messages here (for example, non-delivery reports and messages that are sent to mailing lists).

- **Holding.** Messages are moved from the incoming directory into this directory by the SMTP Delivery Agent.

- **Domains.** When a message is moved into the holding directory, the Delivery Agent creates a subdirectory within the domains directory for each separate domain to which the message is addressed. If the message is for a local user, the Delivery Agent creates a subdirectory called $local$ In each subdirectory it stores routing information and information about the message recipients in that domain. (The message itself stays in the holding directory.)

- **inlog.** This directory contains log files created by the SMTP Receiver.

- **outlog.** This directory contains log files created by the SMTP Delivery Agent.

- **pop3log.** This directory contains log files created by the POP3 Server.

- **lists.** This directory contains subdirectories corresponding to mailing lists. For every mailing list, two directories are created — one corresponding to the list itself, and one corresponding to the -request address for the list.

When you have finished making changes to the configuration, click the OK button. The configuration takes effect the next time you start the affected services. If the services are already running, you must stop and restart them. (The exception to this is mailing lists and aliases. If you've changed the membership of a mailing list or alias, the change is recognized immediately.)

The configuration information is stored in the Windows NT Registry.

Cross Reference

For more information about the Windows NT Registry, see Chapter 7, *Working with the Registry.*

Mailing List Membership

You can use the Mailing List Membership dialog box to manage one specific mailing list in the EMWAC Internet Mail Services.

The following options are available in the Mailing List Membership dialog box:

- **Mailing list name.** This option shows the name of the mailing list in question. If you are creating a new mailing list, you can specify its name here. If you are editing an existing mailing list, you cannot change its name.

- **Non-delivery reports.** If a message to an address on the mailing list cannot be delivered, this specifies what should be done. The options are:

  - Discard the message without generating a non-delivery report (the default).

  - Return a non-delivery report to the message sender.

  - Send the non-delivery report to a specified e-mail address.

- **Moderated List.** You can specify the mail address of a moderator for the list. The moderator controls who can join the list and/or who can leave it:

  - Moderator Control Join. Any JOIN message to this list is forwarded to the moderator.

  - Moderator Control Leave. Any LEAVE message to this list is forwarded to the moderator. If a list is not moderated, anyone can join or leave the list by sending a message with JOIN or LEAVE in its body to the the -request address of the list.

- **Membership.** The dialog box contains a scrolling list of all the addresses on the mailing list. Selecting one and clicking Delete causes the address to be removed from the list. Note that if you join or leave the list using a mail message to the -request address while the dialog box is displayed, the change is lost when you click OK.

- **New Member.** Typing an address in the box and clicking the Add button causes the address to be added to the list.

How To Use Mailing Lists

When SMTPDS receives a message in which the domain name of the recipient address corresponds to the domain name of the system on which SMTPDS is running, it assumes the message is for a local user or for a mailing list. First it checks the mailing lists directory to see if a subdirectory with a matching name exists. If so, the message is temporarily delivered to that directory. If not, it assumes that the message is for a local user. (This means that if a mailing list has the same name as a local user, messages are sent to the mailing list and not to the user.)

SMTPDS "explodes" messages delivered to the mailing lists by sending them onward to all list members. It handles messages delivered to -request directories by parsing them for commands and creating a Journal file which it then returns to the sender.

The SMTP Delivery Agent manages mailing lists. This section explains:

- How to set up a mailing list
- How to join (subscribe to) a mailing list
- How to leave (remove your subscription from) a mailing list
- How to remove a mailing list
- Mailing list processor commands

Setting up a mailing list

Use the Configuration program to create a new mailing list called (for example) foobar. Now, messages directed to foobar@*yourmachine.yourdomain* will be sent to members of the new mailing list (except of course that a newly-created mailing list does not yet have any members).

Joining a mailing list

Anyone can join any mailing list maintained by SMTPDS. To join a list called foobar, send a message to foobar-request@*yourmachine.yourdomain*, containing the word SUBSCRIBE in the message body. SMTPDS responds with a mail message indicating the success or failure of your attempt.

If a list is moderated and Moderator Control Join is enabled, any JOIN message is forwarded to the moderator. Then the moderator determines who can join the list.

Leaving a mailing list

To leave a mailing list called, for example, foobar, send a mail message to foobar-request@*yourmachine.yourdomain*, containing the words UNSUBSCRIBE in the message body.

If a list is moderated and Moderator Control Leave is enabled, any LEAVE message is forwarded to the moderator. The moderator determines who can leave the list.

Removing a mailing list

To remove a mailing list, use MCTRL.EXE.

Mailing list processor commands

The mailing list processor understands the following commands:

HELP	Produce summary of commands
JOIN [listname]	Subscribe to mailing list
LEAVE [listname]	Unsubscribe from mailing list
STOP	Stop processing commands (for example, to avoid processing a signature)
SUBSCRIBE [listname]	Subscribe to mailing list
UNSUBSCRIBE [listname]	Unsubscribe from mailing list

Logging Internet Mail Service Events

You can enable separate logging for each of the services in IMS. When logging for a service is enabled, the service creates a log file in the appropriate logging directory. A new file is created every day, with a name of the form *YYMMDD*.LOG.

Error logging

If an error in the operation of one of the services occurs, the error is logged in the Application Event Log. When a service is started or stopped, Information events are recorded in the log. This log can be viewed with the Event Viewer, which is located in the Administrative Tools program group in the Program Manager. See your Windows NT documentation for details of how to use the Event Viewer.

Note

To interpret messages associated with events, the Event Viewer uses the EXE file for the service in question. Therefore, if you remove the executable file, the events for the corresponding service in your Application Event Log will be unintelligible.

Errors recorded in the Event Log

This section describes some of the error messages that may appear in the Application Event Log. Many of these are self-explanatory.

Windows Sockets library function "bind" failed. The address or port is already in use.

One of the following situations may cause this error:

- The TCP/IP port for the protocol in question is already in use for some other purpose.

- The EMWAC Internet Mail Services are using incorrect IP addresses.

Start the Network Control Panel applet and configure the TCP/IP software to use the correct IP address.

Windows Sockets library function "accept" failed. The call was canceled.

This message indicates that the service terminated abnormally for some reason. Restart the service.

Formal command syntax

The formal description of the syntax for the services is as follows:

Syntax: *servicename* [-REMOVE | -INSTALL] [-VERSION] [-IPADDRESS]

where *servicename* stands for one of the following:

Service name	Description
SMTPRS	The SMTPRS command installs or removes the SMTP Receiver.
SMTPDS	The SMTPDS command installs or removes the SMTP Delivery Agent.
POP3S	The POP3S command installs or removes the POP3 Server.

Options: The formal description of the command options is as follows:

-INSTALL	Adds the service to the list of installed services. Make sure you are executing a copy of SERVICENAME.EXE that you aren't planning to delete later.
-REMOVE	Removes the service from the list of installed services. This command also deletes the service's configuration information from the Registry.
-VERSION	Reports the version number of the service.
-IPADDRESS	Reports the IP addresses and corresponding host names that the service regards as local.

Troubleshooting the Internet Mail Services

When starting the EMWAC Internet Mail Services, you may see one of the following error messages:

Could not start the service name service on \\yourmachine. Error 0002: The system cannot find the file specified.

The Service Manager could not locate the EXE file for the service. This probably means it has been moved or has not been installed correctly. Remove and reinstall the service.

Could not start the service name service on \\yourmachine. Error 0005: Access is denied.

The EXE file for the service is inaccessible to the SYSTEM user. By default, the Service Manager starts the service process running under a user ID of SYSTEM. The executable file for the service must be readable by this user.

Could not start the service name service on \\yourmachine. Error 2140: An internal Windows NT error occurred.

This usually indicates a problem with the initialization of the service. Further information detailing the precise problem is recorded in the Application Event Log, which was discussed earlier.

Registry Entries

The various services comprising the IMS read their configuration information from the Windows NT Registry. Two keys are used by each service: one key for information that is common to more than one service, and one key containing information specific to the service in question.

Common configuration information is stored under the key HKEY_LOCAL_MACHINE\SOFTWARE\EMWAC\IMS. The following values may be stored in the Registry under this key:

- **MailInBoxDir (REG_SZ).** This template defines the location of each local user's incoming mailbox. The default is %HOME%\INETMAIL\INBOX.

- **AutoCreateInboxDir (REG_DWORD).** If this entry is non-zero, POP3S or SMTPDS tries to create a user's mail inbox directory when the user accesses the POP3 Server, or a message addressed to the user is processed by the SMTP Delivery Agent. The default is 1.

- **MailSpoolDir (REG_SZ).** This is the location of the main directory for storing mail in transit. The default is %SystemRoot%\EMWAC\MAIL.

- **Postmaster (REG_SZ).** This is the name of the local user who is acting as postmaster. The default is administrator.

- **Lists (key).** This value contains one subkey for each mailing list under the key HKEY_LOCAL_MACHINE\SOFTWARE\EMWAC\IMS\LISTS. Each mailing list subkey contains the following:

    - **Members (key).** This entry contains one subkey for each e-mail address belonging to the mailing list.

    - **BouncesTo (REG_SZ).** This entry contains the mail address of the person to whom any non-delivery messages should be sent. If empty (the default), non-delivery messages cannot be generated. If this is the special value $SENDER, then non-delivery messages are sent to the person who sent the message to the mailing list.

- **Moderator (REG_SZ).** This entry contains the mail address of the moderator of this mailing list. If empty (the default), the mailing list is not moderated.

- **ModeratorControlJoin (REG_DWORD).** If a list is moderated and this entry is non-zero, any JOIN message to this mailing list is forwarded to the moderator. The default is 0.

- **ModeratorControlLeave (REG_DWORD).** If a list is moderated and this entry is non-zero, any LEAVE message to this mailing list is forwarded to the moderator. The default is 0.

- **Aliases (key).** This key is under the key HKEY_LOCAL_MACHINE\ SOFTWARE\EMWAC\IMS\ALIASES. This key contains one value for each host for which aliases are defined. Currently, only aliases for users at local hosts are supported; therefore this key contains only one value: $local$.

  Each value is a REG_MULTI_SZ that contains multiple pairs of strings. In each pair, the first string is the user name, which is matched against incoming recipient names. The second string is the mapped-to address.

SMTP Receiver

SMTPRS-specific configuration information is stored under the key HKEY_LOCAL_MACHINE\SYSTEM\CurrentControlSet\Services\SMTPRS\Parameters. The following values may be stored in the Registry under this key:

- **CheckLocalRecipient (REG_DWORD).** A non-zero value means that names of local recipients of a mail message are checked when SMTPRS receives the message. If a name does not exist, then that recipient is rejected immediately. If this value is zero, then all local names are assumed valid — the SMTP Delivery Agent checks whether the name is actually correct. The default is 0.

- **InlogEnabled (REG_DWORD).** This value is non-zero if logging is enabled. The default is 0.

- **ProhibitMailRelay (REG_DWORD).** In order for mail addressed to sites other than the local machine to be accepted, this value must be zero. The default is 0.

- **PortNo (REG_DWORD).** SMTPRS listens for incoming connections on this port number. It would be extremely unusual to change this value. The default is 25.

- **MailQueueDir (REG_SZ).** This is the subdirectory of the MailSpoolDirectory into which SMTPRS writes incoming messages. This does not affect SMTPDS, which always uses incoming, so IMS stops working if you set this value. The default is incoming.

SMTP Delivery Agent

SMTPDS-specific configuration information is stored under the key HKEY_LOCAL_MACHINE\SYSTEM\CurrentControlSet\Services\SMTPDS\ Para meters. The following values may be stored in the Registry under this key:

- **OutlogEnabled (REG_DWORD).** This value is non-zero if logging is enabled. The default is 0.

- **Timeout (REG_DWORD).** SMTPDS regularly checks the domain subdirectories to see if it is time to retry any domain. This parameter is the interval in seconds between checks. The default is 120.

POP3 Server

POP3-specific configuration information is stored under the key HKEY_LOCAL_MACHINE\SYSTEM\CurrentControlSet\Services\POP3S\Parameters. The following values may be stored in the Registry under this key:

- **MessageExtension (REG_SZ).** This extension is used for message files. The default is MSG.

- **PortNo (REG_DWORD).** The POP3 Server listens for incoming POP3 connections on this TCP/IP port number. It would be most unusual to change this number. The default is 110.

- **Timeout (REG_DWORD).** This parameter is an inactivity autologout timeout in seconds. The default is 600.

- **Pop3LogEnabled (REG_DWORD).** This value is non-zero if logging is enabled. The default is 0.

Part VII

Appendixes

Appendix A

Remote Access Technical Notes

You can use the SWITCH.INF file (or PAD.INF on X.25 networks) to automate the logon process instead of using the manual RAS Terminal window. Automated scripts are especially useful when you need a constant connection to a remote computer. If a remote connection fails and the RAS entry is configured to use a script, RAS automatically redials the number and reestablishes the connection. However, this is only true for non-SLIP connections.

Scripts are also time savers if you frequently log on to a remote system and do not want to manually log on each time.

Note

RAS does not support automatic redialing upon link failure. Someone must type in the required logon information in the RAS Terminal window.

SWITCH.INF provides a generic script that should work with little or no modification when connecting to many PPP servers. First try to connect using the generic script. If that does not work, you can copy and then modify the generic script to match the logon sequence of the remote computer to which you want to connect.

The first step in automating a remote logon is creating a script in the SWITCH.INF file. Then you must enable the script by selecting it in the Before Dialing or After Dialing check boxes in the Security Settings dialog box. The After Dialing box applies in most cases.

The script language described in this chapter was designed to communicate with other devices, including modems. If you are not familiar with modem scripts, scripting can be difficult to understand. The following text explains how to create scripts.

Creating Scripts for RAS

The SWITCH.INF file is like a set of small batch files (scripts) contained in one file. The SWITCH.INF file can contain a different script for each intermediary device or online service the RAS user calls. A SWITCH.INF script has six elements: section headers, comment lines, commands, responses, response keywords, and macros.

Section headers

Section headers divide the SWITCH.INF file into individual scripts. A section header marks the beginning of a script for a certain remote computer and must not exceed 31 characters. The text of a section header appears in RAS when you activate the script. The section header is enclosed in square brackets. For example,

```
[Route 66 Logon]
```

Comment lines

Comment lines must have a semicolon (;) in the first column and can appear anywhere in the file. Comment lines contain information for those who maintain the SWITCH.INF file. For example,

```
; This script was created by ValdaH January 29, 1996
```

Commands

Each line in a script is a command from your local computer to the remote computer, or it is a response from the remote computer to your local computer. Each command or response is a stream of data or text. For example, the following command sends a user name (ValdaH) and a carriage return (the macro <cr>) to the remote computer.

```
COMMAND=ValdaH<cr>
```

The commands and responses must be in the exact order the remote device expects them. Branching statements, such as GOTO or IF, are not supported.

The required sequence of commands and responses for a specific remote device should be in the documentation for the device or, if you are connecting to a commercial service, from the support staff of that service. If the exact sequence is not available, activate the generic script provided with RAS and modify it to match the logon sequence of the remote computer as described in the section, *Troubleshooting scripts using DEVICE.LOG.*

The COMMAND= command can be used in two additional ways:

```
COMMAND=NoResponse
```

The preceding command is the default and causes an approximate two-second delay. This can be useful when the intermediate device requires a delay.

Or

```
COMMAND=string
```

This command is useful when a device requires slow input. Instead of receiving the whole command string, the device requires characters to be sent one by one. Note that the string is not followed by a carriage return (<cr>).

The following is an example where the intermediary device is so slow that it is only able to receive and process one character of the command PPP at a time.

```
COMMAND=P
NoResponse
COMMAND=P
NoResponse
COMMAND=P
NoResponse
```

Responses

A response is sent from the remote device or computer. To write an automatic script, you must know the responses you will receive from the remote device. If there is a gap of two or more seconds between characters, the received text is sent as a response. This gap is the only cue that a response is over.

Response keywords

The keyword in a response line specifies what to do with the responses you receive from the remote computer:

```
OK=remote computer response<macro>
```

The script continues to the next line if the response or macro is encountered.

```
LOOP=remote computer response<macro>
```

The script returns to the previous line if the response or macro is encountered.

```
CONNECT=remote computer response <macro>
```

This script is used at the end of a successful modem script. It is not generally useful for the SWITCH.INF file.

```
ERROR= remote computer response <macro>
```

This script causes RAS to display a generic error message if the response is encountered. It is useful for notifying the RAS user when the remote computer reports a specific error.

```
ERROR_DIAGNOSTICS= remote computer response <diagnostics>
```

This script causes RAS to display the specific cause for an error returned by the device. Not all devices report specific errors. Use ERROR= if your device does not return specific errors that can be identified with Microsoft RAS diagnostics.

`NoResponse`

This script is used when no response will come from the remote device.

RAS on the local computer always expects a response from the remote device and will wait until a response is received unless a NoResponse statement follows the COMMAND= line. If there is no statement for a response following a COMMAND= line, the COMMAND= line will execute and stop the script at that point.

Macros

Macros are enclosed in angle brackets (<>). Macros perform special functions as described in Table A-1.

Table A-1	Macro Functions
Macro	*Description*
<cr>	Inserts a carriage return.
<lf>	Inserts a line feed.
<match>	Reports a match if the string enclosed in quotation marks is found in the device response. Each character in the string is matched according to upper- and lowercase. For example, <match> "Smith" matches Jane Smith and John Smith III, but not SMITH.
<username>	The user name entered in the RAS Authentication window is sent to the remote computer. This is not supported with SLIP connections. This macro is in Windows NT 3.51 and higher.
<password>	The password entered in the RAS Authentication window is sent to the remote computer. This is not supported with SLIP connections. This macro is in Windows NT 3.51 and higher.
<?>	Inserts a wildcard character, for example, CO<?><?>2 matches COOL2 or COAT2, but not COOL3.
<hXX> (XX are hexadecimal digits)	Allows any hexadecimal character to appear in a string including the zero byte, <h00>.
<ignore>	Ignores the rest of a response from the macro on.
<diagnostics>	Passes specific error information from a device to RAS. This enables RAS to display the specific error to RAS users. Otherwise, a nonspecific error message appears.

Authentication problems

If you run into authentication problems, a Retry Authentication dialog box appears with a message that your logon credentials have failed. This situation occurs if both of the following situations are true:

- You are calling into a system with an intermediary security device. (This situation would generally not apply if you are using RAS to call an Internet provider.)

- After the security device has logged you on successfully, you are attempting to log on to a Windows NT RAS server.

This message appears because the RAS Authentication dialog box user name and password boxes are used by the two new user name and password macros as well as by Windows NT RAS Servers.

For example, if the logon information for an intermediary security device that is plugged in between the Windows NT RAS Server and its modem is user name BB318 and password 34554377, but its Windows NT user name is BB318 and that password is "treehouse," your logon to the intermediary device will succeed, but your logon to Windows NT will fail.

Logon will fail because the security device password 34554377 is different from the Windows NT domain password. Windows NT prompts you with the Retry Authentication dialog box to obtain your proper Windows NT logon credentials, in this case, the password.

To eliminate the Retry Authentication dialog box, you have the following options:

- Make your user name and password identical on both systems. Be aware that doing this defeats the purpose of the security device.

- Avoid using the shared dialog box for the intermediary device logon credentials by entering the user name and password in clear text into the SWITCH.INF file according to the [Generic logon for YourLogonHere] script provided in SWITCH.INF. In order to keep your clear text password confidential, use Windows NT file system (NTFS) file permissions to prevent other users from accessing this file.

An Example Script

This section describes each part of the generic script provided in the SWITCH.INF file included with RAS.

Every script must start with a command to the remote computer followed by one or more response lines. This initial command often may be simply to wait for the remote computer to initialize and send its logon banner. The default initial command is to wait two seconds for the logon banner. It would look like this in the SWITCH.INF file:

```
COMMAND=
```

If the response (the logon banner from the remote computer) is

```
Welcome to Gibraltar Net. Please enter your logon:
```

the corresponding response line in the SWITCH.INF file should be

```
OK=<match>Please enter your logon:
```

You respond by sending a command with the characters in your user name and the carriage return:

```
COMMAND=ValdaH<cr>
```

If the response from the remote computer is

```
Please enter your password:
```

the corresponding response line in the SWITCH.INF file should be

```
OK=<match>Please enter your password:
```

To send your password, you would send the command

```
COMMAND=mUs3naB<cr>
```

On many advanced PPP computers, this script would automatically log you on.

On SLIP systems, you are also required to enter an IP address; so even though you can automate much of the logon sequence, you must manually enter your IP address in the SLIP terminal window. A permanent IP address may be provided to you in advance, or the SLIP Logon Terminal window may provide a different IP address each time you log on. This is why PPP connections are usually easier to use.

Automating logon to SLIP computers

It is possible to fully automate connections to a SLIP provider using the command-line utility RASDIAL.EXE, but only if all of the following conditions are true:

■ The SLIP provider assigns you the same IP address every time you call.

■ You have called at least once using the Remote Access program and filled in the IP address field at the lower right corner of the SLIP Terminal window so that the permanent IP address can be stored by RAS for the next connection with the RASDIAL.EXE utility.

■ The SLIP logon sequence is automated by an After Dialing SWITCH.INF script. Note that the script you create usually would not have to include any commands or responses using the IP address because the IP address is permanently stored by RAS (until you delete your particular Phonebook entry) if you followed the preceding step.

If any of the above conditions are not true, you cannot use the RASDIAL.EXE utility to connect to your SLIP provider because your IP address will not be set correctly.

Note

RASDIAL.EXE is in your \SystemRoot\SYSTEM32 directory. Among several other features, it is missing the Automatic Redial Upon Link Failure feature, which is present in the Remote Access program (RASPHONE.EXE). For help on RASDIAL.EXE, type **RASDIAL /?** at a Windows NT command prompt.

Getting through large blocks of text and two-second gaps

If the remote computer has a two-second gap in the data stream response to your computer, RAS assumes that the gap is at the end of the response. These gaps may occur anywhere, including between words, and can only be detected using DEVICE.LOG. If you write a script that seems to fail for no reason, consult DEVICE.LOG to see if a response ends in the middle of a word. If so, your script must account for the two-second gap. A simple way to do this is to include the command

```
COMMAND=<cr>
```

You can skip to the end of large blocks of text that contain multiple gaps by using the LOOP= keyword and by matching text at the end of a block. For example,

```
COMMAND=<cr>
OK=<match>Enter the service to start:
LOOP=<ignore>
```

In this example, RAS sends a null command (waits two seconds), and then waits for the Enter the service to start: message. If this is a long block of text, RAS does not find the message so it moves to the LOOP command. The LOOP command causes RAS to return to the line above, and RAS waits for the words Enter the service to start: in the second response. In this manner, you can loop though long blocks of text until you reach the text of the desired prompt.

Commands and carriage returns

Usually, you must include <cr>, which indicates a carriage return, at the end of a command. The carriage return causes the remote computer to process the command immediately. If you do not include <cr>, the remote computer may not recognize the command.

In other situations, <cr> cannot be used because the remote computer accepts the command without a carriage return and requires time to process the command. This situation mainly applies when you are sending a series of commands without expecting a response.

Activating SWITCH.INF scripts

After you have created a script in SWITCH.INF, you can configure a RAS entry to execute the script before dialing, after dialing, or both.

To activate a script in Windows NT

1. In Remote Access, select the entry to which you want to connect.

2. Choose the Edit button.

3. Choose the Security button.

4. If the Security button is not visible, choose the Advanced button.

5. In the After Dialing or Before Dialing box in the Security Settings dialog box, select the name of the script.

   By default, None is selected. The section header in SWITCH.INF appears as the name of the script.

6. Select the Accept Any Authentication Including Clear Text option. You only need to configure this for PPP connections.

   Selecting this option turns off the terminal, and the Authentication dialog box appears. To prevent this dialog box from appearing, select the Authenticate Using Current User Name and Password check box, which is in the Edit Phonebook Entry dialog box.

7. Choose the OK button until you return to the main Remote Access screen.

   When you dial this entry, the selected script will execute and complete all communication with the remote device before or after RAS dials the remote host.

Troubleshooting scripts using DEVICE.LOG

Windows NT allows you to log all information passed between RAS, the modem, and the remote device, including errors reported by the remote device. This information allows you to find errors that prevent your scripts from working.

The DEVICE.LOG file is created by enabling logging in the Registry. The DEVICE.LOG file is in the SystemRoot\SYSTEM32\RAS directory.

To create the DEVICE.LOG file

1. Hang up any connections, and then exit from Remote Access.

2. Start the Registry Editor by running the REGEDT32.EXE program.

3. Go to HKEY_LOCAL_MACHINE, and then access the following key:

   \SYSTEM\CurrentControlSet\Services\RasMan\Parameters

4. Change the value of the Logging parameter to 1. When changed, the parameter should look like this:

Logging:REG_DWORD:0x1

5. Close the Registry Editor.

Logging begins when you restart Remote Access or start the Remote Access Server service (if your computer is receiving calls). You do not need to shut down and restart Windows NT.

After you dial a number and connect, a script will start. If an error is encountered during script execution, execution halts. You should exit RAS and then determine the problem by using any text editor to view DEVICE.LOG.

Note

The traces from all calls will be appended to DEVICE.LOG as long as RAS or the Remote Access Server service are not stopped and restarted. If you need to save a DEVICE.LOG file with useful information for later review or troubleshooting, make a copy of the file and give it another name before you restart RAS or the Remote Access Server service.

The following example is of an incomplete script that failed and the DEVICE.LOG file that was created when a connection was attempted.

Example of an incomplete SWITCH.INF script

The following script is incomplete for the service to which the user tried to connect. This script was used with DEVICE.LOG to discover that the remote computer expected additional commands from the script. See the next section, *Sample DEVICE.LOG,* for the complete output that was generated.

```
[Gibraltar Net Logon for ValdaH]
; FIRST COMMAND TO INITIALIZE REMOTE COMPUTER
COMMAND=
; Skip to logon prompt. That is, loop through blocks of text
; separated by 2-second gaps until the logon prompt is encountered.
OK=<match>Logon:
LOOP=<ignore>
; Provide username to remote computer
COMMAND=ValdaH<cr>
; Since no 2-second gap is present, immediately match Password:
OK=<match>Password:
; Provide password to remote computer
COMMAND=mUs3naB
```

Sample DEVICE.LOG

This is the DEVICE.LOG file created by using the sample generic script. Note that DEVICE.LOG comment lines in all uppercase letters are writer comments added after the file was created. These are included to help you understand the contents of the file.

Remote Access Service Device Log 08/23/1996 13:52:21

; THIS SECTION IS THE COMMUNICATION BETWEEN RAS AND THE MODEM
Port:COM1 Command to Device:AT&F&C1&D2 W2\G0\J0\V1 S0=0 S2=128 S7=55
Port:COM1 Echo from Device:AT&F&C1&D2 W2\G0\J0\V1 S0=0 S2=128 S7=55
Port:COM1 Response from Device:
OK
Port:COM1 Command to Device:AT\Q3\N7%COM1
Port:COM1 Echo from Device:AT\Q3\N7%COM1
Port:COM1 Response from Device:
OK
; COMMAND TO DIAL REMOTE COMPUTER AND SUCCESSFUL CONNECTION
Port:COM1 Command to Device:ATDT1 206 555 5500
Port:COM1 Echo from Device:ATDT1 206 555 5500
Port:COM1 Response from Device:
CONNECT 14400/REL
Port:COM1 Connect BPS:19200
Port:COM1 Carrier BPS:14400
; INITIAL NULL COMMAND SENT TO DEVICE
Port:COM1 Command to Device:
Port:COM1 Response from Device:
_[2J_[H
Welcome to Gibraltar Net, a service of: Trey Computing, Inc.
Problems logging on? Call us at 555-5500 between 8:00am and 8:00pm
Mon-Sat.
NOTE: Your software must support VT100 (or higher) terminal emula-
tion!

Port:COM1 Response from Device:P
; THE LINE ABOVE INDICATES A TWO-SECOND GAP IN THE MIDDLE
; OF THE WORD PLEASE IF YOUR SCRIPT FAILED AND DEVICE.LOG ENDED
; AFTER THE RESPONSE ABOVE, YOU WOULD ACCOUNT FOR THIS
; TWO-SECOND GAP IN YOUR SCRIPT BY USING A NULL COMMAND= LINE OR THE
; OK=response AND LOOP=<match> COMBINATION.
Port:COM1 Response from Device:Please turn OFF your Caps Lock if it
is on now.
Please enter your logon name and password at the prompts below.
- Log on as "guest" to take a look around the system.
- Log on as "new" to create an account for yourself.
Logon:
; SEND YOUR USERNAME AS A COMMAND
Port:COM1 Command to Device:ValdaH
Port:COM1 Echo from Device:ValdaH
Port:COM1 Response from Device:
Password:
; SEND YOUR PASSWORD AS A COMMAND
Port:COM1 Command to Device:mUs3naB
Port:COM1 Echo from Device:mUs3naB
; THE LOGON SEQUENCE CONTINUES ON THE REMOTE COMPUTER
; BUT THE SCRIPT DOES NOT CONTINUE FROM HERE.
; THE AUTOMATED LOG ON WOULD FAIL AT THIS POINT.
Port:COM1 Response from Device:
Q-Script 3.5 - Copyright 1995 by Louise Morgan, all rights reserved

This script would be complete for many remote computers, but the remote computer sent more responses and expected a command to start a service. To complete the script, you must know the remainder of the responses from the remote computer. If you logged on manually using RAS Terminal and found the remainder of the logon sequence looked like this:

```
One Net offers you several network services:
Service
_____

SHell
UPload
DOwnload
PAssword
PPP
SLIP
Please enter a service:
```

you would complete the script with these lines:

```
COMMAND=<cr>
OK=<match>Please enter a service:
LOOP=<ignore>
```

If you added the lines above to your script, restarted RAS, and redialed, you would connect successfully.

If the generic script in RAS does not work, these guidelines should help you modify the generic script to work for your connections. I suggest that you first copy the generic script to the end of SWITCH.INF and then modify the copy to work with your connections.

Using scripts with other Microsoft RAS Clients

Microsoft RAS version 1.0 (which runs on LAN Manager) does not have the capability to invoke RAS Terminal or use scripts in .INF files.

Microsoft RAS version 1.1a (which runs on LAN Manager) supports PAD.INF only. Note that the syntax used in the PAD.INF file differs slightly from subsequent versions of Microsoft RAS.

Microsoft RAS for Windows for Workgroups version 3.11 and Windows NT version 3.1 or later support RAS Terminal and scripts in SWITCH.INF and PAD.INF.

Appendix B

Remoteboot Service

T he Remoteboot Service (also called RPL) makes it possible to boot a workstation over the network using software on the server's hard disk instead of the workstation's hard disk. You install and configure the Remoteboot Service on the server and then customize it for your particular network and for your users' needs. This chapter describes how to use Windows NT's Remoteboot Server to remoteboot various clients.

When you start, or boot, a computer, the operating system is loaded into the computer's memory. The Windows NT Remoteboot Service supports MS-DOS and Microsoft Windows personal computers (also called workstations) that boot using software on the server's hard disk instead of the workstation's hard disk. Eliminating the need for a hard disk on each workstation allows the use of diskless workstations. This has several advantages:

- **Enhanced network security**. Workstations that start remotely can only run software made available through the server. Because there are no disk drives to copy data, Remoteboot reduces the risk of viruses.

- **Software version control**. With the Remoteboot Service, it is possible to update many workstations' operating environments by updating the files on a single server.

- **Centralized disk resources**. You can place widely accessed data resources on a single disk instead of a number of individual workstation disks. This also makes it much easier to back up data.

- **Reduced workstation costs**. Diskless workstations are cheaper, but they do have drawbacks. If the server goes off-line, you cannot use the diskless workstation as a stand-alone workstation. Furthermore, diskless workstations increase the traffic on the network because every user is accessing the same files. Windows performance suffers because the system performs paging on the network drive, and the workstations load dynamic link libraries from the network drive. You can offset some of this and still enjoy the benefits of a diskless workstation (such as easy operating system upgrades and the prevention of virus introduction) by using a local hard disk to create the paging file and hold the user's data files (and applications if desired).

Remoteboot Service Operation

In order to remoteboot a workstation, the Windows NT Server that is running the Remoteboot Service must provide two resources to the client:

- A boot block, which contains all of the information needed to start the workstation when it boots

- The Remoteboot profile, which specifies the operating system environment for the workstation to use after it boots

To receive this data, the Remoteboot client must use the RPL ROM chip on its network adapter to communicate with the Remoteboot Server using the Data Link Control (DLC) protocol. The following steps describe this process in two phases: Phase I, Initial Boot Block Download, and Phase II, Operating System Download.

Downloading the initial boot block

During Phase I, the Remoteboot client seeks out a Remoteboot Server and attempts to download the boot block information specific to the client's type of network adapter. The boot block configuration file is stored on the server in the \WINNT\RPL\BBLOCK\NETBEUI\<adapter type>\DOSBB.CNF file. This file is used in Phase II to actually boot the workstation. The following steps outline Phase I:

1. When a Remoteboot client powers up, it initializes the network adapter, and the RPL ROM broadcasts a FIND frame (a boot request), which contains the client's adapter ID.

2. The Remoteboot Server receives the FIND frame and checks the Remoteboot database to see if a client record with this adapter ID already exists. If not, the Remoteboot Server records this adapter ID but does not boot the client workstation. To boot the workstation, the user must use Remoteboot Manager to convert this adapter ID record to a workstation record. If a workstation record with this adapter ID does exist, the Remoteboot Server sends a FOUND frame, containing the server's adapter ID, to the RPL ROM on the client workstation.

3. The client's RPL ROM accepts the first FOUND frame it receives (it may receive more than one if several servers are running the Remoteboot Service) and returns the SEND.FILE.REQUEST frame to the adapter ID of the server that sent the first FOUND frame.

4. When the Remoteboot Server receives the SEND.FILE.REQUEST frame, it uses FILE.DATA.RESPONSE frames to send a boot block to the RPL ROM. The client record in the Remoteboot database specifies which boot block to send.

5. When the RPL ROM receives the last FILE.DATA.RESPONSE frame, it transfers execution to the entry point of the boot block.

Downloading the operating system

Phase II attempts to mimic the MS-DOS boot process. The RPL ROM uses the information from the boot block to load the basic operating system and network and to establish a session with the Remoteboot Server. At this point, the client workstation should display the following logon prompt:

```
Type Remoteboot username, or press enter if it is <workstation>
```

This logon is called the *workstation logon* and is different from the actual user logon. The workstation logon is used to establish the first session with the file server and uses the FIT (File Index Tables) to map the original drive C directories to the file server. The Remoteboot Server creates a special user account for the workstation when its adds the workstation to the Remoteboot database. By default, workstation accounts are set to have no password.

Next, the user completes separate user logons to the domain to gain user-specific permissions on the network.

Once the workstation logon is complete, the workstation can read a boot sector file and boot using the MS-DOS files stored on the server. The operating system is downloaded in the following sequence:

1. Control is first passed to RPLBOOT.SYS, which moves each network driver and RPL disk (RPLDISK.SYS) into high conventional memory (just below 640K). A PROTOCOL.INI file is stored in the same directory as the boot block information.

2. Next, control is passed to RPLSTART.COM, which reads the boot sector.

3. RPLDISK.SYS establishes a NetBIOS session to the file server and reads the boot sector (the boot sector is a normal MS-DOS boot sector).

4. While processing CONFIG.SYS and AUTOEXEC.BAT, the redirector is loaded, initialized, and started.

5. RPLINIT.EXE is run as the first workstation service in LANMAN.INI to establish the following:

   - User identity
   - A session to the file server
   - A connection to drive C

When a client has completed a remoteboot, the current directory is C:\, and drive C is a virtual hard drive, parts of which are mapped to various places on the file server (or on multiple file servers) by the FIT file.

The C:\WKSTA directory contains workstation- and profile-specific configuration files (such as WIN.INI). It is different for each profile to which the workstation is joined. The C:\DATA directory is always the same, regardless of the profile used; the user can create files and directories there.

The C:\DOS and C:\LANMAN.DOS directories provide access to MS-DOS and network utilities. The C:\BINR directory provides access to shared real-mode utilities.

Local hard disks, if present, are assigned drive letters starting with D, unlike the local boot case, where the drive letters start with C.

Once the boot is complete, the user should type a net logon command to log on with his or her own user name and password. This logon establishes user permissions for any network connections made from that point on. The logon does *not* override the workstation logon permissions that were set on the FIT drive mappings such as C:\DOS.

Remoteboot Requirements

The Remoteboot Service is available on Windows NT Server version 3.5x and higher, and supports MS-DOS and Windows 3.1 clients. Windows 3.0 clients may work with Remoteboot, but Remoteboot is not designed to work with Windows 3.0 so this option is not recommended. OS/2 and Windows for Workgroups clients are *not* supported either.

The workstation's network adapter card must have a Remote Program Load (RPL) ROM chip on it. Each RPL ROM chip is made for a specific network adapter; it is not interchangeable. This RPL network adapter broadcasts a request for boot records; the server responds by automatically establishing a connection and loading the MS-DOS startup files into the workstation's memory.

File server disk space

When installing the Remoteboot Service on a server, you need 29–40 MB of free disk space, depending on the type of remote workstations. Table B-1 lists the disk space required to run various Remoteboot software components.

Table B-1	Remoteboot Software Components
Component	*Disk space*
Network Client version 2.2 for MS-DOS	5.1 MB
MS-DOS 3.30	0.7 MB
MS-DOS 4.01	1.5 MB
MS-DOS 5.00	2.8 MB
MS-DOS 6.xx	5.9 MB
Microsoft Windows 3.0	9.6 MB
Microsoft Windows 3.1	12.4 MB

In addition to the space for the basic components, you need room for personal copies of Remoteboot profiles (if needed) and for work directories for each workstation where users can store their own data.

Workstation network adapter cards

The network adapter card must have the correct Remoteboot (RPL) ROM chip made for the adapter. Windows NT Server provides support for the following Ethernet and Token Ring adapters:

3Com Etherlink

3Com Etherlink II

3Com Etherlink Plus

3Com Etherlink /MC

3Com Etherlink III

3Com Racal NI 5210

3Com Racal NI 6510

3Com 3StationAMD Series 2100 Ethernet

HP Ethertwist

IBM Token Ring

IBM Ethernet

Nokia/ICL Ethernet Iie

Intel EtherExpress 16

Novell NE1000

Novell NE2000

Western Digital/SMC Ethernet

Note

Check the README.TXT that ships with Remoteboot to verify if any adapters have been added to the preceding list. Most network adapters work best with the Remoteboot Service when you use the default settings. However, if you need to modify these default settings, the PROTOCOL.INI files are located in the BBLOCK\NETBEUI*adapter*\PROTOCOL.INI directory, where *adapter* is the name of the particular network adapter.

Installing the Remoteboot Service

Installing the Remoteboot Service is a multipart process. First you have to install the service. Then you have to copy the operating systems to the RPL root directories. And finally you have to use the Remoteboot Manager to set the security on these files and check the configurations. After you've done all this, you can create a profile. A profile contains the user configuration. For example, you might have a profile for MS-DOS 5.0 or MS-DOS 6.x, with both profiles being able to run Windows 3.x from the shared installation.

Note

Before you install the Remoteboot Service you should be aware of two points. First, your server name cannot contain any spaces or your MS-DOS clients will not be able to connect to it. And second, you should install the Remoteboot files to an NTFS directory. This is because the FAT file system cannot support more than 100 Remoteboot clients; NTFS can. And with NTFS, you can also specify the correct permissions on the shared files.

To install Remoteboot

1. Choose the Add Software option in the Control Panel Network applet to install the Remoteboot Service. This brings up the Remoteboot Setup dialog box as shown in Figure B-1.

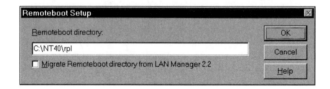

Figure B-1: The Remoteboot Setup dialog box.

2. Choose the drive and directory where the Remoteboot files are to be installed.

   If you intend to migrate a LAN Manager 2.2 Remoteboot directory, check the box and also be sure to point the files to the location of the LM Remoteboot tree. The user needs to run the RPLCNV conversion program after the Remoteboot installation.

The installation process creates the following major directories:

- **RPL.** This is the Remoteboot directory. You specify its location and name during installation. The Administrators group and the SYSTEM group have full access.

- **RPL\BBLOCK.** This directory contains boot blocks for each workstation configuration.

- **RPL\FITS.** This directory contains File Index Table (FIT) files that translate references to a file on the workstation to a true path to the file on the server. For example, a FIT file for a workstation with a shared profile would map C:\CONFIG.SYS to *server*\RPLFILES\PROFILES\ *profile*\CONFIG.SYS, where *server* is the server's name and *profile* is the profile for this workstation.

- **RPL\RPLFILES.** This directory contains files specific to each workstation as well as shared files such as profiles and operating system files. This directory is shared with the name RPLFILES.

- **RPL\RPLFILES\BINFILES.** This directory contains shared files such as profiles and operating system files.

- **RPL\RPLFILES\BINFILES\LANMAN.DOS.** This directory contains the Microsoft Network Client version 2.2 for MS-DOS, the network software used by all Remoteboot workstations.

The first time you start the Remoteboot Service, it creates the RPLUSER group and assigns permissions as appropriate throughout the RPL directory. Note that these permissions are set only if the Remoteboot files are stored on an NTFS partition. Access to the server by Remoteboot clients is through the \\SERVER\RPLFILES share. This share's permissions are set to full access.

The Remoteboot Service is installed as a manual startup service. Use Control Panel Services to configure it to automatic startup if desired.

Starting and stopping the Remoteboot Service

The Remoteboot Service installs as a manual service, meaning that you must start it intentionally each time you want it to run. If you want it to start automatically each time the server starts, you need to configure the service's startup options.

To start or stop the Remoteboot Service

1. In the Control Panel, choose the Services icon.

2. In the Services dialog box, select the Remoteboot Service. You may need to scroll down the list of services to reach it.

3. Choose the Start or Stop button. The Pause and Continue buttons have no effect on the Remoteboot Service.

4. In the Services dialog box, choose the Close button.

You can also use the **net start remoteboot** command to start the Remoteboot Service and **net stop remoteboot** to stop it.

Checking the Remoteboot installation

After you start the Remoteboot Service for the first time, you should verify that it has started without any problems by checking the server's event log for entries related to the Remoteboot Service. Use Event Viewer, located in the Administrative Tools program group, to view the event log.

You should also use Remoteboot Manager's configuration and security checking features after installation and after you add or remove support for an operating system.

To check the Remoteboot configuration

1. From the Configure menu, choose Check Configurations.

2. Choose the Yes button.

Note

This checks which operating systems are available for Remoteboot worksta-tions. Remoteboot Manager offers these as choices when you create a new profile as described next in the section titled *Creating a Profile*.

To check security settings in the Remoteboot directory

1. From the Configure menu, choose Fix Security.

2. Choose the Yes button.

This overwrites permissions throughout the \SYSTEMROOT\RPL directory, creates accounts for Remoteboot workstations and the RPLUSER local account (if they don't already exist), and updates the domain entry in LANMAN.INI files for Remoteboot workstations to match the server's own domain/workgroup.

Creating a Profile

Before a workstation can use the Remoteboot Server, you must use the Remoteboot Manager to create at least one profile that can be assigned to workstations. The Remoteboot Manager is an administrative tool used to configure the Remoteboot Service on either local or remote servers. You must configure a profile with a profile name and specified configuration. When choosing a configuration, you should have a list of network adapter types for each version of MS-DOS that is installed on the server. If the network adapter type of the workstation is not listed, choose the default for the version of MS-DOS that you want. The configuration specifies the version of MS-DOS that the workstation is to run and either lists the type of network adapter or uses the default.

When you use Remoteboot Manager for the first time, you must decide which profiles you need. A profile is the working environment shared by one or more workstations. It consists of the operating system, the workstation and architecture type, the network adapter type, and all of the other infor-mation needed to boot a workstation.

Workstations use profiles in either of two ways: They share a profile or use a personal copy of a profile. In either case, the profile is the same; the only difference is in how the workstation uses the profile.

Note

Remoteboot profiles are completely different from user profiles, which are used elsewhere in Windows NT.

To establish and name profiles, you choose from a list of configurations (which are actually profile templates). You create a profile by copying one of the base configurations. After you define the profiles, you're ready to add workstations.

You can set up a profile so that a group of common users who have similar workstations share it and, therefore, use the same startup information. However, the workstation architecture must be similar enough that the workstations can share startup files. Workstations that share profiles get their environment from a \systemroot\RPL\RPLFILES\PROFILES*profile* directory (where *profile* is the name of the profile).

Sharing profiles is not always practical. For example, a workstation may need customized system configuration files (like CONFIG.SYS). In this case, the workstation should use a personal copy of a profile. Changes to the startup information affect only the single workstation. Workstations that have a personal copy of a profile get their environment from a \systemroot\RPL\RPLFILES\MACHINES*cname**profile*\PRO directory (where *cname* is the computer name and *profile* is the name of the profile). Users can edit any of the files in that directory, such as CONFIG.SYS.

Note

When you upgrade operating systems and make software changes, you need to install them separately to each profile and copy of a profile.

To create a profile

1. From the Remoteboot menu in Remoteboot Manager, choose New Profile. The New Profile dialog box appears as shown in Figure B-2.

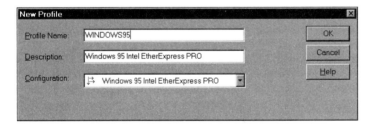

Figure B-2: The New Profile dialog box.

2. For the Profile Name, type a name containing no more than 16 characters, with no spaces or backslashes(\).

    If the server's RPL directory is on a FAT file system, use standard MS-DOS 8.3 format (eight characters, with an optional period and three more characters).

3. For the Description, type a comment for the profile. The description should summarize the profile for easy recognition (for example, MSDOS 6.20 VGA & 3Com 503 EtherLink II adapter).

    If you enter a description before selecting the configuration, the default description will overwrite it. The default description is the same as the configuration you choose.

4. In the Configuration box, choose a configuration.

If the configuration you want is not present, you must install the files for the appropriate operating system and check the configuration as described in the previous section, *Checking the Remoteboot installation.*

5. Choose OK.

6. Repeat Steps 1 through 5 for each profile you want to create.

Note

Before creating profiles, use the Fix Security option to ensure the proper file permissions have been set on the RPL files. This also ensures that the RPLUSERS local group has been created in the Windows NT user accounts database.

Adding a New Workstation

Once you have established at least one profile, you can use Remoteboot Manager to add remote workstations to the Remoteboot Server database.

The server identifies remote workstations by their network adapter IDs, which are unique to each RPL ROM. When you add a workstation, you must provide the adapter ID along with the following information:

- **Workstation Name.** Assign a workstation name to each Remoteboot workstation that is used for the initial workstation logon. This name is added to the user accounts database and the RPLUSERS group. File level permissions are automatically assigned for this account to the RPL directories (if the RPL files are located on an NTFS volume). Because the workstation name is a Windows NT user account, it can have no more than 15 characters, contain no spaces, and must be unique.

- **Password.** Leave this entry blank. This account is only for the workstation to log on to the network and should not need a password. Left null, the workstation automatically boots onto the network. The workstation's user then uses the Net Logon command to log on to the network with a specific user account.

- **Configuration Type (Shared or Personal).** You can configure workstations to share a profile or have a personal copy of a profile.

  Shared profile clients have read-only access to their configuration files, and all shared profile workstations that are assigned the same profile share the same copy of the file.

  Personal profile clients have read/write access to their configuration files; they start with copies of the shared files but are free to modify them without affecting any other workstations. Profile-specific information is kept under the RPLFILES\PROFILES\

(PROFILE) directory for shared profile clients and
RPLFILES\MACHINES*computer**profile*\PRO for personal profile
clients, where *profile* and *computer* are replaced with the profile and
workstation names.

■ **Wksta In Profile.** Choose a profile for this workstation.

■ **TCP/IP Configuration.** By default, Remoteboot workstations running the
TCP/IP protocol use DHCP and WINS. If a DHCP Server is not available on
the network, enter the appropriate IP addresses if the workstation uses
TCP/IP and does not use DHCP for automatic IP address assignment.

To add a new Remoteboot workstation

Create a new Remoteboot database record for the workstation and fill in
the necessary data manually, including the workstation's network
adapter ID number and the profile that you want this workstation to use.
This method is only recommended when you know the network adapter
ID number and you are copying an existing workstation record.

When you copy an existing workstation record, you also copy the
personal configuration information. For example, if the original workstation record uses a personal copy of a profile and has a customized
installation of Microsoft Windows, the profile and the Windows installation will be copied for the new workstation.

Or

Boot the workstation remotely with no special preparation on the
server. This creates an adapter record on the server, which you can then
convert to a workstation record by adding the workstation's name and
profile. This method is easier because you don't need to know the
workstation's network adapter ID number.

Note

No matter which method you choose, the network client for which you want
to create a workstation record must have the computer turned on and be
available to be queried by the Remoteboot Manager; otherwise the process
will fail.

To create a new workstation record manually

1. Start Remoteboot Manager. Remember to log on to a user account that
   belongs to the Administrators local group.

2. From the Remoteboot menu, choose New Workstation. The New
   Remoteboot Workstation dialog box appears as shown in Figure B-3.

   Or

   Select an existing workstation record and choose Copy from the
   Remoteboot menu.

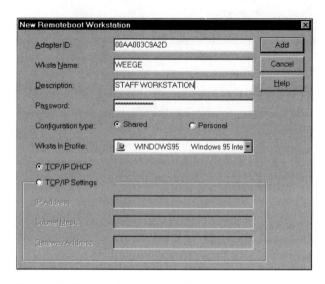

Figure B-3: The New Remoteboot Workstation dialog box.

4. In the Adapter ID box, type the workstation's network adapter ID number. This is a unique number supplied by the network adapter firmware. The adapter ID is 12 hexadecimal digits; the first six digits identify the adapter type. If you don't know the adapter ID, stop this procedure and go to the next procedure.

5. In the Wksta Name box, type a name for the workstation. The name can have no more than 15 characters — with no spaces or backslashes (\). The Remoteboot Service will create a Windows NT user account with this name, not for the user but for the workstation itself.

   If the server's RPL directory is on a FAT file system, use the standard MS-DOS 8.3 format (eight characters, with an optional period and three more characters).

6. In the Description box, type a comment that describes the workstation.

7. In the Password box, type a password for the workstation's account (not for the user using the workstation).

8. Choose a configuration type:

   ■ Shared if this workstation can share its profile with other workstations.

   ■ Personal if this workstation must use a personal copy of a profile so that you can customize the environment for the workstation.

9. In the Wksta In Profile box, choose a profile for this workstation. If none of the profiles are suitable (for example, there are no profiles for this workstation's network adapter), see the section, *Creating a Profile,* for instructions on creating profiles.

10. In the TCP/IP Settings box, enter appropriate addresses only if the workstation will use TCP/IP and will not use DHCP for automatic address handling.

11. Choose the Add button.

To create a new workstation record automatically

1. Start Remoteboot Manager on the server. Remember to log on to a user account that belongs to the Administrators local group.

2. Start the Remoteboot workstation. The workstation does not actually boot, but it does send a boot request to the server. This creates an adapter entry on the server, which you can then modify to reflect the workstation's name and desired profile. This is easiest because there is no need to know the workstation's network adapter ID number.

3. In Remoteboot Manager on the server, choose Refresh from the View menu to refresh the Remoteboot Manager's display as shown in Figure B-4.

4. In Remoteboot Manager, select the adapter record that has appeared with the network adapter ID number in place of the workstation name. From the Remoteboot menu, choose Convert Adapters.

    Or

    Select more than one adapter record (hold down the Ctrl key while clicking with the mouse). From the Remoteboot menu, choose Convert Adapters. You will convert each of the selected records, one at a time.

    Or

    Do not select any adapter records. From the Remoteboot menu, choose Convert Adapters. You convert all of the adapter records to workstation records, one at a time.

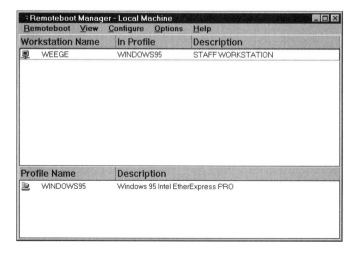

Figure B-4: The Remoteboot Manager dialog box.

Note that you cannot create adapter records; they appear only when a Remoteboot workstation starts and no workstation record exists for that workstation.

5. In the Wksta Name box, type a name for the workstation. The name can have up to 15 characters. The Remoteboot Service will create a Windows NT user account with this name, not for the user but for the workstation itself.

   If the server's RPL directory is on a FAT file system, use the standard MS-DOS 8.3 format (eight characters, with an optional period and three more characters).

6. In the Description box, type a comment that describes the workstation. The box already contains a comment provided by the network adapter itself.

7. Choose a configuration type:

   ■ Shared if this workstation can share its profile with other workstations.

   ■ Personal if this workstation must use a personal copy of a profile so that you can customize the environment for the workstation.

8. In the Wksta In Profile box, choose a profile for this workstation.

   ■ Profiles that are unsuitable for this type of adapter (determined by the first six digits of the network adapter ID number) are marked with a red X.

   ■ If none of the profiles are suitable (for example, there are no profiles for this workstation's network adapter), see the section, *Creating a Profile,* for instructions on creating profiles.

9. In the TCP/IP Configuration box, enter appropriate addresses only if the workstation will use TCP/IP and will not use DHCP for automatic address handling.

10. Choose the Add button.

    If you are converting more than one adapter ID record, the next record appears in the dialog box.

When you add a workstation to the Remoteboot database, a directory is created for that workstation in the WINNT\RPL\RPLFILES\MACHINES\ directory. This directory contains a DATA directory to which the workstation has full rights and also information that is system specific, such as the PROTOCOL.INI.

Backing Up the Remoteboot Database

The Remoteboot database holds the configuration, workstation, and profile records as well as other data for the Remoteboot Service. You should back up and save copies of the database before and after you make significant changes. The Remoteboot Service automatically backs up the database every 24 hours (counting from when you start the service).

Tip

Because the Remoteboot Service makes automatic backups (overwriting the current backup copies) and for good administrative procedure, you should occasionally archive copies of the backup files.

To back up the Remoteboot database

From the Configure menu of Remoteboot Manager, choose Backup Database. The JET.LOG, RPLSVC.MDB, and SYSTEM.MDB files are backed up to the \systemroot\RPL\BACKUP directory.

To restore a backup copy of the Remoteboot database

Copy the files from \systemroot\RPL\BACKUP (or other saved versions of the files) to the RPL directory.

Note

In the event of an emergency (such as a corrupted database), the Remoteboot Service restores automatically from the \systemroot\RPL\BACKUP directory.

Configuring Remoteboot Clients

Once the Remoteboot Service is installed and running, you must configure it before clients can use it. When workstations boot using a Remoteboot Server, they receive a profile, which defines their working environment.

Installing MS-DOS

The first step is to install any versions of MS-DOS that are to be used by Remoteboot clients. Note that there must be a separate, valid software license for each workstation that runs MS-DOS and/or Microsoft Windows.

The WINNT\RPL\RPLFILES\BINFILES directory contains directories for MS-DOS versions 3.3, 4.0, 5.0, 6.0, and 6.21. All of the MS-DOS files (including IO.SYS and MSDOS.SYS) from a workstation have to be copied into the correct directory. This is usually done from a workstation that is running the version of MS-DOS to be installed. The MS-DOS user's manual gives detailed steps for installing MS-DOS from a network client. Here are abbreviated steps from the manual:

1. Log on as an administrator and issue a **net use v: \\<Remoteboot Server>\rplfiles** command.

2. Copy all of the MS-DOS files to the RPL\RPLFILES\BINFILES\DOS*xxx* directory, where *xxx* is the version number (for example, DOS621). Make sure to remove the attributes from the MSDOS.SYS and IO.SYS files or the Remoteboot client will not be able to find them.

3. If DOS versions other than MS-DOS (such as PC-DOS) were used, the system files must be renamed as shown below:

```
rename ibmdos.com msdos.sys
rename ibmbio.com io.sys
```

Enabling Remoteboot on a Workstation's Hard Disk

Before a workstation with a hard disk can be booted remotely, its hard disk must be properly configured for the Remoteboot Service. This does not prevent users from accessing the hard disk after the workstation is booted.

If the Remoteboot workstation has a hard drive installed, you may have to configure the workstation before the Remoteboot Service can work. (Remoteboot assigns the workstation's drive as drive D.) This does not prevent users from accessing the hard disk after the workstation is booted. Use the Microsoft Network Client version 2.2 RPLENABL utility to prepare the workstation to use the Remoteboot Service. Later, if you want to boot the workstation using its hard disk, run the RPLDSABL utility to disable the Remoteboot configuration.

Note

Most RPL ROMs take control of the workstation even though the hard drive is enabled. As a result, you may not need to run the RPLENABL (or RPLDSABL) utility on every workstation. If the RPL ROM has this functionality, the workstation gives you a chance to press H to use the hard drive to boot and then attempt to remoteboot. You can still use RPLDSABL to disable the option to boot from the hard drive.

To configure a workstation's hard disk for the Remoteboot Service

1. Insert a formatted MS-DOS floppy disk in the Remoteboot Server's floppy disk drive.

2. Copy the RPLENABL.EXE and RPLDSABL.EXE programs to the floppy disk by typing

```
copy c:\systemroot\rpl\rplfiles\binfiles\binr\rpl??abl.exe a:
```

where *a:* is the floppy disk drive.

3. Start the Remoteboot workstation, booting MS-DOS from the local hard disk.

4. Put the disk with the RPLENABL.EXE program in the workstation's floppy disk drive and type

```
a:rplenabl
```

where *a:* is the workstation's floppy disk drive.

5. Remove the disk and press Ctrl+Alt+Del.

The Remote Program Load Module information is displayed as the RPL ROM chip initializes the network adapter.

Installing Windows 3.1

Remoteboot systems fully support Windows 3.1. Installing Windows is much like installing the MS-DOS files on the Remoteboot Server. When a Remoteboot workstation boots, it automatically creates a C:\WIN and a C:\WINDOWS directory. The Windows directory (C:\WINDOWS) is unique to each workstation, but the WIN directory (C:\WIN) is mapped to the \WINNT\RPL\RPLFILES\BINFILES\WIN directory. Much like the MS-DOS files, files stored in this WIN directory are accessible from each Remoteboot workstation. To install Windows, use the Workstation Logon to log on as an administrator and do an administrative install (SETUP /A) to the C:\WIN directory from a Remoteboot workstation. This gives all users access to the shared copy of Windows, and user installs (SETUP /N) can be done from there. User installs can be done for each profile or for each workstation.

Note

When using the Windows Setup /A command, the user must have full access to drive C. To gain full access to drive C, use an Administrator account to log on instead of the workstation account. This way, the FIT drive mappings are made using the Administrator account.

Secret

If you run Microsoft Windows 3.1 on a Remoteboot workstation, you must add the following lines to the end of the [386enh] section in the SYSTEM.INI file: TimerCriticalSection=5000 UniqueDosPSP=True PSPIncrement=2.

User Install for a Profile

Using the method described earlier, the system creates a profile that sets up each workstation that joins the profile for Windows. Once the profile is created, assign it to a Remoteboot workstation and then do a user install of Windows to the C:\WINDOWS directory. After you have completed these steps and the workstation can run Windows successfully, use the following command to copy the Windows user files to the workstation's C:\WKSTA.PRO\WIN directory:

```
XCOPY C:\WINDOWS C:\WKSTA.PRO\WIN /E
```

This command maps to the \WINNT\RPL\RPLFILES\MACHINES\<computer>\<profile name>\WKSTA\ WIN directory and is available to all workstations that join the profile.

User Install for an Existing Profile

If you have already created a workstation using a profile that did not have Windows set up, you need to do a Setup /N to the C:\WINDOWS directory on your local system.

Note

To install both the shared and user's Windows files, you must log on to the workstation as an administrator so that you have the correct permissions to create and modify files.

Using Other Protocols

A Remoteboot workstation always runs the NetBEUI protocol. Although NetBEUI is loaded by default and bound statically on remotely booted workstations, you can configure DLC and TCP/IP protocols so that users at Remoteboot MS-DOS workstations can load them dynamically. You can also add Novell NetWare support as shown later in this chapter.

Note

Each of these protocols uses memory and with the aid of extra protocols uses some of the workstation's available conventional memory. In addition, you cannot remove the NetBEUI protocol from Remoteboot workstations.

To enable DLC support

Once the workstation has booted to a C:\ prompt, type:

```
load msdlc
```

Enabling TCP/IP support

When you create workstations in Remoteboot Manager, they use DHCP/ WINS Servers for IP addresses by default. If a DHCP Server is not available on the network (static addresses for Remoteboot workstations), you must configure the workstation before enabling TCP/IP support. To enable TCP/ IP, modify the following files on the Remoteboot Server.

1. Edit the RPL\BBLOCK\NETBEUI*adapter*\DOSBB.CNF file, where *adapter* is the name of the network adapter. Remove the semicolon (;) in front of this line:

   ```
   ;DRV BBLOCK\TCPDRV.DOS /I:C:\LANMAN.DOS ~ ~
   ```

2. For each profile that supports TCP/IP, edit the following files as described:

   In RPL\RPLFILES\PROFILES*profile*\AUTOEXEC.BAT, where *profile* is the name of the profile, enable UMB.COM, NMSTR, and LOAD TCPIP by removing the REM designations at the beginning of each line.

In RPL\RPLFILES\PROFILES*profile*\CONFIG.SYS, where *profile* is the name of the profile, enable NEMM.DOS by removing the REM designation at the beginning of the line.

3. Boot a workstation using one of the profiles altered in the last step.

Enabling Novell NetWare support

When you install NetWare support, you need the Microsoft Network Client version 2.2 NetWare Connectivity disk and the Novell NetWare SHGEN-1 and SHGEN-2 disks (or the WSGEN disk). Directions on how to install NetWare are in the Windows NT Server Remoteboot manual.

Note

Enabling NetWare support on Remoteboot clients only allows them to access either bindery-based NetWare Servers such as a 3.12 Server or NetWare 4.x Servers that are running bindery emulation. In addition, these workstations cannot use the IPX (Internetwork Packet Exchange) protocol to access Windows NT or Windows for Workgroups Servers.

Appendix C

Windows NT Command List

The command prompt is the character-based interface to Windows NT and its subsystems. Any supported command or application can be run at the command prompt regardless of the operating system for which it was designed: Windows NT, Windows 95, Windows 3.1, MS-DOS, MS OS/2 1.x, or POSIX. The command prompt also supports batch programming, redirection between subsystems, cutting and pasting, command line editing, and file management for the NTFS, FAT, and HPFS file systems.

There is a huge benefit to using the Windows NT command prompt: It provides a single interface for seamless operation and integration of applications from different operating systems. I keep several operating systems on a single computer, so it's not unusual to walk into my office and find a command prompt window poised and ready to accept my typewritten command.

This section is for those of you who, like me, still think of the command prompt as a window to the soul of your computer. Even if you prefer the graphical interface, this section might pay off in case your mouse goes on the blink, or you forget where to access a program or command and don't want to waste time pointing and clicking around.

This appendix explains how to use the Windows NT command prompt by providing

- An overview of the Windows NT command prompt

- Lists of available commands

- An explanation of command syntax

- An explanation of command prompt functions

The Command Prompt

The Windows NT command prompt is a major enhancement to the command line interface on most current personal computer operating systems. It allows you to

- Start any Windows NT, Windows 95, Windows 3.1, MS-DOS, character-based MS OS/2 version 1.x, or POSIX-compliant programs.

- Issue Windows NT commands. The command prompt retains and enhances almost all of the commands used in MS-DOS (except new utilities in version 6.x) and contains several new commands.

- Administer or use network resources. Many LAN Manager commands are available.

- Use the Clipboard to cut and paste information between applications.

- Use piping or redirection of data between subsystems.

Start the command prompt by double-clicking on the command prompt icon (located in the Program Manager Main group).

The command prompt window displays the command prompt in monospaced characters followed by a blinking cursor. The default command prompt is the current drive and directory enclosed in brackets.

To quit the command prompt, type **exit** at the command prompt, choose Close from the Control menu, or double-click on the Control-menu box.

If the command prompt (or an application started at the command prompt) fails to respond, do the following:

Choose Settings from the command prompt's Control menu. Then press the Terminate button in the Special box. Use Terminate only as a last resort. Under normal circumstances, you should quit applications by using the application's Quit or Exit command.

Getting Help for the Command Prompt

Online Help is available for all Windows NT commands. Table C-1 shows how to access the different types of help available at the command prompt.

Table C-1	Accessing Help at the Command Prompt
Syntax	*Information*
HELP	Names of native system commands.
COMMAND /?	Description, syntax, parameters, and switches for commands. This syntax also provides help for commands that are not listed when you type **help**.
HELP COMMAND	Description, syntax, parameters, and switches for native system commands.
NET HELP	Names of available network commands.
NET HELP COMMAND	Description, syntax, parameters, and switches for network commands.
NET COMMAND /HELP	Description, syntax, parameters, and switches for network commands.
NET COMMAND /?	Syntax only for network commands.
NET HELPMSG MESSAGE#	Explanation and action for the numbered Help message.

Using Commands

Any supported Windows NT command can be run at the command prompt. Windows NT commands are classified as follows:

- Native commands
- Subsystem commands
- Configuration commands
- TCP/IP utilities
- Special-purpose utilities
- Command symbols

Native commands

Most of the commands you came to know under DOS are also native to Windows NT system commands, but with one difference. These native commands live and work in a 32-bit operating system.

Native commands are commands that exist within Windows NT's environment. They are specific to Windows NT, run under Windows NT only, and are part of the system; they are not added by a third party program. Some commands are internal, residing in memory, and some commands are external executable programs.

Commands like DIR and CHDIR are internal, meaning the command is processed by CMD.EXE and resides in memory at all times. The only way to access and run an internal command is to execute it from the command prompt. Commands like CHKDSK and XCOPY are external, meaning the command is stored in its own file and loads from disk when you use it. You can run external commands several ways: from the command prompt, from the Program Manager dialog box in the File menu, or from the Task List's New Task box. Table C-2 shows you the commands that you can run from the command prompt.

Table C-2	Native Commands
Command	*Purpose*
AT	Schedules commands and programs to run on a computer at a specified time and date.
ATTRIB	Displays or changes file attributes.
BREAK	Sets or clears extended Ctrl+C checking.
CACLS	Displays or modifies access control lists (ACLs) of files.
CALL	Calls one batch program from another (batch command only).

(continued)

Table C-2 *(Continued)*

Command	Purpose
CHCP	Displays or sets the active code page number.
CHDIR (CD)	Displays the name of or changes the current directory.
CHKDSK	Checks a disk and displays a status report.
CLS	Clears the screen.
CMD	Starts a new session of the Windows NT command interpreter.
COMP	Compares the contents of two files or sets of files.
CONVERT	Converts FAT and HPFS disk partitions to NTFS partitions.
COPY	Copies one or more files to another location.
DATE	Displays or sets the date.
DEL	Deletes one or more files.
DIR	Displays a list of files and subdirectories in a directory.
DISKCOMP	Compares the contents of two floppy disks.
DISKCOPY	Copies the contents of one floppy disk to another.
DOSKEY	Edits command lines, recalls commands, and creates macros.
ECHO	Displays messages or turns command echoing on or off.
ENDLOCAL	Ends localization of environment changes in a batch file (batch command only).
ERASE	Deletes one or more files. (See DEL.)
EXIT	Quits the Windows NT command interpreter (CMD.EXE).
FC	Compares two files or sets of files and displays the differences between them.
FIND	Searches for a text string in a file or files.
FINDSTR	Searches for strings in files using literal text or regular expressions.
FOR	Runs a specified command for each file in a set of files.
FORMAT	Formats a disk for use with MS-DOS or Windows NT.
GOTO	Directs Windows NT to a labeled line in a batch program (batch command only).
GRAFTABL	Enables Windows NT to display an extended character set in full-screen mode.
HELP	Provides Help information for Windows NT commands.
IF	Performs conditional processing in batch programs (batch command only).
KEYB	Configures a keyboard for a specific language.

Command	*Purpose*
LABEL	Creates, changes, or deletes the volume label of a disk.
MKDIR (MD)	Creates a directory.
MODE	Configures a system device.
MORE	Displays output one screen at a time.
MOVE	Moves one or more files from one directory to the specified directory.
NET ACCOUNTS	Displays or sets password and logon requirements of servers in a domain.
NET COMPUTER	Adds computers to Windows NT Server domains (available on Windows NT Server only).
NET CONFIG	Displays the controllable services that are running.
NET CONFIG SERVER	Displays or changes settings for the Server service while the service is running.
NET CONFIG WORKSTATION	Displays or changes settings for the Workstation service while it is running.
NET CONTINUE	Reactivates suspended services.
NET FILE	Displays the names of all open shared files on a server and the number of file locks, if any, on each file. This command also closes individual shared files and removes file locks.
NET GROUP	Adds, displays, or modifies global groups (Windows NT Server only).
NET HELP	Provides a list of network commands and topics for which you can get help or provides help with a specific command or topic.
NET HELPMSG	Provides help with a network error message.
NET LOCALGROUP	Adds, displays, or modifies local groups.
NET NAME	Adds, deletes, or displays messaging names on a workstation.
NET PAUSE	Pauses services or shared printers.
NET PRINT	Displays or controls print jobs.
NET SEND	Sends messages to other computers on the network.
NET SESSION	Lists or disconnects sessions between a server and workstations.
NET SHARE	Creates, deletes, or displays shared resources.
NET START	Starts a service or displays a list of started services.*
NET STATISTICS	Displays the statistics log.
NET STOP	Stops a network service.
NET TIME	Synchronizes the computer's clock with that of a server or domain or displays the time for a server or domain.

(continued)

Table C-2 *(Continued)*

Command	Purpose
NET USE	Connects a computer to or disconnects a computer from a shared resource or displays information about computer connections.
NET USER	Adds or modifies user accounts or displays user account information.
NET VIEW	Displays a list of servers or displays resources being shared by a server.
PATH	Displays or sets a search path for executable files.
PAUSE	Suspends processing of a batch file and displays a message (useful only in batch programs).
POPD	Changes to the directory stored by the PUSHD command.
PRINT	Prints a text file while you are using other Windows NT commands.
PROMPT	Changes the Windows NT command prompt.
PUSHD	Stores the current directory for use by the POPD command and then changes to the specified directory.
RECOVER	Recovers readable information from a bad disk.
REM	Records comments (remarks) in batch files. Also available as a configuration command for the MS-DOS and OS/2 subsystems.
RENAME (REN)	Renames a file or files.
REPLACE	Replaces files.
RESTORE	Restores files that were backed up with MS-DOS backup.
RMDIR (RD)	Removes a directory or directory tree.
SET	Displays, sets, or removes Windows NT environment variables.
SETLOCAL	Begins localization of environment changes in a batch file (batch command only).
SHIFT	Shifts the position of replaceable parameters in batch files (batch command only).
SORT	Sorts input.
START	Starts a separate window to run a program or command.
SUBST	Associates a path with a drive letter.
TIME	Displays or sets the system time.
TITLE	Sets the title for the command prompt window.
TREE	Graphically displays the directory structure of a drive or path.
TYPE	Displays the contents of a text file.
VER	Displays the Windows NT version number.

Command	Purpose
VERIFY	Tells Windows NT whether to verify that your files are written correctly to a disk.
VOL	Displays a disk volume label and serial number.
XCOPY	Copies files and directory trees.

*The following services are provided with Windows NT and can be started: Alerter, Client Service For NetWare, Clipbook Server, Computer Browser, DHCP Client, Directory Replicator, Eventlog, FTP Server, Gateway Service For NetWare, LPDSVC, Messenger, Net Logon, Network DDE, Network DDE DSDM, Network Monitoring Agent, NT LM Security Support Provider, OLE, Remote Access Connection Manager, Remote Access ISNSAP Service, Remote Access Server, Remote Procedure Call (RPC) Locator, Remote Procedure Call (RPC) Service, Schedule, Server, Simple TCP/IP Services, SNMP, Spooler, TCP/IP NetBIOS helper, UPS, and Workstation. The following services are available only on Windows NT Server: File Server For Macintosh, Gateway Service For NetWare, Microsoft DHCP Server, Print Server For Macintosh, and Windows Internet Name Service.

Subsystem commands

To maintain compatibility with MS-DOS and other subsystems, Windows NT also includes 16-bit commands.

Some MS-DOS subsystem commands, such as SHARE, perform functions that are now inherent to Windows NT or the MS-DOS subsystem. These commands are accepted by Windows NT to preserve compatibility with existing files, but they have no effect because the functionality is automatic in Windows NT. Table C-3 lists the commands that still have a function in Windows NT.

Table C-3	Subsystem Commands
Command	Purpose
APPEND	Allows programs to open data files in specified directories as if they were in the current directory.
BACKUP	Backs up one or more files from one disk onto another.
DEBUG	Runs Debug, a program testing and editing tool for MS-DOS applications.
EDIT	Starts MS-DOS Editor, which creates and changes ASCII files.
EDLIN	Starts EDLIN, a line-oriented text editor.
EXE2BIN	Converts .EXE (executable) files to binary format.
EXPAND	Expands one or more compressed files.

(continued)

Table C-3 *(Continued)*	
Command	**Purpose**
FASTOPEN	Starts the Fastopen program.
GRAPHICS	Loads a program that can print graphics.
LOADFIX	Loads a program above the first 64K of memory and then runs the program.
LOADHIGH (LH)	Loads a program into the upper memory area.
MEM	Displays the amount of used and free memory for the MS-DOS subsystem.
NLSFUNC	Loads country-specific information.
QBASIC	Starts the QBasic programming environment.
SETVER	Sets the MS-DOS version number that Windows NT reports to a program.
SHARE	Starts the share program.

Configuration commands

You can configure the MS-DOS subsystem under Windows NT with configuration commands such as DEVICE or LASTDRIVE, just as you can configure DOS. Instead of looking for AUTOEXEC.BAT or CONFIG.SYS files, locate the CONFIG.NT file in the \SYSTEMROOT\SYSTEM32 directory. Place configuration commands in CONFIG.NT to set up the MS-DOS subsystem.

Note

The CONFIG.NT file only affects the MS-DOS subsystem. For example, although Windows NT allows you to place commands such as buffers and breaks into the file, it ignores these commands because the MS-DOS subsystem does not use them.

The commands listed in Table C-4 are used to customize the MS-DOS environment. Windows NT reads these commands from the CONFIG.NT file whenever it runs the MS-DOS subsystem.

Table C-4	Configuration Commands
Command	**Purpose**
BUFFERS	Allocates memory for a specified number of disk buffers when the system starts.
CODEPAGE	Specifies which code pages your system is prepared to use (OS/2 only).

Command	Purpose
COUNTRY	Enables a subsystem to use international time, dates, currency, case conversions, and decimal separators.
DEVICE	Loads into memory the device driver you specify.
DEVICEHIGH	Loads into high memory the device driver you specify.
DEVINFO	Specifies the information a device needs in order to use a particular code page (OS/2 only).
DOS	Specifies that the MS-DOS subsystem is to maintain a link to its upper memory area or is to load part of itself in the high memory area (HMA).
DOSONLY	Prevents starting applications other than MS-DOS-based applications from the COMMAND.COM prompt.
DRIVEPARM	Defines parameters for block devices (OS/2 only).
ECHOCONFIG	Displays messages when the MS-DOS subsystem CONFIG.NT file is read.
FCBS	Specifies the number of file control blocks (FCBs) the command prompt can have open at the same time.
FILES	Sets the number of files the command prompt can access at one time.
INSTALL	Loads a memory-resident program into memory.
LASTDRIVE	Specifies the maximum number of drives you can access.
LIBPATH	Specifies the location of OS/2 dynamic-link libraries (OS/2 only).
NTCMDPROMPT	Runs the Windows NT command interpreter, CMD.EXE, rather than COMMAND.COM after running a SPELL OUT TSR (TSR) or starting the command prompt from within an MS-DOS application.
PROTSHELL	Specifies the name and location of the MS OS/2 command interpreter (OS/2 only).
SHELL	Specifies the name and location of the command interpreter for the MS-DOS subsystem.
STACKS	Supports the dynamic use of data stacks to handle hardware interrupts.
SWITCHES	Forces an enhanced keyboard to behave like a conventional one.

TCP/IP utilities

The TCP/IP utilities offer network connections to non-Microsoft hosts such as UNIX system computers. You must have the TCP/IP network protocol installed to use the TCP/IP utilities. Table C-5 lists the commands used with the TCP/IP utilities.

Table C-5	TCP/IP Utilities
Command	*Purpose*
ARP	Displays and modifies the IP-to-Ethernet address translation tables.
FINGER	Displays information about users on a remote system.
FTP	Transfers files to and from a node running FTP service; similar to TFTP.
HOSTNAME	Prints the name of the current host.
IPCONFIG	Displays all current TCP/IP network configuration values.
LPQ	Obtains status of a print queue on a host running the LPD server.
LPR	Prints a file to a host running an LPD server.
NBTSTAT	Displays protocol statistics and current TCP/IP connections using NBT.
NETSTAT	Displays protocol statistics and current TCP/IP connections.
PING	Verifies connections to a remote host or hosts.
RCP	Copies files between computers.
REXEC	Provides remote execution facilities similar to RSH. REXEC is password protected.
ROUTE	Manually manipulates network routing tables.
RSH	Runs commands on remote hosts.
TFTP	Transfers files to and from a node running FTP service using trivial file transfer protocol; similar to FTP.
TRACERT	Determines the route taken to a destination.

Special utilities

Special-purpose utilities are native 32-bit utilities, but they have a very limited purpose and may not appear in future versions of Windows NT. The commands for running these utilities are listed in Table C-6.

Table C-6	Special Utilities
Command	*Purpose*
ACLCONV	Restores OS/2 2.x ACLs to NTFS volumes.
DISKPERF	Starts, stops, and displays system disk performance counter use.
IPXROUTE	Manages the source routing variables of the NWLink protocol on a Token Ring network. This command is available only if the NWLink protocol has been installed.

Command	*Purpose*
MACFILE	Manages Services for Macintosh servers, volumes, files, and directories (Windows NT Server only).
PORTUAS	Converts a LAN Manager user account subsystem to a Windows NT user account database.
RASDIAL	Connects to a RAS server and provides remote access to the server and its network.

Appendix D

Performance Monitor Objects

Performance Monitor is used to monitor the behavior of objects within a Windows NT system. An object is a standard mechanism employed by Windows NT to identify and use a system resource. Windows NT creates objects to represent processes, sections of shared memory, and physical devices.

Performance Monitor is the tool that you need to use if you're serious about performance tuning and monitoring the status of your systems. Deciding which objects and counters to monitor in your quest for greater performance can be a real challenge because Performance Monitor lets you view only one object counter description at a time. For help in implementing a performance tuning plan, refer to Table D-1 which lists all of the standard Performance Monitor object types, object counters, and object descriptions. These entries are written exactly as they appear on the Performance Monitor screen. Use this table to identify the counters that you want to watch and get reports on and then set up Performance Monitor accordingly.

Note

If your system has third-party drivers or system software, there may be additional counters specific to those drivers and software that are not listed here.

Table D-1   Performance Monitor Object Types

Object	Object counter	Description
AppleTalk		
AppleTalk	AARP Packets/sec	Number of AARP packets per second received by AppleTalk on this port.
AppleTalk	ATP ALO Response/sec	Number of ATP at-least-once transaction responses per second on this port.
AppleTalk	ATP Packets/sec	Number of ATP packets per second received by AppleTalk on this port.
AppleTalk	ATP Recvd Release/sec	Number of ATP transaction release packets per second received on this port.
AppleTalk	ATP Response Timeouts	Number of ATP release timers that have expired on this port.
AppleTalk	ATP Retries Local	Number of ATP requests retransmitted on this port.
AppleTalk	ATP Retries Remote	Number of ATP requests retransmitted to this port.
AppleTalk	ATP XO Response/sec	Number of ATP exactly-once transaction responses per second on this port.
AppleTalk	Average Time/AARP Packet	Average time in milliseconds to process an AARP packet on this port.
AppleTalk	Average Time/ATP Packet	Average time in milliseconds to process an ATP packet on this port.
AppleTalk	Average Time/DDP Packet	Average time in milliseconds to process a DDP packet on this port.
AppleTalk	Average Time/NBP Packet	Average time in milliseconds to process an NBP packet on this port.
AppleTalk	Average Time/RTMP Packet	Average time in milliseconds to process an RTMP packet on this port.
AppleTalk	Average Time/ZIP Packet	Average time in milliseconds to process a ZIP packet on this port.
AppleTalk	Bytes In/sec	Number of bytes received per second by AppleTalk on this port.
AppleTalk	Bytes Out/sec	Number of bytes sent per second by AppleTalk on this port.
AppleTalk	Current Nonpaged Pool	The current amount of nonpaged memory resources used by AppleTalk.
AppleTalk	DDP Packets/sec	Number of DDP packets per second received by AppleTalk on this port.
AppleTalk	NBP Packets/sec	Number of NBP packets per second received by AppleTalk on this port.
AppleTalk	Packets Dropped	Number of packets dropped due to resource limitations on this port.
AppleTalk	Packets In/sec	Number of packets received per second by AppleTalk on this port.

Object	Object counter	Description
AppleTalk	Packets Out/sec	Number of packets sent per second by AppleTalk on this port.
AppleTalk	Packets Routed In/sec	Number of packets routed in on this port.
AppleTalk	Packets Routed Out/sec	Number of packets routed out on this port.
AppleTalk	RTMP Packets/sec	Number of RTMP packets per second received by AppleTalk on this port.
AppleTalk	ZIP Packets/sec	Number of ZIP packets per second received by AppleTalk on this port.
Browser		
Browser	Announcements Domain/sec	Rate at which a domain has announced itself to the network.
Browser	Announcements Server/sec	Rate at which the servers in this domain have announced themselves to this server.
Browser	Announcements Total/sec	Sum of Announcements Server/sec and Announcements Domain/sec.
Browser	Duplicate Master Announcements	Indicates the number of times that the master browser has detected another master browser on the same domain.
Browser	Election Packets/sec	Rate of browser election packets that have been received by this workstation.
Browser	Enumerations Domain/sec	Rate of domain browse requests that have been processed by this workstation.
Browser	Enumerations Other/sec	Rate of browse requests processed by this workstation that were not domain or server browse requests.
Browser	Enumerations Server/sec	Rate of server browse requests that have been processed by this workstation.
Browser	Enumerations Total/sec	Rate of browse requests that have been processed by this workstation. This rate is the sum of Enumerations Server, Enumerations Domain, and Enumerations Other.
Browser	Illegal Datagrams/sec	Rate of incorrectly formatted datagrams that have been received by the workstation.
Browser	Mailslot Allocations Failed	Number of times that the datagram receiver has failed to allocate a buffer to hold a user mailslot write.
Browser	Mailslot Opens Failed/sec	Rate of mailslot messages received by this workstation that were to be delivered to mailslots that are not present on this workstation.
Browser	Mailslot Receives Failed	Number of mailslot messages that could not be received due to transport failures.
Browser	Mailslot Writes Failed	Total number of mailslot messages that have been successfully received but were unable to be written to the mailslot.

(continued)

Object	Object counter	Description
Browser	Mailslot Writes/sec	Rate of mailslot messages that have been successfully received.
Browser	Missed Mailslot Datagrams	Number of mailslot datagrams that have been discarded due to configuration or allocation limits.
Browser	Missed Server Announcements	Number of server announcements that have been missed due to configuration or allocation limits.
Browser	Missed Server List Requests	Number of requests to retrieve a list of browser servers that were received by this workstation but could not be processed.
Browser	Server Announce Allocations Failed/sec	Rate of server (or domain) announcements that have failed due to lack of memory.
Browser	Server List Requests/sec	Rate of requests to retrieve a list of browser servers that have been processed by this workstation.
Cache		
Cache	Async Copy Reads/sec	Frequency of reads from cache pages that involve a memory copy of the data from the cache to the application's buffer. The application will regain control immediately even if the disk must be accessed to retrieve the page.
Cache	Async Data Maps/sec	Frequency that an application using a file system such as NTFS or HPFS to map a page of a file into the cache reads the page and does not wait for the cache to retrieve the page if it is not in main memory.
Cache	Async Fast Reads/sec	Frequency of reads from cache pages that bypass the installed file system and retrieve the data directly from the cache. Normally, file I/O requests will invoke the appropriate file system to retrieve data from a file, but this path permits direct retrieval of cache data without file system involvement if the data is in the cache. Even if the data is not in the cache, one invocation of the file system is avoided. If the data is not in the cache, the request (application program call) will not wait until the data has been retrieved from disk but will get control immediately.
Cache	Async MDL Reads/sec	Frequency of reads from cache pages using a Memory Descriptor List (MDL) to access the pages. The MDL contains the physical address of each page in the transfer, thus permitting Direct Memory Access (DMA) of the pages. If the accessed page(s) are not in main memory, the calling application program will not wait for the pages to fault in from disk.

Object	Object counter	Description
Cache	Async Pin Reads/sec	Frequency of reading data into the cache preparatory to writing the data back to disk. Pages read in this fashion are pinned in memory at the completion of the read. The file system will regain control immediately even if the disk must be accessed to retrieve the page. While pinned, a page's physical address will not be altered.
Cache	Copy Read Hits %	Percentage of cache Copy Read requests that hit the cache, that is, did not require a disk read in order to provide access to the page in the cache. A Copy Read is a file read operation that is satisfied by a memory copy from a cache page to the application's buffer. The disk file systems and the LAN redirector use this method for retrieving cache information, as does the LAN server for small transfers.
Cache	Copy Reads/sec	Frequency of reads from cache pages that involve a memory copy of the data from the cache to the application's buffer. The disk file systems and the LAN redirector use this method for retrieving cache information, as does the LAN server for small transfers.
Cache	Data Flush Pages/sec	Number of pages that the cache has flushed to disk as a result of a request to flush or to satisfy a write-through file write request. More than one page can be transferred on each flush operation.
Cache	Data Flushes/sec	Frequency that the cache has flushed its contents to disk as the result of a request to flush or to satisfy a write-through file write request. More than one page can be transferred on each flush operation.
Cache	Data Map Hits %	Percentage of data maps in the cache that could be resolved without having to retrieve a page from the disk, that is, the page was already in physical memory.
Cache	Data Map Pins/sec	Frequency of data maps in the cache that resulted in pinning a page in main memory, an action usually preparatory to writing to the file on disk. While pinned, a page's physical address in main memory and virtual address in the cache will not be altered.
Cache	Data Maps/sec	Frequency that a file system such as NTFS or HPFS maps a page of a file into the cache to read the page.
Cache	Fast Read Not Possible/sec	Frequency of attempts by an Application Program Interface (API) function call to bypass the file system to get at cache data that could not be honored without invoking the file system after all.
Cache	Fast Read Resource Misses/sec	Frequency of cache misses necessitated by the lack of available resources to satisfy the request.

(continued)

Object	Object counter	Description
Cache	Fast Reads/sec	Frequency of reads from cache pages that bypass the installed file system and retrieve the data directly from the cache. Normally, file I/O requests invoke the appropriate file system to retrieve data from a file, but this path permits direct retrieval of cache data without file system involvement if the data is in the cache. Even if the data is not in the cache, one invocation of the file system is avoided.
Cache	Lazy Write Flushes/sec	Frequency that the cache's lazy write thread has written to disk. Lazy writing is the process of updating the disk after the page has been changed in memory, so that the application making the change to the file does not have to wait for the disk write to complete before proceeding. More than one page can be transferred on each write operation.
Cache	Lazy Write Pages/sec	Frequency that the cache's lazy write thread has written to disk. Lazy writing is the process of updating the disk after the page has been changed in memory, so that the application making the change to the file does not have to wait for the disk write to complete before proceeding. More than one page can be transferred on a single disk write operation.
Cache	MDL Read Hits %	Percentage of cache memory descriptor list (MDL) read requests that have hit the cache, that is, did not require disk accesses in order to provide memory access to the page(s) in the cache.
Cache	MDL Reads/sec	Frequency of reads from cache pages that use a memory descriptor list (MDL) to access the data. The MDL contains the physical address of each page involved in the transfer and thus can employ a hardware direct memory access (DMA) device to effect the copy. The LAN server uses this method for large transfers out of the server.
Cache	Pin Read Hits %	Percentage of cache Pin Read requests that have hit the cache, that is, did not require a disk read in order to provide access to the page in the cache. While pinned, a page's physical address in the cache will not be altered. The LAN redirector uses this method for retrieving cache information, as does the LAN server for small transfers. This method is usually used by the disk file systems as well.
Cache	Pin Reads/sec	Frequency of reading data into the cache preparatory to writing the data back to disk. Pages read in this fashion are pinned in memory at the completion of the read. While pinned, a page's physical address in the cache will not be altered.

Object	Object counter	Description
Cache	Sync Copy Reads/sec	Frequency of reads from cache pages that involve a memory copy of the data from the cache to the application's buffer. The file system will not regain control until the copy operation is complete, even if the disk must be accessed to retrieve the page.
Cache	Sync Data Maps/sec	Frequency that a file system such as NTFS or HPFS maps a page of a file into the cache to read the page and requests to wait for the cache to retrieve the page if it is not in main memory.
Cache	Sync Fast Reads/sec	Frequency of reads from cache pages that bypass the installed file system and retrieve the data directly from the cache. Normally, file I/O requests invoke the appropriate file system to retrieve data from a file, but this path permits direct retrieval of cache data without file system involvement if the data is in the cache. Even if the data is not in the cache, one invocation of the file system is avoided. If the data is not in the cache, the request (application program call) will wait until the data has been retrieved from disk.
Cache	Sync MDL Reads/sec	Frequency of reads from cache pages that use a memory descriptor list (MDL) to access the pages. The MDL contains the physical address of each page in the transfer, thus permitting direct memory access (DMA) of the pages. If the accessed page(s) are not in main memory, the caller will wait for the pages to fault in from the disk.
Cache	Sync Pin Reads/sec	Frequency of reading data into the cache preparatory to writing the data back to disk. Pages read in this fashion are pinned in memory at the completion of the read. The file system will not regain control until the page is pinned in the cache, in particular, if the disk must be accessed to retrieve the page. While pinned, a page's physical address in the cache will not be altered.
FTP Server		
FTP Server	Bytes Received/sec	Rate at which data bytes are received by the FTP Server.
FTP Server	Bytes Sent/sec	Rate at which data bytes are sent by the FTP Server.
FTP Server	Bytes Total/sec	Sum of Bytes Sent/sec and Bytes Received/sec. This is the total rate of bytes transferred by the FTP Server.
FTP Server	Connection Attempts	Number of connection attempts that have been made to the FTP Server.
FTP Server	Current Anonymous Users	Number of anonymous users currently connected to the FTP Server.

(continued)

Object	Object counter	Description
FTP Server	Current Connections	Current number of connections to the FTP Server.
FTP Server	Current NonAnonymous Users	Number of nonanonymous users currently connected to the FTP Server.
FTP Server	Files Received	Total number of files received by the FTP Server.
FTP Server	Files Sent	Total number of files sent by the FTP Server.
FTP Server	Files Total	Sum of Files Sent and Files Received. This is the total number of files transferred by the FTP Server.
FTP Server	Logon Attempts	Number of logon attempts that have been made by the FTP Server.
FTP Server	Maximum Anonymous Users	Maximum number of anonymous users simultaneously connected to the FTP Server.
FTP Server	Maximum Connections	Maximum number of simultaneous connections to the FTP Server.
FTP Server	Maximum Non- Anonymous Users	Maximum number of nonanonymous users simultaneously connected to the FTP Server.
FTP Server	Total Anonymous Users	Total number of anonymous users that have ever connected to the FTP Server.
FTP Server	Total NonAnonymous Users	Total number of nonanonymous users that have ever connected to the FTP Server.
Gateway Service For NetWare		
Gateway Service For NetWare	Bytes Received/sec	Rate of bytes coming in to the redirector from the network. It includes all application data as well as network protocol information (such as packet headers).
Gateway Service For NetWare	Bytes Total/sec	Rate at which the redirector is processing data bytes. This includes all application and file data in addition to protocol information (such as packet headers).
Gateway Service For NetWare	Bytes Transmitted/sec	Rate at which bytes are leaving the redirector to the network. It includes all application data as well as network protocol information (such as packet headers and the like).
Gateway Service For NetWare	Connect NetWare 2.x	Counts connections to NetWare 2.x Servers.
Gateway Service For NetWare	Connect NetWare 3.x	Counts connections to NetWare 3.x Servers.
Gateway Service For NetWare	Connect NetWare 4.x	Counts connections to NetWare 4.x Servers.

Object	Object counter	Description
Gateway Service For NetWare	File Data Operations	Rate at which the redirector is processing data operations. One operation includes (hopefully) many bytes. I say "hopefully" here because each operation has overhead. You can determine the efficiency of this path by dividing the Bytes/sec by this counter to determine the average number of bytes transferred/operation.
Gateway Service For NetWare	File Read Operations/sec	Rate at which applications are asking the redirector for data. Each call to a file system or similar Application Program Interface (API) call counts as one operation.
Gateway Service For NetWare	File Write Operations/sec	Rate at which applications are sending data to the redirector. Each call to a file system or similar Application Program Interface (API) call counts as one operation.
Gateway Service For NetWare	Packet Burst IO/sec	Sum of Packet Burst Read NCPs/sec and Packet Burst Write NCPs/sec.
Gateway Service For NetWare	Packet Burst Read NCP Count/sec	Rate of NetWare Core protocol requests for Packet Burst Read. Packet Burst is a windowing protocol that improves performance.
Gateway Service For NetWare	Packet Burst Read Timeouts/sec	Rate at which the NetWare Service has had to retransmit a Burst Read Request because the NetWare Server took too long to respond.
Gateway Service For NetWare	Packet Burst Write NCP Count/sec	Rate of NetWare Core protocol requests for Packet Burst Write. Packet Burst is a windowing protocol that improves performance.
Gateway Service For NetWare	Packet Burst Write Timeouts/sec	Rate at which the NetWare Service has had to retransmit a Burst Write Request because the NetWare Server took too long to respond.
Gateway Service For NetWare	Packets Received/sec	Rate at which the redirector is receiving packets (also called SMBs or server message blocks). Network transmissions are divided into packets. The average number of bytes received in a packet can be obtained by dividing Bytes Received/sec by this counter. Some packets received may not contain incoming data; for example, an acknowledgment to a write made by the redirector would count as an incoming packet.
Gateway Service For NetWare	Packets Transmitted/sec	Rate at which the redirector is sending packets (also called SMBs or server message blocks). Network transmissions are divided into packets. The average number of bytes transmitted in a packet can be obtained by dividing Bytes Transmitted/sec by this counter.

(continued)

Object	Object counter	Description
Gateway Service For NetWare	Packets/sec	Rate at which the redirector is processing data packets. One packet includes (hopefully) many bytes. I say "hopefully" here because each packet has protocol overhead. You can determine the efficiency of this path by dividing the Bytes/sec by this counter to come up with the average number of bytes transferred per packet or you can divide this counter by Operations/sec to determine the average number of packets per operation.
Gateway Service For NetWare	Read Operations Random/sec	Counts the rate at which, on a file-by-file basis, reads are made that are not sequential. If a read is made using a particular file handle and then is followed by another read that is not contiguous, this counter is increased by one.
Gateway Service For NetWare	Read Packets/sec	Rate at which read packets are placed on the network. Each time that a single packet is sent with a request to read data remotely, this counter is incremented by one.
Gateway Service For NetWare	Server Disconnects	Counts the number of times that a server has disconnected your redirector. See also *Server Reconnects*.
Gateway Service For NetWare	Server Reconnects	Counts the number of times that your redirector has had to reconnect to a server in order to complete a new active request. You can be disconnected by the server if you remain inactive for too long. Locally even if all your remote files are closed, the redirector will keep your connections intact for (nominally) ten minutes. Such inactive connections are called Dormant Connections. Reconnecting is expensive in terms of time.
Gateway Service For NetWare	Server Sessions	Counts the number of active security objects managed by the redirector at a given time. For example, a logon to a server followed by a network access to the same server will establish one connection, but two sessions.
Gateway Service For NetWare	Write Operations Random/sec	Rate at which, on a file-by-file basis, writes are made that are not sequential. If a write is made using a particular file handle and then is followed by another write that is not contiguous, this counter is increased by one.
Gateway Service For NetWare	Write Packets/sec	Rate at which writes are being sent to the network. Each time a single packet is sent with a request to write remote data, this counter is increased by one.
ICMP		
ICMP	Messages Outbound Errors	Number of ICMP messages that this entity did not send due to problems discovered within ICMP, such as lack of buffers. This value should not include errors discovered outside the ICMP layer, such as the inability of IP to route the resultant datagram. In some implementations, there may be no types of error that contribute to this counter's value.

Object	Object counter	Description
ICMP	Messages Received Errors	Number of ICMP messages that the entity received but determined as having errors (bad ICMP checksums, bad length, and so on).
ICMP	Messages Received/sec	Rate at which ICMP messages are received by the entity. The rate includes those messages received in error.
ICMP	Messages Sent/sec	Rate at which the entity attempts to send ICMP messages. The rate includes those messages sent in error.
ICMP	Messages/sec	Total rate at which the entity sends and receives ICMP messages. The rate includes those messages received or sent in error.
ICMP	Received Address Mask	Number of ICMP Address Mask Request messages received.
ICMP	Received Address Mask Reply	Number of ICMP Address Mask Reply messages received.
ICMP	Received Destination Unreachable	Number of ICMP Destination Unreachable messages received.
ICMP	Received Echo Reply/sec	Rate of ICMP Echo Reply messages received.
ICMP	Received Echo/sec	Rate of ICMP Echo messages received.
ICMP	Received Parameter Problem	Number of ICMP Parameter Problem messages received.
ICMP	Received Redirect/sec	Rate of ICMP Redirect messages received.
ICMP	Received Source Quench	Number of ICMP Source Quench messages received.
ICMP	Received Time Exceeded	Number of ICMP Time Exceeded messages received.
ICMP	Received Timestamp Reply/sec	Rate of ICMP Timestamp Reply messages received.
ICMP	Received Timestamp/sec	Rate of ICMP Timestamp (request) messages received.
ICMP	Sent Address Mask	Number of ICMP Address Mask Request messages sent.
ICMP	Sent Address Mask Reply	Number of ICMP Address Mask Reply messages sent.
ICMP	Sent Destination Unreachable	Number of ICMP Destination Unreachable messages sent.
ICMP	Sent Echo Reply/sec	Rate of ICMP Echo Reply messages sent.
ICMP	Sent Echo/sec	Rate of ICMP Echo messages sent.
ICMP	Sent Parameter Problem	Number of ICMP Parameter Problem messages sent.

(continued)

Object	Object counter	Description
ICMP	Sent Redirect/sec	Rate of ICMP Redirect messages sent.
ICMP	Sent Source Quench	Number of ICMP Source Quench messages sent.
ICMP	Sent Time Exceeded	Number of ICMP Time Exceeded messages sent.
ICMP	Sent Timestamp Reply/sec	Rate of ICMP Timestamp Reply messages sent.
ICMP	Sent Timestamp/sec	Rate of ICMP Timestamp (request) messages sent.
IP		
IP	Datagrams Forwarded/sec	Rate of input datagrams for [sic] that this entity was not their final IP destination, as a result of which an attempt was made to find a route to forward them to that final destination. In entities that do not act as IP Gateways, this rate will include only those packets that were successfully Source-Routed via this entity.
IP	Datagrams Outbound Discarded	Number of output IP datagrams for which no problems were encountered to prevent their transmission but which were discarded (for example, for lack of buffer space). This counter includes datagrams counted in Datagrams Forwarded if any such packets meet this (discretionary) discard criterion.
IP	Datagrams Outbound No Route	Number of IP datagrams discarded because no route could be found to transmit them to their destination. This counter includes any packets counted in Datagrams Forwarded that meet this "no route" criterion.
IP	Datagrams Received Address Errors	Number of input datagrams discarded because the IP address in their IP header's destination field was not a valid address to be received at this entity. This count includes invalid addresses (for example, 0.0. 0.0) and addresses of unsupported Classes (for example, Class E). For entities that are not IP Gateways and therefore do not forward datagrams, this counter includes datagrams discarded because the destination address was not local.
IP	Datagrams Received Delivered/sec	Rate at which input datagrams are successfully delivered to IP user protocols (including ICMP).
IP	Datagrams Received Discarded	Number of input IP datagrams for which no problems were encountered to prevent their continued processing, but which were discarded (for example, for lack of buffer space). This counter does not include any datagrams discarded while awaiting re-assembly.

Object	Object counter	Description
IP	Datagrams Received Header Errors	Number of input datagrams discarded due to errors in their IP headers, including bad checksums, version number mismatch, other format errors, time-to-live exceeded, errors discovered in processing their IP options, and so on.
IP	Datagrams Received Unknown Protocol	Number of locally-addressed datagrams received successfully but discarded because of an unknown or unsupported protocol.
IP	Datagrams Received/sec	Rate at which IP datagrams are received from the interfaces, including those in error.
IP	Datagrams Sent/sec	Rate at which IP datagrams are supplied to IP for transmission by local IP user protocols (including ICMP). This counter does not include any datagrams counted in Datagrams Forwarded.
IP	Datagrams/sec	Rate at which IP datagrams are received from or sent to the interfaces, including those in error. Forwarded datagrams are not included in this rate.
IP	Fragment Re-assembly Failures	Number of failures detected by the IP re-assembly algorithm (for whatever reason: timed out, errors, and so on). This is not necessarily a count of discarded IP fragments because some algorithms (notably RFC 815) can lose track of the number of fragments by combining them as they are received.
IP	Fragmentation Failures	Number of IP datagrams that have been discarded because they needed to be fragmented at this entity but could not be (for example, because their "Don't Fragment" flag was set).
IP	Fragmented Datagrams/sec	Rate at which datagrams are successfully fragmented at this entity.
IP	Fragments Created/sec	Rate at which IP datagram fragments have been generated as a result of fragmentation at this entity.
IP	Fragments Re-assembled/sec	Rate at which IP fragments are successfully re-assembled.
IP	Fragments Received/sec	Rate at which IP fragments that need to be re-assembled at this entity are received.
LogicalDisk		
LogicalDisk	% Disk Read Time	Percentage of elapsed time the selected disk drive is busy servicing read requests.
LogicalDisk	% Disk Time	Percentage of elapsed time the selected disk drive is busy servicing read or write requests.

(continued)

Object	Object counter	Description
LogicalDisk	% Disk Write Time	Percentage of elapsed time the selected disk drive is busy servicing write requests.
LogicalDisk	% Free Space	Ratio of the free space available on the logical disk unit to the total usable space provided by the selected logical disk drive.
LogicalDisk	Avg. Disk Bytes/Read	Average number of bytes transferred from the disk during read operations.
LogicalDisk	Avg. Disk Bytes/Transfer	Average number of bytes transferred to or from the disk during write or read operations.
LogicalDisk	Avg. Disk Bytes/Write	Average number of bytes transferred to the disk during write operations.
LogicalDisk	Avg. Disk sec/Read	Average time in seconds of a read of data from the disk.
LogicalDisk	Avg. Disk sec/Transfer	Average time in seconds of the disk transfer.
LogicalDisk	Avg. Disk sec/Write	Average time in seconds of a write of data to the disk.
LogicalDisk	Disk Bytes/sec	Rate at which bytes are transferred to or from the disk during write or read operations.
LogicalDisk	Disk Queue Length	Number of outstanding requests on the disk at the time the performance data is collected. It includes requests in service at the time of the snapshot. This is an instantaneous length, not an average over the time interval. Multi-spindle disk devices can have multiple requests active at one time, but other concurrent requests are awaiting service. This counter may reflect a transitory high or low queue length, but if there is a sustained load on the disk drive, it is likely that this will be consistently high. Requests experience delays proportional to the length of this queue minus the number of spindles on the disks. This difference should average less than 2 for good performance.
LogicalDisk	Disk Read Bytes/sec	Rate at which bytes are transferred from the disk during read operations.
LogicalDisk	Disk Reads/sec	Rate of read operations on the disk.
LogicalDisk	Disk Transfers/sec	Rate of read and write operations on the disk.
LogicalDisk	Disk Write Bytes/sec	Rate at which bytes are transferred to the disk during write operations.
LogicalDisk	Disk Writes/sec	Rate of write operations on the disk.
LogicalDisk	Free Megabytes	Displays the unallocated space on the disk drive in megabytes. (One megabyte equals 1,048,576 bytes.)

Object	Object counter	Description
MacFile Server		
MacFile Server	Current Files Open	Number of internal files currently open in the MacFile Server. This count does not include files opened on behalf of Macintosh clients.
MacFile Server	Current Nonpaged memory	Current amount of nonpaged memory resources used by the MacFile Server.
MacFile Server	Current Paged Memory	Current amount of paged memory resources used by the MacFile Server.
MacFile Server	Current Queue Length	Number of outstanding work items waiting to be processed.
MacFile Server	Current Sessions	Number of sessions currently connected to the MacFile Server. Indicates current server activity.
MacFile Server	Current Threads	Current number of threads used by the MacFile Server. Indicates how busy the server is.
MacFile Server	Data Read/sec	Number of bytes read from disk per second.
MacFile Server	Data Received/sec	Number of bytes received from the network per second. Indicates how busy the server is.
MacFile Server	Data Transmitted/sec	Number of bytes sent on the network per second. Indicates how busy the server is.
MacFile Server	Data Written/sec	Number of bytes written to disk per second.
MacFile Server	Failed Logons	Number of failed logon attempts to the MacFile Server. Can indicate whether password guessing programs are being used to crack the security on the server.
MacFile Server	Max Nonpaged Memory	Maximum amount of nonpaged memory resources used by the MacFile Server.
MacFile Server	Max Paged Memory	Maximum amount of paged memory resources used by the MacFile Server.
MacFile Server	Maximum Files Open	Maximum number of internal files open at one time in the MacFile Server. This count does not include files opened on behalf of Macintosh clients.
MacFile Server	Maximum Queue Length	Maximum number of outstanding work items waiting at one time.
MacFile Server	Maximum Sessions	Maximum number of sessions connected at one time to the MacFile Server. Indicates usage level of server.
MacFile Server	Maximum Threads	Maximum number of threads used by the MacFile Server. Indicates peak usage level of server.

(continued)

Object	Object counter	Description
Memory		
Memory	Available Bytes	Displays the size of the virtual memory currently on the Zeroed, Free, and Standby lists. Zeroed and Free memory is ready for use, with Zeroed memory cleared to zeros. Standby memory is memory removed from a process's working set but still available. Notice that this is an instantaneous count, not an average over the time interval.
Memory	Cache Bytes	Measures the number of bytes currently in use by the system cache. The system cache is used to buffer data retrieved from disk or LAN. The system cache uses memory not in use by active processes in the computer.
Memory	Cache Bytes Peak	Measures the maximum number of bytes used by the system cache. The system cache is used to buffer data retrieved from disk or LAN. The system cache uses memory not in use by active processes in the computer.
Memory	Cache Faults/sec	Occurs whenever the cache manager does not find a file's page in the immediate cache and must ask the memory manager to locate the page elsewhere in memory or on the disk so that it can be loaded into the immediate cache.
Memory	Commit Limit	Size (in bytes) of virtual memory that can be committed without having to extend the paging file(s). If the paging file(s) can be extended, this is a soft limit.
Memory	Committed Bytes	Displays the size of virtual memory (in bytes) that has been committed (as opposed to simply reserved). Committed memory must have backing (disk) storage available or must be assured never to need disk storage (because main memory is large enough to hold it). This is an instantaneous count, not an average over the time interval.
Memory	Demand Zero Faults/sec	Number of page faults for pages that must be filled with zeros before the fault is satisfied. If the Zeroed list is not empty, the fault can be resolved by removing a page from the Zeroed list.
Memory	Free System Page Table Entries	Number of Page Table Entries not currently in use by the system.
Memory	Page Faults/sec	Number of page faults in the processor. A page fault occurs when a process refers to a virtual memory page that is not in its Working Set in main memory. A page fault will not cause the page to be fetched from disk if that page is on the standby list, and hence already in main memory, or if it is in use by another process with which the page is shared.

Object	Object counter	Description
Memory	Page Reads/sec	Number of times the disk was read to retrieve pages of virtual memory necessary to resolve page faults. Multiple pages can be read during a disk read operation.
Memory	Page Writes/sec	Number of times that pages have been written to the disk because they were changed since last retrieved. Each such write operation may transfer a number of pages.
Memory	Pages Input/sec	Number of pages read from the disk to resolve memory references to pages that were not in memory at the time of the reference. This counter includes paging traffic on behalf of the system cache to access file data for applications. This is an important counter to observe if you are concerned about excessive memory pressure (that is, thrashing) and the excessive paging that may result.
Memory	Pages Output/sec	Number of pages that are written to disk because the pages have been modified in main memory.
Memory	Pages/sec	Number of pages read from the disk or written to the disk to resolve memory references to pages that were not in memory at the time of the reference. This is the sum of Pages Input/sec and Pages Output/sec. This counter includes paging traffic on behalf of the system cache to access file data for applications. This is the primary counter to observe if you are concerned about excessive memory pressure (that is, thrashing) and the excessive paging that may result.
Memory	Pool Nonpaged Allocs	Number of calls to allocate space in the system Nonpaged Pool. Nonpaged Pool is a system memory area where space is acquired by operating system components as they accomplish their appointed tasks. Nonpaged Pool pages cannot be paged out to the paging file but instead remain in main memory as long as they are allocated.
Memory	Pool Nonpaged Bytes	Number of bytes in the Nonpaged Pool, which is a system memory area where space is acquired by operating system components as they accomplish their appointed tasks. Nonpaged Pool pages cannot be paged out to the paging file but instead remain in main memory as long as they are allocated.
Memory	Pool Paged Allocs	Number of calls to allocate space in the system Paged Pool. Paged Pool is a system memory area where space is acquired by operating system components as they accomplish their appointed tasks. Paged Pool pages can be paged out to the paging file when not accessed by the system for sustained periods of time.

(continued)

Object	Object counter	Description
Memory	Pool Paged Bytes	Number of bytes in the Paged Pool, which is a system memory area where space is acquired by operating system components as they accomplish their appointed tasks. Paged Pool pages can be paged out to the paging file when not accessed by the system for sustained periods of time.
Memory	Pool Paged Resident Bytes	Size of Paged Pool resident in core memory. This is the actual cost of the Paged Pool allocation, because this is actively in use and using real physical memory.
Memory	System Cache Resident Bytes	Number of bytes currently resident in the global disk cache.
Memory	System Code Resident Bytes	Number of bytes of System Code Total Bytes currently resident in core memory. This is the code working set of the pageable executive. In addition, there are another ~300K bytes of nonpaged kernel code.
Memory	System Code Total Bytes	Number of bytes of pageable pages in NTOSKRNL.EXE, HAL.DLL, and the boot drivers and file systems loaded by NTLDR/OSLOADER.
Memory	System Driver Resident Bytes	Number of System Driver Total Bytes currently resident in core memory. This number is the code working set of the pageable drivers. In addition to this, there are another ~700K bytes of nonpaged driver code.
Memory	System Driver Total Bytes	Number of bytes of pageable pages in all other loaded device drivers.
Memory	Transition Faults/sec	Number of page faults resolved by recovering pages that were in transition, that is, being written to disk at the time of the page fault. The pages were recovered without additional disk activity.
Memory	Write Copies/sec	Number of page faults that have been satisfied by making a copy of a page when an attempt to write to the page is made. This is an economical way of sharing data because the copy of the page is only made on an attempt to write to the page; otherwise, the page is shared.

NBT Connection

Object	Object counter	Description
NBT Connection	Bytes Received/sec	Rate at which bytes are received by the local computer over an NBT connection to some remote computer. All of the bytes received by the local computer over the particular NBT connection are counted.

Object	Object counter	Description
NBT Connection	Bytes Sent/sec	Rate at which bytes are sent by the local computer over an NBT connection to some remote computer. All of the bytes sent by the local computer over the particular NBT connection are counted.
NBT Connection	Total Bytes/sec	Rate at which bytes are sent or received by the local computer over an NBT connection to some remote computer. All of the bytes sent or received by the local computer over the particular NBT connection are counted.
NetBEUI		
NetBEUI	Bytes Total/sec	Sum of Frame Bytes/sec and Datagram Bytes/sec. This is the total rate of bytes sent to or received from the network by the protocol, but it only counts the bytes in frames (packets) that carry data.
NetBEUI	Connection Session Timeouts	Number of connections that were dropped due to a session timeout. This number is an accumulator and shows a running total.
NetBEUI	Connections Canceled	Number of connections that were canceled. This number is an accumulator and shows a running total.
NetBEUI	Connections No Retries	Total count of connections that were successfully made on the first try. This number is an accumulator and shows a running total.
NetBEUI	Connections Open	Number of connections currently open for this protocol. This counter shows the current count only and does not accumulate over time.
NetBEUI	Connections With Retries	Total count of connections that were made after retrying the attempt. A retry occurs when the first connection attempt failed. This number is an accumulator and shows a running total.
NetBEUI	Datagram Bytes Received/sec	Rate at which datagram bytes are received by the computer. A datagram is a connectionless packet whose delivery to a remote computer is not guaranteed.
NetBEUI	Datagram Bytes Sent/sec	Rate at which datagram bytes are sent from the computer. A datagram is a connectionless packet whose delivery to a remote computer is not guaranteed.
NetBEUI	Datagram Bytes/sec	Rate at which datagram bytes are processed by the computer. This counter is the sum of datagram bytes that are sent and datagram bytes that are received. A datagram is a connectionless packet whose delivery to a remote computer is not guaranteed.

(continued)

Object	Object counter	Description
NetBEUI	Datagrams Received/sec	Rate at which datagrams are received by the computer. A datagram is a connection-less packet whose delivery to a remote computer is not guaranteed.
NetBEUI	Datagrams Sent/sec	Rate at which datagrams are sent from the computer. A datagram is a connectionless packet whose delivery to a remote computer is not guaranteed.
NetBEUI	Datagrams/sec	Rate at which datagrams are processed by the computer. This counter displays the sum of datagrams sent and datagrams received. A datagram is a connectionless packet whose delivery to a remote computer is not guaranteed.
NetBEUI	Disconnects Local	Number of session disconnections that were initiated by the local computer. This number is an accumulator and shows a running total.
NetBEUI	Disconnects Remote	Number of session disconnections that were initiated by the remote computer. This number is an accumulator and shows a running total.
NetBEUI	Expirations Ack	Number of T2 timer expirations.
NetBEUI	Expirations Response	Number of T1 timer expirations.
NetBEUI	Failures Adapter	Number of connections that were dropped due to an adapter failure. This number is an accumulator and shows a running total.
NetBEUI	Failures Link	Number of connections that were dropped due to a link failure. This number is an accumulator and shows a running total.
NetBEUI	Failures No Listen	Number of connections that were rejected because the remote computer was not listening for connection requests.
NetBEUI	Failures Not Found	Number of connection attempts that failed because the remote computer could not be found. This number is an accumulator and shows a running total.
NetBEUI	Failures Resource Local	Number of connections that failed because of resource problems or shortages on the local computer. This number is an accumulator and shows a running total.
NetBEUI	Failures Resource Remote	Number of connections that failed because of resource problems or shortages on the remote computer. This number is an accumulator and shows a running total.
NetBEUI	Frame Bytes Re-Sent/sec	Rate at which data bytes are re-sent by the computer. This counter only counts the bytes in frames that carry data.

Object	Object counter	Description
NetBEUI	Frame Bytes Received/sec	Rate at which data bytes are received by the computer. This counter only counts the frames (packets) that carry data.
NetBEUI	Frame Bytes Rejected	Rate at which data bytes are rejected. This counter only counts the bytes in data frames (packets) that carry data.
NetBEUI	Frame Bytes Sent/sec	Rate at which data bytes are sent by the computer. This counter only counts the bytes in frames (packets) that carry data.
NetBEUI	Frame Bytes/sec	Rate at which data bytes are processed by the computer. This counter is the sum of data frame bytes sent and received. This counter only counts the bytes in frames (packets) that carry data.
NetBEUI	Frames Re-Sent/sec	Rate at which data frames (packets) are re-sent by the computer. This counter only counts the frames or packets that carry data.
NetBEUI	Frames Received/sec	Rate at which data frames are received by the computer. This counter only counts the frames (packets) that carry data.
NetBEUI	Frames Rejected/sec	Rate at which data frames are rejected. This counter only counts the frames (packets) that carry data.
NetBEUI	Frames Sent/sec	Rate at which data frames are sent by the computer. This counter only counts the frames (packets) that carry data.
NetBEUI	Frames/sec	Rate at which data frames (or packets) are processed by the computer. This counter is the sum of data frames sent and data frames received. This counter only counts those frames (packets) that carry data.
NetBEUI	Packets Received/sec	Rate at which packets are received by the computer. This counter counts all packets processed — control as well as data packets.
NetBEUI	Packets Sent/sec	Rate at which packets are sent by the computer. This counter counts all packets sent by the computer — control as well as data packets.
NetBEUI	Packets/sec	Rate at which packets are processed by the computer. This count is the sum of Packets Sent and Packets Received per second. This counter includes all packets processed — control as well as data packets.

(continued)

Object	Object counter	Description
NetBEUI	Piggyback Ack Queued/sec	Rate at which piggybacked acknowledgments are queued. Piggybacked acknowledgments are acknowledgments to received packets that are to be included in the next outgoing packet to the remote computer.
NetBEUI	Piggyback Ack Timeouts	Number of times that a piggybacked acknowledgment could not be sent because there was no outgoing packet to the remote on which to piggyback. A piggybacked acknowledgment is an acknowledgment to a received packet that is sent along in an outgoing data packet to the remote computer. If no outgoing packet is sent within the timeout period, an acknowledgment packet is sent, and this counter is increased by one.
NetBEUI	Window Send Average	Average number of data bytes that were sent before waiting for an acknowledgment from the remote computer.
NetBEUI	Window Send Maximum	Maximum number of bytes of data that will be sent before waiting for an acknowledgment from the remote computer.
NetBEUI Resource		
NetBEUI Resource	Times Exhausted	Number of times that all of the resources (buffers) were in use. The number in parentheses following the resource name identifies the resource in Event Log messages.
NetBEUI Resource	Used Average	Number of resources (buffers) in use at this time. The number in parentheses following the resource name is used to identify the resource in Event Log messages.
NetBEUI Resource	Used Maximum	Maximum number of NetBEUI resources (buffers) in use at any point in time. This value is useful in sizing the maximum resources provided. The number in parentheses following the resource name is used to identify the resource in Event Log messages.
Network Interface		
Network Interface	Bytes Received/sec	Rate at which bytes are received on the interface, including framing characters.
Network Interface	Bytes Sent/sec	Rate at which bytes are sent on the interface, including framing characters.
Network Interface	Bytes Total/sec	Rate at which bytes are sent and received on the interface, including framing characters.
Network Interface	Current Bandwidth	Estimate of the interface's current bandwidth in bits per second (bps). For interfaces that do not vary in bandwidth or for those where no accurate estimate can be made, this value is the nominal bandwidth.

Object	Object counter	Description
Network Interface	Output Queue Length	Length of the output packet queue (in packets.) If this is longer than 2, delays are being experienced, and the bottleneck should be found and eliminated if possible. Because the requests are queued by NDIS in this implementation, this will always be 0.
Network Interface	Packets Outbound Discarded	Number of outbound packets that were discarded — even though no errors had been detected — to prevent their being transmitted. One possible reason for discarding such a packet could be to free up buffer space.
Network Interface	Packets Outbound Errors	Number of outbound packets that could not be transmitted because of errors.
Network Interface	Packets Received Discarded	Number of inbound packets that were discarded — even though no errors had been detected — to prevent their being delivered to a higher-layer protocol. One possible reason for discarding such a packet could be to free up buffer space.
Network Interface	Packets Received Errors	Number of inbound packets that contained errors preventing them from being delivered to a higher-layer protocol.
Network Interface	Packets Received Non-Unicast/sec	Rate at which non-unicast (that is, subnet broadcast or subnet multicast) packets are delivered to a higher-layer protocol.
Network Interface	Packets Received Unicast/sec	Rate at which unicast (subnet) packets are delivered to a higher-layer protocol.
Network Interface	Packets Received Unknown	Number of packets received via the interface that were discarded because of an unknown or unsupported protocol.
Network Interface	Packets Received/sec	Rate at which packets are received on the network interface.
Network Interface	Packets Sent Non-Unicast/sec	Rate at which packets are requested to be transmitted to non-unicast (that is, subnet broadcast or subnet multicast) addresses by higher-level protocols. The rate includes the packets that were discarded or not sent.
Network Interface	Packets Sent Unicast/sec	Rate at which packets are requested to be transmitted to subnet-unicast addresses by higher-level protocols. The rate includes the packets that were discarded or not sent.
Network Interface	Packets Sent/sec	Rate at which packets are sent on the network interface.
Network Interface	Packets/sec	Rate at which packets are sent and received on the network interface.

(continued)

Object	Object counter	Description
Network Segment		
Network Segment	% Broadcast Frames	Percentage of network bandwidth that is made up of broadcast traffic on this network segment.
Network Segment	% Multicast Frames	Percentage of network bandwidth that is made up of multicast traffic on this network segment.
Network Segment	% Network Utilization	Percentage of network bandwidth in use on this network segment.
Network Segment	Broadcast Frames Received/sec	Number of broadcast frames received per second on this network segment.
Network Segment	Multicast Frames Received/sec	Number of multicast frames received per second on this network segment.
Network Segment	Total Bytes Received/sec	Number of bytes received per second on this network segment.
Network Segment	Total Frames Received/sec	Total number of frames received per second on this network segment.
NWLink IPX		
NWLink IPX	Bytes Total/sec	Sum of Frame Bytes/sec and Datagram Bytes/sec. This is the total rate of bytes sent to or received from the network by the protocol, but it only counts the bytes in frames (packets) that carry data.
NWLink IPX	Connection Session Timeouts	Number of connections that were dropped due to a session timeout. This number is an accumulator and shows a running total.
NWLink IPX	Connections Canceled	Number of connections that were canceled. This number is an accumulator and shows a running total.
NWLink IPX	Connections No Retries	Total number of connections that were successfully made on the first try. This number is an accumulator and shows a running total.
NWLink IPX	Connections Open	Number of connections currently open for this protocol. This counter shows the current count only and does not accumulate over time.
NWLink IPX	Connections With Retries	Total number of connections that were made after retrying the attempt. A retry occurs when the first connection attempt failed. This number is an accumulator and shows a running total.

Object	Object counter	Description
NWLink IPX	Datagram Bytes Received/sec	Rate at which datagram bytes are received by the computer. A datagram is a connectionless packet whose delivery to a remote computer is not guaranteed.
NWLink IPX	Datagram Bytes Sent/sec	Rate at which datagram bytes are sent from the computer. A datagram is a connection-less packet whose delivery to a remote computer is not guaranteed.
NWLink IPX	Datagram Bytes/sec	Rate at which datagram bytes are processed by the computer. This counter is the sum of datagram bytes that are sent and received. A datagram is a connectionless packet whose delivery to a remote computer is not guaranteed.
NWLink IPX	Datagrams Received/sec	Rate at which datagrams are received by the computer. A datagram is a connection-less packet whose delivery to a remote computer is not guaranteed.
NWLink IPX	Datagrams Sent/sec	Rate at which datagrams are sent from the computer. A datagram is a connectionless packet whose delivery to a remote computer is not guaranteed.
NWLink IPX	Datagrams/sec	Rate at which datagrams are processed by the computer. This counter displays the sum of datagrams sent and datagrams received. A datagram is a connectionless packet whose delivery to a remote computer is not guaranteed.
NWLink IPX	Disconnects Local	Number of session disconnections that were initiated by the local computer. This number is an accumulator and shows a running total.
NWLink IPX	Disconnects Remote	Number of session disconnections that were initiated by the remote computer. This number is an accumulator and shows a running total.
NWLink IPX	Expirations Ack	Number of T2 timer expirations.
NWLink IPX	Expirations Response	Number of T1 timer expirations.
NWLink IPX	Failures Adapter	Number of connections that were dropped due to an adapter failure. This number is an accumulator and shows a running total.
NWLink IPX	Failures Link	Number of connections that were dropped due to a link failure. This number is an accumulator and shows a running total.
NWLink IPX	Failures No Listen	Number of connections that were rejected because the remote computer was not listening for connection requests.
NWLink IPX	Failures Not Found	Number of connection attempts that failed because the remote computer could not be found. This number is an accumulator and shows a running total.

(continued)

Object	Object counter	Description
NWLink IPX	Failures Resource Local	Number of connections that failed because of resource problems or shortages on the local computer. This number is an accumulator and shows a running total.
NWLink IPX	Failures Resource Remote	Number of connections that failed because of resource problems or shortages on the remote computer. This number is an accumulator and shows a running total.
NWLink IPX	Frame Bytes Re-Sent/sec	Rate at which data bytes are re-sent by the computer. This counter only counts the bytes in frames that carry data.
NWLink IPX	Frame Bytes Received/sec	Rate at which data bytes are received by the computer. This counter only counts the frames (packets) that carry data.
NWLink IPX	Frame Bytes Rejected/sec	Rate at which data bytes are rejected. This counter only counts the bytes in data frames (packets) that carry data.
NWLink IPX	Frame Bytes Sent/sec	Rate at which data bytes are sent by the computer. This counter only counts the bytes in frames (packets) that carry data.
NWLink IPX	Frame Bytes/sec	Rate at which data bytes are processed by the computer. This counter is the sum of data frame bytes sent and received. This counter only counts the bytes in frames (packets) that carry data.
NWLink IPX	Frames Re-Sent/sec	Rate at which data frames (packets) are re-sent by the computer. This counter only counts the frames or packets that carry data.
NWLink IPX	Frames Received/sec	Rate at which data frames are received by the computer. This counter only counts the frames (packets) that carry data.
NWLink IPX	Frames Rejected/sec	Rate at which data frames are rejected. This counter only counts the frames (packets) that carry data.
NWLink IPX	Frames Sent/sec	Rate at which data frames are sent by the computer. This counter only counts the frames (packets) that carry data.
NWLink IPX	Frames/sec	Rate at which data frames (packets) are processed by the computer. This counter is the sum of data frames sent and data frames received. This counter only counts those frames (packets) that carry data.
NWLink IPX	Packets Received/sec	Rate at which packets are received by the computer. This counter counts all packets processed — control as well as data packets.

Object	Object counter	Description
NWLink IPX	Packets Sent/sec	Rate at which packets are sent by the computer. This counter counts all packets sent by the computer — control as well as data packets.
NWLink IPX	Packets/sec	Rate at which packets are processed by the computer. This count is the sum of Packets Sent and Packets Received per second. This counter includes all packets processed — control as well as data packets.
NWLink IPX	Piggyback Ack Queued/sec	Rate at which piggybacked acknowledgments are queued. Piggybacked acknowledgments are acknowledgments to received packets that are to be included in the next outgoing packet to the remote computer.
NWLink IPX	Piggyback Ack Timeouts	Number of times that a piggybacked acknowledgment could not be sent because there was no outgoing packet to the remote on which to piggyback. A piggybacked acknowledgment is an acknowledgment to a received packet that is sent along in an outgoing data packet to the remote computer. If no outgoing packet is sent within the timeout period, an acknowledgment packet is sent, and this counter is increased by one increment.
NWLink IPX	Window Send Average	Average number of data bytes that were sent before waiting for an acknowledgment from the remote computer.
NWLink IPX	Window Send Maximum	Maximum number of bytes of data that will be sent before waiting for an acknowledgment from the remote computer.
NWLink NetBIOS		
NWLink NetBIOS	Bytes Total/sec	Sum of Frame Bytes/sec and Datagram Bytes/sec. This is the total rate of bytes sent to or received from the network by the protocol but only counts the bytes in frames (packets) that carry data.
NWLink NetBIOS	Connection Session Timeouts	Number of connections that were dropped due to a session timeout. This number is an accumulator and shows a running total.
NWLink NetBIOS	Connections Canceled	Number of connections that were canceled. This number is an accumulator and shows a running total.
NWLink NetBIOS	Connections No Retries	Total number of connections that were successfully made on the first try. This number is an accumulator and shows a running total.

(continued)

Object	Object counter	Description
NWLink NetBIOS	Connections Open	Number of connections currently open for this protocol. This counter shows the current count only and does not accumulate over time.
NWLink NetBIOS	Connections With Retries	Total number of connections that were made after retrying the attempt. A retry occurs when the first connection attempt failed. This number is an accumulator and shows a running total.
NWLink NetBIOS	Datagram Bytes Received/sec	Rate at which datagram bytes are received by the computer. A datagram is a connectionless packet whose delivery to a remote computer is not guaranteed.
NWLink NetBIOS	Datagram Bytes Sent/sec	Rate at which datagram bytes are sent from the computer. A datagram is a connectionless packet whose delivery to a remote computer is not guaranteed.
NWLink NetBIOS	Datagram Bytes/sec	Rate at which datagram bytes are processed by the computer. This counter is the sum of datagram bytes that are sent as well as received. A datagram is a connectionless packet whose delivery to a remote computer is not guaranteed.
NWLink NetBIOS	Datagrams Received/sec	Rate at which datagrams are received by the computer. A datagram is a connectionless packet whose delivery to a remote computer is not guaranteed.
NWLink NetBIOS	Datagrams Sent/sec	Rate at which datagrams are sent from the computer. A datagram is a connectionless packet whose delivery to a remote computer is not guaranteed.
NWLink NetBIOS	Datagrams/sec	Rate at which datagrams are processed by the computer. This counter displays the sum of datagrams sent and datagrams received. A datagram is a connectionless packet whose delivery to a remote computer is not guaranteed.
NWLink NetBIOS	Disconnects Local	Number of session disconnections that were initiated by the local computer. This number is an accumulator and shows a running total.
NWLink NetBIOS	Disconnects Remote	Number of session disconnections that were initiated by the remote computer. This number is an accumulator and shows a running total.
NWLink NetBIOS	Expirations Ack	Number of T2 timer expirations.
NWLink NetBIOS	Expirations Response	Number of T1 timer expirations.
NWLink NetBIOS	Failures Adapter	Number of connections that were dropped due to an adapter failure. This number is an accumulator and shows a running total.
NWLink NetBIOS	Failures Link	Number of connections that were dropped due to a link failure. This number is an accumulator and shows a running total.

Object	Object counter	Description
NWLink NetBIOS	Failures No Listen	Number of connections that were rejected because the remote computer was not listening for connection requests.
NWLink NetBIOS	Failures Not Found	Number of connection attempts that failed because the remote computer could not be found. This number is an accumulator and shows a running total.
NWLink NetBIOS	Failures Resource Local	Number of connections that failed because of resource problems or shortages on the local computer. This number is an accumulator and shows a running total.
NWLink NetBIOS	Failures Resource Remote	Number of connections that failed because of resource problems or shortages on the remote computer. This number is an accumulator and shows a running total.
NWLink NetBIOS	Frame Bytes Re-Sent/sec	Rate at which data bytes are re-sent by the computer. This counter only counts the bytes in frames that carry data.
NWLink NetBIOS	Frame Bytes Received/sec	Rate at which data bytes are received by the computer. This counter only counts the frames (packets) that carry data.
NWLink NetBIOS	Frame Bytes Rejected/sec	Rate at which data bytes are rejected. This counter only counts the bytes in data frames (packets) that carry data.
NWLink NetBIOS	Frame Bytes/sec	Rate at which data bytes are sent by the computer. This counter only counts the bytes in frames (packets) that carry data.
NWLink NetBIOS	Frame Bytes/sec	Rate at which data bytes are processed by the computer. This counter is the sum of data frame bytes sent and received. This counter only counts the bytes in frames (packets) that carry data.
NWLink NetBIOS	Frames Re-Sent/sec	Rate at which data frames (packets) are re-sent by the computer. This counter only counts the frames or packets that carry data.
NWLink NetBIOS	Frames Received/sec	Rate at which data frames are received by the computer. This counter only counts the frames (packets) that carry data.
NWLink NetBIOS	Frames Rejected/sec	Rate at which data frames are rejected. This counter only counts the frames (packets) that carry data.
NWLink NetBIOS	Frames Sent/sec	Rate at which data frames are sent by the computer. This counter only counts the frames (packets) that carry data.

(continued)

Object	Object counter	Description
NWLink NetBIOS	Frames/sec	Rate at which data frames (or packets) are processed by the computer. This counter is the sum of data frames sent and data frames received. This counter only counts those frames (packets) that carry data.
NWLink NetBIOS	Packets Received/sec	Rate at which packets are received by the computer. This counter counts all packets processed — control as well as data packets.
NWLink NetBIOS	Packets Sent/sec	Rate at which packets are sent by the computer. This counter counts all packets sent by the computer — control as well as data packets.
NWLink NetBIOS	Packets/sec	Rate at which packets are processed by the computer. This count is the sum of Packets Sent and Packets Received per second. This counter includes all packets processed — control as well as data packets.
NWLink NetBIOS	Piggyback Ack Queued/sec	Rate at which piggybacked acknowledgments are queued. Piggybacked acknowledgments are acknowledgments to received packets that are to be included in the next outgoing packet to the remote computer.
NWLink NetBIOS	Piggyback Ack Timeouts	Number of times that a piggybacked acknowledgment could not be sent because there was no outgoing packet to the remote on which to piggyback. A piggybacked acknowledgment is an acknowledgment to a received packet that is sent along in an outgoing data packet to the remote computer. If no outgoing packet is sent within the timeout period, an acknowledgment packet is sent, and this counter increases by one increment.
NWLink NetBIOS	Window Send Average	Average number of data bytes that were sent before waiting for an acknowledgment from the remote computer.
NWLink NetBIOS	Window Send Maximum	Maximum number of bytes of data that will be sent before waiting for an acknowledgment from the remote computer.
NWLink SPX		
NWLink SPX	Bytes Total/sec	Sum of Frame Bytes/sec and Datagram Bytes/sec. This is the total rate of bytes sent to or received from the network by the protocol, but it only counts the bytes in frames (packets) that carry data.
NWLink SPX	Connection Session Timeouts	Number of connections that were dropped due to a session timeout. This number is an accumulator and shows a running total.
NWLink SPX	Connections Canceled	Number of connections that were canceled. This number is an accumulator and shows a running total.

Object	Object counter	Description
NWLink SPX	Connections No Retries	Total number of connections that were successfully made on the first try. This number is an accumulator and shows a running total.
NWLink SPX	Connections Open	Number of connections currently open for this protocol. This counter shows the current count only and does not accumulate over time.
NWLink SPX	Connections With Retries	Total number of connections that were made after retrying the attempt. A retry occurs when the first connection attempt failed. This number is an accumulator and shows a running total.
NWLink SPX	Datagram Bytes Received/sec	Rate at which datagram bytes are received by the computer. A datagram is a connectionless packet whose delivery to a remote computer is not guaranteed.
NWLink SPX	Datagram Bytes Sent/sec	Rate at which datagram bytes are sent from the computer. A datagram is a connectionless packet whose delivery to a remote computer is not guaranteed.
NWLink SPX	Datagram Bytes/sec	Rate at which datagram bytes are processed by the computer. This counter is the sum of datagram bytes that are sent as well as received. A datagram is a connectionless packet whose delivery to a remote computer is not guaranteed.
NWLink SPX	Datagrams Received/sec	Rate at which datagrams are received by the computer. A datagram is a connectionless packet whose delivery to a remote computer is not guaranteed.
NWLink SPX	Datagrams Sent/sec	Rate at which datagrams are sent from the computer. A datagram is a connectionless packet whose delivery to a remote computer is not guaranteed.
NWLink SPX	Datagrams/sec	Rate at which datagrams are processed by the computer. This counter displays the sum of datagrams sent and datagrams received. A datagram is a connectionless packet whose delivery to a remote computer is not guaranteed.
NWLink SPX	Disconnects Local	Number of session disconnections that were initiated by the local computer. This number is an accumulator and shows a running total.
NWLink SPX	Disconnects Remote	Number of session disconnections that were initiated by the remote computer. This number is an accumulator and shows a running total.
NWLink SPX	Expirations Ack	Number of T2 timer expirations.
NWLink SPX	Expirations Response	Number of T1 timer expirations.

(continued)

Object	Object counter	Description
NWLink SPX	Failures Adapter	Number of connections that were dropped due to an adapter failure. This number is an accumulator and shows a running total.
NWLink SPX	Failures Link	Number of connections that were dropped due to a link failure. This number is an accumulator and shows a running total.
NWLink SPX	Failures No Listen	Number of connections that were rejected because the remote computer was not listening for connection requests.
NWLink SPX	Failures Not Found	Number of connection attempts that failed because the remote computer could not be found. This number is an accumulator and shows a running total.
NWLink SPX	Failures Resource Local	Number of connections that failed because of resource problems or shortages on the local computer. This number is an accumulator and shows a running total.
NWLink SPX	Failures Resource Remote	Number of connections that failed because of resource problems or shortages on the remote computer. This number is an accumulator and shows a running total.
NWLink SPX	Frame Bytes Re-Sent/sec	Rate at which data bytes are re-sent by the computer. This counter only counts the bytes in frames that carry data.
NWLink SPX	Frame Bytes Received/sec	Rate at which data bytes are received by the computer. This counter only counts the frames (packets) that carry data.
NWLink SPX	Frame Bytes Rejected/sec	Rate at which data bytes are rejected. This counter only counts the bytes in data frames (packets) that carry data.
NWLink SPX	Frame Bytes Sent/sec	Rate at which data bytes are sent by the computer. This counter only counts the bytes in frames (packets) that carry data.
NWLink SPX	Frame Bytes/sec	Rate at which data bytes are processed by the computer. This counter is the sum of data frame bytes sent and received. This counter only counts the bytes in frames (packets) that carry data.
NWLink SPX	Frames Re-Sent/sec	Rate at which data frames (packets) are re-sent by the computer. This counter only counts the frames or packets that carry data.
NWLink SPX	Frames Received/sec	Rate at which data frames are received by the computer. This counter only counts the frames (packets) that carry data.
NWLink SPX	Frames Rejected/sec	Rate at which data frames are rejected. This counter only counts the frames (packets) that carry data.

Object	Object counter	Description
NWLink SPX	Frames Sent/sec	Rate at which data frames are sent by the computer. This counter only counts the frames (packets) that carry data.
NWLink SPX	Frames/sec	Rate at which data frames (packets) are processed by the computer. This counter is the sum of data frames sent and data frames received. This counter only counts those frames (packets) that carry data.
NWLink SPX	Packets Received/sec	Rate at which packets are received by the computer. This counter counts all packets processed — control as well as data packets.
NWLink SPX	Packets Sent/sec	Rate at which packets are sent by the computer. This counter counts all packets sent by the computer — control as well as data packets.
NWLink SPX	Packets/sec	Rate at which packets are processed by the computer. This count is the sum of Packets Sent and Packets Received per second. This counter includes all packets processed — control as well as data packets.
NWLink SPX	Piggyback Ack Queued/sec	Rate at which piggybacked acknowledgments are queued. Piggybacked acknowledgments are acknowledgments to received packets that are to be included in the next outgoing packet to the remote computer.
NWLink SPX	Piggyback Ack Timeouts	Number of times that a piggybacked acknowledgment could not be sent because there was no outgoing packet to the remote on which to piggyback. A piggybacked acknowledgment is an acknowledgment to a received packet that is sent along in an outgoing data packet to the remote computer. If no outgoing packet is sent within the timeout period, an acknowledgment packet is sent, and this counter increases by one.
NWLink SPX	Window Send Average	Average number of data bytes that were sent before waiting for an acknowledgment from the remote computer.
NWLink SPX	Window Send Maximum	Maximum number of bytes of data that will be sent before waiting for an acknowledgment from the remote computer.
Objects		
Objects	Events	Number of events in the computer at the time of data collection. This is an instantaneous count, not an average over the time interval. An event is used when two or more threads have to synchronize execution.

(continued)

Object	Object counter	Description
Objects	Mutexes	Counts the number of mutexes in the computer at the time of data collection. This is an instantaneous count, not an average over the time interval. Mutexes are used by threads to ensure that only one thread is executing some section of code.
Objects	Processes	Number of processes in the computer at the time of data collection. This is an instantaneous count, not an average over the time interval. Each process represents the running of a program.
Objects	Sections	Number of sections in the computer at the time of data collection. This is an instantaneous count, not an average over the time interval. A section is a portion of virtual memory created by a process for storing data. A process may share sections with other processes.
Objects	Semaphores	Number of semaphores in the computer at the time of data collection. This is an instantaneous count, not an average over the time interval. Threads use semaphores to obtain exclusive access to data structures they share with other threads.
Objects	Threads	Number of threads in the computer at the time of data collection. This is an instantaneous count, not an average over the time interval. A thread is the basic executable entity that can execute instructions in a processor.
Paging File		
Paging File	% Usage	Percentage of time that the Page File instance is in use. See also *Process: Page File Bytes*.
Paging File	% Usage Peak	Percentage of time that Page File is at peak usage. See also *Process: Page File Bytes Peak*.
PhysicalDisk		
PhysicalDisk	% Disk Read Time	Percentage of elapsed time that the selected disk drive is servicing read requests.
PhysicalDisk	% Disk Time	Percentage of elapsed time that the selected disk drive is servicing read or write requests.
PhysicalDisk	% Disk Write Time	Percentage of elapsed time that the selected disk drive is servicing write requests.
PhysicalDisk	Avg. Disk Bytes/Read	Average number of bytes transferred from the disk during read operations.
PhysicalDisk	Avg. Disk Bytes/Transfer	Average number of bytes transferred to or from the disk during write or read operations.

Object	Object counter	Description
PhysicalDisk	Avg. Disk Bytes/Write	Average number of bytes transferred to the disk during write operations.
PhysicalDisk	Avg. Disk sec/Read	Average time in seconds of a read of data from the disk.
PhysicalDisk	Avg. Disk sec/Transfer	Time in seconds of the average disk transfer.
PhysicalDisk	Avg. Disk sec/Write	Average time in seconds of a write of data to the disk.
PhysicalDisk	Disk Bytes/sec	Rate bytes are transferred to or from the disk during write or read operations.
PhysicalDisk	Disk Queue Length	Number of requests outstanding on the disk at the time the performance data is collected. It includes requests in service at the time of the snapshot. This is an instantaneous length, not an average over the time interval. Multi-spindle disk devices can have multiple requests active at one time, but other concurrent requests are awaiting service. This counter may reflect a transitory high or low queue length, but if there is a sustained load on the disk drive, it is likely that this will be consistently high. Requests are experiencing delays proportional to the length of this queue minus the number of spindles on the disks. For good performance, this difference should average less than 2.
PhysicalDisk	Disk Read Bytes/sec	Rate at which bytes are transferred from the disk during read operations.
PhysicalDisk	Disk Reads/sec	Rate of read operations on the disk.
PhysicalDisk	Disk Transfers/sec	Rate of read and write operations on the disk.
PhysicalDisk	Disk Write Bytes/sec	Rate at which bytes are transferred to the disk during write operations.
PhysicalDisk	Disk Writes/sec	Rate of write operations on the disk.
Process		
Process	% Privileged Time	Percentage of elapsed time that this process's threads have have spent executing code in Privileged Mode. When a Windows NT system service is called, the service will often run in Privileged Mode to gain access to system-private data. Such data is protected from access by threads executing in User Mode. Calls to the system may be explicit, or they may be implicit such as when a page fault or an interrupt occurs. Unlike some early operating systems, Windows NT uses process boundaries for subsystem protection in addition to the traditional protection of User and Privileged modes. Therefore, some work done by Windows NT on behalf of your application may appear in other subsystem processes in addition to the Privileged Time in your process.

(continued)

Object	Object counter	Description
Process	% Processor Time	Percentage of elapsed time that all of the threads of this process used the processor to execute instructions. An instruction is the basic unit of execution in a computer, a thread is the object that executes instructions, and a process is the object created when a program is run. Code executed to handle certain hardware interrupts or trap conditions may be counted for this process.
Process	% User Time	Percentage of elapsed time that this process's threads have spent executing code in User Mode. Applications execute in User Mode, as do subsystems like the window manager and the graphics engine. Code executing in User Mode cannot damage the integrity of the Windows NT Executive, Kernel, and device drivers. Unlike some early operating systems, Windows NT uses process boundaries for subsystem protection in addition to the traditional protection of User and Privileged modes. Therefore, some work done by Windows NT on behalf of your application may appear in other sub-system processes in addition to the Privileged Time in your process.
Process	Elapsed Time	Total elapsed time (in seconds) that this process has been running.
Process	Handle Count	Total number of handles currently open by this process. This number is the sum of the handles currently open by each thread in this process.
Process	ID Process	Unique identifier of this process. ID Process numbers are reused, so they only identify a process for the lifetime of that process.
Process	Page Faults/sec	Rate of page faults by the threads executing in this process. A page fault occurs when a thread refers to a virtual memory page that is not in its working set in main memory. This will not cause the page to be fetched from disk if it is on the standby list and hence already in main memory, or if it is in use by another process with which the page is shared.
Process	Page File Bytes	Current number of bytes that this process has used in the paging file(s). Paging files are used to store pages of memory used by the process that are not contained in other files. Paging files are shared by all processes, and lack of space in paging files can prevent other processes from allocating memory.
Process	Page File Bytes Peak	Maximum number of bytes that this process has used in the paging file(s). Paging files are used to store pages of memory used by the process that are not contained in other files. Paging files are shared by all processes, and lack of space in paging files can prevent other processes from allocating memory.

Object	Object counter	Description
Process	Pool Nonpaged Bytes	Number of bytes in the Nonpaged Pool, which is a system memory area where space is acquired by operating system components as they accomplish their appointed tasks. Nonpaged Pool pages cannot be paged out to the paging file, but instead remain in main memory as long as they are allocated.
Process	Pool Paged Bytes	Number of bytes in the Paged Pool, which is a system memory area where space is acquired by operating system components as they accomplish their appointed tasks. Paged Pool pages can be paged out to the paging file when not accessed by the system for sustained periods of time.
Process	Priority Base	Current base priority of this process. Threads within a process can raise and lower their own base priority relative to the process's base priority.
Process	Private Bytes	Current number of bytes that this process has allocated that cannot be shared with other processes.
Process	Thread Count	Number of threads currently active in this process. An instruction is the basic unit of execution in a processor, and a thread is the object that executes instructions. Every running process has at least one thread.
Process	Virtual Bytes	Current size in bytes of the virtual address space that the process is using. Use of virtual address space does not necessarily imply corresponding use of either disk or main memory pages. Virtual space is finite, and by using too much, the process may limit its ability to load libraries.
Process	Virtual Bytes Peak	Maximum number of bytes of virtual address space that the process has used at any one time. Use of virtual address space does not necessarily imply corresponding use of either disk or main memory pages. Virtual space is finite, and by using too much, the process may limit its ability to load libraries.
Process	Working Set	Current number of bytes in the Working Set of this process. The Working Set is the set of memory pages touched recently by the threads in the process. If free memory in the computer is above a threshold, pages are left in the Working Set of a process even if they are not in use. When free memory falls below a threshold, pages are trimmed from Working Sets. If they are needed, they will then be soft-faulted back into the Working Set before they leave main memory.

(continued)

Object	Object counter	Description
Process	Working Set Peak	Maximum number of bytes in the Working Set of this process at any point in time. The Working Set is the set of memory pages touched recently by the threads in the process. If free memory in the computer is above a threshold, pages are left in the Working Set of a process even if they are not in use. When free memory falls below a threshold, pages are trimmed from Working Sets. If they are needed they will then be soft-faulted back into the Working Set before they leave main memory.
Processor		
Processor	% DPC Time	Percentage of elapsed time that the processor spent in Deferred Procedure Calls. When a hardware device interrupts the processor, the Interrupt Handler may elect to execute the majority of its work in a DPC. DPCs run at lower priority than interrupts and so permit interrupts to occur while DPC is being executed. Deferred Procedure Calls are executed in Privileged Mode, so this is a component of Processor: % Privileged Time. This counter can help determine the source of excessive time being spent in Privileged Mode.
Processor	% Interrupt Time	Percentage of elapsed time that the processor spent handling hardware interrupts. When a hardware device interrupts the processor, the Interrupt Handler will execute to handle the condition, usually by signaling I/O completion and possibly issuing another pending I/O request. Some of this work may be done in a Deferred Procedure Call (see *% DPC Time*). However, time spent in DPCs is not counted as time in interrupts. Interrupts are executed in Privileged Mode, so this is a component of Processor: % Privileged Time. This counter can help determine the source of excessive time being spent in Privileged Mode.
Processor	% Privileged Time	Percentage of processor time spent in Privileged Mode in non-Idle threads. The Windows NT service layer, the Executive routines, and the Windows NT Kernel execute in Privileged Mode. Device drivers for most devices other than graphics adapters and printers also execute in Privileged Mode. Unlike some early operating systems, Windows NT uses process boundaries for subsystem protection in addition to the traditional protection of User and Privileged modes. Therefore, some work done by Windows NT on behalf of your application may appear in other subsystem processes in addition to the Privileged Time in your process.

Object	Object counter	Description
Processor	% Processor Time	Percentage of the elapsed time that a processor is busy executing a non-Idle thread. It can be viewed as the fraction of the time spent doing useful work. Each processor is assigned an Idle thread in the Idle process which consumes those unproductive processor cycles not used by any other threads.
Processor	% User Time	Percentage of processor time spent in User Mode in non-Idle threads. All application code and subsystem code executes in User Mode. The graphics engine, graphics device drivers, printer device drivers, and the window manager also execute in User Mode. Code executing in User Mode cannot damage the integrity of the Windows NT Executive, Kernel, and device drivers. Unlike some early operating systems, Windows NT uses process boundaries for subsystem protection in addition to the traditional protection of User and Privileged modes. Therefore, some work done by Windows NT on behalf of your application may appear in other subsystem processes in addition to the Privileged Time in your process.
Processor	APC Bypasses/sec	Rate at which kernel APC interrupts were short-circuited.
Processor	DPC Bypasses/sec	Rate at which Dispatch interrupts were short-circuited.
Processor	DPC Rate	Average rate at which DPC objects are queued to this processor's DPC queue per clock tick.
Processor	DPCs Queued/sec	Rate at which DPC objects are queued to this processor's DPC queue.
Processor	Interrupts/sec	Number of device interrupts that the processor is experiencing. A device interrupts the processor when it has completed a task or when it otherwise requires attention. Normal thread execution is suspended during interrupts. An interrupt may cause the processor to switch to another, higher-priority thread. Clock interrupts are frequent and periodic and create a background of interrupt activity.
RAS Port		
RAS Port	Alignment Errors	Total number of Alignment Errors for this connection. Alignment Errors occur when a byte received is different from the byte expected.
RAS Port	Buffer Overrun Errors	Total number of Buffer Overrun Errors for this connection. Buffer Overrun Errors occur when the software cannot handle the rate at which data is received.
RAS Port	Bytes Received	Total number of bytes received for this connection.

(continued)

Object	Object counter	Description
RAS Port	Bytes Received/sec	Number of bytes received per second.
RAS Port	Bytes Transmitted	Total number of bytes transmitted for this connection.
RAS Port	Bytes Transmitted/sec	Number of bytes transmitted per second.
RAS Port	CRC Errors	Total number of CRC Errors for this connection. CRC Errors occur when the frame received contains erroneous data.
RAS Port	Frames Received	Total number of data frames received for this connection.
RAS Port	Frames Received/sec	Number of frames received per second.
RAS Port	Frames Transmitted	Total number of data frames transmitted for this connection.
RAS Port	Frames Transmitted/sec	Number of frames transmitted per second.
RAS Port	Percent Compression In	Compression ratio for bytes being received.
RAS Port	Percent Compression Out	Compression ratio for bytes being transmitted.
RAS Port	Serial Overrun Errors	Total number of Serial Overrun Errors for this connection. Serial Overrun Errors occur when the hardware cannot handle the rate at which data is received.
RAS Port	Timeout Errors	Total number of Timeout Errors for this connection. Timeout Errors occur when an expected signal is not received in time.
RAS Port	Total Errors	Total number of CRC, Timeout, Serial Overrun, Alignment, and Buffer Overrun Errors for this connection.
RAS Port	Total Errors/sec	Total number of CRC, Timeout, Serial Overrun, Alignment, and Buffer Overrun Errors per second.
RAS Total		
RAS Total	Alignment Errors	Total number of Alignment Errors for this connection. Alignment Errors occur when a byte received is different from the byte expected.
RAS Total	Buffer Overrun Errors	Total number of Buffer Overrun Errors for this connection. Buffer Overrun Errors occur when the software cannot handle the rate at which data is received.
RAS Total	Bytes Received	Total number of bytes received for this connection.

Object	Object counter	Description
RAS Total	Bytes Received/sec	Number of bytes received per second.
RAS Total	Bytes Transmitted	Total number of bytes transmitted for this connection.
RAS Total	Bytes Transmitted/sec	Number of bytes transmitted per second.
RAS Total	CRC Errors	Total number of CRC Errors for this connection. CRC Errors occur when the frame received contains erroneous data.
RAS Total	Frames Received	Total number of data frames received for this connection.
RAS Total	Frames Received/sec	Number of frames received per second.
RAS Total	Frames Transmitted	Total number of data frames transmitted for this connection.
RAS Total	Frames Transmitted/sec	Number of frames transmitted per second.
RAS Total	Percent Compression In	Compression ratio for bytes being received.
RAS Total	Percent Compression Out	Compression ratio for bytes being transmitted.
RAS Total	Serial Overrun Errors	Total number of Serial Overrun Errors for this connection. Serial Overrun Errors occur when the hardware cannot handle the rate at which data is received.
RAS Total	Timeout Errors	Total number of Timeout Errors for this connection. Timeout Errors occur when an expected signal is not received in time.
RAS Total	Total Errors	Total number of CRC, Timeout, Serial Overrun, Alignment, and Buffer Overrun Errors for this connection.
RAS Total	Total Errors/sec	Total number of CRC, Timeout, Serial Overrun, Alignment, and Buffer Overrun Errors per second.
Redirector		
Redirector	Bytes Received/sec	Rate of bytes coming in to the redirector from the network. It includes all application data as well as network protocol information (such as packet headers).
Redirector	Bytes Total/sec	Rate at which the redirector is processing data bytes. This includes all application and file data in addition to protocol information (such as packet headers).
Redirector	Bytes Transmitted/sec	Rate at which bytes are leaving the redirector to the network. It includes all application data as well as network protocol information (such as packet headers and the like).

(continued)

Object	Object counter	Description
Redirector	Connects Core	Number of connections to servers running the original MS-Net SMB protocol, including MS-Net itself, Xenix and Vax.
Redirector	Connects Lan Manager 2.0	Number of connections to Lan Manager 2.0 servers, including LMX servers.
Redirector	Connects Lan Manager 2.1	Number of connections to Lan Manager 2.1 servers, including LMX servers.
Redirector	Connects Windows NT	Number of connections to Windows NT computers.
Redirector	Current Commands	Number of requests to the redirector that are currently queued for service. If this number is much larger than the number of installed network adapter cards, the network(s) and/or server(s) being accessed will be seriously bottlenecked.
Redirector	File Data Operations/sec	Rate at which the redirector processes data operations. One operation includes (hopefully) many bytes. I say "hopefully" here because each operation has overhead. You can determine the efficiency of this path by dividing the Bytes/sec by this counter to determine the average number of bytes transferred per operation.
Redirector	File Read Operations/sec	Rate at which applications ask the redirector for data. Each call to a file system or similar Application Program Interface (API) call counts as one operation.
Redirector	File Write Operations/sec	Rate at which applications send data to the redirector. Each call to a file system or similar Application Program Interface (API) call counts as one operation.
Redirector	Network Errors/sec	Number of serious unexpected errors, which generally indicate that the redirector and one or more servers are having serious communication difficulties. For example, an SMB (server manager block) protocol error will generate a Network Error. These errors result in an entry in the system Event Log, so look there for details.
Redirector	Packets Received/sec	Rate at which the redirector is receiving packets (also called SMBs or server message blocks). Network transmissions are divided into packets. The average number of bytes received in a packet can be obtained by dividing Bytes Received/sec by this counter. Some packets received may not contain incoming data; for example, an acknowledgment to a write made by the redirector would count as an incoming packet.
Redirector	Packets Transmitted/sec	Rate at which the redirector is sending packets (also called SMBs or server message blocks). Network transmissions are divided into packets. The average number of bytes transmitted in a packet can be obtained by dividing Bytes Transmitted/sec by this counter.

Object	Object counter	Description
Redirector	Packets/sec	Rate at which the redirector is processing data packets. One packet includes (hopefully) many bytes. I say "hopefully" here because each packet has protocol overhead. You can determine the efficiency of this path by dividing the Bytes/sec by this counter to determine the average number of bytes transferred per packet, you can divide this counter by Operations/sec to determine the average number of packets per operation.
Redirector	Read Bytes Cache/sec	Rate at which applications on your computer are accessing the cache using the redirector. Some of these data requests may be satisfied by merely retrieving the data from the system cache on your own computer if it happened to have been used recently and there was room to keep it in the cache. Requests that miss the cache will cause a page fault (see *Read Bytes Paging/sec*).
Redirector	Read Bytes Network/sec	Rate at which applications are reading data across the network. For some reason, the data was not in the system cache, and these bytes actually came across the network. Dividing this number by Bytes Received/sec will indicate the efficiency of data coming in from the network, because all of these bytes are real application data (see *Bytes Received/sec*).
Redirector	Read Bytes Non-Paging/sec	Bytes read by the redirector in response to normal file requests by an application when those bytes are redirected to come from another computer. In addition to file requests, this counter includes other methods of reading across the network such as Named Pipes and Transactions. This counter does not count network protocol information, just application data.
Redirector	Read Bytes Paging/sec	Rate at which the redirector is attempting to read bytes in response to page faults. Page faults are caused by loading of modules (such as programs and libraries), by a miss in the cache (see *Read Bytes Cache/sec*), or by files directly mapped into the address space of applications (a high-performance feature of Windows NT).
Redirector	Read Operations Random/sec	Rate at which, on a file-by-file basis, reads are made that are not sequential. If a read is made using a particular file handle and then is followed by another read that is not contiguous, this counter increases by one increment.
Redirector	Read Packets Small/sec	Rate at which reads less than one-fourth of the server's negotiated buffer size are made by applications. Too many of these could indicate a waste of buffers on the server. This counter is increased by one increment for each read. It does not count packets.

(continued)

Object	Object counter	Description
Redirector	Read Packets/sec	Rate at which read packets are being placed on the network. Each time a single packet is sent with a request to read data remotely, this counter is increased by one increment.
Redirector	Reads Denied/sec	Rate at which the server is unable to accommodate requests for Raw Reads. When a read is much larger than the server's negotiated buffer size, the redirector requests a Raw Read which, if granted, permits the transfer of the data without a lot of protocol overhead on each packet. To accomplish this, the server must lock out other requests, so the request is denied if the server is really busy.
Redirector	Reads Large/sec	Rate at which reads over twice the server's negotiated buffer size are made by applications. Too many of these could place a strain on server resources. This counter is increased by one increment for each read. It does not count packets.
Redirector	Server Disconnects	Number of times that a server has disconnected your redirector. See also *Server Reconnects*.
Redirector	Server Reconnects	Number of times that your redirector has had to reconnect to a server in order to complete a new active request. You can be disconnected by the server if you remain inactive for too long. Locally even if all your remote files are closed, the redirector will keep your connections intact for (nominally) ten minutes. Such inactive connections are called Dormant Connections. Reconnecting is expensive in terms of time.
Redirector	Server Sessions	Number of active security objects that the redirector is managing. For example, a logon to a server followed by a network access to the same server will establish one connection, but two sessions.
Redirector	Server Sessions Hung	Number of active sessions that are timed out and unable to proceed due to a lack of response from the remote server.
Redirector	Write Bytes Cache/sec	Rate at which applications on your computer are writing to the cache using the redirector. The data may not leave your computer immediately but may be retained in the cache for further modification before being written to the network. This saves network traffic. Each write of a byte into the cache is counted here.
Redirector	Write Bytes Network/sec	Rate at which your applications are writing data across the network. Either the system cache was bypassed, as for Named Pipes or Transactions, or else the cache wrote the bytes to make room for other data. Dividing this counter by Bytes Transmitted/sec will indicate the efficiency of data written to the network, because all of these bytes are real application data (see *Bytes Transmitted/sec*).

Object	Object counter	Description
Redirector	Write Bytes Non-Paging/sec	Rate of the bytes that are written by the redirector in response to normal file outputs by an application when they are redirected to go to another computer. In addition to file requests, this counter includes other methods of writing across the network such as Named Pipes and Transactions. This counter does not count network protocol information, just application data.
Redirector	Write Bytes Paging/sec	Rate at which the redirector is attempting to write bytes changed in the pages being used by applications. The program data changed by modules (such as programs and libraries) that were loaded over the network are "paged out" when no longer needed. Other output pages come from the cache (see *Write Bytes Cache/sec*).
Redirector	Write Operations Random/sec	Rate at which, on a file-by-file basis, writes are made that are not sequential. If a write is made using a particular file handle and then is followed by another write that is not contiguous, this counter is increased by one increment.
Redirector	Write Packets Small/sec	Rate at which writes are made by applications that are less than one-fourth of the server's negotiated buffer size. Too many of these writes could indicate a waste of buffers on the server. This counter is increased by one for each write — it counts writes, not packets.
Redirector	Write Packets/sec	Rate at which writes are being sent to the network. Each time that a single packet is sent with a request to write remote data, this counter is increased by one increment.
Redirector	Writes Denied/sec	Rate at which the server is unable to accommodate requests for Raw Writes. When a write is much larger than the server's negotiated buffer size, the redirector requests a Raw Write which, if granted, would permit the transfer of the data without a lot of protocol overhead on each packet. To accomplish this, the server must lock out other requests, so the request is denied if the server is really busy.
Redirector	Writes Large/sec	Rate at which writes are made by applications that are over twice the server's negotiated buffer size. Too many of these writes could place a strain on server resources. This counter is increased by one increment for each write — it counts writes, not packets.
Server		
Server	Blocking Requests Rejected	Number of times that the server has rejected blocking SMBs due to insufficient count of free work items. Indicates whether the maxworkitem or minfreeworkitems server parameters need tuning.

(continued)

Object	Object counter	Description
Server	Bytes Received/sec	Number of bytes the server has received from the network. Indicates how busy the server is.
Server	Bytes Total/sec	Number of bytes the server has sent to and received from the network. This value provides an overall indication of how busy the server is.
Server	Bytes Transmitted/sec	Number of bytes the server has sent on the network. Indicates how busy the server is.
Server	Context Blocks Queued/sec	Rate at which work context blocks had to be placed on the server's FSP queue to await server action.
Server	Errors Access Permissions	Number of times open on behalf of clients that have failed with STATUS_ACCESS_DENIED messages. Can indicate whether somebody is randomly attempting to access files to get at something that was not properly protected.
Server	Errors Granted Access	Number of times that access to files opened successfully was denied. Can indicate attempts to access files without proper access authorization.
Server	Errors Logon	Number of failed logon attempts to the server. Can indicate whether password guessing programs are being used to crack the security on the server.
Server	Errors System	Number of times an internal server error was detected. Unexpected errors usually indicate a problem with the server.
Server	File Directory Searches	Number of searches for files currently active in the server. Indicates current server activity.
Server	Files Open	Number of files currently open in the server. Indicates current server activity.
Server	Files Opened Total	Number of successful open attempts performed by the server on behalf of clients. Useful in determining the amount of file I/O, the overhead for path-based operations, and the effectiveness of oplocks.
Server	Logon Total	Total number of interactive logons, network logons, service logons, successful logons, and failed logons since the machine was last rebooted.
Server	Logon/sec	Rate of all interactive logons, network logons, service logons, successful logons, and failed logons.
Server	Pool Nonpaged Bytes	Number of bytes of nonpageable computer memory the server is currently using. Can help in determining good values for the maxnonpagedmemoryusage parameter.

Object	Object counter	Description
Server	Pool Nonpaged Failures	Number of times allocations from nonpaged pool have failed. Indicates the computer's physical memory is too small.
Server	Pool Nonpaged Peak	Maximum number of bytes of nonpaged pool the server has had in use at any one point. Indicates how much physical memory the computer should have.
Server	Pool Paged Bytes	Maximum number of bytes of paged pool the server has had allocated. Indicates the proper sizes of the page file(s) and physical memory.
Server	Pool Paged Failures	Number of times allocations from paged pool have failed. Indicates the computer's physical memory of page file is too small.
Server	Pool Paged Peak	Number of bytes of pageable computer memory the server is currently using. Can help in determining good values for the maxpagedmemoryusage parameter.
Server	Server Sessions	Number of sessions currently active in the server. Indicates current server activity.
Server	Sessions Errored Out	Number of sessions that have been closed due to unexpected error conditions. Indicates how frequently network problems are causing dropped sessions on the server.
Server	Sessions Forced Off	Number of sessions that have been forced to logoff. Can indicate how many sessions were forced to logoff due to logon time constraints.
Server	Sessions Logged Off	Number of sessions that have terminated normally. Useful in interpreting the Sessions Timed Out and Sessions Errored Out statistics — allows percentage calculations.
Server	Sessions Timed Out	Number of sessions that have been closed due to their idle time exceeding the autodisconnect parameter for the server. Shows whether the autodisconnect setting is helping to conserve resources.
Server	Work Item Shortages	Number of times that STATUS_DATA_NOT_ACCEPTED was returned at receive indication time. This occurs when no work item is available or can be allocated to service the incoming request. Indicates whether the initworkitems or maxworkitems parameters need tuning.
Server Work Queues		
Server Work Queues	Active Threads	Number of threads currently working on a request from the server client for this CPU. The system keeps this number as low as possible to minimize unnecessary context switching. This is an instantaneous count for the CPU, not an average over time.

(continued)

Object	Object counter	Description
Server Work Queues	Available Threads	Number of server threads on this CPU not currently working on requests from a client. The server dynamically adjusts the number of threads to maximize server performance.
Server Work Queues	Available Work Items	Every request from a client is represented in the server as a *work item*, and the server maintains a pool of available work items per CPU to speed processing. This is the instantaneous number of available work items for this CPU. A sustained near-zero value indicates the need to increase the MinFreeWorkItems registry value for the server service. This value will always be 0 in the Blocking Queue instance.
Server Work Queues	Borrowed Work Items	Every request from a client is represented in the server as a *work item*, and the server maintains a pool of available work items per CPU to speed processing. When a CPU runs out of work items, it borrows a free work item from another CPU. An increasing value of this running counter may indicate the need to increase the MaxWorkItems or MinFreeWorkItems registry values for the server service. This value will always be 0 in the Blocking Queue instance.
Server Work Queues	Bytes Received/sec	Rate at which the server is receiving bytes from the network clients on this CPU. This value is a measure of how busy the server is.
Server Work Queues	Bytes Sent/sec	Rate at which the server is sending bytes to the network clients on this CPU. This value is a measure of how busy the server is.
Server Work Queues	Bytes Transferred/sec	Rate at which the server is sending and receiving bytes with the network clients on this CPU. This value is a measure of how busy the server is.
Server Work Queues	Context Blocks Queued/sec	Rate at which work context blocks had to be placed on the server's FSP queue to await server action.
Server Work Queues	Current Clients	Instantaneous count of the clients being serviced by this CPU. The server actively balances the client load across all of the CPUs in the system. This value will always be 0 in the Blocking Queue instance.
Server Work Queues	Queue Length	Current length of the server work queue for this CPU. A sustained queue length greater than four may indicate processor congestion. This is an instantaneous count, not an average over time.
Server Work Queues	Read Bytes/sec	Rate at which the server is reading data from files for the clients on this CPU. This value is a measure of how busy the server is.
Server Work Queues	Read Operations/sec	Rate at which the server is performing file read operations for the clients on this CPU. This value is a measure of how busy the server is. This value will always be 0 in the

Object	Object counter	Description
Server Work Queues	Total Bytes/sec	Rate at which the server is reading and writing data to and from the files for the clients on this CPU. This value is a measure of how busy the server is.
Server Work Queues	Total Operations/sec	Rate at which the server is performing file read and file write operations for the clients on this CPU. This value is a measure of how busy the server is. This value will always be 0 in the Blocking Queue instance.
Server Work Queues	Work Item Shortages	Every request from a client is represented in the server as a *work item*, and the server maintains a pool of available work items per CPU to speed processing. A sustained value greater than zero indicates the need to increase the MaxWorkItems registry value for the Server service. This value will always be 0 in the Blocking Queue instance.
Server Work Queues	Write Bytes/sec	Rate at which the server is writing data to files for the clients on this CPU. This value is a measure of how busy the server is.
Server Work Queues	Write Operations/sec	Rate at which the server is performing file write operations for the clients on this CPU. This value is a measure of how busy the server is. This value will always be 0 in the Blocking Queue instance.
SNA Adapter SnaDlc1		
SNA Adapter SnaDlc1	Adapter Failures	Number of times since startup that a network adapter has encountered an error condition.
SNA Adapter SnaDlc1	Connection Failures	Number of times since startup that a connection has encountered an error condition.
SNA Adapter SnaDlc1	Data Bytes Received/sec	Number of data bytes received per second.
SNA Adapter SnaDlc1	Frames Received/sec	Number of data frames received per second. A frame is an information structure recognized by one of the various protocols related to SNA. Frames contain multiple bytes of data.
SNA Adapter SnaDlc1	Frames Transmitted/sec	Number of data frames transmitted per second. A frame is an information structure recognized by one of the various protocols related to SNA. Frames contain multiple bytes of data.

(continued)

Object	Object counter	Description
SNA Adapter SnaDlc1	Successful Connects	Number of times since startup that a successful connection has been made.
SNA Adapter SnaDlc1	Throughput Bytes/sec	Total number of bytes flowing through the SNA Server per second. This includes both incoming and outgoing bytes and is a good indicator of your SNA Server load.
SNA Adapter SnaDlc1	Throughput Frames/sec	Total number of data frames flowing through the SNA Server per second. This includes both incoming and outgoing frames and is a good indicator of your SNA Server load.
SNA Logical Unit Sessions		
SNA Logical Unit Sessions	Data Bytes Received/sec	Number of data bytes received per second.
SNA Logical Unit Sessions	Data Bytes Transmitted/sec	Number of data bytes transmitted per second.
SNA Logical Unit Sessions	Throughput Bytes/sec	Total number of bytes flowing through the SNA Server per second. This includes both incoming and outgoing bytes and is a good indicator of your SNA Server load.
SQL Server		
SQL Server	Cache – Avg. Free Page Scan	Average number of data cache buffers scanned by the Lazy Writer each time it searches for unused buffers to replenish the free pool.
SQL Server	Cache – Max. Free Page Scan	Maximum number of data cache buffers scanned by the Lazy Writer while searching for unused buffers to replenish the free pool.
SQL Server	Cache – Number of Free Buffers	Number of data cache buffers currently in the free pool.
SQL Server	Cache Hit Ratio	Percentage of time that a requested data page was found in the data cache (instead of being read from disk).
SQL Server	I/O – Batch Average Size	Average number of 2K pages written to disk during a batch I/O operation. The checkpoint thread is the primary user of batch I/O.
SQL Server	I/O – Batch Max Size	The maximum number of 2K pages written to disk during a batch I/O operation. The checkpoint thread is the primary user of batch I/O.
SQL Server	I/O – Batch Writes/sec	Number of 2K pages written to disk per second using batch I/O. The checkpoint thread is the primary user of batch I/O.

Object	Object counter	Description
SQL Server	I/O – Lazy Writes/sec	Number of 2K pages flushed to disk per second by the Lazy Writer.
SQL Server	I/O – Log Writes/sec	Number of log pages physically written to disk per second.
SQL Server	I/O – Outstanding Reads	Number of physical reads pending.
SQL Server	I/O – Outstanding Writes	Number of physical writes pending.
SQL Server	I/O – Page Reads/sec	Number of physical page reads per second.
SQL Server	I/O – Single Page Writes/sec	Number of single page writes performed per second (does not include log writes, cache flushes (Lazy Writer), or batch writes).
SQL Server	I/O – Trans. per Log Record	Number of transactions that were packed into a log record before the log record was written to disk.
SQL Server	I/O – Transactions/sec	Number of Transact-SQL command batches executed per second.
SQL Server	NET – Command Queue Length	Number of client requests that are waiting to be handled by the SQL Server working threads.
SQL Server	NET – Network Reads/sec	Number of tabular data stream (TDS) packets read from the network.
SQL Server	NET – Network Writes/sec	Number of tabular data stream (TDS) packets written to the network.
SQL Server	User Connections	Number of open user connections.
SQL Server Locks		
SQL Server Locks	Extent Locks – Exclusive	Number of exclusive extent locks.
SQL Server Locks	Extent Locks – Shared	Number of shared extent locks.
SQL Server Locks	Extent Locks – Total	Total number of extent locks.
SQL Server Locks	Intent Locks – Exclusive	Number of exclusive intent locks.
SQL Server Locks	Intent Locks – Shared	Number of shared intent locks.
SQL Server Locks	Intent Locks – Total	Total number of intent locks.
SQL Server Locks	Page Locks – Shared	Number of shared page locks.

(continued)

Object	Object counter	Description
SQL Server Locks	Page Locks – Total	Total number of page locks.
SQL Server Locks	Page Locks – Update	Number of update page locks.
SQL Server Locks	Page Locks – Exclusive	Number of exclusive page locks.
SQL Server Locks	Table Locks – Exclusive	Number of exclusive table locks.
SQL Server Locks	Table Locks – Shared	Number of shared table locks.
SQL Server Locks	Table Locks – Total	Total number of table locks.
SQL Server Locks	Total Blocking Locks	Total number of locks blocking other processes.
SQL Server Locks	Total Demand Locks	Number of all demand locks.
SQL Server Locks	Total Exclusive Locks	Number of all exclusive locks.
SQL Server Locks	Total Locks	Total number of locks being used by the SQL Server.
SQL Server Locks	Total Shared Locks	Total number of shared locks.
SQL Server Log		
SQL Server Log	Log Size (MB)	Amount of space allocated to the transaction log.
SQL Server Log	Log Space Used(%)	Percentage of the transaction log that is used.
SQL Server Users		
SQL Server Users	CPU Time	Cumulative CPU time for a user connection (and checkpoint process).
SQL Server Users	Locks Held	Number of locks held by a user connection.
SQL Server Users	Memory (2K pages)	Amount of memory (in 2K pages) allocated to a user connection.
SQL Server Users	Physical I/O	Number of disk reads and writes for the current statement.
System		
System	% Total DPC Time	Sum of % DPC Time of all processors divided by the number of processors in the system. (See *Processor: % DPC Time* for details.)

Object	Object counter	Description
System	% Total Interrupt Time	Sum of % Interrupt Time of all processors divided by the number of processors in the system. (See *Processor: % Interrupt Time* for details.)
System	% Total Privileged Time	Average percentage of time spent in Privileged mode by all processors. On a multi-processor system, if all processors are always in Privileged mode, this is 100%; if one-fourth of the processors are in Privileged mode, this is 25%. When a Windows NT system service is called, the service will often run in Privileged mode in order to gain access to system-private data. Such data is protected from access by threads executing in User mode. Calls to the system may be explicit, or they may be implicit such as when a page fault or an interrupt occurs. Unlike some early operating systems, Windows NT uses process boundaries for subsystem protection in addition to the traditional protection of User and Privileged modes. Therefore, some work done by Windows NT on behalf of an application may appear in other subsystem processes in addition to the Privileged Time in the application process.
System	% Total Processor	Average percentage of time that all of the processors on the system are busy executing non-idle threads. On a multi-processor system, if all of the processors are always busy, this is 100%; if all of the processors are busy half the time, this is 50%; and if all processors are busy one-fourth of the time, this is 25%. This number can be viewed as the fraction of the time spent doing useful work. Each processor is assigned an Idle thread in the Idle process which consumes those unproductive processor cycles not used by any other threads.
System	% Total User Time	Average percentage of time spent in User mode by all processors. On a multi-processor system, if all processors are always in User mode, this is 100%; if all processors are in User mode half the time, this is 50%; and if all the processors are in User mode one-fourth the time, this is 25%. Applications execute in User mode, as do subsystems like the window manager and the graphics engine. Code executing in User mode cannot damage the integrity of the Windows NT Executive, Kernel, and device drivers. Unlike some early operating systems, Windows NT uses process boundaries for subsystem protection in addition to the traditional protection of User and Privileged modes. Therefore, some work done by Windows NT on behalf of an application may appear in other subsystem processes in addition to the Privileged Time in the application process.
System	Alignment Fixups/sec	Rate of alignment faults fixed by the system.

(continued)

Object	Object counter	Description
System	Context Switches/sec	Rate of switches from one thread to another. Thread switches can occur either inside of a single process or across processes. A thread switch may be caused either by one thread asking another for information, or by a thread being preempted by another, higher-priority thread becoming ready to run. Unlike some early operating systems, Windows NT uses process boundaries for subsystem protection in addition to the traditional protection of User and Privileged modes. Therefore, some work done by Windows NT on behalf of an application may appear in other subsystem processes in addition to the Privileged Time in the application. Switching to the subsystem process causes one Context Switch in the application thread. Switching back causes another Context Switch in the subsystem thread.
System	Exception Dispatches/sec	Rate of exceptions dispatched by the system.
System	File Control Bytes/sec	Aggregate of bytes transferred for all file system operations that are neither reads nor writes. These operations usually include file system control requests or requests for information about device characteristics or status.
System	File Control Operations/sec	Aggregate of all file system operations that are neither reads nor writes. These operations usually include file system control requests or requests for information about device characteristics or status.
System	File Data Operations/sec	Rate at which the computer is issuing read and write operations to file system devices. It does not include file control operations.
System	File Read Bytes/sec	Aggregate of the bytes transferred for all of the file system read operations on the computer.
System	File Read Operations/sec	Aggregate of all of the file system read operations on the computer.
System	File Write Bytes/sec	Aggregate of the bytes transferred for all of the file system write operations on the computer.
System	File Write Operations/sec	Aggregate of all of the file system write operations on the computer.
System	Floating Emulations/sec	Rate of floating emulations performed by the system.
System	Processor Queue Length	Instantaneous length of the processor queue in units of threads. This counter is always 0 unless you are also monitoring a thread counter. All processors use a single queue in which threads wait for processor cycles. This length does not include the threads that are currently executing. A sustained processor queue length greater than 2 generally indicates processor congestion. This is an instantaneous count, not an average over the time interval.

Object	Object counter	Description
System	System Calls	Frequency of calls to Windows NT system service routines. These routines perform all of the basic scheduling and synchronization of activities on the computer and provide access to non-graphical devices, memory management, and name space management.
System	System Up Time	Total time (in seconds) that the computer has been operational since it was last started.
System	Total Interrupts/sec	Rate at which the computer is receiving and servicing hardware interrupts. Some devices that may generate interrupts are the system timer, the mouse, data communication lines, and network interface cards. This counter indicates how busy these devices are on a computer-wide basis. See also *Processor: Interrupts/sec.*
TCP		
TCP	Connection Failures	Number of times that TCP connections have made a direct transition to the CLOSED state from the SYN-SENT state or the SYN-RCVD state, plus the number of times that TCP connections have made a direct transition to the LISTEN state from the SYN-RCVD state.
TCP	Connections Active	Number of times that TCP connections have made a direct transition to the SYN-SENT state from the CLOSED state.
TCP	Connections Established	Number of TCP connections for which the current state is either ESTABLISHED or CLOSE-WAIT.
TCP	Connections Passive	Number of times that TCP connections have made a direct transition to the SYN-RCVD state from the LISTEN state.
TCP	Connections Reset	Number of times that TCP connections have made a direct transition to the CLOSED state from either the ESTABLISHED state or the CLOSE-WAIT state.
TCP	Segments Received/sec	Rate at which segments are received, including those received in error. This count includes segments received on currently established connections.
TCP	Segments Retransmitted/sec	Rate at which segments are retransmitted, that is, segments containing one or more previously transmitted bytes.
TCP	Segments Sent/sec	Rate at which segments are sent, including those on current connections, but excluding those containing only retransmitted bytes.
TCP	Segments/sec	Rate at which TCP segments are sent or received using the TCP protocol.

(continued)

Object	Object counter	Description
Thread		
Thread	% Privileged Time	Percentage of elapsed time that this thread has spent executing code in Privileged mode. When a Windows NT system service is called, the service will often run in Privileged mode in order to gain access to system-private data. Such data is protected from access by threads executing in User mode. Calls to the system may be explicit, or they may be implicit such as when a page fault or an interrupt occurs. Unlike some early operating systems, Windows NT uses process boundaries for subsystem protection in addition to the traditional protection of User and Privileged modes. Therefore, some work done by Windows NT on behalf of your application may appear in other subsystem processes in addition to the Privileged Time in your process.
Thread	% Processor Time	Percentage of elapsed time that this thread used the processor to execute instructions. An instruction is the basic unit of execution in a processor, and a thread is the object that executes instructions. Code executed to handle certain hardware interrupts or trap conditions may be counted for this thread.
Thread	% User Time	Percentage of elapsed time that this thread has spent executing code in User mode. Applications execute in User mode, as do subsystems like the window manager and the graphics engine. Code executing in User mode cannot damage the integrity of the Windows NT Executive, Kernel, and device drivers. Unlike some early operating systems, Windows NT uses process boundaries for subsystem protection in addition to the traditional protection of User and Privileged modes. Therefore, some work done by Windows NT on behalf of your application may appear in other subsystem processes in addition to the Privileged Time in your process.
Thread	Context Switches/sec	Rate of switches from one thread to another. Thread switches can occur either inside of a single process or across processes. A thread switch may be caused either by one thread asking another for information, or by a thread being preempted by another, higher-priority thread becoming ready to run. Unlike some early operating systems, Windows NT uses process boundaries for subsystem protection in addition to the traditional protection of User and Privileged modes. Therefore, some work done by Windows NT on behalf of an application may appear in other subsystem processes in addition to the Privileged Time in the application. Switching to the subsystem process causes one Context Switch in the subsystem thread. Switching back causes another Context Switch in the subsystem thread.
Thread	Elapsed Time	Total elapsed time (in seconds) that this thread has been running.
Thread	ID Process	Unique identifier of this process. ID Process numbers are reused, so they only identify a process for the lifetime of that process.

Object	Object counter	Description
Thread	ID Thread	Unique identifier of this thread. ID Thread numbers are reused, so they only identify a thread for the lifetime of that thread.
Thread	Priority Base	Current base priority of this thread. The system may raise the thread's dynamic priority above the base priority if the thread is handling user input, or the system may lower it toward the base priority if the thread becomes computer bound.
Thread	Priority Current	Current dynamic priority of this thread. The system may raise the thread's dynamic priority above the base priority if the thread is handling user input, or the system may lower it toward the base priority if the thread becomes computer bound.
Thread	Start Address	Starting virtual address for this thread.
Thread	Thread State	Current state of the thread. It is 0 for Initialized, 1 for Ready, 2 for Running, 3 for Standby, 4 for Terminated, 5 for Wait, 6 for Transition, 7 for Unknown. A Running thread is using a processor; a Standby thread is about to use one. A Ready thread wants to use a processor but is waiting for a processor because none are free. A thread in Transition is waiting for a resource in order to execute, such as waiting for its execution stack to be paged in from disk. A Waiting thread has no use for the processor because it is waiting for a peripheral operation to complete or a resource to become free.
Thread	Thread Wait Reason	Only applicable when the thread is in the Wait state (see *Thread State*). It is 0 or 7 when the thread is waiting for the Executive, 1 or 8 for a Free Page, 2 or 9 for a Page In, 3 or 10 for a Pool Allocation, 4 or 11 for an Execution Delay, 5 or 12 for a Suspended condition, 6 or 13 for a User Request, 14 for an Event Pair High, 15 for an Event Pair Low, 16 for an LPC Receive, 17 for an LPC Reply, 18 for Virtual Memory, 19 for a Page Out; 20 and higher have not been assigned at the time of this writing. Event Pairs are used to communicate with protected subsystems (see *Context Switches*).
UDP		
UDP	Datagrams No Port/sec	Rate of received UDP datagrams for which there was no application at the destination port.
UDP	Datagrams Received Errors	Number of received UDP datagrams that could not be delivered for reasons other than the lack of an application at the destination port.
UDP	Datagrams Received/sec	Rate at which UDP datagrams are delivered to UDP users.

(continued)

Object	Object counter	Description
UDP	Datagrams Sent/sec	Rate at which UDP datagrams are sent from the entity.
UDP	Datagrams/sec	Rate at which UDP datagrams are sent or received by the entity.
WINS Server		
WINS Server	Failed Queries/sec	Total number of Failed Queries/sec.
WINS Server	Failed Releases/sec	Total number of Failed Releases/sec.
WINS Server	Group Conflicts/sec	Rate at which group registration received by the WINS Server resulted in conflicts with records in the database.
WINS Server	Group Registrations/sec	Rate at which group registrations are received by the WINS Server.
WINS Server	Group Renewals/sec	Rate at which group renewals are received by the WINS Server.
WINS Server	Queries/sec	Rate at which queries are received by the WINS Server.
WINS Server	Releases/sec	Rate at which releases are received by the WINS Server.
WINS Server	Successful Queries/sec	Total number of Successful Queries/sec.
WINS Server	Successful Releases/sec	Total number of Successful Releases/sec.
WINS Server	Total Number Conflicts/sec	Sum of the Unique and Group Conflicts/sec. This is the total rate at which conflicts were seen by the WINS Server.
WINS Server	Total Number of Registrations/sec	Sum of the Unique and Group Registrations/sec. This is the total rate at which Server registrations are received by the WINS Server.
WINS Server	Total Number of Renewals/sec	Sum of the Unique and Group Renewals/sec. This is the total rate at which renewals are received by the WINS Server.
WINS Server	Unique Conflicts/sec	Rate at which unique registrations or renewals received by the WINS Server resulted in conflicts with records in the database.
WINS Server	Unique Registrations/sec	Rate at which unique registrations are received by the WINS Server.
WINS Server	Unique Renewals/sec	Rate at which unique renewals are received by the WINS Server.

Appendix E

Using the CD-ROM

The following instructions are for installing the various software files included in the CD that accompanies this book.

Camellia Software

In Windows Explorer, open the Camellia Software directory on the CD. Double-click the SETUP.EXE file and follow the on-screen prompts to set up the software.

Executive Software's Diskeeper

In Windows Explorer, open the Executive Software directory on the CD. Double-click the SETUP.EXE file and follow the on-screen prompts.

EMWAC Files

In the Gopher, HTTP and WAIS subdirectories, you'll find several versions of the EMWAC software for alpha, I386 and mips processors. Create an EMWAC directory with Gopher, HTTP and WAIS subdirectories and copy the files from the subdirectories on the CD into the matching subdirectory on your hard drive. Run the executable files from the subdirectories.

WinZip 6

Double-click the WINZIP95.EXE file in the WinZip6 subdirectory on the CD. Follow the on-screen prompts to set up the software.

Index

(continued)

(continued)

(continued)

(continued)

(continued)

(continued)

(continued)

(continued)

(continued)

IDG BOOKS WORLDWIDE LICENSE AGREEMENT

4. Limited Warranty. IDG warrants that the Software and disc are free from defects in materials and workmanship for a period of sixty (60) days from the date of purchase of this Book. If IDG receives notification within the warranty period of defects in material or workmanship, IDG will replace the defective disc. IDG's entire liability and your exclusive remedy shall be limited to replacement of the Software, which is returned to IDG with a copy of your receipt. This Limited Warranty is void if failure of the Software has resulted from accident, abuse, or misapplication. Any replacement Software will be warranted for the remainder of the original warranty period or thirty (30) days, whichever is longer.

5. No Other Warranties. To the maximum extent permitted by applicable law, IDG and the author disclaim all other warranties, express or implied, including but not limited to implied warranties of merchantability and fitness for a particular purpose, with respect to the Software, the programs, the source code contained therein and/or the techniques described in this Book. This limited warranty gives you specific legal rights. You may have others which vary from state/jurisdiction to state/jurisdiction.

6. No Liability For Consequential Damages. To the extent permitted by applicable law, in no event shall IDG or the author be liable for any damages whatsoever (including without limitation, damages for loss of business profits, business interruption, loss of business information, or any other pecuniary loss) arising out of the use of or inability to use the Book or the Software, even if IDG has been advised of the possibility of such damages. Because some states/jurisdictions do not allow the exclusion or limitation of liability for consequential or incidental damages, the above limitation may not apply to you.

7. U.S.Government Restricted Rights. Use, duplication, or disclosure of the Software by the U.S. Government is subject to restrictions stated in paragraph (c) (1) (ii) of the Rights in Technical Data and Computer Software clause of DFARS 252.227-7013, and in subparagraphs (a) through (d) of the Commercial Computer—Restricted Rights clause at FAR 52.227-19, and in similar clauses in the NASA FAR supplement, when applicable.

Replacement Disc. If a replacement CD-ROM is needed, please write to the following address: IDG Books Disc Fulfillment Center, Attn: *Windows NT Server 4.0 Secrets,* IDG Books Worldwide, 7260 Shadeland Station, Indianapolis, IN 46256, or call 800-762-2974.